SEEING THE WORLD AND KNOWING GOD

Seeing the World and Knowing God

*Hebrew Wisdom and Christian Doctrine
in a Late-Modern Context*

PAUL S. FIDDES

OXFORD
UNIVERSITY PRESS

OXFORD

UNIVERSITY PRESS

Great Clarendon Street, Oxford, OX2 6DP,
United Kingdom

Oxford University Press is a department of the University of Oxford.
It furthers the University's objective of excellence in research, scholarship,
and education by publishing worldwide. Oxford is a registered trade mark of
Oxford University Press in the UK and in certain other countries

First Edition published in 2013

Published in the United States of America by Oxford University Press
198 Madison Avenue, New York, NY 10016, United States of America

British Library Cataloguing in Publication Data
Data available

ISBN 978-0-19-964410-0

For Pamela Sue Anderson
Scholar, Colleague, and Friend

Preface

This book is a greatly expanded form of the Bampton Lectures, which I delivered from the pulpit of the University Church of St. Mary the Virgin, Oxford, on successive Sunday mornings in Hilary and Trinity Terms 2005. I am very grateful to the Heads of House of the University for electing me to this historic Lecturership, and to the hospitality of the University Church and its Vicar. Since then, I have given revised versions of some of the Lectures in Union University, Tennessee; Samford University (Martha H. Holley Lectures); the International Baptist Theological Seminary, Prague (Nordenhaug Lectures); Duke University Divinity School; Baylor University; Syracuse University; and the University of Gloucestershire. I am grateful for the welcome given me by all these institutions, and for the comments of the audiences which have helped in the shaping of this book in its present form. In addition, I want gladly to acknowledge many conversations with my research students over the last decade, during which the ideas in this book have been developed and refined; among these friends I especially mention Cyrus Olsen, Daniel Miller, Brandon Gallaher, Julia Meszaros, Kathryn Bevis, and Andrew Dunstan, and I thank them warmly for their contributions to my thought.

During the period of revision of these lectures an important influence has been dialogue with members of a research network for 'Critical Theory and Spiritual Practice', and among these especially with my colleague at Regent's Park College, Dr Pamela Sue Anderson, Reader in Philosophy of Religion in the University. She has in addition read and offered valuable comments on some of the following chapters in draft. I hope that the dedication of this book to her will indicate my considerable debt for her scholarly insights and friendly encouragement over the years. Special thanks are due to my editor at the Oxford University Press, Mr Tom Perridge, for his skills, patience, and generosity in accepting a work which, like wisdom, has been ever-expanding. To this I want to add similar thanks to Lizzie Robottom at the Press for her painstaking work in production of the volume.

This book has its remoter origin in a doctoral thesis in Old Testament studies, titled 'The Hiddenness of Wisdom in the Old Testament and Later Judaism', which I wrote in Oxford nearly forty years ago and which remains unpublished. I am delighted to take the opportunity now to salute my supervisor, the Rt Revd John Baker, former Bishop of Salisbury, author of a truly groundbreaking book on divine wisdom called *The Foolishness of God*. Shortly after writing the thesis I moved into the area of Systematic Theology, and my teaching, research, and publication since then has largely been in that discipline. However, I have continued to reflect on the issues raised about hidden wisdom in my early research, at the very beginning of my career, and it seems clear to me now that I have been living with them ever since in everything I have done.

Contents

Abbreviations and Acknowledgements

ANET   *Ancient Near Eastern Texts Relating to the Old Testament*, ed.
        J. B. Pritchard, Second edition (Princeton, Princeton University Press)

MT   Masoretic Text.

NEB   New English Bible (Oxford University Press/Cambridge University Press,
        1970). ©1970 by the Delegates of the Oxford University Press and the
        Syndics of the Cambridge University Press.
        All quotations from the Apocrypha in English are taken from the NEB,
        except where otherwise indicated, and used by permission.

NRSV   New Revised Standard Version of the Bible (New York/Oxford: Oxford
        University Press, 1989). ©1989 by Division of Christian Education of the
        Churches of Christ in the United States of America.

All quotations from the Hebrew Bible in English are taken from the NRSV,
except where otherwise indicated, and used by permission.

Quotations from the Jerusalem Bible are ©1996, 1967 and 1968 by Darton,
Longman & Todd and Doubleday & Company, used by permission.

Excerpts from *Choruses from 'The Rock'* in *The Complete Poems and Plays of
T. S. Eliot* 1909–1962 by T. S. Eliot © 1969 by Valerie Eliot, are reprinted
by permission of Faber and Faber Ltd. Also from *Collected Poems 1909–1962* by
T. S. Eliot. Copyright 1936 by Houghton Mifflin Harcourt Publishing Company.
Copyright © renewed 1964 by Thomas Stearns Eliot. Reprinted by permission
of Houghton Mifflin Harcourt Publishing Company. All Rights Reserved.

Excerpts from 'Song of the Soul' in *The Poems of St John of the Cross*, English
translations by John Frederick Nims © 1959, 1968, 1979 by John Frederick
Nims are reprinted by kind permission of The University of Chicago Press. All
Rights Reserved.

Excerpts from 'Three Meetings' in *Vladimir Solovyov's Poems of Sophia* ©
1996 Boris Jakim and Laury Magnus are reprinted by kind permission of the
Variable Press.

The excerpt from 'A Confession' by C.S. Lewis is copyrighted by the Executors
of the Estate of C.S. Lewis, 1964.

Please note that, as a guide to pronunciation by the general reader, the author
has used his own form of simplified transliteration from Hebrew, which
therefore does not exactly follow the now standard SBL convention. For
instance, the -ah endings sufficiently imply a long 'a' without marking the
vowel. Note also that š is pronounced 'sh', ṣ is pronounced 'ts', and ḥ is
pronounced as a guttural h, as in the 'ch' of the Scots word 'loch'.

Part One

Setting the Scene

1

The Cry for Wisdom

The age in which we are living is sometimes called 'the knowledge revolution'. A less complimentary description might be 'information overload'. We are bombarded by 24-hour news, multi-channel satellite TV, and myriad websites offering us advice, consumer choice, down-loadable essays for students, and down-loadable sermons for clergy. In the face of this constant flow of information, of invitations to a knowledge which is instantly accessible, the term 'wisdom' has marked something of a reaction. One often hears it said that what is needed is 'less knowledge and more wisdom'. The appeal to find 'wisdom' is also heard in situations where science has made many procedures possible (say) in medicine, bio-technology, and weapons-production, but where human beings seem incapable of making moral choices which will foster life both individually and socially. T. S. Eliot, writing in an age before the modern information-explosion, still felt compelled to protest:

> All our knowledge brings us nearer to our ignorance,
> All our ignorance brings us nearer to death,
> But nearness to death no nearer to GOD.
> Where is the Life we have lost in living?
> Where is the wisdom we have lost in knowledge?
> Where is the knowledge we have lost in information?[1]

The lament for something lost and desired called 'wisdom' is characteristic of an age which has been critical of the project for human mastery as popularized in the European Enlightenment. In our 'late-modern' era, the privileging of the conscious mind as controller of the world around it has come under sustained attack. A significant project of modernity was the attempt to subjugate the natural world with all its mysterious and threatening aspects to the control of the consciousness that—it was supposed—defines humanity. This has led, we can now see, to a split between subject and object, to a gulf opening up between the mind as subject and the world as mere object, something to be

---

[1] T. S. Eliot, *Choruses from 'The Rock'*, I, in *The Complete Poems and Plays of T. S. Eliot* (London: Faber & Faber, 1969), p. 147.

investigated and mastered—not to say exploited. Destruction of the environment inevitably follows. One small sign of the great divide is the expansion of the adventure-holiday industry, as people attempt to re-connect with the natural world from which they feel alienated. They try to journey into their environment and thereby—ironically—inflict more damage on it, leaving, for instance, empty meal cartons scattered all over Mount Everest.

In this context 'wisdom' has become an all-purpose word to denote a way of living in the world which aims to transcend the self as a merely thinking subject. This wisdom must have a place within it for knowledge as collecting information about the world, and especially for reason as careful reflection on the world, but it is always exceeding these faculties. The term 'wisdom' thus contests the attempt of the subject to use cognition for the sake of controlling other things and people, and indicates alternative ways of relating the self to the world. It is associated with other terms such as 'embodiment', 'connectedness', and 'participation'. We recognize that in our *bodies* we are deeply immersed into our physical surroundings. We recognize that human beings are *connected* with other living beings in a world community in which all things influence each other. Perhaps above all we recognize that we *participate* in lives beyond our own, especially through sympathy and empathy. A guiding thread is the sense that wisdom is about living in tune with the world in which we are placed, in all its differences and otherness. From a religious point of view, 'seeing the world' (through reason and knowledge) can be a means of knowing others in a truly relational way, and finally knowing God.

DIFFERENT KINDS OF WISDOM

In this seeking of 'wisdom' as a step beyond the mere gathering of knowledge, appeal is often made to the Ancient Greek concept of *phronēsis*. While Aristotle considered *technē* as exercise of a skill or craft that can secure success in life, he developed the idea of *phronēsis* as a higher order of wisdom: *phronēsis* is the virtue of practical reason, the capacity to make moral judgements and to regulate other virtues and skills in a particular situation.[2] To take an example of modern appeal to this ancient concept, specialists in business management have recently complained that business schools have 'lost their way' in concentrating on teaching a 'scientific-rationalist approach' to strategic management and in neglecting the fostering of skills of judgement based on 'wisdom and experience'.[3] Thus, they have urged, what needs to be

---

[2] Aristotle, *Nichomachean Ethics*, trans. D. Ross (Oxford: Oxford University Press, 1980), 1140a.20, 1140b.6.

[3] Warren G. Bennis and James O'Toole, 'How Business Schools Lost their Way', *Harvard Business Review* 83/5 (2005), pp. 1–11 (esp. p. 6).

recovered is a 'phronēsis' which offers 'a relational mode of knowing',[4] or a 'knowledge acquired from practical experience that enables one to make prudent decisions and take action appropriate to each situation, guided by values and ethics'.[5]

To take another example, there has been an increasing volume of voices in healthcare circles about the need for 'wisdom' in medicine. Usually, what is meant by 'wisdom' here is the clinical judgement of the practitioner, shaped by his or her experience over the years, and this is often contrasted with 'evidence-based' medicine or EBM. EBM approaches rely on guidelines supplied by databases of evidence culled from tests and from observed outcomes over a wide range of the population. All discussion in the medical literature acknowledges that an element of EBM is essential for successful and responsible practice. But there has been an anxiety that a purely scientific approach has begun to *dominate* medical decision-making at the expense of more human and social factors, and so to threaten the 'art' or wisdom of medicine. It is proposed that regard to an Aristotelean *phronēsis* involves taking into account what the *technē* of EBM cannot, that is, 'a wide range of imponderables, but especially a patient's own (perhaps irrational) perspective'.[6] When doctors have to come to a decision about treatments for individual patients, or in other words, have to make value-judgements relating to what is good or bad for a particular person in a particular situation, practitioners perceive that 'this is not the same as making judgements about what is or is not the case . . . the judgements of the good clinician must be more than technical; they must show practical wisdom'.[7]

Such talk of wisdom outside Christian theology, reflecting the uneasiness of a late-modern world about a merely rational self, has thus often focused on the Greek idea of *phronēsis*, or 'practical wisdom'.[8] My proposal in this book is to shift attention to another concept of wisdom, recovering the Hebrew idea of

---

[4] Elena P. Antonacopoulou, 'Making the Business School More "Critical": Reflexive Critique Based on Phronesis as a Foundation for Impact', *British Journal of Management* 21 (2010), pp. 6–25 (esp. p. 7).

[5] Ikujiro Nonaka and Ryoko Toyama, 'Strategic Management as Distributed Practical Wisdom (Phronesis)', *Industrial and Corporate Change* 16/3 (2007), pp. 371–94 (esp. p. 378).

[6] Jane Macnaughton, 'Evidence and Clinical Judgement', *Journal of Evaluation in Clinical Practice* 4/2 (1998), p. 92; cf. Fredrik Svenaeus, 'Hermeneutics of Medicine in the Wake of Gadamer: The Issue of Phronesis', *Theoretical Medicine* 24 (2003), pp. 407–31.

[7] Ricca Edmondson and Jane Pearce, 'The Practice of Health Care: Wisdom as a Model', *Medicine, Health Care and Philosophy*, 10 (2007), p. 237.

[8] A further example is in the social sciences. Bent Flyvbjerg coined the term 'phronetic social science' in his *Making Social Science Matter: Why Social Enquiry Fails and How it can Succeed Again* (Cambridge: Cambridge University Press, 2001), introducing the idea pp. 2–4 and offering a case study on regional planning, pp. 141–61. Sanford Schram reviews the position with his 'Phronetic Social Science: An idea Whose Time Has Come' in Bent Flyvbjerg, Todd Landman, and Sanford Schram, *Real Social Science: Applied Phronesis* (Cambridge: Cambridge University Press, 2012), pp. 15–26.

ḥokmah (wisdom, חכמה) which develops into the *sophia* of the New Testament. Inside Christian theology, talk of living a life of wisdom has been influenced by a renewed interest in the range of literature in the Hebrew Bible and inter-testamental books called 'wisdom literature', and so in the concept of *ḥokmah*. The literature mainly in view comprises the books of Proverbs, Koheleth (Ecclesiastes), and Job in the Hebrew Bible, together with the Wisdom of Jesus Ben Sira (translated from Hebrew into Greek by his grandson, also called Ben Sira)[9] and the Wisdom of Solomon (written in Greek)[10] in the Greek Septuagint. My project is to bring this Hebraic *ḥokmah* into conversation with a Christian theology which is aware of its context in a late-modern world, and to some extent already in conversation with it, to see whether this way of doing theology might throw some light on a general situation in which there is a quest for wisdom.

In fact, there are two features of Hebrew wisdom that make us suspect immediately that it *will* be useful in exploring concerns of our own time. The first concerns the different kinds of wisdom to which we are alerted by the discussion of Aristotle about *phronēsis*, and to understand this we need to clear our way for a while through a tangled thicket of terms that have grown up around the word 'wisdom' itself.

Aristotle usefully distinguishes not only between *technē* and *phronēsis*, but between *phronēsis* and *sophia*. By *sophia* Aristotle means the ability to discern what is ultimately real, lasting, universal, and true, with the combined help of both the intelligence (*nous*) and the process of reasoning (*epistēmē*).[11] *Sophia* and *phronēsis* have thus sometimes been contrasted as 'theoretical' and 'practical' wisdom respectively. The approximate counterpart of Aristotle's *sophia* in the Western, Latin Christian tradition was often named *sapientia* (wisdom). It indicated a knowledge of God as the final reality, and was characterized by contemplation and a disposition in which knowing and loving God were inseparable. Its context was the monastery and a life of prayer, and its main tool was a spiritual reading of Scripture (*lectio divina*). While the Christian idea of 'wisdom' (*sapientia*) was to some extent influenced by Aristotle's *sophia* (largely assuming, for instance, that the ultimate reality to be contemplated was timeless and unchanging), it derived more directly from the *sophia* of the New Testament, identifying Christ as the true 'Wisdom of God',[12] and

---

[9] About two-thirds of the original Hebrew text is extant, in a number of fragments. See Roland E. Murphy, *The Tree of Life. An Exploration of Biblical Wisdom Literature* (Grand Rapids: Eerdmans, 1996), pp. 67–9. The Hebrew text was written in Jerusalem between 190–175 BCE, and the Greek translation was made in Alexandria after 132 BCE.

[10] Written to the Jewish community in Alexandria in the first century BCE. In addition, I will be referring to a poem in praise of wisdom in Baruch 3:9–4:4, a Greek text that probably originated in the first century BCE, possibly from an earlier Hebrew original.

[11] Aristotle, *Nichomachean Ethics* 1141a.19–20.

[12] Colossians 2:1–3, I Corinthians 2:1–10.

believing that the Holy Spirit can inspire wisdom within those who seek to have 'the mind of Christ'.[13] Indeed, the New Testament seems to show a distinct hostility towards the *sophia* of Greek philosophy, as a form of human self-aggrandizement; we shall see later how the positive celebration of *sophia* in early Christian thinking is grounded in the wisdom of the Hebrew Bible.

With the growth of the universities from the twelfth century, however, another mode of knowing God appeared which may be called *scientia*. Characterized by speculation and a disposition of knowing *about* God, its context was the lecture room and argument, and its main tool was a dialectic of question and answer. It may appear that wisdom (*sapientia*) was being pitched against science (*scientia*). While *scientia* has resonances with the *epistēmē* of Aristotle, it also has its successor in the modern notion of a *Wissenschaft*, which became the official ideology of German universities in the nineteenth century. In the *Wissenschaftlich* approach, stress is laid upon a systematic organization of knowledge and a method of study in which the learners discover knowledge for themselves rather than being dependent on tradition, and theology is counted among the *Wissenschaften*.[14]

In older theological accounts of learning in the Middle Ages, *sapientia* and *scientia* were customarily polarized, and opposed to each other. Regret was often expressed for a supposed overshadowing of divine wisdom (*sapientia*) by human, rational knowledge. It is more usual now to recognize blurred edges between these two spheres. Thomas Aquinas, for instance, has often been regarded as the archetypal representative of *scientia* (while Bonaventure was nominated as representing *sapientia*), but it is clear that Aquinas was also a 'sapiential' theologian, concerned with the integration of knowledge with love of God and having a strong contemplative streak. It is still possible, however, to recognize two trends of approach to knowing God, which might be combined in one *habitus* or disposition of life, or which might appear in distinct forms with their own emphases.

In recent theological writing, the appeal to 'wisdom' is often a renewal of Christian *sapientia*, as seems to be the main emphasis in the project of David Ford to recover a Christian wisdom for living in the twenty-first century.[15] Ford claims 'The richest wisdom has been found in God's love of creation for its own sake and a responsive human love of God for God's sake and of other people for their own sake'. Wise living before this God thus 'involves a faith that above all acknowledges being desired and loved by God, like Jesus at his

---

[13] 1 Cor 2:14–16.

[14] Further, see Chapter 11, the section called 'Wisdom, Pedagogy and the Puzzle of Rejection'.

[15] David Ford, *Christian Wisdom. Desiring God and Learning in Love* (Cambridge: Cambridge University Press, 2007). Nevertheless, Ford makes a place for both *scientia* and *phronēsis*, as evidenced in a chapter on wisdom in the modern research university (pp. 304–49) on which I comment in Chapter 11.

baptism, and that in response desires and loves God',[16] guided—as in the Christian sapiential tradition—by a repeated reading of Scripture which seeks both the 'plain' sense and multiple layers of meaning. Within Scripture, Ford pays attention to the Jewish wisdom literature, especially to the 'cries' to God for justice found within it, and affirms that his proposal for wise living is in accord with the ancient wisdom movement. However, he acknowledges that, in setting out his project, he has only dealt at length with one text from the 'wisdom literature in the scholarly sense', namely the Book of Job.[17] My own project in this book is a complementary one, precisely to engage in close interaction with an extensive range of texts from the literature of *ḥokmah*.

It is not surprising that in a late-modern age, suspicious as it is that systems of thought can be concealed power-games, there has been a reaction against *scientia* in its exaggerated modern versions. Alongside the recalling of the Christian tradition of *sapientia*, response to the dominance of *scientia* has taken the form of a stress on 'practice' over against 'theory', and this is a mood which we can discern outside Christian theology as well as within it. The discussion of 'practices' by Alasdair MacIntyre has struck a chord in several places, not only theological.[18] He observes that 'practice' is 'any coherent and complex form of socially established cooperative human activity through which goods internal to that form of activity are realized in the course of trying to achieve those standards of excellence which are appropriate to, and partly definitive of, that form of activity'.[19] Human identity will consist in engaging in certain practices, reflecting upon them and allowing virtuous character to be formed within them. With regard to the Christian community, David Kelsey has claimed that there is a mode of wisdom here that has always been present alongside *sapientia* and *scientia*, though it has received particular stress in our age. He judges that for Scotus, for instance, 'because understanding God culminates in precisely will's love of God, it must begin here and now neither solely in reason's *sapientia* nor solely in its *scientia*, but in will's deliberate and conscious action, that is, in praxis'.[20] Kelsey thus argues that the 'wisdom' of Christian theology consists in holding a set of practices in relation to God; we can understand God only 'indirectly by way of' other activity.[21]

---

[16] Ford, *Christian Wisdom,* p. 380.

[17] Ford, *Christian Wisdom,* p. 120.

[18] See, for example, Geoff Moore, 'On the Implications of the Practice-Institution Distinction: MacIntyre and the Application of Modern Virtue Ethics to Business', *Business Ethics Quarterly* 12/1 (2002), pp. 19–32.

[19] Alasdair MacIntyre, *After Virtue: A Study in Moral Theory*, Second Edition (London: Duckworth, 1985), p. 187.

[20] David Kelsey, *To Understand God Truly: What's Theological about a Theological School* (Louisville: Westminster John Knox, 1992), p. 46.

[21] Kelsey, *To Understand God Truly*, pp. 123–9. Similarly, he finds that the Israelite wise know God through the practices of daily life in his *Eccentric Existence: Theological Anthropology*, 2 Volumes (Louisville, Westminster John Knox, 2009), vol. 1, pp. 211–14, 311–21.

Self-critical reflection arises within practices, and so out of engaging deliberately in certain practices there emerges a knowing of oneself, the world and God.

Talk of 'practices' is, of course, in the same area as *phronēsis*, or 'practical wisdom', as Daniel Treier perceives.[22] By advocating a Christian form of *phronēsis*, he proposes to re-think the relation between practice and knowing God, taking a different direction from Kelsey. According to Treier, a Christian *phronēsis* is utterly dependent on Christian *sophia* (or *sapientia*). He argues that *phronēsis*, or ethical discernment in practical situations, is entirely enabled by *sophia*, or by seeing God in Christ through revelation, as normatively found in Scripture. While the noun *phronēsis* is infrequent in the New Testament, Treier points to the use of the verbal form (*phroneō*) to indicate a mindset or orientation, as in the injunction 'let this mind be in you that was in Christ Jesus' (Phil. 2:5).[23] For Treier, the Scripture thus forms the *person* in *phronēsis* rather than providing comprehensive material for application to particular judgements. *Phronēsis* is a gift from God, and 'is nurtured by the Spirit in response to prayer, who hones it though habits of obedience, and informs it by scripture . . .'.[24] While the exercise of *phronēsis* forms ecclesial communities of virtuous living to counter-balance the communities of intellect (*scientia*) in the universities, Treier argues that it also enables the church to take Christian knowledge into the public space and engage in debate.[25]

By a winding trail we have now arrived at our first significant reason why the Hebrew concept of wisdom has so much to offer in our late-modern world. Reviewing the story of *phronēsis*, *sophia*, *sapientia*, *scientia*, and *praxis*, we may say that the writers of ancient Israelite wisdom literature offer a unique integration of *phronēsis* and *sophia*. On the one hand, wisdom is about exercising practical judgement when faced by situations of everyday life. As they show themselves to us in their writings, the 'wise' aim to cope with experience through careful observation of how things are. From their own experiments in living, and from the reports of others back through the generations, they can judge the thing to do which will make for the 'good' and for human well-being in any particular circumstances. Their technique is to collect and pass on deductions from experience, on the assumption that the natural and human world is open to being understood by patient investigation, built up over many years. From this observation of the world, sometimes in the face of extreme adversity, the wise find patterns of meaning and detect regularities that can offer guidance to those who are willing to listen to their teaching. Their observations are fixed in proverbs, riddles, and lists of

---

[22] Daniel J. Treier, *Virtue and the Voice of God. Towards Theology as Wisdom* (Grand Rapids: Eerdmans, 2006), pp. 61–4, 95–8.

[23] Treier, *Virtue and the Voice of God*, pp. 54–7. Other instances are of the verb are: Phil. 2:2; 3:15, 19; 4:2; Rom. 12:3, 16; 14:6; 15:5 and 1 Cor. 4:2.

[24] Treier, *Virtue and the Voice of God*, p. 55.

[25] Treier, *Virtue and the Voice of God*, pp. 65–6.

natural phenomena, by which they begin to bring some order to a vast and complex area of investigation. When the wise have to cope with a situation, to 'steer' their way through the maze of events, they appeal to the guidelines gleaned from experience: these represent order won from the chaos of life. So the opening to the Book of Proverbs urges us:

> For gaining instruction in wise dealing,
> righteousness, justice and equity . . . .
> let the wise hear and gain in learning,
> and the discerning *acquire skill*,
> to understand a proverb and a figure,
> the words of the wise and their riddles. (Prov. 1:3, 5–6)

This exercise of practical wisdom (roughly equivalent to *phronēsis*) thus also contains a larger element of *scientia* than in the Greek concept, at least with regard to a systematic understanding of the world. In this book I am going to call this dimension a 'wisdom of observation', and I will explore it in more detail in Chapters 4 and 5.

On the other hand, 'wisdom' is about something that lies in the area of Greek *sophia* and Christian *sapientia*, some contemplative knowledge of final reality, some gesturing towards our 'ultimate concern'. This dimension of wisdom is indicated by a personified figure, usually depicted as an attractive and enticing woman, who walks along the paths of the world. Lady Wisdom is out on the road of life, issuing an invitation to those who are foolish to come and live and learn with her.[26] She cries out her invitation in the streets and in the marketplace, like a wisdom teacher setting out a prospectus, inviting pupils into her school; 'You who are simple' she cries, 'turn in here' (Prov. 9:4). This wisdom danced on the earth at the beginning of creation when God made the mountains and the seas; she played on the earth and delighted in the company of newly created human beings (Prov. 8:30–1). This wisdom walks through the world here and now, seeking for somewhere to dwell, longing for those who will make their home with her. She looks for those who will walk with her, for 'her ways are ways of pleasantness, and all her paths are peace' (Prov. 3:17). In this book I am calling this dimension of wisdom a 'wisdom of participation', and I intend to consider it in more detail in Chapter 6. In a way that is yet to be explored, this wisdom belongs to God and expresses God's own creativity.

In the Israelite wisdom literature, these two dimensions of wisdom interweave in quite different ways from the Aristotelean *phronēsis* and *sophia*. Both Kelsey and Treier, in their appeal to the relevance of Israelite wisdom literature

---

[26] An alternative title to 'Lady Wisdom' would be 'Woman Wisdom', as used by Claudia Camp in her *Wisdom and the Feminine in the Book of Proverbs* (Sheffield: Almond, 1985). I prefer 'Lady' as an equivalence to the metaphor of 'Lord' attributed to God in Jewish–Christian tradition, and as evocative of the title 'Lady Philosophy' usually ascribed to the figure who appears in Boethius and Dante.

in the contemporary world, have something to contribute here. As Kelsey suggests, a knowledge of God (a 'wisdom of participation' in my description) always emerges indirectly from the practice of wisdom in daily life (my 'wisdom of observation'). Knowing God is inseparable from 'seeing' the world, where 'seeing' may be taken as a metaphor for an exploration of the world which is not restricted to the literal use of the eyes.[27] But in this literature there is also an element of the self-disclosure of divine wisdom, which Treier highlights over against Kelsey's account. There is some truth in Treier's insistence that *phronēsis* is *formed* by *sophia*, although we shall see that the exercise of practical judgement does not simply *derive* from a revelation of wisdom as he rather dogmatically proposes.

How these dimensions are related, how 'seeing the world' is connected with 'knowing God' must await the unfolding of argument and exposition of Scripture texts in the chapters to come. Here I merely want to observe that we cannot meet the cry for wisdom in late-modern culture without both dimensions of wisdom. The 'cry' we hear is not only for the wisdom of knowing what judgements will result in human well-being, but for the wisdom of participating in the whole, cosmic environment in which we are set. Not all people in our age will include God in that wider context in which we make our daily decisions, but there is a feeling outside the Christian community that we must learn to live 'in tune' with the rhythms of a reality that is larger than ourselves, and which transcends our everyday preoccupations. Christian wisdom-theology will then be at least coherent with the desires and anxieties of a secular culture, and the reason why this coherence is possible at all will emerge in the process of our study.

One major reason for drawing on ancient Israelite wisdom literature to make Christian doctrine anew in the context of the preoccupations of our late-modern world is, thus, the potential it offers for integrating different kinds of wisdom. But there is another reason, also, which does not rely on an explicit appeal to wisdom or its lack in contemporary culture. There is, generally, a common ground between the mood of Hebrew wisdom and the late-modern mind, especially as the latter is expressed in a number of thinkers usually identified as 'postmodern'. I mean that wisdom literature, unlike other literature in the Hebrew Bible, has a central concern with thinking about the relation between the self and the observable world around; this relation is in turn bound up with a relation to God. In our late-modern world, there is also a concern to re-think the relation of self to world, in the light of losing old certainties about the self as a subject which can control its own destiny. We might even say that there is a crisis about the place of the self in the world. While, outside religious communities, this self-world relation is not usually

---

[27] See Chapter 6.

orientated towards a notion of a personal God, it is (often surprisingly) open to a sense of transcendence, to some ultimate reality or final Good which challenges the status quo in political and social life, and which 'comes' to interrupt all attempts to construct the world as an extension of the self. The relation of self, world, and transcendence is thus a marked feature of both ancient wisdom and the late-modern world. Furthermore, both wisdom and late-modernity register a strong sense of the elusiveness or hiddenness of the self and the world. Both the self and the world, while apparently open to observation, escape our scrutiny, for reasons that I intend to explore in this study. As one wisdom teacher expressed it, 'Three things are too wonderful for me; four I do not understand...' (Prov. 30:18), and another, 'I have not learned wisdom, nor have I the knowledge of the Holy One (Prov. 30:3)'.

An elusive self and an elusive world are thus equally matched with an elusive sense of transcendence. Neither in ancient wisdom nor in late-modern thinking can the ultimate reality that 'goes beyond' human life and strikes into it be objectified like any object in the world. In the language of Heidegger, Being itself (*Sein*) cannot be confused with beings (*Seiendes*).[28] Nor can transcendent reality be defined by a reversal from the immanence of the 'here and now'. There is some Other which calls us to account, but which cannot be categorized as non-immanence: it is the Other which is always in the midst. This, as we shall see, is what Jacques Derrida means with his gnomic dictum that 'there is nothing outside the text'.[29]

In this book, then, I am aiming to make a Christian wisdom-theology which *connects* with its context in the intellectual and cultural life of the late-modern world. Systematic theology, I have argued elsewhere, is not a tight, self-enclosed scheme of thought but 'connectional theology', connecting themes of doctrine with each other and allowing this process to be shaped by a connection with the world in which theology is made.[30] This will mean opening up horizons between the ancient world-view of the Hebrew wisdom movement, with its continuation in Hellenistic–Jewish literature and the New Testament on the one hand, and late-modern understandings of the relation of the self to the world on the other. Because this is an exercise in Christian theology, the world will be understood as a *created reality*. We are not just concerned with living in tune with this world; we are thinking about what it means to be attuned to the world *and* to its creator, and so I shall be proposing a doctrine of creation which is firmly rooted in participation in a God who exists in triune relations, and who relates to what is created in all its diversity.

---

[28] Martin Heidegger, *Being and Time*, trans. J. Macquarrie and E. Robinson (Oxford: Blackwell, 1973), pp. 22, 32–5.

[29] Jacques Derrida, 'Afterword', trans. S. Weber, in *Limited Inc* (Evanston: Northwestern University Press, 1988), p. 148.

[30] Paul S. Fiddes, 'Concept, Image and Story in Systematic Theology', *International Journal of Systematic Theology* 11/1 (2009), pp. 3–23.

Such a venture should be fruitful in shaping Christian theology for a late-modern age. It may also, however, allow Christian theologians to keep a conversation going with others outside the church, and to occupy a public space (in the academy at least) alongside late-modern thinkers who do not share a Christian view of the world.

THE STORY OF WISDOM IN ANCIENT ISRAEL

But what is this 'wisdom movement' in Ancient Israel to which I have been referring? While this is not the place for an extensive historical account of its origins and development, we need a sufficient outline to make sense of the texts we are examining—mainly Proverbs, Job, Koheleth (or 'Ecclesiastes'), The Wisdom of Jesus Ben Sira (or 'Ecclesiasticus'), and the Wisdom of Solomon. In particular, there is a question of the relation of 'wisdom' to the Yahwistic religion of Israel. As is often pointed out, until Ben Sira in the second century BCE the wisdom literature contains no explicit reference to the salvific 'mighty acts of God' in the history of the Hebrew people, nor to the making of covenant, nor to God's self-disclosure to the prophets and significant leaders of the nation. Until Ben Sira, wisdom literature passes over the great names of Israelite tradition in silence: there is no trace of Abraham, Isaac, Jacob, Moses, and David.

A significant point of distinction from prophetic and priestly groups in Israel is an emphasis upon 'seeing' the world. The prophets characteristically bid their audience to 'hear' the word of the Lord which they themselves have heard God speak to them, perhaps in a flight of ecstasy, perhaps in a moment of intuition as they reflect upon their society. The priests bid their worshippers to 'hear' the commandments of God (Torah) which they hold as guardians from the past, or which they formulate in their own day as they reflect on their tradition. The wise, however, bid their disciples to cultivate the art of 'looking' at the world around. There is, of course, no exclusive use of isolated senses here. On the one hand the language of 'hearing' is present in the wisdom material; learners are to 'listen' to instruction from their parents and teachers, and in the later period of wisdom education there is a merging of wisdom with the observation of Torah, so that learners are now to listen to the 'commandments'.[31] As a proverbial saying puts it, 'The hearing ear and the seeing eye—the Lord has made them both' (Prov. 20:12). On the other hand, the prophets often hear their word in a moment of *vision*, and the earliest prophets were called 'seers'. But the characteristic cast of mind which persists from the

---

[31] As found in the 'Instruction' genre of Proverbs, for example 2:1–6; 3:1–8.

earliest to the latest period of wisdom is one of observing the details and particularities of the human and natural world, and deducing patterns of similarity and typical behaviour from what the eye has seen. Whereas the prophet is inclined to say 'the Lord *showed* me . . . ',[32] appealing to a moment of divine revelation, the wise person simply says 'I saw', recalling the exercise of a human faculty of vision. The teacher in Proverbs 7 'looks out' through his lattice, and tells his disciples that:

> I *saw* among the simple ones,
> I *observed* among the youths,
> a young man without sense (v. 7)

The foolish youth is taking the road to the prostitute's house, rather than to the house (school) of wisdom, and brings disaster upon himself. Passing by the field of a lazy person, overgrown with thorns, the teacher recalls that 'I saw and considered it, I looked and received instruction' (Prov. 24:32). 'Do you *see* persons wise in their own eyes?' asks the teacher of Proverbs 26:12. 'There is more hope for fools than for them'. The teacher called Koheleth tells us of all that he 'saw done under the sun': he has 'seen' the business that preoccupies people, evil, oppressions, futility, and yet also the enjoyment that daily work can bring.[33] Reflecting on the avidity of human perception, another teacher urges that:

> Sheol and Abaddon [i.e. the underworld and destruction] are never satisfied and human eyes are never satisfied (Prov. 27:20).

This is also, we notice, a remark about the elusiveness of wisdom, a theme to which we shall return many times in this study. Even more than the direct use of the verb 'to see', however, the proverbial literature is full of lovingly crafted observations of the world, little cameo pictures that are held up to view: the king's face appears to be like the clouds that bring the spring rain, those who linger late over wine have red eyes and 'see strange things', the person who sleeps during harvest invites nothing but shame.[34]

The framework for this attentive seeing of the natural world and other people is an understanding of creation which is rather different from the perspective of the account of creation in Genesis 1–3. As Kelsey has pointed out, following Claus Westermann, this Genesis account is 'bent under the pressure of the narrative logic of the stories of God relating to reconcile';[35] human beings are presented there as losing an original paradisial state through sin, with the promise that they will be redeemed within the history of God's

---

[32] E.g. Amos 7:1, 4, 7 cf. Ezek. 37:2, Jer. 18:2.

[33] Koheleth (Ecclesiastes) 1:14; 2:3, 13, 24; 3:10, 16; 4:3, 7–8; 5:13, 18; 6:1; 7:15; 8:9–10, 16; 9:11, 13; 10:5.

[34] Prov. 16:15; 23:29, 33; 10:5.

[35] Kelsey, *Eccentric Existence*, vol. 1, p. 162; see Claus Westermann, *Genesis 1–11. A Commentary*, trans. J. Scullion (Minneapolis: Augsburg, 1984), pp. 64–7.

activity among them. Wisdom, Kelsey suggests, presents the world as a created reality in its own right, not subject to a narrative of redemption. God is generously hospitable, present to the world in a freedom that allows created reality to be itself, attentively delighting in its otherness.[36] Wisdom has a creation theology of God's pleasure in the 'quotidian' (the everyday world),[37] and 'The real you is simply the quotidian you.' Human sin has not brought about some ontological change in creation, but is 'an inappropriate response' to God's relating creatively to all reality other than God.[38] There is no paradigm of a perfect human being in a pre-fall state, but 'the real human person is God's good creature precisely in his or her quotidian everydayness and finitude'.[39]

Wisdom thus lays stress on the flourishing of the human self in its inter-connection to other persons and the natural world. The relation between self and world is at the heart of wisdom, and this makes it, I suggest, an appropriate conversation-partner with thinkers of our late-modern period. As Kelsey puts it, human beings are 'born into complex networks of other beings that interact with one another',[40] and wisdom's creation theology invites us to describe the quotidian in terms of human 'practices', including practices of interaction with non-human creatures, other human creatures, and social institutions.[41] Human beings are thus invited to attend to fellow creatures with a 'compassionate and just gaze'.[42] With this account of the creation-theology of wisdom, it is easy to see why Kelsey proposes that knowledge of God emerges 'indirectly' from human practices. I suggest that this is indeed an accurate account of 'wisdom as observation' within the wisdom movement, but that it does not fully describe the dimension of 'wisdom as participation' with which we will also be concerned in our study.

The particular emphases of the wisdom movement within Yahwism to which I have drawn attention are perhaps due to its international setting. Similar proverbial, instructive and reflective material is to be found in Egyptian, Assyrian, and Babylonian literature. For example, the formal similarity of Proverbs 1–9 to Egyptian Instruction literature has been demonstrated by several scholars,[43] and it seems clear that Proverbs 22:17–24:22 is indebted to

---

[36] Kelsey, *Eccentric Existence*, vol. 1, pp. 174–5.

[37] Kelsey, *Eccentric Existence*, vol. 1, p. 191.

[38] On this lack of response, see my Chapter 11 on the rejection of wisdom.

[39] Kelsey, *Eccentric Existence*, vol. 1, p. 207.

[40] Kelsey, *Eccentric Existence*, vol. 1, p. 160.

[41] Kelsey, *Eccentric Existence*, vol. 1, pp. 193–4.

[42] Kelsey, *Eccentric Existence*, vol. 1, p. 200.

[43] Christa Kayatz, *Studien zu Proverbien 1–9* (Neukirchen-Vluyn: Neukirchener Verlag, 1966), pp. 15–17; R. N. Whybray, *Wisdom in Proverbs: The Concept of Wisdom in Proverbs 1–9:45* (London: SCM, 1967), pp. 33–70; William McKane, *Proverbs. A New Approach* (London: SCM, 1970), pp. 262–7.

the Instruction of Amen-em-Opet in particular.[44] The world to which the wisdom self is related is thus a wide one, crossing the borders of Israel. To some extent, this affinity is to be expected, as the search for personal well-being and the transmission of the results of experience to successive generations in a proverbial form is found in virtually all cultures. There may, however, be a more specific reason in the case of Israel and its neighbours, as the wisdom method of education seems to have been used in Egypt and Mesopotamia, not only for the education of royal rulers, but for the training of a scribal class, to cope with the demands of bureaucracy in a centralized state which required literacy and numeracy for political administration and trading interests. The technique of 'wisdom' learning, as is now widely agreed, was the recording and classifying of experience in order to produce educational material which was both a tool for the teaching of literary skills (by the copying out of inherited sayings) and a collection of guidelines for successful living.[45]

Attempts have thus been made to demonstrate the existence of a distinct social class in Israel called 'wise men', a profession alongside prophets and priests, servicing the bureaucracy of the state and entirely responsible for the writings we have identified as 'wisdom literature'. Appeal is often made to the saying in Jeremiah 18:18 that 'instruction shall not perish from the priest, nor counsel from the wise (ḥākām), nor the word from the prophet'.[46] The beginning of 'the wise' has even been traced to the reign of Solomon and his pressing need for trained scribes in his centralized kingdom, establishing itself as a trading nation with its neighbours; to provide this expertise, it is suggested, he imported 'wisdom' techniques and set up schools, triggering a fabled reputation for wisdom and (much later) three pseudonomous books

---

[44] R. J. Williams denies the influence runs the other way, in 'The Alleged Semitic Original of the Wisdom of Amenemope', *Journal of Egyptian Archaeology* 47 (1961), pp. 100–6. See also James L. Crenshaw, *Old Testament Wisdom. An Introduction*. Revised and Enlarged (Louisville: Westminster/John Knox, 1998), pp. 60–2.

[45] For the experiental method of wisdom, see e.g. Walther Zimmerli, 'The Place and Limit of the Wisdom in the Framework of the Old Testament Theology', *Scottish Journal of Theology* 17 (1964), pp. 146–58; William McKane, *Prophets and Wise Men* (London: SCM, 1965), pp. 46–51; H. H. Schmid, *Wesen und Geschichte der Weisheit* (Berlin: de Gruyter 1966), pp. 155–60; R. E. Murphy, 'The Interpretation of Old Testament Wisdom Literature', *Interpretation* 23 (1969), pp. 293–7; R. B. Y. Scott, *The Way of Wisdom* (New York: Macmillan, 1971), pp. 48–59; Gerhard von Rad, *Wisdom in Israel*, trans. J. D. Martin (London: SCM, 1972), pp. 24–34, 74–87, 113–24; Crenshaw, *Old Testament Wisdom*, pp. 55–66; Leo G. Perdue, *Wisdom & Creation: The Theology of Wisdom Literature* (Eugene, Wipf and Stock, 2009), pp. 49–59. A challenge to the idea of a distinctive educational technique has, however been mounted by N. Whybray, *The Intellectual Tradition in the Old Testament* (Berlin: de Gruyter, 1974), pp. 69–70.

[46] So McKane, *Prophets and Wise Men*, pp. 42–4; more cautiously, Katharine Dell, *'Get Wisdom, Get Insight': An Introduction to Israel's Wisdom Literature* (London: Darton, Longman and Todd, 2000), p. 87.

attributed to him among the wisdom literature,[47] together with three collections assigned to him in the Book of Proverbs.[48] William McKane has found evidence for a distinct class of 'wise men' in traces of conflicts between the prophets and those who they dub 'the wise', especially in the ministry of Isaiah: it is significant that Isaiah complains, 'Ah, you who are wise in your own eyes, and shrewd in your own sight (Isa. 5:19–21).[49] McKane also finds these polemics to be evidence that early wisdom was essentially secular, or was a 'disciplined empiricism' of statecraft in which religious idealism had no place, which necessarily came into conflict with prophetic insistence about the will of Yahweh for the nation.[50]

We notice, however, that the contents of the wisdom literature itself are much less directed towards specific success in a scribal career than in Egypt or Babylon. It is feasible that a wisdom education was conventional for people in the higher classes of society regardless of their intended professions, so that even some of those concerned with the writing of sacral history could have been schooled by wisdom methods of gaining literacy, while those destined for government service could also have acquired more specialized wisdom techniques for their careers. Thus all those endebted to wisdom approaches need not have been wisdom scribes proper. Nor should we even assume that 'wisdom schools' were the only place where literacy could be gained, as it is unfortunately impossible to reconstruct the Israelite school system.[51] It is thus

---

[47] Koheleth, the Wisdom of Solomon, and the 'Song of Songs' if this is to be counted among the wisdom literature. I follow the majority of scholars of Israelite wisdom in not including the Song in my discussion here; William Horbury points out that it became central to mystical thinking about wisdom only after the Second Temple period: Horbury, 'The Books of Solomon in Ancient Mysticism' in David Ford and Graham Stanton (eds), *Reading Texts, Seeking Wisdom* (London: SCM, 2003), pp. 185–201.

[48] See the superscriptions at Proverbs 1:1, 10:1, 25:1. In support of the origins of wisdom education in government of the Solomonic era see: E. W. Heaton, *Solomon's New Men* (London: Thames and Hudson, 1974), *passim*; Walter Brueggemann, 'The Social Significance of Solomon as Patron of Wisdom' in John G. Gammie and Leo G. Perdue (eds),*The Sage in Israel and the Ancient Near East* (Winona Lake: Eisenbrauns, 1990), pp. 117–32, and (cautiously), Perdue, *Wisdom & Creation*, pp. 71–3. R. B. Y. Scott, 'Solomon and the Beginnings of Wisdom in Israel' in Martin Noth and D. Winton Thomas (eds), *Wisdom in Israel and the Ancient Near East*. Supplement to *Vetus Testamentum* 3 (Leiden: Brill, 1955), pp. 262–79, locates the beginnings of scribal wisdom in the reign of Hezekiah rather than Solomon (pp. 274–9), but has modified his position in *Way of Wisdom*, pp. 13–15.

[49] Cf. Isaiah 10:1–3, 19:11–13, 30:1–2, 31:1–2.

[50] McKane, *Prophets and Wise Men*, pp. 53–54, 69–71; see earlier, J. Fichtner, 'Isaiah among the Wise' in James L. Crenshaw (ed.), *Studies in Ancient Israelite Wisdom* (New York, KTAV, 1976), pp. 434–7.

[51] In support of the existence of scribal schools, see Heaton, *Solomon's New Men* (1968), pp. 74–5; André Lemaire, 'The Sage in School and Temple' in Gammie and Perdue, *The Sage in Israel*, pp. 165–81. G. I. Davies, 'Were there schools in Ancient Israel?' in John Day, Robert P. Gordon, H. G. M. Williamson (eds), *Wisdom in Ancient Israel: Essays in Honour of J. A. Emerton* (Cambridge: Cambridge University Press, 1998), pp. 209–11 gives qualified assent. Those proposing a variety of schools (in private homes, government buildings, sanctuaries, gates, and courtyards) include H. J. Hermisson, *Studien zur israelitischen Spruchweisheit*

Setting the Scene

probably better to regard the literature we have as collections of material which have emerged from several social and cultural contexts within Israelite society, but which share a basic method of learning and view of the world, recording and transmitting packets of experience and assuming that the world is amenable to attentive and appreciative investigation. We might then speak of a 'wisdom movement' or 'wisdom mood' rather than a 'wisdom school' (just as I am suggesting a 'late-modern mood' in our present world). Some of this material must indeed have come from scribal schools, but (as Scott suggests),[52] other has come from accumulated folk wisdom, some from education in the home, some from the work of counsellors to the royal court, and some from unidentified thinkers who had an intellectual curiosity about their physical environment and a moral concern for human life. Finally, in a later development (probably from the time of the Exile), existing literary and oral forms of wisdom were adapted for the purpose of religious instruction in the Torah.

The impact of this last convergence can be seen on later material in Proverbs (especially in parts of the Instruction of Chapters 1–9), in some additions to the books of Job and Koheleth,[53] on the Septuagintal wisdom books and in a number of late Psalms. In older material from the Hebrew Bible, wisdom themes have been identified in passages such as the 'Joseph Narrative', the 'Succession Narrative', and the prophets;[54] in fact the hunt for wisdom high and low in recent scholarship has probably been pursued with excessive enthusiasm. If these *are* genuine traces of wisdom thinking, then they may be explained either as evidence of a power-struggle between 'realpolitik' wisdom on the one hand and the prophetic movement and priestly establishment on the other (as McKane proposes), or simply as evidence of the widely diffused mood of wisdom. My own preference is for the latter explanation. Where criticism of 'wisdom' appears (such as perhaps in the fall story of Genesis 3),[55] this may not be an attack on a professional class, or on the

---

(Neukirchen-Vluyn: Neukirchener Verlag, 1968), pp. 98–103, von Rad, *Wisdom,* pp. 16–18, Perdue, *Wisdom & Creation,* pp. 72–3. The existence of any scribal schools at all is challenged by Whybray, *Intellectual Tradition,* pp. 33–43.

[52] R. B. Y. Scott, 'The Study of the Wisdom Literature', *Interpretation* 24 (1970), p. 29.

[53] These will be explored later in this book. See the end of the section 'Wisdom as Torah' in Chapter 10.

[54] See e.g. R. N. Whybray, *The Succession Narrative* (London: SCM, 1968), pp. 56–95; Gerhard von Rad, 'The Joseph Narrative and Ancient Wisdom' in von Rad, *The Problem of the Hexateuch and Other Essays,* trans. E. T. Dicken (Edinburgh: Oliver & Boyd, 1966)), pp. 292–300; Samuel Terrien, 'Amos and Wisdom' in Crenshaw (ed.), *Studies in Ancient Israelite Wisdom,* pp. 448–55; Luis Alonso-Schökel, 'Sapiential and Covenant Themes in Genesis 2–3' in Crenshaw (ed.), *Studies in Ancient Israelite Wisdom,* pp. 468–80; A. A. Mackintosh, 'Hosea and the Wisdom Tradition' in Day, Gordon and Williamson (eds), *Wisdom in Ancient Israel,* pp. 14–31. For some useful criticisms, see James L. Crenshaw, 'Method in Determining Wisdom Influence upon "Historical" Literature', *Journal of Biblical Literature* 88 (1969), pp. 129–42.

[55] So Treier, *Virtue and the Voice of God,* pp. 36–40; Alonso-Schökel, 'Sapiential and Covenant Themes', p. 53.

methods of wisdom education in general, but on the kind of wisdom that has no orientation towards the presence and activity of Yahweh in creation. Suffice it to say, in the light of my advocacy of a wisdom 'mood' or 'movement', that when I use the term 'the wise' in this book, I mean not a single class of people but all those involved in teaching from a wisdom perspective, whose work is enshrined in the wisdom books of the Hebrew Bible and the Septuagint.

I have already suggested that common ground exists between ancient Hebrew wisdom and the late-modern world in a sense of the elusiveness of the self and the world. In sketching the story of wisdom, we must note that this sense increases as time goes by. Wisdom begins as a fairly confident enterprise, assuming that the world and the human self are for the most part open to exploration, yielding their secrets to a loving attentiveness. Scepticism increases in later products of the movement in the post-Exilic period, showing a loss of confidence in the results of the wisdom approach to experience: this is expressed notably in wrestling with the problem of suffering in Job, in Koheleth's sense of futility, in the despair of Proverbs 30:1–5, and classically in the cry of Job Chapter 28:

> But where shall wisdom be found?
> And where is the place of understanding?
> Mortals do not know the way to it . . .
> It is hidden from the eyes of all living. (Job 28:12–13, 21)

This loss of confidence seems to be met by the exalting of Torah as an accessible form of wisdom in Ben Sira, and by the presentation of wisdom as the immanent divine Spirit in the Wisdom of Solomon.

But we should avoid supposing *either* that there was an absolute and sudden change from an attitude of confidence to a sense of hiddenness, *or* that there was no shift of consciousness at all. Those who lay stress on a shift from optimism to pessimism find an overall reason for it in such factors as the failure of a doctrine of retribution any longer to be convincing,[56] an increasing sense of the transcendence of God,[57] and the shock of the exile.[58] Although

---

[56] O. S. Rankin, *Israel's Wisdom Literature* (Edinburgh: T & T Clark, 1936), pp. 93–7; J. Coert Rylaarsdam, *Revelation in Jewish Wisdom Literature* (Chicago: University of Chicago, 1946), pp. 74–7; Zimmerli, 'Place and Limit', p. 158; Schmid, *Wesen und Geschichte der Weisheit*, pp. 246–8; Murphy, 'Interpretation', pp. 299–301; John L. McKenzie, 'Reflections on Wisdom', *Journal of Biblical Literature* 86 (1967), p. 4.

[57] Rylaarsdam, *Revelation*, pp. 88–92; Norman Snaith, *The Book of Job* (London: SCM, 1968), pp. 94–9; Martin Hengel, *Judaism and Hellenism. Studies in their Encounter in Palestine during the Early Hellenistic Period*, 2 Volumes, trans. J. Bowden (London: SCM, 1973), vol. 1, p. 121.

[58] Burton L. Mack, 'Wisdom, Myth and Mythology', *Interpretation* 24 (1970), pp. 56–8; Mack, *Logos und Sophia: Untersuchungen zur Weisheitstheologie im hellenistischen Judentum* (Göttingen: Vandenhoeck & Ruprecht, 1973), pp. 45–9; cf. James L. Crenshaw, 'Popular Questioning of the Justice of God in Ancient Israel', *Zeitschrift für die Alttestamentlichen Wissenschaft* 82 (1970), pp. 384, 389–94.

such views may concede the presence of less confident elements in earlier wisdom, they judge that the change in attitude is more significant than any continuity. On the other hand, it has been argued (notably by Gerhard von Rad) that there is a blend of confidence with acknowledgement of limitations at every stage of the wisdom tradition: 'every period has its own conflicts with reality...there is always something that cannot be accommodated'.[59] The relatively early practical wisdom of Proverbs (especially 16:1–9) recognizes limitations in the wisdom method, and this argument gains strength from the presence already in international wisdom literature of pessimistic as well as confident works. The increasing emphasis upon the limitations of wisdom in Israel, urges von Rad, is simply the treating of mystery as an object of study rather than an aspect to be allowed for in studying other things: the attention given to it, but not the quality of its pessimism, increases. But to take a view which sees no heightening of a sense of elusiveness within wisdom means that such a work as Koheleth has to be treated as untypical of the wisdom schools, as an eccentric individual, since he has certainly abandoned any confidence in interpreting the face of the world. Von Rad concludes, 'This work is not the expression of any school; we are rather justified in considering him as an outsider completely free of tradition.'[60] Yet Koheleth cannot be dismissed so easily from the Israelite wisdom movement as an 'outsider': his evident familiarity with the style and manner of earlier proverbial literature in Israel and the breaking out of something very like his point of view in Proverbs 30:1–5 are only two indications that his lack of confidence in the wisdom method may very well be connected with that found elsewhere in the post-exilic period. As we draw upon the wisdom tradition, we shall explore the way that a sense of the elusiveness of the world and the self as objects of study continues throughout the period, and yet is radicalized as time passes, and we will ask why this should be so.

Another contested question I have already raised in mentioning McKane's stress on the 'secularity' of wisdom is the place of the wisdom movement within Israel's Yahwistic faith. While some commentators have argued for faith in Yahweh as an essential component of wisdom in Israel from the beginning,[61] others have observed the detachment of wisdom from the tradition of God's saving acts in history, and concluded that it was at first entirely

---

[59] Von Rad, *Wisdom*, p. 110.

[60] Von Rad, *Wisdom*, p. 235.

[61] Von Rad, *Wisdom*, pp. 53–73; Berend Gemser, 'The Spiritual Structure of Biblical Aphoristic Wisdom' in *Adhuc Loquitur: Collected Essays*, ed. A. van Selms and A. S. van der Woude (Leiden: Brill, 1968), pp. 138–49; Harmut Gese, *Lehre und Wirklichkeit in der alten Weisheit: Studien zu den Sprüchen Salomos und zu dem Buche Hiob* (Tübingen: Mohr, 1958), pp. 35–50; R. E. Clements, *Wisdom in Theology* (Carlisle: Paternoster, 1992), pp. 151–9; Crenshaw, *Old Testament Wisdom*, pp. 76–82; Stuart Weeks, *Early Israelite Wisdom* (Oxford: Clarendon Press, 1994), pp. 57–73.

separated from Israel's faith and only later incorporated into it.[62] Those on both sides of this complex question make some assumptions which we shall be querying as our study progresses. The first assumption is related to the increasing sense of the limits of wisdom. It is assumed that the limitations recognized within the practical wisdom material of Proverbs must inevitably be an acknowledgement of the sovereign activity of God. Thus, those who draw a picture of wisdom as Yahwistic from the first claim the sense of limitation as evidence for this picture.[63] On the other hand, those who argue for the secularity of early wisdom find that material which speaks of limitations (e.g. 16:1–9) necessarily excludes itself as late.[64] Indeed, McKane suggests a wholesale reinterpretation of early secular sayings by sayings which now mention Yahweh. But it may well be that there are reasons for the elusiveness of the world as an object of study in the nature of the world itself, and in the relation of the self to it. Even if texts which associate a sense of human uncertainty with the activity of Yahweh are late, we have not said all there is to say about the hiddenness of wisdom.

Further, when the Yahwistic character of early wisdom is being claimed or denied, it is tacitly assumed that what is under discussion is whether instruction is the revealed gift of Yahweh. This is assumed even when distinctions are rightly drawn between the religious attitudes of wisdom, prophecy, and priesthood: Gemser speaks, for example, of the wise having a 'horizontal' view of revelation (through experience) rather than 'vertical' (through prophetic word and priestly Torah).[65] With even less regard for distinction of attitude, von Rad speaks of the wise supposedly listening for the word of God spoken in the depths of creation (the 'Voice of Primeval Order'[66]). But we must be alert to the possibility that wisdom may, at some stages in its development at least, have a place for God in its approach to the world without any idea at all of *receiving* instruction from God, even in a form mediated through creation. As we have already seen with its distinctive approach to creation, wisdom may be Yahwistic in its own way and add a totally new dimension to Yahwism which is not apparent in either prophetic or priestly religion. Correspondingly, while it may be possible to demonstrate that

---

[62] McKane, *Prophets and Wise Men*, pp. 48–54; McKane, *Proverbs* pp. 1–22; J. Fichtner, *Die Altorientalische Weisheit in ihrer israelitisch-jüdischen Ausprägung* (1933), pp. 24–7; R. B. Y. Scott, *Proverbs - Ecclesiastes*, The Anchor Bible (New York: Doubleday, 1965), pp. 17–18, and Scott, 'Wise and Foolish, Righteous and Wicked' in *Studies in the Religion of Ancient Israel*. Supplement to *Vetus Testamentum* 23 (Leiden: Brill, 1972), pp. 146–65; cf. Whybray, *Wisdom in Proverbs*, pp. 21–6: early wisdom was 'by no means opposed to religion but was based on human reason and so was basically anthropocentric rather than theocentric'.

[63] Von Rad, *Wisdom*, pp. 98ff.; Rylaarsdam, *Revelation*, pp. 71–4; Schmid, *Wesen und Geschichte der Weisheit*, p. 147.

[64] McKane, *Proverbs*, pp. 15–16, 495–7; Scott, *Proverbs-Ecclesiastes*, p. 17.

[65] Gemser, 'Spiritual Structure', p. 148, endorsing Rylaarsdam, *Revelation*, p. 55.

[66] Von Rad, *Wisdom*, pp. 154–66.

wisdom sayings which speak of teaching as being *given* by Yahweh are late, this does not in itself mean that there are no religious elements in early wisdom.

AN ENCOUNTER WITH MANY VOICES AND MANY EYES

My intention is to develop a wisdom-theology for the age in which we are living, connecting with the mood of our late-modern world, and drawing upon the wisdom literature of Ancient Israel, inter-testamental Judaism, and early Christianity. Inevitably, using the form of a book, this will be an encounter between texts. I have suggested that this is not a merely arbitrary meeting-place since there is a quest for 'wisdom' in our time, and because the ethos of ancient wisdom and the mood of late-modernity have in common an interest in—perhaps even an anxiety about—the relation between the self and the world, as well as in the possibility of finding traces of an ultimate reality that transcends the self and yet is embodied in this interaction. Religious people name this final reality God; Christians believe that the inexhaustible depths of this name call for expression as a communion of relationships, or Trinity. But beyond any claim for relevance, all encounters between texts are going to be full of rich possibilities, inspired by what Mikhail Bakhtin called 'the dialogic imagination'.

In his early work on Dostoevsky, Bakhtin observed that 'a plurality of independent and unmerged voices and consciousnesses, a genuine polyphony of fully valid voices is in fact the chief characteristic of Dostoevsky's novels.'[67] From this critique he developed a general theory of literature in which no utterance, word, or text is ever spoken or written in isolation, but always calls to mind other utterances, words, or texts which either precede it or come after it in response.[68] In fact, he extends this principle beyond literature to life itself, writing that in the make-up of nearly every utterance of everyday living 'a significant number of words can be identified that are implicitly or explicitly admitted as someone else's', so that 'an intense interaction and struggle between one's own and another's word is being waged'.[69] He explains:

> The word, directed toward its object, enters a dialogically agitated and tension-filled environment of alien words, value judgments and accents, weaves in and

---

[67] Mikhail M. Bakhtin, *Problems of Dostoevsky's Poetics*, ed. and trans. C. Emerson (Minneapolis: University of Minnesota Press, 1984), p. 6.

[68] See 'Discourse in the Novel' in Mikhail M. Bakhtin, *The Dialogic Imagination: Four Essays*, ed. and trans. C. Emerson and M. Holquist (Austin: University of Texas Press, 1981), pp. 259–422.

[69] Bakhtin, 'Discourse', p. 354.

out of complex interrelationships, merges with some, recoils from others, intersects with yet a third group: and all this may crucially shape discourse, may leave a trace in all its semantic layers, may complicate its expression and influence its entire stylistic profile.[70]

As Juliana Claassens comments, 'He argues that the text comes alive only by coming into contact with another text (with context). At this point of contact between texts, it is as if a light flashes that illuminates both the posterior and the anterior.'[71] Thus, Bakhtin is of the opinion that the real meaning of a text develops on the boundary between texts: 'The word lives, as it were, on the boundary between its own context and another, alien, context.'[72] Meaning is to be found, not in one text alone, but in the midst of the dialogue of interacting voices. This process happens over many years, or in what Bakhtin calls 'the great time', or the 'infinite and unfinalized dialogue in which no meaning dies'.[73] Great works such as Shakespeare continue to live in the distant future, and 'in the process of their posthumous life they are enriched with new meanings, new significance'. This theory is thus not just about discerning what might be happening within a particular text, but about the work of the reader as author constructing an 'imaginary dialogue' out of 'dialogic imagination'.

In Chapter 10 I intend to take up the insight that 'the word lives on the boundary' in exploring the relationship between the Bible and other texts, but here I want to apply Bakhtin's theory to the whole project of this book. Elsewhere I have used the model of 'dialogue' to bring creative literature together with theology,[74] and although the concept of dialogue for this kind of project has come under attack in recent years[75] it still seems useful in affirming that each discipline must be allowed to be truly itself, not manipulated by the other, while contributing to a mutual illumination and the emergence of new meaning. As Hans-Georg Gadamer puts it, who also develops the method of dialogue:

> What emerges in its truth is the logos, which is neither mine nor yours and
> hence so far transcends the subjective opinions of the partners to the dialogue

---

[70] Bakhtin, 'Discourse', p. 276.

[71] Juliana M. Claassens, 'Biblical Theology as Dialogue: Continuing the Conversation on Mikhail Bakhtin and Biblical Theology', *Journal of Biblical Literature* 122 (2003), p. 130. I am much indebted to this article.

[72] Bakhtin, 'Discourse', p. 284.

[73] Mikhail M. Bakhtin, *Speech Genres and Other Late Essays*, ed. C. Emerson and M. Holquist, trans. V. W. McGee (Austin: University of Texas Press, 1986), p. 169.

[74] Paul S. Fiddes, *Freedom and Limit: A Dialogue between Literature and Christian Doctrine* (Basingstoke: Macmillan, 1991), pp. 27–46.

[75] Georg Langenhorst, *Theologie und Literatur: Ein Handbuch* (Darmstadt: Wissenschaftliche Buchgesellschaft, 2005) prefers 'encounter' to 'dialogue', on the grounds that only people can participate in dialogues.

that even the person leading the conversation is always ignorant . . . [dialogue] is the art of the formation of concepts as the working out of the common meaning.[76]

In connecting theology with texts of our late-modern world, I am therefore wanting to allow these texts to speak in their own right. Though my aim is to develop a theology, I aim not to manipulate these texts to make them serve theological ends, but expect that the voices within them will shape the theology itself. However, because I am engaging in a three-way exercise of bringing together modern theology, ancient Israelite wisdom, and the context of the late-modern world, it might be better to use Bakhtin's alternative language of 'polyphony', and to speak of a conversation with many participants. There are many layers of dialogue going on at once and 'many voices' seems appropriate.

This principle lies behind the shape of most of the chapters in parts two and three of this book. Each begins by identifying some aspect of the intellectual context of our late-modern world, or some feature of the postmodern condition. The central section engages in an exegesis of texts from ancient wisdom material in the Bible, sometimes in considerable detail. Finally, I stage a conversation in which voices from late-modern texts, the biblical material, and Christian theology interact in a polyphony, with the purpose of making a Christian wisdom theology.[77] Before embarking on this process, the next two chapters will sketch the intellectual mood of the late-modern world rather generally, opening up themes that will be continued at the beginning of each of the chapters in parts two and three.

Some justification may be needed for beginning each of these chapters with some aspect of the mood of the late-modern world. Is this, a hostile critic may ask, an instance of the method of correlation rather than dialogue or conversation? The term 'correlation' was made familiar by Paul Tillich who proposed it as a tool for the 'reading' of a culture, with culture raising questions in its own style and theologians offering answers from their resources in Christian symbols, which are themselves rooted in revelation.[78] Cultural movements, urged Tillich, represent a common human vocabulary for the questions of anxiety, death, guilt, forgiveness, and redemption to which theologians can give responses. Those who followed Tillich saw the need for revision in what seemed to be a one-way street between culture and theology. David Tracy, for example, insists that culture and the Christian tradition must be allowed to

---

[76] Hans-Georg Gadamer, *Truth and Method*, English Translation (London: Sheed & Ward), p. 331.

[77] The exception to this structure is Chapters 4 and 5, where the scheme is present but spread out over the two chapters.

[78] Paul Tillich, *Systematic Theology*. Combined Volume (London: James Nisbet), vol. 1, pp. 67–73.

interrogate each other, both parties posing questions and answers, both illuminating and correcting the other.[79] But, in defence of Tillich, I suggest that there is already a basis for this revised view of correlation in Tillich's own thinking, since he believes that human beings only ask questions about ultimate meaning because they are already seized and held by the 'spiritual presence'. At its roots, thought Tillich, culture is linked to the depths of Being, so that God is in our asking of questions about meaning as much as in the answers.[80]

This is admittedly a theological basis for dialogue, but then Christian theology will inevitably look for a theological reason for the polyphony I have identified. In both poetic and philosophical speech, the mind reaches out towards mystery, towards a reality for which we feel an ultimate concern, but which eludes empirical investigation. As Jacques Derrida proposes, the consciousness transcends itself towards something other than the world which it treats so often as an object to be dominated; it is open to something which both promises and threatens to 'come' into our present moment without ever being possessed.[81] With Kant, we might regard this movement towards the absolutely Other merely as a plumbing of the depths of our own feelings. But we might also regard this Other as the mystery of God, and think that our very capacity for self-transcendence is being prompted by the self-opening of the mystery to us. As Paul Tillich expresses it, we have ultimate concerns because what is ultimate—God as Being itself—is already participating in our existence. Symbols which are apparently non-religious thus open up a way into a final reality which is already present in our experience, though in a hidden way.[82] Similarly, Karl Rahner observes that the human spirit appears to have a natural openness to the infinite. A person experiences himself or herself as a 'transcendent being', able to go on asking questions endlessly about existence: 'the infinite horizon of human questioning is experienced as a horizon which recedes further and further the more answers man can discover'.[83] In fact, however, Rahner maintains that this openness to mystery can never be separated from God's own openness to us in gracious self-communication. The movements of grace and nature are always bound up together, so that God's offer of God's self to us is prior to all human freedom and

---

[79] David Tracy, *The Analogical Imagination* (London: SCM, 1981), p. 64.

[80] Tillich, *Systematic Theology*, vol. 1, pp. 88–93, 181–4; vol. 2, pp. 203–4; vol. 3, pp. 235–7.

[81] Jacques Derrida, 'Of an Apocalyptic Tone Newly Adopted in Philosophy', trans. J. Leavey, in Harold Coward and Toby Foshay (eds), *Derrida and Negative Theology* (Albany: State University of New York Press, 1992), pp. 63–6.

[82] Paul Tillich, *Theology of Culture*, ed. R. C. Kimball (New York: Oxford University Press, 1959), pp. 54, 72–3.

[83] Karl Rahner, *Foundations of Christian Faith: An Introduction to the Idea of Christianity*, trans. W. V. Dych (London: Darton, Longman and Todd, 1978), p. 32.

self-understanding.[84] To be a person is actually to take part in 'the event of a supernatural self-communication of God'.

There is then, Rahner suggest, a universal revelation giving rise to a knowledge of God which is non-conceptual and non-objective; Rahner identifies this as 'transcendental' revelation, a 'pre-apprehension' (*Vorgriff*) of God which happens in the human orientation towards mystery. By contrast, there are also moments when the self-giving of God takes form in historic events and gives rise to deliberate concepts (what Rahner calls 'categorical' revelation).[85] Some events 'stand out' as decisive moments of disclosure, insisting that they be noticed and calling for a whole reorientation of life from the participant. They also demand conceptualization in an attempt to understand them, and doctrine emerges. At the centre of particular revelation like this, Christians find the 'final' revelation of God in the life of Christ and the historical events surrounding it. 'Final' indicates of course not 'last' in time, but a completeness in the light of which all other revelations are to be interpreted.

Beginning, therefore, with the late-modern context is not at all 'allowing the world to set the agenda for theology' as other critics may protest. It is giving the first voice to non-theological writers of our present age, but in the conviction that there is *already* a conversation going on in which they are involved. In Bakhtin's sense, this is because every word or utterance is responding to utterances or texts that have preceded it, and because every word or utterance is related also to responses that are going to be made. Bakhtin argues that texts are always constructed in anticipation of possible responses to them.[86] In the case of the whole range of late-modern writers I consider in this book, there is a clear intention to enter into conversation with theology, whether there is the throwing down of the challenge that 'God is dead', or whether there is an interest in using God-language to 'save the name'[87] of 'otherness' that breaks open the 'sameness' of the self. Indeed, some philosophers have complained that recent continental philosophy has made such a 'turn to the theological' that the achievements of phenomenology are being undermined by language such as 'an opening to the invisible, to the Other, to a pure "givenness" and to "archi-revelation"'.[88] Now, beneath what Baktin identifies as this kind of ongoing conversation, the theologian, from the perspective

---

[84] Rahner, *Foundations*, p. 127.

[85] Rahner, *Foundations*, pp. 153–62.

[86] Bakhtin, *Speech Genres*, p. 94.

[87] Jacques Derrida, *On the Name*, ed. Thomas Dutoit (Stanford: Stanford University Press, 1995), p. 58.

[88] Dominique Janicaud, 'The Theological Turn of French Phenomenology' in Janicaud (ed.), *Phenomenology and the 'Theological Turn': The French Debate*, trans. B. G. Prusak (New York: Fordham University Press, 2000), p. 17.

of belief in a self-revealing God, will also find a participation in another conversation, the utterance of the divine word.

It should be remembered, however, that 'word' is only one metaphor for the self-giving of God. The language of 'polyphony' must not lead us into privileging the spoken word over the 'seeing' to which wisdom alerts us. Here I suggest we will have to diverge a little from Bakhtin. His theory of intertextuality was based on the conviction that the basic linguistic unit was the spoken utterance, since he judged that it was this that anticipated a response and engaged the speaker in dialogue.[89] The voice, he thought, is prior to writing. As my study proceeds I shall be offering reasons to doubt this prejudice which stems from Plato. For now, it is sufficient to recognize (with Bakhtin himself) that the word is, in fact, not only heard but seen, as an image inscribed on a page, and that it bears witness to the world as a network of signs. Polyphony of voice can be complemented by an interweaving of many lines of vision, by what Jacques Lacan describes as an 'interlocking gaze' in which seer and seen only have partial sight of the other when looking from their individual perspective.[90]

Our exploration of wisdom will throw new light on how a universal participation in the self-disclosure of God might be happening. Whether or not this theological perspective results in the 'manipulation' of others will be shown, I suggest, in how much theology allows itself to be shaped by exterior speech, alien eyes, and non-theological texts, rather than expecting to be merely re-affirmed in its own set habits of thought.

[89] Bakhtin, *Speech Genres*, pp. 67–75.
[90] Jacques Lacan, *The Four Fundamental Concepts of Psychoanalysis*, trans. A. Sheridan (New York: Norton, 1981), p. 106.

2

The Mood of the Late-Modern World

It is doubful whether we can properly speak of the age in which we live as 'postmodern', though the label is often used, and has a limited usefulness. The force of the prefix 'post' is in the widespread rejection of many aspects of 'modernity', a period which is usually reckoned to begin with the European Enlightenment. However, it is questionable whether we have as yet left modernity entirely behind, and a spate of neologisms such as 'metamodernism', 'digimodernism', 'altermodernism', or 'transmodernism'[1] only serve to reinforce this suspicion. On the one hand, many of the aspects of modernity persist in present-day culture. While there is some scepticism about the 'assured results' of the scientific method, for example, this has not shaken a general reliance on technology, and the picture is an ambiguous one as physical scientists themselves are ready to admit areas of mystery in their craft (as we shall see in a later chapter). Again, suspicion about 'grand narratives' inside the academy has not undermined reliance outside it on a global theory of free markets, or on an uncritical acceptance of the structure of international corporations. On the other hand, so-called 'postmodern thinking' remains indebted to philosophies that developed in the modern period; as we shall see, it owes a large debt to Kant, Nietzsche, Saussure, and Husserl, among others. The term 'late-modern' acknowledges that the situation is a mixed one – elements of modernity remain alongside, sometimes muddled up with, a deconstruction of much of the modern mindset.[2]

[1] See Timotheus Velmeulen and Robin van den Akker, 'Notes on Metamodernism', *Journal of Aesthetics & Culture* 2 (2010), open access, aesthetics&culture.net; Paul C. Vitz, 'From the Modern and Postmodern Selves to the Transmodern Self', in Paul C. Vitz and Susan M. Felch (eds), *The Self. Beyond the Postmodern Crisis* (Wilmington: ISI Books, 2006), pp. xi–xxii.

[2] See Jürgen Habermas, 'The Unfinished Project of Modernity' in Maurizio Passerin d'Entrèves and Seyla Benhabib, *Habermas and the Unfinished Project of Modernity: Critical essays on the philosophical discourse of modernity* (Cambridge, Mass: MIT, 1997), pp. 38–55.

SELF AND THE WORLD IN MODERNITY

In sketching the mood of the late-modern world, we need to begin with its attack on the 'self' of modernity, a critique which is a basic element of our late-modern ethos, making clear that we cannot recover the former innocence of a self in control of its own destiny. To clarify use of terms, I suggest it is appropriate to distinguish between the project of the self in 'modernity' on the one hand, and 'modernism' on the other, the latter indicating a cultural movement from about 1850 to the mid-twentieth century.

'Modernism', involving artists, poets, philosophers, and theologians, was a natural successor to Romanticism, representing a rejection of many certainties of the Enlightenment – especially its assumptions about rational order. Sensitive to radical changes happening in society, it was characterized by either an overturning or a reformulation of traditions, and prioritized dislocation and fragmentation over harmony in art and life. It was (in T. S. Eliot's words) 'time for a thousand visions and revisions'.[3] However, it continued the Enlightenment focus on the subject, with a central interest in the nature of self-consciousness.[4] While questioning the identification of consciousness with reason alone, detecting currents of desire, deceptions, illusions, and fantasy beneath the surface (with the help of Freud), it still placed subjectivity in the foreground. We might then regard 'modernism' as a later phase in modernity. The 'postmodern' challenge to the dominance of the self over the world can thus be regarded as a reaction against both modernity and modernism, but since 'modernity' is the longer and more basic project it might be more accurate to speak of 'the postmodern mood' or 'postmodernity'. The late-modern age, I am suggesting, is strongly but not exclusively characterized by this postmodernity.

My interest is not in a general account of either modernity or postmodernity, but in the particular issue of the relation of the self to the world. I propose then to identify three forms of this self–world relation in modernity, three attempts to negotiate the relation of subject to object. The postmodern mood seeks to negate these attempts, gaining its character from this denial, and in this study I aim to show that the tradition of Israelite wisdom has already anticipated much of this reaction. The first two forms, I suggest, belong to 'modernity' as a whole, and the third to 'modernism'. In the first, the world is an object that is detached from the subject; in the second, it is an object that necessarily expresses the subject; and in the third it is a threat to the subject. Each of these forms has prompted a kind of theological version of itself, bringing self, world, and God into a certain configuration which has shaped

---

[3] T. S. Eliot, 'The Love Song of Alfred J. Prufrock' in *Complete Poems and Plays*, p. 14.
[4] See Patricia Waugh, *Practising Postmodernism, Reading Modernism* (London: Edward Arnold, 1992), pp. 73–81.

theology, and which still makes a valuable contribution to the theological enterprise. Each of them, however, fails sufficiently to attend to the world in its own right, and each fosters the tendency of the self to try and control or absorb the world around it.

(a) *The world as detached from the self*

The first form of this relation is the making of a division, not just a distinction, between subject and object. It has become widespread in *theological* accounts of the 'modern self' to trace the detachment of self from the world, and the consequent pretensions of self to master the world, to the influence of the thought of Descartes and—a century later—Kant.[5] This analysis has been supported by a number of philosophers, including Hannah Arendt and Charles Taylor.[6] For the most part I intend to subscribe to this account, although it should become clear that I do not think it follows that theology should move entirely behind the Enlightenment (and especially Kant) in a kind of nostalgic retreat to a mediaeval world-view. We should also be alert to parodies of Descartes and Kant which present exaggerated versions of their thought about the thinking and ethical self.

Descartes was haunted by the problem of certainty. He could not find this in knowledge of the world, since any representation of the world within the mind seemed unreliable, and he concluded that certainty was only to be found in the process of thinking itself; within thought, indeed, there was room for radical doubt. 'I think', famously said Descartes, 'therefore I am.' Or to put it another way, 'the proposition *I am, I exist*, is necessarily true whenever it is put forward by me or conceived in my mind.'[7] God was not to be found through orientation to moral values which supposedly existed in some order of reality outside the mind, but through the engagement of the self with moral issues within its own reason. The subject thinks God and the world because God creates these thoughts in the human mind.[8] For a person to follow virtue, he thus proposes,

[5] E.g. Jürgen Moltmann, *Theology of Hope: On the Ground and Implications of a Christian Eschatology*, trans. J. W. Leitch (London: SCM, 1967), pp. 45–50, 62–6; Anthony C. Thiselton, *Interpreting God and the Postmodern Self: On Meaning, Manipulation and Promise* (Edinburgh, T & T Clark, 1995), pp. 49, 120–3; Helmut Thielicke, *The Evangelical Faith, Volume I. Prolegomena: The Relation of Theology to Modern Thought Forms*, trans. G. Bromiley (Grand Rapids: Eerdmans, 1974), pp. 32–5, 140–2, 152–3; Kelsey, *Eccentric Existence*, vol. 1, pp. 84–92; cf. Wolfhart Pannenberg, *Anthropology in Theological Perspective*, trans. M. J. O'Connell (Edinburgh: T & T Clark, 1985), pp. 33, 85–6, 214–20 (critique qualified by appreciation for Kant's account of radical evil).
[6] Charles Taylor, *Sources of the Self. The Making of Modern Identity* (Cambridge: Cambridge University Press, 1989), pp. 143–58, 355–67; Hannah Arendt, *The Human Condition*. Second Edition (Chicago: University of Chicago Press, 1998), pp. 155–8, 254, 284, 295–7.
[7] René Descartes, *Meditations on First Philosophy. With Selections from the Objections and Replies*, trans. J. Cottingham (Cambridge: Cambridge University Press, 1986), Meditation II, p. 17. Cf. already Augustine, *City of God* XI.26.
[8] Descartes, *Meditations*, III, pp. 26–8; *Objections and Replies*, III, pp. 76–8.

is 'never to fail of his own will to . . . execute all the things which he judges to be the best'.[9] Taylor judges that 'Descartes' ethic, just as much as his epistemology, calls for disengagement from world and body and the assumption of an instrumental stance towards them.'[10] Modernity has been characterized by a 'turn to the subject', and this was given formative expression in Descartes' distinction between the *res cogitans* and the *res extensans*, a fundamental dualism between the cognitive self and its physical embodiment and environment. This meant, stresses Taylor, that the world and the body were not simply objects to the subject, but were 'objectified': he judges that 'where the Platonic soul realizes its eternal nature by becoming absorbed in the supersensible, the Cartesian discovers and affirms his immaterial nature by objectifying the bodily'.[11] Knowledge of the world, while falling short of certainty, does at least offer control over the world; so Descartes writes in his *Discourse on Method* that

> it is possible to attain knowledge which is very useful in life, and , , , we may find a practical philosophy by means of which, knowing the force and the action of fire, water, air, the stars, heavens and all other bodies that environ us . . . we can in the same way employ them in all those uses to which they are adapted, and *thus render ourselves the masters and possessors of nature.*[12]

Hannah Arendt judges that the legacy from Descartes has been 'an exclusive concern with the self . . . an attempt to reduce all experiences, with the world as well as other human beings, to experiences between man and himself'[13] and that 'the Cartesian solution was to choose as ultimate point of reference the pattern of the human mind itself, which assures itself of reality and certainty within a framework of mathematical formulas which are its own products'.[14] It is possible here to produce a caricature of a Descartes who withdraws into the lonely seclusion of the rational self, and perhaps Arendt is guilty of this, writing of the Cartesian mind as being 'shut off from all reality'.[15] Descartes may make what Taylor calls an 'ontological cleft' between self and the material world,[16] but he also aims to overcome it, affirming that the mind needs to take account of, and even conform to, the dispositions of things that we find in the world or in our own bodies. But we get the sense that taking such account of the world is not because it commands our respect for its own sake, but because

---

[9] *The Philosophical Works of Descartes*, trans. E. S. Haldane and G. R. T. Ross (Cambridge: Dover, 1955), I.401–2.

[10] Taylor, *Sources*, p. 155.

[11] Taylor, *Sources*, p. 146.

[12] *Descartes, Philosophical Works*, I.119. My italics.

[13] Arendt, *Human Condition*, p. 254. See, more extensively, Chapter 4.

[14] Arendt, *Human Condition*, p. 284.

[15] Arendt, *Human Condition*, p. 284.

[16] Taylor, *Sources*, p. 145.

it is the rational thing to do, so that 'the new model of rational mastery which Descartes offers presents it as a matter of instrumental control' (Taylor).[17]

The nature of objective knowledge of the world is developed by Kant in his 'transcendental deduction' of the pure a priori categories of the understanding, expressed in the first *Critique*. For Kant, the world of phenomena presents sense impressions to the understanding, which perceives objects through applying to these impressions (or 'intuitions' of the sensibility) a set of concepts which pre-exist the act of cognition in the mind. These concepts of the understanding are a set of a priori categories which we all share: without them our intuitions would be, in Kant's terms, 'blind',[18] since things cannot be known 'in themselves' as 'noumena'.[19] The fact that we *do* have sense experience of phenomena means for Kant that we have to assume the necessary conditions for this experience, that is our set of already-existing categories. Phenomena are, to take a significant example, determined by the pre-existing category of causality;[20] this causality is necessary for our *experiences* of the world as a reality characterized by cause and effect, so that we classify causality as a 'law of nature'. Phenomena then are consigned to a realm of natural laws, bound by the necessities of cause and effect.[21] On the other hand, the subject has its freedom over against the world of objects through the exercise of its moral reason. The subject has autonomy in acting to carry out its moral duty, and so affirms itself against the constraints of both its own physical body and the physical world. As a 'noumenal' moral agent, the subject acts freely in a world of objects.[22] The religious implication of such a world-view is that God cannot be known as an object of perception, since God is not a phenomenon in the world to be presented to the understanding through the senses, and realities 'in themselves' are unknowable. Nevertheless, there is a place for religion in providing a motivation for moral action and moral struggle, with the postulation of a God as the supreme moral law-giver of the universe.[23] While in theory the moral will needs no other incentive than itself, there is a kind of practical necessity of religious motivation in the actual world in which we live, marked as it is by radical evil, and given that there are 'mysteries' within the moral will itself.[24] In the drive of the reason towards synthesis, the

---

[17] Taylor, *Sources*, p. 149.

[18] Immanuel Kant, *Critique of Pure Reason*, trans. N. Kemp Smith (London: Macmillan, 1933), p. 93.

[19] Kant, *Critique of Pure Reason*, pp. 87, 149.

[20] Kant, *Critique of Pure Reason*, pp. 223–4.

[21] Kant, *Critique of Pure Reason*, pp. 409–11.

[22] Kant, *Critique of Practical Reason*, trans. L. W. Beck (Indianapolis: Bobbs-Merrill, 1956), pp. 47–51, 59–63.

[23] Kant, *Critique of Practical Reason*, pp. 137–9, 142–6.

[24] Kant, *Religion within the Boundaries of Mere Reason and Other Writings*, ed. and trans. Alan Wood and George di Giovanni (Cambridge: Cambridge University Press, 1998), pp. 33–4, 140–7.

concept of God as Creator (together with the idea of the world 'as a whole') also provides motivation for exploration of natural phenomena.

Now, we could exaggerate the distinction in Kant between two worlds of 'practical reason' and 'theoretical reason', or between morality and nature, and so over-widen the gulf between subject and object. David Kelsey, for instance, depicts the Kantian moral agent as caught in a 'struggle against nature', rather as Sartre portrays the subject (for which, see further below), and finds that 'in exercising moral freedom, a subject as spirit is in conflict with itself as nature'.[25] To the contrary, it might be claimed that Kant is simply describing the way that the mind operates in the natural world, living in a tension between determinism and freedom. His theory of cognition does achieve an impressive integration between the mind, acting in its function as pure reason, with the empirical world, even though the cost is a certain determinism. Moreover, with regard to the moral function of the reason, a caricature of the Kantian ethical subject circulates as an isolated mind acting entirely independently, as if a hero of the moral imperative is doing abstract moral geometry in a room shut away from all human company. If, as moral philosophers have proposed, autonomy in Kant must be understood in the context of respecting all persons as 'ends rather than means', this places autonomy in the midst of a community of similarly rational beings, with an individual's decisions being subject to wider criticism.[26] It allows for elements of emotion and imagination in moral judgements. However, I suggest that the basic structure of an ontological gap between the ethical self and world remains, even if those set against the world are a community of justice rather than lonely individuals.

Kant, we may say, *contributes* to a modern mindset in which the self is seen as being both detached from nature and the controller of physical nature,[27] although he himself is more subtle in his analysis. His very notion that 'rational nature exists as an end in itself'[28] does imply, as Taylor suggests, that 'everything else in the universe can be treated as a mere means to our goals, whatever they are... their value is instrumental'.[29] As Kant puts it, other things have either a 'market value' or a 'fancy value', but only rational agents have 'dignity' (*Würde*).[30] In his third *Critique* Kant himself admits that

---

[25] Kelsey, *Eccentric Existence*, vol. 1, pp. 87–8. Here he seems to run Kant and theological Neo-Kantians such as Albrecht Ritschl together.

[26] See Onora O'Neill, *Constructions of Reason. Explorations of Kant's Practical Philosophy* (Cambridge: Cambridge University Press, 1989), pp. 105–6; Pamela Sue Anderson and Jordan Bell, *Kant and Theology* (London: T & T Clark, 2010), pp. 78–9.

[27] Cf. Iris Murdoch, *Sovereignty of Good* (London: Routledge and Kegan Paul, 1970), p. 80: the 'Kantian man-god' is 'increasingly aware of his alienation from the material universe which his discoveries reveal.'

[28] Kant, *Fundamental Principles of the Metaphysics of Ethics*, trans. T. Kingsmill Abbott Lewis (London: Longmans, 1969), p. 56.

[29] Taylor, *Sources*, p. 365; so also Arendt, *Human Condition*, p. 156.

[30] Kant, *Fundamental Principles*, p. 63.

'between the realm of the natural concept, as the sensible, and the realm of the concept of freedom, as the supersensible, there is a great gulf fixed, so that it is not possible to pass from the former to the latter by means of the theoretical employment of reason'.[31] He believes, nevertheless, that there must be a transition from one to the other, proposing to bridge this gulf (*Kluft*) with his idea of aesthetic judgement. Derrida, examining the bridge over the 'crack, cleavage, abyss',[32] finds its structure to be decidedly rickety—among other reasons because Kant in his view has failed to reconcile subject and object: the faculty of judgement has a subjective rule—it gives itself its own norms—yet judgements apparently make universal and so objective claims about the external world.[33]

A more central place for God than in Kant was found by Schleiermacher, who offers an alternative to Kant's dichotomy between knowing (phenomena) and doing (moral actions). He appeals to a third way, that of 'feeling' (*das Gefühl*), where God is still not an object of knowing, but is the 'whence' of the self's 'feeling of absolute dependence'.[34] The self is conscious of being relatively dependent on many relations in the finite world—with other people and with objects in nature. It is also, he argued, conscious of being absolutely dependent, and this is a 'God-consciousness' that orientates the self towards the final reality of the universe as a whole. In a distinctively Christian emphasis, Schleiermacher stresses that Christ, as a person who uniquely had perfect God-consciousness, clarifies and shapes the consciousness of others in community.[35] But, despite dependence on the world, the result of this account of the subject is actually to continue the gap set up between subject and world initiated by Descartes and continued by Kant. The world is not given attention in its own right, but only indirectly as the content of one's self-consciousness. Awareness of objects outside the self is always mediated through the subject's immediate awareness of *itself*.

Both Kant and Schleiermacher have gifted much to theology. Kant is surely right that God is not an object to be known like other objects in the world, and all theology after Kant has had to cope with his challenge. Indeed, this is already a perception inherent in Descartes' thought. In my own making of theology in this study, I will be resisting any idea that the triune God can be known as an object, even in subtle theological variations on the theme (such as

---

[31] Kant, *The Critique of Judgement*, trans. J. C. Meredith (Oxford: Clarendon Press, 1952), Introduction, p. 14.

[32] Jacques Derrida, 'Parergon' in Derrida, *The Truth in Painting*, trans. G. Bennington and I. McLeod (Chicago: University of Chicago Press, 1987), p. 35.

[33] Derrida, 'Parergon', p. 42.

[34] Friedrich Schleiermacher, *The Christian Faith*. Second Edition, trans. H. R. Mackintosh and J. S. Stewart (Edinburgh, T & T Clark, 1928), pp. 12–26.

[35] Schleiermacher, *Christian Faith*, pp. 52–8, 385–90.

that God makes God's-self an object to us).[36] Kant has also rightly affirmed human responsibility, and prompted theologians to take more seriously the insight of the Apostle Paul that in Christ humanity has 'come of age'.[37] In terms of my own theologizing in this study, human beings can and must cultivate a wisdom of responsible decision-making, using their substantial (if not absolute) freedom to be creative.

Schleiermacher has rightly identified the place of human experience in all talk about God, and his stress on 'feeling' points us to other dimensions of 'knowing' than the mere making of concepts. Moreover, he makes an important step towards a deeper recognition of the 'other' by applying a hermeneutic simultaneously to the interpretation of *texts* and to the understanding of *selfhood*.[38] As Anthony Thiselton has emphasized, for Schleiermacher hermeneutics means encountering a text or another self '*before* we have taken the step to subsume the alien or other within our own horizons of the familiar and pigeon-holed it within the prior categorizations of our expectations'.[39] As well as perceiving that other persons and objects in the world are 'texts' to be read, this is a significant advance towards respect for the otherness of the other *as* other. It invites engagement with the other and not a detached observation. As Thiselton puts it again, 'Schleiermacher's model of understanding texts and selfhood was along the lines of empathy between friends.'[40] Schleiermacher's extension of hermeneutics to the interpretation of human persons, or of what is 'other' in human life, was to be taken up by Dilthey, who affirmed that lessons learnt in critical reflection on the reading of texts could be a resource for understanding 'life' (*Leben*) lived in the experience of time.[41]

For all this, however, neither Kant nor Schleiermacher escape the danger of presenting some kind of detachment of the object from the subject. Schleiermacher's presentation of the subject must not be read as individualism, since relationality is essential for his hermeneutics, as well as for the experience of Christ as the 'redeemer' of consciousness in the midst of community. But the world of objects is subordinated to the human consciousness, and is not yet being given attention for what it is in itself. While Schleiermacher avoids making the 'texts' of other *selves* mere passive objects to be manipulated, *non-human* texts are (after the initial shock of the strange) assumed into the control of the subject. As for Kant, Iris Murdoch has probably gone too far

---

[36] Karl Barth, *Church Dogmatics*, transl. & ed. G. W. Bromiley and T. F. Torrance. 14 Volumes (Edinburgh: T & T Clark, 1936–77), II/1, pp. 21–3.

[37] Galatians 4:1–7.

[38] F. Schleiermacher, *Hermeneutics. The Handwritten Manuscripts*, trans. H. Kimmerle (Missoula: Scholars Press, 1977), pp. 97–8, 101, 109, 150–1.

[39] Thiselton, *Interpreting God*, p. 50.

[40] Thiselton, *Interpreting God*, p. 49.

[41] See Wilhelm Dilthey, 'The Rise of Hermeneutics' (1900), trans. Fredric Jameson, *New Literary History* 3 (1972), pp. 229–44, esp. pp. 232–4.

in judging that 'Kant is afraid of the particular, he is afraid of history' and that he 'does not tell us to respect whole particular tangled-up historic individuals, but to respect the universal reason in their breasts';[42] yet there is some truth in the judgement that the phenomenal world is downgraded to an instrument of the reason. Moreover, God in both accounts can easily become a sanction for human subjectivity, a dominating authority validating human mastery over the world, even if neither Kant nor Schleiermacher conceive of God as a supreme Thinker in the way that Descartes does.[43]

(b) *The world as expression of the self*

With Hegel we do, however, take the step of conceiving God as absolute mind coming to self-consciousness through relation to the world. Despite Hegel's professed intention to close the ontological gap between subject and object, the result is ironically a second form of lack of attention to the world as it is, since the world is merely an expression of the thinking subject. Hegel asserts against Kant that it is possible to know God, because Kant's human reason is actually a relative form of an Absolute Mind (*Geist*) or self-thinking Idea;[44] 'God' is thinking God's thoughts through finite consciousness embodied in a physical world, and since the Absolute Mind is also the Whole, it will come to full self-awareness through a universal community of minds.[45] Just because they are centres of self-critical reason, human subjects are thus not isolated from the context of the non-human world.

The idealist account of the universe means that an interior subjectivity is necessarily integrated into the external objectivity of physical, cultural, and social contexts. The human subjective spirit is becoming objective in nature and history, through physical embodiment, the creation of artefacts, and the progressive development of social and political institutions.[46] Through this objectification, the mind or spirit is coming to full actualization and awareness of itself, returning to itself as enriched through its exposure to what is *not* itself. In this, finite spirits participate in the movement of Absolute Spirit itself, which goes out of itself into the alienation and 'non-being' of the finite world, in order to return to itself with enhancement of being.[47] Moreover, this journey of God in creation has its basis in an inner movement of Spirit,

---

[42] Iris Murdoch, 'The Sublime and the Good' in Murdoch, *Existentialists and Mystics*, ed. Peter Conradi (London: Chatto & Windus, 1997), pp. 214–15.

[43] 'This entire universe can be said to be an entity originating in God's thought, that is, an entity created by a single act of the divine mind': Descartes, *Meditations*, pp. 83–4.

[44] G. W. F. Hegel, *The Phenomenology of Mind*, trans. J. Baillie (London: George Allen & Unwin, 1949), pp. 80–2.

[45] G. W. F. Hegel, *The Christian Religion: Lectures on the Philosophy of Religion Part III*, trans. P. C. Hodgson. American Academy of Religion, Texts and Translations 2 (Missoula: Scholars Press, 1979), pp. 256–7.

[46] Hegel, *Phenomenology of Mind*, pp. 531–41.

[47] Hegel, *Phenomenology of Mind*, pp. 81, 769–70; *Christian Religion*, pp. 89–91, 109–12.

diversifying itself from oneness into difference and returning to itself in communion, symbolized in the image of Trinity.[48] The Father begets the Son, and is fulfilled in the communion of the Spirit. The progress of Spirit through history to consummation is further aptly symbolized in the story of the death of Christ, who endures the non-being and strangeness of an utterly alienating death ('"God himself is dead" it says in a Lutheran hymn'),[49] but who comes to a fuller self through the continuing of his spirit in the community of the church, combining resurrection and Pentecost.

There are several lasting contributions which Hegel makes to Christian theology through this comprehensive account which he regarded as the 'final philosophy'. He affirms a self-emptying or kenotic nature of God, overturning centuries of Christian belief in the impassibility of God, in a way that proved attractive to many theologians in the twentieth century.[50] He affirms the manifestation of unity in difference, apparently giving value to the concrete particularities of the world. He affirms a commitment of God to time and history, and revelation can be understood, not as the communication of propositions, but as the self-manifestation of God in the whole of history. Most significant for our present study, he appears to overcome the divide between subject and object, spirit and nature; he has the key perception that self-identity depends on relation to the 'other'. But on closer inspection, it is here that he finally fails. The objectivity of the world is nothing other than an expression of the subject, of a mind which is self-aware. It is doubtful then whether the world and even other persons are really 'alien' and 'strange' to the journeying mind at all. 'Others' are seen to be simply 'more of the same'. This means that even horrific evils are to be reconciled with the Spirit as a necessary part of its self-alienating pilgrimage, part of the machinery of the dialectical process.

It may be argued that until the consummation of all things there is nevertheless a difference between the Spirit and its objective forms, since until the coming of full self-awareness, the objectively lived worlds of subjects are inadequate manifestations of the subject. Human works of art and social institutions are always distorted expressions of the self, and must be so in order to keep the engine of the dialectic turning to the third movement of return to the self and thence to a further objectification. Ironically, this introduces some of the element of the 'gulf' between subject and object that we saw in Kant. It does explain why the subject is always mysterious and elusive, escaping from full explanation by scientific analysis, and this mystery

---

[48] Hegel, *Phenomenology of Mind*, pp. 765–9; *Christian Religion*, pp. 48–9, 86–7.

[49] Hegel, *Christian Religion*, p. 218, cf. pp. 212–17; cf *Phenomenology of Mind*, pp. 776–8, 780.

[50] See Paul S. Fiddes, *The Creative Suffering of God* (Oxford: Clarendon Press, 1988), pp. 23–43; Jürgen Moltmann, *The Crucified God: The Cross of Christ as the Foundation and Criticism of Christian Theology*, trans. R. A. Wilson and J. Bowden (London: SCM, 1974), pp. 252–5.

has been picked up in postmodern accounts of the self. But it is a mystery in which we fall back again into a great divide between self and the world. We shall see that the perspective of wisdom will give us other ways to conceive of this mystery.

(c) *The world as a threat to the self*

A third form of relation between self and the world is found in the period of modernity we have called 'modernism'. The existential approach to the self, as expressed most clearly by Jean-Paul Sartre, emphasizes the aspiration of the human agent to become (in the words of Kierkegaard) a truly 'existing individual' with a passionate interest in being. The human subject, Sartre proposes, is 'being-for-itself', 'being-in-itself' and 'being-for-others'. In being for-itself, the human subject constructs itself as an individual through choosing itself; this means building deliberate acts of consciousness, which are grounded in an implicit self-consciousness, into a single 'project' of life which is originally formed during childhood. The project is created by a choice which is 'a fundamental act of freedom'.[51] In Sartre's novel *Nausea*, Roquentin's abandonment of his project brings with it the end of his subjectivity: 'suddenly the I pales, pales and goes out'.[52] As Iris Murdoch puts it, for Sartre the pure, free moment of moral choice enervates a consciousness which otherwise in itself lies inert.[53] This freedom exists in tension with the limits and boundaries to the subject constituted by objects in the world around, which are thus felt as hindrances to freedom. This contradictory situation, causing anxiety, must simply be accepted as an absurdity. There is thus a profound alienation between the subjective consciousness and the contingent objects of the world, a relationship in which there is no inherent meaning. Earlier in *Nausea* Roquentin, sitting under a chestnut tree in the public gardens, realizes that the sheer existence of this object constitutes a threat to his radical freedom: 'The word Absurdity is now born beneath my pen . . . how can I put that into words? Absurd: irreducible . . .'[54] All the human agent can do is take the courage to be, to affirm its freedom in the face of the absurd.

In the case of other persons the threat of the world is even greater. The 'for-itself' of the consciousness depends for its existence on 'being-in-itself', including physical embodiment, and this in turn only exists in relation to something other than itself ('being-for-others'). Here Sartre adopts what he calls 'Hegel's brilliant intuition' that 'I depend on the Other in my being.'[55] He

[51] Jean-Paul Sartre, *Being and Nothingness. An Essay on Phenomenological Ontology*, trans. H. E. Barnes (London: Routledge, 2003), p. 461.

[52] Jean-Paul Sartre, *Nausea*, trans. R. Baldick (Harmondsworth: Penguin, 1963), p. 241.

[53] Iris Murdoch, *Metaphysics as a Guide to Morals* (London: Chatto & Windus, 1992), pp. 154–5.

[54] Sartre, *Nausea*, p. 185.

[55] Sartre, *Being and Nothingness*, p. 237.

explains the dependence by undermining the old certainties about the 'self', which he clearly distinguishes from the conscious 'subject'. While our freedom establishes our consciousness, it is an illusory idea that we possess a stable entity called the 'self' which is the self-sufficient object of our inner conscious reflection (as in 'I know *myself*'). The true self is a project, a work in progress, an unstable reality continually created by the subject in relation to its sur- roundings. The 'me' or 'self', he proposes, only exists as an object of others, who therefore represent us to our selves.[56] We are at others' mercy insofar as their consciousness of our self effectively determines our being: we fear that what there is to us is exhausted by how we appear to them. The insecurity that results from this dependency prompts an existential dread in the 'for-itself', and this in turn results in a conflict of consciousnesses wanting to control and possess each other.[57] Since no consciousness can exist without the other, the for-itself can only 'recover its own Being [in itself] by directly or indirectly making an object out of the other', that is,' by 'enslaving the Other' who possesses me 'by making me be'.[58] 'Being-for-others' thus means not allowing the world to be felt as a weight, imposing its objectivity on the subject, and not capitulating to the way that others conceive or treat us as objects. The objective world is necessary for the identity of the subject, but is also felt as a threat.

Sartrean existentialism has certainly contributed to Christian theology. The tension between human freedom and human limits does cause anxiety, as Kierkegaard had already recognized,[59] but theologians drawing on this analy- sis propose to cope with anxiety through faith in God rather than an assertion of human freedom. This, Paul Tillich asserts, is the true 'courage to be'.[60] Moreover, Sartre's recognition that the self is not a substantial, stable, ready- made and complete entity strikes notes of agreement with a theological critique of human self-sufficiency, although theology will place the dynamic project of the 'making of the self' in the context of relationship with God and others. However, more negatively, the existential split betweeen subject and object, which Sartre does not solve, can lead to the theological view that the authenticity of the subject is to be found in response to a presence of God which is restricted to inner subjectivity; this leads to abandonment of any talk about the activity of God in the natural world as 'mythological'.[61] By a curious

---

[56] Sartre, *Being and Nothingness*, p. 364.

[57] Sartre, *Being and Nothingness*, p. 237.

[58] Sartre, *Being and Nothingness*, p. 364.

[59] Søren Kierkegaard, *The Concept of Anxiety*, trans. R. Thomte (Princeton: Princeton University Press, 1980), pp. 41–6.

[60] Paul Tillich, *The Courage to Be* (London: Collins/Fontana, 1962), pp. 137–45, 167–72; Tillich, *Systematic Theology*, vol. 2, pp. 38–45; cf. John Macquarrie, *Principles of Christian Theology*. Revised Edition (London: SCM, 1977), pp. 64–5, 86–7.

[61] So Rudolf Bultmann, *Jesus Christ and Mythology* (London: SCM Press, 1960), 62, 65–8.

route we seem to have arrived at the same situation described by Kant, with a dualism between a phenomenal and noumenal world.

THE SELF AND THE WORLD IN POSTMODERNITY

We have arrived at the point where we can understand what 'postmodern' thinkers are reacting against, as they are constantly in conversation with the self or subject of modernity. While postmodern thinking emerges at the somewhat rarified heights of academic debate, it does reflect a more popular 'mood' to which it is responding and to some extent affecting. The mood with which I want Christian theology to connect is articulated by a number of thinkers in the academy on whom we will mainly be concentrating, but I hope not to lose sight of the larger context of popular culture. In the realm of critical thought, then, I suggest that four sets of ideas have flowed into the world-view that we can call 'postmodern': immersion in the world, a hermeneutic of suspicion, openness of meaning, and the impact of the sublime. Together they contribute to what Norman Denzin identifies as 'a shattering of innocent confidence in the capacity of the self to control its own destiny', signalling 'a loss of trust in global strategies of social planning, and in universal criteria of rationality'.[62] David Harvey's diagnosis is similar: the postmodern self lives daily with fragmentation, indeterminacy, pluralism, and intense distrust of all universalizing and totalizing discourses.[63] Here I want to make a brief sketch of a complex terrain that we shall be exploring in more detail as our venture proceeds, and to hint at the way that each of these four sets of ideas makes late-modern thinking potentially open to conversation with a theology that draws substantially on the Jewish–Christian wisdom tradition.

(a) *Immersion in the world*

First in the kaleidoscope of postmodernity there is the idea that the self is always and already immersed into the world. The world is 'given' to the subject from the moment of its inception, and even before it. It is thus a pseudo-problem to ask how to bridge a gap between subject and object, between the world 'in the consciousness' and the 'world out there'. There is no gap between the world and the *res cogitans*, or the moral reason, or the self-consciousness, as respectively envisaged by Descartes, Kant, and Schleiermacher. This per-spective was greatly indebted to the movement of 'phenomenology,' largely

---

[62] Norman K. Denzin, *Images of Postmodern Society: Social Theory and Contemporary Cinema* (London: Newbury Park, 1991), p. vii.

[63] David Harvey, *The Condition of Postmodernity: An Enquiry into the Origins of Cultural Change* (Oxford: Blackwell, 1990), pp. 44–9.

initiated by Edmund Husserl, which insisted that consciousness is always consciousness *of* the world. Objects 'appear' in the consciousness *as* they are thought about, hoped for, or desired. Meaning (given by the mind) and being (the object in the world) are always implicated in each other, so that multiple things in the world appear in the light of the consciousness.

Husserl give us the example of looking at an apple tree: 'Let us suppose that in a garden we regard with pleasure a blossoming apple tree, the freshly green grass of the lawn . . . '[64] He points out that we not only regard the tree, but regard it *with pleasure*. There is no question of having to bridge a gap between the knowing subject and the object which is known, between the person walking in the garden, relishing its sights and smells, and the blossoming tree. The attitude taken towards the object is inseparable from it, so that consciousness is always 'consciousness of', and the object is always 'perceived as'. This inseparability is what Husserl calls 'intentionality', so that observation is always 'intentional' and things are 'intentional objects'. The subject and object of traditional philosophy are 'only abstractions' from this primary reality.[65] Emmanuel Levinas, who played a large part in introducing the work of Husserl to the French philosophical scene, comments that there *is* no objectivity that would be 'indifferent to the very existence of a subjectivity'.[66] The world is always and already given to the subject. Perception does not isolate the subject from the world but immerses the self in it. Levinas, moreover, extended the range of 'intending' an object beyond cognition into 'all our relations with the world', including our desires, actions, loves, and satisfactions. The world, as he puts it, is 'a sensed and wanted world'.[67] In the language of Heidegger, the self is constituted by 'situatedness' (*Befindlichket*), 'historicality' (*Geschichtlichket*) or 'being-there' (*Dasein*).[68]

There is great gain in refusing to start from the assumption that we have to 'mind the gap', as the platform announcement warns us on the underground (or subway for those outside the UK). To take a metaphor from this form of transport, we do not have to step over a gap between the stable platform of the self and the carriage of the world, brightly lit, crammed full of other people, and always in motion. I am going to argue throughout this book that in the 'wisdom' tradition there is similarly no gap between the observing mind of the wise and the observed world; moroever, there is no gap to 'mind' between God and the world, no ontological abyss that has to be bridged for God to be present and active in the world.

---

[64] Edmund Husserl, *Ideas Pertaining to a Pure Phenomenology and to a Phenomenological Philosophy*, trans. F. Kersetn (Dordrecht: Kluwer Academic Publishers, 1983), p. 214.

[65] Emmanuel Levinas, *The Theory of Intuition in Husserl's Phenomenology* [1930], trans. A. Orianne (Evanston: Northwestern University Press, 1973), p. 48.

[66] Levinas, *Theory of Intuition*, p. 6.

[67] Levinas, *Theory of Intuition*, p. 45.

[68] Heidegger, *Being and Time*, pp. 172–88.

However, there are at least two problems, equal and opposite with this assertion of a primal engagement between self and world. In the first place, it might reduce the reality of the world to the consciousness itself, or at least subordinate it. Husserl does not deny the existence of the actual tree in the 'transcendent world' beyond the consciousness, but in the phenomenological attitude (in which the consciousness is the original and primary phenomenon), the actuality of the world is placed in parenthesis or 'bracketed'.[69] By a special process of reflection or 'reduction', judgement is suspended about the external reality of the 'intentional object' in order to grasp its essence intuitively as pure phenomenon, or as an appearance in the consciousness uncontaminated by any prior assumptions or intellectual schemes. Ironically, given the new perspective on self and world, the result may be the detachment of a 'transcendental ego', as Derrida warns;[70] this would be a kind of idealism, and fall under the same criticisms to which we saw that Hegel is liable. Iris Murdoch detects an escape from the variety of phenomena as they are in themselves in the world, and urges that we should be attending to these rather than to the essences and 'deep structure' of our own mental activity.[71] Philosophers who might be called 'postmodern' have generally welcomed Husserl's insistence on immersion into the world, but have rejected the tendency to elevate the consciousness over the contingency of events in time and space. Levinas, for instance, wants to make other persons an exception to the process of reduction; they cannot be 'bracketed out' in themselves since, as transcendent to the self, they drive the subject out of self-absorption into a sense of radical responsibility for the other.

The opposite tendency, again beginning from the inseparability of subject and object and from immersion in the world, is to envisage the self as determined by its social context. The self may be perceived as largely the creation of social conventions and especially the structures of language that precede the emergence of the self and shape it. The self may thus be envisaged as a de-centred construct within the system of signs that constitutes corporate life. Following the insights of Freud, this construction of the self may also include pre-conscious forces within the psyche, especially the impulses of desire. It is a mark of our late-modern world to regard the self as not properly equipped to make the conscious, existential decisions that Sartre endowed it with, or to act as the supreme moral agent promoted by Kant as superior over nature.

The self which exercises 'virtues' has, it seems, often collapsed into a product of social, linguistic, and psychological forces. According to the concise

---

[69] Husserl, *Ideas Pertaining*, p. 215.

[70] Jacques Derrida, *Speech and Phenomena And Other Essays On Husserl's Theory of Signs*, trans. D. B. Allison (Evanston: Northwestern University Press, 1973), p. 78.

[71] Murdoch, *Metaphysics*, pp. 232–42.

description of Anthony Thiselton, 'The self of postmodernity...no longer regards itself as an active agent carving out possibility with the aid of natural and social sciences, but as an opaque product of variable roles and performances which have been imposed upon it by the constraints of society and by its own inner drives or conflicts.'[72] To this account we should add the creative power of systems of signs and language. At the level of popular culture, there is a sense that the self 'has become caught up in a prior agenda as a performer of pre-determined roles'[73], at the mercy of political, economic, and commercial forces in the roles of consumer, or citizen, or borrower. (At the time of writing, ordinary working people in the European community feel helpless in face of a vast national debt for whose size they feel instinctively they are not directly responsible, but which is now directly shrinking their income, benefits, and pensions and reducing the quality of daily life.) This situation is inevitably undermining the sense of having a self which can direct a person's own affairs.

I suggest, nevertheless that we should be cautious about talking of '*the* self of postmodernity' in quite the general way that commentators (including Thiselton) do. Anything like a total loss of self is an extreme of the postmodern mood. At times, perhaps, we can find a tendency towards it in Michel Foucault. In his study of the history of madness and the growth of institutions to cope with mental illness, he shows how the institutions of society rest on social situatedness already present, including networks of language and symbols.[74] The *cogito*, the sense of 'I think', rests on the same foundations, and these are constantly moving. As society is not a stable entity, neither is the self; it 'shimmers' as ethical norms, social habits, and forms of language are always changing and moving on. Don Cupitt accentuates this view, in his account of the postmodern age: 'Reality becomes a beginningless, endless shimmering interplay of signs on a flat surface', so that all that is left is 'devised, ironical'.[75] Language, he concludes, 'is transience: it slips by at such a rate that the object of our desire never fully arrives'.[76] In short, 'there is no substantial individual self'.[77] But the total collapse of the self into a construct is not characteristic of some of the thinkers usually regarded as apostles of postmodernism, such as Derrida, Levinas, and Julia Kristeva. What postmodern thinkers have taken seriously is immersion into the world, making this their starting point rather than a gap of either knowing (an epistemological gap) or being (an ontological gap). This

---

[72] Thiselton, *Interpreting God*, p. 121.

[73] Thiselton, *Interpreting God*, p. 122.

[74] Michel Foucault, *Madness and Civilization* (New York: Random House, 1973), pp. 187–98, 227–34, 253–60; Michel Foucault, *The Order of Things*, English translation (London: Routledge, 2002), pp. 324–7, 339, 357. But for another mood in Foucault, see my Chapter 9.

[75] Don Cupitt, *Lifelines* (London: SCM, 1986), pp. 1–2.

[76] Don Cupitt, *After All: Religion without Alienation* (London: SCM, 1994), p. 57.

[77] Cupitt, *Lifelines*, p. 10.

means that they cannot adopt any of the easier certainties about the self. But many are still intensely interested in talking about a self which is called to responsibility for the world and particularly other persons.

There is, to be sure, a resistance to conceiving any principle or reality that can be thought to exist independently of the signs that indicate it, that can float free of the text and the differentiation of signs from each other. This leads as much to a critique of Husserl's 'pure experiences' of the psyche which are a direct and unmediated awareness of the present moment,[78] as to the self of Descartes or Sartre. This is the danger of a word like 'spirit', which may indicate just such a free-floating transcendent entity, and in his book *Of Spirit* Derrida at first conjures the concept up in order to exorcize it;[79] nevertheless, like Heidegger (whose use of the concept of 'spirit' he examines in this book), he also ends by re-interpreting it. The point he recognizes is that some concept of a responsible human self is necessary to maintain human freedom in the face of totalitarian onslaughts such as Nazism, and to maintain common human identity in the face of racism; 'spirit', he admits, seems an indispensable way of expressing this.[80]

(b) *A hermeneutic of suspicion*

If the sense of being immersed into the world reaches back to Husserl, a second mark of 'postmodern' thought is rooted even further back, in the thought of Friedrich Nietzsche. Nietzsche suspects that claims to truth often represent disguised attempts to legitimate self-interest and uses of power. He attacks the 'truths' propounded by both philosophy and theology as being means of manipulation to which the weak and uncertain are vulnerable in their desire to cope with life.[81] Language, he suspects, often provides the material by which a bid for power over others can be disguised. Significantly, in his essay 'On Truth and Falsehood' he asserts that all truth-claims in language are metaphors for reality which we have forgotten are only metaphors:

> What then is truth? A mobile army of metaphors, metonymics, anthropomorphisms... Truths are illusions of which one has forgotten that they *are* illusions; worn out metaphors which have become powerless to affect the senses.[82]

---

[78] Edmund Husserl, *Cartesian Meditations*, transl. D. Cairns (Dordrecht: Kluwer, 1950) pp. 31–9; see the critique of Derrida, *Speech and Phenomena*, pp. 8–9, 39–41.

[79] Jacques Derrida, *Of Spirit. Heidegger and the Question*, trans. G. Bennington and R. Bowlby (Chicago: University of Chicago Press, 1991), pp. 15–22.

[80] Derrida, *Of Spirit*, pp. 39–40. Cf. 99–113.

[81] Friedrich Nietzsche, *Human, All-Too-Human*, Part 1, paras. 1–9, Part 2, maxims and opinions, 5, 20, 32, 96, 182, 225, 318, in *Complete Works of Nietzsche*, ed. O. Levy, 18 Volumes (London: Allen & Unwin, 1909–13), vols. 6–7.

[82] Nietzsche, 'On Truth and Falsehood in their Ultramoral Sense', in Levy (ed.), *Complete Works*, vol. 2, p. 180.

Those who want power over others exalt metaphors into universal truths, but 'all that exists consists of interpretations'.[83]

Influential thinkers in the late-modern world have inherited this Nietzschean suspicion, and tend to interpret all universal conceptual schemes as concealed power games. Roland Barthes, for instance, examines the influential stories and ideologies of the twentieth century in his book *Mythologies*, and exposes them as manipulative bids by powerful interests. Derrida quotes Nietzsche on 'a mobile army of metaphors' in his essay 'White Mythology';[84] traversing the history of Western philosophy he proposes that philosophers have failed to notice the part played by metaphor in their discourse, and have confused metaphors with universal problem-solving truths. Talk of a 'ground' of an idea, or one concept 'depending' on another, or 'flowing' from another, are all metaphorical expressions.[85] There is, however, a hint in his account that, unlike Nietzsche, he can also see a positive side to the imaginative use of language in philosophy (an insight more enthusiastically proposed by Michèle Le Doeuff).[86] We shall return to the question of metaphor later in our study.

Above all, Jean-François Lyotard stands as successor to Nietzsche's critique of universal truths, finding the rejection of 'grand narratives' or 'metanarratives' to be characteristic of the 'postmodern condition'. He proposes that attempts to find an explanatory framework, or narrative, that can be applied universally to all situations can no longer convince, and must be seen as the pretensions of a 'metasubject'. Whether the narrative is scientific, political, religious, or economic (one is reminded here of the often-used phrase by former British Prime Minister Margaret Thatcher, 'There is no alternative'), it is in fact 'the mechanism of developing a Life that is simultaneously Subject'.[87] That is, grand-narratives are nothing other than a self-presentation of the subject that develops them, and represent the desire to dominate others. Metanarratives, or totalizing discourses, are abusive in setting out to suppress the small stories, or the local narratives. Truth inheres not in the large systems, but in local goals and values. Lyotard supports his perspective by appeal to Wittgenstein's concept of 'language games', or the way that language is used in a particular context, supposing that Wittgenstein is envisaging multiple

---

[83] Nietzsche, *The Will to Power*, vol. 2:12, aphorism 481, in Levy (ed.), *Complete Works*, vol. 15.

[84] Derrida, 'White Mythology. Metaphor in the Text of Philosophy' in Derrida, *Margins of Philosophy*, trans. A. Bass (New York: Harvester, 1982), p. 217.

[85] Derrida, 'White Mythology', pp. 224–9.

[86] Her book, *The Philosophical Imaginary* (London: Continuum, 2002), offers a series of examples of the way that philosophers think in images, e.g. pp. 21–8, 92–8.

[87] Jean-François Lyotard, *The Postmodern Condition: A Report on Knowledge*, trans. G. Bennington and B. Massumi (Manchester: Manchester University Press, 1986), p. 34.

autonomous games, or localized linguistic activities which remain incapable of translation into each other.[88]

Lyotard's sweeping attack on 'grand narratives' can be criticized from several angles. Quickly (and perhaps too cheaply), the riposte can be made that the declaration 'there are no metanarratives' is itself a metanarrative, a postulated universal truth. Or Lyotard's use of Wittgenstein can be questioned, since Wittgenstein actually speaks of linguistic activities as 'overlapping and criss-crossing'; as Thiselton points out, Wittgenstein sees 'the common behaviour of mankind' or 'the whole hurly-burly of human actions' as 'the system of reference by means of which we interpret an unknown language'.[89] Or Lyotard can be shown to be inconsistent; while wanting to protect the rights of local narratives against all-consuming grand narratives, he is also strongly opposed to 'tribal narratives' that bring about war, using the Nazis as an example of what a tribal narrative such as the myth of the Aryan race can produce.[90] But, as David Bentley Hart suggests, a particular narrative can only be judged as socially evil or unjust from the perspective of a metanarrative; even more, vicious metanarratives can only be overthrown by more peaceful ones, not by small stories.[91]

For all this, however, Lyotard and others are right to be suspicious of the manipulative intentions that lurk behind large-scale narratives. As Levinas puts it, totalizing discourses reduce other persons and objects in the world to more of 'the same', nothing other than oneself.[92] On the level of popular culture, it also seems to be true that small, local narratives are likely to catch people's imagination and loyalty more than large schemes of thought. Popular culture shows in its own way a turning away from comprehensive viewpoints and theories. There is a preference for single-issue social campaigns (the disposal of nuclear or industrial waste, the construction of a by-pass road, the building of a new runway at an airport) rather than allegiance to political parties with wide-ranging programmes. There is the continual shifting of images on television, moving quickly from one visual impact to another so that the mind and eye cannot dwell on any one too long, even on the news. This is a culture of the disposable image and sound-bite, which is not congenial to stories with universal claims. In the area of religion, a turning from the comprehensive narrative is likely to manifest itself as a 'pick-and-mix' spirituality, in which people construct their own religion out of a mixture of

[88] Lyotard, *Postmodern Condition*, pp. 10–11, 40–1.

[89] Thiselton, *Interpreting God*, pp. 34–5.

[90] Jean-François Lyotard, *The Differend: Phrases in Dispute*, trans. G. van den Abbeele (Minneapolis: University of Minnesota Press, 1988), p. 105.

[91] David Bentley Hart, *The Beauty of the Infinite: The Aesthetics of Christian Truth* (Grand Rapids: Eerdmans, 2003), pp. 425–7.

[92] Emmanuel Levinas, *Totality and Infinity: An Essay on Interiority*, trans. A. Lingis (Pittsburgh: Duquesne University Press, 1965), pp. 43, 47.

cultural elements in a spiritual free market.[93] A person, for instance, may have her children baptized, marry in church, and attend the festivals of Easter and Christmas, but to these she adds some astrology, Zen meditation, and some use of crystals for communing with nature; she also arranges the furniture and plans the decoration in her house according to the art of *Feng Shui*, a practice which promises to promote health and wealth and which has attracted corporate clients in the UK such as the Body Shop, Marks and Spencer, and Queen's Park Rangers Football Club.

By contrast, the Christian faith presents a metanarrative, a story that purports to cover the progress of the universe from conception to consummation, and which ventures to interpret human experience in every temporal and cultural setting. The central doctrine of the Christian faith, the Trinity, is itself a 'grand narrative', which aims to speak both of God in God's self in eternity (the 'immanent Trinity'), and the activity of God in history ('the economic Trinity'). It is, moreover, a metaphorical account, drawing on the basic image of a 'father' who sends out a 'son', both in an eternal 'birthing' ('eternal generation') and on a historic mission of salvation into the world. Metaphor is indispensable, as it is not possible to speak of a God who is unique, unclassifiable, and self-existent literally; any categories drawn from our knowledge of the world can be used only analogically. Finally, the metanarrative of the Trinity can be said to be 'metaphysics', insofar as this term refers to a comprehensive, conceptual account of reality which *exceeds* a merely empirical analysis of the physical world, and which relies on some appeal to analogy between an uncreated creator and created realities that are also creative. With regard to the doctrine of Trinity, 'metaphysics' means discerning some connection between the relationality of God and the relational nature of the universe. In my qualified use of the term, however, I recognize that there are senses of 'metaphysics' with which Christian theology can be as critical as the philosophers who, beginning with Nietzsche, announce the end of the project altogether. I hope it will become clear in the process of this book that I am working with an 'open metaphysics' (Colin Gunton's term),[94] which does not denigrate the body in its particularities of time and space in favour of some realm of spiritual universals, and which is not characterized by merely speculative reason, divorced from practical human experience.

In the light of the use of metanarrative, metaphor and a qualified metaphysics in Christian theology, the postmodern mood sets it a challenge to present this metanarrative in a way that the hearer will be convinced is not

---

[93] *The Search for Faith and the Witness of the Church.* An exploration by the Missionary Theological Advisory Group of the Church of England (London: Church House Publishing, 1996).

[94] Colin Gunton, *The One, the Three and the Many: God, Creation and the Culture of Modernity* (Cambridge: Cambridge University Press, 1993), p. 157.

dominating, abusive of local narratives, or a rhetoric of power projected by the corporate 'self' of the Christian institution.

(c) *The openness of meaning*

To the components of immersion into the world and a hermeneutic of suspicion the postmodern mood adds another element drawn from earlier in the twentieth century—that is the insights of 'structuralism' into the importance of 'difference'. However, by giving a twist to this insight, the third element is often called 'poststructuralism' or 'deconstruction'. The founder of structuralism, Ferdinand de Saussure, had seen the meaning of a verbal sign as being established through its relational difference from another sign. As he puts it, 'two signs a and b are never grasped as such by our linguistic consciousness, but only the difference between a and b'.[95] As Saussure demonstrated, a sign draws its meaning from what it is *not* ('its non-coincidence from the rest').[96] To invent an example, the meaning of the signifier 'snowflake' is not established by any similarity of the sound or the shape of the word on the page to the actual physical appearance of a snowflake in a snowy scene on a winter's day. The word takes its meaning from its difference from other signifiers such as a flower-petal or a leaf, and the fact that it can be named metaphorically as both in a poem[97] underlines the difference between signs rather than dissolving it.

So for Saussure and the structuralists who follow him, a written text is a sealed world of its own. The network of verbal signs within it does not directly imitate the everyday world, but must be studied as an inter-related system in its own right. A literary text has an autonomy: it is not owned even by the author, and so its meaning is not to be found by investigating the author's intention. For structuralists, the meaning of words and phrases comes from their relation to each other, and particularly their difference from each other. Now, Derrida extends this proposal, pointing out that a relation of difference can be infinitely expanded as all signs differ from all others. So *différence* in the spatial sense of distance between things becomes *différence* in the temporal sense of 'deferment' or postponement of meaning. Derrida coins the word *différance* (with an *a*) to evoke both these senses of difference at once—*differing* and *deferring*—without simply combining them; *différance* hovers between the two and cannot be trapped in any category, but it certainly results

---

[95] Ferdinand de Saussure, *Course in General Linguistics,* transl. R. Harris (London: Duckworth, 1983), p. 116.

[96] Ferdinand de Saussure, *Course in General Linguistics*, p. 116.

[97] 'Storm flakes were scroll-leaved flowers, lily showers': from Gerard Manley Hopkins, 'The Wreck of the Deutschland' in *The Poems of Gerard Manley Hopkins*, Fourth Edition, ed. W. H. Gardner and N. H. Mackenzie (Oxford University Press, London, 1967), p. 58. On metaphor and difference see Derrida, 'White Mythology', pp. 218, 228, 242–3.

in a dispersal of meaning.[98] So if we accept the insights of structuralism itself about the network of language, we can never reach any final point in interpretation of a text. It is endlessly open in meaning. Extending the structuralist insight has in fact undermined it, since structuralism searches for a 'deep structure' in a text, discerning archetypes and primal patterns beneath the surface of the world of signs.

According to deconstructionists, meaning is not immediately present in a sign. Because signifiers become the signified to which new signifiers point, meaning is dispersed down an infinite chain of signs.[99] When we read a sentence, final meaning is suspended or postponed: it is still to come. As Roland Barthes puts it, 'The text practises the infinite deferral of the signified'.[100] There can certainly be no 'transcendental signifier', that is, one signifier that acts as a foundation or unity for all others, whether this be Reason, class warfare or the Oedipus Complex (so dismissing the metanarratives of Kant, Marx, and Freud). Nor can there be a 'transcendental signified'—that is a concept which is present even without signifiers and which exceeds the chain of signs, so acting as the cause of all meaning in the text.[101] God has been conceived like this in some past Christian thinking (although I am going to argue for a different concept of God in this book). *Différance* itself is not a concept that can be *thought*; there is a continual 'flickering, spilling and defusing of meaning' which 'can *show* us something about nature of meaning and signification which it is not able to formulate as a proposition.'[102]

A verbal sign is what it is only because it is *not* something else. It can be called a 'trace', first because it does not correspond to a 'thing in itself' in the world, but only offers a clue or a hint to it (as structuralists had stressed), and second because it contains the mark of what it differs from, or of what is still to come. It traces out a future track for the reader, throwing itself forward in reference to other traces which are yet to be.[103] In this way a text, as Barthes stresses, involves the reader in generating a plurality of meanings; it draws the reader in to share in the pleasurable play which it produces in the absence of either the author or the referent.[104] For Derrida, the trace is thus 'foundational

[98] Jacques Derrida, 'Différance' in Derrida, *Margins of Philosophy*, pp. 6–15.

[99] Jacques Derrida, *Of Grammatology*, trans. G. C. Spivak (Baltimore and London: Johns Hopkins University Press, 1976), p. 7.

[100] Roland Barthes, 'From Work to Text' in Josué V. Harari (ed.), *Textual Strategies: Perspectives in Post-Structuralist Criticism* (Ithica: Cornell University Press, 1979), p. 76.

[101] Jacques Derrida, *Positions*, trans. A. Bass (Chicago: University of Chicago Press, 1981), pp. 19–20; cf. Derrida, *Of Grammatology*, pp. 49–50.

[102] Terry Eagleton, *Literary Theory. An Introduction* (Minnesota: Minneapolis, 1983), p. 134.

[103] Derrida, *Speech and Phenomena. And Other Essays on Husserl's Theory of Signs*, trans. D. Allison (Evanston: Northwestern University Press, 1973), pp. 135–41.

[104] Roland Barthes, *The Pleasure of the Text*, trans. R. Miller (London: Jonathan Cape, 1976), pp. 78–80.

absence'. But we ourselves are not exempted from this world of traces that stand 'under erasure': our selfhood also is in question.[105] Because we always use verbal signs, even when we search our own minds, we are creatures of traces, never fully present to others or to ourselves. The project of modernity had been to establish the presence of the self—to itself and to the world. The being of the self was defined as its ability to impose its presence on others, and Derrida's project is to deconstruct such a 'metaphysics of presence', which he describes as 'Presence of the thing to the sight as *eidos*, presence as substance/ essence/existence [*ousia*] . . . the self-presence of the cogito, consciousness, subjectivity.'[106] In a later chapter we are going to tackle this critique of any full or immediate presence of the self, which in some versions of decon-struction (but not in Derrida himself) has become an onslaught on the very idea of 'presence' altogether.

An emphasis on difference led the structuralist critics to find a deep underlying pattern of myths and images through constructing alternatives and polarities which are supposedly indicated by the text—good or evil, higher or lower, inside or outside, male or female, presence or absence. Poststructur-alists point out that the alternative, the disruptive Other which is excluded, will always re-emerge. It just cannot be suppressed. Deconstructive criticism thus looks for tensions, fissures, and self-contradictions in a text which alerts us to a possible explosion of meaning. Some kind of untidiness, some impasse will occur in the narrative which upsets the closure so that the end is ruptured. Like the pod of a plant bursting open and scattering its seeds, the end of a text bursts and spreads its words.[107] There is always 'surplus' of meaning.

Roland Barthes moved towards this kind of criticism from an originally structuralist viewpoint by careful reading of a number of biblical texts. A turning point was his reading of the story in Genesis 32:22–32 of Jacob wrestling all night with a mysterious stranger, whom Jacob finally identifies with God ('for I have seen God face to face', v. 30),[108] and from whom Jacob exacts a blessing ('I will not let you go unless you bless me', v. 26).[109] Barthes begins his account by mentioning features of the story that would interest a structuralist critic, such as the folklorist theme of the crossing of a river, and draws diagrams to illustrate the structure of the text. However, he then remarks that even at the beginning of the story there is ambiguity and

---

[105] Jacques Derrida, *Writing and Difference*, trans. A. Bass (London: Routledge, 1978), pp. 221–31.

[106] Derrida, *Of Grammatology*, p. 12. Cf. Derrida, *Speech and Phenomena*, p. 39.

[107] Jacques Derrida, 'Limited Inc abc', *Glyph* 2 (1977), p. 197; cf. Derrida, *Writing and Difference*, trans. A. Bass (London: Routledge & Kegan Paul, 1978), pp. 298–9.

[108] The identification of the stranger as an angel in Hosea 12:4 is doubtless a euphemism for God.

[109] Roland Barthes, 'Struggle with the Angel' in Barthes, *Image/Music/ Text*, trans. Stephen Heath (London: Collins/Fontana, 1993), pp. 125–41.

contradiction within the text: we cannot be sure from the account whether Jacob does indeed cross the ford of Jabbok, or on which side of the river the wrestling takes place. One verse declares that he crossed the ford, another that he sent his family across and 'remained alone'. Barthes is not interested in the source-critical question of whether there is a combination of two originally separate sources here, but only in the shape of the final narrative, in which there are 'frictions, breaks, discontinuities'.[110] The text pauses, hovers, and stumbles at its very threshold.

Structural criticism can be used to analyse three sequences in the story—the crossing, the wrestling, and the naming—and to find mythical patterns in them. But Barthes' structural analysis collapses into 'poststructuralism'. He notes several points of internal conflict, in addition to the location of the wrestling-match, which produce a sense of surprise, giving the impression of an 'open network which is the very infinity of language'.[111] The one who strikes the decisive blow does not win but is defeated; Jacob is marked out by his new name not as a hero but as a limping survivor; the old structural types of a 'sender' of the quest-hero and an 'opponent' are confused, as the sender (God, according to Gen 31:13) turns out to *be* the opponent; God is exposed as a cheat, striking an illegal blow, and thereby taking on the identity of Jacob who cheated his brother; finally, Jacob's request for the divine name is apparently refused, but it is still given indirectly ('I have seen the face of El'). Criticism, urges Barthes, is called to the task of showing how the text 'is unmade, how it explodes, disseminates', so that as we read the text we do not 'reduce the text to a signified, whatever it may be (historical, economic, folkloric, or kerygmatic), but . . . keep its signifying power open'.[112]

Such a multivalent, open reading of the biblical text is actually in line with the Christian tradition of interpretation, which has always found several levels of meaning in the text, which were finally tidied up into the mediaeval 'fourfold exegesis' of literal, allegorical (usually doctrinal), tropological (moral), and tropological (spiritual) meanings.[113] Earlier, Augustine had understood the nature of the biblical text to be polysemic, believing that it was God's intention for different readers to find different meanings in the text. With regard to Genesis, for example, others might disagree with his own exegesis, but 'through [Moses] God has tempered the sacred books to the interpretation of many, who could come to see a diversity of truths'.[114]

---

[110] Barthes, 'Struggle with the Angel', p. 94.
[111] Barthes, 'Struggle with the Angel', p. 85.
[112] Barthes, 'Struggle with the Angel', p. 94.
[113] See Gerhard Ebeling, 'The New Hermeneutics and the Early Luther', *Theology Today* 21 (1964), pp. 34–46.
[114] Augustine, *Confessions* XII.31.42, trans. Henry Chadwick (Oxford: Oxford University Press, 1992), p. 271.

Recently, David Ford has maintained that a 'wisdom interpretation' of Scripture is attentive to multiple meanings, since it is a hermeneutic based on a desire to find the wisdom of God in life now; there must be an abundance of interpretations, both because of the 'abundance of grace of God in Christ' and because reading takes place in a whole variety of communities with their different 'cries' of need. There is, he urges, a 'huge surplus of meaning', and rereadings are 'not systematizable under some "master" theory, theology or metanarrative'.[115] Later I intend to argue that there is a commonality between the hermeneutics of a sacred text and *all* texts, but even a Christian approach to Scripture which is 'sophianic' (in the sense explained by my opening chapter) shows that there is a basic sympathy with postmodern insights into openness of meaning. In a theological perspective, this openness is held in tension with the boundaries set up by doctrinal concepts (such as Ford's own belief that God is at work through divine wisdom in history), but theology must always be ready for these parameters to be broken open by the surprise that comes from image and narrative.[116]

Derrida's perception that all signs contains only a 'trace' of the other to which they point can, of course, be exaggerated into a *total* fluidity of meaning and a *total* loss of any reference beyond the sign that is much less amenable to a dialogue with the Jewish–Christian tradition of wisdom. Baudrillard, for instance, undertands signs as being only signs of other signs: they are 'simulacra' or a self-referring virtual reality. We live, he declares in an era where we experience a simulation of reality, which has destroyed the original reality that it has replaced. He writes: 'to simulate is not simply to feign. . . . feigning or dissimulation leaves the reality intact . . . whereas simulation threatens the difference between 'true' and 'false,' between 'real' and 'imaginary'.[117] I will be suggesting in this study that God can never be conceived *without* the signs of the world, but Baudrillard poses the question: 'what if God himself could be simulated, that is to say, *reduced* to the signs which attest his existence? Then the whole system becomes weightless . . . never again exchanging for what is real, but exchanging in itself in an uninterrupted circuit.'[118] Reflecting on the deliberate creation of signs in human society, Baudrillard suggests that these are simply another level of simulation, one that simulates simulating in order to deceive us into thinking that there is something 'real' beyond the glittering surfaces of the simulacra. He appeals to the simulations of Disneyland as the prime example of this phenomenon: 'Disneyland is presented as imaginary in order to make us believe that the rest is real, when in fact Los Angeles and the

---

[115] Ford, *Christian Wisdom*, pp. 52, 56, 71.

[116] See Fiddes, *Freedom and Limit*, pp. 45–6.

[117] Jean Baudrillard, *Simulations*, trans. P. Foss, P. Patton, P. Beitchman (NewYork: Semiotext(e), 1983), p. 5.

[118] Baudrillard, *Simulations*, p. 10. My italics.

America surrounding it are no longer real, but of the order of the hyperreal and of simulation.'[119]

Even if we do not interpret the sign-making in our present culture to this degree of nihilism, there is a pervasive mood around in which verbal and visual signs can be felt to be self-enclosed, an autonomous web. The net can close in upon itself. A reader can find the world of the text to be open to nothing outside itself, as a crisis of confidence befalls our culture about whether words can represent anything—God, the self, or the world around. In his book *Real Presences*, George Steiner refers to this crisis as a shattering of trust, a breaking of a contract.[120] However slippery and fragile words might be, Western civilization has in the past lived with a trustfulness that there is some kind of relationship between the word and the world. It is this contract of trust—we might prefer to use Steiner's alternative term 'covenant'—that has now broken down. A 'crisis of representation' has befallen the academic and artistic community, but it is not absent from popular culture. Television gives us many examples of advertisements which scarcely refer to the product any longer, but entice us instead into the inner world occupied by the persons portrayed; watching a beautiful girl assert her identity by driving a car, or a young man washing his jeans in a launderette, we exclaim in bewilderment: 'what was that advert all *about*?'

Such a popular mood can be created by the postmodern perception of the fragility of signs, but at the same time I suggest that this can be an important ground for conversation with a Christian theology of *sophia*, which is also (as we shall see) only too aware of the uncertain relation between sign and world. Meanwhile, we turn to a fourth set of ideas that has fed into the ethos of late-modern thinking.

(d) *The challenge of the sublime*

If the first set of ideas reaches back to Husserl, the second to Nietzsche, and the third to de Saussure, the fourth is rooted in a reading of Kant. Kant followed the lead of Edmund Burke (1757)[121] in overturning a long tradition of conceiving the sublime as an intensification of the beautiful, and in replacing it by a contrast of one with the other. For Kant, the sense of the beautiful is a result of harmony between the imagination and the understanding, while the feeling of sublimity is the result of a conflict between the imagination and the reason. Kant considers the sublime, unlike the beautiful, to be connected with both emotion and morality. Sublimity results from a conflict between

---

[119] Baudrillard, *Simulations*, p. 25.

[120] George Steiner, *Real Presences. Is There Anything in What We Say?* (London: Faber and Faber, 1991), pp. 90–2.

[121] Edmund Burke, *A Philosophical Enquiry into the Origin of our Ideas of the Sublime and Beautiful*, ed. Adam Phillips (Oxford: Oxford University Press, 1990).

imagination and reason (as distinct from understanding which applies categories to sensations) and is occasioned by what is vast, limitless, and formless
in nature, or by what is immensely powerful. Reason demands that we place
what we see in the world within a totality or systematic wholeness. Reason
imposes the law that things must make a whole. But confronted with lofty
mountains, a sky full of stars, a great waterfall, or a stormy sea, imagination
strives to its utmost to satisfy the requirement of reason for wholeness, and
fails.[122] The result is a mixture of feelings: as Iris Murdoch puts it in her
summary of Kant's sublime, 'on the one hand we experienced distress at this
failure of imagination to compass what is before us, and on the other hand we
feel exhilaration in our consciousness of the absolute nature of reason's
requirement and the way in which it goes beyond what mere sensible imagination can achieve.'[123] So the experience of the sublime is a 'negative pleasure',[124] shocking us into realizing that we are not trapped in the senses, that we
have a 'supersensible faculty'[125] and a supersensible destiny.

This mixed experience, Kant remarks, is very like the experience of respect
for the moral law, which he calls *Achtung*.[126] In *Achtung* we feel frustrated at
the thwarting of our sensuous nature by a moral requirement, but at the same
time we are elated by the consciousness of our rational nature. We are exhilar-
ated by a sense that we have freedom to conform to the absolute requirements
of reason. So Murdoch draws the conclusion that for Kant the experience of
the sublime, resembling as it does the exercise of the will in moral judgement,
is actually an experience of moral freedom: 'the freedom of sublimity does not
symbolize, but *is* moral freedom, only moral freedom not practically active but
only, as it were, intuiting itself in an exultant manner'.[127] For Kant, then, the
experience of the sublime underlines the superiority of the moral subject over
against the objectivity of the world. Indeed, the sublime is a renewal of
spiritual power of the self arising from observing the vast formless strength
of the natural world.

Through a winding path of its appearance in the Romantics, the sublime has
now had a new flowering in our late-modern era. Like its use in Kant, the
experience of the sublime is to be placed in contrast to the experience of the
beautiful, or of particular forms in the world that we contemplate with
pleasure. The postmodern sublime runs contrary to Kant, however, in introducing an actual *opposition* betweeen the sublime and the beautiful, and
reinforcing an attack on the dominant consciousness of the subject. Linking
with scepticism about the ability of the sign to refer directly to the world, the

---

[122] Kant, *Critique of Judgement*, §26, pp. 98–109.
[123] Murdoch, 'Sublime and the Good', p. 208.
[124] Kant, *Critique of Judgement*, §§23, 29, pp. 91, 120.
[125] Kant, *Critique of Judgement*, §25, p. 97.
[126] Kant, *Critique of Judgement*, §§25, 29, pp. 96, 123.
[127] Murdoch, 'Sublime and the Good', p. 209.

sublime appears as the 'thrill of the void', an event of nothingness and absence that overturns the realm of representation, presence, and stability. Appealing to the notion of the sublime, Jean-François Lyotard finds 'narratives of the unrepresentable' everywhere in the philosophy of our age.[128] The 'unrepresentable', whether it be called 'difference' (Jacques Derrida), 'chaos' (Gilles Deleuze), 'being' (Martin Heidegger), 'otherness' (Emmanuel Levinas), or infinity, is presented as offering a challenge to the representable. Each of these disturbing elements will make their entrance into my own narrative as this book proceeds. But in summary, there is an aspect of the late-modern mood which proposes that what is true, good, and just lies beyond the surface of things and enters to break up the conventional structures of objects in the world.

The opposition between the sublime and the beautiful is intense in Lyotard, who reads Kant as proposing that 'the aesthetic of the sublime . . . brings about the overturning, the destruction, of the aesthetics of the beautiful'. Using a striking image, he declares that 'the marriage' between the imagination and the understanding 'is broken by the sublime',[129] and even that the sublime does 'violence' to an imagination that delights in the beautiful forms of the world.[130] Sublimity is an erotic impulse that evokes a thinking of what cannot be represented in signs and images, and which Lyotard enlists as part of his war against all totalizing kinds of thought, including a universal aesthetic. For Christian theology, and for the tradition of wisdom in particular, the problem with this appeal to the sublime is that it seems to be a negation of a finite creation where the glory of God shines out in all the multiple details of the world. In Gregory of Nyssa, for instance, the infinity of God appears as a kind of excessiveness in the world. According to his commentary on *The Song of Songs* (sometimes regarded as part of the Hebraic wisdom literature) the finite participates in the infinite which inflames our desire and draws us into an endless display of beauty in both God and the world; the God who is 'beyond the beyond' is also intimately present in creation whose forms thus display a beauty which always exceeds itself.[131] As David Bentley Hart affirms, the infinite horizon of beauty is not an orientation towards a formless absolute or towards a sublime that surpasses the aesthetic; rather, objects of attention and love are open to an infinity of perspectives, allowing for ceaseless supplementation, expansion of meaning and re-composition.[132] Though Iris

---

[128] Jean-François Lyotard, *Lessons on the Analytic of the Sublime: Kant's 'Critique of Judgment*, trans. E. Rottenberg (Stanford: Stanford University Press, 1994), pp. 50–8; Lyotard, *The Postmodern Condition*, p. 81.

[129] Jean-François Lyotard, *The Inhuman. Reflections on Time*, trans. G. Bennington and R. Bowlby (Stanford: Stanford University Press, 1988), pp. 136–7.

[130] Lyotard, *Lessons*, p. 239.

[131] Gregory of Nyssa, *In Canticum Canticorum* 2. 8.

[132] Hart, *Beauty of the Infinite*, p. 19.

Murdoch does not have a theistic framework, she is in agreement in finding the sublime to lie in the boundless particularities of the world. The sublime shocks and amazes us, she writes, but 'what stuns us into a realization of our supersensible destiny is not, as Kant imagined, the formlessness of nature, but rather its unutterable particularity'.[133]

While Hart's main aim is to *replace* the postmodern sublime with attention to the beautiful, I suggest that—while recognizing the dangers of loss of the particular forms of the world—the sublime also offers common ground for theology and thinkers of the late-modern world to explore a sense of transcendence. The sense of the sublime alerts us, as Derrida puts it, to 'what comes in'. In his essay 'Of an Apocalyptic Tone Newly Adopted in Philosophy', Derrida reflects on the appeal to 'come' which resonates through the Revelation of St John the Divine. It points, he suggests, to an event of 'coming' (*venir*) which is an 'event of the other', a 'breaking out' into the open in which the cry 'come' (*viens*) is for something new that shatters the horizon of sameness and challenges us with the need for justice.[134] While Derrida does not use the actual term 'sublime' here,[135] this 'coming' clearly functions as a signal of the sublime. As John Caputo comments, 'The very structure of the *Viens* is to disturb the horizon of the present with the call of the impossible... the *viens* calls for a step beyond that it is structurally impossible to complete... *Viens* does not let itself be brought before any court of reason... *Viens* is a certain structural wakefulness or openness to an impossible breach of the present, shattering the conditions of possibility by which we are presently circumscribed'.[136]

Derrida confesses that he has become intrigued by the resonance of the appeal 'Come!' throughout the text of the Book of Revelation (though he had also previously found the imperative *viens* in Maurice Blanchot).[137] The invitation accompanies the opening of the first four of the seven seals (Revelation 6:1–8), the showing of the judgement of the Great Harlot (17:1), and the showing of the bride of the Lamb in the heavenly Jerusalem (21:9). Above all, the book ends with the invitation 'Come' issued by the Spirit and the bride, to which the visionary responds 'Come, Lord Jesus'. The text shows the multivalency of meaning that a deconstructive critic finds in all texts, since—according to Derrida's exegesis—it is unclear to the reader who the

---

[133] Murdoch, 'Sublime and the Good', p. 215.

[134] Jacques Derrida, 'Of an Apocalyptic Tone', pp. 54–5, 64–7.

[135] But see his extended analysis of the Kantian sublime in his 'Parergon', pp. 119–47, as 'conflict, disharmony, counterforce' (p. 129) and 'between the presentable and the unpresentable' (p. 143).

[136] John Caputo, *The Prayers and Tears of Jacques Derrida: Religion without Religion* (Bloomington: Indiana University Press, 1997), pp. 95–6.

[137] See Caputo, *Prayers and Tears*, pp. 77–81, and Jacques Derrida, *Parages* (Paris: Galilée, 1987), p. 66.

speaker or author of the invitation is. Jesus is on the face of it the one who says 'stay awake, I am coming soon' (22:7, 12, 20); he is the narrative voice which is heard from behind John's back (1:9–11). But throughout the text Derrida finds a 'differential multiplication of messages', a complex interaction of narrative voices and narrating voice so that one is often not clear who speaks or writes, or who addresses what to whom.[138] There is an interlacing of 'narrative sending', which Derrida evidently identifies as an open series of signifiers and signified. At the very beginning of the book, for instance, God is said to give a revelation to Christ, who gives it to his angel, who gives it to John, who gives it to the reader (Rev. 1:1–2). Yet all this is summed up as somehow being 'the testimony *of* Jesus Christ'. The confusion as to who is speaking also comes out into the open in the final chapter, with the mingled voices of the angel, Jesus, John, the Spirit, the Bride, and 'the one who testifies', but every time someone speaks in the book he does so through a narrator who is apparently not simply John. Derrida concludes that the recurrent invitation 'Come' thus resists any assimilation to ideology, and 'tolerates no metalinguistic citation',[139] since one cannot deduce its origin and so the issuing authority. 'Come' cannot be made into an object to be examined or categorized: it points to an absent place which is not described, and it is addressed to recipients who are not identified in advance.

'Come' is the apocalyptic tone itself, 'the apocalypse of the apocalypse', without message, without messengers, without senders or destinations.[140] In this single word Derrida is thus able to sum up deconstructionist convictions about the *absences* of the writer and the referent from a text, that enable the reader to find inexhaustible meaning within it. 'Come' breaks open the ending of the narrative. When we think that everything is neatly wrapped up through the Last Judgement into either the heavenly Jerusalem or the lake of fire, there is heard once more the word 'Come!' The invitation is issued to drink of the water of life. The apocalypse breaks into the apocalypse, so that even the ending deconstructs itself, and disperses meaning rather than completing it. But the word 'come' also takes us *beyond* deconstruction. In *Psyche: Inventions of the Other*, Derrida affirms that deconstruction is only the preparation for something else, 'to prepare oneself for the coming of the other'.[141] Here Derrida distinguishes between two sense of 'invention': a 'discovery' of the same, and a coming-in (*invenir*) of the other. 'Invention of the same' is discovery of what is already embedded in the system, the programme, the existing order, with no surprises. 'Invention of the other' is based on

---

[138] Derrida, 'Apocalyptic Tone', pp. 52–6.
[139] Derrida, 'Apocalyptic Tone', p. 65.
[140] Derrida, 'Apocalyptic Tone', p. 66.
[141] Jacques Derrida, 'Psyche, Inventions of the Other', trans. C. Porter, in Lindsay Waters and Wlad Godzich (eds), *Reading de Man Reading* (Minneapolis: University of Minnesota Press, 1989), p. 56.

deconstruction of prevailing concepts and practices of discovery.[142] Taking 'difference' seriously beckons us 'toward another coming. . . . of which we dream, the invention of the wholly other (*tout autre*), the one that allows the coming of a still anticipatable alterity'.[143]

The plea 'come!' points to a place and a time which cannot be contained by philosophy, metaphysics, or theology. This coming is an *in-venir*, an incoming of the wholly other which cannot be objectified and possessed and which is always 'yet to come'.[144] The advent of the other is to be distinguished, Derrida says, from a 'theological order', by which he means an 'ontotheology'[145] in which God establishes a pre-given order of things where the only 'invention' (*in-venir*) is for us to 'discover' it, where we can only fill in the details to a predetermined scheme, and where 'nothing comes to the other or from the other'.[146] Theology is, I suggest, not interested in such a God either, but in a creator who enables what is created to be genuinely creative and so to exercise 'wisdom'. Deconstruction, Derrida avers, is a discourse that works at not being enclosed by 'the same' but which dreams of 'the absolute surprise', 'allowing the adventure or the event of the *tout autre* to come'.[147] Yet deconstruction can only prepare for the advent of the other: it cannot effect it or bring it about. I suggest that when the process of discerning and affirming 'difference' is related to the radical difference of alterity, theology can work with this sense of a sublime disturbance, as a kind of transcendence. At the same time this is a transcendence which is always immanent, as the difference of the 'other' can never be disconnected from the differential network of signs that constitutes the world.

This last of the four strands that contribute to the late-modern mood illustrates particularly well the way that they are woven together. We could, in fact, begin with any one of the four and show their interconnections. For instance, beginning from immersion into the world, we could analyse the influences that construct the self as being both oppressive ideologies and the prevenient structures of language, both of which in turn are brought into question (though in different ways) by the 'sublime'. But there is an advantage in beginning with the incoming of 'alterity' in the sublime: this requires 'difference', which is at the basis of openness of meaning in texts. The

---

[142] Derrida, 'Psyche', 43–5.

[143] Derrida, 'Psyche', p. 55.

[144] See also Derrida, *Parages*, p. 66.

[145] As used by Derrida, following Heidegger, 'ontotheology' means equating God as a Supreme Being (a projection of existent beings) with Being itself, or with the first principle and ground of all reality. See Derrida, 'Différance', p. 6; Martin Heidegger, 'The Onto-theo-logical Constitution of Metaphysics' in *Identity and Difference*, trans. J. Stambaugh (Chicago: Chicago University Press, 2002), p. 58. For my own rejection of ontotheology in this sense, see Chapter 5, the section called 'The Complex Being of the Triune God'.

[146] Derrida, 'Psyche', p. 60.

[147] Derrida, 'Psyche', p. 61.

affirming of difference, like the experience of the sublime, undermines totalizing 'grand stories' which are only concealed ideologies imposed by dominant subjects, whose isolated subjectivity is questioned by the immersion of self into the world. This is the setting in which I intend to construct a theology of wisdom, or perhaps one might say it is the social network in which I aim to have a conversation of many voices.

3

'Where Were You'? Self and Other

THE QUEST FOR THE SELF

One constantly hears of a 'death of the self' or 'total loss of the self' which is supposed to appear in postmodern thinking. I have already questioned this sweeping generalization, and would rather speak of a 'quest' for the self in its relation to the world. There is a widespread *tendency* to absorb the self into structures of language, or society, or into boundless desire, but only some thinkers of this period (Deleuze, Lacan, and Žižek, for example)[1] portray anything like a death of the self. In others, alongside the tendency there is also a resistance to it on behalf of a self which is responsible in the face of the other.

The 'other' might be identifiable as the neighbour, as in Levinas, or might remain sublimely unrepresentable, as in Derrida, but (as Edith Wyshogrod has proposed) there cannot be an alterity without some kind of identity or 'singularity' of the subject who is open to the other.[2] The question is how to express it. The late-modern mood is good at negatives here, since there is certainly the loss of a certain *kind* of self. This has become clear through reflecting on the various strands of influence that I isolated in the last chapter. As we have seen, there is, first, an attack on the dominant, controlling subjectivity of modernity, set over against an objective world. There is, second, a denial of any self that is transcendent in the sense of being detached from the signs of the world. And, third, there is the loss of self as any kind of objective, stable entity that we can *observe* and possess, in favour of the self as a project that is always to be made.

This third point deserves expansion, especially in the context of the mood of wisdom literature, which is that of 'seeing' the world. On an initial glance,

---

[1] On the 'empty self' in Žižek and Lacan, see Slavoj Žižek, *How to Read Lacan* (London: Granada, 2006), Chapter 3, *passim*. For the self in Deleuze, see six paragraphs further on.

[2] Edith Wyschogrod, *Saints and Postmodernism: Revisioning Moral Philosophy* (Chicago; University of Chicago Press, 1990), pp. 236, 252–7, distinguishing 'singularity' from individuality or particularity. See Jacques Derrida, *The Gift of Death*, trans. D. Wills (Chicago: University of Chicago Press, 1995), p. 66, on 'the absolute singularity of the other' for whom God is the name.

there seems to be a conflict here between two partners in dialogue I am staging, since there is a deep suspicion in late modernism of either the world or the self as objects of observation. Emphasis on the ability to observe things is suspected of becoming an adulation of the human mind as a God-like spectator of the material world, bringing everything into a unified viewpoint with a detached, disembodied 'Cartesian perspectivalism'.[3] In a later chapter I am going to consider whether this critique can be reconciled with the wisdom emphasis on cultivating the craft of looking at the world, but here we need to consider the results of this 'ocular regime' on the nature of the self—for the self too can be understood as an entity to be observed. The image of the *camera obscura*, drawn from the expanding field of the science of optics, became a powerful philosophical metaphor during the age of Enlightenment. The *camera obscura* was a dark chamber on whose walls images of the outside world appeared, projected by the entrance of rays of light through a small hole. When applied to the human mind, first by Locke and later implicitly by Descartes,[4] this image not only separated the 'inside' of the mind from the 'outside' of the world, and deprived the things seen of any significance other than being playthings of the observer. It also envisaged the self as an inner spectator, inhabiting the dark chamber or theatre of the mind as a *homunculus*, a human-like figure, who could muse upon images abstracted from the world of the senses.[5] That is, the ego as a disembodied spectator could observe the 'self' with the mind's eye.

The impact of this image was to suppose that the reflexive 'self' (myself) was a stable, self-sufficient entity that could be possessed by the subject ('I'); it was an empirical phenomenon open to exploration and investigation. Hume, for instance, assumed that one could look within oneself to perceive a succession of mental perceptions (though the result was to make him doubt how stable the self actually was). This confidence has been undermined by the claims of Nietzsche and Freud that the process of inner perception is absolutely concealed from us because of the mechanisms of self-delusion in which we are caught. Moreover, our apparent observation of the self can be dismissed as a mere internalizing of the hostile gaze turned on us by others; we are

---

[3] Martin Jay's phrase, in his *Downcast Eyes: The Denigration of Vision in Twentieth-Century French Thought* (Berkeley: University of California Press, 1994), pp. 76–8, 186–7. Cf. Stephen Pattison, *Seeing Things: Deepening Relations with Visual Artefacts* (London: SCM, 2007), pp. 33–7.

[4] John Locke, *An Essay concerning Human Understanding*, ed. Alexander Campbell Fraser, 2 Volumes (New York: Dover, 1959), vol. 1, pp. 211–12; René Descartes, *Discourse on Method, Optics, Geometry and Meteorology*, trans. P. Olscamp (Indianapolis: Hackett, 2001), pp. 87–90. See Dalia Judovitz, *Subjectivity and Representation in Descartes* (New York: Cambridge University Press, 1988).

[5] See Maurice Merleau-Ponty, 'Man and Adversity' in Merleau-Ponty, *Signs*, trans R.C. McCleary (Evanston: Northwest University Press, 1964), p. 240: 'a second man behind the retinal image . . . responsible for seeing the first [the image on the retina]'.

conscious of ourselves as victimized and objectified by the gaze of others who seek to reduce and control us by their look. Sartre especially had a relentless critique of the gaze, which led him to dismiss the self as an 'illusion'. 'I am possessed by the Other', Sartre writes; 'the Other's look fashions my body in its nakedness, produces it as it is, sees it as I shall never see it. The Other holds a secret—the secret of what I am.'[6] In his play *The Flies*, King Aegisthus complains that his image of himself is only the image others have of him:

> I have come to see myself *only as they see me*. I peer into the dark pit of their souls and there, deep down, I see the image that I have built up. I shudder, but I cannot take my eyes off it. Almighty Zeus, who am I? Am I anything more than the dread others have of me?[7]

The lighted inner theatre has become a dark pit. For Sartre, as we have seen, in the face of the illusion of the self the consciousness can still make its spontaneous acts of freedom, but even this subjectivity is lost in some thinkers of the truly late-modern era.

We may take Deleuze as one portrayal of a radical loss of the subject. He picks up Freud's perception that the self is swayed by conflicting impulses of desire, which he links to Nietzsche's insistence that the self is motivated towards fullness of being by the will to power. His conclusion, however, is that desire is not an attribute of the subject at all, but is the force that circulates within an economy and is socially apportioned in accordance with specifiable laws of distribution. Desire is a kind of commodity, streaming without restriction on the 'plane' or 'collectivity' of existence, and it 'produces' desiring persons.[8] The 'body without organs' (freed from all inhibiting organizations) is manufactured through practices of desire, and is conceived as transpersonal and cosmic, with multiple capacities for experience.[9] This body is deprivatized as the possession of the individual, and its surface is inscribed (indeed, wounded) with the codes of social alliance without which there would be no culture and no memory, and which are more primordial than any individual biological codes. In this endless flow of desire between persons without boundaries, there is no 'lack'. Desire is usually understood to be an intention aimed at what is absent, and which one wishes to be present. As Edith Wyschogrod points out, in postmodern thought, which stresses 'difference', there is a real alterity because the 'other' who is desired is absent and felt to be lacking. But in this 'pleromatic' or 'ecstatic postmodernism' (which Wyschogrod also detects in the *jouissance* of Lacan), any lack is suppressed by

⁶ Sartre, *Being and Nothingness*, p. 445.
⁷ Sartre, *The Flies*, trans. S. Gilbert, in *Altona; Men Without Shadows; The Flies* (Harmondsworth: Penguin, 1965), p. 291.
⁸ Gilles Deleuze and Félix Guattari, *Anti-Oedipus: Capitalism and Schizophrenia*, trans. R. Hurley, M. Seem, H. R. Lane (London: Continuum, 2004), pp. 31–8.
⁹ Deleuze and Guattari, *Anti-Oedipus*, pp. 153–6.

interpreting desire quasi-materially as a process of flow and production, with unrestricted access to the basic raw material—desire itself.[10] Desire does not lack an object: what is missing is any fixed subject that does the desiring. Deleuze explains:

> If desire produces, its product is real . . . as autoproduction of the unconscious. Desire does not lack anything; it does not lack its object. It is, rather, the subject that is missing in desire, or desire that lacks a fixed subject; there is no fixed subject unless there is repression.[11]

By contrast, we may take Derrida as representing the kind of qualified loss of the self in the threefold form I have described above—loss of the dominating self, loss of the sign-less self, and loss of the observed self. Commenting on Husserl's notion of a 'transcendental ego' that can see the essences of things that appear in the self-consciousness, Derrida denies that there is any such 'metaphysical phantom of the empirical ego'; indeed, he goes on, 'this leads us to take the ego—as absolute spectator of its own psychic self—to be but a theoretical image and metaphor.'[12] Neither an ego-subject that observes the self, nor a self that is observed, are actual. What remains after these denials is a *quest* for the human self, which Derrida roughly indicates in the term 'life'. In a late interview Derrida proposes this quest in a riddling, paradoxical way, affirming that 'everything I oppose, so to speak, in my texts, everything that I deconstruct—presence, living, voice and so on—is exactly what I'm after in life. I love the voice, I love presence, I love . . . ; there is no love, no desire without it.'[13] No wonder that in the last recorded interview with him, entitled *Learning to Live Finally* (his own phrase taken from his *Spectres of Marx*),[14] he confesses 'I am at war with myself, it's true, you couldn't possibly know to what extent.'[15] Just as deconstruction prepares for the 'in-coming of the other', so 'life' somehow precedes deconstruction, and remains in tension with it. That this 'life' implies more of a self than Deleuze's economy of desire is clear from his statement of the tension in which he lives, that 'I insist on the fact that there is no pure presence . . . nevertheless there is a desire for presence and intimacy.'[16]

Derrida's word for the quest for the living self is the 'secret'. Reflecting on the story of Abraham, when God calls him to sacrifice his son Isaac (Genesis 22), Derrida finds the name 'God' to be a place-holder for every other who

---

[10] Wyschogrod, *Saints and Postmodernism*, p. 199.

[11] Deleuze and Guattari, *Anti-Oedipus*, p. 28.

[12] Derrida, *Speech and Phenomena*, pp. 11–12.

[13] Michael Payne and John Schad (eds), *Life. After. Theory* (London: Continuum, 2003), p. 8.

[14] Jacques Derrida, *Spectres of Marx: The State of the Debt, the Work of Mourning and the New International*, trans. P. Kamuf (New York: Routledge, 1994), p. xvii.

[15] Jacques Derrida and Jean Birnham, *Learning to Live Finally*, trans. P.-A. Brault and M. Naas (Hoboken: Melville House, 2007), p. 47.

[16] Payne and Schad (eds), *Life. After. Theory*, p. 9.

makes a demand upon us: *tout autre est tout autre*—'every other is wholly other'.[17] In accord with both Kierkegaard and Levinas, Derrida claims that the demand of the other for one's own self-sacrifice is outrageous to all forms of institutional ethics. Unlike Levinas, Derrida is willing to extend the irreducible ethical claim of the other upon us beyond human persons to all objects in the world—'just as well places, animals, language'.[18] Now, this demanding and infinite singularity of the other implies the singularity of one's own self, but this is a 'secret', just as the singularity of the other is a secret. Thus Abraham in the story is reduced to silence when Isaac questions him, for his response— 'God will provide the lamb'—is a non-response. Abraham cannot share his absolute secret with us, since it is also a secret to him: 'Abraham doesn't know anything.'[19] Here Derrida is clearly referring to Kierkegaard's 'secret' of subjectivity, to which Heidegger also seems to refer as he reflects on the way that one's own 'particular Dasein' can get 'levelled down' in the experience of the everyday, so that 'Every secret loses its force.'[20] Derrida reflects that:

> God, as the wholly other, is to be found everywhere there is something of the wholly other. And since *each of us*, everyone else, *each other* is infinitely other in its absolute singularity . . . not originarily present to my ego . . . then what can be said about Abraham's relation to God can be said about my relation without relation to every other as wholly other, in particular my relation to my neighbour or my loved ones who are as inaccessible to me, as secret and transcendent as Yahweh.[21]

We share the 'secret' of being responsible for the other, a demand that we cannot communicate to others or even examine within ourselves; so while we share it (we all have the secret) we *cannot* share it. This, I suggest, is a never-ending 'quest' for the self in relation to the world. Now, as Caputo recognizes,[22] for Derrida, this secret of subjectivity 'passes over into the deconstructive secret' with the question:

> What is a secret that is a secret about nothing and a sharing that doesn't share anything? Such is the secret truth of faith as absolute responsibility and as absolute passion, the 'highest passion' as Kierkegaard will say.[23]

Elsewhere, Derrida links Kierkegaard's 'passion' of the existing individual with the passion that generates literature, the secret passion that sees to it that literature always makes new beginnings, so that the secret is writing itself:

---

[17] Derrida, *Gift of Death*, p. 68.
[18] Derrida, *Gift of Death*, p. 71.   [19] Derrida, *Gift of Death*, p. 80.
[20] Søren Kierkegaard, *Concluding Unscientific Postscript*, trans. H. V. and H. E. Hong (Princeton: Princeton University Press, 1992), pp. 79–80; Heidegger, *Being and Time*, p. 165. Caputo makes this connection, *Prayers and Tears*, p. 107.
[21] Derrida, *Gift of Death*, p. 80. My italics.
[22] Caputo, *Prayers and Tears*, p. 209.   [23] Derrida, *Gift of Death*, p. 80.

> There is in literature, in the exemplary secret of literature, a chance of saying everything without touching upon the secret . . . the secret impassions us. Even if there is none, even if it does not exist, hidden behind anything, whatever. Even if the secret is no secret, even if there has never been a secret.[24]

Deconstruction works on the fact that 'the readability of the text is structured by the unreadability of the secret, that is by the inaccessibility of a certain intentional meaning'.[25] There is no secret in the sense of a hidden reality behind the tissue of texts, no fixed semantic content which has to be brought to light, only a passion of always beginning again: the exemplary secret means that 'something will have begun'.[26] With the idea of the secret, as with the 'come' of apocalyptic, deconstruction opens the way for the alterity. The secret of the text is bound up with the secret of subjectivity, and this is an 'absolute responsibility' which has no fixed content but whose call we cannot ignore.

Christian theology, and wisdom theology in particular, can work with the elusiveness of the self as portrayed in such late-modern thinking as Derrida's. Wisdom knows that 'the purposes in the human mind are like deep water' (Prov. 20:5). Theology is sympathetic to the overturning of the self as a dominating, sign-less, and possessable reality. In fact, it agrees with Sartre that the self is always open to being shaped by the other, but regards this situation, not with Sartre's fear and loathing, but with delight. The self is a dynamic project, always in process of becoming what it is in relation to God and the world in which it is set. It cannot be 'observed' as an individual, a-priori interior substance, just because it is always being formed in relation to the other. With Paul Tillich, we may register a dialectic of 'individuation' and 'participation': 'every life-process unites a trend toward separation with a trend towards reunion'.[27] Life is marked by a desire for reunion with that from which one has separated. God is no exception: the identification of Being-Itself as love amounts to 'apply[ing] the experience of separation and reunion to the divine life'.[28] To return to the symbol of the Trinity, which I have already mentioned as the Christian 'metanarrative', each hypostasis in this dynamic network of relations is distinct only because of relation to another. This insight was first clearly articulated by Athanasius—finding the difference between 'persons' in God in their relationship of origin to each other. Athanasius could not get very enthusiastic about what the philosophical

---

[24] Jacques Derrida, *On the Name*, trans. T. Dutoit (Stanford: Stanford University Press, 1995), pp. 29–30.

[25] Jacques Derrida, *Given Time: I. Counterfeit Money*, trans. P. Kamuf (Chicago: University of Chicago Press, 1994), p. 152.

[26] Derrida, *On the Name*, p. 142, n.12.

[27] Tillich, *Systematic Theology*, I, p. 310.

[28] Tillich, *Systematic Theology*, I, p. 310.

difference might be between a *hypostasis* and an *ousia*.[29] He was more captivated by the relations of Father, Son, and Spirit. To the sceptical Arian question as what the difference could be between the persons if they are one in divine essence (*ousia*), he gave a different kind of answer: the Father is 'other' (*heteros*) in that he alone begets the Son, the Son is 'other' in that he alone is begotten, and the Spirit is 'other' in that he alone proceeds from the Father.[30] They are different in the way that they are related to each other.

OPENING A CONVERSATION WITH WISDOM: 'WHERE WERE YOU'?

My brief sketch of the reaction against the self or subject of modernity in late-modern thinking will be extended and filled out in the following pages as I venture to make a theology which both connects with this context and is shaped by the Jewish–Christian tradition of wisdom. This venture does not require that late-modern thinkers explicitly comment on wisdom texts. However, it is appropriate to open the conversation, as well as to reflect further on features of late-modernity as outlined in this chapter and the last, by considering the reactions of two late-modern thinkers to one such text. One of these thinkers may be reckoned postmodern—Emmanuel Levinas—and the other—Paul Ricoeur—either rejected such a label or acknowledged it only in a modified sense.[31]

In his reflections on the Book of Job, Levinas takes as a key verse the question posed by Yahweh to the hapless Job: 'Where were you when I laid the foundations of the earth?' (Job 38:4) In the context of this ancient poem, Job has been afflicted with the greatest suffering, losing his family, his riches, and his health. Accused by his so-called friends of hidden sins which have, in their view, prompted divine punishment as retribution, he not only protests his innocence, but demands that God should come 'into court' with him to present his case against him (Job 13:3, 14–22). He is confident that if Yahweh appears, he will be acquitted, vindicated, and restored. The question identified by Levinas is the point when Yahweh does actually finally confront Job in person in a theophany:

---

[29] In fact, for some while he treated them as identical; see *Contra Arianos* 1.11; *De Decretis* 27; *De Synodis* 41.

[30] Athanasius, *Contra Arianos* 3.4–6, cf. 1.9, 39, 58.

[31] He acknowledged that his 'enterprise could be called postmodern if this qualification can apply to reconstruction and not (or not only) to deconstruction': André LaCocque and Paul Ricoeur, *Thinking Biblically. Exegetical and Hermeneutical Studies*, trans. D. Pellauer (Chicago: University of Chicago Press, 1998), p. 116.

Then the LORD answered Job out of the whirlwind:
'Who is this that darkens counsel by words without knowledge?
Gird up your loins like a man,
I will question you, and you shall declare to me.
Where were you when I laid the foundation of the earth? (Job 38:1–4)

The first question is followed by many others, extending over four chapters, enquiring whether Job has the same first-hand knowledge of the vastness of the world, in all its heights and depths, that God has. As scholars and readers have perceived ever since, this 'answer to Job' is not an 'answer' to human suffering at all, but leaves the problem open as a mystery for which no rational solution can be satisfactory. This is a book to which we shall return many times, but for the moment we shall focus on Levinas' engagement (in three different places)[32] with the question of Job 38:4.

Levinas thinks that the poem is written in a way that is critical of its central character, Job, and here he is somewhat at odds with much modern biblical scholarship which views Job simply as the victim of undeserved suffering.[33] Levinas here, however, has the poet William Blake on his side, who sees Job—though essentially innocent of the charges his friends bring against him—to be in need of redemption from legalistic adherence to received wisdom.[34] Job, it seems, has the same perspective as his friends: he assumes that the world runs by a law of retribution, and merely differs from his friends in seeing it as failing to operate properly in his case—hence his concern to get God into the law-court to rectify a miscarriage of justice. The Accuser's question in the prose prologue to the poem is all too relevant: 'Does Job serve God for nothing?'—or does he assume that a comforting order of reward and retribution operates in the universe? From a late-modern perspective, Levinas sees Job's attitude as a misplaced confidence that the world ought to be controllable within a theory of the ego: Job and his friends both try to trace the origins of his misery by an internal examination of his faults—they simply draw different conclusions. Thus Levinas reads *The Book of Job* as exemplifying a critique of the dominating, observable self of modernity.

This brings us to the first major meaning that Levinas finds in the question, 'Where were you when I laid the foundations of the earth?' The question, he

---

[32] In order of original publication: Emmanuel Levinas, 'As Old as the World?' in *Nine Talmudic Readings*, trans. A. Aronowicz (Bloomington: Indiana University Press, 1994) [1968 & 1977], p. 85; Levinas, *Otherwise Than Being: Or Beyond Essence*, trans. A. Lingis (Pittsburgh: Duquesne University Press, 1998), p. 122 [1974]; Levinas, 'Postface: Transcendence and Evil' in Philippe Nemo, *Job and the Excess of Evil: With a Postface by Emmanuel Levinas*, trans. M. Kigel (Pittsburgh: Duquesne University Press, 1998) pp. 165–82 [1978].

[33] See, for example, David Clines, *Job 1–20*. Word Biblical Commentary 17 (Dallas: Word Books, 1989), pp. xxxviii–xlvii.

[34] This view is expressed in his engravings to the Book of Job: see Christopher Rowland, *Blake and the Bible* (New Haven: Yale University Press, 2010), pp. 15–16.

maintains in *Otherwise than Being*, limits the freedom of the ego-self, under-standing it in the sense that 'you have come late to the world':

> We have been accustomed to reason in the name of the freedom of the ego—as though I had witnessed the creation of the world, and as though I could have only been in charge of a world that would have issued out of my free will. These are presumptions of philosophers, presumptions of idealists! That is what scripture reproaches Job for. He would have known how to explain his miseries if they would have devolved from his faults! . . . But the subjectivity of a subject come late into a world which has not issued from his projects does not consist in projecting, or in treating this world as one's project.[35]

In *Nine Talmudic Readings*, Levinas writes similarly, '"Where were you when I created the World?" the Holy One asks [Job]. You are a self, certainly. But even if you are free you are not the absolute beginning. You come after many things and many people.'[36] There is a hint here that 'coming late to the world' includes facing a world full of multiplicity and diverse phenomena, and this too is a limit on the rational freedom of the ego. Levinas agrees with Philippe Nemo in his book *Job and the Excess of Evil* that 'evil is excess in its very quiddity'. In the 'Postface' he writes to Nemo's book he asserts that the suffering which befalls Job is a manifestation of the 'non-integratability of the non-integratable',

> As if, to synthesis, even the purely formal synthesis of Kant's 'I think' which is capable of reuniting data, as heterogeneous as they may be—there still stands opposed, under the species of evil, the non-synthesizable, more heterogeneous still than any heterogeneity subject to being embraced by the formal which exposes heterogeneity in its very malice.[37]

Even if we were to suppose that the heterogeneity of the world, its sheer diversity, could be embraced by Kant's reasonable subject (and this is a concession by Levinas, as is clear from elsewhere), the excess of evil 'exposes' a heterogeneity that baffles the mind. One cannot make any totality that would include evil; in another essay, Levinas describes this non-integrability as the 'uselessness of suffering'.[38] The phenomenon of suffering, its excessiveness and its physicality, defeats any attempt of the subject to categorize the world, or to separate the self from body. But at the same time, the monstrous excessiveness of evil 'ruptures' the everyday life of the world, and so becomes an indicator of 'transcendence'.[39] The 'ex-' in 'excess' is the ex- of exteriority,

---

[35] Levinas, *Otherwise than Being*, p. 122.

[36] Levinas, 'As Old as the World?', p. 85.

[37] Levinas, 'Postface', p. 173.

[38] Emmanuel Levinas, 'Useless Suffering' in Robert Bernasconi and David Wood, *The Provocation of Levinas: Rethinking the Other* (London: Routledge, 1988), p. 163.

[39] So also Paul D. Janz, *God, the Mind's Desire* (Cambridge: Cambridge University Press, 2004), pp. 171–2.

of the wholly other, not merely an opposition of the interior and the imma-nent. Transcendence, moreover, seems to 'shine in the face of other person: alterity of the non-integrateable, of that which does not let itself be gathered into a totality'.[40] The excessiveness of evil alerts us to something else that cannot be integrated in the 'same' of the self—the infinite demand of the other.

This has brought us to the second meaning that Levinas finds in the question, 'Where were you when I laid the foundations of the earth?' It can be read as a 'record of truancy',[41] as if to say 'Where were you when you were needed?' The question only makes sense, reflects Levinas, 'if the humanity of the human being stands in fraternal solidarity with Creation, that is to say, if man is responsible for what was neither his "I" nor his work... which is impossible without pain'.[42] Although the freedom of human subjectivity is limited, writes Levinas in *Otherwise than Being*, the 'lateness' with which it comes to creation ('Where were you?') is not 'insignificant': 'To be responsible over and beyond one's freedom is certainly not to remain a pure result of the world.' The subject is destined to the responsibility of being held 'hostage' to the other's demand, which 'he cannot evade without denying himself, and by virtue of which he is *unique*'.[43] In his *Talmudic Readings* Levinas writes, 'You are a self, certainly' but just because 'you come after many things and many people... you are bound to others beyond your freedom'.[44] Self and subject-ivity is thus established through responsibility to the other, and in the face of the human other we catch a trace of God. Levinas, comments Derrida in his reflection on the story of Abraham, playfully moves about in 'the difference between the face of God and the face of my neighbour, between the infinitely other as God and the infinitely other as human',[45] between two but unique 'wholly others'; this is a difference between two infinities, the infinity of other persons visited upon us in ethical experience and the infinity of God as the trace we can glimpse on the face of the other as God withdraws from the world to leave us to exercise our own responsibility.

In the light of this responsibility, Levinas finds an even sharper critical edge to the question, 'Where were you...?' when it is understood as implying 'when you were needed?' Levinas points out that in the poem Job only wrestles with the problem of his own suffering. The problem of the relationship between the suffering of the 'I' and the suffering that an 'I' can feel of the suffering of another human being never appears in the foreground of either the poem or the commentary by Nemo to which Levinas is writing the 'postface'.[46] Job, it seems, shares the perspective of the friends—the problem for them all (Nemo included!) is the justice or otherwise of one's own

---

[40] Levinas, 'Postface', pp. 173–4.   [41] Levinas, 'Postface', p. 180.
[42] Levinas, 'Postface', p. 180.   [43] Levinas, *Otherwise than Being*, p. 122.
[44] Levinas, 'As Old as the World?', p. 85. (NTR 85).
[45] Derrida, *Gift of Death*, p. 84.   [46] Levinas, 'Postface', p. 180.

suffering. While the text of the book does not explicitly make this criticism of Job, Levinas asks, 'would there not be in this very silence some secret indication?' and suggests that the question of 38:4 implies it. Levinas is in effect re-writing the question as 'Where *are* you?' and—though he does not make the linkage himself—the answer to the question is surely his famous cry of response to the other, *'me voici'*—'I am here.'[47]

In finding the identity of the self before the face of others to be an 'I' which is not a totalizing, dominant self, Levinas *does* approve of the way that Nemo uses the phenomenological method for exploring the problem of suffering. In line with what I suggested in the last chapter was one influence on postmodernity, namely immersion into the world, Levinas finds that the only way to read Job is of a suffering person embedded in the everyday world of 'lived experience', and he commends Nemo for reading it this way. Rather than analysing 'formal structures of being' in order to explain the presence of suffering in the world, the reader needs to examine the 'concrete content' of a consciousness embodied in the world.[48] Here, we may say, there is no gap between the subject and the object, whether this object is the body in pain or things in the world that are causing suffering. If we give attention to the primordial moods that arise from this basic engagement with the world, then we are brought up against a mood of acute anxiety, which leads us towards transcendence.[49] For Husserl, points out Levinas, it indicates a transcendence of the ego and its 'essences' over the empirical self. For Heidegger, Levinas explains, this sense of anxiety in face of the threat of 'nothingness' prompts us into noticing the reality of Being itself which is always neglected in the attention we give to beings; this is in fact the line that Nemo himself takes in his study.[50] But Levinas proposes that Job shows us that attention to the anxieties of lived experience take us in a different direction.

In the first place, we are directed to a transcendence of 'evil that pursues and touches me'; we are alerted to the sheer excessiveness of evil. But sometimes what appears to us, in our state of anxiety, to be an evil is in fact a 'persecution' of us by the other for our own good. The transcendence to which we should be alerted is the infinite demand of the need of the other, who for Job is symbolized in a God who seems to be Job's enemy. Levinas here refers to the place in Nemo's study where he is commenting on those passages where Job protests against being harassed by God, interpreting his suffering as a divine persecution. Among the passages cited by Nemo are the following:[51]

---

[47] Emmanuel Levinas, *Difficult Freedom: Essays on Judaism*, trans. Seán Hand (Baltimore: Johns Hopkins University Press, 1990), p. 89.

[48] Levinas, 'Postface', pp. 180–1, cf. pp. 176–7.

[49] Levinas, 'Postface', pp. 168–9.   [50] e.g. Nemo, *Job*, pp. 103–5.

[51] Nemo, *Job*, pp. 113–14.

Will you not look away from me for a while,
let me alone until I swallow my spittle?
If I sin, what do I do to you, you watcher of humanity?
Why have you made me your target?
Why have I become a burden to you? . . . . . (7:19–20)

Bold as a lion you hunt me;
you repeat your exploits against me.
You renew your witnesses against me
and increase your vexation towards me;
you bring fresh troops against me. (10:16–17)

You have turned cruel to me;
with the might of your hand you persecute me. (30:21)

Levinas' comment on Job's experience is that 'God hurts me and does evil to me in order to . . . hold me up as unique and exceptional', creating 'through the hurt within me, my awakening to myself'.[52] While Nemo understands the 'good' revealed by anxiety to be simply the opposite of evil, Levinas understands the language of persecution to indicate that the good is always a radical *demand* upon us, and in this sense the divine 'law'.[53]

Beginning from phenomenology, we have arrived at a breach with phenomenology in Levinas' idea of self-transcendence. On the one hand, there is a constant appeal to the givenness of lived experience, but on the other Levinas is willing to explore those elements of human experience which remain as an excess over and above the phenomenological reduction. In the midst of seeing phenomena which appear in our consciousness as they are, illuminated in the 'world of light', we come across situations which alert us to the fact that we cannot transcend ourselves from our own initiative—moods like insomnia, disturbing images in modern art, Shakespearean tragedies, and 'useless evil'.[54] We discover that, in the very moment of 'standing out' from being as existents, we are still chained to being, still in slavery, riveted to the self, needing redemption. Like Michaelangelo's half-finished statues of the *Slaves*, we might say, we are struggling out of the stone from which we are emerging, but still embedded in it.[55] Levinas is clear that there is no transcendence of the subject here, in the 'horror of the night "with no exits"'.[56] But it is just here that we can notice the initiative being taken by another, the imperative call to us from outside, from the other, which enables us to transcend ourselves. The event of the other person, beyond all being, is an ethical awakening which in fact *predates* the

[52] Levinas, 'Postface', pp. 177, 175.
[53] Nemo takes up this challenge by Levinas in *Job*, pp. 83–203.
[54] Emmanuel Levinas, *Existence and Existents*, trans. A. Lingis (Pittsburgh: Duquesne University Press, 2001), pp. 47–64.
[55] Levinas himself appeals to the sculpture of Rodin at this point: *Existence and Existents*, p. 70.
[56] Levinas, *Existence and Existents*, p. 58.

subject, although it is only *discovered* 'after the event' of subjectivity. This 'disturbance of the Self by the Other'[57] is, I suggest, a kind of ethical 'sublime'.[58]

The commitment to the other, which is a doing of the law, is an unconditional 'yes.' The origin of the free subject lies in responsibility to the other who is infinitely 'different' to the self, making a demand which is always prevenient, overturning all structures of being and totality with a force like the sublime. Here, the approach of Levinas shows the influence of all four of the elements of postmodernity outlined in the last chapter.[59] But for Levinas this means that to be free is already to be held hostage to another, and—echoing Job—he is prepared to call this demand of the other upon us an 'accusation' and 'persecution' of the self, driving it out of its home into exile.[60] What Job portrays as the accusation of the divine Other, the heavenly hunter, is in fact the demand upon us of all others in the world. It is a call for us to substitute ourselves completely for the other. The relation to the other is thus 'not a harmonious relation of communion' but 'a relationship with a Mystery';[61] it is not mutuality or reciprocity, such as Martin Buber explores in his notion of I and Thou.[62] Levinas judges that this would undermine our responsibility to the absolute demand of the other, and turn it into a comfortable give-and-take. Generosity for the other, asserts Levinas, positively 'requires an ingratitude of the Other':[63] we must expect and want nothing in return. He prefers to think of relationship as the 'proximity' of our neighbour, not an empathetic engagement. In the 'asymmetrical' ethical relation one must not even notice the colour of another's eyes,[64] lest our gaze makes the other an extension of the self, just more of the same. This lack of sympathy in relationship with another has incurred the scorn especially of feminist critics, such as Luce Irigaray, who comments:

> He knows nothing of communion in pleasure. Levinas does not ever seem to have experienced the transcendence of the other which becomes an immediate ecstasy (extase instante) in me and with him—or her. For Levinas, the distance is always maintained with the other in the experience of love.[65]

---

[57] Levinas, 'Postface', p. 182.

[58] Levinas identifies the self-removal of God from the world in favour of the ethical demand as 'sublime': see Emmanuel Levinas, 'Ethics of the Infinite' in Richard Kearney, *States of Mind* (New York: New York University Press, 1995), p. 197. Hart, *Beauty of the Infinite*, pp. 75–92, regards Levinas' demand of the other as a form of the 'postmodern sublime', but rejects it as authentic transcendence.

[59] With regard to 'difference', this is exemplified by the difference between the infinity of the other and that of God.

[60] Levinas, *Otherwise than Being*, pp. 110–12.

[61] Emmanuel Levinas, *Time and the Other*, trans. R. A. Cohen (Pittsburgh: Duquesne University Press, 1987), p. 75.

[62] Levinas, *Totality and Infinity*, pp. 194–201; 'Postface' p. 177.

[63] Levinas, 'Meaning and Sense' in A. Peperzak, S. Critchley, R. Bernasconi (eds), *Levinas. Basic Philosophical Writings* (Bloomington: Indiana University Press, 1996), p. 49.

[64] Emmanuel Levinas, *Ethics and Infinity*, trans. R. Cohen (Pittsburgh: Duquesne University Press, 1985), p. 85.

[65] Luce Irigaray, 'Questions to Emmanuel Levinas' in Margaret Whitford (ed.), *The Irigaray Reader* (Oxford: Blackwell, 1991), p. 180.

Christian theology has warmed to Levinas' theme of responsibility before the face of the other, and the trace this gives of the face of God.[66] The self is to be established only in response to the demand of the infinitely Other. We have already found a similar theme in Derrida, except that Levinas is more definite about the identity of both the other and of the self, both of which remain a 'secret' in Derrida's more deconstructive approach. Levinas' radical sense of the demand of the neighbour is understandable in the light of his own history, interned as a Jew during the Second World War, with close family killed by the SS; the shadow of the Holocaust and its 'useless suffering' hovers over all his work, underlining the horrific consequences of a failure to attend to the moral demand of the other. But Christian theology will want to speak more of Irigaray's 'communion' and Buber's 'reciprocity'. Buber is in fact clear that reciprocity is not a symmetrical 'give and take'; there is an element of being 'overwhelmed' by the other person in any personal relationship, as the core of the subject is broken open by the ethical demand which the other makes.[67] The essence of the I-Thou relation lies in the space 'between' persons, not in an exactly matching and equal response of each person,[68] and yet there is a genuine mutuality as each treats the other as a 'thou' rather than an 'it'.

It may be that in the dialogue between Levinas and *Job*, the book itself has not been allowed sufficiently to speak. The climax of the poem is in the moment when Job acknowledges that he has a personal encounter with God:

> I had heard of you by the hearing of the ear,
> but now my eye sees you. (42:6)

The problem of suffering has not been solved, but it is enough for Job to know that he has not been deserted by God in the midst of it. As one commentator, H. H. Rowley, puts it: 'It is of the essence of [the poem's] message that Job found God *in* his suffering.'[69] There is an intimacy and communion adumbrated here which is more than knowing God as the hunter whose cruel visage is glimpsed in the face of the needy other. Moreover, Job repents—not of asserting his innocence which is upheld by God, but of insisting that God should work by a scheme of retribution. It is only while Job insists on his just deserts that suffering takes on the illusory face of a God who is his enemy.

---

[66] See e.g. David Ford, *Self and Salvation: Being Transformed* (Cambridge: Cambridge University Press), pp. 45–72.

[67] Martin Buber, *I and Thou*, trans. R. Gregor Smith (Edinburgh: T & T Clark, 1937), pp. 51–4, 111–12.

[68] Martin Buber, *Between Man and Man*, trans. R. Gregor Smith (London: Collins/Fontana, 1961), pp. 19–22, 32–3.

[69] So H. H. Rowley, *Job*. The New Century Bible (London: Nelson, 1970), p. 20.

AN ALTERNATIVE CONVERSATION: 'ONESELF
AS ANOTHER'

A somewhat different dialogue with Job emerges from the pages of Paul Ricoeur,[70] and a different approach to the question of the self in the world, while still being critical of aspects of modernity. He begins, however, where Levinas does, in finding the divine question of Job 38:4 ('Where were you when I laid the foundations of the earth'?) to be an undermining not only of a retributive view of suffering, but of the kind of concept of the self developed in the Enlightenment. His understanding of the question is—in effect— 'Where were you when I made a world that does not revolve around you?' The succeeding questions of Yahweh, such as the ones about Behemoth and Leviathan ('Can you take [them]with hooks?') point to things in the world that do not concern Job personally,[71] and yet they are vestiges of the chaos that Yahweh has overcome in bringing order. Job is invited, points out Ricoeur, to 'look at a world composed without him, where the role of man is . . . practically zero.'[72] The display of the vast diversity of creation in these chapters calls for:

> the sacrifice of the demand that was at the beginning of [Job's] recrimination, namely the claim by himself to form a little island of meaning in the universe, an empire within an empire.[73]

Ascribing to the law of retribution had led Job, judges Ricoeur, to 'an explanation in proportion to his existence, a private explanation . . .'[74]

When it comes to a proper understanding of the self, however, Ricoeur wants to establish a subject which is 'at an equal distance' from advocacy of the Cartesian cogito and from the postmodern 'shattering' of the cogito.[75] In his

---

[70] The more significant references to Job in Paul Ricoeur are: *The Symbolism of Evil*, trans. E. Buchanan (Boston: Beacon Press, 1969), pp. 85–6, 314–22; 'The Hermeneutics of Symbols and Philosophical Reflection I', trans. D. Savage, in Don Ihde (ed.), *The Conflict of Interpretations* (Evanston: Northwestern University Press, 1974), p. 309; 'The Demythization of Accusation', trans. P. McCormick, in *Conflict of Interpretations*, p. 351; 'Religion, Atheism and Faith', trans. C. Freilich, in *Conflict of Interpretations*, p. 461; 'On the Exegesis of Gen. 1.1–2.4a' in Mark I. Wallace (ed.) *Figuring the Sacred*, trans. D. Pellauer (Mineapolis: Fortress Press, 1995), pp. 82–3; 'Towards a Hermeneutic of the Idea of Revelation' in Essays on Biblical Interpretation, ed. and trans. Lewis S. Mudge (Philadelphia; Fortress Press, 1980), pp. 86–8. Some of these instances are reviewed by Loretta Dornisch, 'The Book of Job and Ricoeur's Hermeneutics', *Semeia* 19 (1981), pp. 3–22.

[71] Ricoeur, *Symbolism of Evil*, pp. 320–1; 'Religion, Atheism and Faith', p. 461.

[72] Ricoeur, 'Exegesis of Gen. 1.1–2.4a', p. 138, quoting a commentary by P. Beauchamp (p. 135).

[73] Ricoeur, *Symbolism of Evil*, p. 321.

[74] Ricoeur, *Symbolism of Evil*, p. 321.

[75] Paul Ricoeur, *Oneself As Another*, trans. K. Blamey (Chicago: Chicago University Press, 1994), pp. 4, 21.

view, the self is fragile, fallible, and wounded, but it is still a 'capable' self.[76] This is a self which has a 'narrative identity', understanding it to have—and to be—a story within the frame of a temporal relation between the past, present, and future. Such a story only makes sense in the context of a larger story, so that the identity of the 'real self' emerges only in relation to purposes which transcend the individual self. Leaning on Dilthey's idea of the 'connectedness of life',[77] this is an idea of the self which contradicts the 'little island' of the cogito, while maintaining an identity which (we may say) contradicts the 'body without organs' of Deleuze, is firmer than the mere 'secret' of Derrida, and is even more distinct than the persecuted self of Levinas. Moreover, the story-like quality of the self means that it need not be stuck in the limitations, habitus, and conventionalities which belong to the present inscriptions that society writes on the body: the story can be 're-configured', re-written from new perspectives.

One significant way that Ricoeur sees this happening is through stories in literature. Ahead of entering into a text, we carry around in our minds a model of reality, or a representation of the world to ourselves (*mimēsis*$_1$); it is the 'story' we tell ourselves, an orientation which is 'pre-figurative' in the sense of preceding the narrative in any written story, and which shows the capacity of human imagination to exist and act in the world. The writer takes this everyday story and 'configures' or recomposes it (*mimēsis*$_2$, now linked with *poiēsis* or creativity), so that readers can 'reconfigure' their own stories in the light of it (*mimēsis*$_3$), as they enter the world of the text: as Ricoeur writes: 'We are following the destiny of a *prefigured* time that becomes a *refigured* time through the mediation of a *configured* time.'[78]

Job stands for Ricoeur as an instance of this 're-enactment' of the human story. Taking a typical tragic narrative of the innocent sufferer, the story is re-written with an unexpected twist at the ending: the one who is innocent repents, with a 'wholly internal re-enactment which is no longer a restoration of an earlier happiness, but re-enactment of the present unhappiness'.[79] Replacing Ricoeur's term 're-enactment' (which echoes Kierkegaard's 'repetition') with his later hermeneutical tool, we may say that the whole story has been 'configured' from this perspective; the repentance is a 're-enactment of misfortune which illuminates it with a sombre light.'

---

[76] Paul Ricoeur, 'Asserting Personal Capacities and Pleading for Mutual Recognition' in Brian Treanor and Henry Isaac Venema, *A Passion for the Possible: Thinking with Paul Ricoeur* (New York: Fordham University Press, 2010), pp. 22–6.

[77] Ricoeur, *Oneself As Another*, p. 141.

[78] Paul Ricoeur, *Time and Narrative*, 3 Volumes, transl. K. McLaughlin, K. Blamey, D. Pellauer (Chicago and London: University of Chicago Press, 1984–88), vol. 1, p. 54.

[79] Ricoeur, *Symbolism of Evil*, p. 322.

> 'Who is that hides counsel without knowledge?'
> Therefore I have uttered what I did not understand,
> things too wonderful for me, which I did not know . . .
> I had heard of you by the hearing of the ear,
> but now my eye sees you;
> therefore I despise myself,
> and repent in dust and ashes. (42:3–6)

Of course, Job has no need to repent of maintaining his innocence, in which God has vindicated him. The 're-enactment' surely lies in a repentance for insisting on the moral law of retribution. Yet the repentance is presented in an open way, without qualification. We are faced with a 'tragic wisdom of the "re-enactment" that triumphs over the ethical vision of the world'.[80] Ricoeur suggests that Job is really repenting for 'his supposition that existence does not make sense', and thereby opening up 'an unsuspected meaning which cannot be transcribed by speech or logos a human being has at his disposal'. What is being revealed, he maintains, 'is the possibility of hope in spite of . . .'[81] The configuring of a narrative plot projects a 'possibility' which readers can work upon with their own fecund possibilities to refigure their own stories and make a new future.[82] Thus, in this response of Job, suggests Ricoeur, faith confronts the accusation of the judging consciousness. 'It is faith itself that fulfills the task that Freud called "renunciation of the Father".' Job receives no explanation of his suffering; 'his faith is simply removed from every moral vision of the world'. Ricoeur goes on to conclude that 'a path is opened' into the future: 'I renounce my viewpoint; I love the whole as it is.'[83] Job assumes an 'active quality of suffering' which opens up new possibilities rather than the closed resignation of the victim.[84]

Outside his exegesis of Job, Ricoeur sums up this story-like quality of the human self by characterizing it as more *ipse* than *idem*. The identity of 'oneself' is not a static substance, the unchanging core of personality which was typical of Enlightenment thinking, but rather temporal, with a narrative. It is not just *idem*—the 'same' thing (*même*). It is *ipse*, the self which is identical through changing states in our past, present, and future. It is selfhood and not mere sameness. In Ricoeur's definitive phrase 'oneself as another' (*soi-même comme un autre*), the term 'oneself' does not have the connotation 'one's same-self'. Ricoeur admits that the presence of *même* in *soi-même* (oneself) is misleading since it could imply sameness, but within the limits of the French language it should simply be taken as reinforcing and emphasizing the *soi*.[85]

---

[80] Ricoeur, *Symbolism of Evil*, p. 322.
[81] Ricoeur, 'Towards a Hermeneutic', p. 87, cf. p. 89.
[82] Paul Ricoeur, *Time and Narrative*, vol. 1, pp. 52–90; vol. 2, pp. 100–52; vol. 3, pp. 60–156.
[83] Ricoeur, 'Demythization', p. 351.
[84] Ricoeur, 'Towards a Hermeneutic', p. 86.   [85] Ricoeur, *Oneself As Another*, pp. 2–3.

The term *soi-même* (oneself) will lead us—by a slightly winding route—back to Ricoeur's exegesis of Job. The subject ('I think', 'I am')[86] is first and always reflexive—it is 'oneself' *(soi-même)*, and to indicate this priority Ricoeur chooses to use this reflexive pronoun as a *personal* pronoun. But the subject or consciousness cannot constitute itself as a 'free-floating subjectivity'.[87] Since the self is not an unchanging core which can be possessed, the subject is always 'mediated' to itself through reflection on 'a universe of signs', symbols, and myths, as well as other persons and even 'works, institutions and monuments.'[88] Thus Ricoeur sees himself as continuing the tradition of the reflexive self, as in Descartes and Kant, but unlike both of them he sees reflection as mediated through a turn to the world and to language. This is a decisive rejection of Descartes' inward turn to the individual self, which supposed that one could 'start anew all by oneself'.[89] The subject, contrary to Descartes' assertion, does not have 'an immediate intuition of his existence as a thinking being' but is formed by 'mediated reflection'.[90]

Symbols play a key part in this mediation of *soi-même*, and so we return to Job as an example of the tragic symbol which is offered to us so that we can know ourselves 'as another'. In his early book on *The Symbolism of Evil*, Ricoeur identifies two primal symbols. On the one hand there is the 'Adam' symbol which is 'anti-tragic' in so far as the expulsion from the garden follows on from a sin which is openly confessed and for which human beings are rightly accused. On the other hand there is the 'tragic symbol' where there is a clash between innocent suffering and a God who is meant to maintain the ethical order of the universe: there is a 'shattering of the moral vision of the world', and 'it becomes possible to turn the accusation back against God, against the ethical God of the accusation.'[91]

Job represents the tragic symbol, which Ricoeur notes can also be found in Babylonian wisdom writing such as 'I will Praise the Lord of Wisdom', 'A Pessimistic Dialogue between Master and Servant' and 'A Dialogue about Human Misery'. However, in Israel, 'since the "ethicization" of the divine had nowhere else been carried as far . . . the crisis of that vision of the world was nowhere else as radical'.[92] The degree of the crisis can be measured by what happens to the image of the absolute sight ('regard') of God, and here Ricoeur picks up the interest of wisdom in 'seeing', to which I have already

---

[86] Ricoeur, *Oneself As Another*, p. 1.

[87] Ricoeur, *Oneself As Another*, p. 7.

[88] Ricoeur, 'Towards a Hermeneutic', p. 106; Ricoeur, *Freud and Philosophy: An Essay on Interpretation*, trans. D. Savage (New Haven: Yale University Press, 1970), pp. 43–4.

[89] Paul Ricoeur, 'On Interpretation' in *From Text to Action: Essays in Hermeneutics II*, trans. K. Blamey and J. B. Thompson (Evanston: Northwestern University Press, 1991), pp. 12–15.

[90] Ricoeur, 'Towards a Hermeneutic', pp. 105–6, 108.

[91] Ricoeur, *Symbolism of Evil*, pp. 314–15.

[92] Ricoeur, *Symbolism of Evil*, p. 317.

drawn attention. Previously in the faith of Israel, the absolute sight of God into the truth of the human situation had been not only an acknowledgement of human sin but also a source of wonder and a reassurance of the compassion of God. 'That is why this seeing, far from preventing the birth of the self, gives rise to self-awareness; it enters into the field of subjectivity as the task of knowing oneself better . . . I desire to know myself as I am known (Ps. 139:23–4).'[93] This divine seeing does not turn the human self into a mere object. But now the force of the tragic symbol is to raise severe doubt about this seeing, 'which suddenly reveals itself as the seeing of the hidden God who delivers man up to unjust suffering . . . [the seeing] of the Hunter who lets fly the arrow'.[94] This is how Ricoeur reads the protests of Job against being 'seen' by God to which Levinas also refers, as in Job 7:17–19:

> What is man, that you make so much of him,
> that you fix your attention on him,
> that you inspect him every morning,
> that you scrutinize him every instant?
> Will you ever stop looking at me
> For the length of time it takes to swallow my spittle?[95]

Adherence to a law of retribution, stemming from the Adamic symbol, makes this situation of tragedy more extreme, and the sense of God's hostile 'spying' more acute. This particular aspect of the tragedy can be resolved through dismissal of an inflexible law of retribution, as Job does in his repentance and to which we may assume the author of the book assents. But, Ricoeur affirms, the larger tragedy of God, caught between ethics and human suffering, and the mystery of *Deus Absconditus* remains unresolvable by reason,[96] and becomes the occasion for a penetration 'beyond any ethical vision to a new dimension of faith, the dimension of *unverifiable* faith'.[97] This persistent value of the tragic symbol in coming to knowledge of the self means that Ricoeur finds that even the human accusation against God, as long as it remains in the form of invocation of God, is valuable for coming to self-awareness:

> the discovery of the hostile Seeing is always inscribed within a relationship in which the absolute Seeing continues to be the foundation of truth for the view that I have of myself . . . this Seeing preserves the reality of my existence.[98]

Like Levinas, it seems that the 'accusation' of the self by another establishes the self. But for Ricoeur, the sense of persecution by the other (here, God) is subordinated to a more compassionate relationship of 'being seen', and within the tragic symbol there is a mutuality between being accused and accusing.

---

[93] Ricoeur, *Symbolism of Evil*, p. 85.   [94] Ricoeur, *Symbolism of Evil*, p. 86.
[95] Translation as in Ricoeur, *Symbolism of Evil*, p. 318, not NRSV. Cf. Job 14:3.
[96] Ricoeur, *Symbolism of Evil*, pp. 322–3.   [97] Ricoeur, *Symbolism of Evil*, p. 319.
[98] Ricoeur, *Symbolism of Evil*, p. 86.

This observation brings us back to the central dimension of 'oneself' *(soi-même)* as Ricoeur develops it; fundamental to the reflexiveness of the subject is knowing oneself by way of 'the other'. The 'oneself' as an *ipse*-identity which is not mere 'sameness-identity' involves a dialectic between the self and other than self. This is a kind of otherness that is not merely a comparison with the self, but which is 'constitutive of selfhood as such'. The phrase 'oneseself as another' suggests that selfhood 'implies otherness to such an intimate degree that one cannot be thought of without the other, that instead one passes into the other'. The 'as' in 'oneself as another' has the strong implication of 'oneself *inasmuch as* being other'.[99]

Here Ricoeur is critical of the relation between self and other which Levinas conceives, objecting that the supposed initiative of the other in fact 'establishes no relation at all, to the extent that the other represents absolute exteriority with respect to an ego defined by the condition of separation.'[100] He asks, 'whose face' appears, according to Levinas, in the face of the other? The face, he concludes 'is that of a master of justice, of a master who instructs and who does so only in the ethical mode.' What strikes one immediately, he comments, is 'the contrast between the reciprocity of friendship and the dissymetry of the injunction. To be sure, the self is summoned to responsibility by the other, but since the initiative of the injunction comes only from the other, the self is called 'in the accusative mode alone.' Central to the good life, argues Ricoeur, is friendship (the Aristotelean *philia*) which is based on the mutual activity of giving and receiving.[101] This reciprocity is certainly missing from Levinas' account, though we ought not to ignore his warmer portrayals of an 'imperative of gratuitous love', which takes hold of the human person, pulling him or her into an ethical subjectivity which is displayed in acts of justice.[102]

In reading the Book of Job, Ricoeur thus finds a different picture of the self from the 'little island' of an isolated cogito. With its story-like quality, the *ipse* comes to a mediated self-awareness through powerful symbols in culture (including a tragic symbol), and through relation with the 'other' who calls us to responsible action by 'seeing' us with compassion rather than (as with Levinas) accusing us. In the Book of Job as Ricoeur reads it, this other is God, while Levinas finds God merging together with the human other as the demand that awakens the self. Indeed, another difference that Ricoeur detects generally between himself and Levinas is that Levinas moves easily as a philosopher between the infinite other of the neighbour and the infinite other of God while Ricoeur doubts whether this is a move defensible strictly by philosophy. The 'philosopher *as* philosopher' must leave the identity of the Other open:

---

[99] Ricoeur, *Oneself As Another*, p. 3.
[100] Ricoeur, *Oneself As Another*, pp. 188–9.   [101] Ricoeur, *Oneself As Another*, p. 188.
[102] Emmanuel Levinas, *Of God Who Comes to Mind*, trans. B. Bergo (Stanford: Stanford University Press, Stanford, 1998), p. ix.

Perhaps the philosopher as philosopher has to admit that one does not know and cannot say whether this Other, the source of the injunction, is another person whom I can look in the face or who can stare at me . . . Or God—living God, absent God—or an empty place. With this aporia of the Other, philosophical discourse comes to an end.[103]

On the other hand, when commenting on Scripture as a religious thinker Ricoeur finds a dialogue between self and divine Other, with a mutuality that Levinas denies. He finds that in Job the poem moves from complaint and lament to the 'rhetorical voice of God', and so to dialogue in the mood of supplication and praise.[104] The dialogue, he comments, is one in which God 'does not speak of Job; he speaks to Job; and that alone is sufficient . . . dialogue is in itself a mode of consolation'. Although Job has been displaced from his own centre by the word of God, this displacement is in itself 'the fundamental possibility of consolation', since Being itself is no longer relegated to something at the disposal of the human subject, and emerges as the wholeness of reality to which humans 'belong' as speaking beings.[105] This 'belongingness' is another way of expressing the constitution of the self by the other, indicating a relation that already 'carries' us, prior to any split between subject and object. In opposition to 'Husserlian idealism', Ricoeur affirms that:

> the problematic of objectivity presupposes as prior to itself an inclusive relation which englobes the allegedly autonomous subject and the allegedly adverse object. It is this inclusive or englobing relation that I call participation or 'belonging to'.[106]

Here Ricoeur envisages human dialogue with God in the context of 'belonging in' the world, as Job's dialogue takes place in the context of a vision of the whole of creation. Like Levinas he stresses immersion of the subject into concrete experiences of the world. However, he develops this with the idea that 'testimony' has a place in seeing the world and knowing God, and testimony—like the process of mediation—undermines the posturings of the subject. He writes, 'recourse to testimony occurs in a philosophy of reflection when such a philosophy renounces the pretension of consciousness to constitute itself'. Testimony happens at the point when self 'lets itself go', renouncing not only control over empirical objects ordered by reason, but also 'those transcendental objects of metaphysics that might still provide support for thinking the unconditioned'. It is this movement of letting go that testifies to 'encounter with contingent signs of the absolute which the absolute in its generosity allows to appear'.[107]

---

[103] Ricoeur, *Oneself As Another*, p. 355.
[104] Ricoeur, 'Towards a Hermeneutic', p. 89.
[105] Ricoeur, 'Religion, Atheism and Faith', pp. 461–2.
[106] Ricoeur, 'Towards a Hermeneutic', p. 107.
[107] Ricoeur, 'Towards a Hermeneutic', p. 111.

Thus, in looking at external signs and objects in the world, the subject can testify to finding traces of the absolute as it 'gives of itself'.[108] There is a dialectic here between the 'witness' and the 'things seen'; thus, testimony is linked with participation or 'belonging: 'to be a witness is to have participated in what one has seen and to be able to testify to it'. The reflection of the subject abandons the illusions of a sovereign consciousness and does so 'by internalizing the dialectic of testimony from which it records the trace of the absolute in the contingency of history'.[109] This detection of the 'trace of the absolute' provides a horizon, suggests Ricoeur for the specifically religious and biblical experience of revelation, to which confession of faith bears witness.[110] Revelation is not a communication of propositions, but the manifestation in contingent events of God's design or purpose for human life,[111] and non-religious 'testimony' similarly finds a trace of purpose, giving meaning to the narrative self from beyond itself.

The discussion of 'testimony' from which I am quoting is not related explicitly by Ricoeur to the Book of Job, but takes place in an article where Ricoeur has discussed Job, and evidently connects with what he has written about Job elsewhere. When he refers to a sense of 'belonging to an order of things which precedes our capacity to oppose ourselves to things taken as objects opposed to a subject',[112] we recall that he ascribes to Job this sense of belonging following his repentance. When he suggests that archetypes of the martyr, witnessing at the cost of his life, arise in the course of history, and names the Suffering Servant, 'the persecuted righteous', Socrates and Jesus, we recall that he has previously included Job among the suffering innocent. When he refers to witness to contingent events in which we can detect the trace of God, we recall his discussion of the diversity of things in creation in Job: 38–41 in which he finds 'a witness to the power and wisdom of God', as distinct from such accounts of creation as Genesis 1 which have human salvation as their theme.[113]

'Mediation' and 'testimony' taken together reconfigure, thinks Ricoeur, the Kantian autonomy of the self. Ricoeur approves of Kant's portrayal of autonomy, in his *What is the Enlightenment?*: '*Sapere aude!* Dare to Learn, Taste, Savour for Yourself!'[114] But this venture of the self in morality and politics should, he urges, always be in community with other persons and in the context of justice in society—'for and with others in just institutions'.[115]

---

[108] Ricoeur, 'Towards a Hermeneutic', p. 112.
[109] Ricoeur, 'Towards a Hermeneutic', p. 113.
[110] Ricoeur, 'Towards a Hermeneutic', p. 117.
[111] Ricoeur, 'Towards a Hermeneutic', pp. 79–80, 84–5.
[112] Ricoeur, 'Towards a Hermeneutic', p. 101.
[113] Ricoeur, 'Exegesis of Gen. 1.1–2.4a', pp. 131–2.
[114] Ricoeur, *Oneself As Another*, p. 296.
[115] Pamela Sue Anderson argues that the basis for Ricoeur's reconfigured autonomy is already in Kant himself: see her 'Ricoeur's Reclamation of Autonomy: Unity, Plurality and Totality' in

Autonomy as a moral capacity and exercise of responsibility is tied up with interdependence, or inter-personal life. In his chapter significantly titled on 'The Self and *Practical Wisdom*', he proposes that rather than beginning with a formal principle of autonomy, we should start with responsible actions for others and with others, and only from this point reflect back on the autonomy of selfhood, or the *ipse*. This compares interestingly with his statement earlier that among the wise of Ancient Israel, 'Nothing is further from the spirit of the sages than the idea of an autonomy of thinking', on the basis that 'intimacy with Wisdom is not to be distinguished from intimacy with God', symbolized in the 'transcendent feminine figure' of wisdom.[116] The wisdom which Ricoeur relates to his revised autonomy is the Greek *phronēsis*, and so we may assume that he distinguishes this from Hebraic wisdom.[117] But I have already suggested in my first chapter that there is an affinity between Greek *phronēsis* and one strand in Hebrew *ḥokmah*, and during the progress of this book we will indeed find something like Ricoeur's 'autonomy' in the wisdom literature. This is supported by the fact that Ricoeur's stress on 'testimony to things seen' has a strong resonance with the observational methods of wisdom. Ricoeur's reference to 'intimacy with God' and the feminine figure of wisdom in Hebraic wisdom are, I have suggested, elements of what might be called wisdom as *sophia*, but these are always intertwined with something like *phronēsis* or practical wisdom.

In the next two parts of this book, in which I venture to shape a theology which connects both with the wisdom tradition and the thought of the late-modern world, I will be using the words 'subject' and 'self' basically in Ricoeur's sense. The subject ('I', as in 'I am', 'I think', 'I see') is a self (having distinct identity) only in the Ricoeurian sense of 'oneself' (*soi-même, ipse*), that is a subject with a narrative history, always mediated to itself through reflection on signs, symbols, other persons, and objects in the world. With Ricoeur, as well as Derrida, Levinas, and other late-modern thinkers (including the 'modernist' Sartre), I maintain that a stable and self-sufficient self which can be observed empirically by the subject is an illusion. As Sartre emphasizes, the self is a fluid project in development. With Levinas and Ricoeur, I am proposing that a relation to the other precedes the being of the subject, so that the self is always 'oneself as another.' We shall find that the nature of this relation is better understood through Ricoeur's reciprocity than through Levinas' 'accusation' by the other. In all this, a wisdom theology for today will withstand any pretensions of the self to master or dominate the

---

John Wall, William Schweiker, and W. David Hall (eds), *Paul Ricoeur and Contemporary Moral Thought* (New York: Routledge, 2002), pp. 15, 27. Also see Chapter 2, the section called 'Self and the World in Modernity', sub-section a.

[116] Ricoeur, 'Towards a Hermeneutic', p. 88.

[117] Ricoeur, *Oneself As Another*, pp. 174–9, 261, 290–1, 352.

world and others, a trend which has unfortunately marred the sense of the subject in modernity, and which both Levinas and Ricoeur oppose through their exegesis of Job.

In making a wisdom theology for today, I shall be exploring the way that the self participates in the divine Other through immersion into the contingent details of the world, or how *phronēsis* becomes *sophia*—in short, how seeing the world is knowing God. In their own way, Levinas and Ricoeur consider this issue through their reflections on two areas in the Book of Job—the theophany of chapters 38–41, and the passages in which Job protests against the God who 'sees' and pursues him. I aim to show that participation in the divine Other, which is inseparable from responsibility for human others, occurs when the self is mediated through the Christian symbol of the Trinity, and through the personal reality it expresses.

Part Two

Wisdom as Observation
and Participation

4

The Elusiveness of the World and the Limits of Wisdom

WORLD ALIENATION AND EARTH ALIENATION

Hannah Arendt opens her book *The Human Condition* with a striking image. It is 1957 when she is writing, and the Russians have just launched their 'sputnik' into space, the first satellite to orbit the earth. She notes that an American newspaper reporter has remarked that he feels a sense of relief in this making of the first 'step towards escape from men's imprisonment to the earth'.[1] What, she asks, has become so inhospitable about the world that humankind should desire to leave it? She believes that human beings them-selves have made the world a place that no longer feels like home, so that our reaction is to flee from it. In fact, there has been a long history of attempting to escape from the world, of which the 'sputnik' is only the most recent example, and it is precisely this turning away that has *made* the world the inhospitable place it is. We are in a condition, she diagnoses, of 'world alienation' and 'earth alienation'.

I began this book by observing that the modern attempt to subjugate the world (as object) to the human mind (subject) has resulted in a sense of alienation from the world, both the world of nature and of other persons. This sense may be expressed in an existential way, feeling the world as a threat to the uninhibited freedom of consciousness, or in a Marxist form, finding that we (or at least all workers) have been alienated from the works of our hands because the resources of the world and the products of our work have been appropriated and exploited by owners of capital.[2] 'Postmodern' thinkers have consequently made an assault on the manipulative self, fostered as it was by Enlightenment confidence in human rationality, which is perceived to be at the bottom of the problem of the human place in the world. As Arendt puts it,

---

[1] Cit. Arendt, *Human Condition*, p. 1.

[2] Karl Marx, *Collected Works: Karl Marx and Friedrich Engels*, 50 Volumes (London: Law-rence and Wishart, 1975–), ed. and trans. Jack Cohen, Maurice Cornforth, vol. 3 (1975), p. 272.

one of the most persistent trends in modern philosophy has been 'an exclusive concern with the self . . . an attempt to reduce all experiences, with the world as well as with other human beings, to experiences between man [*sic*] and himself.'[3] She concludes that 'World alienation, and not self-alienation, as Marx thought, has been the hallmark of the present age'. Arendt, a thinker who cannot easily be classified by established labels, sits on the boundary between modernism and the postmodern, as will become evident, and so is a significant example of what I have called the 'mixed' mood of late-modernity. We shall stay with her diagnosis of 'world alienation' and 'earth alienation' for a while as we further explore the context for a wisdom-theology today. In a situation of male-dominated thought, it also behoves us to listen to a woman speaking.

In her book *The Human Condition*, Arendt finds a key example of world-alienation at the inauguration of the modern age, in the discovery of America and the subsequent exploration, charting, and mapping of the entire earth. While this was apparently an expansion of the known geographical area, it had the unexpected result of shrinking distances and of abolishing space. Everything was scaled down to the human mind, for 'nothing can remain immense if it can be measured'.[4] Through the use of numbers, symbols, and models, the mind condensed earthly distance 'down to the size of the human body's natural sense and understanding'.[5] At the same time as a geographical shrinkage, an 'economic shrinkage' was taking place. Through the event of expropriation of church and monastic land at the time of the Reformation, there was an uprooting of the peasant class which had tilled the land, a 'deprivation for certain groups of their place in the world'.[6] Alienation from the world was thus a long story of turning away from the open spaces of the world into the inner, narrow confines of the human mind.

By 'world', Arendt means a symbiosis between the *natural* world and the *human-made* world, the latter an area full of artefacts created by the work of *homo faber* which give stability to what would otherwise be a transient process of life. 'Men, their ever-changing nature notwithstanding, can retrieve their sameness, that is, their identity, by being related to the same chair and the same table.'[7] A human public life, a common space, occupies the space of the world, and its objectivity does not only consist of artefacts, but stable political institutions with a regard for permanence, together with public buildings, parks, monuments, and public stories. Arendt thinks of the 'world' as the

---

[3] Arendt, *Human Condition*, p. 254.

[4] Arendt, *Human Condition*, p. 250.

[5] Arendt, *Human Condition*, p. 251. Harvey, *The Condition of Postmodernity*, pp. 284–307 argues that postmodernity has accentuated the compression of space (and time) that was typical of modernism.

[6] Arendt, *Human Condition*, p. 254.

[7] Arendt, *Human Condition*, p. 137.

earth, a natural space filled with natural objects, which is ingathering and giving a home to the public 'world' of the polis which is filled with human-made objects. In this concern for a 'world of things', Arendt thus claims a 'materialism' which, provocatively, she accuses Marx of neglecting in a concern for the subjective processes of work rather than its products—hence her comment that he is really concerned with 'self-alienation.' While we have seen the recognition of 'alterity' to be typical of late-modern thinking, Arendt adds a particular dimension by stressing the 'otherness' of things rather than the otherness of persons.

Arendt offers an analogy for this objective structure. Public life is like a table around which people are sitting: 'To live together in the world means essentially that a world of things is between those who have it in common, as a table is located between those who sit around it; the world, like every in-between, relates and separates men at the same time.'[8] A public, civic life is thus the means by which people manifest their separateness or distinctiveness (their 'plurality') as well as their interdependence. If the table were to vanish 'through some magic trick', the people sitting round it would be no longer separated, 'but also would be entirely unrelated to each other by anything tangible'.[9] Now, Arendt's point is that the trick has in fact happened in recent human history. In many ways the 'spaces'—natural and manufactured—have been shrunk, and the public structures have collapsed. There has been a withdrawal into the 'intimacy' of the isolated subject, which is not the same as a proper privacy. Alienated from the objective world, political life has become stultified and replaced by the 'social sphere', which means the projection into society of what used to be concerns of the private household, and especially by an obsession with economics or a preoccupation with sheer survival over creating what is truly human. A sense of the permanent has been lost, the fleeting nature of human experience has been magnified, and no products of human hands are expected to last. We live in a society of conspicuous consumption where goods are devoured and constantly replaced.

Alongside 'world-alienation', Arendt sets 'earth alienation'. While these two ideas tend to flow into each other, the latter has a distinct image attached to it. Together with the discovery of America and the appropriation of church land, Arendt identifies a third great event which 'stands at the threshold of the modern age'—the invention of the telescope. The effect of this invention by Galileo was not only to give human beings a clearer view of the universe beyond the earth, but to make possible an imaginary point outside the earth from which to look back and view the earth itself. Recalling Archimedes' remark that if he were given a lever long enough, and a point outside the

---

[8] Arendt, *Human Condition*, p. 52.   [9] Arendt, *Human Condition*, p. 53.

earth on which to stand, he could lift the very earth itself, Arendt writes that whatever we do in modern physics,

> we always handle nature from a point in the universe outside the earth. Without actually standing where Archimedes wished to stand (*dos moi pou sto*), still bound to the earth through the human condition, we have found a way to act on the earth and within terrestial nature as though we dispose of it from outside, from the Archimedean standpoint. And even at the risk of endangering the natural life process we expose the earth to universal, cosmic forces alien to nature's household.[10]

The telescope gave a sense that human beings could understand the secrets of the universe, and could make their home in the cosmos beyond the earth. The result has been to engender a certain attitude towards the earth, an Archimedean stance in which science can 'handle' and manipulate nature from a superior perspective, assisted by a science which has freed itself from the shackles of spatiality—that is, from geometry—and has acquired the tools of abstract mathematics.[11] With this non-spatial symbolic language, required for a universal, astrophysical viewpoint, human beings 'since Descartes' have been escaping from the earth into a rational mind which—as Descartes perceived— claimed to carry the Archimedean point within itself.[12]

This alienation from the earth and flight into the mind was accentuated by another aspect of the use of the telescope: whether used on earth or directed to the stars it cast doubt on the appearances of things to the human eye, since an instrument was needed to see accurately. Arendt suggests that this experience was at the basis of Descartes' 'doubt about everything' which led him to the only certainty that he existed—the very fact of a doubting and therefore thinking mind: 'You cannot doubt...and remain uncertain whether you doubt or not.'[13] This doubt about a world available to the senses has been radically extended, Arendt proposes, in modern physics. Science uses its instruments to search for a supposedly 'real world' beyond the appearances, a 'true reality' which can be conceived only mathematically in the mind. This itself means a loss of the objective world. Moreover, since there is a limit to the accuracy of all measurements obtainable by humanly devised instruments in an effort to find 'mysterious messengers from the real world',[14] while hunting for 'objective reality' the human being has discovered (in Heisenberg's words) that he always only 'confronts himself alone'.[15]

---

[10] Arendt, *Human Condition*, p. 262.   [11] Arendt, *Human Condition*, p. 265.

[12] Arendt, *Human Condition*, p. 284; Arendt cites Descartes, 'un point fixe et immobile', n. 45. See Chapter 2, section a, in 'The Self and the World in Modernity'.

[13] Arendt, *Between Past and Future: Six Exercises in Political Thought*. Enlarged Edition (New York: Viking, 1968), p. 300, n.22.

[14] Arendt, *Between Past and Future*, pp. 276–7.

[15] Arendt, *Between Past and Future*, p. 277, citing Werner Heisenberg's phrase in his *The Physicist's Conception of Nature* (New York; Harcourt Brace, 1958), p. 24.

So we return to the sputnik and its more ambitious successors. In an article later than *The Human Condition*, Arendt observes that human beings can now hope to journey to the Archimedean point which before they only anticipated in their minds:

> It is as though Einstein's imagined 'observer poised in free space'—surely the creation of the human mind and its power of abstraction—is being followed by a bodily observer who must behave as though he were a mere child of abstraction and imagination.[16]

There is the danger, therefore, that such journeys will only end where they began, in the 'mere' mind and its powers of mathematical abstraction, 'as though we disposed of terrestial nature from outside'.[17] The symptoms can be seen in nuclear technology and genetic manipulation, 'when we release energy processes that ordinarily go on only in the sun, or attempt to initiate in a test tube the processes of cosmic evolution, or build machines for the production and control of energies unknown in the household of earthly nature'.[18] Human productivity as *homo faber* has become violation, a matter of conducting oneself as 'lord and master of the whole earth', an atttitude which Arendt suggests contradicts the spirit of the creation story of Genesis, according to which Adam 'was put into the garden of Eden to serve and preserve it.'[19]

THE SELF-REVEALING WORLD AND THE SELF-CONCEALING EARTH

For Arendt, the earth-world takes on a problematic appearance in face of human alienation from it, and to understand this we need to pursue further the concepts of 'world' and 'earth'. 'World-alienation' denotes an escape from the world into the solitary self; 'earth alienation' is apparently an escape–first imaginary and then partly realized–into outer space, but only finally once again into the self and its mental activity. Both alienations involve taking up a position to exercise control over the natural world and both mean that the world is not taken seriously in its objectivity. It is not surprising that the two concepts tend to merge in Arendt's description. But there are indications in Arendt's thought of a significant distinction between 'world' and 'earth', which

---

[16] Arendt, *Between Past and Future*, p. 274.
[17] Arendt, *Between Past and Future*, p. 279.
[18] Arendt, *Between Past and Future*, p. 279.
[19] Arendt, *Human Condition*, p. 139, and n.3.

(as David Macauley suggests)[20] we may trace to the influence of Heidegger. As has often been observed, Arendt both depends on Heidegger for the point of departure for much of her thought, and ends up by developing his ideas in her own way or even contradicting them. Here, the relation between world and earth is illuminated by Heidegger's use, as well as offering an intersection with Hebrew wisdom literature that we shall shortly be exploring. Just as Arendt speaks of the 'world' (a symbiosis of the human and the natural) as occupying space within the open spaces of the 'earth', so Heidegger writes that 'World and earth are essentially different from one another and yet are never separated. The world grounds itself on the earth, and earth juts through the world.'[21] Earth is 'the serving bearer, blossoming and fruiting…'[22]

Now, for Heidegger, the world is 'self-revealing', while the earth is 'self-concealing'. The world in which the human being (*Dasein*, 'being there') is immersed is a place of the self-disclosure of Being. Following a phenomenological description, it is where things 'appear' in the consciousness, and Being will also appear in the 'clear space' of *Dasein* if we do not forget about it in focussing on the many beings that surround us. We ourselves, as beings, can make an 'ecstatic' movement into Being. The 'earth', however, denotes the experience that things—and especially Being—are also concealed from the consciousness, always elusive. Reflecting upon the form of an art-object, as a product of human work, Heidegger finds it to 'set forth the the earth' in the sense of bringing it 'into the Open as the self-secluding'. The sculptor uses stone, 'but he does not use it up', and the poet used the word in such a way that the word is not exhausted but 'remains truly a word'.[23] This alerts us to a fundamental distintion:

> The world is the self-disclosing openness of the broad paths of the simple and essential decisions in the destiny of an historical people. The earth is the spontaneous forthcoming of that which is continually self-secluding and to that extent sheltering and concealing… The world, in resting upon the earth, strives to surmount it. As self-opening, it cannot endure anything closed. The earth, however, as sheltering and concealing, tends always to draw the world into itself and keep it there.[24]

The self-seclusion of the earth is not 'a uniform, inflexible staying under cover, but unfolds itself in an inexhaustible variety of simple modes and shapes'.[25] So

---

[20] David Macauley, 'Hannah Arendt and the Politics of Place: From Earth Alienation to Oikos', in Macauley (ed.), *Minding Nature: The Philosophers of Ecology* (New York: Guildford Press, 1996), pp. 100–11.

[21] Martin Heidegger, *Poetry, Language, Thought*, trans. A. Hofstadter (New York: Harper-Collins/Perennial, 2001), p. 47.

[22] Heidegger, *Poetry*, p. 147.   [23] Heidegger, *Poetry*, p. 46.

[24] Heidegger, *Poetry*, p. 47.   [25] Heidegger, *Poetry*, p. 46.

Arendt writes that the earth is 'effortless', 'inexhaustible and indefatigable'.[26] Characterized by biological and geological rhythms, the earth persists in an endless flux, a movement which is a threat to the world of human stability. As Heidegger declares that 'the opposition of world and earth is a striving' (but not 'discord' and 'disorder'),[27] Arendt writes that:

> Only we who have erected the objectivity of a world of our own from what nature gives us, who have built it into the environment of nature so that we are protected from her, can look upon nature as something 'objective.' Without a world between men and nature, there is eternal movement, but no objectivity.[28]

We can now, then, view the phenomena of 'earth alienation' and 'world alienation' from another perspective. Faced by an earth-world which is both amenable to cooperative work and resistant to our investigation, the human tendency is to retreat to the inner 'Archimedean point' of the mind to exercise control over this world, with the consequent loss of a common home within it. Moreover, loss of a sense of the objective products of our work means that work (as homo *faber*) degenerates into mere labour (as *animal laborans*), a struggle for survival which is a capitulation to the repetitive rhythms of the earth, now made more inhuman by enslavement within the automated cyclic processes of machines which parody the 'rhythm of the life process'.[29] Arendt aptly cites the ancient wisdom writer Koheleth that 'Vanity of vanities; all is vanity . . . There is no new thing under the sun' (Eccl. 1:2, 9) and could well have continued with the quotation: 'What do people gain from the toil at which they toil under the sun?' (Eccl. 1:3). This is a despairing observation to which we will return in detail later.[30] The balance between self-disclosure and self-concealment in the earth-world has been badly upset by alienation, so that humankind has lost a sense of being at home within it.

THE SELF AND AN ALIENATED WORLD

As far as Arendt offers a way forward (and her analysis of the situation is more extended than any solutions), it is to recover a sense of public space, and so the objectivity of the world, through her favoured means of political 'action'. Action is not motivated by a comprehensive ideology, but is an activity that takes place 'between' human beings when they form and test their opinions (*doxa*) in public. First they seek to persuade fellow human beings in the to and

---

[26] Arendt, *Between Past and Future*, pp. 42, 213.
[27] Heidegger, *Poetry*, pp. 47–8.
[28] Arendt, *Human Condition*, p. 137.
[29] Arendt, *Human Condition*, pp. 144–7.
[30] See Chapter 9, the section called 'The Whole as a Sum'.

fro of public debate, and then having found others to join them they initiate new things in the world without the guarantee of a predictable end, but with the hope of renewing a sense of community and create public space.[31] To act is to 'take an initiative, to begin . . . to set something into motion'; here Arendt cites Augustine: 'that there be a beginning, man was created before whom there was nobody'—with humanity the principle of beginning or 'natality' itself comes into the world.[32] Action is related to the 'plurality' of human beings, which does not just mean alterity but a distinctiveness which persons disclose to each other in the process of speaking and acting.[33]

Here, as Richard Bernstein stresses, Arendt radically modifies Heidegger, since for all his writing about 'disclosure', there is nothing that 'even approximates to what Arendt means by plurality'.[34] For Arendt, Heidegger's discussion of *Mitsein* (being-with) and *Mitdasein* (being-there-with) in *Being and Time* fails to lift the solitary self out of isolation into the world of 'they' (and here Levinas agrees with her).[35] Despite her evident debt to Heidegger for the concepts of 'earth' and 'world', she tells us that 'Later . . . Heidegger has drawn on mythologizing and muddled concepts like "folk" and "earth" in an effort to supply his isolated Selves with a shared common ground to stand on.'[36] While Arendt seems over-severe with regard to the dialectic between *Mitsein* and *Dasein* in the two parts of *Being and Time*, Bernstein seems just in judging that for Heidegger 'being-with' (*Mitsein*) is a characteristic belonging to 'being there' (*Dasein*), rather than describing the actual situation of mutual disclosure between persons in speaking and acting that Arendt has in mind.[37]

Arendt's concept of action attempts to protect the public sphere as a civic community. She understands the *polis* to be based on active citizenship, civic engagement, cooperation of interest groups, direct political action and direct democracy. In her version of communitarianism she seems curiously both modernist and postmodern. She has been claimed as postmodern for her vigorous assault on the controlling self and suspicion of 'consciousness', her disavowal of any ideological programme in political action, her suspicion of technology, her denial of any goal (*telos*) envisaged for action with a stress on 'plurality' and unpredictability, and her general emphasis on the self as immersed into the 'world'. However, she can be claimed as 'modernist', having

---

[31] Arendt, *Human Condition*, pp. 188–91.

[32] Arendt, *Human Condition*, p. 177.

[33] Arendt, *Human Condition*, p. 179.

[34] Richard J. Bernstein, 'Procovation and Appropriation: Hannah Arendt's Response to Martin Heidegger', *Constellations* 4 (1997), p. 159; cf. Bernstein, *Radical Evil. A Philosophical Interrogation* (Cambridge: Polity Press, 2002), pp. 212–13.

[35] Bernstein, 'Procovation and Appropriation', p. 171, n.14; Levinas, *Time and the Other*, pp. 39–41, 62–4.

[36] Bernstein, 'Procovation and Appropriation', p. 171, n.15.

[37] Bernstein, 'Procovation and Appropriation', pp. 166–8.

a kind of metanarrative of the public space and its relation to both 'earth' and 'world', placing emphasis on structures and a materialist stress on the making of products which supply a stability 'over against' the self. As I suggested earlier, she stands as an effective representative of the mixed mood of late-modernism.

However, her tentative solution to the problem of earth alienation and world alienation, in the face of an earth-world which is both open and self-concealing, also runs into problems. First, as Margaret Canovan points out (and as Arendt herself recognizes),[38] there are inevitable dangers in actions of a 'plurality' which have no clear aim *(telos)* in view. The 'miraculous' and joyous unpredictability of plural actions, when one cannot forsee the effects of one's initiatives, necessarily means a lack of control over them, and this can lead to the damaging not only of the human community but nature itself. Forgiveness can cover the some of the unintended results of action in society, but there is no remedy through forgiveness for—to take an example—'an "action into nature" that sets off a nuclear reaction or causes the extermination of the species'.[39] Second, as George Kateb has suggested, Arendt's concentration on objectivity at the expense of the subjective may make it difficult to regenerate community and ensure that the environment is habitable for all. Arendt's flight from inwardness in her criticism of world-alienation, her refusal to discuss the consciousness in the context of the renewal of public life, and her strident separation of contemplation and action, may—he argues—limit her concept of politics in a crippling way.[40] One of my main concerns in this book is the problem of the dominating subject and the consequent gap between subject and object; I suggest that this will not be solved by failing to explore the selfhood at all. By 'objectivity' Arendt means allowing things and people a real identity over against us, not of course the treating of them as mere objects, but this 'otherness' will not be achieved without some recognition of the subject. Third, as Jennifer Ring has suggested, Arendt shows a distrust of the biological rhythms of the self and nature.[41] Arendt's assertion that we need 'protection' from 'the eternal movement of nature' implies a hostility between the objective worlds of human culture and the earth which seems curiously Sartrean.[42]

Nevertheless, Arendt's analysis of an earth-world which is both cooperative and 'intransigent' is a significant point of dialogue with a wisdom theology. She alerts us to the context of late-modern thought which finds the world to be

---

[38] Arendt, *Human Condition*, pp. 220–1, 236–443.

[39] Margaret Canovan, introduction to Arendt, *Human Condition*, pp. xviii–xix.

[40] George Kateb, *Hannah Arendt: Politics, Conscience, Evil* (Totowa: Rowman and Allenhead, 1984), pp. 94–5, 108–9; so also Jennifer Ring, 'On Needing both Marx and Arendt: Alienation and the Flight from Inwardness', *Political Theory* 17 (1989), pp. 442–3, 445.

[41] Ring, 'On Needing both Marx and Arendt', p. 442.

[42] See Chapter 2, section a, in 'The Self and the World in Modernity'.

full of contingent things which—in different ways—elude investigation by the rational mind when it is thought to reign supreme in the world. If the human self tries to control and dominate the earth, then the earth's natural self-concealment and resistance to investigation will be accentuated. Her sense of the elusiveness of the world has remarkable resonances with the outlook of ancient wisdom, to which we now turn.

THE CONFIDENCE AND CAUTION OF WISDOM

Reading the Hebrew wisdom literature, we catch a glimpse of a class of people called 'the wise', probably—as I suggested in the first chapter—a diverse group of scribes, teachers, and royal advisors. We surmise from their writings that the wise approach the world with a fair degree of confidence. Spending time and effort in observing things and people around them, they aim to cope with the challenges of their experience, 'steering' (*taḥbulōt*, תחבלות Prov. 1:5) their way through life. To their own direct experiments in living they add reports of the experience of others over the years, contained in proverbial sayings or more formal instructions transmitted to them by their teachers, and so aim to deduce what might be the most successful thing to do in any particular circumstance. As they have collected the wisdom of others, so they pass it on, at the same time using the copying out of this material as a technique to teach skills of reading and writing. Their assumption in all this is that the natural and human world is amenable to being understood by patient investigation. From this observation of the world, the wise find patterns of meaning and detect regularities that can offer guidance to those who are willing to listen to their teaching. They fix their conclusions in proverbs, riddles, instructions, numerical sayings, and lists of natural phenomena (*onomastica*), by which they begin to bring some order to a vast and complex area of investigation. So, for example, they note *analogies* between events in the natural and human world, pointing out that 'this is like that'. For example:

> Three things are stately in their tread;
> four are stately in their stride:
> the lion, which is mightiest among beasts
> and does not turn back before any;
> the strutting cock, the he-goat,
> and a king striding before his people. (Prov. 30:29–31 RSV)

The lion, the cock, and the goat are all like a king leading his people; however, we can hardly miss the tone of social satire in this saying when the analogy is turned back on the human actor (as Ellen Davis puts it, 'even the king looks remarkably like a strutting rooster—if you squint').[43]

Most frequently the wise observe *consequences*, or the link between cause and effect, warning that 'if you do this, then that will happen'. For instance:

> Pride goes before destruction
>> and a haughty spirit before a fall. (Prov. 16:18)

> Laziness brings on deep sleep;
>> an idle person will suffer hunger. (Prov. 19:15)

It is these cause–effect patterns from experience that have the largest place in the 'sentence literature' of the Book of Proverbs, so called because wisdom is presented in short, complete units in contrast to the discursive and imperative teaching that can be found in the 'instruction literature' of chapters 1–9. The sentence literature now occupies most of chapters 10–29 of the book,[44] which overall is a kind of textbook of wisdom, containing collections from different sages, appearing possibly in successive editions, and gathered together over hundreds of years.

Sayings can combine both the elements of analogy and consequence, as does this one:

> The beginning of strife is *like* letting out water;
>> so stop before the quarrel breaks out. (Prov. 17:14)

The consequences of allowing a quarrel (or perhaps litigation in the law-court)[45] to get under way are, it is implied, as disastrous as the small trickle of water from a dam which, if not mended, will become a flood.

Thus, when the wise have to cope with a situation, to 'steer' their way through the maze of events, they appeal to the guidelines gleaned from experience; these represent order won from the chaos of life, as the opening to the instruction literature of Proverbs 1–9 asserts (1:1–6). But there is a dual mood in this wisdom literature. Alongside confidence there is a strong note of caution. For all the hard discipline, the teacher of wisdom was prepared to recognize an element of the unpredictable in all calculations: there are unknown factors which the wise person must reckon with. The multiplicity and variety of the world order with which the wise are dealing can never be completely mastered, and always have the capacity to surprise. The elusiveness of the physical world lies in its sheer extent, and also in its complexity, as this numerical saying admits:

---

[43] Ellen E. Davis, *Proverbs, Ecclesiastes and the Song of Songs* (Louisville: Westminster John Knox, 2000), p. 148.

[44] 22:17–24:22 is modelled on the genre of international instruction; 31:1–9 is also of the instruction genre; 30 and 31:10–31 contain numerical sayings and poems combining elements of sentence and instruction.

[45] See McKane, *Proverbs*, p. 505.

> Three things are too wonderful for me;
> four I do not understand:
> the way of an eagle in the sky,
> the way of a snake on a rock,
> the way of a ship on the high seas,
> and the way of a man with a girl. (Prov. 30:18–19)

This beautiful little piece is an attempt to catalogue similar phenomena, namely the movement of something through some element: the eagle through the air, the snake over rock, the ship through water, and the human being in and through the body. It draws an analogy between human and natural life; we might say from a modern perspective that it attempts to unify biology, physics, and social behaviour. It stands near to the analogy between animal and human leaders (the lion, the cock, the goat, and the king), but unlike that piece it registers a sense of uncertainty. Despite a confidence in cataloguing, the wise person here admits a limit in understanding. 'Three things are too wonderful for me, four I do not understand.' The wise, then, are aware of the incalculabilities that arise out of the very material they are dealing with. To use the language of Heidegger and Arendt with which we began this chapter, the world is both 'self-revealing' and 'self-concealing', it is both 'open' and 'inexhaustible'.

CAUTIOUSNESS AND GOD IN THE SENTENCE
LITERATURE OF PROVERBS

Now it is in this situation that, for wisdom, talk about God gets started. There are unknown factors with which the wise must reckon, and it is in this context that it becomes appropriate to talk about God. In a significant group of sayings in the sentence literature there is a recognition of something which cannot be calculated in experience, and in this connection the name of Yahweh, God the Lord, is invoked—referring to Yahweh's presence or purpose or activity.[46] This cluster of sayings connects Yahweh explicitly with the *limits* of human wisdom. Here is an example from Proverbs 16:

> The plans of the mind belong to mortals,
> but the answer of the tongue is from the LORD [Yahweh].[47] (16:1)

So one can plan to say something in one's mind, but there is always something that cannot be controlled about the way that the words actually come out, and

---

[46] Prov. 16:1, 2, 3, 9, 20, 33; 19:14, 21; 20:12, 24; 21:30, 31.
[47] The NRSV uses the typographical convention of indicating the divine name YHWH (יהוה), usually vocalized as 'Yahweh', with the upper-case LORD.

God has a part to play there. Similar sayings are 16:2, 3, 9, 20, 33; 19:14, 21; 20:12, 24 and 21:30, 31. In each case some uncertainty is detected in the process of 'steering' one's way through life on the basis of experience, which is the art of wisdom: there is something that cannot be absolutely guaranteed, however technically perfect one's mastery might be of wisdom's guidelines and Yahweh is given his place in that area of the unknown—in, for example, the achievement of happiness (16:20), victory in battle (21:31), and choice of a right wife (19:14). In the last case the saying begins with what is certain, and then moves to the uncertain:

> House and wealth are inherited from parents:
> but a prudent wife is from the LORD.

I aim to show that this association of Yahweh with the limits of human wisdom is not a matter of locating God merely in the 'gaps' of human ignorance, but it will take an exploration of the sentence literature over the next few pages to get to that point.

This small group of 'Yahwistic limitation sayings' (as we might call them) have their context in a much larger number of sayings with a religious content in the sentence literature which we may conveniently classify into five categories. First, the 'Yahwistic limitation' sayings are the only sentences about Yahweh which balance human enterprise against the limitations of wisdom within the structure of the individual saying itself. I am suggesting that they are a key within our present discussion. Second, there are sayings which appeal to a 'fear of Yahweh', seven examples of the formula with the noun 'fear' (*yir'ah*, יראה)[48] and two with the verb 'to fear' (*yārē'*, ירא).[49] Third, there are many other sayings which mention Yahweh as active in human experience (another forty-one, plus two references to El and two to 'Maker') and which we might call 'Yahweh-sayings'. Fourth, there are a number of sayings which contrast the behaviour and fate of the 'righteous' person (*ṣaddīq*, צדיק) with that of the 'wicked' (*rāšā'*, רשע), or which use synonyms for these antitheses. Most of these antitheses must be considered religious in tone, but some, notably in chapters 16 onwards carry the neutral, forensic meaning of 'innocent' and 'guilty', either within the law-court or from the standpoint of the social judgement of the community. Finally, there are a small number of extra sentences which employ religious vocabulary but are not included in the above four groups.[50]

These religious sayings are found in juxtaposition with the 'secular' sayings which form the bulk of the sentence literature. In employing the term 'secular' here I am intending no relation to modern sociological categories; it is merely descriptive of the appearance of these sayings, leaving for the moment as an

---

[48] 10:27; 14:27; 15:16; 15:33; 16:6; 19:23; 22:4.   [49] 14:2; 14:26.
[50] E.g. 10:16; 13:6; 13:22; 28:13; 28:20.

open question whether there are any religious motivations or convictions *behind* their use. They display a characteristically wisdom approach to experience, observing the 'world' (the *saeculum*) and noting consistent patterns of behaviour and consequences of actions, while they make no explicit appeal to God or piety. In their pragmatic approach they evoke an experimental ethos in old wisdom, though this need not imply a ruthlessness of morality. Now, this juxtaposition of sayings with a religious and secular content, and especially the presence of the 'Yahwistic limitation sayings' in the setting of secular sayings, presents an ambiguous appearance.

On the one hand it could be interpreted as evidence of the religious nature of the wisdom enterprise from its very inception in Israel.[51] Gerhard von Rad takes this view, arguing that the very parallelism of statements about 'experience of the world' and 'experience of Yahweh' demonstrates that the wise did not find these two approaches to the world incompatible. He suggests that with the new empirical approach to the world in the 'Enlightenment' under Solomon, the old faith in Yahweh remained strong, so that the wise found their experience of the world to be dialectical, both religious and secular ways of speaking about it being equally valid. 'Indeed,' he proposes, 'it was precisely because this knowledge of Yahweh was so strong . . . that Israel was able to speak of the orders of the world in quite secular terms.'[52] In line with this view, von Rad finds that the group of 'Yahwistic limitation sayings' were a way in which the wise defined the relationship between the two sides of the dialectic: while the two types of saying—secular and credal—were otherwise never fused in one statement, in this small group 'God and man were mentioned in one breath.' The relationship between the secular and the credal was achieved by recognizing that 'the continuity between human intentions and actual realisation' was broken, and 'the unpredictable area which lay between these two they regarded as the specific domain of Yahweh'.[53]

Other scholars, however, have maintained that this kind of observation is a development in Israelite wisdom, not typical of the early period in which wisdom was an essentially secular venture; it is wisdom getting religious as time goes on. Since the sentence literature is a collection, it is likely that the sayings contained in it come from different stages of the wisdom tradition, and so it is possible that the secular sayings represent the deposit of the original wisdom approach to the world, while the Yahwistic sayings reflect the assault which orthodox Yahwism made later upon the self-confidence of the wisdom method, finally re-interpreting the approach of old wisdom for the benefit of Yahwistic faith. This is basically the conclusion of William McKane, who lays emphasis upon the pragmatic quality of the art of statesmanship for which the early wisdom schools were founded: 'The Israelite *sōpᵉrîm* or

---

[51] See Chapter 1, the section called 'The Story of Wisdom in Ancient Israel'.
[52] Von Rad, *Wisdom*, p. 63.   [53] Von Rad, *Wisdom*, p. 105.

ḥᵃkāmîm... were not necessarily hostile or indifferent to religious belief and morality, but... they were persuaded that the world in which they had to operate and take decisions was not amenable to the assumptions of religious belief or to a black and white ethical terminology'.[54] He finds therefore that the sentences of Proverbs 10–29 fall into categories which reflect the Yahwizing of an original pragmatic wisdom: he suggests Class A sayings which come from old wisdom, and are concerned with the education of the individual for a successful and harmonious life; Class B, which are similarly old wisdom but concerned with the health of the community; and Class C sayings, which are religious and re-interpret old wisdom in the interests of Yahwistic piety.[55] The small group of 'Yahwistic limitation sayings' I have identified above fall into this latter class, as part of a 'Yahwistic riposte to the claims of old wisdom and a severe circumscribing of the powers exercised by its practitioners'.[56]

In the absence of any effective external controls, this fundamental disagreement about the interpretation of the sentence literature can only resolved by internal literary criticism. Here, R. B. Y. Scott has usefully built upon the proposals made by McKane, arguing that secular sayings have been taken as the *basis* for the construction of Yahwistic versions, correcting or modifying them. My own observations that follow are indebted in general to Scott's method, while extending and varying his results.[57] If we concentrate on the 'Yahwistic limitation sayings', I suggest that we do indeed find evidence of their being a deliberate *modification* of secular sayings. For example, 16:1 has marks of being corrective both in its similar structure and proximity to secular sayings. With the saying

> The plans of the mind belong to mortals,
> but the answer of the tongue is from the LORD.

we may compare the secular 15:23:

> To make an apt answer is a joy to mortals,
> and a word in season, how good it is!

---

[54] McKane, *Prophets and Wise Men*, p. 47.
[55] McKane, *Proverbs*, p. 11.   [56] McKane, *Proverbs*, p. 495.
[57] Scott, 'Wise and Foolish, Righteous and Wicked', pp. 152–3, compares 13:14/16:22 with 14:27/10:11; 15:17/17:1 with 16:8/15:16; 28:21/18:5 with 17:15; elsewhere, pp. 162–4, he draws attention to other examples which we may perceive as being in the same category: 15:23 with 16:1; 15:22/20:18/21:5 with 16:3/19:21; 20:24/16:30 with 16:9; 10:27 with 28:16; 18:12 with 15:33. Some comparisons which Scott does not note are: 10:17 with 19:23; 16:9 also with 16:25; 18:12 with 22:4; 20:18 also with 21:30–1; 20:26 with 20:27; 28:4 with 28:5; 28:16 with 10:27. Scott further suggests that Yahweh sayings are found in the immediate context of secular sayings which they correct or supplement: he compares 10:3 with 10:4; 11:20 with 11:21; 15:9 with 15:10; 15:16 with 15:17; 18:10 with 18:11; 22:2 with 22:7 (see p. 162). He does not note the comparison of 19:20 with 19:21; 22:11 with 22:12; 10:27 with 10:28; 12:1 with 12:2; 20:26 (cf. 20:5) with 20:27; 29:13 with 29:14; 28:4 with 28:5 (and the dogmatic 10:16 may also be compared with 10:17). Some of the examples in this note are discussed in my main text as the argument develops.

Also the characteristic ideas of secular wisdom modified in 16:1 appear again in the near context of 16:23 in a secular form:

> The mind of the wise makes their speech judicious
> and adds persuasiveness to their lips.

There is a close interaction, moreover, between several secular and Yahwistic sayings here in their use of the vocabulary of education wisdom. The 'plans' (*maḥᵃšābōt*, מחשבות) of 16:3,

> Commit your work to the LORD
> and your plans will be established.

are a Yahwistic version of the secular 'plans' (same word) in 15:22:

> without counsel, plans go wrong,
> but with many advisors they succeed.

The 'answer' (*maʿᵃneh*, מענה) of the tongue in 16:1b which comes 'from Yahweh' comments on the secular 'answer' (same word) of 15:23: 'to make an apt answer is a joy to mortals'. The 'way' (*derek*, דרך) which lies under the eye of Yahweh in 16:2 also echoes the 'way' (same word) which the wise take in 15:24, so that the three secular themes of the 'plans' the 'answer' and the 'way' in 15:22–24 are given a Yahwistic version in 16:1–3.

Another example of this Yahwistic modification is 16:33, which is clearly based on 18:18. In 18:17–18 we have the picture of two well-trained lawyers, equally skilled in the wisdom method, who are arguing opposite sides of a case; how can one decide who is right? In this situation, we read, there is only one thing to do—cast lots, or 'toss a coin'.

> Casting the lot puts an end to disputes
> and decides between powerful contenders. (18:18)

The saying of 16:33 now offers a Yahwistic version of this secular saying:

> The lot is cast into the lap
> but the decision is wholly from the LORD. (16:33)

19:20–21 provides an example of correction of a secular saying by immediate context:

> Listen to advice (*ʿēṣah*, עצה) and accept instruction
> that you may gain wisdom for the future.

> The human mind may devise many plans,
> but it is the purpose (*ʿēṣah*, עצה) of the LORD that will be established.

In the light of other similar examples a merely 'stitchword' principle is surely an inadequate explanation for this editorial positioning. The 'Yahwistic limitation sayings' demonstrate not merely a complementary approach to secular wisdom, as Von Rad proposes, but a modification of it.

It could, of course, be urged that the chronological gap between secular sayings and Yahwistic sayings based upon them is only relative, and that all the time secular insights might have been converted *immediately* into Yahwistic ones. This would not be impossible in itself (and we shall see that something like this continual shift was happening in Egyptian wisdom) but the actual literary evidence is against it. If it were the case, it is curious that the secular and Yahwistic sayings remain so separate for the most part, and the style of the re-use of vocabulary in the Yahweh sayings does seem to be corrective, though not as pejorative as McKane maintains.[58] It would, however, be in accordance with this evidence to suppose that the compilers of Proverbs 10–29 used some Yahweh sayings which were indeed as old as the secular sayings, but which for a long period had been a kind of 'minority report' of the wisdom movement and which now came into their own, as well as using (and coining) new ones. The likelihood of this situation is increased, I suggest, when we add to the modification of secular sayings a *continuity* we can detect between sayings in the wisdom collections of Proverbs which do not mention God, and those which do. This observation has a significance, as we shall see, far beyond questions of chronology.

Here our small group of Yahwistic limitation sayings provides an important focus, since an underlying continuity can be found precisely in a sense of limitation upon human wisdom, and a cautiousness in using the guidelines of experience. If we return to the saying of 18:18 about 'tossing a coin,' which has a Yahwistic revision in 16:33, the recommendation contains within itself an admission of the uncertainty of conflicting evidence when presented persistently by 'powerful opponents', and this is exactly the point made also in the preceding secular sentence:

> He who states his case first seems right
> until the other comes and cross-examines. (18:17)

This urges caution in the first place as a matter of successful technique: the good judge waits for all evidence before deciding. But there is also the possibility raised of not knowing which of the two skilful speakers is right, for two possessing impressive skills in speech may simply end in deadlock.

Again, we found that the Yahwistic qualification of 'the plans of the mind' in 16:1 was followed immediately by a qualification of the 'way' of wisdom (referrring to the 'plans' and 'way' in the secular sayings 15:22–24):

> All one's ways may be pure in one's own eyes,
> but the LORD weighs the spirit. (16:2)

---

[58] McKane, *Proverbs*, p. 17.

Yahweh is also described as limiting human plans in 16:9, and this is equated with 'directing of the way':

> The human mind plans the way
> but the LORD directs the steps.

This may be compared with the many secular sayings which take the theme of 'the way', among them and in this near context 15:24 and 16:25. While the Yahwistic limitation sayings refute the confidence of secular sayings in this manner, we find a note of caution already underlying secular approaches to the 'establishing of plans' and the planning of the 'way'. The secular saying 16:25 which looks as if it has been taken as the basis for the Yahweh-limitation saying 16:2 and whose idea is echoed in 16:9 points out itself that:

> There is a way that appears to someone to run straight forward,
> yet it ends as the way to death.[59]

A way may begin by looking advantageous, but the wise person must always be ready to find other factors arising that could not have been planned for, and not just stick to the planned course. Even after everything has been taken into consideration in the beginning, there is still some uncertainty. I cannot agree with the commentators who restrict the application of this phrase to the incorrigible man or the evil man[60] but I find its basic meaning to be a neutral description of the unpredictability of events, and so a warning against pride to all. It is therefore similar to another secular limiting saying in 27:1:

> Do not boast about tomorrow
> For you do not know what a day may bring.

The meaning of 16:25 proposed here is underlined by its other occurrence at 14:12, where it is juxtaposed with the saying:

> Even in laughter the heart may be sad
> and the end of joy may be grief. (14:13)[61]

Something begins in one way—straight (16:25; 14:12) or joyous (14:13) – but ends in another—death (16:25; 14:12) or grief (14:13).[62] This is not a simple pessimism or fatalism, but the recognition of the unexpected factor that the wise person will need to take into account, and which may even be

---

[59] My translation.

[60] So e.g. McKane, *Proverbs*, p. 490; C. H. Troy, *Proverbs*. International Critical Commentary (Edinburgh: T & T Clark, 1899), p. 289; André Barucq, *Le Livre des Proverbes* (Paris: Gabalda, 1964), p. 127. But in accord with my argument, see C. T. Fritsch, *Proverbs*. Interpreter's Bible (New York: Abingdon, 1955), p. 863: 'The way which promises happiness, prosperity and success may lead for one reason or another to destruction.'

[61] My translation.

[62] So Norman Whybray, *Proverbs*. Cambridge Biblical Commentary (Cambridge: Cambridge University Press, 1972), p. 83.

incalculable. The need to reckon with the immediately unknown is always shading into the long-term unknown, and even into the always to be unknown. Another secular saying that qualifies the confidence of human 'plans' is 21:5, which recognizes the difficulty of balancing the need to take decisive action and the need to wait; caution must replace destructive haste, and yet some compromises with certainty have to be made or nothing will get done:

> The plans of the man who acts decisively will lead to success,
> yet everyone who is hasty comes only to want.[63]

The continuity that we have so far elucidated between secular and Yahwistic sayings about human limitations may also be found between secular sayings and the *wider* Yahweh sayings that comment upon them. For instance, the greatest area of uncertainty that the wise person recognizes is the unfathomability of another person's mind, the mystery of another person's personality that introduces the element of incalculability into the best counsel. The Yahweh saying 17:3 corrects the apparent confidence of the secular 27:21:

> The crucible is for silver, and the furnace is for gold;
> so a person is tested by being praised. (27:21)

> The crucible is for silver, and the furnace is for gold,
> but the LORD tests the heart. (17:3)

But the confidence of 27:21, that someone may be assessed by the reputation which the society gives him,[64] is *already* placed in juxtaposition with other secular reflections that admit more uncertainty in perception. Thus in the nearby 27:19,

> As in water face [answers] to face
> so [answers] the heart of a man to a man.[65]

G. R. Driver aptly paraphrases, 'As a man sees his and no other face reflected in water, so he will see only his own nature reflected in his companion's heart.'[66] The saying of 27:7 strikes the same note about the subjectivity, and so the uncertainty, of judgement:[67]

> The person who is satiated loathes honey,
> but to one who is hungry everything bitter is sweet.

---

[63] My translation. Cf. Prov. 21:25, 27:13.

[64] *Proverbs*, p. 606.

[65] Literal translation, not NRSV.

[66] G. R. Driver, 'Problems in Proverbs', *Zeitschrift für die alttestamentliche Wissenschaft* 50 (1932), pp. 146ff.

[67] My translation. This is a common reflection in proverbial wisdom: cf. *Ahikar* xxii.188 (ANET, p. 430); Onchsheshonqy 14:14; 15:11–12 (S. R. K. Glanville, *The Instruction of Onchsheshonqy*; Catalogue of Demotic Papyri in the British Museum. 2 Volumes [London: British Museum, 1955], vol. 2, pp. 25, 37; W. G. Lambert, *Babylonian Wisdom Literature* (Oxford: Clarendon Press, 1960), p. 249.

Further to the water image of 27:19, the slightly different image of deep water as representing the mind, the words and especially the wisdom of someone is to have a considerable future in the wisdom tradition; it contains the possibility of ambiguity between the ampleness and unfathomability of things. Water can be both vast (especially in the sea) and unsearchable. Thus, while 20:5 expresses confidence in the wisdom techniques for plumbing the 'deep water' of a person's heart, 18:4 may well admit the obscurity of the 'deep waters' of a person's words:[68]

> The words of the mouth are deep waters;
> the fountain of wisdom is a gushing stream.

The essential impenetrability of another person's mind is similarly expressed, though without the image of water, by 14:10 ('the heart knows its own bitterness').[69] That the function of 27:19 (one sees only one's own face in the water of the mind) is to qualify 27:21 (the confident assessment of a person by the community) is confirmed also by the intervening saying 27:20. This is again about the uncertainty of perception:

> Sheol and Abaddon are never satisfied
> and human eyes are never satisfied.

This is a sentence of immense significance for our theme of hiddenness in the world order; there is no end to what persons can see, and so there is no end to their quest for discovery.[70] Human beings have an unsatisfied hunger for looking at the world, just as the underworld, Sheol, has a never-ending appetite for receiving the dead. The elusiveness of the visible world lies in its extent. The thought of lack of satisfaction is to be picked up later by Koheleth:

> All things are wearisome,
> More than one can express;
> the eye is not satisfied with seeing,
> or the ear filled with hearing. (Eccl. 1:8)

In its immediate application in context the non-satisfaction of Proverbs 27:20 seems to be applied to the world of human relationships, but it obviously has an application also to the physical world, as in Ecclesiastes 1:8b.

The theme of the limits to enquiring human sight expressed in the secular sayings of Proverbs 27:19–20 has continuity with Yahwistic adaptations in 20:12 and 15:11. Human beings are never satisfied with their observations, because they cannot see everything, but God has an unlimited capacity to see:

---

[68] So R. B. Y. Scott, *Proverbs-Ecclesiastes*, p. 114.

[69] The context is also that of other sayings about uncertainty: vv. 12, 13, 16.

[70] It is unnecessary to restrict this sentence to a statement of unsatisfied desire here, as do several commentators: Scott, *Proverbs-Ecclesiastes*, p. 162; Troy, *Proverbs*, p. 490; McKane, *Proverbs*, p. 618.

The hearing ear and the seeing eye—
the LORD has made them both. (20:12)

Sheol and Abaddon lie open before the LORD,
how much more human hearts! (15:11)

The mysterious nature of another's mind is a common theme in other Ancient Near Eastern wisdom and an important example occurs in the Aramaic Wisdom of Ahikar:

Many are the stars of heaven whose names man knows not;
so man knows not men. (VIII.116)[71]

The stars cannot be known for their multiplicity, and no less complex is human personality. Here is an equation between multiplicity (here, stars) and profundity (here, human beings) that we shall find many times in the Israelite wisdom tradition. That is, the second half of the saying is not concerned with the number of human beings but, as McKane perceives, with 'The difficulty which one man has in penetrating the mystery of another's personality.'[72]

The religious proverbs I have cited, and especially the Yahwistic limitation sayings, urge that in every area of life there needs to be caution that amounts to humility before God. This humble approach to life can take the form of admonitions about 'the fear of the Lord', a phrase that appears, as we have seen, some nine times in the sentence literature of Proverbs. The primary meaning of the phrase 'the fear of the Lord' is thus a humility in the midst of calculations. But this humble 'fearing' takes not only a religious but a secular form, and it seems that there is a shifting borderline between them. One saying (Proverbs 14:16), for instance, simply commends 'fearing', in a kind of secular version of the 'fear of the Lord':

A wise man is a fearer (*yārē'*, יָרֵא) and turns away from evil
but a fool throws off restraint and is careless.[73]

In this secular saying of old wisdom, the wise man is presented as a 'fearer', that is cautious, slow to speak and slow to act in contrast to the fool who is hasty and impetuous (14:15–18). The reason for caution as exemplified in this sentence literature is no doubt to achieve more effective action, to give opportunity to choose exactly the right word to fit the occasion, to reflect carefully upon the course of action to take: that is, caution improves the

---

[71] A. E. Cowley, *Aramaic Papyri of the Fifth Century BC* (Oxford: Clarendon Press, 1923), pp. 223–4.

[72] McKane *Proverbs*, p. 167. This is obscured by H. L. Ginsberg's translation of the line as 'no man knows mankind', in J. B. Pritchard (ed.), *Ancient Near Eastern Texts Relating to the Old Testament.* Second edition (Princeton, Princeton University Press), henceforth cited as ANET, p. 429.

[73] My translation.

technique of 'steering', and the fool is the man who does not take the trouble to do this.[74] But lying behind this is the realization that some things are initially deceptive, and may not be known for a long time, while other things may never be known at all. The wise person is aware that his or her conclusions might after all be wrong, for 'the whole story' cannot be known. This sense of limitation is a secular 'fearing' (14:16) and not by itself a God-fearing attitude, yet there is a continuity between the two moods.

In fact, cautiousness in secular wisdom sayings merges into humility:

> When pride comes, then comes disgrace
> but wisdom is with the humble. (11:2, cf. 16:18; 21:23–4; 29:1, 23).

This atttitude may be expressed as 'not being wise in one's own eyes' (26:5, 12, 16; 28:11, 26). Such a quality of humility is a willingness to submit to further wisdom instruction, and a willingness to wait to act or speak despite provocation if the effective time has not come. In the light of the material we have examined, we can add that the willingness to admit that one may never know some things fully inhibits boasting (27:1). This is not a religious humility in itself, but one can see how religious sayings are easily built upon it, such as 22:4 (which builds on the phrases of the secular 29:23 and 18:12):

> The reward for humility and fear of the LORD
> is riches and honour and life.

Now, the discovery that there is a sense of limitation, expressed explicitly as humility, on the two levels of secular pragmatism and piety, has important consequences for our understanding of the nature of that limitation. If, like von Rad, we locate the sense of limitation *entirely* in the explicitly religious sayings of Proverbs, then we will tend to think of human experience of divine 'interventions' into an otherwise calculable order. Von Rad pictures these limitations as areas of divine mystery whose 'frontiers' or 'boundaries . . . man comes up against in his investigations'.[75] But when we recognize the limitation's arising out of the very material which secular wisdom concerns itself with, then we picture it not as a 'boundary' *beyond* which God is, but as the continual *extension* of known material into the unknown. It is a question of complexity and multiplicity, of limitation consisting in the 'limitless' scope of things which cannot be grasped. It is not a boundary, but boundlessness that defeats wisdom.[76] In perhaps the least religious of the Egyptian instructions, *Ptah-hotep*, we read:

---

[74] E.g. 10:8; 11:12; 12:15–16, 23; 13:16; 14:29; 18:7.

[75] Von Rad, *Wisdom*, pp. 72–3, 99–106. Cf. his *Old Testament Theology*, trans. D. M. G. Stalker. 2 Volumes (Edinburgh: Oliver and Boyd, 1962), vol. 1, pp. 438–40.

[76] I argue this at length in my 'Hiddenness of Wisdom', pp. 23–30, 178–88.

Let not thy heart be puffed up because of thy knowledge: be not confident because thou art a wise man . . . The full limits of skill cannot be attained: there is no man equipped to his full advantage.[77]

Later Israelite wisdom puts the situation in similar terms: 'No man has ever fully known wisdom' (Ben Sira 24:28). This is the continuity in the wisdom tradition, although the balance between a sense of confidence in dealing with the world and a sense of limitation will obviously shift under different pressures. While in the early stages of the Israelite wisdom movement, wisdom is thought to be *not totally accessible* to man, we shall see that in the less confident wisdom of the post-exilic period it is *not totally inaccessible* either. Von Rad denies (contrary to our present argument) that this limitation is grounded in 'limitation of man's range of vision' or 'the quantitative limitation of human capabilities';[78] he maintains that it is only because the sense of limitation has a religious origin in trust in Yahweh that 'a veil of resignation' does not lie over the wisdom enterprise.[79] But this view fails to reckon with the vigorous willingness to compromise with uncertainty that we have discerned in secular wisdom. The secular sense of limitation need not lapse into fatalism since it arises within an active application of skills, and is indeed thought to be an essential part of those skills.

Further, the continuity between secular and religious caution we have elucidated tends to confirm our earlier suggestion about the development of religious wisdom sayings. Since secular wisdom is—by its character of cautious humility—potentially Yahwistic, it can be seen how easily the shift could be made by some wise who wanted to bring their wisdom methods into conformity with a more explicit Yahwism. While the evidence we have examined indicates that such a regular shift was a relatively later state in the wisdom movement, it is possible that a minority made it from early on; then their work would have been included by the compilers of Proverbs 10–29, who must by the time of its composition have had a more confessional Yahwistic approach as shown by the bias in their editing. We ought perhaps then to reckon with a diversity in the religion of the wisdom movement rather than a strict progression.

Finally, this continuity in a sense of caution and humility in face of the world leads us to a certain interpretation of the association of Yahweh with wisdom's limits. The point of the 'Yahwistic limitation sayings' is not that God suddenly intervenes to trip the wise person up, or that God *only* acts where there are 'gaps' in human knowledge. Rather, the sayings affirm that God has the perfect wisdom to operate successfully in *all* areas, *including* those where human wisdom falters through lack of grasp on the situation. Where the

---

[77] *Ptah-hotep*, trans. J. A. Wilson, ANET, p. 412.
[78] Von Rad, *Wisdom*, pp. 100, 102.   [79] Von Rad, *Wisdom*, p. 101.

human capacity to see is limited, God has total vision of everything that is there to be seen:

> Sheol and Abaddon lie open before the LORD [i.e. to Yahweh's sight],
> how much more human hearts! (Prov. 15:11)

God is always on the scene, always immediately involved in the world, including all those situations where the wise *are* confident in their appraisal of the world and their consequent actions. The moments when a sense of the limits of wisdom is sharpest are simply reminders of what is always the case, points of focus. We have found that the limitation of the wisdom method arises out of the very material which wisdom concerns itself with; so we can picture this limit not as a boundary *beyond* which God resides, but as a boundlessness of the human personality and the natural world. Wisdom is limited by the scope of its material—its diversity, multiplicity, and complexity that can never be fully grasped by human minds. The transcendence of God, or the infinite difference between the uncreated and the created, does not consist in God's dwelling beyond a boundary located between two spheres of reality; rather, God is at home in the boundless expanse of the world in a way that we are not.

Israel's proverbial wisdom thus finds an *opportunity* for talk about God as creator and sustainer of the world at the points where the world is found to be most complex and elusive, although God is not to be confined to those points. The wisdom scribes pride themselves on their craft in words, but they also recognize the frailty of words ('the answer of the tongue is from Yahweh!'), aware that there is no simple correspondence between the verbal sign and the world of objects.[80] Analogies can always break down and truth is not always deducible from observation. In this situation they urge trust in God without *restricting* God to gaps in human knowledge. While perceiving, as Arendt does many centuries later, the self-concealing nature of the world and its exacerbation by a lack of humility, the wise also open up the possibility of thinking about the divine purpose (*telos*) in this situation.

ORDER IN EGYPTIAN WISDOM AND 'ORDERING'
IN ISRAELITE WISDOM

Given the international scope of the wisdom movement in the Ancient Near East, and the presence of 'borrowed' pieces of Egyptian wisdom in Proverbs, it is of no little interest that Egyptian wisdom literature reveals a duality between a stand-alone 'cautiousness' about the limits of wisdom and an expression of

---

[80] See further Chapter 8, the end of the sections called 'Hiddenness and Interpretation in Modern Thought' and 'Disruption and Empathy'.

the same idea in terms of 'the plan of the god'. This bears a striking similarity to the juxtaposing of 'secular' and 'Yahwistic' sayings in the sentence literature of Proverbs. In Egyptian wisdom there seems to be a range of possibilities for expressing a sense of limitation, some more religious than others. Throughout the instructions, from the less religious (*Ptah-hotep*, *Amen-em-het*) to the more religious (*Meri-ka-Re*, *Ani*, *Amen-em-Opet*), there is a consistent sense of the limits of knowledge, expressed in terms of the hiddenness of 'Ma'at', or the 'Order' of things.

At first sight it might appear that this fact settles the question as to the religious nature of early wisdom in Israel. It has been argued that it would be impossible for Israel not to take over and emphasize the view of those Egyptian sayings that give place to faith in God.[81] However, there is a fundamental difference between Egyptian and Israelite religion in this matter of 'Order'. In Egyptian wisdom, the framework of 'Ma'at' provides an inherent link between the less and more religious sayings from the beginning, as well as the context for a duality between confidence and caution. The keystone of the religious basis of 'Order' (Ma'at) in Egyptian thinking was the king, who preserved through his divine functions the order of the human society that participated in the divinely created Order of the world. The Israelite kingship ideology did not provide such a firm basis for a theology of Order. In accord with this, there is no exactly comparable term for 'Ma'at' in Israelite wisdom; there are approximations which indicate the idea of world Order—'righteousness' (*ṣᵉdāqah*, צדקה), 'judgement/justice' (*mišpāṭ*, משפט), 'wisdom' itself (*ḥokmah*, חכמה)—but no one ter acting as the focus for a consistent theology of Order as in Egypt.

In Egyptian wisdom the acknowledgement of the limits of wisdom stands against the background of the confidence which the concept of Ma'at as a stable, right order in society and nature gave to the wise in their providing of instruction. There were two strands in this confidence. First, a stable and perceptible structure makes possible the application of the wisdom method: patterns of experience can be detected in order to participate in right ones which are health-giving ('doing Ma'at'),[82] both by means of instruction inherited from the past[83] and by a certain freedom in discovering for oneself

---

[81] See e.g. Rylaarsdam, *Revelation*, pp. 70–1: Gemser, 'Spiritual Structure', pp. 146–7; Weeks, *Early Israelite Wisdom*, pp. 67–9.

[82] Reference to 'doing' or 'speaking Ma'at' are found in *Ptah-hotep*, text following 640 (ANET, p. 414), *Meri-ka-Re*, text following 45 (ANET, p. 415), *Amen-em-Opet* xx.14f., xxi.5f (F. Ll. Griffith, 'The Teaching of Amenophis', *Journal of Egyptian Archaeology* 12 [1926], p. 218), *Onchsheshonqy* 13.15 (Glanville, *Instruction*, p. 33), *Protests of the Eloquent Peasant* B.1.209f., 300ff. (A. H. Gardiner, *Journal of Egyptian Archaeology* 9 [1923], pp. 16–17), cf. the funerary inscription of *Kagemni*, cit. Siegfried Morenz, *Egyptian Religion*, trans. A. E. Keep (London: Methuen, 1973), p. 112. For an account of the nature of Ma'at, see Morenz, *Egyptian Religion*, pp. 112–136.

[83] *Ptah-hotep*, text following 510 (ANET, p. 414), *Meri-ka-Re*, text following 35 (ANET, p. 415), *In Praise of Learned Scribes* (ANET, pp. 431–2).

what it means to live in tune with Ma'at.[84] Second, there is a confidence that derives from the influence of Ma'at upon a man's career. Ma'at exerts an inexorable pressure upon a man, so that he is bound to rise to the limit of his worth[85] unless he is lazy or careless. He has a place assigned to him in the Order which the Order itself will ensure he reaches provided that he acts in tune with it. This belief in the pressure of Ma'at is largely responsible for the attractive ethos of tranquillity in Egyptian instruction: it is impossible to force the pace of things, and self-restraint will achieve what assertiveness will not. This statement of people's progress to their proper place is usually expressed in religious terms, since Ma'at is established and preserved by God, although the relationship between Ma'at and God is complex: 'God' in this context may mean the creator God, the local god, the king, who possesses the 'ba' or 'soul' of the god, or any combination of these. In many sayings, then, the activity of Ma'at and God, though not identical is practically interchangeable—it is a perpetual force or influence upon a man's course:

> It is God who assigneth the foremost place,
> but one attaineth nothing with the elbow.[86]

Despite the formal similarity of such sayings with Israelite sayings like Proverbs 16:3, 7 the thought is not really parallel since the whole context of the pressure of Ma'at is missing in Israelite wisdom.

While these two aspects of Ma'at—stability and influence—give confidence to the activity of the wise man, at the same time he recognizes limitations on his wisdom which can be expressed in various degrees of religious attitude. A lack of absolute certainty about how a person is related to the Order is common to all instructions: a person does not fully know the exact workings of Ma'at as they affect him, and to which his action should be attuned. In the quite religious *Meri-ka-Re* the knowledge of having infringed Ma'at is presented as sometimes delayed until the judgement after death, whereas in the less religious *Ptah-hotep* a man knows by the immediate consequences when he has done so;[87] but in neither case can wisdom ensure that a man will never

---

[84] Stressed by Morenz, *Egyptian Religion*, pp. 117–19.

[85] *Ptah-hotep*: 'It is God who makes [a person's] quality, and he defends him [even] while he is asleep.' (ANET, p. 413). Cf. *Kagemni*: 'The cautious man flourisheth ..., but knives are prepared against one that forceth a path' (Battiscombe Gunn, *The Instruction of Ptah-hotep and the Instruction of Ke'gemni* [London: Methuen, 1906], p. 62). *Meri-ka-Re*, text following 50 (ANET, p. 415); *Amen-em-Opet* i.9–10 (Griffith, 'Teaching', p. 195); *Amen-em-Opet* ix.10–15; x.10–11 (Griffith, 'Teaching', p. 206), *Onchsheshonqy* 6.12 (Glanville, *Instruction*, p. 19). There is an important discussion of this point in McKane, *Proverbs*, pp. 60–2, cf. Heaton, *Solomon's New Men*, pp. 117–19.

[86] *Ptah-hotep*, in A. Erman, *The Literature of the Ancient Egyptians*, trans. A. Blackman (London: Methuen, 1926), p. 59. Cf. the prayer to the Aton in *Amen-em-Opet* x.12–15, following a description of the silent man's progress in x.10–11 (Griffith, 'Teaching', p. 206).

[87] *Meri-ka-Re*, text following 50 (ANET, p. 415) cf. Gese, *Lehre und Wirklichkeit*, pp. 17–19, Morenz, *Egyptian Wisdom*, pp. 127–8.

infringe Ma'at in the first place and act in total conformity to it. Indeed, this only 'relative explicitness' of Ma'at (the phrase is Morenz's)[88] is inherent in the very nature of the wisdom method, which is less concerned with the production of absolute definition of Ma'at than with living in tune with it.

The range of expression of this lack of certainty takes three basic forms. First, there may be acknowledgement of a lack of total grasp of the nature of Ma'at which stands on its own, without further religious support. For example, *Ptah-hotep* expresses a humility about the limitations of speech:

> Let not the heart be puffed up because of thy knowledge; be not confident because thou art a wise man. Take counsel with the ignorant as well as the wise. The full limits of skill cannot be attained, and there is no skilled man equipped to his full advantage. Good speech is more hidden than the emerald, but it may be found with maidservants at the grindstones.[89]

The imperfections of even the best craftsman in words should lead him to seek out the unexpected verbal gem where it may be hidden even among the ignorant. We must not overestimate this note of caution, and expressions of confidence about effective speech in *Ptah-hotep* and *Meri-ka-Re* put it in perspective: the wise are 'craftsmen' in 'speaking Ma'at'[90] but it is admitted that something may escape them.

Ptah-hotep raises the familiar theme of the obscurity of a person's heart to the observer:

> Laugh after he (i.e. 'the great man') laughs, and it will be very pleasing to his heart: no one can know what is in the heart.[91]

The last phrase concedes that the wise man cannot be certain of the success of his social ploy, though again we must balance this against confidence in a technique for eliciting what is in a person's heart: 'Test his heart with a bit of talk.'[92]

In conversation generally, the wise man should be reticent, as he does not know fully the state of affairs. Moreover, he can afford to be patient because the force of Ma'at will carry his opponent to his destination anyway: 'Do not answer in a state of turmoil... his time has never failed to come.'[93] But the later *Amen-em-Opet* explicitly offers another reason for silence in dispute (which may well be implied in the earlier instruction also), and this brings us to a second major form of expression of uncertainty: no person can fully

---

[88] Morenz, *Egyptian Religion*, p. 117.

[89] *Ptah-hotep*, text following 50 (ANET, p. 412).

[90] *Meri-ka-Re*, text following 33 (ANET, p. 415), *Ptah-hotep*, text following 510 (ANET, p. 414).

[91] *Ptah-hotep*, text following 130 (ANET, p. 412).

[92] *Ptah-hotep*, text following 465 (ANET, p. 414).

[93] *Ptah-hotep*, text following 475 (ANET, p. 414).

comprehend the 'plan of god' for him. After the advice, 'Leave it to him that he may empty his innermost soul' i.e. let your opponent in dispute give himself away, four lines are repeated that have already appeared in the previous section of the teaching:

> For surely thou knowest not the plans of god
> Lest thou (be ashamed) on the morrow.
> Sit thou down at the hands of god
> and thy tranquillity will throw them down.[94]

The two ways of expression, the first more pragmatic and the second more theological, are not as distinct as Israelite secular and Yahwistic sayings, since the force of Ma'at in the first can be equated with the will of god in the second. We have seen two examples from Ptah-hotep where a note of caution stands without appeal to the plan of god, but in other passages the two ways of expressing limitation stand together. For instance, at meals the officials will receive favour from the great man in a way that they cannot calculate or engineer: the host will give bread to those within reach, and those to whom he reaches (perhaps 'further')[95] are favoured through his acting the impulse of his *ka* (natural vitality):

> As for the great man when he is at meals, his purposes conform to the dictates of his ka. He will give to the one whom he favors. The great man gives to the man whom he can reach, but it is the ka that lengthens out his arms.[96]

To this naturalistic explanation of the unpredictability of a man's vital impulses is then added a more theological explanation:

> The eating of bread is under the planning of god—it is (only) a fool who would complain of it.

However, the two viewpoints are inseparable, due to the underlying concept of Ma'at: the ka prompts social behaviour which is part of the Order which is sustained by god (whether creator, local god, or king) so that the wise man submits to the pressure of ka-Ma'at-god[97] upon him. There is a whole consistent context of social order here which is lacking in Israelite wisdom.

Again, the pragmatic warning is given that, 'One does not know what may happen so that he may understand the morrow',[98] and thus a man is advised to

---

[94] *Amen-em-Opet* xxiii.4–5 (Griffith, 'Teaching', p. 220).

[95] So Erman, *Literature*, p. 51.

[96] The idea of the 'ka' (vitality) is too complex for us to assume a simple identity between ka and the god. Cf. Jaroslav Cerny, *Ancient Egyptian Religion* (London: Hutchinson, 1952), pp. 81–2 and Morenz, *Egyptian Religion*, p. 204, who draws an important distinction between the 'ka' and the 'ba' of heavenly origin.

[97] Cf. 'Follow thy ka so long as you livest': *Ptah-hotep*, in Erman, *Literature*, p. 58.

[98] *Ptah-hotep*, text following 43 (ANET, p. 413).

cover all unpredictable contingencies (by satisfying his clients so that they will come to his help). But at the same time prosperity is described as being 'favoured' by the god.[99]

The reference to the unknown morrow significantly comes even from this earliest of the instructions extant, from the relatively stable Old Kingdom (V Dynasty). The balance between a sense of predictability and randomness will, of course, shift according to social climate, and there is an increasing note of uncertainty in other instructions which can be located in times of social upheaval.[100] From *Amen-em-Opet* comes perhaps the classic expression of the incalculable activity of god, conjoined with the pragmatic warning about the incalculable morrow:

> Do not spend the night fearful of the morrow.
> At day-break, what is the morrow like?
> Man knows not what the morrow is like.
> God is (always) in his success
> Whereas man is in his failure;
> One thing are the words which men say,
> Another is that which the god does.[101]

The final two lines seem especially close to Proverbs 16:1–9, but the context of Ma'at gives the activity of the god an inflexibility and a weight of destiny which is not characteristic of the Israelite sayings.

A third kind of expression for the sense of limitation of wisdom is a more mythological form of the explicitly religious one. While there are only rare references to mythological stories of divine activity such as creation,[102] there is present in instructions later than Ptah-hotep the mythopoetic picture of the divine observing of the world, mainly in the person of the sun-god (there being also a lunar eye, Thoth). So *Meri-ka-Re* describes the perfect vision of Re, in this instance following reference to the act of creation:

> Well directed are men, the cattle of the god ... he sails by in order to see them ... the god knows every name.[103]

Now in contrast man's observation and so his coordination with world order is limited. The order that 'the eye (of man) can see' is in fact subject both to the

---

[99] Ibid. For another example, see *Amen-em-Opet* x.10–11 and 12–15 already cited.

[100] *Meri-ka-Re* can be located in the first Intermediate Period, X Dynasty; *Amen-em-Het* probably at the time of the breaking up the Middle Kingdom; *Amen-em-Opet* probably at the time of the breaking up the of national unity in XXII–XXIII Dynasties.

[101] *Amen-em-Opet* xix.10–17, trans. J. A. Wilson (ANET, p. 423).

[102] *Meri-ka-Re* 130–5 (ANET, p. 417), *Amen-em-Opet* xviii.2–3 (ANET, p. 423), xii.15f. (Griffith, 'Teaching', p. 208).

[103] *Meri-ka-Re* 130–5 (ANET, p. 417). Also *Ani* vii.12–17 (ANET, p. 420), *Amen-em-Opet* xviii.23–xix.3, xxv.17–20 (Griffith, 'Teaching', pp. 215–23), *Onchsheshonqy* 26:11 (Glanville, *Instruction*, p. 59). Cf. similarly Thoth or lunar eye in *Amen-em-Opet* iv.19, vii.18, xvii.9–12 (Griffith, 'Teaching', pp. 214, 200–4).

god's perfect vision and to his invisible control which is described by recourse to the (popular) etymology of Amon as 'hidden':

> Generation passes generation among men, and the god, who knows (men's) characters, has hidden himself. (But) there is none who can withstand the Lord of the Hand; he is the one who attacks what the eye can see.[104]

The concept of Amon-Re's surveying the world was particularly congenial to wisdom which was concerned with the art of observing. Further, the presentation of the judgement after death in *Meri-ka-Re* is in accord with the perfect grasp of Ma'at possessed by the observer god. The fact of death is not just the supreme warning about the limiting 'morrow'[105] but is the time of judgement, at this stage in Egyptian religion presided over by the sun-god (as 'Lord of Ma'at' according to extra-wisdom texts[106]) when the full nature of a person's place in, and attunement to, Ma'at is disclosed to him. McKane aptly summarizes:

> The judgement does not presuppose an order which has been inoperative in a this worldly context. Its function is to clear up finally the unresolved ambiguities of a man's relation to the order, and to reveal to him in a moment of truth the ultimate worth of his life measured against the demands of the order.[107]

As we shall see in the next chapter, the idea of divine observation is also central to Israelite wisdom, but there is no place for the idea of divine judgement after death anywhere in Israel's faith until the very late apocalyptic material (second century BCE) such as Daniel 12:2.

Some conclusions may now be drawn about the sense of limitation contained in this Egyptian material. First, the expression of limitation in both mainly pragmatic and mainly religious terms confirms the fact that, as in Israelite wisdom, limitation is a lack of full awareness of the nature of the order of things (Ma'at) rather than divine intervention. In Egypt however, the pragmatic and religious approaches can be fully integrated because of the underlying framework of Ma'at as an inevitable 'pressure' exerted upon a person's course, a binding force not present in early Israelite wisdom. Therefore no straight transfer can be assumed between the religious way of expressing limitation in Egypt and the sense of limitation in Israel. Because of the inherently religious nature of Ma'at, David Kelsey is surely incorrect to maintain that Egyptian wisdom, unlike Israelite, can appeal to Ma'at without reference to God.[108] But he argues correctly that the Israelite sense of order is an active 'ordering' that is social, teleological (working out some purpose or

---

[104] *Meri-ka-Re* 120–5 (ANET, p. 417).
[105] e.g. *Ani* 4:14ff (ANET, p. 420), *Onchsheshonqy* 12.5 (Glanville, *Instruction*, p. 31).
[106] As cit. Morenz, *Egyptian Religion*, p. 129.
[107] McKane, *Proverbs*, p. 72.
[108] Kelsey, *Eccentric Existence*, vol. 1, p. 239.

intention), and personal. It is not a static and impersonal structure of order that is universally normative, such as is found either in Egyptian Ma'at or in the later Hellenistic cosmic principle of Logos. Yahweh *does* justice and *acts* righteously according to his wisdom.[109] One might say that a general assumption about the 'order' of things lies behind the experimental method of wisdom, but the Israelite wise seem to have had no theology for it until the point when there was explicit reflection on the activity of Yahweh, and then the sentence literature in Proverbs evokes a personal relationship between human beings and a God who is ever-present in the world of daily affairs. The limitation of wisdom arises from the extent of its material, not from divine interruption, but God is at work immediately and intimately in the whole expanse of the world. 'Attunement' to divine wisdom, which is to be a central theme as our study proceeds, is not a matter of conformity to an inevitable pressure on life as with Ma'at, but a cooperation with a personal influence.

Returning to Arendt's diagnosis of the human predicament with which we began this chapter, in face of the elusiveness of the world she is suspicious of imposing any *telos* by a human agent, let alone a divine *telos*. Egyptian wisdom typifies all she rejects, envisaging an immanent and irresistible *telos* (in Ma'at). Israelite wisdom, however, opens up the possibility of thinking of a divine *telos* that works in ways that cannot be dogmatically defined.

AN ALTERNATIVE ROUTE OF WISDOM: THE DOGMA OF THE RIGHTEOUS AND THE WICKED

Our conclusion about the lack of an impersonal, inflexible order of things (Ma'at) in Israelite wisdom may appear to be undermined by what seems to be a dogma about the outcome of two classes of people, contrasting the 'righteous' (*ṣaddīq*, צדיק) person and the 'wicked' (*rāšā'*, רשע). For example:

> The memory of the righteous is a blessing,
> but the name of the wicked will rot. (10:7)

> When the tempest passes, the wicked are no more,
> But the righteous are established for ever. (10:25)

There is a preponderance of such sayings, mostly antithetical, in chapters 10–15 and so, without espousing any theory of separate collections, it is a sensible formal procedure to consider the 'righteous–wicked' material in chapters 10–15 in separation from that elsewhere in the sentence literature (16–22:16; 25–29). Those who argue that these antitheses belong to the earliest

---

[109] Kelsey, *Eccentric Existence*, vol. 1, pp. 171, 239–41.

stage of wisdom[110] urge a link between the concept of Ma'at in Egyptian wisdom, and that of 'righteousness' ($s^e d\bar{a}qah$, צדקה) in Hebrew: the wise man who 'does Ma'at' is—they suggest—easily translatable into the man who 'does $s^e d\bar{a}qah$'.[111] On the other hand, there are arguments in favour of a later date: there is a pervasive sense of dogma in the classification of people into two classes, righteous and wicked, that belongs uneasily in the atmosphere of experimental wisdom, and a thorough-going theory of retribution applied to two classes of people is not known in Egyptian wisdom, where it is rather individual actions that bring consequences in their train.

An attempt to reconcile these two conflicting points, and to save the righteous-wicked antitheses for early wisdom in Israel, has been made by H. Schmid,[112] who suggests that the sayings taken individually need not bear the sense of a class dogmatically determined, but could refer to specific acts. It is the later compiler who is responsible for understanding 'the righteous' as a *class* with guaranteed benefits, and has expressed this view both by grouping the separate sayings together, and by including other antitheses containing synonyms for 'righteous'and 'wicked'. Some support for the view that the sayings in themselves are early might be found in the fact that there are very few sayings which mention Yahweh together with the righteous and wicked. Of 37 righteous–wicked sayings in chapters 10–15 (35 actual antitheses), only three mention Yahweh (10:3, 15:9, 15:29). For example,

> The LORD [Yahweh] does not let the righteous go hungry,
> but he thwarts the craving of the wicked. (10:3)

Among sixteen antithetical sayings which use a synonym either for the righteous or the wicked, or for both, only two mention Yahweh (15:8, 15:26). One further saying contrasts the wicked with 'the fear of Yahweh' (10:27).

> The fear of the LORD [Yahweh] prolongs life,
> but the years of the wicked will be short.

Thus only three instances in total among these fifty-four sayings relate Yahweh to the 'righteous'. If the basic formula contrasting the righteous with the wicked had been created in the first place as part of the process of Yahwizing earlier wisdom, it is curious that the antitheses do not appeal more often to the sanction of Yahweh upon the righteous and wicked, as is so common elsewhere in Yahwism. On the other hand we must give full weight

---

[110] So Rankin, *Israel's Wisdom Literature*, pp. 69–75; Udo Skladny, *Die ältesten Spruchsammlungen in Israel* (Göttingen : Vandenhoeck & Ruprecht, 1962), pp. 7–9, 71–4; Barucq, *Proverbes*, p. 17; Schmid, *Wesen und Geschichte der Weisheit*, pp. 159–64.

[111] Schmid, *Wesen und Geschichte der Weisheit*, p. 169.

[112] Schmid, *Wesen und Geschichte der Weisheit*, pp. 159–72.

to the tone of religious dogmatism that most of the sayings display, without recourse to that specific sanction.

It is surely possible then that within the formal structure of the sayings there is content from different stages of Israelite wisdom. The actual form of the righteous-wicked antithesis could be original to the earliest wisdom (though infrequent), and later on, increasing numbers could have been built on these occasional examples in the direction of a Yahwistic dogmatism; finally a few sayings actually mentioning Yahweh could have been created. The term 'righteous' (*ṣaddîq*, צדיק) may carry a merely secular meaning when applied in a legal situation ('in the right' over against an opponent) and also in a wider social situation when applied to individuals and to factions who are applauded by the judgement of the community.[113] The same is true, conversely, of 'wicked' (*rāšā'*, רשע).

This reading of the situation is confirmed by the material about the righteous-wicked in the sentence literature outside chapters 10–15, where there is a similarly low proportion of such sayings that mention Yahweh. Out of a fairly wide semantic field of forty-seven sayings about the righteous and the wicked, or one or the other, or antitheses using a synonym for one term, only five mention Yahweh and only three of these conjoin Yahweh and the righteous (17:15, 18:10, 21:3).[114] Further, although there are far fewer actual righteous–wicked antitheses than in chapters 10–15—only eight, none mentioning Yahweh—it is much easier to detect among them sayings that seem older, five of them carrying a forensic or social connotation (especially in chapters 28–29). For example:

> When the righteous are in authority, the people rejoice;
> but when the wicked rule, the people groan. (29:2)
>
> The righteous know the rights of the poor;
> the wicked have no such understanding. (29:7)[115]

Since there are otherwise far more 'Yahweh sayings' in chapters 16 and following than in 10–15, we may conclude that in these two sections of sentence literature we have broad (not exclusive) emphases on two ways of Yahwizing older material: in 10–15 by dogmatizing righteous-wicked sayings, and in the remaining literature by constructing other Yahweh sayings alongside sayings that do not mention Yahweh.

The very distribution of the righteous-wicked sayings between chapters 10–15 and 16 onwards contributes to the conclusion that we have two lines

---

[113] Cf. Elizabeth Achtemeier, 'Righteousness in the Old Testament' in *Interpreter's Dictionary of the Bible*, 4 Volumes (Nashville: Abingdon, 1962), Vol. 4, p. 80, paras. 2–3; von Rad, 'Righteousness and Life in the Cultic Language of the Psalms', in *The Problem of the Hexateuch*, p. 249.

[114] The other two Yahweh sayings are 16:4 and 28:5.

[115] The other instances are Prov. 28:12, 28:28, 29:16.

of development in the process of Yahwizing older, 'secular' wisdom. This two-fold development in the face of a vast and complex world reflects a continual tension—between resorting to the conversion of flexible guidelines into dogma, and recognizing that there is need for an openness towards perplexing experience. While the development of a dogma of retribution about the righteous and the wicked would tend to lead to a fixity of mind, this would be continually challenged by the cultivation of sayings that stress the hidden-ness of things, and which associate this limitation with the presence and acts of Yahweh. Being aware of this challenge might also lead to treating the respective fates of the righteous and the wicked as a 'rule of thumb', or as a mere observation of what often happens, rather than an inevitable outcome. Even the contrast between the destinies of the righteous and the wicked does not, then, create an ethos similar to the stable and universal order of Ma'at. Reading the development of wisdom in this way means that Job appears less as a denial of traditional wisdom than as a recalling of wisdom to its ancient well-springs. It also makes possible the sense of a divine purpose (*telos*) that is not an inflexible and eternal law, but which is open to cooperation with the created world, and especially human beings.

CAUTIOUSNESS IN THE INSTRUCTION LITERATURE OF PROVERBS

In the instruction literature of Proverbs 1–9, we find further stages in the sense of limitation on wisdom which is associated with Yahweh. While some of the material, which I will label as 'A', expresses a similar kind of cautiousness and check on human confidence to that found in the sentence literature, other material—which I will label 'B'—takes a step into affirming that human limits can be overcome by being *taught* wisdom by Yahweh. In the 'B' instruction wisdom is now a gift of God, and there also appear the early traces of a conviction that true wisdom is the Torah (the revealed law of God). In both sets of material we find the theme of the 'fear of the Lord' which has already appeared in the sentence literature, but we shall find a change in its meaning from 'A' to 'B'.

The formal similarity of Proverbs 1–9, 22:17–24:22 and 31:1–9 to Egyptian instruction literature has now been adequately demonstrated by several scholars.[116] Whybray, however, points out that there are types of material present in Proverbs 1–9 which are strange to the Egyptian instruction genre. First, 'wisdom' is treated as a distinct object, mostly personified, or otherwise

---

[116] See Chapter 1, footnote 43.

depicted as a precious thing; in Egypt Ma'at appears as a feminine figure only in texts designed for religious rituals, not in the sapiential material. Second, this wisdom is portrayed as Yahweh's creation, possession and gift to human beings.[117] Whybray further makes the important discovery that all this new material belongs together: nearly all the material which identifies wisdom as the creation or gift of God is embedded in the material which presents wisdom as a personification or a precious object. Thus, 1:29 is embedded in 1:20–33; 2:5–8 in 2:1–15; 3:19–20 in 3:13–20; 8:22–31 in 8:1–36; 9:1–6 in 9:1–12[118] (1:7 is a special case, belonging to the preface). This is the material that I am designating 'B'. For Whybray, it represents additions to an original body of instruction, which is most of the remaining material in chapters 1–9, corresponding to my 'A'; this 'original' material, he argues, resembles Egyptian models in its form and content, and he concludes that the new material has been added to integrate the original (foreign-derived) instruction into mainstream Yahwism. McKane[119] sharply disagrees with this analysis, maintaining that the whole of Proverbs 1–9 bears the marks of Yahwistic re-interpretation, and so an original stratum cannot be quarried out.

My concern at this point is with the 'A' material, which does not portray wisdom as either a personification or a precious object. I shall be returning to the 'B' instruction, which does, in chapters 6 and 10. Whybray has usefully separated out types of material in Proverbs 1–9, although to recognize this does not necessarily imply following his suggestions about dating. While Whybray has probably under-estimated the amount of distinctively Yahwistic content in 'A', McKane does not recognize that that there are, nevertheless, differences in the way that the relationship of Yahweh to wisdom is described in 'A' and 'B'.

The interest of what I am calling 'A' instruction in Proverbs 1–9 is that it presents a sense of limitation upon wisdom which is thoroughly associated with reverence for Yahweh. There is a total lack of a sense of limitation expressed in purely secular terms, and here it differs both from Egyptian instruction and the sentence literature of Proverbs. It is unlikely, then, to be of an early date (*pace* Whybray) and it is hard to conceive of its being put together in its present form before the process visible in Proverbs 10 onwards was completed. However, my concern is not with establishing a date of origin, or even arguing that 'A' is earlier than 'B'. I simply want to show that there can be a body of instruction that is thoroughly Yahwistic and yet which still has a view of human limit arising from the scope of what is being observed. This 'A' instruction expresses a sense of human limit without any need to appeal to the idea that wisdom is a revealed gift of God. If it is of the same period as 'B'

---

[117] Whybray, *Wisdom in Proverbs*, pp. 72–6.
[118] Whybray, *Wisdom in Proverbs*, p. 73.
[119] McKane, *Proverbs*, pp. 279–81.

then we see that two religious views of wisdom can exist side by side, each complementing the other, neither to be absorbed into the other.

Thus, for example, in 3:5–10 the activity of Yahweh represents a limit on wisdom with which human beings must reckon:

> Trust in the LORD [Yahweh] with all your heart,
> and do not rely on your own insight.
> In all your ways acknowledge him,
> and he will make straight your paths.
> Be not wise in your own eyes;
> fear the LORD and turn away from evil.
> It will be a healing for your flesh
> and a refreshment for your body.
> Honour the LORD with your substance
> and with the first fruits of all your produce;
> then your barns will be filled with plenty,
> and your vats will be bursting with wine.

This is the view of Yahweh's activity contained in the 'Yahwistic limitation sayings' of chapters 16 onwards (compare 3:5–6 with 16:1–9) and, as there, parallels can be easily found in the Egyptian instruction: for example, 'steer not with thy tongue alone' (*Amen-em-Opet* xx.3). It does not say that Yahweh will *give* insight or instruction as to how to walk the paths of life. Whatever the degree of piety here, the wisdom technique of inherited instruction (3:1 'My child, do not forget my teaching') and experiment is not contradicted. But a wise man will not simply rely on his wisdom instruction: he must also trust in God to act for him in those areas where his wisdom fails, and trusting includes the doing of religious duties (3:9–10). This is essentially the view of *Meri-ka-Re*: 'Act for the god, that he may act similarly for thee.'[120]

The pious wise man trusts that Yahweh is acting for him, straightening his paths (compare the relationship between 16:25 and 16:9), giving health and filling his barns: none of these things can be absolutely guaranteed by his own insight (3:5) and so he must not neglect piety. Having made that concession to the unknown, however, the wise remain confident in the efficacy of their instruction (3:23; 4:11–12; 6:22).

The old injunction to a cautious humility, 'Be not wise in your own eyes' (3:7a), is firmly interpreted as 'fearing Yahweh' (3:7b), a making religious of secular caution that we have already seen in the 'fear of Yahweh' sayings in the sentence literature. This is underlined by the similar depiction of Yahweh as observer: he who sees all paths is best able to straighten them, being at work in those areas where human vision is deficient:

---

[120] *Meri-ka-Re*, text following 125 (ANET, p. 417).

> For human ways are under the eyes of the LORD,
> and he examines all their paths. (5:21, cf. 3:6)

Such a reading of the wisdom attitude in 3:5–10 would be difficult to maintain if 3:3 were to be taken as referring to covenant law, which would then, of course, be instruction from Yahweh (as several commentators in fact believe).[121]

> Do not let not loyalty and faithfulness forsake you:
> bind them around your neck,
> write them on the tablets of your heart.

While 3:1–2 and 3:4 clearly have wisdom instruction in view, it is argued (by, for example, McKane)[122] that v. 3 re-interprets this as instruction belonging to the covenant between God and Israel. But the phrase 'loyalty and faithfulness' (*ḥesed we'met*, חסד ואמת) is not necessarily covenantal; the terms appear as the solidarity of human friendship in 20:6 and as qualities the King requires from his subjects in 20:28. The clauses about attaching loyalty and faithfulness to the neck (as an amulet) and the heart, have several parallels in this instruction material, all referring to wisdom instruction, either scholastic or parental: 3:21–2 (neck), 4:4 (heart), 4:21 (heart), 6:21 (heart and neck), 7:3 (fingers and heart). The closeness of these phrases to Deuteronomy 6:8 and 11:18 has often been noted,[123] and Proverbs 6:20–2 seems especially close to Deuteronomy 6:6–8:[124]

> When you walk [your father's commandments] will lead you;
> when you lie down they will watch over you;
> when you awake they will talk with you. (Prov. 6:22)

> Keep these words I am commanding you today in your heart . . . Talk about
>   them . . .
> when you lie down and when you rise. (Deut. 6: 6–7)

If the influence is presumed to flow simply from Deuteronomy to Proverbs, then we might conclude that 3:3 does refer to the (Deuteronomic) covenant law: but the overwhelming occurrence of the phrases in contexts which betray no other references to covenant law makes it more likely that in this case the

---

[121] Barucq, *Proverbes*, p. 61, Helmer Ringgren and Walter Zimmerli, *Sprüche. Prediger. Das Alte Testament Deutsch* (Göttingen : Vandenhoeck & Ruprecht, 1962), p. 20; McKane, *Proverbs*, pp. 290–1.

[122] McKane, *Proverbs*, p. 291.

[123] See A. Robert, 'Les Attaches Litteraires Bibliques de Prov. i–ix', *Revue Biblique* 43 (1934), pp. 51, 67–8; J. Malfroy, 'Sagesse et Loi dans le Deuteronome', *Vetus Testamentum* 15 (1965), p. 58; Moshe Weinfeld, *Deuteronomy and the Deuteronomistic School* (Oxford: Clarendon Press, 1972), pp. 299–305.

[124] I accept that Prov. 6:22 is in place here; however, NEB and Scott, *Proverbs-Ecclesiastes* transfer 6:22 to follow 5:19.

influence is the other way round, as has been cogently argued by Moshe Weinfeld.[125]

I judge then, that the Yahwistic content of the instruction in 3:1–10 does not extend to the replacing of the 'teaching and commandments' (v. 1) of wisdom by covenant law. The criticism of the adequacy of 'insight' (v. 5) and 'wisdom' (v. 7) continues wisdom's inherent sense of caution. This understanding of Yahweh's acting for, or towards, people where they cannot fully see the situation, is precisely the point where wisdom's understanding of the activity of Yahweh has its own particular place within Yahwism. It has some similarity to the expectation that Yahweh will act in the cultic law-suit, but does not include the revelation which is provided in priestly instruction and prophetic word. It does not provide a way of discovering from Yahweh what the situation *is* in any case: that is to be discovered through the experiental method. It is a further step to receive 'instruction from Yahweh', a step which is taken in the material in Proverbs 1–9 that I have labelled B, which portrays the divine creation and gift of wisdom, and where 'fear of Yahweh' has now become equivalent to keeping the Torah (1:7, 1:29, 2:5, 9:10). I will be exploring this material in chapter 10.

It is therefore misguided to find a progression from earlier to later views of Yahweh's *activity*, in terms of a supposed movement from Yahweh's impersonal upholding of a world order to an acting out of his personal will.[126] It is not an understanding of Yahweh's relation to the world order that fundamentally changes, but the human technique for perceiving what the world is—moving from a cautious confidence in wisdom method (sentence literature) to reverence for Yahweh (sentence literature and instruction 'A'), then to seeking the gift of wisdom from Yahweh (instruction 'B'), and finally to identifying this gift with the instruction of the Torah (some instruction 'B').

In the 'A' material of Proverbs 1–9, the contrast between the rewards of the righteous and the wicked is a persistent theme. We have seen that the sense of the limitations of wisdom would encourage the testing of such a dogmatic guideline by fresh experience, and in this instruction material the same tension persists between dogma and uncertainty. However, the antithesis of the righteous/wicked threatens to become more rigid here (2:20–2; 3:32–3; 4:14–19; 5:22–3), appearing more forceful because of the extended, discursive nature of the instruction in contrast to the fragmentary units of the sentence literature. Proverbs 3:11–12, in the context of 3:1–10,

---

[125] Weinfeld, *Deuteronomy*, p. 301, against Robert, 'Les Attaches Litteraires'. The same direction of influenced may be proposed for the similarity of 3:3c and 7:3 to Jeremiah 31:33, since the phraseology (at least) of this oracle has been shaped by the Deuteronomic school: see Ernest W. Nicholson, *Preaching to the Exiles* (Oxford: Blackwell, 1970), pp. 82–5.

[126] So Whybray, *Wisdom in Proverbs*, pp. 92–5; Gese, *Lehre und Wirklichkeit*, pp. 37–40; Skladny, *Die ältesten Spruchsammlungen*, pp. 23, 41, 71–5.

offers an example of a tension which remains but which inclines towards the victory of the dogmatic:

> Honour the LORD with your substance
> and with the first fruits of all your produce;
> then your barns will be filled with plenty,
> and your vats will be bursting with wine. (vv. 9–10)

> My son, do not despise the LORD's discipline
> or be weary of his reproof,
> For the LORD reproves the one he loves,
> as a father the son in whom he delights. (vv. 11–12)

The fresh invocation 'My son' is probably an indication that 3:11–12 is an addition to 3:1–10,[127] offering an immediate comment on vv. 9–10 which promise that the one who trusts in Yahweh will have filled barns and overflowing wine vats. The prevailing dogmatism here may be being put under question by the word translated 'discipline' (*mūsār*, מוסר), since this could point to the occurrence of suffering as a *corrective* to the view confidently expressed that God will always work for the wise and pious man in the area of what is incalculable (a good harvest). As has been pointed out by Weinfeld,[128] the idea of the discipline of a father in Deuteronomy 8:5 derives from wisdom, rather than vice versa. However, this concept of the educational nature of suffering might itself easily become an inflexible explanation of suffering, reinforcing a general dogmatism.

Our conclusion that a limiting 'fear of Yahweh' existed at first without any idea of revelation is confirmed by the other main grouping of instruction in Proverbs, 22:17–24:22, which there is no reason to doubt is based upon the Egyptian *Amen-em-Opet*[129] (at least 22:17–23:11) and which also shows familiarity with instruction that appears in the Aramaic *Words of Ahikar* (in 23:12–24:22).[130] Nowhere in this collection of instruction literature is Yahweh said to *give* wisdom-teaching, though reverence for Yahweh is commended several times. Rather, in the preface the wisdom-teacher urges attention to his own teaching (22:17–18, 20–1) in terms close to the introduction to *Amen-em-Opet*, making one concession to piety (v. 19a), 'That your trust may be in Yahweh.' I cannot agree with McKane that this phrase indicates that 'the wisdom teacher is entirely occupied with Yahweh's business; he inculcates trust and supplies guidance like a priest'.[131] Rather, instruction comes from accumulated human wisdom, but the only proper attitude in which to receive

---

[127] So Ringgren, *Sprüche*, p. 19.

[128] Weinfeld, *Deuteronomy*, p. 303.

[129] Ringgren, *Sprüche*, pp. 90–2 conveniently discusses unsuccessful challenges to this view.

[130] So Scott, *Proverbs-Ecclesiastes*, pp. 136, 143; Berend Gemser, *Sprüche Salomos* (Tübingen: Mohr 1963), p. 85.

[131] McKane, *Proverbs*, p. 376.

it is remembering the 'fear of Yahweh', that is with caution, and trust in Yahweh's unknown activity (23:17, 'always continue in the fear of Yahweh'). This reading of the matter is underlined by the concluding saying of the group (24:21–22), which exactly captures the cautious note of wisdom at this stage. There are, admittedly linguistic and textual difficulties for translation, but we may essentially follow the Septuagint:[132]

> My son, fear Yahweh and the king
> and do not disobey either of them;
>
> For disaster comes from them suddenly
> and who knows the ruin that both can bring?

The reactions of God and the king cannot be absolutely predicted, so a cautious obedience is best; there is a close parallel to this dangerous opaqueness of both God and the king in the Aramaic *Words of Ahikar*.[133] Other references to Yahweh have this quality of warning:

> [the orphans'] redeemer is strong;
> he will plead their cause against you (23:11, cf. 22:23)

and there is the characteristic depiction of Yahweh as the perfect observer of all things:

> If you say, 'Look, we did not know this'—
> Does not he who weighs the heart perceive it?
> Does not he who keeps watch over your soul know it? (24:12, cf. 24:18)

This piece of instruction literature preserves more of the secular sense of caution than does Proverbs 1–9[134] and this, together with a concern for the training of pupils for official posts[135] that is missing in 1–9, might argue that this piece of instruction is relatively earlier than the other. However, it is similar to the 'A' material of Proverbs 1–9 in providing an example of the appeal to religious caution without tracing instruction to Yahweh as its revealer and giver.

There will, of course, be a place for revelation in the full development of wisdom thinking in Israel, placing the self-disclosure of wisdom alongside the experiential method. It is this whole vision of wisdom that will be most useful for creating a Christian wisdom for the present day. But we shall not be able to understand the purpose (*telos*) of Yahweh in the world unless we appreciate the difference between reverence for Yahweh in exercising a wisdom of

---

[132] So NRSV, reading against MT in 21b, but with Scott, *Proverbs-Ecclesiastes*, p. 146; Gemser, *Sprüche*, p. 88.

[133] Ahikar vii.104–9, ANET pp. 428–9.

[134] e.g. warning against over-hasty speech, Prov. 22:24.

[135] Prov. 23:24; 24:15–22.

observing the world on the one hand, and the self-gift of divine wisdom herself on the other; that is, the difference between the 'A' and 'B' approaches of Proverbs 1–9. Only by discerning the difference between them will we be able to appreciate the blend of both, the integration of observation with participation or – in the terms of our first chapter—*phronēsis* with *sophia*.

COPING WITH AN ELUSIVE WORLD

I began this chapter with reflections of a late-modern thinker on the loss of a balance between the self-disclosure and self-concealment of the earth-world. In face of an alienation between self and the world, the earth-world seems increasingly to conceal itself. For both the late-modern Arendt and the ancient wise, concealment is rooted in the complexity and inexhaustibility of the natural world. But an assertion of the subject's mastery of the world (criticized by Arendt) or an over-confident exercise of wisdom without humility (criticized by Israelite wisdom) will only intensify the elusiveness of the world to human exploration and make it seem an inhospitable place. Arendt's solution of political action is, I suggested, problematic in at least three ways: without a clear *telos* it can result in damage to the world; in celebrating objectivity it avoids any reflection on the self; and it shows a distrust of the 'indefatigable' rhythms of nature.

An instructive contrast on all counts may be drawn with another woman philosopher (also novelist), Iris Murdoch, writing at a similar period. Like Arendt, she celebrates the 'thinginess' of the world, and believes that giving attention to both art-objects and natural objects—such as the stones that litter her novels—will draw the subject out of its self-seclusion. In one of her novels an artist, Tim, confronts the 'great face' of a rock, and reflects: 'There was absolute truth *in the thing*, something of wholeness and goodness which called to him from outside the dark tangle of himself . . . That it should have been accidental [i.e. contingent] did not dismay him.'[136] In another novel, Dora is prone to getting trapped in self-absorption; as an antidote she looks at her favourite pictures in the National Gallery, and sees them as 'something real outside herself, which spoke to her kindly and yet in sovereign tones', destroying 'dreary, trance like solipsisms'.[137] Murdoch suggests that reflection upon art is a kind of religious experience, since it:

> perhaps provides for many people, in an unreligious age without prayer or sacraments, their clearest experience of something grasped as separate and

---

[136] Iris Murdoch, *Nuns and Soldiers* (London: Chatto & Windus, 1980), p. 272. My italics.
[137] Iris Murdoch, *The Bell* (Harmondsworth: Penguin, 1972), p. 190.

precious and beneficial and held quietly and unpossessively in the attention. Good art which we love can seem holy and attending to it can be like praying.[138]

This observation hints at a *telos* which is missing in Arendt. For Murdoch, through the sublimity of the many contingent objects of the world the self is orientated towards the transcendent Good, and we can break out of an artificial world we construct around ourselves. For Murdoch, the self is turned towards the Good and stripped of its self-centredness by paying attention to a multiplicity of objects that remain in their own integrity ('truth in the thing'). At the same time, Murdoch has learnt from Freud that the self is full of impulses of desire, and she believes that this energy of eros can sink towards a degraded state or be purified and point towards a higher eros of loving the Good for no reward.[139] Rather than ignoring the consciousness, as in Arendt, a re-orientation of its desires through paying attention to objects in the world can lead to a true ascesis, a flaying away of the self for the sake of the Good.

But we note that for Murdoch there is no question of a reciprocal response of the Good, which like Levinas' God is elusive, 'above being, non-personal, non-contingent, and not a particular thing among other things'.[140] She is adamant that the 'traditional' God, whom she understands to be an 'answering judging rewarding Intelligence and a comforting flow of love' does not exist.[141] As a Platonist, she thinks that we cannot encounter the Good in itself, or make direct relation with it, but intimations of the transcendent Good are 'scattered' in the world, and the beauty of objects is 'a clue' to this good, so that 'as we refine our conception of beauty we discover good'.[142] This perspective of a Good whose traces can be found in the many things of the world means, however, that no opposition is set up (as in Arendt) between natural objects belonging to the cycle of nature and objects that are products of human work—between (we may say) the rock face and the pictures in the National Gallery.

Murdoch's concern for transcendence plays no part in Arendt's approach to overcoming world-alienation.[143] By contrast, as ancient Hebrew wisdom litera-ture reflects on objects in the world there is a key place for transcendence, but— unlike Murdoch's Good—this is the 'otherness' of a personal creator who relates immanently to a reality that is not God's self. The self-concealment of the world

---

[138] Iris Murdoch, *The Fire and the Sun: Why Plato Banished the Artists* (Oxford: Clarendon Press, 1977), pp. 76–7.

[139] Murdoch, *Sovereignty of Good*, pp. 75, 102–3; *Metaphysics*, pp. 494–6.

[140] Murdoch, *Metaphysics*, p. 37.

[141] Murdoch, *Metaphysics*, p. 344.

[142] Murdoch, *Metaphysics*, pp. 343–4.

[143] I am passing no comment here on what might have been Arendt's religious beliefs. On Jewish religious influence on Arendt, who declared herself to be a non-religious thinker, see Jennifer Ring, *The Political Consequences of Thinking, Gender and Judaism in the Work of Hannah Arendt* (Albany: SUNY Press, 1997), esp. pp. 6–7, 276–8.

calls for a humility of approach; this is a 'fear of the Lord' within which there is a proper confidence about 'steering' one's way through life. The objection may be made that a religious humility towards the purpose (*telos*) of God only results in projecting a divine subjectivity, which in turn bolsters up a domineering human subjectivity over against the world. Whether this must be the case is a question we shall be pursuing in the next chapter, beginning from late-modern concepts of complexity in the world.

5

The Complexity of the World and the Extent of Wisdom

The plans of the mind belong to mortals, but the answer of the tongue is from Yahweh.

(Prov. 16:1)

For the wise who have given us the sentence and instruction literature of Proverbs, complexity arises both in the physical world and in the signs with which they attempt to represent it. As we have seen in the last chapter, they admit uncertainty both in their grasp of an inexhaustible world in which Yahweh acts with ease, and in the adequacy of human words that are meant to bring order to diffuse phenomena. In our late-modern age we are well aware of both kinds of complexity, which we increasingly perceive to be interwoven. Both science and semiotics, and physics and philosophy have their contribution to make to an awareness of a world which is complex and multiple in its self-presentation.[1]

Athough 'postmodern' critique of metanarratives is often pitched against science, a suspicion which Hannah Arendt shares in her account of *The Human Condition*,[2] scientists themselves have a certain humility about the grand story they can tell. First I intend to sketch the way that the modern scientific enterprise identifies the sources of complexity, as a matching piece to the proto-scientific approach of wisdom explored in the last chapter. If there are doubts whether a theologian should be venturing onto ground which is not

---

[1] Recent 'complexity theory', or the study of complex systems rooted in 'chaos theory' (see subsection a) and using computer simulations, may be applied to such areas as mathematics, strategy of organizations, art, ecology, and economics: see Kees van Kooten Niekerk and Hans Buhl, 'Comprehending Complexity' in Niekerk and Buhl, *The Significance of Complexity: Approaching a Complex World through Science, Theology and the Humanities* (Aldershot; Ashgate, 2004). My own approach is largely independent of 'complexity theory' as such, which has shown no interest in the tradition of wisdom.

[2] See the beginning of Chapter 4.

his own expertise, I can only respond that theology can hardly talk about 'the world' in our age without at least attempting to connect with the way that science sees the world, since this is such a shaping force in our culture. Then we shall look at complexity from another angle, that of the world as a network of signs to be read. Finally, we shall see what kind of talk about God might be appropriate in this double situation for a wisdom theology today.

THE COMPLEXITY OF THE WORLD IN MODERN SCIENCE

The modern scientific view of a complex world belongs in the period I am calling 'late modernity', which is a blend of the modern and 'postmodern'. Elements of postmodernity may be traced in complexity theories: there is an interest in a diversity of local rules which are only loosely connected with 'universal' laws of physics,[3] and the world is conceived as a cluster of fluid networks, opening up differences, and open to many avenues of development.[4] Modernity persists in a certain confidence in the self's ability to investigate and classify this complex world, yet the recognition of complexity also creates an awareness of limits on human knowledge, and this prompts a certain caution and even humility.

(a) *Complexity arising from initial, elusive conditions*

The first kind of complexity identified by the modern scientific enterprise is a complexity in a physical event which is due to initial factors which either cannot be fully observed, or which cannot be accurately measured. Right at the beginning of the event there are a number of things happening which escape our attention. At the macroscopic level an obvious example is the *chaotic system*, a non-linear dynamic state which is more popularly dubbed 'the butterfly effect'.[5] Chaotic systems are peculiarly sensitive to their initial conditions, and highly irregular effects can be produced from quite specific causes. Weather systems are the most obvious example of chaos, and the instance is often given of a butterfly flapping its wings in Tokyo and the result being a hurricane in Florida a month later. Such chaotic behaviour looks completely

---

[3] See Paul Colliers, *Complexity and Postmodernism: Understanding Complex Systems* (London: Routledge, 1998).

[4] See the avowedly postmodern theologian Mark Taylor, *The Moment of Complexity: Emerging Network Culture* (Chicago: Chicago University Press, 2001), p. 72.

[5] Ian Stewart, *Nature's Numbers: Discovering Order and Pattern in the Universe* (London: Wedenfeld and Nicholson, 1995), pp. 112–13, 124–5. Stuart Kauffman describes complexity as the behaviour of networks 'at the edge of chaos': Kauffman, *At Home in the Universe. The Search for Laws of Complexity* (Harmondsworth: Penguin, 1995), p. 87.

random, but it is only apparently without any pattern at all. We just cannot see how the flapping of the wings causes some small change which gradually impacts on the whole building of the system.

The consequences of initial factors such as the flapping of a butterfly appear to be haphazard, but in fact they happen within a limited range of possibilities which can be mapped onto a graph. The set of curves which represent future options of the system converge to a certain portfolio of possibility, which is called a 'strange attractor'.[6] The swirling curves of the graph filling the 'phase space' of the system present a 'portrait' in which a limited range of contingencies is being explored. Though the future behaviour of a chaotic system such as the weather is unknowable in detail, certain things can be reliably said about it in general (which is why weather forecasters still have jobs). It might then be called 'deterministic chaos'. The complexity is hard to grasp, both because the system reacts to the slightest disturbance at the initial stage, and also because any errors in measurement at this early point are amplified. To take a simpler chaotic system, the dripping of a tap, the measurement of the first drop to an error of ten decimal places will grow by one place every further drop (this experiment has actually been done, and reputations have been made by it).[7]

At the microscopic level of sub-atomic particles, we enter a shadowy and unreliable world. In the strange world of the quantum, we can find no cause for the decay of the nucleus of a radioactive atom (say, uranium) at any particular moment. There appears to be no difference at all between a radioactive atom that is just about to decay and one that is not. We can calculate a probability for such a decay taking place within a specified period of time, but we cannot say for certain when it will happen, or which half of a collection of radioactive atoms with a half-life will *give up* their life. Conventional quantum theory regards this as a real indeterminacy, not just ignorance: most quantum researchers think that there is just no cause for individual events in the quantum world. This would take us to a second kind of complexity, to be considered shortly below. But for the moment, we should consider the possibility that there *are* causes, but they are hidden from us. This theory has been propounded by David Bohm, though it has not won wide acceptance.[8] In this case the decay of a nucleus would be like deterministic chaos: there would be hidden variables in the initial conditions. I prefer to follow the majority scientific view that there is real indeterminacy here, but it seems likely that there are at least *some* causes present that we cannot now discern.

---

[6] Stewart, *Nature's Numbers*, pp. 117–18; James Gleick, *Chaos* (London: Minerva 1966), pp. 133–44.

[7] Stewart, *Nature's Numbers*, pp. 110–11.

[8] David Bohm and D. J. Riley, *The Undivided Universe* (London: Routledge, 1993), pp. 35–8.

In human biology there are also elusive initial conditions which give rise to enormous complexity. In the relation *between* cells, chaos theory has been appealed to for the understanding of both destructive and creative events. On the negative side, heart fibrillation and epileptic fits, which appear random, can be seen as the reaction of sensitive systems—whether the body's mechanical pump or its electrical circuits—to tiny initial disturbances.[9] On the positive side, psychologists have speculated that the intellectual and artistic creativity of the mind may be due to an underlying chaotic process: very small fluctuations in the firing of synapses in the brain may be amplified until they become large-scale mental states experienced as new ideas.

On the level of the *inner* life of a cell, the cell-division and combination which is necessary for the growth of complex life may be due to another kind of dynamic system than chaos, but one also sensitive to initial conditions. This is the kind of open system which is 'far from equilibrium':[10] push it far enough to a crisis point, and small triggers will generate large-scale patterns. Structures are formed which begin to swim against the dissipative tide of increasing entropy, and order is produced instead of disorder.[11] Self-organization begins to emerge: in a universe which is constantly running down to a low level of energy according to the second law of thermodynamics, life actually *evolves*. These systems can be observed in the macroscopic world, but living beings certainly exist in 'far from equilibrium' states: to take just one small example, the flow of potassium and sodium ions across the membrane of a nerve cell happens in sudden pulses or 'glugs' rather than a regular flow. One can see how the incredible complexity of life could emerge from such self-organizing chemical systems.[12]

(b) *Complexity arising from uncertainty*

The first type of complexity thus arises from the reaction of non-linear systems to initial conditions. We find events to be unpredictable and surprising because certain formative factors are hidden from us, or we find it difficult to measure them. A second kind of complexity arises from actual uncertainty, or indeterminacy. If the first can be dubbed the butterfly effect, this is the dice effect, as in Einstein's comment when facing early quantum physics: 'God does not throw dice.'[13] Today scientists disagree, at least on the issue of throwing

---

[9] Gleick, *Chaos*, pp. 4, 109, 280–4.

[10] John Polkinghorne, *Science and Creation: The Search for Understanding* (London: SPCK, 1989), pp. 44–6.

[11] Ilya Prigogine and Isabelle Stengers, *Order out of Chaos: Man's New Dialogue with Nature* (London: Heinemann, 1984), Chapter 5.

[12] See Stephen Wolfram's studies of cellular automata in Wolfram, *A New Kind of Science* (Champaign: Wolfram Research, 2002), *passim*.

[13] Letter to Max Born (4 December 1926), in *The Born-Einstein Letters*, ed. & trans. Irene Born (New York: Walker and Company, 1971).

dice. At the microscopic level of sub-atomic particles, in the 'quantum' world, most researchers accept—despite Einstein—that there is a real indeterminism. It is not just that we cannot see all the causes. To take another instance from this fitful and strange world, Werner Heisenberg showed famously that an electron could have position (we can know where it is) or momentum (we can know what it is doing), but not both at once.[14] As Paul Davies puts it, 'Atomic uncertainty is truly intrinsic to nature: the rules of clockwork might apply to familiar objects such as snooker balls, but when it comes to atoms, the rules are those of roulette.'[15] Niels Bohr, the philosopher of the quantum world, did entertain the thought in passing that there might actually be no quantum world at all, but 'only abstract quantum physical description'.[16] However, if we think that the models of science indicate some kind of realism, however critically we must regard it, then we are plunged into a world in which the motion of an electron has a wave function which has the potential either for position or momentum, but not both simultaneously. It is a world in which possibilities are no less real than actualities. And this also indicates an indeterminism at the heart of reality.

Hannah Arendt thinks that the uncertainty disclosed by Heisenberg should have some effect in shaking human confidence that we occupy an Archimedean point, alienated from the earth, from which to survey and master nature.[17] However, there is a question whether the principle of uncertainty generated at the quantum level can be extended into the large-scale world, or macro-world. Does it really make any difference in the world of solid and full-size objects in which we experience living? It might be urged that so-called chaos only confirms that the world as we know it runs by deterministic laws. Events at the quantum level, within systems that are sufficiently large scale, seem to lose nearly all of their indeterminacy and appear to behave as Newton would expect them to. This effect, called *decoherence* seems to reinstate classical mechanics for most human purposes. As Ian Stewart puts it, the performance of horses in a race is not unpredictable because of quantum mechanics but because of hidden variables, such as what kind of hay they had for breakfast.[18] We seem to have returned to deterministic chaos.

Some thinkers have suggested, by contrast, that chaotic systems might be actually indeterminate after all, because quantum uncertainty may be magnified in some mysterious way at the macro-level. A macro-scopic openness might be quantum openness, amplified by chaos. One of the initial conditions

---

[14] Werner Heisenberg, *Philosophic Problems of Nuclear Science* (New York: Pantheon, 1952), p. 73.

[15] Paul Davies, *God and the New Physics* (London: Dent, 1983), p. 102.

[16] Bohr in private conversation, as cited in John Polkinghorne, *The Quantum World* (London: Longman, 1984), p. 79.

[17] Arendt, *Between Past and Future*, pp. 276–9.

[18] Stewart, *Nature's Numbers*, p. 110.

of a chaotic system might actually be an indeterminate detail of the quantum world, and the whole system might be vulnerable to this vanishingly small disturbance. So there might be uncertainty at the heart of chaos after all.[19] However, we really have little idea about the way that the micro- and macro-worlds lock together. The very difficulty of measuring quanta shows us this, since the measuring instruments belong to the macro-world, as do the human beings who measure. Here, at the interface, there seems to be a great deal of mystery.

This does not mean, however, that there is no element of indeterminacy at all in a chaotic system. We might instead look to the aspect of the random *within limits*, that is within the field of the 'strange attractor'. While there is a limited range of possible trajectories along which the system might develop, there is still an intrinsic unpredictability which leaves the system open to being 'nudged along' by external influences.[20] The system reacts not only to initial conditions, but to disturbances met along the way; it may also be responding to the influence of the whole community of the world on its parts—a kind of 'top-down' causality described first by Arthur Peacocke and then adopted by John Polkinghorne,[21] and to which I want to return. This would be a real novelty in the state of the system, not contained in the initial conditions, as it would not simply be the collection of 'bottom-up' details. The fact that the indeterminate (on this account) would be within limits or boundaries of possibilities would not make it less open. Moreover, this limited openness might combine with the openness of other systems to amplify a real freedom within nature.

The operation of chance within limits certainly seems to be characteristic of the emerging of complexity on the biological level. Evolution requires a combination of chance and necessity. According to the Neo-Darwinian account of evolution, which combines Mendel with Darwin—genetics with natural selection—random mutations in the genes are perpetuated through the mechanisms of preservation and selection. Chance differences of development, in very small incremental steps, build into amazingly complex life through aiming at survival in a stable environment of lawful necessity. This is what Richard Dawkins calls 'tamed chance' rather than 'pure naked chance'.[22] For him, this is witness to nature as a 'Blind Watchmaker', making a purposeful creator redundant. There is no reason, to think, however, that

---

[19] See John Polkinghorne, tentatively, in *Belief in God in an Age of Science* (Yale: Yale Univesity Press, 1998), p. 63; Joseph Ford, 'What is Chaos that We Should Be Mindful of it?' in Paul Davies (ed.), *The New Physics* (Cambridge: Cambridge University Press, 1989), pp. 348–72.

[20] Polkinghorne, *Belief in God*, pp. 61–2.

[21] Arthur Peacocke, *Creation and the World of Science* (Oxford: Clarendon Press, 1979), pp.134–43; Polkinghorne, *Belief in God*, pp. 56–9.

[22] Richard Dawkins, *The Blind Watchmaker* (London: Longman, 1986), pp. 43–51.

this interaction of chance and necessity is the whole story. John Polkinghorne writes, 'I think that a number of physical scientists feel uneasiness about whether the Neo-Darwinian accumulation of small improvements is the whole story of how such intricacy came to be in the time available.' He adds that 'there may be more to the story than the Neo-Darwinists tell us. If so, it is the task of science to seek out what that extra might be.'[23]

(c) *Complexity arising from interaction*

Beginning to explore what Polkinghorne calls the 'extra' brings us to a third kind of complexity recognized in modern science: a complexity *arising from interaction*. I might say 'social interaction', as long as this is understood in the widest sense of relations within the whole community of the natural world, not just among human beings. But human life does offer us a startling example of complexity, in the relation between the brain and the mind, physical and mental life. While we can trace this back, to some extent, to emergence at the genetic level from cell divisions, it also seems to be due to interactions with other brains.

One aspect of this complexity is the development of altruism or self-giving within the personality. The giving of ourselves to others, our self-sacrifice for others, is a highly complex activity. While we think of this as being character-istically human, we can in fact see comparable behaviour throughout living creatures. The 'honey pot' worker ants, for example, do nothing but hang from the ceiling of the colony, acting a receptacles or storage jars for honey which the colony draws on when needed. This seems to be a self-sacrificing act indeed! It can partly be explained by evolutionary theory: genes favouring altruism ensure the survival of the gene pool in the social group, and so they will make sure that they get reproduced down the generations. However, some biologists[24] insist that complex organisms are not simply the sum of their genes, and urge that we ought not to limit the discussion to a 'bottom up approach' from the physical basis of life and behaviour. This is where inter-action with others becomes significant. There is a kind of 'top-down' causation in which the community itself—whether ants or humans—will nurture the development of altruistic behaviour.[25] This is especially the case where the community as a whole values self-giving. So what we think and do in commu-nity can actually shape or 'sculpt' the physical structure of the brain, the neural substrate, as the whole affects the parts.

---

[23] John Polkinghorne, *One World: The Interaction of Science and Theology* (London: SPCK, 1986), p. 53.

[24] Malcolm Jeeves, 'The Nature of Persons and the Emergence of Kenotic Behaviour' in John Polkinghorne (ed.), The *Work of Love. Creation and Kenosis* (Grand Rapids: Eerdmans, 2001), pp. 75–86; Stephen J. Gould, 'Message from a Mouse', *The New York Times*, 13 September 1999, p. 64.

[25] Jeeves, 'The Nature of Persons', p. 86.

The complexity of brain and personality may then come at least partly from relations with others in society. I have already referred to a similar top-down causation that Polkinghorne and Peacocke think is operative in complex systems in the macro-world, and especially in dissipative and chaotic systems. Complexity may be caused not only by exponential growth from the bits and pieces of original conditions, but by holistic influences which help to form patterns. Some of these holistic agencies will be energetic (making a physical impact on a system), and others will be purely informational, bringing about the formation of a structured pattern of future dynamical behaviour. For the informational kind, Polkinghorne finds an analogy in the 'pilot wave' of Bohm's version of quantum theory; this encodes information about the whole environment, and influences the motion of a quantum entity, bringing about an 'enfolding' of the whole into every part.[26] Now, if these holistic agencies are to bring something really new into the situation, then there must be room for them to manoevre, real opportunities in the structure of inter-actions between the bits and pieces from below, and so an actual indetermin-ism. There must be a space for top-down causality to fit into. Complexity type three, we may say, thus builds on type two.

Another major example of this third kind of complexity at quantum level is the very relation between the human observer and the quanta being observed. I have already mentioned that this is a mysterious interface. How do we actually get a determinate result from measuring the indeterminate? How does this come to be objectified in the dependable everyday world? It seems that in some way the act of measuring, and so the intervention of conscious-ness, contributes to the nature of the particle which before this exists in a potential state. This, then, brings us to a fourth kind of complexity.

(d) *Complexity that belongs to possibilities*

In a book significantly called *The End of Certainty*, Ilya Prigogine sums up the revolution that has taken place in thought about the basic nature of the world, when he comments that 'we have come to a new formulation of the laws of nature, one that is no longer built on certitudes, as is the case for deterministic laws, but rather on possibilities'.[27] This in turn means that the flow of time is taken seriously as a range of possibilities are actualized unpredictably in irreversible processes. The arrow of time is not an illusion, as Einstein tended to think; not only systems but the future is open, continually under construc-tion. Classical science emphasized order and stability, a certainty that belonged to laws that could exactly predict future events, and to equations

---

[26] David Bohm, *Wholeness and the Implicate Order* (London: Routledge and Kegan Paul, 1980), p. 177; see Polkinghorne, *One World*, p. 84; *Science and Creation*, p. 83.

[27] Ilya Prigogine, *The End of Certainty: Time, Chaos and the New Laws of Nature* (New York: The Free Press, 1997), p. 29.

that were time-reversible. So-called scientific laws now sketch out a range of possibilities, all of which are valid and which issue in different kinds of reality.

We have already seen possibility at the heart of the chaotic system, with the portrait of the strange attractor. At the quantum level, particles have the potential to act either as waves or particles. Even more strangely, it seems that before they are measured by instruments and a human consciousness, electrons have a ghostly existence known as a 'superposition of states'. They have a property of spin, rotating like a ball either in one direction or another; but before being actually measured for spin, it appears that an electron has a ghostly dual existence in which it is spinning in both directions at the same time. The point here is that possibilities are not unreal until they become actualities, and so are to be subordinated to what is actual. They have a reality of their own. Such a perception may even be applied to the initial state of the universe. Perhaps, before the Big Bang, there was a fluctuating vacuum in a quantum field containing many possible states of matter or potentials of particles.[28] While there would be no permanent particles present, particles might transiently appear and disappear. One fluctuation like this might have been the very dense singularity from which the whole universe expanded.

In the realm of human biology there is an interesting similar emphasis on open possibilities. It is not just a fertilized egg or zygote that is a potential human being. It is not even just the gametic material of the egg or the sperm on its own which has this potential. Cloning through substitution of the nucleus has demonstrated that any cell in the human body has the potential to become a new person. Since the birth of 'Dolly the sheep' from a cloning process it has become clear that any cell containing a nucleus with forty-six chromosones is potentially a germ line cell, and so capable of becoming a person.

Here then is a typology of complexity in the thought of modern science: complexity arising from elusive initial states, from indeterminacy, from inter-action, and from open possibilities. The four types do, of course, overlap with each other as I have shown, and together they create a sense of limitation about human knowledge. The wisdom writers of Ancient Israel knew, in their own way, about the limits that a complex world imposes, and it was in this context that talk about God got going. They affirmed that God was unlike human observers in seeing everything: nothing is hidden from the divine gaze, as a psalm (possibly influenced by wisdom thinking)[29] confesses: 'you saw me when my unformed limbs were being made in the womb' (Psalm 139:16). But is the modern sense of complexity and uncertainty a similarly fruitful context for thinking about God as creator and sustainer of the universe? Is it a

---

[28] Prigogine, *The End of Certainty*, 175–82.

[29] Otto Eissfeldt, *The Old Testament: An Introduction*, trans. P. R. Ackroyd (Oxford: Blackwell, 1966), p. 15, classifies it as a wisdom poem.

situation in which we can talk about the purpose (*telos*) of God, as the Hebrew wise did? The point is not, of course, to try and *prove* God out of complexity, but to talk about God in this context. I believe that we can, but only if we have a concept of God as *complex* being, rather than the *simple* divine being Christians have often conceived, stressing belief in one God. A complex God is the most appropriate creator of a complex world.[30] This means that Christian wisdom in the present day will be about attunement to a creator who is certainly one God, but essentially *triune*. As Karl Rahner has stressed, Trinity can be no mere afterthought to monotheism, as if it is simply an optional variation on the theme.[31]

THE COMPLEXITY OF SIGNS IN THE WORLD

The appropriateness of talking about God as Trinity will also become clear—in due course—if we think about complexity from the perspective of language. Thinkers such as Jacques Derrida point out that the whole world around us can be envisaged as a system of signs—or signifiers—which we 'read' in order to make sense of our place in the world and through which we relate to others. 'Text' does not have to be written down on paper, or appear on the screens of computers and mobile phones, but consists of all material forms which we refer to, and which in turn point beyond themselves to something or someone else. Derrida, whom I take as the key example of this approach, explains:

> the concept of text I propose is limited neither to the graphic, nor to the book, nor even to discourse, and even less to the semantic, representational, symbolic, ideal or ideological sphere. What I call 'text' implies all the structures called 'real,' 'economic', 'historical', 'socio-institutional', in short: all possible referents. Another way of recalling once again that 'there is nothing outside the text'.[32]

We only have to think of the notion of 'body language' to see the truth of this: we communicate not just through words but through gestures, physical reactions, and the way we dress. We cannot, then, escape from being involved in textuality. In former ideas about language and signs, it has been assumed that there were subjects with consciousness—especially human beings, and very especially God—who existed behind or beyond the signs and who imposed their presence on others by merely *using* signs. The signs in the world, and words in particular, were simply tools that could be employed to control the

---

[30] Similarly, Niels Henrik Gregson, 'Complexity: What is at Stake for Religious Reflection?' in Niekerk and Buhl, *Significance of Complexity*, pp. 159–63, but without exactly relating complexity to Trinity.

[31] Karl Rahner, *The Trinity*, trans. J. Donceel (London: Burns & Oates, 1975), pp. 15–24.

[32] Derrida, 'Afterword', p. 148.

world. In this way, the individual mind could use words to dominate and impose its will on others. We now see, however, that the relation between the individual self and signs is more complicated than this. Language is there ahead of all individuals who live in the world, and helps to shape them and the way that they live in community. We are born into a world whose signs are already there before us.

Derrida in particular is waging a war against an attractive but misleading appeal to *simplicity* in the subject's observation and talk of the world. The fact that the meaning of any sign is constituted by a play of differences[33] between this sign and all others 'supposes, in effect, syntheses and referrals which forbid at any moment, or in any sense, that *a simple element be present* in and of itself, referring only to itself'.[34] This 'radically destroys any possibility of the *simple self-identity*' of a present thing, person, or moment.[35] If 'difference' itself is conceived as the source of the interplay of differences, then it is 'the nonfull, *nonsimple origin*'.[36] This undermining of simplicity relates both to the objects of perception and the perceiving subject.

In the first place, nothing can be 'simply' and immediately present to the consciousness (as Husserl, for instance, supposed). There is never a simple 'signified' which avoids the 'detour of signs':[37] when something or someone is present to us there is always an intermediate sign. Moreover, since this sign draws its meaning from its difference from other signs, it always carries 'a trace within it of the other elements of the chain or system' of signifieds.[38] A book, we might say, gives out its particular message to those who see it because it is *not* a newspaper or a CD ROM or a portable e-book reader. Each sign contains the trace of another, of what is *not* present. Difference or 'otherness' must be respected, whether in words or in people: it cannot be simply reduced in a desire to force our presence on others and to be the master of all we survey. Complexity is thus increased by the element of absence within the sign—the trace of what is not present—as well as by its position in time, since it does not exist in an eternal present tense but contains the traces of the past and the future where it is *not*. It is even less 'simple' since, in carrying the trace of another, it is not just something signified (or referred to) but is also a signifier in its turn, pointing to something other: 'every concept [signified] is necessarily and essentially inscribed in a chain or system, within which it refers to another . . . by the systematic play of differences'.[39] There can be no 'transcendent signified' which could be a presence 'outside and before the

---

[33] See Chapter 2, the section called 'The Self and the World in Postmodernity', sub-section c.
[34] Derrida, *Positions*, p. 26. My italics.
[35] Derrida, *Speech and Phenomena*, pp. 65–6. My italics.
[36] Derrida, 'Differance', in *Speech and Phenomena*, p. 141. My italics.
[37] Derrida, 'Differance', in *Speech and Phenomena*, p. 138.
[38] Derrida, *Positions*, p. 26.
[39] Derrida, 'Differance', in *Speech and Phenomena*, p. 140.

process of signification'.[40] Rather than a rigorous distinction between signifier and signified, there is an endless chain of each becoming the other, a process in which the full presence of the signified is always being put off, or deferred. 'Difference' is a movement, a 'play of differences, of the traces of differences'.[41] There is a semiotic form here of what science has identified as 'open possibilities'.

If an object is not 'simply' present to the subject or consciousness, equally— according to Derrida—the subject is not 'simply' present to itself. In the thinking of the Enlightenment, the subject is 'self-identical' in the sense that 'as the face of pure intelligibility, it refers to an absolute logos to which it is immediately united'. This logos is both the human word or reason and 'the face of God'.[42] In this inherited way of thinking, the subject, with the stability and permanence of the logos, is both present to the self and identical with the self as something 'signified' internally:

> consciousness in all its modifications is conceivable only as self-presence, a self-perception of presence. And what holds for consciousness also holds here for what is called subjective existence in general. Just as the category of subject is not and never has been conceivable without reference to presence as *hypokeimenon* [substratum] or *ousia* [substance], etc., so the subject as consciousness has never been able to be evinced otherwise than as self-presence.[43]

At the same time, this 'presence' is conceived as existing in 'the living present'—in a simple unity of the self and time. As I have already insisted, this critique of a concept of the self-identical subject does not mean that Derrida has abolished the subject altogether.[44] Like Levinas, he is being critical of a view of the simplicity of the subject as 'selfsame in the presence of self-relationship'.[45] By contrast, in Derrida's view, 'there is no subject who is agent, author, and master of *différance*'.[46] For the subject is a kind of event or happening within the field of *différance*, and to understand this we have to return to Derrida's wide view of text which 'implies all the structures called "real"'.

Presence, whether of the subject or object, is the result of the movement of *différance*—of continual relation to the other who/which is absent and of the interplay between signs. This movement can also be called 'writing', which refers both to the actual inscribing of a sign on some medium (paper, canvas, stone, glass) and to the play of *différance* which is to be found in inscribed

---

[40] Derrida, *Positions*, p. 31.   [41] Derrida, *Positions*, p. 27.
[42] Derrida, *Of Grammatology*, p. 13.
[43] Derrida, *Speech and Phenomena*, p. 147.
[44] See Chapter 3, the section called 'The Quest for the Self'.
[45] Derrida, *Of Grammatology*, pp. 68–9.
[46] Derrida, *Positions*, p. 29.

signs and which makes all inscription possible in the first place.[47] If writing conditions the 'whole field of linguistic signs' (graphic or spoken), then it makes sense to use the word 'text' to describe any 'fabric of signs' which constitutes presence.[48] The term 'sign' is inclusive of anything to which we might refer and which in turn signifies something else. Not just literal books and manuscripts, but the whole world is a network of signs, or a weaving together of texts which can be read and interpreted. Seeking to make clear his statement that 'there is nothing outside the text', which has been taken up with unbalanced enthusiasm by some of his followers, Derrida explains:

> That does not mean that all referents are suspended, denied, or enclosed in a book, as people have claimed, or been naive enough to believe and to have accused me of believing. But it does mean that every referent, all reality has the structure of a differential trace, and that one cannot refer to this 'real' except in an interpretive experience.[49]

Earlier he has already tried to explain his much traduced phrase (*il n'ya pas de hors-texte*), which 'for some has become a kind of slogan, in general so badly understood, of deconstruction': it means 'nothing else' than that 'there is nothing outside context'.[50] Every text is situated alongside or within another text, so that it has a 'context' (a 'with-text'). Particular groupings of signs form a text, but this is always related to other texts in the movement of *différance*. This is the complexity of the world from a semiotic standpoint: 'the finiteness of a context is never secured *or simple*, there is an indefinite opening of every context, an essential nontotalization.'[51] Contexts are 'constantly being re-framed' and there is 'an incessant movement of recontextualization'.[52]

The boundaries of texts are always open. Written texts such as books, letters, and emails can help to open us up to a sense of difference and otherness. The words within a book take their meaning from the whole network of words in which they are placed, and this differential meaning can never be fixed and completed; since words contain traces of each other, and since there is an endless process of interaction between them, new meaning is always being created, and there is always a surplus or excess.[53] Yet there is a further layer of complexity because these texts are open to other texts, including 'social institutions' and other structures in the world.[54] There can be no exact correspondence between one system of signs and another, as if one can be a mirror-image of another—as if, for example, a written text can represent the world in any *exact* way. Yet there is an interleaving of one text with another; otherwise the written or electronic text becomes a mere fantasy of what we desire. Despite

---

[47] Derrida, Of Grammatology 44.   [48] Derrida, *Of Grammatology* 14.
[49] Derrida, 'Afterword', p. 148.   [50] Derrida, 'Afterword', p. 136.
[51] Derrida, 'Afterword', p. 137.   [52] Derrida, 'Afterword', p. 195–6.
[53] Derrida, *Positions*, p. 26; Derrida, *Of Grammatology*, p. 62.
[54] Derrida, 'Afterword', p. 136.

some of his followers, Derrida does not usually deny representation altogether:[55] representations, Derrida maintains, are 'sendings' (*envois*) which
never reach their final destination, or never reunite with the object they
represent.[56] Because of their wandering or 'erring' (*desinerrance*) they can
never be replaced by the 'pure' or simple presence of what they re-present.
However, as Martin Jay justly comments, 'Neither can their difference from the
"things" they represent be completely effaced in the name of a realm of pure
simulacra entirely without a trace of reference (as theorists like Baudrillard
were to argue).'[57]

It is in this situation of inter-textuality that we can, Derrida thinks, understand the activity of the subject. The subject is indeed the 'product' of *différance*
in society and language, rather than being a stable 'substance' or 'substratum'.
The subject is 'the finite experience of non-identity to self...inasmuch as it
comes from the other, from the trace of the other'.[58] Nevertheless the 'who' of a
subject is a 'singularity', although it is 'not the individuality of a thing that
would be identical to itself'.[59] Earlier in my discussion of late-modernity,
I maintained that the identity of the self in Derrida and some other postmodern thinkers derives from its relation to the other.[60] Now we can place
this alterity in the 'context' of a complex world. Daniel Miller has rightly
suggested that 'the subject becomes something like an event', and that 'the
movement of *différance* opens every (con)text beyond itself, creating the
"space" for movement on the part of the subjects inscribed within it'.[61]
Because of the open boundaries of texts to each other, the subject is unstable,
not possessing the 'solid substance' of an older metaphysics of presence, and
yet this very instability is the ground for the agency and moral responsibility
of the 'singular' self.

The endless openness of contextuality is what Derrida calls 'undecidability',
as distinct from a 'calculability' that would belong to a static, substantial self.
But this very undecidability provides an open field for ethical-political decision-making, whereas a subject fully present to itself would reduce everything

---

[55] Derrida does refer to 'a reference without a referent' in Jacques Derrida, 'The Double
Session' in *Dissemination*, trans. B. Johnson (Chicago: University of Chicago, 1981), p. 206, but
this discussion of Mallarmé is not necessarily to be generalized.

[56] Derrida, 'Sending: On Representation', *Social Research* 49 (1982), p. 322.

[57] Jay, *Downcast Eyes*, p. 508.

[58] Jacques Derrida, '"Eating Well", or the Calculation of the Subject', trans. P. Connor and
A. Ronell in Elisabeth Weber (ed.), *Points...Interviews 1974–1994* (Stanford: Stanford University Press, 1982), p. 266.

[59] Derrida, 'Eating Well', p. 261.

[60] See Chapter 3, the section called 'The Quest for the Self'. The same argument holds for
Levinas and—I argue later—Kristeva.

[61] Daniel Miller, 'Church Textuality and the Shaping of Christian Subjectivity', unpublished
M.St. thesis, University of Oxford, Trinity Term 2004, p. 18. I am indebted to this thesis, which
both exegetes and extends my own work on Derrida.

to a calculable programme and the imperative of 'petty or grand inquisitors'.[62] Thus the very complexity of the world, with its interacting texts and differential signs, calls for the action of a responsible subject:

> this particular undecidable opens the field of decision of decidability. It calls for decision in the order of ethical-political responsibility. It is even its necessary condition. A decision can only come into being *in a space that exceeds the calculable programme* that would destroy all responsibility by transforming it into a programmable effect of determinate causes. There can be no moral or political responsibility without this trial and this passage by way of the undecidable.[63]

This location of the identity of the subject in its freedom to decide sounds a little like the existentialism of Jean-Paul Sartre, but it differs in that the freedom can only be established *within* the context of the world, not in opposition to it.

COMPLEXITY, WISDOM, AND GOD

Modern science and postmodern semiotics provide us with complementary accounts of a complex world, which is (in Derrida's words) 'a space that exceeds the calculable programme'. Science locates this complexity in physical factors, while the semiotics of Derrida locates it in the network of signs that constitutes the 'real'. Actually, the difference is not as great as might appear, as scientists themselves recognize that the mathematical models they use to talk about the world, especially at the microcosmic level, can only approximate to reality, and the measurements they make at least partly create it.[64] Aspects of both the scientific method and the semiotic approach are to be found in Israelite wisdom, which is aware both of the inexhaustible and ummeasurable extent of the world, and of the fragility of words with which they try to capture it.

In its blend of confidence in calculation, and yet caution about what is incalculable, Israelite wisdom perhaps stands closer to the world-view of modern science. However, there is something like this blend in Derrida's thought. In sketching out the possibilities for understanding the 'freeplay' or 'game' (*jeu*) of 'undecidability', Derrida emphasizes that 'undecidability' cannot be said to be 'complete', since this after all would be a totalization,

---

[62] 'Eating Well', p. 286.

[63] Derrida, 'Afterword', p. 116. My italics.

[64] Lee McIntyre, 'Complexity. A Philosopher's Reflections', *Complexity* 3 (1998), pp. 29–30 entirely reduces ontology to epistemology, which is not my argument. Closer is Ian Barbour's espousal of 'critical realism' in his *Myths, Models and Paradigms* (London: SCM, 1974), pp. 45–9.

no less than complete self-presence; 'I never spoke', he asserts, 'of complete freeplay'.[65] The 'incompleteness' of undecidability might lie in the fact that decisions are prompted by it, and Derrida evidently prefers this particular meaning of incompleteness; but he recognizes that there is another meaning of the 'game', which is to affirm incompleteness as 'the *limits* of decidability, of calculability or of formalized completeness' while still remaining 'within the order of the calculable'.[66] This (which Derrida does not rule out) would certainly be closer to the ancient mood of wisdom, at least until the period of Koheleth.

Where wisdom does obviously stand close to the semiotic approach is in its stress on the immersion of the subject into the world. Derrida affirms that every signified becomes a signifier in its turn, creating a never-ending chain of meaning; he also finds the common ground between the subject and the object through notions of 'difference' and 'the trace of the other'. Ancient Israelite wisdom expresses similar ideas in the very notion of *ḥokmah* ('wisdom'), which itself crosses the boundaries between subject and object. In the last chapter I used the English word 'wisdom', translating *ḥokmah* (חכמה) as a convenient short-hand term for the whole educational enterprise represented by the Book of Proverbs at all its stages. This practice has been subjected to some intensive criticism by Whybray,[67] but no harm will be done if we are aware of the actual occurrence of the term in the text, and as long as we do not assume that the 'wise' we have in view constituted a distinct social class that always went by that name. In the sentence and instruction literature of Proverbs, 'wisdom' is actually one term among several—although the most frequent—for the intellectual activity commended, some other relevant terms being: 'discernment/understanding' (*bīnah*, בינה /*t*ᵉ*būnah*, תבונה), discrimination (*lehābīn*, להבין), admonishment or discipline (*mūsār*, מוסר), guidance (*da'at*, דעת), successful wisdom/competence (*tūšīyah*, תושיה), prudence (*haskēl*, השכל), instruction (*tōrah*, תורה), shrewdness (*'ormah*, ערמה), resourcefulness (*m*ᵉ*zimmah*, מזמה), judgement (*mišpāṭ*, משפט), commandment (*miṣwah*, מצוה), and righteousness (*ṣ*ᵉ*dāqah*, צדקה). Of these terms, *mišpāṭ* and *miṣwah* carry immediate associations of Yahwistic piety and religious instruction, while all the other terms might be found in material that is both 'secular' and Yahwistic.[68]

This profusion of terminology persists in the later instruction of Proverbs chapters 1–9, but the emergence of the term *ḥokmah* ('wisdom': חכמה) as a precious object (Prov. 2:1–10) and finally as a personification with a name indicates, together with the continued frequency of the term, an increasing desire for a single comprehensive term to describe the educational enterprise. In the major

---

[65] Derrida, 'Afterword', p. 115.   [66] Derrida, 'Afterword' p. 116.
[67] Whybray, *Intellectual Tradition*, pp. 3–5; also see von Rad, *Wisdom*, p. 53.
[68] Against McKane, *Proverbs*, p. 265, *ṣ*ᵉ*dāqah* can also carry a less religious meaning.

speeches of personified wisdom she is identified clearly as 'wisdom' (*ḥokmah*, חכמה: Prov. 1:20, 8:1, 8:12, 9:1), and while many alternative terms for education continue in later literature, it is evident that they are now synonyms for wisdom (see, for example, Job 28:12, 20). In the books of Jewish wisdom in Greek (Ben Sira, Wisdom of Solomon) wisdom appears under the name of *sophia* (σοφια), but she should not be confused with Aristotelean, gnostic or later Christian *sophia*. The *sophia* of these books carries with her the identity of the Hebrew *ḥokmah*, blending practical wisdom with the knowledge of God. In the terminology I introduced earlier, she integrates elements both of *phronēsis* and what *will* be called *sophia* in the Christian tradition.[69]

In fact, *ḥokmah* (חכמה) was particularly useful in the flexibility of its meaning, a characteristic not possessed by the Egyptian Ma'at and its nearest equivalents in Israel, 'righteousness' (*ṣᵉdāqah*) and 'justice/judgement' (*mišpāṭ*). The word *ḥokmah* stands on the one hand for a faculty of mind, a 'skill' of approach gained through experience (Prov. 1:5), an ability to 'steer' through life. A person is wise (*ḥākām*, חכם), or has wisdom:

> Wisdom is at home in the mind of one who has understanding
> but it is not known in the heart of fools. (Prov. 14:33)

On the other hand it stands for the area of knowledge itself, a 'body' of instruction. It is subject *and* object. The body of instruction can, further, itself be two things. It can be the *thoughts* within the mind of the person who exercises wisdom, which are spoken out loud and recorded for future generations in a written text:

> My child, be attentive to my wisdom;
> incline your ear to my understanding . . .
> do not depart from the words of my mouth. (Prov. 5:1, 7)

But wisdom as the body of knowledge is also something not yet known to a person, something to be 'found', knowledge which waits exploration within the world order itself, an area of knowledge corresponding to the world, or the world as an object of study:

> Happy are those who find wisdom
> and those who get understanding. (Prov. 3:13)

> I have not learned wisdom . . .
> Who has ascended to heaven and come down? (Prov. 30:3)

---

[69] See Chapter 1, the section called 'Different Kinds of Wisdom'. In this study, although 'wisdom' can be a proper name for personified wisdom, I am printing wisdom throughout with a lower-case 'w' so as not to obscure the constant flow of meaning between practical wisdom and the wisdom which invites relationship. Context, and the occasional use of 'Lady Wisdom', should make clear where personified wisdom is intended.

Thus those who 'have' wisdom (as a faculty) apply their minds to 'knowing' wisdom (in the mind and the mouth) and 'searching for wisdom' (in the world). Although one sense might be more prominent, the three senses interweave in each of the examples given above, as they do in the words of Koheleth:

> I said to myself, 'I have acquired great wisdom, surpassing all who were over Jerusalem before me; and my mind has had great experience of wisdom and knowledge'. And I applied my mind to know wisdom. (Eccl. 1:16–17)

This ambiguity of the term 'wisdom' is to be of central importance in my discussion, continually transgressing the distinctions between subject and object, and in itself expressing the immersion of the self into the world. The mind of someone wise can never stand above and beyond the world of signs. Now, it is in this very context, as well as in the context of a complex world revealed to us by science, that talk about God becomes appropriate. God, the wisdom literature affirms, is supremely wise. If this affirmation is to have any power of analogy with what human beings know as wisdom, God must be always committed to the signs of the material world, always involved in its text as God's 'context'. God too must 'search wisdom out' (Job 28:27). Indeed, God must be deeply immersed in the time and history in which signs exist. If we follow through this thought seriously, we shall be critical of the theological tradition in which God is 'simple being'.

To be God at all, to be a creator and not created, God must exist *a se*—that is, God cannot owe God's being to anything or anybody else than God's own self. But the self-existence (aseity) of God has been traditionally understood as also implying a *self-sufficiency*, in which God as absolute Being is defined as being totally uncaused and unconditioned by any created reality. This notion is rooted in the doctrine of divine simplicity, denying any kind of composition in God. As Aquinas states, quoting Augustine, 'God is the most truly simple thing there is (*vere et summe simplex est*).[70] Such a 'simple' divine Being cannot suffer at the hands of the world, cannot change in any way, and cannot include the finite within its infinity. To complete the picture of a 'pure act' (*actus purus*) which is also 'simple being', God cannot have any potentials which are not actualized,[71] and must exist in an eternity which is conceived as a simultaneous moment, knowing past, present, and future in one instant flash of perception. Such a God supports the 'metaphysics of presence' that Derrida wants to deny for the human consciousness, in which 'to be' is to be fully present in self-identity. We have seen how much of relation to others is excluded from this view of total presence. God, traditionally conceived as 'simple', grounds an individual human consciousness which is 'simply' present

---

[70] Aquinas, *Summa Theologiae*, 1a.3.7.
[71] Aquinas, *Summa Theologiae*, 1a.2.3; 1a.3.7; 1a.9.1–2.

to itself and to the world. God as Logos, validating human reason or logos, is present to God's own self without needing to take account of the signs of the world and is self-identical in an absolute present moment. As Derrida puts it, God on this reckoning is 'the name and the element of that which makes possible an absolutely pure and absolutely present self-knowledge'.[72]

Talk about God which takes its departure from the complexity of the world will oppose all such notions of simple being. Talk about God properly conceives God as both self-existent and *actus purus*, but this need not imply either self-sufficiency or *actus simplex*. As Keith Ward suggests, 'It is quite coherent, however, to suppose that God, while indivisible, is internally complex.'[73] Such complexity would allow us to conceive of God as exhibiting infinity, not in excluding the finite, but including it as part of the divine Being. Further, Karl Barth suggests that if God is the God whom God chooses to be, whose freedom of will constitutes the divine Being, then aseity need not mean self-sufficiency: '[He] ordains that He should not be *entirely* self-sufficient as He might be,'[74] writes Barth. To affirm that God is self-sufficient for the fact of God's existence does not necessarily mean that God is self-sufficient for the whole mode of divine life. We can think of a God who determines God's self and yet also allows a creation to participate in the causes of God's own becoming. As Barth puts it, God has a freedom to choose to be affected by the world and to suffer in sympathy with the world:

> According to the biblical testimony, God has the prerogative to be free without being limited by His freedom from external conditioning, free also with regard to His freedom . . . God must not only be unconditioned but, in the freedom in which He sets up this fellowship [i.e. with humankind], He can and will also be conditioned.[75]

A final blow against the notion of God as 'simple' Being is delivered by the process theologian Charles Hartshorne, who maintains that it is quite coherent to conceive of a God who knows the possibilities for what God and the world can achieve together in cooperation and co-creativity, but cannot experience them as actualities until they happen. Possibility and actuality are not to be fused, but in each case God has perfect vision (omniscience) where we do not.[76]

---

[72] Derrida, *On Grammatology*, p. 98, cf. pp. 279–80.

[73] Keith Ward, *Rational Theology and the Creativity of God* (Oxford: Blackwell, 1982), p. 216, cf. p. 71.

[74] Barth, *Church Dogmatics* II/2, p. 10.

[75] Barth, *Church Dogmatics* II/1, p. 303.

[76] Later we will have to define more carefully what it means for God to 'know' all possibilities; there must be room for new possibilities to emerge in the interaction between God and the world which God will not 'know' until they appear. See Chapter 12, the section called 'The Body and Music'.

He is the Whole in every categorial sense, all actuality in one individual actuality, and all possibility in one individual potentiality. This relatively simple idea was apparently too complex for most of our ancestors to hit upon.[77]

The ancestor he has especially in his sights is Aquinas, who maintained that as pure and simple Being, God actualizes all divine potentials simultaneously. But, insists Hartshorne, 'possibility is in principle inexhaustible: it could not be fully actualized'.[78] Such a concept of God brings theology close to both the scientific understanding of open possibilities and the Derridean semiotics of undecidability, making clear that God participates in time rather than a timeless present. A God of temporal simplicity would not have the power to act in the world, as a timeless being could hardly sustain a temporally extended universe, or respond to temporal beings in a meaningful relationship.[79] To understand God as temporal does not, of course, mean that God must be subject to exactly the same frustrations of passing time as we are, nor that God is confined to the particular time-scale of the universe with which we are familiar.[80] Further, unlike Hartshorne and with Barth, we need not locate these divine limitations only within the processes of reality, but root them in the eternal desire of God to be a creator. This is the desire, not of a monadic absolute, but of a God who lives in a communion of love, and so we come to the point in our conversation where we must think more explicitly of Trinity.

THE COMPLEX BEING OF THE TRIUNE GOD

The doctrine of the Trinity has sometimes been presented as a kind of numerical puzzle in which God is supposedly one individual being and three individual beings at the same time. This is not a complexity but a contradiction, and falls into the trap of making the being of God a mere projection of finite being, even if at the top of an ontological tree (what Heidegger dismissed as 'ontotheology'). The ancient formula of the Trinity, created by the Church Fathers, refers to 'three persons (*hypostases*) in one essence'. They did not intend to speak of three 'persons' in the modern sense of three self-conscious individuals, as if asserting that these were also, by some paradox, one

---

[77] Charles Hartshorne, *A Natural Theology for our Time* (La Salle: Open Court, 1967), pp. 20–1.

[78] Harthorne, *Natural Theology*, p. 21; cf. Hartshorne, *Man's Vision of God* (Hamden: Archon Books, 1964), pp. 121–3.

[79] See Richard Swinburne, *The Coherence of Theism* (Oxford: Clarendon Press, 1977), p. 221; Nelson Pike, *God and Timelessness* (London: Routledge & Kegan Paul, 1970), pp. 97–119. I argue the point in more detail in Fiddes, *The Promised End: Eschatology in Theology and Literature* (Oxford: Blackwell, 2000), pp. 124–7.

[80] See Fiddes, *Promised End*, pp. 138–40, 177–9, and Chapter 12 of this volume, the section called 'The Body and Music').

individual as well. They aimed to speak of a divine life which was rich in relationships and which escaped literal description. By *hypostasis* the Fathers meant a 'distinct reality' which has being, and the hypostases were entirely characterized by being in relation with each other and the world that God had created. Athanasius, for example, was scarcely bothered to define any philosophical difference between a *hypostasis* and an *ousia* (essence).[81] Instead he found the nub of the matter in the relations of Father, Son, and Spirit. He met the hostile question as to what the difference could be between the persons if they are one in divine essence (*ousia*) with a different style of theological speech: the Father is 'other' (*heteros*) in that he alone begets the Son, the Son is 'other' in that he alone is begotten, and the Spirit is 'other' in that he alone proceeds from the Father.[82] These realities are different in the way that they are related to each other, notably in their origin. This doctrine of relations was taken up by the Cappadocians in the East—who spoke of paternity, filiation, and spiration (begetting, being begotten, and being breathed out)—and by Augustine in the West.[83] Trinity, then, is a vision of God as three interweaving relationships of ecstatic, outward-going love, giving and receiving.

Here I intend to take this patristic emphasis on relations more radically than the Fathers did themselves: I urge that the *hypostases* (which are not distinct beings) should not even be understood as subjects or agents, but as relations which are as real as any subjects who *have* relations.[84] The Church Fathers took one step towards this when they affirmed that the persons of Father, Son, and Spirit are wholly *constituted* by their relationships with each other.[85] They perceived that relationship is not something merely added on to a person, as if a core of *hypostasis* could exist without or before the relationships in which a person is engaged.[86] The being of God is communion, and the Fathers used the verb *chōreō* to express the way that each person 'penetrated', 'filled', or was 'contained' in the others.[87] Somewhat later this was expressed in a noun, *perichōrēsis* (first used, it seems, in a trinitarian context by Pseudo-Cyril in the sixth century, followed by John of Damascus in the eighth),[88]

---

[81] In fact, for most of his theological career he treated them as identical; see *Contra Arianos* 1.11; *De Decretis* 27; *De Synodis* 41.

[82] Athanasius, *Contra Arianos* 3.4–6, cf. 1.9, 39, 58.

[83] See e.g. Gregory Nazianzen, *Orationes* 29.16; Augustine, *De Trinitate* 5.6–13.

[84] For the following, I am drawing on material from my book *Participating in God. A Pastoral Doctrine of the Trinity* (London: Darton Longman and Todd, 2000), pp. 34–40, 72–4.

[85] We can observe this conflation happening in e.g. T.F. Torrance, *Trinitarian Perspectives* (Edinburgh: T & T Clark, 1994), pp. 33, 49; Leonardo Boff, *Trinity and Society* (London: Burns & Oates, 1988), pp. 88, 92.

[86] See John Zizioulas, *Being as Communion* (London: Darton, Longman and Todd, 1985), pp. 27–41.

[87] So Hilary (*De Trinitate* 9.69); Cyril of Alexandria (*Dial. de Trinitate* 3.467C).

[88] Pseudo-Cyril, *De Sacrosancta Trinitate*, 24; John of Damascus, *De Fide Orthodoxa* 1.14.

which had the advantage of emphasizing reciprocity and exchange in the mutual indwelling and penetration of the persons.

The term *perichōrēsis* thus expresses the permeation of each person by the other, their coinherence without confusion. It takes up and develops the words of Jesus in the Fourth Gospel: 'believe me that I am in the Father and the Father is in me' (John 14:11). Two Latin translations were used which together bring out quite well the sense of the Greek term. First, *circuminsessio* means that one person is contained in another—literally 'seated' in another, filling the space of the other, present in the other. This stresses a state of being, and was preferred by Thomas Aquinas.[89] Second, *circumincessio* is a more active word, evoking a state of doing, the interpenetrating of one person in another; it captures the sense of a moving in and through the other, and was preferred by Bonaventure among other theologians in the West.[90]

However, I suggest that we should go even further in the direction of a relational understanding of God than this, and think of the 'persons' in God as not simply *formed* by their relations, but as *being* no more and no less than the relations themselves.[91] The *hypostases* are 'distinct realities' *as* relations and the *perichōrēsis* is an interweaving of relations. This idea was already hinted at by Augustine when he declared that 'the names, Father and Son do not refer to the substance but to the relation, and the relation is no accident'.[92] Aquinas then gave formality to the notion with the term 'subsistent relations', stating that 'divine person signifies relation as something subsisting... relation is signified... as hypostasis'.[93] While Augustine's approach was experimental[94]—even playful—Aquinas unfortunately explained the subsistence or self-existence of the relations by claiming that relations in God must be identical with the essence of God, since God is simple being.[95] In his view, they subsist because they are the same as the one divine substance, thus giving grounds for the suspicion of Eastern theologians that such talk is simply in aid of the typical Western stress on the unity of divine essence, with the consequent loss of real threeness and 'otherness' in God. We can, however, free the idea of subsistent relations from its Neoplatonic and Aristotelean settings in Augustine and Aquinas. Taking a clue from Barth's insistence that 'with regard to the being of God, the word

---

[89] Aquinas, *Summa Theologiae* 1a.42.5.

[90] Bonaventura, *Liber Sententiarum* I, Dist.19, 1.1.4, concl.

[91] A similar case for taking subsistent relations seriously is made by David Cunningham, *These Three are One: The Practice of Trinitarian Theology* (Oxford: Blackwell, 1998), pp. 59–71; cf. pp. 168–9. But Cunningham still refers to 'addressing' or 'speaking to' the relations (p. 72) rather than 'speaking in' the flow of relations.

[92] Augustine, *De Trinitate* 5.6.

[93] Aquinas, *Summa Theologiae*, 1a.29.4.

[94] He was grappling with the alternatives presented to him by the Arians that the persons of the Trinity must be distinguished either by substance (hence tritheism) or accident (so lacking the enduring nature of divinity).

[95] Aquinas *Summa Theologiae* 1a.29.4; cf. 1a.3.6; 1a.27.4.

"event" or "act" is final',[96] we may speak of God as an event of relationships, or three *movements* of relationship subsisting in one event. Focusing on relations rather than personal agents who *have* relations takes us from an ontology of substance to one of event. It is in this complex sense that God is *actus purus*.

I intend to develop and justify this form of 'subsistent relations' further as this study proceeds (and especially in Chapter 7), but for now we should note that with this perspective, talk of the triune God ceases to be a language of observation and becomes one of participation. For of course it is not possible to visualize, paint or etch in glass, three interweaving 'relationships' without any personal agents who exercise them. We cannot 'see', even in our mind's eye, three movements of being which are characterized by relationship. But then this ought to be a positive advantage in thinking about God, who (as Kant pointed out)[97] is not an object in the world. Talk of God as Trinity is not the language of a spectator, but the language of a *participant*. It only makes sense in terms of involvement in the complex network of relationships in which God happens. In the case of finite beings we can still still distinguish between subject and object, although both ancient wisdom and postmodern thinking aim to overcome the alienation between them, especially that caused by the dominance of the subject. The language of 'subsistent relations' suggests that it is inappropriate to refer to God, as infinite and uncreated being, in terms of either subject or object, and experience of participation in this God may help to overcome the divisiveness and hostility between subject and object in the world.

To refer to God as 'Father' thus does not mean to represent or objectify God as a father-figure, but to *address* God as Father, and by using this invocation to enter into a movement of a relationship which, by analogy, we can say is like a relationship between a son and a father. The Christian practice of prayer is one place where this participation comes alive. The cry of 'abba, Father' in prayer fits into a movement of speech like that between a son and a father; our response of 'yes' ('Amen') leans upon a filial 'yes' of humble obedience,[98] glorifying the Father, a response which is already there. At the same time, we find ourselves involved in a movement of self-giving like that of a father sending forth a son, a movement which the early theologians called 'eternal generation' and which has its outworking in the mission ('sending') of the Son by the Father in history to achieve the reconciliation of all things. In this moment we discover that these movements of response and mission are undergirded by movements of suffering, like the painful longing of a forsaken son towards a father and of a desolate father towards a lost son; here Jürgen Moltmann speaks of God as 'the event of Golgotha' and to the question 'can one pray to an event?' rightly answers that one can 'pray *in* this event.'[99] These

---

[96] Barth, *Church Dogmatics* II/1, p. 263.   [97] See the first section in Chapter 2.
[98] 2 Cor. 1:19–21; cf. Heb. 5:7–10.   [99] Moltmann, *Crucified God*, p. 247.

two directions of movement, sending and response, are interwoven by a third, as we find that they are continually opened up to new depths of relationship and to the new possibilities of the future by a movement for which Scripture offers impressionistic images—a wind blowing, breath stirring, wings beating, oil trickling, water flowing, fire burning. The traditional formulation that the Spirit 'proceeds from the Father through the Son' points to movement which renews all relations 'from' and 'to' the other. In the language of the New Testament, we are praying to the Father, through the Son and in the Spirit.[100]

Thus, through our participation, we can identify three distinct movements which are like speech, emotion, and action within relationships 'from father to son', 'from son to father', and a movement of 'deepening relations'. They are mutual relationships of ecstatic, outward-going love, giving and receiving. Actively they are such moments as originating, responding, opening; passively they are moments of being glorified, being sent, being breathed. So far in describing them I have followed the form of address that Jesus himself taught his disciples, 'Abba, Father' (Matthew 6:9), offering the image 'from son to father' for the movement of response that we lean upon. But these movements of giving and receiving cannot in themselves be restricted to a particular gender, as is quite clear with the images for the movement of Spirit. They will also, in appropriate contexts, give rise to feminine images; for instance, the nature of our participation may require us to say that we are engaging in a flow of relationships like those originating in a mother (cf. Isa. 49:14–15), especially in experiences of being spiritually nurtured and fed,[101] or like those which characterize the response of a daughter.

Participation in the relations of the Trinity undermines any concept of God as the 'transcendental signified' opposed by Derrida. The triune God cannot be a kind of remote mind that stands beyond the signs in the world and their differences from each other in a complexity such as semiotics uncovers. Talk about God as Trinity begins from encounter with God in the world. We can only experience divine relations in and through the multiple relations we find in the world, whether human or in the wider scene of nature. In the present, Trinity-talk begins from Christian practices such as prayer, and from engagement in the lives of others. In the memory of the church it begins from a person, Jesus, who is fully open in trust to God his Father in a responsive life, in a pattern of relationship that becomes revelatory of the love of God. There can be no triune God other than the one who opens the divine *perichōrēsis* of relations for human beings to participate within it. In creation and redemption God opens space within the interweaving of movements of relation, so that the created universe exists 'in' God, immersed into the flow.

---

[100] See e.g. Mt. 6:6, Jn. 14:16, Heb. 7:25, Eph. 6:18.
[101] See Michael Jacobs, *Living Illusions: A Psychology of Belief* (London: SPCK, 1993), pp. 68–71.

Indeed, from a trinitarian perspective the world with its complexity of signs exists within the 'difference' which is God, in a communion of love which is entirely characterized by difference. Aquinas thought that, although there might be a kind of 'conceptual commonness' in the word 'person' when applied to the *hypostases* of the Trinity, the particularity of each person in relation to the others meant that there could be no 'real commonness'.[102] Karl Rahner thus suggests that for Aquinas the single word 'person' is only a stopgap, as it were; one really needs the three different words 'Father', 'Son', and 'Spirit' to do justice to the difference between the distinct modes of being in God.[103] Heribert Mühlen rightly considers this difference in the context of love, observing that in human relationships we only become truly close to someone when we experience the other person as different from us. As our encounter with someone deepens, we become more and more aware of the uniqueness of the other, and only from this awareness of this difference from ourselves can the relationship take on a new depth of nearness. So by analogy in God, who is perfect love, Mühlen suggests we may say that:

> The distinction of the divine persons, in so far as they are distinct modes of being, is so great that it could not be conceived of as greater, while their unity is so intensive that it could not be conceived of as more intensive.[104]

That is, the modes of God's being are so closely united with each other that they must be infinitely different from each other. Hans Urs Von Balthasar similarly suggests that:

> God as the gulf of absolute love contains in advance, eternally, all the modalities of love, of compassion, and even of a 'separation' motivated by love and founded on the infinite distinctions between the [persons]—modalities that may manifest themselves in the course of a history of salvation involving sinful humankind.[105]

In the difference between the persons, in the distances between the movements of love, there is room to take in the painful experience of relationlessness in death. God can enter with empathy into the human experience of the breaking of relations because God lives in relationships which have a difference and otherness about them.

---

[102] Aquinas *Summa Theologiae* 1a. 30. 4;.

[103] Rahner, *The Trinity*, pp. 104ff.

[104] Heribert Mühlen, *Die Veränderlichkeit Gottes als Horizont einer zukünftigen Christologie* (Münster: Aschendorf, 1969), p. 26. Cf. Adrienne Von Speyr, *The Word: A Meditation on the Prologue to St John's Gospel*, trans. A. Dru (London: Collins, 1953), pp. 60–1: 'Their estrangement [i.e. of the Father and Son] is a form of their supreme intimacy.' Also, Eberhard Jüngel, *God as the Mystery of the World*, transl. D. Guder (Edinburgh: T & T Clark, 1983), pp. 317–20, 374–5.

[105] Hans Urs von Balthasar, *Mysterium Paschale*, trans. A. Nichols (Edinburgh: T & T Clark, 1990), p. ix.

Derrida does associate 'difference' with the concept of God, writing that 'God himself is, and appears as what he is, within difference, that is to say as difference and within dissimulation.'[106] However, by 'difference' Derrida does not intend a trinitarian conceptuality, which he identifies with the absolute self-differentiating Subject of Hegel, so that, for Derrida, Trinity is the symbol of a circular, harmonious rhythm of suffocating closure.[107] Derrida means that the concept of God is an 'example' of difference, in so far as we can only conceive God as the rupturing of a fullness of presence, a separation of God from God's self that would turn us in the direction of what is radically Other *(tout autre)* or the 'sacred'. There is thus an 'essential experience of divinity or deity' *before* those ideas are captured by the religious tradition and solidified into the presence of a God.[108] Derrida finds some parallel here with the theology of Meister Eckhart, in which there is 'deity' beyond 'God',[109] but he complains that Eckhart—and all negative theology with him—finally relapses into enclosing this deity within a dogmatic Trinitarian scheme. The 'difference' of God must be the alienation of God from any concept of an absolute and personal subject, so that human beings have the freedom to be themselves, and to 'take words upon ourselves'.[110] It is only in God's difference from God's self that creation can come to be. Commenting on the imagery of the Jewish poet Edmond Jabès, Derrida judges that 'God separated himself from himself in order to let us speak, in order to astonish and interrogate us'.[111] Now, this means a rejection of classical metaphysical statements about the unity and 'simplicity' of God. Provocatively, Derrida puts this in terms of the 'dissimulation' or 'duplicity' of God:

> If God opens the question in God, if he is the very opening of the Question, there can be no simplicity of God. And, thus, what was unthinkable for the classical rationalists here becomes the obvious itself. Proceeding within the duplicity of his own questionability, God does not act in the simplest ways: he is not truthful, he is not sincere. Sincerity, which is simplicity, is a lying virtue.[112]

Human beings take words on themselves, in the 'desert' space of writing, an empty place where God is separated from God's self.

With Robert Magliola, I suggest that Derrida could take Trinity as 'difference' more seriously. He argues that, whereas Derrida views the Trinity as the epitome of self-enclosed identity, in fact the doctrine shows that the Christian God is made up of real, differentiated relations. The revelation in Christ offers

---

[106] Derrida, *Writing and Difference*, p. 74.
[107] Derrida, *Dissemination*, p. 352.
[108] Derrida, *Writing and Difference*, pp. 145, 319.
[109] Derrida, *Writing and Difference*, pp. 146–7.
[110] Derrida, *Writing and Difference*, p. 68.
[111] Derrida, *Writing and Difference*, p. 67.
[112] Derrida, *Writing and Difference*, p. 68.

us a 'Trinity which is sacred differance'.[113] The revelation of Christ and the teaching of the church 'deconstruct trinitarian theories which propose a self-enclosed entitative triadic model'.[114] The Trinity, Magliola argues, is constituted by 'purely negative or relational differences' as 'a God of perpetual alterity'.[115] But if we are indeed to reject a God of 'simplicity', and find that a God of difference is our 'access' into difference and complexity in the world, I suggest that we also have to abandon any notion of persons as 'subjects' in God, to which Magliola at least is still attached in his adherence to the teaching of the Catholic Magisterium. If we understand the 'persons' to indicate movements of relation in which we participate, then we would find a 'truth' in God of a different kind from simplicity. If there is no simple message from a simple God, we will experience the complexity of the world as an *ambiguous* witness to God rather than as 'lying', a hiddenness (but not absence) of God which does indeed give the room for our responsible action that both Derrida and Levinas require.[116]

We can explore the same issues from the perspective of a language of Being. For Derrida, there is an Otherness to the world which cannot be encapsulated in any concepts ('a radical trembling can only come from the outside'),[117] and which at the same time cannot be separated from the 'inside' of the world: the terms 'sacred' and 'divinity' can be attached to this reality, as well as 'différ-ance', none of these terms being categories but only indicators of what cannot be classified. This *différance* 'is the non-full, *non-simple*, structured and differentiating origin of differences' for which the usual concept of 'origin' is thus no longer suitable.[118] The sacred is to be distinguished from the concept of 'God', which always exists within a framework of beliefs and dogmas, such as Trinity. Now, in his earlier work, in *Writing and Difference*, Derrida thinks that 'Being' as used by Heidegger in absolute difference from 'beings' can also indicate this sacred Otherness. Levinas' critique and rejection of 'Being' in Heidegger in favour of the ethical demand of the 'other' is (thinks Derrida) misplaced, since Heidegger does not intend Being as a totalizing foundation of beings, which robs them of their otherness. Thinking of Being does not make the other a species of the simple genre Being, subordinating the other to a pre-existing abstract unity. Rather, because Being cannot be classified or categorized, and because it 'lets beings be', it precedes all concepts, and the thought of Being is actually necessary to preserve 'the irreducibility of the existence and

---

[113] Robert Magliola, *Derrida on the Mend* (West Lafayette: Purdue University Press, 1984), p. 134.

[114] Magliola, *Derrida on the Mend*, p. 135.

[115] Magliola, *Derrida on the Mend*, p. 149.

[116] Derrida, *Writing and Difference*, pp. 168–9; Levinas, *Difficult Freedom*, pp. 143–5.

[117] Derrida, *Margins*, p. 134.

[118] Derrida, 'Différance', in *Margins*, p. 11.

essence of the other, and [its] consequent responsibility'.[119] Derrida thinks that the experience of the 'sacred' is when we think Being as 'promise', where Being is not a static foundation of the world but 'an elusive, fleeting reality'[120] that only emerges in and as language, time, and difference.[121] Here, Derrida quotes Heidegger, apparently with approval: 'It is only on the basis of the truth of Being that the essence of the Sacred can be thought. It is only on the basis of the Sacred that the essence of Divinity must be thought.'[122]

In the same context Derrida, however, dismisses Eckhart's concept of 'Deity beyond God', on the grounds that Eckhart confesses that he attributes to God 'a more elevated being'. Similarly, in a later essay, Derrida accuses both Eckhart and Pseudo-Dionysius of 'seeking a hyperessentiality, a being beyond Being',[123] so that they relapse into 'ontotheology'. This is why, he asserts, he wants to separate his own thinking about difference and otherness from negative theology. Is it consistent, then, for Derrida to approve of Heidegger's use of 'Being' for 'the Sacred'? Heidegger's writing of Being with a cross through it, 'under erasure', disrupts conventional ideas of dividing being into subject and object, but still retains the notion of Being as unclassifiable and unique, and Derrida appears to approve of this use.[124] Derrida, I suggest, means by 'elevated being' and 'hyperessentiality' any notion of Being which is an intensification of existent beings in the world; he understands Christian mystics to be intending by *hyperousios* 'the ineffable transcendence of an infinite existent',[125] and this is why he rejects it. For Derrida, indications that 'Being' is being used in this illegitimate way, as equivalent to 'a being', however elevated, are: an affirming of a 'simple' origin for the world ('the solitary and pure unity of God'),[126] an application of trinitarian language, an assumption of 'fullness of presence', and the possibility of participation in Being. For Derrida, such 'hyperessentiality' confuses the Sacredness and the Deity of 'Otherness' with 'a God'.

Both Heidegger and Derrida thus distinguish between 'Being' and 'God'.[127] As Steven Shakespeare summarizes it, 'Being comes before God as the emergence of life and difference within which the idea of God can do its work.'[128]

---

[119] Derrida, *Writing and Difference*, p. 140.

[120] Steven Shakespeare's phrase, in his *Derrida and Theology* (London: T & T Clark, 2009), p. 92.

[121] Derrida, *Writing and Difference*, p. 145.

[122] Derrida, *Writing and Difference*, pp. 145–6.

[123] Derrida, 'How to Avoid Speaking. Denials' in Coward and Foshay (eds), *Derrida and Negative Theology*, p. 77.

[124] Derrida, 'How to Avoid Speaking', p. 126.

[125] Derrida, *Writing and Difference*, p. 146.

[126] Derrida, 'How to Avoid Speaking', p. 120.

[127] Derrida, *Writing and Difference*, p. 143; Heidegger, 'Onto-theo-logical Constitution of Metaphysics', pp. 58–9; Heidegger, *Being and Time*, pp. 125–7.

[128] Shakespeare, *Derrida and Theology*, p. 93.

However, Shakespeare is right to comment that this distinction between Being and God is 'unstable'. With regard to Derrida's objections to 'hyperessentiality' listed above, we may agree that notions of a 'simple' origin are quite incoherent with a complex world. Later I shall be defending notions of presence (though not full and simple presence) and participation with regard to the God who is infinitely Other, but here I want to continue a reflection on trinitarian language. Once Being is understood in the dynamic sense that Derrida gives it, and once we understand God not as 'a being' or even a 'subject' or 'agent', but as a trinitarian difference of relations, then there is no reason to make a separation between 'Being' and 'God'. That is, there is no reason why 'Being' as 'the emergence of difference' should not be used as one symbol among others for the ultimate creative reality that is God.[129] If God, like Derrida's concept of the infinite Other, cannot be talked about literally, but only in metaphors and symbols, then a whole range of language becomes available and appropriate. Derrida himself uses 'the Sacred', 'deity', '*différance*'—and later 'flame', '*khōra*', and 'the promise'[130]—for encounter with a transcendence which is nevertheless embodied in the signs of the world. To these symbols we can surely add 'divine relations' and 'Being' (but not 'a being'). We may agree with Jean-Luc Marion that the Thomist language of God as Being (*ipsum esse subsistens*) is too restrictive to encompass the experience of God's absurdly generous self-revelation of love,[131] and that language such as 'gift', 'excess', 'face', and 'icon' is needed to understand this divine generosity. But to speak of 'God without being' may deprive us of one useful symbol among others.

The language of Being has a usefulness, in the Heideggerian sense of 'Being that lets be'. John Macquarrie has re-employed the Heideggerian distinction between Being and beings in this way, identifying God with Being (or 'Holy Being', Being that invites trust)[132] in a way that Heidegger resists. Macquarrie argues that language of God as 'Being' has capacity for expressing both transcendence and immanence, since we cannot think of Being directly but only as that which supports and sustains beings.[133] Macquarrie points to experiences of awe and wonder that we can identify as encounters with 'Holy Being'; however, since Being is unique and incomparable, we only come to notice the presence of 'Being' indirectly through a contrast with experiences of 'non-being', when facing the shock of death or falling into moods of anxiety when the world sinks to nothing. With Heidegger, Maquarrie comments that 'For the first time our eyes are opened to the wonder of

---

[129] I return to this claim in Chapter 7, the section called 'The Search for a No-Place'.

[130] For 'flame', see three paragraphs further on; for '*khōra*' and 'promise' see Chapter 7.

[131] Jean-Luc Marion, *God Without Being. Hors-Texte*, trans. T. A. Carlson (Chicago: University of Chicago Press, 1995), pp. 78–83.

[132] Macquarrie, *Principles of Christian Theology*, p. 121.

[133] Macquarrie, *Principles of Christian Theology*, pp. 115–22, 142–5.

Being, and this happens with the force of revelation.'[134] Language of Being thus has the advantage of capturing the ambiguity of unveiling and veiling in the revelation of meaning in the world and–for a theologian–revelation of God. For Macquarrie, this in turn leads to a re-fashioning of trinitarian Persons as 'Primordial Being, Expressive Being and Unitive Being,' which are three 'movements', 'acts', or 'energies' of God.[135] For Karl Barth, a theologian who begins from another perspective altogether, from the Word of God revealed in Scripture, language of Being is also useful in stressing that God is 'event' or 'happening', and so Trinity can be conceived as 'three modes of Being' (*Seinsweise*) rather than three personal subjects.[136] Paul Ricoeur, reflecting on the 'capability' and 'potentiality' of human life, comes naturally to the language of 'Being-as-the-power-of-the-possible',[137] so much so that Ricoeur confesses in a late conversation that 'I am [now] not sure about the absolute irreconcilability between the God of the Bible and the God of Being.'[138]

Despite the usefulness of the symbol of Being, we must however resist any privileging of it over other symbols, and especially over the personal language of relations in God. Macquarrie and Tillich make Being the formative analogy for God, and regard 'person' as a symbol *for* Being (though at times it is not clear whether they remember that 'Being' too must be symbolic and not literal language for our 'ultimate concern'),[139] regarding the language of personal relations as more restrictive than that of Being. Language of personal relations is not considered to be useless, having an indispensable place in public and private prayers. God, after all, is 'not less than personal' because Being lets persons be and so Being has 'the power of personality'.[140] However, in strictly theological terms, language about personal relationship with—and in—God is judged to be only 'remotely analogous' to the self-disclosure of Being.[141] By contrast, I am arguing that the most adequate, or least inadequate, symbol for God is that of personal relations. This is a capacious language, encompassing transcendence and immanence, since the idea of Trinity as an interweaving of relations—rather than a community of persons who 'have' relations—refers to

---

[134] Macquarrie, *Principles of Christian Theology*, p. 87.

[135] Macquarrie, *Principles of Christian Theology*, pp. 200–2.

[136] Barth, *Church Dogmatics*, I/1, pp. 360–3.

[137] In Richard Kearney, *Debates in Continental Philosophy* (New York: Fordham Press, 2004), p. 43.

[138] In Kearney, *Debates*, p. 25.

[139] See Tillich, *Courage to Be*, pp. 173–9; *Systematic Theology*, vol. 2, pp. 9–12; Macquarrie, *Principles of Christian Theology*, pp. 140–3.

[140] Tillich, *Systematic Theology*, vol. 1, p. 271; Macquarrie, *Principles of Christian Theology*, p. 204.

[141] Macquarrie, *Principles of Christian Theology*, pp. 93–4.

a God who is unique and incomparable while also being immanent, embracing all created relations. God as 'an event of relations' escapes an objectifying conceptuality as effectively as terms like 'the Sacred'. Personal language used in this way can grasp the complexity of God that is called for by a complex world.

In commenting on Heidegger's concept of Spirit, Derrida picks up his use of the symbol of flame, borrowed from the poet Trakl: the 'Spirit in-flames', owned by nobody, is a 'trace on the way,' which 'writes itself right in the flame'. This 'archi-originary' movement of burning is not simple—it is a spirit that 'inscribes itself, retires, or retracts. It belongs to the flame it divides.'[142] It is a 'spirituality of promise' which Derrida judges that Heidegger would find foreign to Christianity, despite the theologians' protest that they honour 'The God of flame and fire-writing in the promise'. On behalf of Heidegger, Derrida asserts that he wants to think the 'basis' that makes all religious ideas of God and divine Spirit possible; determinate religion comes after the thinking of 'flame' in all its untamed risk.[143] I suggest that this 'archi-originary spirit' can be thought as a movement of relation as much as a movement of flame; the first escapes determination as much as the second does, neither of them surely doing so totally.

Taking the complexity of both the world and God seriously begins to meet the objection of Derrida to Christian prayer. Derrida finds prayer a meaningful act as an 'address to the other', an appeal to an Otherness that is not yet defined by one orthodoxy or another, an invocation that resists total comprehension in any discourse.[144] Yet Christian theology, he complains, turns this address into an 'enconium', into a praise of God which determines the prayer in a certain direction, towards a supreme subject who may—in the thought of negative theology—be 'beyond Being', and yet who is still trapped in the self-enclosure of the Trinity, and who claims 'full presence' as hyper-Being. Even in the thought of a negative theologian like Pseudo-Dionysius, prayer is still addressed to a 'trinitary and hyperessential God'. Derrida is looking for an 'address to' which is not also an 'address *about*' God, as exemplified in his cry 'come!'[145] But I am maintaining that the prayer 'to the Father, through the Son and in the Spirit' is an '*address in*' the triune God, invoking God only as a means of participating in the movements of relationship in God which cannot be reduced to either subject or object.

---

[142] Derrida, *On Spirit*, pp. 104—6.
[143] Derrida, *On Spirit*, p. 111.
[144] Derrida, 'How to Avoid Speaking', p. 111.
[145] See the subsection in Chapter 2 called 'The challenge of the sublime'.

THE COMPLEX ACTIVITY OF THE TRIUNE GOD

Engagement in the triune God is a mode of knowing God which will warn the participant against opening the kind of gap between subject and object in the world in which the subject dominates and controls. It is this complex life of God that also matches the complex life of the world that science and semiotics explore, as late-modern versions of the complex world discerned by the wise of Ancient Israel. The triune God enjoys a richness of life which results precisely from the infinite difference between Father, Son, and Spirit, and this God is committed unconditionally to the world of signs for which room is made within the fellowship of the divine life. Any idea that God acts in the world must thus connect with the complexities of indeterminism and interaction, as science conceives them and as I have already described them.

A creator who makes a world in which complexity arises from the indeterminate and the uncertain, in which chance plays a major role, gives considerable freedom to creation: such a God gives the world its own freedom to be self-organizing and self-creating. This means giving the world freedom to make its own mistakes and to develop its own tragedies. A God like this must be patient and vulnerable, willing to work with the long, painful process of growth and to have at least short-term purposes frustrated. The action of such a God will not be unilateral but cooperative. It will not be coercive, but seeking to achieve the purpose of love through persuasion. We can then conceive of God's influencing created beings, or luring them with love, to cooperate with divine aims. There is no mechanical causality here, no inevitable link between cause and effect. To return to the vision of Trinity I proposed earlier, this divine persuasion is based in attraction, in the attractiveness of *movements* of love, rhythms of a dance[146] into which we are swept up, so that our actions follow the same divine purpose. We are offered, or presented with, aims through being engaged in the purposeful flow of the divine love.

Here we learn from the witness of the ancient wisdom writers. They were not, of course, working with the image of God as Trinity, although they gave hints of complexity in God by speaking of a God who somehow embraced wisdom and the spirit. But they were always thinking of the world in a continuous relation with its creator. This is the point of the sayings from the

---

[146] Several modern theologians associate the *perichōrēsis* of the Trinity with a 'dance': see Edmund Hill, *The Three-Personed God* (Washington: University of America Press, 1982), p. 272; Catherine M. LaCugna, *God For Us: The Trinity and Christian Life* (San Francisco: Harper Collins, 1991), p. 271; Elizabeth Johnson, *She Who Is: The Mystery of God in Feminist Theological Discourse* (New York: Crossroad, 1993), pp. 220–1; Paul S. Fiddes, *Participating in God: A Pastoral Doctrine of the Trinity* (London: Darton, Longman and Todd, 2000), pp. 72–81. This is a modern play on words: *perichōrēsis* derives from *perichōrēo* (to interpenetrate), which sounds similar to—but is not etymologically connected with—*perichōreuo* (to dance around).

sentence literature of Proverbs which caution the hearer to respect limits, and with which we were occupied in the last chapter: God is deeply involved in the events of daily life, even those (but not only those) which human beings cannot see:

> Honest balances and scales are Yahweh's;
> all the weights in the bag are his work. (Prov. 16:11)

> The human spirit is the lamp of Yahweh,
> searching every innermost part. (Prov. 20:27)

If we think of this from the perspective of God as Trinity, we can say that in creation God makes room for created beings to indwell the fellowship of the divine life, and that in redemption God draws them ever more deeply into God's own communion of relationships. These are actions of self-giving, self-limiting love. The triune God is then the total environment within which complex systems develop; everything that exists is embraced within relational movements of self-giving and self-realizing love.

As David Kelsey rightly perceives, ancient wisdom theology is 'indifferent' to any idea of divine cause and effect in the world. We will be in accord with its approach if we 'rule out every effort to explain causally the dynamics of divine productivity of reality other than God and to attend instead to characterizing the ongoing relation that obtains between the Creator and creatures'.[147] God is freely present to reality other than God 'in order to constitute, sustain and respect this reality's otherness to God' as well as to sustain a 'genuine other-ness' of things and persons to each other'.[148] The technique of wisdom teaching is not to impose instruction on another, but to evoke wisdom within the hearer and so form a wise person. The aim of the sayings which are collected and passed on is to make the hearer wise, but this can only be by the non-violent and non-coercive means of arousing wisdom in the pupil; this is clear from the fact that the Wise are aware, especially in the 'instruction literature' that their teaching is vulnerable to being neglected or rejected, and needs to be held fast with love:

> My child, keep my words
> and store up my commandments with you:
> keep my commandments and live;
> keep my teachings as the apple of your eye....
> say to wisdom 'You are my sister,'
> and call insight your intimate friend. (Prov. 7:1–4)

Now, the very fact that God is said to create the world 'by his wisdom' evokes, as again Kelsey points out, an action in which God gives life and well-being by

---

[147] Kelsey, *Eccentric Existence*, vol. 1, p. 169.
[148] Kelsey, *Eccentric Existence*, vol. 1, p. 168.

'calling, inviting and evoking wisdom in us in ways that do not violate our integrity as human creatures'.[149] God acts as does a wisdom teacher, with a pedagogy of persuasion.

Some Christian thinkers are content to speak of God's loving persuasion in the human consciousness, and especially in what we have been calling the subjective exercise of wisdom, but can only conceive of God's action within physical matter (the objective scope of wisdom) as purely unilateral. But we can surely have no such dualism. If human beings are psychosomatic unities and are truly involved in their environment, it makes no sense to speak of persuasive action in human consciousness and coercive action everywhere else, whether in the human body or the many bodies of the world. If the mind is not separable from the physical substratum of the brain (though this is not the same thing as saying that mind is simply reducible to brain),[150] and the physical brain is embedded in the materiality of the world, then we cannot have any duality in the activity of God. If we are to conceive God's action in and through human wisdom as persuasive, then we must also conceive God as working in this way within the whole of nature, guiding it patiently, offering innovation through the influence of the Holy Spirit and calling out response from it. In the world as an organic community all its members work together, affecting each other. If the human mind can respond to God, then it is not unreasonable to think that there must be something at least akin to response to God at all levels of creation, some 'family-likeness' within the cosmos. Even if we cannot describe exactly how this relationship between God and the physical world works, we do have various kinds of language to point to the mystery.

One kind of language is offered by 'process theology', which envisages all entities in the world as having the capacity for feeling enjoyment, and reaching after satisfaction. In the process vision, 'actual entities' are the smallest building-blocks of the universe, sub-atomic particles in the process of becoming; they aggregate together to form larger scale objects or 'societies', whether persons or inanimate objects such as stones. All entities are 'dipolar', with a mental as well as a physical dimension, though at this lowest level of reality 'mind' has not yet reached consciousness as it has in persons. Individual entities and 'societies' work together in the organic community of the world, influencing and being influenced by others, moving towards the achievement of value and beauty.[151] God offers an aim—or at least parameters for development—to every entity in creation to enable it to grow into fulness of life, and

---

[149] Kelsey, *Eccentric Existence*, vol. 1, p. 170.

[150] See Richard Swinburne, *The Evolution of the Soul* (Oxford, Clarendon Press, 1986), pp. 29–31, 298–300.

[151] A. N. Whitehead, *Process and Reality: An Essay in Cosmology* (New York: Macmillan, 1967), pp. 27–39, 163–6, 373–5.

because there is a mental element (or a 'feeling' aspect) in everything, all can accept, reject or modify the divine purpose.[152]

While thorough-going adherents of process philosophy take this picture of the world as a scientific description, I suggest that it may be better to regard it as metaphor, pointing to an underlying reality which is finally inexpressible. Wisdom literature has poetic ways of including all creation in a covenantal relation to Yahweh; as we have already seen in the question 'Where were you?' of Job 38:4, the wise envisage an activity of Yahweh with the world which is not reducible to human concerns. Yahweh speaks to the sea ('Thus far shall you come'), walks in the deep, accompanies the sun on its rounds, guides the stars, provides for the ravens, is present with the wild deer when they give birth, accompanies the wild hinds when they calve, and plays with the sea-monster.[153]

Another pathway of thought, based on more recent physics than process philosophy, concerns the 'top-down' influence of holistic causation on systems which I have already mentioned in relation to two kinds of complexity— 'chaos' and social interaction. One example, I suggested, is the way that a wider community helps to shape altriusm in a species. Now, some theologians, and notably John Polkinghorne, have suggested that while creaturely acts involve a mixture of energetic and informational causalities, God acts through making a pure entry of information into nature. This is a holistic kind of causation, affecting the patterns of whole, large-scale systems, which then have an influence on their smaller component parts.[154] I suggest that we can place this 'pattern-inducing' activity in the context of the triune life of God. As I have been proposing, the triune God acts in the world through being in movement within God's self, and by drawing created realities into the momentum of divine relationships.

We can thus take up the insight of 'pattern making', though without having to restrict it to the particular scientific language of an 'input of information'. Nor do we have to adopt the notion of causation, in which—as I have observed—ancient wisdom theology is not interested. We can envisage the influence of the patterns of the divine 'dance' of relationships (an image for the traditional doctrine of *perichōrēsis*) on the patterns of behaviour of natural

---

[152] Lewis S. Ford, The *Lure of God: A Biblical Background for Process Theism* (Philadelphia: Fortress Press, 1978), pp. 82–5; Charles Hartshorne, *The Divine Relativity: A Social Conception of God* (New Haven: Yale University Press, 1976), pp. 134–8.

[153] Job 38:11, 16, 19–20, 32, 41; 39:1; 41:5.

[154] John Polkinghorne, *Belief in God*, pp. 62–4; also, Arthur Peacocke, 'God's Interaction with the World' in R. J. Russell, N. Murphy and A. R. Peacocke (eds), *Chaos and Complexity: Scientific Perspectives on Divine Action* (Vatican City State: Vatican Observatory/Berkeley: Center for Theology and Natural Sciences, 1995), pp. 263–4, 272–5, 285–7.

systems, human persons, and human societies.[155] Since patterns in nature are being shaped by participation in the movements of relational love in the divine life, 'top-down' influence does not seem the most suitable term, and we might rather speak of an 'all-embracing' persuasion. God acts by the influence of the divine movements and actions that surround all finite movements and actions, enticing them and inducing them to conform to the purposes of love. Conversation with ancient Hebrew wisdom sets us the challenge of conceiving of a divine *telos* or purpose[156] which is appropriate to a complex world. Conversation with late-modern science and semiotics makes clear that a God of 'simple being' will not meet the challenge, but a God of triune relations surely fits the picture.

The last chapter began with Hannah Arendt's account of the intransigence and self-concealment of the earth-world in the face of human alienation from it. While she sees science as a perpetrator of earth-alienation, beginning with the telescope and progressing in her time to space flight, she judges that science can still be a means for a reintegration of human beings into the world, if certain conditions are fulfilled. First, humanity must recognize that there are limits to the search for knowledge, and especially to discovery of the universe. Otherwise human beings will only search for one new 'Archimedean point' of observation after another, from which to look back on where they have just arrived, and they will only get lost in the immensity of the universe, for the only true Achimedean point would then be an 'absolute void behind the universe'.[157] We might see this admission of limitation as equivalent to the 'humble approach' commended in ancient wisdom. Second, if the journey to the 'Archimedean point'—by space-craft or in the imagination—were undertaken in such a mood of humility, exploration of the universe could actually be a means of opening up the public space that has been shrunk on earth, and which is necessary to hold persons together; humans alone, in distinction from other living things, 'desire to be at home in a "territory" as large as possible'. But third, experience of this larger space together with a recognition of limitation by it will bring human beings back to earth with a new perspective, seeing the earth 'as the centre and home of mortal men', and recognizing the limits of human mortality rather than exalting 'man as the highest being there is'.

Arendt is not hopeful that science will bring about this beneficial development, as it is still fixated (in her view) on 'disposing of terrrestial nature from

---

[155] Here Graham Buxton, in his *Trinity, Creation and Pastoral Ministry: Imaging the Perichoretic God* (Milton Keynes: Paternoster, 2005), pp. 130–42 has taken up and extended my argument in my *Participating in God*, pp. 146–7.

[156] 'ēṣah, עֵצָה: Prov. 19:21. Cf. Isa. 5:19, the 'policy' of Yahweh attacked by opponents of the prophet; see McKane, *Prophets and Wise Men*, pp. 65–8.

[157] Arendt, *Between Past and Future*, p. 278.

outside', handling nature 'from a point in the universe outside the earth'.[158]
She does not look for any transcendent reality that might enable human beings
to experience the humbling sense of the 'wider space' that she desires. However, her insight that moving into a larger space can enable us to overcome
alienation on earth and find ourselves at home here is surely what is affirmed
theologically by the image of the Trinity. Finding ourselves in a space 'as large
as possible', in the room opened up for us between movements of relation that
are infinitely different from each other, we can heal the breach between
ourselves and the earth. In that complex world known by ancient wisdom,
explored by modern science and affirmed in postmodern theory of signs, the
triune God moves all things precisely by being in movement, and by attracting
the world into formation by the complex patterns of the divine dance. So if 'the
fear of the Lord is the beginning of wisdom', this fear is not only humility
before the limits of the unknown, but fascination with the beauty of the sacred.

[158] Arendt, *Between Past and Future*, p. 278.

6

The Seeing Self and Wisdom as Observation

THE SELF AS OBSERVER

The ability to observe the world around us has long been associated with being truly human. The image of the seeing eye is at the heart of the scientific enterprise, the reflections of the philosopher, and the work of the artist. In science, for instance, cosmologists find it highly significant that a human mind has evolved which can *observe* the origin of the universe; through radio-telescopes, cameras on space-probes, electron colliders, and spectrum analysis we can now 'see' the Big-Bang, or at least the state of the universe a micro-second after it. The universe is thus a 'self-observing system', and scientists think this offers evidence that there must be interconnnections between the various forces and principles of physics. The universe, we may say, participates in itself. One scientist, writing in a collection on the theme of complexity, ventures into the domain of the artist and produces a picture of the universe in which a huge eye—in the manner of Salvador Dali—contemplates the tail of its own curved stalk, or its own point of beginning.[1]

Then, in philosophy, there is a tradition since Plato which has used the analogy of sight for the human intellect, and we readily use terms such as 'insight', 'point of view,' theory (from the Greek *theoria*, sight) and 'world-view' for our grasp on reality. 'Have you considered', asks Plato, 'how lavish the maker of our senses was in making the power to see and be seen?'[2] The phenomenon of vision has given rise to metaphors, images and concepts that shape thought, as the Western intellectual tradition has drawn on the inter-action between light, reason, and sight in Greek philosophy. Hannah Arendt remarks that:

---

[1] John Wheeler, 'Information, Physics, Quantum: the Search for Links', in W. H. Zureck (ed.), *Complexity, Entropy and the Physics of Information* (Redwood City: Addison-Wesley, 1990), p. 8.
[2] Plato, *Republic* 507c, 508b.

> From the outset in formal philosophy, thinking has been thought of in terms of *seeing*... The predominance of sight is so deeply embedded in Greek speech, and therefore in our conceptual language, that we seldom find any consideration bestowed upon it, as though it belonged among things too obvious to be noticed.[3]

More negatively, in his essay 'White Mythology', Derrida identifies the imagery of sight as an example of the way that truth claims in texts of philosophy often turn out to be only inherited metaphors which are now being manipulated to serve human interests. The 'white' in the title evokes the light often associated with the faculty of vision, and exposes a world where the 'whiteness' of light becomes a symbol for prejudice in many different cultural contexts: 'The white man takes his own mythology, Indo-European mythology, his own *logos*, that is the *mythos* of his idiom for the universal form of that which he must still wish to call Reason.'[4]

In the realm of the visual arts, there is an awareness that the eye penetrates beyond the mere surface of perception. In his novel, *The Vivisector*, Patrick White explores the way that the eye of the artist is like a scalpel, cutting away the outer skin of things and people to penetrate to the inner core. His central character, Hurtle Duffield, is regenerated in his creative imagination through his tempestuous sexual relationship with Nance Lightfoot; as he transfers her body to oil and canvas,

> A sense of freedom started him whistling and singing, until he realised the wrestling match was on: to recreate the body as he saw it without losing the form of flesh... What he conceived that day was vegetable in form and essence... Like all human vegetables she was offering herself to the knife she only half suspected.[5]

The image of the knife is central to White's view of the artistic vision, and is reflected in the title of the book. Duffield is born 'with a knife in his eye', and his half-sister Rhoda accepts as she goes to live with him in old age that it will mean being 'vivisected afresh, in the name of truth—or art'.[6] To get at the reality of his subject, the artist must uncover layers of protection, and so runs the risk of destroying what he loves. Similarly, in an essay of 1929 simply called 'Eye', Bataille explored anxieties engendered by the experience of surveillance by the eye of the artist. The slitting of the eye in the film *Un Chien Andalou* by Luis Buñuel and Salvador Dali symbolized, he claimed, the way that the eye was related to cutting, both as perpetrating violence and suffering it.[7]

---

[3] Hannah Arendt, *The Life of the Mind* (New York: Harcourt Brace Jovanovich, 1978), pp. 110–11.

[4] Derrida, 'White Mythology', in *Margins*, p. 213.

[5] Patrick White, *The Vivisector* (Harmondsworth: Penguin Books, 1973), pp. 199–200.

[6] White, *The Vivisector*, p. 445.

[7] Georges Bataille 'Eye' in *Visions of Excess: Selected Writings 1927–1939*, ed. Allan Stoekl, trans. A. Stoekl, C. R. Lovitt, D. M. Leslie (Minneapolis: University of Minnesota Press, 1985), p. 19.

There are, indeed, problems when the human subject is typified as an observer of its context. In earlier chapters we explored the way that the wisdom writers of Ancient Israel regarded the practice of wisdom as observation of the world, bidding pupils 'Look, look there!'[8] We have found, however, that the wise are well aware that there are always limits to the power of observation, due to the complexity and extent of the material to be surveyed, and that this is recognized by modern as well as ancient thought. Another modern caution over the seductive image of seeing is the warning against projecting an illusory 'self' that can be supposedly observed by the inner eye of the mind, in detachment from relation to the world and others.[9] But perhaps an even greater danger, exposed by a great deal of late-modern thought, is that an eye which sees all, a self which surveys all, will tend to dominate and exploit the world, and especially other persons.

The 'cutting gaze' may have a therapeutic aspect when it comes from an artist such as White depicts, but Emmanuel Levinas points out that the faculty of sight can be employed for a totalizing approach to life in which everything is subordinated to a particular theory or ideology.[10] This is an instance of what cultural theorists call a 'scopic regime', when social practices of vision are closed down into one ruling vision.[11] Totalitarian thinking aims to gain a panoramic view of all things, fitting other persons into an all-embracing point of view, such as in a system of absolute Spirit or universal Being. Systems of totality assume that selves are all 'the same', often conceived as rational selves within an all-inclusive reason. Others are then seen either as extensions of the observing self, 'more of the same', or as objects to be manipulated for the advantage of the individual or the social unit: 'it is incontestable that objectification operates in the gaze in a privileged way'[12] writes Levinas, and 'The light, brightness, is intelligibility itself; making everything come from me.'[13] But, urges Levinas, this viewpoint does not do justice to others as we meet them for the first time in their strangeness, face to face.[14] They inhabit their own world, and are 'altogether other', with hidden depths of alien existence. The self is thus confronted with the challenge of the altogether other, which is infinite in being unlimited, and which shatters our expectations. This is an 'infinity', an infinite demand, which must not be confused with 'totality'.

---

[8] See Chapter 4, the section called 'Cautiousness in the Instruction Literature of Proverbs', and Chapter 4, the section called 'The Confidence and Caution of Wisdom'.

[9] See the beginning of Chapter 3.

[10] Levinas, *Totality and Infinity*, pp. 188–91, 295–7.

[11] See Hal Foster, introduction to Foster (ed.), *Vision and Visuality* (Seattle: Bay Press, 1988), p. ix.

[12] Levinas, *Totality and Infinity*, p. 188.

[13] Levinas, *Time and the Other*, p. 68.

[14] Levinas, *Totality and Infinity*, pp. 194–7.

We are tempted to 'open our eyes and enjoy the spectacle'.[15] But if we are to have 'regard' for others in the sense of caring for them, then we must keep our eyes shut, and in the face of infinity our 'orientation towards the Other can lose the avidity proper to the gaze only by turning into generosity.'[16] For Levinas, the space between the self and the other, between the self and the world, cannot be bridged by the faculty of sight. It can only be filled with language, and especially the spoken word. The questioning glance of the other, the 'face' of the other, is calling for a response which must be made in words. 'I' must be ready to put my own world into words and to give it to the other in an act of sheer generosity. While Levinas here uses a visual image of 'face', he immediately reinterprets it in terms of 'expression', especially in verbal terms, exceeding any attempts to measure what is seen by the standard of the observing self: 'The face of the Other at each moment destroys and overflows the plastic image it leaves me, the idea existing in my own measure...It *expresses itself.*'[17] It is this that leads Levinas to what seems a scandalous disinterest in particularity: in the ethical relation one must not even notice the colour of another's eyes,[18] lest our gaze makes the other an extension of the self, just 'more of the same'. Levinas proposes that, while the Hebrew Bible suggests a visible 'face-to-face' encounter between Moses and God on Sinai, what the text really relates is an exposure to the divine verbal command, since all God promises to show is his back (Ex. 33:23).[19] Levinas links ethics firmly to the Hebraic prohibition of visual images, and contrasts it favourably with the Greek obsession with connecting light, sight, and visible form.[20]

The Good, asserts Levinas, comes before any totalizing system of Being.[21] Where an all-inclusive system is concerned, even the *sacrifice* of self to it can offer no escape from egotism, or from a domineering subjectivity. But in conversation with others there is room for growth through the dynamics of question and answer. In speaking to others we pay attention to them, and become aware, both of the ultimate ethical demand they make upon us and our own inner egocentric attitudes.[22] This was a philosophy that Levinas developed in the context of the European Holocaust, when the Jewish Other was being subjected to an objective rational system or 'final solution'. Levinas is thus prepared to think that there is one practice among the arts that belongs

---

[15] Levinas, *Totality and Infinity*, p. 130.

[16] Levinas, *Totality and Infinity*, p. 50.

[17] Levinas, *Totality and Infinity*, p. 51.

[18] Emmanuel Levinas, *Ethics and Infinity*, p. 85.

[19] Emmanuel Levinas, 'Revelation in the Jewish Tradition' in Levinas, *Beyond the Verse. Talmudic Readings and Lectures*, trans. G. D. Mole (London: Continuum, 2007), p. 141.

[20] 'Reality and its Shadow' in Seán Hand (ed.), *The Levinas Reader* (Oxford: Blackwell, 1989), pp. 141–2.

[21] Levinas, *Otherwise than Being*, pp. 122–3.

[22] Levinas, *Totality and Infinity*, pp. 72–7.

to the realm of the personal other; this is the practice of poetry, that relies on *sound* rather than vision. Poetry and the ethical are both forms of 'saying' (*Le Dire*). In contrast to sight, which attempts to construct the world, sound is a mode of transcendence. He writes:

> There is . . . in sound—and in consciousness understood as hearing—a shattering of the always complete world of vision and art. Sound is all repercussion, outburst, scandal. While in vision a form espouses a content and soothes it, sound is like the sensible quality overflowing its limits, the incapacity of form to hold its content.[23]

In his protest against the imperialism and illusion of vision, Levinas represents a widespread trend of a suspicion about visuality in twentieth-century French philosophy. 'More than any other sense', writes Luce Irigaray, 'the eye objectifies and it masters.'[24] Discourse about the 'eye' and 'the gaze' is related to the Cartesian observing subject which detaches itself from the world and seeks to dominate it; this is a pervasive model of knowledge in the 'Enlightenment', a term which is itself a visual metaphor. Alongside the picture of the mind as a *camera obscura*,[25] a key image appealed to here is the 'Panoptikon' proposed by Jeremy Bentham in 1791. Outlining a plan for an ideal prison, Bentham envisioned a circular arrangement of cells, all of which were to be visible to a jailor in a tower in the centre, who was himself hidden by an ingenious arrangement of shutters from the prisoners' own gaze. In the thought of Foucault and others, the Panoptikon (the 'Seeing All') was a symbol of the Enlightenment project to subject everything to the oversight of an unreciprocal and rational gaze; the setting of the prison underlines that the apparatus of spectacle and surveillance is central to the maintenance of disciplinary and repressive power in the modern world.[26]

Amid this rejection of 'ocularcentric discourse',[27] Derrida sounds a more moderate tone, especially in his dialogue with Levinas. On the one hand he is sympathetic with Levinas' rejection of the centrality of ocular metaphors in the phenomenological project of Husserl, with its emphasis on 'the world of light'. Summing up and agreeing with Levinas' critique, Derrida writes: 'Therefore, there is a soliloquy of reason and a solitude of light. Incapable of respecting the Being and meaning of the other, phenomenology and ontology would be philosophies of violence.'[28] Derrida criticizes Husserl's privileging of an

---

[23] Levinas, *Outside the Subject*, trans. M. B. Smith (London: Athlone Press, 1993), pp. 147–8.

[24] Luce Irigaray, interview in Marie-Françoise Hans and Gilles Lapuge (eds), *Les Femmes, la Pornographie et l'Erotisme* (Paris: Seuil, 1973), p. 493.

[25] See the beginning of Chapter 3.

[26] Foucault, *Discipline and Punish. The Birth of the Prison*, trans. A. Sheridan (New York, 1979), p. 217.

[27] Jay, *Downcast Eyes*, p. 3, chooses this form of expression for his comprehensive study, to which I am endebted.

[28] Derrida, *Writing and Difference*, pp. 91–2.

Augenblick—a timeless instant, a 'blink of an eye' in which the 'scene of ideal objects' appears intuitively to the consciousness.[29] This appears to Derrida to be confusing the presence of the self with 'the immediate present', in which the *eidos* or visual idea assumes the 'self-same identity of the actual now'; this not only undermines the movement of time but confirms a metaphysics of absolute presence, in which something is 'beingful' by imposing its presence violently on the world and others.

However, Derrida is equally critical of Levinas' replacement of 'seeing' by 'speaking and hearing'. In Hussserl's project itself, Derrida points out, the presence of the self is secured by the observer's hearing his own voice within: 'This self-presence of the animating act . . . this inwardness of life with it-self . . . supposes, then, that the speaking subject hears himself in the present.'[30] By the *phōnē* (voice), expressed in spoken language, the self attempts to bring what is signified into a 'relationship of essential and immediate proximity to the mind'.[31] In verbal speech, thought seems to be present in an unmediated way to the consciousness because 'the phenomenological "body" of the signifier seems to fade away at the very moment it is produced; it seems already to belong to the element of ideality.'[32] So speakers may try to get *behind* the signs or text of the world, *beyond* the messages given out by myriad things in their differences from each other—whether these signs are in body language or actual words. 'Self-presence must be produced', comments Derrida critically, 'in the undivided unity of a temporal present, so as to have nothing to reveal to itself by the agency of signs.'[33] This means that speaking can be as tyrannical as surveillance with the eye. Derrida underlines that for Husserl the voice which seeks to bring the signified into the direct presence of consciousness is a 'wilful activity' of the subject. Derrida here translates Husserl's statement that the subject 'means' (*bedeuten*) to say something as 'wills' (*vouloir-dire*) to express itself.[34] Thus he suggests that people can use their voice to command or cajole others into conformity to themselves or their system. The 'voice' may be a symptom of the fact that they are trying to impose themselves, asserting an immediate presence which ignores the world of difference (embodied in signs) which is shaping them.

To be sure, Levinas is proposing that we should be listening to the voice of the *other*, and Derrida can invoke the 'ear of the other' as undercutting the assumed authority of the author or speaker and their self-authenticating self-signing, for 'it is the ear of the other that signs'.[35] But Derrida thinks that the 'conversation' Levinas commends is nevertheless always in danger of being

---

[29] Derrida, *Speech and Phenomena*, p. 62.   [30] Derrida, *Speech and Phenomena*, p. 78.
[31] Derrida, *Of Grammatology*, p. 11.   [32] Derrida, *Speech and Phenomena*, p. 77.
[33] Derrida, *Speech and Phenomena*, p. 60.
[34] Derrida, *Speech and Phenomena*, pp. 18, 36.
[35] Jacques Derrida, *Ear of the Other: Otobiography, Transference, Translation*, ed. Christie McDonald, trans. P. Kamuf and A. Ronell (Lincoln: University of Nebraska Press, 1982), p. 51.

used to support the presence of the self, validating the ear as 'the articulated organ that produces the effect of proximity . . . the idealizing erasure of organizing difference'.[36]

Negatively, then, 'speaking' is as likely to be manipulative as 'seeing'. Positively, Derrida wants to give sight a place in the commerce between the self and the world. This is inevitable since Derrida gives 'writing' priority over the voice, maintaining this against both Husserl and Plato,[37] and writing is bound to be related to a visual experience. As writing takes form both in physical signs in the world ('real objects') and in marks on the page, the grapheme must be visible. Derrida is constantly critical of those who want to suppress the materiality of the sign, including its visibility, and to understand it merely as a transparent window onto some world of purely mental discourse.[38] Theatricality and 'spectacle' cannot be entirely replaced by a 'community of speech where all the members are within earshot'.[39] Indeed, the play on words central to his thinking between 'difference' and 'deferral' can only be expressed through visual rather aural means:[40] the 'a' in *différance* cannot be heard, but is there to be seen in its idiosyncratic spelling. As Jay perceptively comments, 'As such, *différance* performatively enacts Derrida's "grammatological" resistance to the putative primacy of speech over the written word.'[41]

The significance of the visual also appears in his essay 'Parergon', where Derrida assumes and adapts the distinction which Kant makes between the 'beautiful' and the 'sublime'. The form of the beautiful requires a visible bounding, framing, or limitation—*parergon*—to supplement the lack at its heart, whereas it seems that the sublime defeats the imagination just because it is formless, excessive, or boundless. The sublime thus 'cannot inhabit any sensible form'[42] and presumably escapes visualization, but as if to undermine this dictum Derrida nevertheless includes in the text several paintings by Goya of the figure of a colossus, which he has been using as a cipher for the sublime. By contrast, a 'column' is an example of the framing (*parergon*) of a beautiful object, in this case a building. He now suggests that the colossus and the column have much in common, beyond their etymology root in *kol-*, hinting that even the sublime may have a *parergon*, so constantly defeating our tendency to differentiate between the 'inside' and 'outside' of a constellation of signs.[43] The sublime is 'between the

---

[36] Derrida, 'Tympan', in *Margins*, p. xvii.
[37] Derrida, 'Plato's Pharmacy' in *Dissemination*, pp. 65–84.
[38] Derrida, *Of Grammatology*, pp. 32–4.
[39] Derrida, *Of Grammatology*, p. 136.
[40] See Derrida, 'Différance', in *Margins*, p. 3.
[41] Jay, *Downcast Eyes*, p. 504.
[42] Jacques Derrida, 'Parergon', in *Truth in Painting*, p. 131.
[43] Derrida, 'Parergon', pp. 119–21, 141–5.

presentable and the unpresentable'.[44] In a similar deconstruction of his own critique of the visual, his essay 'White Mythology' demonstrates—as Geoffrey Hartman suggests—that 'the blackness of ink or print suggests that *écriture* is a hymn to the Spirit of the Night',[45] so that we cannot escape from black marks inscribed on a page.

On the other hand, the visuality of a sign will always be limited: what is visible on the surface cannot exhaust the hidden depths of 'difference' that make it what it is, so that a sign can only be a 'trace', or a 'trace of a trace', not a full representation of what is signified. Reflecting on the metaphors of light and vision in the West within the tradition of the university, Derrida makes clear that:

> It is not a matter of distinguishing here between sight and non-sight, but rather between two ways of thinking of sight and light, as well as between two conceptions of listening and voice. But it is true that a caricature of representational man, in the Heideggerian sense, would readily endow him with hard eyes permanently open to a nature that is to dominate, to rape if necessary, by fixing it in front of him, or in swooping down on it like a bird of prey.[46]

The eye that stares without eyelids in the full glare of the light of reason will 'dominate' and 'rape' the world. But it is possible, Derrida muses, to use the eyes in a different way, knowing when to blink or shut them, and when to look appropriately.[47] Perhaps, then, it may be possible to envisage a *seeing* of the world which is not totalizing and dominating, fitting everything into the perspective of the observer.

Taking this conversation between Derrida and Levinas as our starting point, we return now to the wisdom tradition of Israel. Within this context, the paradigm of seeing is central. Through holding a dialogue with this tradition, we may well find clues to a healthy relation between self and others in a seeing the world which avoids manipulation and yet retains a reflexive self that both sees and hears. Because this is a theological dialogue, the place of the triune God within this non-coercive relation will be crucial: is belief in a God who sees all (is 'omniscient') a validation of human visual oppressiveness, or a means of using vision to enable others to flourish? We turn, then, to some passages in the wisdom literature which are concerned with wisdom as the art of observing.

---

[44] Derrida, 'Parergon', p. 143.

[45] Geoffrey Hartman, *Saving the Text: Literature, Derrida, Philosophy* (Baltimore: Johns Hopkins University Press, 1981), p. xix.

[46] Jacques Derrida, 'The Principle of Reason: The University in the Eyes of its Pupils', *Diacritics* 13 (1983), p. 10.

[47] Derrida, 'Principle of Reason', p. 20.

WISDOM AS OBSERVER: PROVERBS 8:22-31

Three passages from different stages of the wisdom movement present wisdom as a female figure who is active on a cosmic scene and who makes herself available to human beings; significantly, she is also some kind of supreme observer of the world. We find these portrayals in Proverbs 8:22–31, The Wisdom of Jesus Ben Sira 24:1–22 and the Wisdom of Solomon chapters 6–9. In the last passage she is portrayed as one who 'spans the world . . . from end to end' and is 'all-surveying' (7:23). She knows and understands all things (9:11), and shares with God the faculty of being a 'witness' and a 'true overseer' of the heart and tongue of human beings (1:6). This portrait of an observer, as we shall see, is in continuity with the picture of wisdom in the earlier two passages.

Now, these passages stand alongside others that portray wisdom in a rather different guise, either as something hidden and inaccessible (Job 28, Ben Sira 1:1–10, Baruch 3:9–4:4), or as something that was once present to hand but has now disappeared or vanished (Proverbs 1:20–33, 1 Enoch 42, 4 Esdras 4:5–5:13, 2 Baruch 48:33–36).[48] The assumption has been made by several scholars, following Rudolf Bultmann,[49] that these three kinds of passages—wisdom as available, hidden and vanished—can be bundled together in order to produce a single underlying 'wisdom myth'. The passages about a *hidden* or *vanished* wisdom are said to be a reflection of an original myth where wisdom comes from heaven, searches for a home, is rejected by human beings and consequently hides herself back in heaven. The passages about an *available* wisdom figure, like the three we are examining in this chapter, are said to represent an adaptation of this myth for Jewish use; in this version, although wisdom is rejected elsewhere, she is is welcomed in Israel as the elect people.[50] Basic to the shape of this presumed myth, we notice, is the notion of wisdom as a kind of mediator between heaven and earth, bridging a gap between two orders of reality. Many scholars and commentators now simply refer to 'the ancient Jewish wisdom myth' as if it were an established fact.[51] Others who

---

[48] Hans Conzelmann has made this useful three-fold classification of available, hidden, and vanished wisdom in 'Paulus und die Weisheit', *New Testament Studies* 12 (1965-66), p. 236; cf. Conzelmann, 'The Mother of Wisdom' in James M. Robinson (ed.), *The Future of our Religious Past* (London: SCM, 1971), pp. 230–43; see esp. p. 240, n.7.

[49] Rudolf Bultmann 'Der Religionsgeschichtliche Hintergrund des Prologs zum Johannesevangelium', originally in *Gunkel-Festschrift* 2 (1923), pp. 3–26; reprinted in *Exegetica. Aufsätze zur Erforschung des Neuen Testaments*, ed. Erich Dinkler (Tübingen: Mohr Siebeck, 1967), pp. 10–35.

[50] Bultmann, *Exegetica*, pp. 15–18; See Ulrich Wilckens, Art. σοφία, in *Theological Dictionary of the New Testament*, ed. Gerhard Kittel, Geoffrey Bromiley, Wilhelm Friedrich. 10 Volumes (Grand Rapids, Eerdmans, 1964–76), vol. 5, p. 509.

[51] e.g. Wilckens, Art. σοφία, p. 508; Wilckens, *Weisheit und Torheit* (Tübingen: Mohr, 1959), pp. 139–70; Conzelmann, 'Mother of Wisdom', 230–43; Felix Christ, *Jesus Sophia: Die Sophia-Christologie bei den Synoptikern* (Zürich: Zwingli Verlag, 1970), pp. 31–42 (adding 11QPs[a]XVIII,

doubt the existence of a single, comprehensive, proto-Gnostic myth in Judaism still find traits and fragments of mythical accounts of wisdom which are gathered together for the theological needs of the moment; such mythical components include being a heavenly mediator and being rejected by humanity.[52]

But we must take serious note of the fact that in the three accounts of 'available' wisdom we are considering in this chapter, in all of which a figure of wisdom offers herself to those who want to learn, there is no hint that she has earlier been rejected by anybody or is hidden in any way. We must examine these portrayals by themselves without any presupposition of a supposed myth, and see what kind of a wisdom they *do* present. In the next chapter I want to examine the picture of a wisdom which is indeed said to be hidden, and in Chapter 11 we shall consider passages about a wisdom that has 'disappeared', but in this chapter we are concerned with the figure of a wisdom who makes herself openly available.

The place to start is with the the earliest version of the story in Proverbs chapter 8. Here wisdom is depicted as a young child, rejoicing, perhaps playing, in the presence of Yahweh when he created the world. Here I have opted for the translation of the Hebrew *'āmōn*, אמון in 8:30 as 'child' or 'darling' (NEB), although there is dispute over this identification since the term could also be rendered as 'master-workman' (NRSV) or 'architect'.[53] The reasons for my choice should become evident in due course, as we get a firmer understanding of what the picture presents:

> The LORD created me at the beginning of his work,
> the first of his acts of long ago. . . .
> When he established the heavens I was there,
> when he drew a circle on the face of the deep,
> when he made firm the skies above,
> when he established the fountains of the deep,

12–15 from Qumran texts); R. G. Hamerton-Kelly, *Pre-Existence, Wisdom and the Son of Man: A Study of the Idea of Pre-Existence in the New Testament* (Cambridge: Cambridge University Press, 1973), pp. 206–15; Rudolf Schnackenburg, 'Logos Hymnus und johanneischen Prolog', *Biblische Zeitschrift* 1 (1957), pp. 69–109. cf. C. H. Dodd, *Historical Tradition in the Fourth Gospel* (Cambridge: Cambridge University Press, 1968), pp. 274–5.

[52] So Burton Lee Mack, 'Wisdom, Myth and Mytho-logy', pp. 47–8, 56–7; *Logos und Sophia*, pp. 16–20, 60–2; M. Jack Suggs, *Wisdom, Christology and Law in Matthew's Gospel* (Cambridge: Harvard University Press, 1970), p. 44; Ben Witherington III, *Jesus the Sage. The Pilgrimage of Wisdom* (Minneapolis; Fortress, 2000), pp. 253–6.

[53] R. B. Y. Scott, 'Wisdom and Creation: The *'āmôn* of Prov. 8:30', *Vetus Testamentum* 10 (1960) provides a good survey of the discussion. 'Workman', from an Akkadian loanword [*ummānu*] is followed by the ancient versions and tradition of interpretation: e.g. LXX, ἁρμόζουσα; Vulg., 'cuncta componens'; Wisdom 7:21and 8:6, τεχνῖτις, Midrash Ber. Rabb. I.1 prefers among four explanations the rendering 'architect' (אומן), taking Torah as architectural plans.

> when he assigned to the sea its limit,
> so that the waters might not transgress his command,
> when he marked out the foundations of the earth,
> then I was beside him like a young child (*'āmōn*)
> and I was daily his delight,
> rejoicing before him always,
> rejoicing in his inhabited world
> and delighting in the human race.
> And now, my children, listen to me:
> happy are those who keep my ways. (Proverbs 8: 22–32).[54]

Several mythological candidates have been proposed as a model for the wisdom who speaks in this poem, including the sexually attractive Canaanite-Phoenician Astarte.[55] The most serious contender for the role is the Egyptian goddess Ma'at, daughter of Atum-Re, the sun-god. Since the *principle* of Ma'at, or 'right order' in the world, is fundamentally important for the wisdom writings of Ancient Egypt,[56] and these have had some influence on the development of Israelite wisdom, on the face of it there seems to be something in the suggestion that the worship of Ma'at in the Egyptian cult may have shaped the figure of wisdom in Israel, and especially in this poem in the book of Proverbs. Those who urge this resemblance refer to a spell in an Egyptian mortuary text which refers to the relationship between Ma'at and the creator-god Atum before the act of creation:

> Nu said to Atum: Kiss your daughter Ma'et, put her at your nose, that your heart may live, for she will not be far from you; Ma'et is your daughter and your son is Shu whose name lives. Eat of your daughter Ma'et; it is your son Shu who will raise you up.[57]

At first sight this may seem a striking parallel to Proverbs 8:22–31: Ma'at is a beloved child before Atum, as wisdom is a child before Yahweh, and the parallel apparently confirms the translation 'child' for *'āmōn* in Proverbs 8 as well as supporting the interpretation of vv. 30–1 as that of a child 'playing'. Christa Kayatz therefore concludes that the Egyptian presentation of Ma'at as a 'beloved child of the gods' has served as a model for the Israelite wisdom

---

[54] NRSV except for translation of *'āmōn*; NRSV has 'master workman'.

[55] Helmer Ringgren, *Word and Wisdom: Studies in the Hypostatization of Divine Qualities and Functions in the Ancient Near East* (Lund: H. Ohlssons Boktrycken, 1947), p. 136; but Astarte/Ishtar does not fit with the picture of some kind of 'bringing forth' of wisdom (Prov. 8: 24).

[56] See Chapter 4, the section called 'Order in Egyptian Wisdom and "Ordering" in Israelite Wisdom'.

[57] I quote the translation of Spell 80 by Raymond O. Faulkner, *The Ancient Egyptian Coffin Texts.* Vol. I , Spells 1–354 (Warminster: Aris & Phillips 1973), pp. 3–85.

child playing before Yahweh:[58] Von Rad has, among others, accepted this suggestion.[59] But a number of objections can be raised against this supposed parallel. Neither in this mortuary text, nor in any extant Egyptian text, does Ma'at use the I–style of address ('I was there ... listen to me') as wisdom does characteristically. Further, the Egyptian spell is not actually about the 'playing' of Ma'at at all; Atum kisses *both* Shu (the air-god) and Ma'at, and the kiss is related to the setting of Ma'at and Shu 'at his nose', which is not a playful game but concerns the cosmic authorization of these divinities. Finally, we ought to give some weight to our previous discovery (Chapter 4) that there is no straightforward identification made between Egyptian Ma'at and a sense of order in Israelite wisdom.

There is, in fact, something less obscure than this supposed parallel in a single text, a solution that the figure of Ma'at also points us towards. In many Egyptian texts Ma'at rides in the solar barque of the sun-god, Re; she directs his course, and Re establishes Ma'at ('right order') in his daily solar circuit, rejoicing in her and living by her:

> O Re, Lord of Ma'at! O Re who lives by Ma'at!
> O Re, who rejoices over Ma'at!
> ... O Re, who established Ma'at after he had created her,
> Joyful is your heart when you see her.[60]

Because of being a travel-companion with Re, in later texts she is celebrated as 'the female sun'.[61] Now, I suggest that in the poem of Proverbs 8 the figure of wisdom appears herself to be a traveller on the circuit of the sun; she recounts her journey of witness at creation as following the path of the sun, which in ancient Near Eastern thought traverses the three dimensions of heaven, earth, and underworld:

> when he drew a circle on the face of the deep,
> when he made firm the skies above ...
> when he assigned to the sea its limit ...
> then I was beside him, like a young child. (8:27–30)[62]

Further, by claiming to be 'the first of Yahweh's acts of old' (v. 22) wisdom describes her place in the created order in terms which are reminiscent of the sun in the thought of the time. It is the sun above all in Egyptian texts which is

---

[58] Christa Kayatz, *Studien zu Proverbien 1–9* (Neukirchen-Vluyn: Neukirchener, 1966), pp. 93–5.

[59] Von Rad, *Wisdom*, p. 153.

[60] Cit. Kayatz, *Studien*, p. 97. Compare the 'offering of Ma'at' ritual in Alexandre Moret, *Le Rituel du Culte Divin Journalier en Éypte* (Paris, E. Leroux, 1902 1902), pp. 138–47.

[61] Cit. Ringgren, *Word and Wisdom*, p. 46.

[62] NRSV except for translation of *'āmōn*.

described as the 'first-born' in order of creation.[63] Confirming the reading 'child' for *'āmōn*, the morning sun which appears over the horizon each day is portrayed as the 'young sun', beginning as a child or young man. In Egyptian mythical thinking the sun was a child in the morning, a grown man at midday, and an old man in the evening.[64] An Egyptian ascription praises the emerging sun as 'The goodly beloved youth to whom the gods give praise.'[65] The hymns to the rising sun in the Egyptian Book of the Dead have the constant motif of a child being rejoiced over by the gods.[66] So it is said 'Re, born early every day.'[67] Thus the continuing emergence of the young sun each day was conceived as a repetition of creation; the first-born of creation is a young child again each day:

> The idea of a new beginning each day is expressed not only in the emergence of the sun–god from the primeval ocean, but also in the idea of him as a new-born child who within the span of a single day lives out his life . . . each day nature starts quite afresh, as at the first time.[68]

So wisdom in this poem declares that *every day* (v. 30) she was at the side of Yahweh as a young child, that she was his delight and rejoiced in the inhabited world. Here wisdom is not only the cause of joy, but herself rejoices. Again in the hymns to the sun in the Book of the Dead the rejoicing of the sun is a fixed item.[69] The widespread nature of these motifs can be seen from Psalm 19, where the sun at the beginning of the day is presented as young (though older than a child), rejoicing, and ready to travel:

> In the heavens he has set a tent for the sun,
> > which comes forth like a bridegroom leaving his chamber,
> > and like a strong man runs his course rejoicing . . .
> Its rising is from the end of the heavens,
> and its circuit to the end of them,
> and nothing is hid from its heat. (vv. 4–6).[70]

The description here is admittedly closer to the emergence of the Babylonian sun-god, Shamash, as a hero than to the Egyptian conception,[71] but this only

---

[63] E.g. 'A Hymn to Amon-Re', trans. J.A. Wilson, ANET, p. 365a; 'Universalist Hymn to the Sun', ANET, 368a.

[64] 'The God and His Unknown Name of Power', ANET, p. 13b: 'I am Khepri in the morning, Re at noon, and Atum who is in the evening'. See Morenz, *Egyptian Religion*, p. 145.

[65] *Hymn to Amon-Re*, ANET, p. 365a.

[66] E. A. Wallis Budge, *The Book of the Dead*. 3 Volumes (London: Kegan Paul, 1901), vol. 1, p. 11, 'Thou beautiful and beloved man-child'; cf. pp. 4, 13, 14, 15, 16.

[67] 'Hymn to Amon-Re', ANET, p. 367a.

[68] Morenz, *Egyptian Religion*, p. 168. Cf. 'Hymn to the Gods as a Single God', ANET, p. 372a.

[69] Budge, *Book of the Dead*, vol 1, pp. 8, 11, 17 (although rejoicing is due mainly to defeat of the chaos dragon).

[70] NRSV, but v.4 altered.

[71] So A. A. Anderson, *Psalms*. 2 Volumes. New Century Bible (London: Oliphants, 1972), vol. 1, pp. 169–70. See Lambert, *Babylonian Wisdom Literature*, pp. 129–30.

shows that we are dealing with a widespread image which Israel inherited from several sources—Egyptian, Canaanite, and Babylonian. The advantage of the image of the solar circuit in hymnology is that it is readily comprehensible, and requires no detailed mythological background at all.

It seems likely then that the same simple picture lies behind *both* Ma'at (i.e. order) in Egypt and personified wisdom in Israel—the pattern of the movement of the sun. Any similarities between wisdom and Ma'at do not come from a modelling of wisdom on Ma'at (or any goddess), but the fact that both are depicted as following the path of the sun.[72] The reason for clothing personified wisdom in Proverbs 8 in the garments of the sun is not to present her as a sun-goddess. She is portrayed as treading the path of the sun in order to endow her with a key solar function, that of being the great observer of everything that takes place in the world.

Egyptian wisdom literature pictures a world 'under the eye of Re' the sun-god, who perfectly establishes Ma'at (good order).[73] Later in Israel, Koheleth repeatedly speaks of a world 'under the sun', meaning a world which is there to be seen and to be the object of investigation by wisdom:

> I applied my mind to search out by wisdom all that is done under heaven . . . I have seen everything that is done under the sun. (Eccl. 1:13–14)[74]

A similar expression, 'in the eyes of this sun,' appears in a judgement context in the Succession Narrative,[75] which probably bears the marks of wisdom influence. As we have read in Psalm 19, 'nothing is hid from its heat'.

The fact that the relationship of wisdom to Yahweh is not being modelled on the relationship of Ma'at to Re (against Christa Kayatz) is made clear by transfer of imagery applied elsewhere to the sun (first-born, new born every morning, rejoicing) directly to personified wisdom. There is no myth here, no relation of a daughter-goddess to a father-god, but only a cluster of poetic images; what matters is the imagery of the *solar circuit* itself. The fact that the sun-god, Re, in Egypt is male is no objection to the atttribution of solar imagery to the female figure of wisdom in Israel; what is being applied is imagery that could *become* a myth, but in itself is simply a simile ('like the

---

[72] An extended argument for the solar imagery of wisdom can be found in Paul S. Fiddes, 'The Hiddenness of Wisdom and Later Judaism', unpublished DPhil thesis, University of Oxford, 1976, pp. 92–112. Now see Edward L. Greenstein, 'The Poem on Wisdom in Job 28' in Ellen Van Wolde (ed.), *Job 28: Cognition in Context* (Leiden: Brill, 2003), pp. 256–8, who identifies a solar image for wisdom shaped by the Babylonian Shamash, but concludes—contrary to my stress on availability—that 'Wisdom is as remote as the sky; it is in a divine realm.'

[73] See Chapter 4, the section called 'Order in Egyptian Wisdom and "Ordering" in Israelite Wisdom'.

[74] Also Eccl. 1:3, 1:9, 2:11, 2:17, 2:18, 2:19, 2:20, 2:22, 4:1, 4:3, 4:15, 5:18, 6:12, 8:9, 8:13, 8:15, 8:17, 9:3, 9:6, 9:9. Direct references to 'seeing' or searching out' under the sun are: 3:16, 4:7, 5:13, 6:1, 8:17, 9:11, 9:13, 10:5.

[75] 2 Samuel 12:11–12. Cf. 21:6, 9. For the idea generally, see Ben Sira 17:15–19, 23:19, 42:16.

journey of the sun'). Thus, the portrayal of wisdom as walking the path of the sun confirms that in the poem of Proverbs 8 she is a personification, not a distinct person or hypostasis independent (or even partly independent) of Yahweh. Wisdom is an extension of Yahweh's own personality, since sun-imagery is above all applied to Yahweh. *He* is the great cosmic observer, as is made clear in Psalm 104, where all the living things of the world are given life and joy by the over-watching deity:

> These all look to you to give them their food in due season:
> When you hide your face, they are dismayed . . . (vv. 27–9)

This psalm contains a theme which also appears in Egyptian and Babylonian hymns to the sun on its daily course, namely a review of all the vegetation and creatures of the world which flourish under the gaze of the deity.[76] The similarity is particularly close to the Hymn to the Aton[77] and the inclusion of the sun itself as an item in the created order which God has made (vv. 19, 22) does not refute this connection: the transference to Yahweh emphasizes his superiority in both teaching the sun its course and exercising the functions elsewhere ascribed to a sun-god.

While elements of an Egyptian hymn to the sun-god have probably been transferred to Yahweh in this psalm, the general theme of a world under the eyes of Yahweh is pervasive throughout Israel's hymnody, and the imagery of 'over-seeing' has probably been gathered from the Canaanite cult of the high-god El (once established in Jerusalem) as well as from Egyptian and Babylonian religion.[78] However, when wisdom in Israel has begun to merge with teaching of the Torah, and when the Psalms in the post-exilic period begin to reflect wisdom concerns, it is this already-established area of Yahweh's vision of the world that forms a link between earlier psalmic material and wisdom materials. This can be seen, for instance, in Psalm 33:

> The LORD looks down from heaven:
> he sees all humankind.
> From where he sits enthroned he watches
> all the inhabitants of the earth. (vv. 13–14)

This confession accords with many other Psalms (for example, 2:4, 9:8, 10:14, 11:4, 14:2, 26:2, 102:19). It is emphasized that Yahweh knows the hearts of all.

---

[76] 'Hymn to Amon-Re', ANET, p. 366; 'A Universalist Hymn to the Sun, ANET, p. 368a; Lambert, *Baylonian Wisdom Literature*, pp. 127–29, 137.

[77] 'Hymn to the Aton', ANET, pp. 370–1. A direct literary debt is argued by J. H. Breasted *The Dawn of Conscience* (New York: Scribner's, 1934), pp. 366–9.

[78] See H.-J. Kraus, *Psalmen*. Biblische Kommentar. 2 Volumes (Neukirchen: Neukirchener Verlag, 1960), vol. 1, pp. 197–205; vol. 2, pp. 709, 713. William F. Albright, *Yahweh and the Gods of Canaan* (New York: Doubleday, 1968), pp. 193–94, is more cautious. Aubrey R. Johnson, 'The Role of the King in the Jerusalem Cultus', in S. E. Hooke (ed.), *The Labyrinth* (London: SPCK, 1935), pp. 83ff identifies Elyon as a solar deity.

But this then introduces a reflection on the limitations of human preparations which parallels Proverbs 21 :31, and just as there it gives a specific example of what has been said about the futility of human 'counsel and plans' against Yahweh (v. 10 cf. Proverbs 21: 30):

> The war horse is a vain hope for victory
> and by its great might it cannot save (Ps. 33:17)

> The horse is made ready for the day of battle
> but the victory belongs to Yahweh (Prov. 21:31)

The Psalm concludes with typical wisdom injunctions to 'fear' Yahweh and to 'wait for him' (vv. 18–20, cf. Proverbs 16:3, 6), addressed to those who live under 'the eye of Yahweh'. In a Psalm, therefore, which shows a continuity with other earlier Psalms of praise about Yahweh's omniscience, the characteristic wisdom theme is introduced of human complementary lack of vision and control over events.[79] Similarly, in Psalm 19 an old lyric about the overseeing sun ('there is nothing hid from its heat' v. 6) is immediately followed by a new theme: direction really comes from the 'law of Yahweh' (v. 7) calling for 'the fear of Yahweh' (v. 9).

Psalm 139 is also illuminating in this regard. It is rarely classified as a 'wisdom psalm',[80] and has the form of a 'judgement doxology' used in a plea for vindication, where the accused suppliant in a cultic lawsuit invokes the divine examination of hearts in order to establish his innocence. A central part of this cultic act is the doxology which confesses the perfect vision of God, and it has been suggested that this doxology is rooted in the Jerusalem tradition of El as world-ruler and overseer.[81] Similar appeals to the testing of Yahweh are found in Psalms 7:9, 17:3, 26:1, 44:21, Jer. 11:4, 12:3. Here, however, I suggest that we find that the doxology is marked strongly by the features of the solar circuit, perhaps inheriting this same imagery from the Jerusalem tradition.

The suppliant confesses that he cannot escape God's searching gaze even if he travels in the tripartite dimensions of the world: heaven, Sheol, and 'the farthest limits of the sea', that is, the extremity of the earth disc:

---

[79] Psalm 33 is not usually classified as a wisdom psalm; but Morna Hooker, 'Where is Wisdom to be Found?', in Ford and Stanton (eds), *Reading Texts*, p. 119, rightly draws a parallel with Proverbs 8.

[80] Eissfeldt, *Introduction*, p. 15; Roland Murphy, 'A Consideration of the Classification "Wisdom Psalms"', Supplement to *Vetus Testamentum* 9 (1962), p. 156, n.8, notes this but does not follow him. Samuel Terrien, 'Amos and Wisdom', in James L. Crenshaw (ed.) *Studies in Israelite Wisdom* (New York: KTAV, 1976), p. 451, classifies Psalm 139 as 'a hymnic meditation of the sapiential type' and proposes that it has 'come from a milieu strongly influenced by the Joban poetic school'.

[81] So E. Würthwein, 'Erwägungen zu Psalm 139', *Vetus Testamentum* 7 (1957), pp. 165–82 and Kraus, *Psalmen*, vol. 2, pp. 915–17. Cf. 1 Sam. 2:3, Josh. 7:19.

O Lord, you have searched me and known me . . .
Where can I go from your spirit?
Or where can I flee from your presence?
If I ascend to heaven, you are there;
if I make my bed in Sheol, you are there.
If I take the wings of the morning
and settle at the farthest limits of the sea,
even there your hand shall lead me . . . .(vv. 1, 7–10)

I suggest that this travelling is described as following the path of the sun: the psalmist takes 'the wings of the morning', that is starts at the east with the morning sun[82] and goes to dwell in the 'farthest limits of the sea', that is crosses to the western horizon. There follows a passage about the illuminating of the night ('even the darkness is not dark to you'), which commentators have had difficulty with. But surely the image of the path of the sun is continuing: the traveller descends into the underworld where there is darkness,[83] but the sun traverses the underworld during the night after setting in the west, and brings light even to that realm ('night is as bright as the day').[84] If the Egyptian solar sequence is in mind, then the description is even more striking, since in Egyptian thought it is by way of the west ('farthest limits of the sea') that the dead make their way into the underworld. Even, then, if the Psalmist were to travel with the sun he could not escape Yahweh's observation: the implication is that Yahweh sees as perfectly as the sun, indeed more completely. So the poem expands on the area of depth (vv. 12–16): Yahweh who can see into Sheol (Job 17:13, 26:6, Prov. 15:11) can also see into the depths of a mother's womb (v. 13) which is like the earth, mother of all living things: 'when I was being made in secret,/ intricately woven in the depths of the earth/Your eyes beheld my unformed substance' (vv. 15–16).

While imagery of the sun and divine observation, applied to Yahweh, have no doubt been inherited from doxologies in the cult, here they are now employed for a wisdom end. At the beginning and end of the psalm it is stressed that Yahweh's powers of observation expose the limited vision of humanity:

Such knowledge is to wonderful for me;
It is so high that I cannot attain it. (v. 6)

. . . . your thoughts, O God!

---

[82] Cf. Malachi 4:2. With the wings we may compare the popular icon of a winged solar disc, found in Judah from the reign of Josiah; see McKay, *Religion in Israel under the Assyrians* (London: SCM, 1973), pp. 52–3, 115. The wings of the disc probably derive from Horus, who combines with Re to form Re-Harakhti, 'the horizon-dweller, Horus of the east', 'Hymn to Amon-Re', ANET, 367a.

[83] Cf. Job 17:11–13 where the 'bed in Sheol' is in parallel with darkness.

[84] Morenz, *Egyptian Religion*, p. 208. See ANET, p. 368a: 'thou has completed the hours of the night'; 372a: 'conducting the mysteries of the underworld'.

How vast is the sum of them!
I try to count them – they are more than the sand;
If I were to complete the count I would have to be continually with you.
    (vv. 17–18)[85]

As in Psalm 33, humanity is not simply under the eye and so the judgement of Yahweh, but must recognize that human grasp of the vast expanse of the world is limited. With the confession 'I would have to be continually with you' we may compare the boast of wisdom herself in Proverbs 8:30: 'I was beside him . . . daily'. We notice however, that it is *possible* to compare human vision with divine vision, however despairing the result: the two activities have something in common. The psalmist can envisage himself travelling, at least to some extent, on the path of the sun, and he can try to count the works of God. We may contrast this typically wisdom sense of limitation with another judgement doxology – that in Amos 9:2–4 ('Though they dig into Sheol . . . though they climb up to heaven . . . though they hide from my sight at the bottom of the sea'); although this is expressed in overtly similar terms to Psalm 139, the only point made is the impossibility of escaping from Yahweh's gaze. There is no sense of the human sapiential project.[86]

We conclude then that the portrayal of Lady Wisdom as a young child in Proverbs 8:22–31, as a personification of Yahweh's wisdom, and so as the perfect observer, has a background in Israelite worship. But as in a number of psalms, the solar imagery is being re-employed for the purposes of wisdom instruction.

DIVINE AND HUMAN SEEING

When we identify the basic pattern of a solar circuit in the movements of personified wisdom we can come to some important conclusions. The first is that divine and human wisdom differ vastly, but only in degree. There is a sharing in the same enterprise–that is, seeing the world; there is a divine *and* human seeing which always exist together. This is made clear by the peda-gogical setting of the picture of Lady Wisdom.

The figure of wisdom in Proverbs 8 belongs in the context of other presen-tations of wisdom either as a personification or as a valuable object[87] in the instruction and sentence literature of Proverbs. Once we have disposed of the

---

[85] V. 18 my translation: emending MT הקיצתי ('I awake') to הקצותי ('I come to an end, complete'), with BH margin, NEB, NRSV; so also Kraus, *Psalmen*, vol. 2, p. 914.
[86] Terrien, 'Amos and Wisdom', pp. 450–1, notes that only wisdom material, Psalm 139 and Amos 9:2 refer to Yahweh's vision of Sheol.
[87] Proverbs 2:4, 3:15, 14:24, 13:14, 16:16, 16:22, 23:23, 24:3, 24:14.

idea that there is a goddess-myth behind the figure of Proverbs 8, then we shall cease to look for fragments of the myth in other presentations; we shall be open to see diverse expressions of both human and divine wisdom, and a shifting boundary between them. Some of the portrayals are literary objectifications or personifications of a *human* teacher's wisdom, depicted as a precious thing or precious person. So the teacher urges a 'father's instruction':

> Let your heart hold fast *my* words;
> keep *my* commandments and live.
> Get wisdom; get insight: do not forget, nor turn away
> from the words of *my* mouth.
> Do not forsake *her*, and *she* will keep you;
> love *her*, and *she* will guard you . . . .
> Prize *her* highly and *she* will exalt you;
> *she* will honour you if you embrace *her*. (Prov. 4:5–8. My italics).

There is a natural shift here from 'my' to 'her' and 'she', from the wise man to Lady Wisdom. Such a wisdom is the guardian of the paths of life ('when you walk it will lead you', 6:22), which is what one would expect from wisdom as the art of observation. In 2:1–5 the command of the teacher 'accept my words and treasure up my commandments' is followed by an objectification of wisdom as a precious object (like silver and treasure); but in 7:1–5 the instruction 'My child, keep my words' is followed by a personification: 'Say to wisdom, "You are my sister"'. The very fact that *ḥokmah* is a feminine noun in Hebrew (like *sophia* in Greek) may have helped to prompt this imaginative move to embodiment in a female form.

Other appearances of the figure of wisdom are more clearly personifications of the wisdom of *God* who has perfect vision of the world, and they invoke divine authority. In 1:20–33 wisdom first 'cries out' her invitation, but then 'laughs' (*śāḥaq*, שׂחק) at the calamity of the obstinate which recalls the mocking laughter of the heavenly observer in Psalms 2:4 ('He who sits in the heavens laughs') and 37:13. This laughter has a joyful counterpart in wisdom's pleasure in observing the created world in Prov. 8:30, where the same verb is used (*śāḥaq*, שׂחק).[88] Another indication of a personification of divine wisdom is the use of the 'I'-style of address by wisdom, which has resonances of the 'presentation formula' of a god found widely in the Ancient Near East, and notably in the 'I' speeches of Yahweh in Second Isaiah (to which we shall return). Such 'I'-speeches are found in Prov. 1:20–33 (the wisdom who cries out and laughs), 8:1ff (the wisdom who takes her stand at the crossroads) and 9:1ff (the wisdom who builds her house). Most obviously, the wisdom of Proverbs 8:22–31 presents herself in the first person: 'The Lord created me at the beginning of his work.' There is no reason why mythological colouring should not have been added to

---

[88] Cf. Psalm 104:26.

the figure of wisdom, whether representing human or divine wisdom, at all stages of development; for example, detail may have been 'borrowed'[89] from the sexually-attractive Ishtar in the personifications of human wisdom in 4:6–9 and 7:4 as well as in the I–style personifications of wisdom in 8:1–21 and 9:1ff, in order to counter the worldly attractions of the 'strange woman'. But this colouring does not mean that the personifications are *based* on a myth, and this kind of borrowing seems totally out of place in the wisdom of the poem in Proverbs 8:22–31, where the predominant imagery is that of birth and childhood.

Boundaries are thus blurred between personifications of human and divine wisdom. Moreover, while the poem of Proverbs 8:22ff presents the figure of a divine wisdom, the purpose appears to be to commend the authority of the wisdom being taught by *human* teachers. When the same wisdom continues

> Hear instruction and be wise,
> and do not neglect it.
> Happy is the one who listens to me,
> watching daily at my gates,
> waiting beside my doors . . . (8:33–4)

it is the actual doors of the wisdom school that are being evoked. As in 8:1ff and 9:1ff Lady Wisdom is offering the pupil an invitation to learn in a school, as a life-giving alternative to the house of the prostitute. The wisdom of God and humanity is the same kind of faculty, differing only in degree. While human beings are warned to respect the limits of their vision, Lady Wisdom's skills of observation are stressed so that there is common ground between human and divine activity. The same point is made, though in a different way, by the provision of a matching portrait to that of Lady Wisdom in the 'Capable Wife' of 31:10–31. As Claudia Camp has suggested, the present collection of the Book of Proverbs has been structured by final redaction into literary and theological form by the frame of 'Woman Wisdom' (her title for Lady Wisdom) at the beginning (chapters 1–9) and the ode to the Capable Wife at the end, with many verbal similarities between them.[90] Like Wisdom, for instance, the Wife is more precious than jewels (3:15; 31:10), she 'laughs' at calamity to come (1:26; 31:25), and opens her mouth to speak what is wise (8:6–7; 31:26). Here a human practitioner of wisdom is painted in the same colours as the Lady Wisdom who is a personification of God's own wisdom.

It is in this context that von Rad's intriguing theory of the nature of personified wisdom cannot be sustained. Based on a parallel with Ma'at, he suggests that the wisdom in Proverbs 8 is not a divine attribute at all, but is the 'orderliness' which God has implanted in creation, 'something which . . . now

---

[89] Ringgren's term: see *Word and Wisdom*, pp. 134–5, 149.
[90] Claudia V. Camp, *Wisdom and the Feminine*, chapter 6, *passim*.

mysteriously inhabits it', and which could also be described as 'world reason' or 'meaning'. This 'order' he suggests is depicted in personal terms because that is the best way to fix in words the human experience of being addressed by this order, of hearing an 'organizing voice' which is described in the other appeals of personified wisdom in Proverbs 1–9.[91] But the problem with this theory (apart from the fact that the primary concern of wisdom is not with hearing but with seeing) is that it detaches the *figure* of wisdom entirely from the *faculty* of wisdom, whether divine or human. As we have seen, the Israelite concept of 'wisdom' is not directly to be equated with the Ma'at (world-order) of the Egyptian instructions;[92] *ḥokmah* is both the subjective faculty of perceiving and the object of that perception, continually transgressing the boundary between the self and world. Wisdom thus cannot simply be some aspect of the world. Moreover, identifying it as 'orderliness' loses the ambiguity and overlap between divine and human exercise of wisdom which the figure of Lady Wisdom expresses.

David Kelsey appears to offer a more nuanced version of von Rad's theory. He rightly stresses that Israelite 'order' is very different from Egyptian Ma'at: there is no static order in creation, but an active process of 'ordering' in which God is personally engaged. Reality which is other than God is 'sufficiently orderly' to be a reliable context in which living creatures can flourish, but it is not the fixed order of either Egyptian Ma'at or Hellenistic *Logos*, so that when order is discerned it is 'localized, ad hoc and patchy', only to be formulated in 'rules of thumb'.[93] This is an 'ambiguity of the observable scene'[94] which corresponds to the need for humility I have myself expounded. However, he still denies that the figure of Lady Wisdom (or 'Woman Wisdom') is a personified attribute of God, and aligns it/her only on the side of creation: 'Wisdom personified is not God. Rather she represents creation'.[95] She 'lies at the foundation of the creaturely realm, to which she gives abundant life and the guarantee that creation is understandable'.[96] So while not representing fixed principles of order, she is 'a quasi-personal socially teleological ordering of the contexts and networks of our own personal agencies', maintaining the sorts of order that 'make for the well-being of human life'.[97] This looks like a sophisticated version of Von Rad's theory. But Kelsey then modifies his account in what seems to me to be a crucial way. He asserts that God 'relates to [Woman Wisdom] and to all creatures through her' and 'her relation back

---

[91] Von Rad, *Wisdom*, pp. 55–6.
[92] See Chapter 4, the section called 'Order in Egyptian Wisdom and 'Ordering' in Israelite Wisdom'.
[93] Kelsey, *Eccentric Existence*, vol. 1, p. 173.
[94] Kelsey, *Eccentric Existence*, vol. 1, p. 211.
[95] Kelsey, *Eccentric Existence*, vol. 1, p. 163.
[96] Kelsey, *Eccentric Existence*, vol. 1, p. 225.
[97] Kelsey, *Eccentric Existence*, vol. 1, p. 239.

to God is a trope for the how creation generally ought to relate to the Creator'. What matters, he maintains, 'is to stress the relationships in which she stands'.[98] Woman Wisdom is a trope, then, for the way that God relates to the world and the way that world relates to God, living in tune with the call to wisdom.

In terms of the poetic form of Proverbs 8 there seems then no reason to deny that Lady Wisdom appears here as a personified attribute of God. She is indeed the way that God deals with the world. To deny this is to neglect the interaction in *hokmah* between subject and object, between wisdom as faculty and wisdom as the 'order' in the world. It also obscures the common ground between human and divine wisdom, which Kelsey himself wants to maintain. It does not matter that, as Kelsey objects, Lady Wisdom is said to be 'created' by God (v. 22). This passage is not presenting a mythical theogenesis, but a poetic personification, and any number of metaphors might be drawn upon to describe the relation between wisdom and God; the image of creation is immediately balanced by those of being 'set up' and being born ('brought forth'). When we come to think theologically about divine wisdom, then indeed the notion of a 'trope of relating' is helpful. The triune God cannot be conceived as a superior Mind with wise thoughts, and we should understand a divine 'attribute' of wisdom as a movement of relating to the world which draws out a 'vocation to be wise for the well-being of creation'.[99]

One suspects that there is something more behind Kelsey's denial that Lady Wisdom in this poem represents an attribute of God. This in fact appears in his assertion that 'in creating, God precisely does not give us Godself. To the contrary, what God gives in creating is thoroughly-other-than-God'.[100] Kelsey's point is that God's gift in creation is the quotidian, or everyday reality, 'gratuitously given to each human creature and each human creature gratuitously given to the quotidian'. This is the context into which we are born, a network of relations in which we engage in practices of interaction with the natural world, other humans, and God.[101] Through these practices, as Kelsey explains in an earlier book, knowledge of God arises indirectly.[102] I agree that knowledge of God only arises through being in the world, but this is not the whole story. I suggest that this knowledge emerges precisely because in daily practices, in a created context which is 'other-than-God', we are participating in a self-giving movement of God. This is a giving of God's self which is aptly pictured in the dancing and travelling of Lady Wisdom, who is thus portrayed as an attribute of God. This is why seeing the world is knowing God.

---

[98] Kelsey, *Eccentric Existence*, vol. 1, p. 225.
[99] Kelsey, *Eccentric Existence*, vol. 1, p. 224.
[100] Kelsey, *Eccentric Existence*, vol. 1, p. 214.
[101] Kelsey, *Eccentric Existence*, vol. 1, p. 193.
[102] Kelsey, *To Understand God Truly*, pp. 123–9. See the first section of Chapter 1.

NO WISDOM MYTH: BEN SIRA 24:1–22

If the first result of identifying the pattern of the sun in the wisdom of Proverbs 8 is to underline the common project of divine and human seeing, the second is to make redundant the kind of wisdom myth suggested by Bultmann. Those who ascribe to a hypothetical 'ancient wisdom myth' look for an ancestor of the figure of wisdom who supposedly appears there (a 'Mother of Wisdom'),[103] and think they have found her in the traces of a goddess who speaks in this poem. On the contrary, we have seen that the poem gives us a *picture* of the sun, not a *myth* of a cosmic mediator. Nevertheless, to back up the idea of a widespread myth, some have claimed that yet another model underlies the portrayal of wisdom in these Hebrew poems, namely the Egyptian and Hellenistic goddess Isis. Some commentators have found her traces in the poem of Proverbs 8 itself,[104] and rather more detect her presence in the way that wisdom presents herself in our second passage, Ben Sira chapter 24.[105] Here wisdom speaks thus:

> I am the word which was spoken by the Most High;
> it was I who covered the earth like a mist.
> My dwelling-place was in high heaven;
> my throne was in a pillar of cloud.
> Alone I made a circuit of the sky
> and traversed the depths of the abyss.
> The waves of the sea, the whole earth,
> every people and nation were under my sway.
> Among them all I looked for a home . . . . . . (vv. 3–7)

The Isis of Hellenistic texts similarly praises herself in speeches in the first person: 'I am Isis, sovereign of every land' she declares.[106] Her supporters also

---

[103] Conzelmann, 'Mother of Wisdom', pp. 332–3. Bruce Vawter, 'Prov. 8, 22: Wisdom and Creation', *Journal of Biblical Literature* 99 (1980), p. 206, argues for a 'wisdom-myth' without pronouncing on its provenance.

[104] W. L. Knox, 'The Divine Wisdom', *Journal of Theological Studies* 38 (1937), pp. 230–7; B. L. Mack, *Logos und Sophia*, pp. 38–42 integrates Isis with Ma'at as a compound Ur-goddess of wisdom; cf. Leo G. Perdue, *Wisdom Literature. A Theological History* (Louisville: Westminster John Knox, 2007), pp. 74–5.

[105] e.g. Joseph Blenkinsopp, *Wisdom and Law in the Old Testament* (Oxford: Oxford University Press, 1983), pp. 143–5. Ringgren, *Word and Wisdom*, p. 144, rejects the parallel with Isis for Prov. 8, but accepts it for Ben Sira 24; so also von Rad, *Wisdom*, p. 160. Johann Marböck, *Weisheit im Wandel: Untersuchungen zur Weisheitstheologie bei Ben Sira* (Bonn: Peter Hanstein, 1971), p. 49 accepts it definitely for Ben Sira 24, and only tentatively for Proverbs 8. Against this identification, see Eckhard J. Schnabel, *Law and Wisdom from Ben Sira to Paul: A Tradition Historical Enquiry into the Relation of Law, Wisdom and Ethics* (Tübingen: Mohr Siebeck, 1985), pp. 19–20, citing my thesis, 'The Hiddenness of Wisdom', p. 132.

[106] Aretalogy line 3 from Cyme; as cited in Werner Peek, *Der Isishymnus von Andros und Verwandte Texte* (Berlin: Weidmann, 1930), p. 122, who collects the different versions of the aretalogies extant from Cyme, Ios, and Cyrene (fragment), together with the Isis-hymn from Andros. Kayatz, *Studien*, pp. 86–92, has laid particular stress on the parallel between the aretalogies and the speeches of Wisdom.

point out that she makes a journey in a circuit throughout the cosmos,[107] that she is called the 'first-born' of the gods,[108] and that she is engaged in a search.[109] She is actually looking for her consort, Osiris, but if this is interpreted as a search for a home (which seems to be stretching matters more than a little) then there might be some parallel with wisdom here. We read on in the poem of Ben Sira:

> Among all [nations] I looked for a home:
> In whose territory was I to settle?
> Then the Creator of the Universe laid a command upon me;
> My Creator decreed where I should dwell.
> He said, 'Make your home in Jacob;
> find your heritage in Israel' . . . . .
> Thus he settled me in the city he loved
> and gave me authority in Jerusalem. (vv. 7–11)

By identifying wisdom with Isis, some scholars thus find support for a primal myth of wisdom as suggested by Bultmann—namely a widespread story of wisdom's descent to earth, search for a home and return to heaven, especially as Isis is portrayed as departing to heaven after being metamorphosized with Osiris into gods. This outline has supposedly been adapted and extended in a Jewish way by the settling of wisdom in Jerusalem instead. Conzelmann concludes confidently: 'Sirach 24:3ff is an especially clear example of the adaptation of the wisdom-myth to Jewish thought: this is obviously beyond dispute.'[110]

But it should be clear by now that there is no need to find an echo of Isis either in Proverbs 8 or in Ben Sira 24. Any similarities come from a simple, common, underlying pattern, the movement of the sun through the cosmos, for Isis like Ma'at rides in the sun-boat of Re. Indeed, in later Isis theology she has taken over the functions of the sun-god altogether. The process of transference is described in a Temple inscription from Philae:

> Sun–goddess in the circle of the sun . . . second sun,
> Ruler of all under the gods.
> Her father Re gave to her his light-hill and his throne
> that she might rule his kingdom in heaven and on earth.[111]

While Osiris officially replaced Re in the new Hellenistic–Egyptian cult, and Isis as his consort was often thought of correspondingly as the moon-goddess,

---

[107] Conzelmann, 'Mother of Wisdom', 236–8; cf Cyme 3 (Peek, p. 122), Cyrene 4 (Peek, p. 129).

[108] 'Eldest daughter of Chronos': see Knox, 'Divine Wisdom', p. 232; Cyme 5 (Peek, p. 122).

[109] Knox, 'Divine Wisdom', pp. 232–4, citing Plutarch *de Iside et Osiride*, 356e.

[110] Conzelmann, 'Mother of Wisdom', p. 234.

[111] H. Junker, *Der Grosse Pylon des Tempels der Isis in Philā* (Wien: Rohrer, 1958), pp. 53.17, 56.17, 57.14–15.

in fact her popularity outstripped him and she was thought of as exercising solar functions as well.[112] This is described in the Isis-aretalogies first in implicit terms, speaking of a worldwide power of rule and observation:

> I am Isis, sole ruler for ever, and I oversee the ends of the earth and sea: I have authority, and though I am but one I oversee them.[113]

Then more explicitly she declares: 'I am in the beams of the sun'[114] and 'I draw up the courses of the sun and the moon.'[115] In accordance with this claim, her initiates repeat the circuit of the sun in the mystery rites.[116]

The female figure of wisdom in the Hebrew poems is Israel's *own* use of a basis solar theme, which is used in differing ways in the Egyptian Ma'at and the later Isis. There is, of course, no reason why the Israelite development (wisdom) and the Egyptian–Hellenistic one (Isis) should not have coalesced at some stage; there might be some evidence of this in the Wisdom of Solomon, to which we shall come shortly, but there is no reason to suspect it in Ben Sira 24. The 'circuit' of earth and heaven that is implied in Proverbs 8:22ff is clearly stated in Ben Sira 24:4–6, and as in the former poem, the three dimensions of sky, earth disc, and abyss are reviewed. We have already exposed the basic solar pattern that underlies this: wisdom is a figure treading the path of the sun. This picture is, however, one of a series of metaphors describing wisdom. The opening self-predications of wisdom as something coming from the mouth of God (v. 3a) and as 'mist' (v. 3b) have no parallel in the Isis-aretalogies. The issuing of the divine word recalls a number of Israelite accounts, such as Genesis 1:3;[117] the 'mist' is more difficult to locate, but it may well be a combination of Genesis 1:2 and 2:6.[118] There is no need to find the solar pattern in these opening self-predications. Wisdom is defined first as a divine wisdom that can be expressed in words: Yahweh spoke and breathed out wisdom at the very beginning. The content of that wisdom is then described in terms of a perfect grasp of the world, by means of the image of the sun's circuit. Only if we insist on wisdom's being a hypostasis or modelled on a goddess does this progression of images confuse. While the image of

---

[112] E.g. Apuleius, *Metamorphoses* 11.2 ('thy feminine light...according to the wanderings, near or far, of the sun'); cf. 11.4, Isis as moon.

[113] Cyrene 4. Also Isidore, *Etymologiae* III.24–5, in *Supplementum Epigraphicum Graecum*, 550: 'Thou dost mount the chariots of the swift-running sun and traverse the world completely, looking down and observing the awful works of ungodly and godly men . . .'; cit. Conzelmann, 'Mother of Wisdom', p. 238, n.37.

[114] Cyme 44, cf. 45 (Peek, p. 124).

[115] Cyme 14 (Peek, p. 122).

[116] Apuleius, *Metamorphoses*, 11.6, 23.

[117] Also Gen 1:6 (including the creating of the primal light), Ps. 33:6, Ps. 147:15, 18, 19; Isa. 45:23, 48:3, 55:11.

[118] So G. H. Box and W. O. E. Oesterly, *Sirach*, in R. H. Charles (ed.), *Apocrypha and Pseudepigrapha of the Old Testament*. 2 Volumes (Oxford: Clarendon Press, 1913), vol. 1, pp. 396–7; Marböck, *Weisheit im Wandel*, p. 59.

'mist' (water-vapour) points forward to the image of wisdom as abundant water (v. 25, recalling the four rivers of Genesis 2), it is perhaps significant that the intent of 'mist' image is the same as the solar pattern—total comprehension of the earth: 'I covered the earth like a mist'. The self-predication of wisdom in verse 4 sites her in the heavens, whence she treads her circuit:

> My dwelling–place was in high heaven;
> My throne was in a pillar of cloud.

The pillar of cloud recalls the exodus cloud (cf. Wisdom of Solomon 10:17), providing a link between distinctive images taken from the Israelite Torah and the pattern of the over-watching sun. It is only if, like Conzelmann, we are already convinced that this poem is originally a hymn to Isis that we will read this 'pillar' as a papyrus stalk on which Isis sits as the Crown Goddess of Lower Egypt.[119] Nor will we interpret, like Conzelmann, wisdom's 'walking the circuit of the world' as 'Isis creates the cosmos.' Wisdom certainly rules the cosmos but she does not, unlike Isis, claim to be a creator. As in Proverbs 8 she is an observer, travelling through the three dimensions of heaven, earth, and abyss, or height, breadth, and depth.

What seems to be the most striking parallel between Lady Wisdom and Isis, and the feature that has most persuaded scholars about an association, is the common style of self-predication between the two figures, a self-praise in the first person:

'I came from the mouth of the Most High . . .
I made a circuit of the sky.' (Ben Sira 24)

'Ages ago I was set up . . .
then I was beside [Yahweh] like a young child . . .
delighting in human beings.' (Prov. 8)

'I am Isis, sole ruler for ever, and I oversee the ends of the earth and the sea.'
(Isis-aretalogy, Cyrene 4)

'I am (ἐγω εἰμι) Isis, Sovereign of every Land . . .
I am she who found corn for men.' (Isis-aretalogy, Cyme 3, 7)

However, there is an extensive record of an I-style of speech by gods or divinities in use throughout the Ancient Near East, long before the Isis-aretalogies. Following Bultmann's classification,[120] we may note that a *presentation* formula (the god introduces himself: 'I am . . .') is often followed by a *qualification* formula (the god praises himself by relating his attributes and

---

[119] Conzelmann, 'Mother of Wisdom', p. 236.

[120] Rudolf Bultmann, *The Gospel of John*, trans. G. R. Beasley-Murray (Oxford: Blackwell, 1971), pp. 225–26. Cf. Walther Zimmerli, 'Ich bin Yahwe', in Zimmerli, *Gottes Offenbarung* (München: Kaiser, 1963), pp. 14–16, 33–5, who distinguishes similarly between *Selbstvorstellungsformel* and *Selbstprädikationsformel*.

deeds). In the Hebrew Bible the presentation formula 'I am Yahweh' or 'I am He' usually introduces a qualification which takes the form of a word of salvation or (and) law:[121]

> I am Yahweh your God, who brought you out of the land of Egypt, out of the house of slavery; you shall have no other gods before me. (Exodus 20:2–3)

It might be observed that there is a difference between the self-presentation of wisdom in Proverbs 8:22–31 and most of the self–presentations of Yahweh elsewhere in the Old Testament. While the latter are concerned with the actions of Yahweh in the history of Israel, both in backward glances to past actions and in promise of future saving action, Proverbs 8 is concerned with timeless, unhistorical, and cosmological reflections upon the place of wisdom in the order of the world and its health-giving nature.[122] Kayatz has thus argued that there is reason to associate Proverbs 8 with Isis and her reign in the cosmos, with implications for Ben Sira 24 as well. But we may reply that the difference is least between Proverbs 8 and the qualificatory speeches of self-praise in Second Isaiah.[123] There—in dispute with the gods of Babylon—Yahweh makes an appeal to his cosmological activity in creation:

> I am Yahweh, and there is no other.
> I form light and I create darkness. (Isa. 45:6–7)

While this admittedly still differs from Proverbs 8 in that creation here is envisaged in continuity with the *Heilsgeschichte* of Israel, the Isis-aretalogies also contain claims of Isis to have acted in people's history.

Now, some of the qualification-formulae spoken by Yahweh in Second Isaiah have the character of *recognition* formulae (to continue to use the classification supplied by Bultmann). In the context of the lawsuit with the Babylonian gods, Yahweh asserts that 'it is he' who has 'performed and done this' (41:4). In the 'recognition' formula the speaker identifies himself with someone or something that is already known, or expected, or awaited: but that thing or person is now recognized as having been the speaker all the time. This claim for recognition as part of the self–praise can take the form of the phrase, 'It is I who, . . .' Examples can be found for Isis,[124] but also—and earlier—for Yahweh in Second Isaiah: 'In that day they shall know that it is I who speak; here am I' (52:6).[125] The claim for recognition may also simply take the form

---

[121]   e.g. Gen. 15:7f, 17:1f, Ex. 20:1f, Lev. 18:30, 19:14; Gen. 26:24, 28:13, Ex. 3:6, Hosea 13:4f, Ezek. 36:23, Isaiah 41:10, 13, 14, 43:3–5, 46:4, 51:12.

[122]   This is stressed by Kayatz, *Studien*, p. 92.

[123]   For identification of the speeches, see Claus Westermann, *Isaiah 40–66*, trans. D. M. G. Stalker (London: SCM, 1966), p. 26. Relevant texts are 41:4, 43:13, 44:6, 44:24, 45:5–7, 45:18–22, 46:9, 48:12.

[124]   Cyme 9 (Peek, p. 122); also Cyme 7, 10 (Peek, p. 122). For further Greek examples, see Bultmann, *Gospel of John*, p. 226.

[125]   Bultmann, *Gospel of John*, p. 226, gives as other examples of the recognition-formula Isaiah 41:4, 43:10, Deut. 32:39, to which we must surely add Isa. 48:10.

'I am (he)' ('*ᵃnī hū*', אֲנִי הוּא) followed or preceded by clauses of self-praise. The assertion has a natural place in a dispute,[126] and it is often introduced by a question ('Who is this?' 'Who has done this?'). This is the case in Isaiah 41:4, though here the question is voiced by the claimant himself (Yahweh) rather than by the other party in the dispute.[127]

> Who has performed and done this?
> . . . I, Yahweh, the first,
> and with the last I am he ('*ᵃnī hū*', אֲנִי הוּא)[128]

In Second Isaiah, God enters this claim for recognition over against the Babylonian deities, and with reference to the events of creation with which his hearers are familiar. He claims recognition as *that* creator God whose activity is familiar in the creation myths of Babylon with which the exiles are surrounded:[129]

> I am he ('*ᵃnī hū*'); I am the first
> and I am the last.
> My hand laid the foundations of the earth,
> and my right hand spread out the heavens (48:13)

We might translate: 'It was *my* hand that laid the foundations of the earth . . .' Now, this example of speeches of self-praise used to claim recognition in Second Isaiah is illuminating for the speeches of wisdom in Proverbs 8 and Ben Sira 24. In Proverbs 8 wisdom claims *recognition* as having been all the time what has been ascribed to the sun: 'I was beside him, a young child.' That is, wisdom is making the claim: 'It was *I* who was a young child beside him', or 'it was not the rising sun, but I'. We may compare also v. 27: 'When he established the heavens, there was I'—i.e. 'I was there, not the sun as you thought.'

A similar use of the I-style of self-praise to claim recognition with what is already familiar to the hearer can be seen in Ben Sira 24:3–4. There wisdom refers to items of divine activity from sacral history, and we might translate:

> I am that word which was spoken by the Most High;
> It was I who covered the earth like a mist . . .
> it was I who was enthroned in the pillar of cloud.

And so we can read, 'Mine was the dwelling-place in high heaven', i.e. not the sun. This surely is the force of the next phrase: 'alone (μονη) I made a circuit of

---

[126] So Bultmann, *Gospel of John*, p. 226, for the Johannine examples of ἐγω εἰμι. Raymond E. Brown, *The Gospel According to John*, I–XII, Anchor Bible (New York: Doubleday, 1966), p. 537, suggests that they are direct recollections of Second Isaiah.

[127] In the terminology of Westermann, 'Bestreitung' rather than 'Streitgespräch' proper: 'Sprache und Struktur der Prophetie Deuterojesajas' in Westermann, *Forschung am Alten Testament* (München, Kaiser Verlag, 1964), pp. 124–34.

[128] cf. Isa. 45:21.

[129] cf. Westermann, *Isaiah 40–66*, pp. 23, 56–7.

the sky'. Rather than being a direct transfer from Isis' claim that she 'alone ($\mu o\nu\eta$) oversees the ends of the earth' (as is claimed),[130] the adverb 'alone' carries the force: 'It was I on my own who made the circuit of the sky, not the sun'. The sun, of course makes a circuit of the earth, but it does not exercise this particular circuit of oversight and rule.

The speeches of personified wisdom in Proverbs 8:22ff and Ben Sira 24 have, then, a similar form to the speeches of Yahweh in Second Isaiah, in that creation traditions are used for speeches of self-praise which are of the 'recognition' kind. Moreover, the images of creation themselves recall the the tradition of the High God who has perfect vision of the world. This is well exemplified in Isaiah 40, which contains a series of questions which belong to the pattern of a recognition-formula within a dispute, although the recognition claim is being made by the prophet on Yahweh's behalf rather than directly by Yahweh:

> 18   To whom then will you liken God? . . .
>
> 21   Have you not known, have you not heard?
>   Has it not been told you from the beginning? . . .
>
> 22   *It is he who* sits above the circle of the earth
>   and its inhabitants are like grasshoppers;
>   who stretches out the heavens like a curtain,
>   and spreads them like a tent to live in . . .
>
> 25   To whom then will you compare me,
>   or who is my equal? says the Holy One.
>
> 26   Lift up your eyes on high and see: who created these?
>   He who brings out their host and numbers them.

The participial clauses in vv. 22 and 26 ('he who sits', 'he who brings out') have the force of claims for recognition, answering the disputation questions in vv. 18 and 25. In this dispute there is place for the worldwide vision of the High God: the inhabitants of the earth are like grasshoppers when seen by the one who sits above the circle (*ḥūg*, חוג) of the earth. With this, we may compare Proverbs 8:27:

> When he established the heavens *I was there*
> When he drew a circle (*ḥūg*, חוג) on the face of the deep

In both passages the claim for recognition (in italics) is combined with the idea of observation, using the distinctive term 'circle' (*ḥūg*) which occurs only here and in Job 22:14 and 26:10.

---

[130] Conzelmann, 'Mother of Wisdom', p. 238, 'the cardinal point . . . is the remarkable $\mu o\nu\eta$', p. 238; see Cyrene 4.

We conclude then that the mere incidence of the 'I–am' formula fails to confirm the influence of Isis aretalogies upon Israelite wisdom texts. Positively, the use of the qualification-formula in a way which is a claim for recognition helps to confirm the image of personified wisdom as the cosmic observer we have already discerned, since wisdom claims identity with an image with which the reader is already familiar—the pattern of movement of the sun. It may be that another claim for recognition is also going on. I have already suggested that the poem of Proverbs 8 operates as an authentication for human wisdom, claiming antiquity for the wisdom of the teacher. The 'I'-form might then be seen as formula in which the human teacher asks to be recognized as having the same kind of vision of the world as divine wisdom.

In both Proverbs 8 and Ben Sira 24, wisdom offers herself to human beings with no hint that she might have been previously rejected, but the difference between the two poems is that in Ben Sira wisdom comes from her cosmic circuit to dwell in Jerusalem. In the poem itself it is assumed that this indwelling is in the form of the Torah, the written law of the covenant which is Israel's possession (vv. 8–12). The comment of Ben Sira which follows the poem (vv. 23ff) makes this identification explicit:

> All this is the covenant book of God Most High,
> the law which Moses enacted to be the heritage of the assemblies of Jacob . . .
> No man has ever fully known wisdom;
> from first to last no one has fathomed her.

Those who postulate a widespread 'myth of wisdom' propose that this coming to dwell in Jerusalem is a Jewish adaptation of an ur-myth in which the search of wisdom for a home is frustrated. If we align wisdom with Isis we will struggle to find any point of connection here, since in the Isis aretalogies there is no mention of searching for anything. The myths and festivals of Isis do speak of her quest for Osiris,[131] but this is hardly a search for a place to dwell. There is, in fact, no need to find a precedent in any postulated myths for the idea of the descent of wisdom from her cosmic pathway, either resulting in frustration or success. Her coming to earth is likely to be a *new* mythologizing, a way of speaking about the special gift of wisdom to Israel in the Torah.[132] The poem presupposes that the identification of wisdom with Torah has by now been made in the development of wisdom thinking, and it builds upon the already existing picture of wisdom as a solar traveller in order to express it.

---

[131] 'Hymn to Osiris', cit. Erman, *Literature of the Ancient Egyptians*, p. 143. The most complete account is Plutarch, *de Iside* 356e. Cf. the searching of Psyche (Apuleius, *Metamorphoses* 5.28) and Demeter (Herodotus, *Histories* 2.59) with whom Isis was identified.

[132] C. T. R. Hayward, 'Sirach and Wisdom's Dwelling Place' in Stephen C. Barton (ed.), *Where Shall Wisdom be Found?* (Edinburgh: T & T Clark, 1999), p. 36 suggests that Wisdom's journey is modelled on the journeying of Israel throught the desert with the ark.

The wisdom who is well known to walk the path of the sun (but is not literally the sun) takes up permanent residence in Jerusalem.

Before she comes to dwell in Jerusalem, we notice that wisdom is not portrayed as a transcendent reality, dwelling in heaven and inaccessible to human beings as the proposed myth is thought to say. As in Proverbs 8 she is a personification of the wisdom that is exercised by wisdom teachers, and pre-eminently by God. As such, she is close at hand to all people. Dwelling in Jerusalem is a metaphor for becoming even more accessible to readers of the Torah; but there is no reason to suppose that she ceases to walk the paths of the world, and this becomes apparent in our next text.

WISDOM AS SURVEYING AND PERMEATING ALL: WISDOM OF SOLOMON 6-9

The third poem about an accessible Lady Wisdom is in the Wisdom of Solomon chapters 6–9 (not of course a book literally *by* Solomon, but by an author building in the first century BCE on the story of a famously wise monarch). The portrait of wisdom here exhibits a continuity of pattern with the figures of Proverbs 8 and Ben Sira 24:

> She is more radiant than the sun, and surpasses every constellation; compared with the light of day she is found to excel; for day gives place to night, but against wisdom no evil can prevail. She spans the world in power from end to end, and orders all things benignly. (Wisd. 7:29–8:1)

A later passage confesses that human beings are unable to grasp the vast scope of heaven and earth with their bewildering variety of contents, and so need the aid of wisdom who can (9:16–18). As in Proverbs 8, wisdom has perfect knowledge of the world because she was present at the creating of it by God:

> And with you is wisdom who is familiar with all your works and was present at your making of the world, who knows what is pleasing *in your eyes*. (9:9)[133]

So the solar symbols continue as images of vision; as in the earlier poems wisdom is a figure who 'spans the world' in the path of the sun, and who is 'all-surveying' (7:23). But in this portrayal there is a strengthening of the invitation to a community of life with wisdom, which is already implied in the portrayal of an 'available' wisdom in Proverbs 8 and Ben Sira 24, and which is under-lined by the invitations to learn in Proverbs 1–9.

This new emphasis on communion with wisdom comes partly from the description of wisdom as *permeating* all as well as observing all. In one and the

---

[133] My translation.

same phrase she is said to be 'all-surveying' and 'permeating all spirits' (7:23). Two images are drawn upon by the writer to express this duality—spirit and light. In the first place, the term 'permeation' belongs to the language of spirit, and in her pervading presence in the world wisdom resembles the Stoic world-soul. But unlike the Stoic world-soul this pervading aspect is set off against a personified 'spirit of wisdom' who is 'with God' and can be sent 'from God' (7:8, 9:17).[134] For the first time wisdom is being equated with the Holy Spirit of Yahweh. Speaking about wisdom as Spirit can therefore retain the idea of a wisdom who is 'over against' the world as an observer, while also presenting wisdom within the world as a means of coherence. Both ways of presentation testify to wisdom's grasp of the nature and contents of the world order. This duality is hinted at in 1:6–7, where verse 6 speaks of wisdom-as-spirit sharing God's position as an observer on high, and verse 7 speaks of the divine spirit that permeates all things:

> 1:6 Wisdom is a spirit devoted to man's good, and she will not hold a blasphemer blameless for his words, because God is a witness of his innermost being, who sees clear into his heart ['is a true overseer', $\dot{\epsilon}\pi\iota\sigma\kappa\sigma\pi\sigma s$] and hears every word he says.
> 1:7 For the spirit of the Lord fills the whole earth, and that which holds all things together is well aware of what men say.

This same link between the pervading and the observing presence of wisdom is made in the imagery of light, and here we return to our familiar solar imagery. Light can either be the sun which surveys the world (5:6, 8:1) or the beams of the sun's light which suffuse the world (6:12, 7:25–6). In the former function, wisdom as light belongs to the solar pattern as contained in Proverbs 8, Ben Sira 24. The younger Ben Sira, associating the glory and the wisdom of God, uses the idea of glory in a similar way (Sir. 42:16–18):

> As the sun in its brilliance looks down[135] on everything (observing)
> so the glory of the Lord fills[136] his creation.   (permeating)
> Even to his angels the Lord has not given the power
> to tell the full story of his marvels
> which the Lord Almighty has established
> so that the universe may stand firm in his glory.[137]   (permeating)
> He fathoms the abyss and the heart of man . . . .   (observing)
> and observes the signs of all time.

---

[134] So Hermann Kleinknecht, in Kittel (ed.), *Theological Dictionary of the New Testament*, vol. 6, Art. $\pi\nu\epsilon\upsilon\mu\alpha$ (*Pneuma*), p. 339. Knox, 'Divine Wisdom', p. 237 and J. M. Reese, *Hellenistic Influence on the Book of Wisdom and its Consequences* (Rome: Biblical Institute, 1970), p. 361, unnecessarily find an Alexandrian Stoic-Platonist conflation to explain this duality of wisdom.

[135] Hebrew: 'is revealed'.

[136] Hebrew: 'is over all'.

[137] Hebrew: 'God establishes his hosts to stand firm in his glory'.

Interestingly, the younger Ben Sira, translating the book of his grandfather into Greek, has probably introduced this duality, which is not there in the extant Hebrew text.[138]

We must not make this duality into a systematic polarity between transcendence and immanence, as if we are dealing with a paradox of two realms of being—one 'out there' and another 'in here'. What is refreshing about the wisdom tradition is a natural lack of working with such categories. The duality is closer to the double sense of wisdom I have already remarked upon: wisdom is both a faculty of mind and the field of investigation that lies out in the world, ready to be explored, so crossing the boundary between subject and object. Wisdom as the faculty belonging to God is also there in the world, drawing near to her devotees on the path of daily life; she offers them communion with her, inviting them to walk with her on her own circuit through the cosmos. This is observation that is also sympathetic participation.

In addition to language of 'permeation', communion with Lady Wisdom is expressed in the personal terms of love, and this may indicate that here, finally, we have an association between wisdom and Isis that is missing in the earlier Hebrew poems. If so, the pattern of Lady Wisdom as 'walking the path of the sun' is so firmly established by this time, that there can be no possibility of an Isis myth as having shaped it, or any earlier 'ur-myth' of wisdom. It is the increasing stress on communion with Lady Wisdom which may account for the possibility at this point of a merging between the path of wisdom and the world-circuit of Isis.[139] It may well have a polemical intent, to counter the attraction of the Isis cult for the Jewish community in Alexandria. The popularity of the Isis religion lay in the assurance which her rites offered of comfort in the present by personal union with her, and an assurance about immortality which was grounded in that union. As one scholar of Egyptian religion writes, 'The rite endeavours to bring the person to be initiated into communion with the deity through acts of a most personal kind.'[140] The mortuary rituals of the older Egyptian religion which were effective only for the afterlife were now replaced by 'mortuary rituals' relating in the first place to this life, and only consequently to the life to come. The account of the rites in Apuleius makes significant reference to the course of the sun:

> 'Thou shalt live blessed in this world, thou shalt live glorious by my guide and protection, and when after thine allotted space of life thou descendest to hell, there thou shalt see me in that subterranean firmament shining (as thou seest me now) in the darkness of Acheron'...

---

[138] See three previous notes.

[139] For further suggested similarities see Reese, *Hellenistic Influence*, pp. 46–9. Cf. J. S. Kloppenborg, 'Isis and Sophia in the Book of Wisdom', *Harvard Theological Review* 75 (1982), pp. 57–84.

[140] Morenz, *Egyptian Religion*, p. 247.

I approached near unto hell, even to the gates of Proserpine, and after that I was ravished through all the elements I returned to my proper place. About midnight I saw the sun brightly shine...I was adorned like unto the sun.[141]

As has been suggested by both Reese and Osty,[142] the plague of darkness in Wisdom of Solomon chapter 17 is described in terms of a descent into Hades. We may go further and suggest that it reflects the initiates' descent into the infernal region, where for the 'idol worshippers' the light did *not* shine: it shone for Israel (17:14, 20–1; 18:1) in the pillar of fire (18:3, 'a sun that would not scorch them') and the Torah (18:4). Once more we can trace the persistent picture of the sun that travels through the heavens and below the earth (cf. Psalm 139: 8–12).

It seems then that the emphasis of the Isis cult upon personal communion has encouraged the association of wisdom with Isis in this book, when earlier there was little connection. Where the erotic attractions of wisdom earlier are designed to lead to discipline as a pupil,[143] here they lead also to an almost mystical union in a 'community of life' (6:12–14, 7:28, 8:2–18). The association is further confirmed by the concern of the Wisdom of Solomon about immortality, a concern not found in previous Jewish wisdom writings, but strongly connected to communion with Isis. The argument of the author is best summed up in the sorites of 6:17–19:

> The true beginning of wisdom is the desire to learn,
> and a concern for learning means love towards her;
> the love of her means keeping of her laws,
> to keep her laws is a warrant of incorruption,
> and incorruption brings nearness to God.[144]

The incorruption which is a qualifying state for immortality[145] derives from a right conduct which is grounded fundamentally in personal communion with wisdom: 'In fellowship with wisdom lies immortality' (8:17–18).[146] This unfailing communion is rooted in the pursuit of wisdom, which is nothing less than communion with wisdom herself. The point is not that human beings have an immortal soul, but that they can have a love-affair with wisdom that even death cannot bring to an end. Solomon is presented as the key

---

[141] Apuleius, *Metamorphoses* 11.6, 23, 24, trans. W. Adlington and S. Gaselee, Loeb Classical Library (Harvard, Heinemann, 1924), pp. 549–51, 581–3.

[142] Reese, *Hellenistic Influence*, p. 101; E. Osty, *La Livre de la Sagesse* (Paris, Éditions du Cerf, 1957), p. 101.

[143] e.g. Proverbs 4:6–8, 8:17, 9:1, Ben Sira 14:20–7, 15:2; 51. The erotic content of Ben Sira 51 is subdued in LXX, as can be seen in 11QPsᵃ Sirach, *The Psalms Scroll of Qumran Cave 11*, ed. J. A. Sanders (Oxford: Oxford University press, 1965), pp. 79–85.

[144] V. 19 is emended from NEB.

[145] Reese, *Hellenistic Influence*, pp. 64–8, detects a rebuttal of the Epicureans.

[146] Cf. the 'incorruptible light of the law' (18:4), also a guide to immortality.

example of such a lover, and his relationship with wisdom is sketched in erotic language that is reminiscent of the *Song of Solomon*.[147] Here, perhaps, is warrant for including the *Song* among the books of the wisdom literature.[148]

It is possibly an association of Lady Wisdom with Isis that leads to the presentation of personified wisdom as not simply an observer of creation, but a participant in the activity of creating. Her position goes beyond being the 'first-born' of Proverbs 8 and Ben Sira 24 (though that is included in 8:3 and 9:9); she is the Maker (7:21, 8:6) and the one who performs all things (8:5). It may be that the author understands the title *'āmōn* (אמון) in Proverbs 8:30 as meaning 'workman'. Like Isis she creates, also expressed as being the 'mother' of nature[149] and the 'separator'[150] of creation. She is the throne partner of Yahweh (9:4, 9:10 $\pi\alpha\rho\epsilon\delta\rho os$/*paredros*) who lives with him (8:3, $\sigma\upsilon\mu\beta\iota\omega\sigma\iota\varsigma$/*symbiōsis*), the underlying mythological picture being that of wife, not daughter.

It is perhaps because of the recognizable outlines of Isis that the author is careful to define the relationship between wisdom and Yahweh as a subordinate one: wisdom is not allowed to become an independent goddess. The relationship is defined in terms which echo the image of the sun, following the predominant symbolism: wisdom is the 'pure effluence ($\dot{\alpha}\pi o\rho\rho o\iota\alpha$/*aporroia*) from the glory of the Almighty' (7:25b) and the 'effulgence ($\dot{\alpha}\pi\alpha\upsilon\gamma\alpha\sigma\mu\alpha$/*apaugasma*) from everlasting light' (7:26a). There is no simple analogy here, however, of God as the sun and wisdom as its beams of light. This would undermine the celebration of wisdom as sun, and destroy her dual nature as solar body (observing all) and solar rays (pervading all) that we have already detected. Rather, wisdom is the light or sun which is an outshining of that eternal light which is God.

The language of emanation in 7:25–8:1 is clearly indebted to Greek philosophy, but it is unlikely to be a direct reproduction of a whole system.[151] It is more likely to be making its own original commentary, in partly Greek terms, upon the Hebrew tradition of wisdom, along with veilings of the divine glory in 'masks' such as the cloud and the Angel of the Lord, and other extensions of the divine personality in word and (especially) spirit. This is an early venture, tentative and playful, into the concept of emanation (*aporroia*), pre-dating the

---

[147] Murphy, *The Tree of Life*, p. 89.

[148] Strongly urged by Ford, *Christian Wisdom*, pp. 382–9.

[149] Wisdom 7:12: reading $\gamma\epsilon\nu\epsilon\tau\iota\nu$ (*genetin*) against the alternative textual reading $\gamma\epsilon\nu\epsilon\sigma\iota s$ (*genesis*) followed by NEB, 'beginning'. For Isis as mother of all see Plutarch, *de Iside* 43; Apuleius, *Metamorphoses* 11.5; cf. Cyme 7 (Peek, p. 122).

[150] Wisdom 8:4 $\alpha\dot{\iota}\rho\epsilon\tau\iota s$ (*airetis*) so transl. by H. F. Weiss as cited by Mack, *Logos und Sophia*, p. 70, n.44; cf. Cyme 12 (Peek, p. 122), Plutarch, *de Iside* 62. But if the translation 'chooses among his works' is correct (cf. NEB) this is apt for a perfect wisdom's ability to cope with the multiplicity of creation.

[151] For instance, a philosophical interpretation of the Isis–Osiris mythology advocated by Mack, *Logos and Sophia*, pp. 70–1.

Neoplatonic doctrine of the emanation of Logos from the One or God. The boldness of the usage here, and yet its profound difference from the Neoplatonic scheme to come, is well set out in the lines immediately following the poetic statement of wisdom's emanation from God's power, glory and goodness:

> Though she is only one she can do everything;
> and abiding in herself she can do all things;
> generation by generation she enters into holy souls
> and renders them friends of God and the prophets. (7:27)[152]

Wisdom is both one and many ('only one, she can do everything'), echoing the previous ascription 'unique in her kind yet manifold' (v. 22, *monogenes, polymeres*). Similar contrasting attributes appear in the aretalogies honouring Isis,[153] but these occurrences do not determine the meaning here. Nor is the meaning that of the later Neoplatonic concept, where the Logos, reflecting the unity of the supreme principle, is an intermediary between the One and the many created entities which exist at a lower level of reality. The phrase 'abiding in herself she can do all things' would be understood in a Neoplatonic context as the capacity of the Logos to give rise to an effect (in the many) by emanation from itself while remaining unmoving and unaltered as a more direct emanation of the One.[154] But the point being made by our author here is not that wisdom, as an image of the One, provides a way for the many to return to the unmoving One from which they have unfortunately fallen away. Rather, wisdom as an image of the goodness of God provides a means for her disciples or 'friends' to explore the many aspects of the world; this is a *positive* celebration of the many wonders of creation, a relishing of its variety and multiplicity.

Wisdom shares in the generous creativity of God, giving rise to endless delights of diversity. She does not offer a flight from the many to the alone, but a journey into the manifold aspects of the world which she knows intimately, both because she surveys them and because she pervades them. Thus 'Solomon' claims to have received through her an encyclopedic knowledge of the world, in all its facets: cosmology, time, astronomy, zoology, meteorology, psychology, botany, and pharmacy (7:17–21). 'I learnt it all', he declares, 'hidden and manifest, for I was taught by her whose skill made all things.' She is 'one and many' in a sense distinctive to the wisdom tradition (and in a sense which we will see is to re-appear in John 1:16–18).[155]

As in the two previous Hebrew poems, the availability of wisdom, walking out on the open road, stands alongside the sense of the wise that much about

---

[152] My translation.   [153] Isis aretalogies, Cyrene 6, 15 (Peek, p. 129).
[154] E.g. Plotinus, *Enneads* 3.2.1.45, drawing on Plato, *Timaeus* 42E.
[155] See Chapter 10, the section called 'Christ as Focus of Wisdom'.

the world remains hidden to them. In face of the endlessness and elusiveness of the world, the personification of wisdom is a way of inviting human beings into a personal relationship with a wisdom which is both divine and human. No myth of a searching and hidden wisdom is needed to account for the shape of this story of Lady Wisdom who treads the paths of the sun and is thus near to all who dwell under her influence. Living in tune with wisdom will enable the wise person to enter into the diversity of phenomena of the world, and— although there is no possibility of mastering it entirely—to live with it and flourish within it. In Proverbs 9 we find that the personifying of wisdom as a beautiful woman bidding pupils to receive her instruction, and so to receive life, is a device by which the wise, as envoys of wisdom, seek to advertise their curriculum and attract pupils to their schools:

> 'You that are simple, turn in here!'
> To those without sense she says,
> 'Come, eat of my bread
> and drink of the wine I have mixed.' (Prov. 9:4–5)

The relationship of this welcoming female host to the cosmic wisdom of the poem in chapter 8 of Proverbs, the woman who takes the paths of the sun, is only hinted at in Proverbs 8–9. But here in the Wisdom of Solomon the two are fused; the one who observes all in the world is the same one who offers communion and an everlasting friendship. This surely symbolizes a discovery made by the wise, that there is something *participatory* about wisdom. Confronted by the complexity of the world and the limits of their instructions, the wise seek to align themselves to what the author of the Wisdom of Solomon finally calls 'the spirit of wisdom'. However elusive it might be, it was possible to have a relationship with wisdom, expressed in the image of 'walking in the paths of wisdom' (Prov. 8:22). There are tracks through the complexity of life which wisdom treads, and it is possible to develop an approach to the world in sympathy with her movements. So the author of this book says about wisdom:

> She herself ranges in search of those who are worthy of her; on their daily path she appears to them with kindly intent, and in all their purposes meets them half-way. (Wisd. 6:16)

PARTICIPATION NOT MEDIATION

The portrait of Lady Wisdom, in these three poems, makes clear that observing the world cannot be separated from participating in God. Seeing the world, the viewing self finds itself being drawn into a communion of life with wisdom, and so shares in a *divine* movement of seeing. The human self can see *as God sees*. In the Christian tradition, this idea of sharing the vision of God has often been associated with light, and so with the image of the sun which is such a central metaphor in the wisdom literature. According to Aquinas, for instance, the human intellect throws light on the world around as the sun does, and can see the essences of things because it participates in the uncreated light of God:

> We see everything in God and judge everything by him in the sense that it is by sharing ['participating'—*per participationem*] in his light that we are able to see and judge, for the natural light of reason is a sort of sharing [*participatio*] in the divine light. We might say in the same sense that we see and judge all sensible things in the sun—i.e. by the light of the sun. Hence Augustine says, *The lessons of instruction can only be seen as it were by their own sun*, namely God. Just as we can see sensible things without seeing the essence of the sun, so we can see things intellectually without seeing the essence of God.[156]

However, in the thought of Aquinas and other scholastics, this participation in God is strictly limited. Unlike the communion daringly described between the wise and Lady Wisdom, God does not in fact see the world as mortal eyes do, because—according to Aquinas—God has no need of the *phantasmata*, or the images of things created in the mind by the senses. God does not need to 'turn to the image' of the world, since he perceives the essences of things directly in his mind as the one who has created them.[157] We might say that God, according to Aquinas, is the supreme phenomenologist, immediately intuiting things in the divine mind.

Aquinas offers a careful account of how finite creatures can participate, in a limited way, in the uncreated God. For Aquinas, knowledge occurs when an object, or the image of it, exists immaterially in the mind of the observer: 'vision is made actual', he writes, 'only when the thing seen is in a certain way in the seer'.[158] Because of the divide between created and uncreated being, it is not possible for the essence of God to be contained in the mind of any created likeness of God (as we read in the extract above). Aquinas looks then for the gift of the 'light of glory', or created grace, to raise the intellect above its nature in order to make it capable of a direct vision of the uncreated essence.[159] For this gift, once again he employs the image of the sun: 'in some things we find the light from the sun as an abiding form, as though it had become connatural to them, as in the stars, rubies, and things of this sort'.[160] Such 'abiding' of the

---

[156] Aquinas, *Summa Theologiae* 1a.12.11, reply 3; transl. Herbert McCabe, Blackfriars Edition (London: Eyre and Spottiswoode, 1964), p. 39.

[157] Aquinas, *Summa Theologiae* 1a.14.5.

[158] Aquinas, *Summa Theologiae* 1a.12.2, reply.

[159] Aquinas, Summa Contra Gentiles 3.53.

[160] Aquinas, *Questiones Disputatae de Veritate*, transl. R. Mulligan, J. McGlyn, R. Schmidt. 3 Volumes (New York: Henry Regnery, 1952–4), vol. 2, q.13, art.2., contra.

light of glory is, however, an eschatological hope. During a person's lifetime there may be very rare and temporary anticipations of the final beatific vision, which Aquinas again compares to the light of the sun: 'in other things, the light from the sun is received as a passing impression, as light in the air'.[161] Thus 'participation' does not generally mean, ahead of the beatific vision in heaven, direct vision or engagement in the essence of God. Creatures 'participate' in the pure being of God through an analogy of being, so reflecting aspects or properties of God, and in particular the likeness of the light of reason to the uncreated light of God. Here Aquinas follows Plato in a doctrine of analogy with the Good. So particular entities, as embodied actualizations of forms, participate in God in two senses: 'participation' means that they *resemble* God, and that they are *caused* by God who has created all forms.[162] In this earthly life, God can be known only indirectly, through seeing created things, as the light of the intellect shines upon them and abstracts their universal form from their particularities.

Direct participation of the created in the uncreated remains for Aquinas only an eschatological hope, and this itself is a distinctly intellectual vision, depending on a view of the mind as the aspect of humanity that most resembles God. Moreover, this is an account which, unfortunately, hardly requires a trinitarian theology. Ideas of participation through resemblance, causation, and deification seem to require no more than an account of God as one substance, or one self-existent being. That is, there is no obvious link between God's participation in God's own self in the life of the Trinity, and human participation in God. Aquinas, admittedly, comes *close* to this with his view of analogy. There is a likeness between the pattern of divine self-movement in which the Father eternally generates the Son with the aim of creating the world on the one hand, and—on the other—the movement in which the human mind generates a word and 'illuminates' the world in order to know God.[163] But Aquinas does not think of any 'merging' of these movements into one activity. By contrast, the depictions of wisdom in our three poems from Hebrew wisdom literature offer a much more direct kind of participation, a sharing of the human observer in the very movement of divine seeing. The conclusion we have to draw from Aquinas' account is that this kind of claim for wisdom is only possible if we abandon 'being' or essence as a controlling metaphor in thinking about the triune God. Only then can we walk with Lady Wisdom on the path of the sun.

The question now arises, however, as to whether this image of the sun for the divine wisdom has made more acute the problems of domination raised by

---

[161] Aquinas, *Questiones Disputatae de Veritate*, vol. 2, q.13, art.2., contra.
[162] Aquinas, *Summa Theologiae*, 1a.6.4, reply; 1a. 44.1.1; I.a.3.3.2 and reply; *Summa Contra Gentiles* 3.97.3.
[163] Aquinas, *Summa Contra Gentiles* 4.11.18, cf. 4.12.5.

the 'ocular' metaphors (sight, light) with which I began this chapter. Aquinas, though not our wisdom materials, is dependent with the whole Western intellectual tradition on the thought of Plato, for whom 'as light and sight may be truly said to be like the sun, and yet not to be the sun, so . . . science and truth may be deemed to be like the good, but not the good',[164] and who envisages human beings as sitting in the 'prison-house of the world of sight', struggling out of darkness to see the bright sun of the world of ideas.[165] The sun has been the dominant image of sight and hence the intellect, both because of a parallel drawn (first by Plato) between the eye and the sun, and second because the sun is the primary source of light. The late-modern thinkers who have protested against the hegemony of reason through the symbol of vision have thus fundamentally rejected sun-imagery. For Derrida, the 'white mythology' he exposes has privileged the sun as the dominant symbol of signification: 'value, gold, the eye, the sun etc . . . the exchange dominates the field of rhetoric and of philosophy'.[166] The solar metaphor, evoking the alternation of day and night has encouraged a host of prejudices and polarities: the oppressive oppositions of truth and appearance, disclosure and hiddenness, presence and absence, light and dark, mind and body. To this list we may add, with Irigaray, male and female.[167] In this way, Derrida comments, it 'structures the metaphorical space of philosophy'.[168]

Further, Derrida judges, the apparent return of the sun each day after a trip around the earth, and the human identification with this daily progress across the sky, reinforces the idea of the 'sameness' of phenomena, and so a suppression of difference and otherness. This supports the imposing of a system of regularity on what is seen, and the regarding of the world as an extension of the interior self which creates order. 'The tenor of the dominant metaphor [the image of the sun on its circuit] supports the major "signified" of ontotheology: the circle of the heliotrope.'[169] As we have already observed, Derrida finds the same circularity and closure in the image of the Trinity.

The objection of Levinas to the totalizing tendencies of the eye is only intensified, in his opinion, by the effect of heliotropic images. 'In the Cartesian tradition', he writes, 'clear and distinct ideas still receive light from Plato's intelligible sun', but the clarity comes 'from a certain arrangement . . . into a system.'[170] If we think of our mind as 'illuminating' other persons and things in the manner of the sun casting its rays, as we have found in Aquinas, then

---

[164] Plato, *The Republic* VI.508D. Translation by Benjamin Jowett, *The Republic of Plato* (Oxford: Clarendon Press, 1888).

[165] Plato, *The Republic*, VII.517B.

[166] Derrida, 'White Mythology', p. 218.

[167] Luce Irigaray, *Speculum of the Other Woman*, trans. G. C. Gill (New York: Ithaca University Press, 1985), p. 303.

[168] Derrida, 'White Mythology', p. 251.   [169] Derrida, 'White Mythology', p. 266.

[170] Levinas, *Otherwise than Being*, p. 133.

they become simply an extension of the consciousness which throws its light over them. 'The light makes the thing appear by driving out the shadows; it empties space', writes Levinas, and so the light-giver appears to raise the thing observed from nothingness.[171] This is a critique of Heidegger's thesis that the typical human attitude to the world consists in a 'bringing to light', which Levinas maintains rests on a 'panoramic' vision of existence.[172] It also exposes a collusion between rationality and power. Where in Plato's myth of the cave and the sun, the soul rises towards 'the universal author of all things beautiful and right, parent of light and of the lord of light in this visible world, and the immediate source of reason and truth in the intellectual',[173] Levinas reads an exaltation of a privileged intellectual elite in society, who are to become the leaders in the state. The light of the metaphysical order is simply confirming the absolute identity of the individual, in violent political competition with others to extend its sovereignty. In short, this sun is the 'black light' of war.[174]

Levinas' invocation of a 'dark sun' resonates with others who have used a similar symbol in reaction against the dominating sun of Western intellect. Bataille, for instance, referred to the 'rotten sun' in an essay of 1930. While the sun is a benign and illuminating power for those who prudently decline to stare into it, Bataille suggests that it is an aggressive destroyer for those who dare to look at it openly in the face, and are blinded by it. These two ways of conceiving the sun are, he suggests, represented in the myth of Icarus who seeks the sun of elevated beauty, but is destroyed by the sun of burning heat.[175] Jay is surely right that Bataille associates staring at the 'rotten sun' with artistic creativity;[176] commenting on Blake's *The Tyger*, Bataille writes, 'Never have eyes as wide open as these stared at the sun of cruelty.'[177] Perhaps what is intended by this symbol is the revolt of the artist against the organizing and oppressive forms of the intellect (the elevated sun), and the consequent discovery of a new kind of source of light and heat in the darkness of uninhibited passions.

All these deep suspicions about the concealed intentions of those who use solar imagery, as well as artistic revolution against them, bring us to reconsider the Hebrew image of Lady Wisdom, clothed in the garments of the

---

[171] Levinas, *Totality and Infinity*, p. 189, cf. p. 191 'light as fire and as sun'.

[172] Levinas, Totality and Infinity, p. 294.

[173] Plato, Republic, VII.517C, trans. Jowett.

[174] Levinas, *Totality and Infinity*, p. 21, cf. p. 225. I am indebted to Kathryn Bevis for suggesting in conversation that a reference to Plato's cave lies behind this passage about the 'black light'.

[175] Georges Bataille, 'Rotten Sun' in *Visions of Excess*, p. 57.

[176] Jay, *Downcast Eyes*, p. 224. See the novel by Julian Barnes, *Staring at the Sun* (London: Picador, 1986), p. 155.

[177] Georges Bataille, *Literature and Evil*, trans. Alastair Hamilton (New York, 1973), p. 73.

sun. Does the invitation to walk through the world, and look at all things with her, and thus with God, amount to a call to manipulate the world and dominate others with the dazzling powers of one's mind? I suggest that there is in fact no oppressive divine gaze here that we are called to share, but only a communion of life which enables us and others to be what they are. The clue lies in the nature of the participation depicted by this figure, and the first dimension to be noticed is that personified wisdom is not a cosmological mediator. This is the significance of failing to find a 'myth of wisdom' buried in the three wisdom poems we have explored, whether this be a myth of Ma'at or Isis, or Bultmann's ur-myth of wisdom. Such myths presume an ontological gap between two worlds, between a transcendent world of the divine and the material world of human persons, which has to be bridged by some kind of intermediate principle. These are metanarratives of domination, since the intermediary claims the absolute authority of absent divinity, and demands obedience on the grounds of having sole powers of access to the divine.

Christianity in its early years was strongly influenced by this kind of narrative of mediation, and developed a habit of mind which just (and happily) fell short of being absorbed by it. I mean that the figure of Christ, in whom the New Testament writers find God to be uniquely disclosed, and who acts as a mediator in *relationship* between a righteous God and sinful human beings,[178] was reconfigured as a *cosmic* mediator. As early as Justin Martyr we find the assumption of a Platonic world-view in which there are two ontological spheres—a world of unchanging, intellectual Being and a world of transient, material Becoming (or a re-writing of the biblical heaven and earth). This is nothing other than the drama of Plato's cave, with a great separation between the world of intellectual light and the shadows of the prison-house. In Plato's own thought, the sun shining beyond the cave is a symbol for the supreme Idea of the Good, or in religious language, 'the Father and Maker of all'—though 'Maker' should be understood as 'Shaper', since Plato has no concept of *creatio ex nihilo*. In the Platonic cosmos, the soul is the intermediary principle, belonging to the higher world and able to contemplate the ideas or intellectual forms of Being, while operating in the lower world to imitate these ideas as best as it can in shaping intransigent matter. Plato envisages individual souls of human beings, and alongside them a kind of 'world-soul', or soul embedded in the whole material cosmos.[179] The scene is now set for the more syncretistic and religious form of Platonism that the Church Fathers knew, usually denoted 'Middle-Platonism.' The 'world-soul' of Plato has been conflated with the Stoic 'Logos' – or the reason active as an informing agent in the cosmos. This Logos-Soul contemplates the eternal Ideas, which are now

---

[178] 1 Tim. 2:5, Hebrews 8:6, 9:15, 12:24.
[179] Plato, *Timaeus* 34A–35A, 41D–42D.

thoughts in the mind of a supreme God, modelled after Aristotle's *Nous* or 'Unmoved Mover'.[180]

It was almost irresistable for early Christianity, moving out from Palestine into a Graeco-Roman milieu, to take up these popular philosophical ideas and put Christ into the available role of the Logos/World Soul, mediating between two ontological realms. As Justin explains to the (possibly fictitious) Jew, Trypho, it must have been Christ who appeared to Moses in the burning bush of Exodus 3, since 'he who has but the smallest intelligence will not venture to assert that the Maker and Father of all things, having left all supercelestial matters, was visible on a little portion of earth'.[181] The supreme divine reality needs, Justin argues, a mediator to engage with finite beings in a material, temporal world. In another writing, Justin finds a reference to the crucified Christ in Plato's mythological account of the impressing of the world soul on the cosmos by the 'Father and Maker of all': 'Which things Plato reading and not accurately understanding . . . said that the power next to the first God was placed crosswise in the universe'.[182]

Of course, the early Christian theologians had to modify the concept of an intermediate Logos to make it fit what they wanted to affirm of Christ; this mediator was not an inferior semi-divine principle as in Platonism but fully one with God. Against Middle-Platonists they thus affirmed that the Christ-Logos did not simply *contemplate* the ideas in the mind of God (as Middle-Platonists thought of the Logos), but was *identical* with those ideas. Adopting the Stoic human psychological sequence of a thought immanent in the mind being extrapolated externally as a spoken word, they proposed that Christ was the eternal Idea in God's mind spoken out, or sent forth to mediate for the sake of bringing creation into being and redeeming it when fallen: 'God begot before all creatures a Beginning who was a certain rational power proceeding from himself, who is called by the Holy Spirit [i.e. in Scripture] now the Glory of the Lord, now the Son, again Wisdom, again an Angel, then God, and then Lord and Logos.'[183] Early theologians lived with the paradox of a mediator who was, at the same time, one and equal with the being of God (except when Arius drew the logical conclusion that a mediator had to be a created reality, although the 'highest of the creatures'). They re-interpreted the Word of John's Gospel (Jn. 1:1–18), which had originally been modelled on the Hebraic concept of wisdom, as the Greek philosophical *logos*, but they also continued

---

[180] Albinus, *Epitome of the Teachings of Plato* X.3; see Richard A. Norris, *God and the World in Early Christian Theology* (London: A & C Black, 1965), pp. 27–30.

[181] Justin Martyr, *Dialogue with Trypho* 60, in Alexander Roberts and James Donaldson (eds), *The Ante-Nicene Fathers*, 10 Volumes (Grand Rapids: Eerdmans, 1975), vol. 1, p. 227.

[182] Justin Martyr, *First Apology* 60, in Roberts and Donaldson (eds), *Ante-Nicene Fathers*, vol. 1, p. 183.

[183] Justin Martyr, *Dialogue with Trypho* 61.

to insist on the scandalous belief that the Logos had become a human being in Jesus of Nazareth (Jn. 1:14).

By such means the early Christian theologians were launched towards the doctrine of the Trinity, or one God who lives in complex relationships. In this, I suggest that their contextualization in their culture served them well. However, they were left with the habit of thinking of the Son of God as a mediator bridging an abyss between two worlds of reality,[184] and this image has persisted in Christian thinking ever since. It has resulted in the tension of ascribing to God the philosophical atributes proper to unchanging Being – impassibility, immutability, non-temporality—while at the same time upholding the biblical picture of a God who has a compassionate love for the world. While Christian thought broke free from a rigid Platonic separation of two worlds it never quite detached itself from the idea of a Logos which is projected to span a gap, as if God has to speak out a word as a messenger from heaven to earth.

Colin Gunton has rightly argued that a mediatorial world of eternal ideas or rational principles (whether derived from Aristotle or Plato) standing between Being and Becoming is bound to denigrate the world of physical matter, which is pushed right down to the bottom of a scale of being. It will also lead to a loss of interest in particular things in the world, as the mind will always be trying to find the universal form of things. He maintains that the bridging of the gap between two worlds by the mediation of intellectual forms and causes was due to a loss of belief in Christ as mediator. In the trinitarian perspective, he argues, God is related to the world by the material body of the incarnate Christ.[185] However, while releasing Christ from identity with a supreme intellectual idea, his continued use of the paradigm of mediation means that he has still not escaped from the trap of separating two orders of reality.

This is, in the end, a narrative of domination, a story that validates oppression. For if a cosmic mediator is needed, it is a short step to reproducing this mediator on the earthly scene in the person of an absolute monarch or a supreme ecclesiastical ruler. Bishop Eusebius of Caesarea, for example, achieved this kind of theology for his Emperor. He affirmed that there is one transcendent God who is the 'Supreme Sovereign'; there is one divine Logos or Word of God who governs the universe, and who is yet indistinguishable in essence from the one God; and there is one human monarch who governs the earth as God's representative. The last in this succession, of course, is Constantine, who regards himself as the image on earth of the Logos,

---

[184] See further, Irenaeus, *Adversus Haereses* IV.6.7, cf. V.18.2; Athanasius, *Contra Gentes* 40–1, *Contra Arianos*, III.63–4.

[185] Colin Gunton, *The Triune Creator* (Grand Rapids: Eerdmans, 1998), pp. 43–64.

'deriving his imperial authority from above'.[186] Levinas is right to trace a route from the metaphysics of Plato's cave to political oppression.

In describing the generation of the Logos from God the Father, Justin (as we have seen) identifies Christ as Logos with a number of instances of the personification of God, or extensions of the divine personality which are contained in the Hebrew Bible, including the Wisdom of God: 'God begot before all creatures . . . a certain rational power proceeding from himself, who is called . . . Wisdom.' While these personified attributes of God (glory, wisdom, word) actually affirm God's direct presence in the world, as is the case with Lady Wisdom, Justin appeals to them to substantiate his view of mediation. In this he is followed by later Christian thinkers, including Aquinas who compares the descent of wisdom 'from higher to lower things' bearing its image with the way that the sun's rays descend to 'touch the earth'.[187] However, the Hebrew wisdom literature does not at all present wisdom as a mediator between different levels or spheres of reality. There is no myth of mediation, and when the writer of the Wisdom of Solomon celebrates wisdom as 'one and many' ('abiding in herself she can do all things') he is not thinking of a bridge between a transcendent One and the plurality of a finite world, but a wisdom who enables her friends to enjoy the manifold phenomena among which they live. Wisdom is not projected or extrapolated from a remote deity in order to make contact with a world of change and decay. Wisdom does not in any way bridge a gap between transcendence and immanence, between creator and created. Rather, we have seen that the spirit of wisdom which stands over against the world as its observer is also the *same* spirit which is within the world, holding all things together. We might say that wisdom flows forth from God so that human beings can participate in that same flowing movement. The image of the 'emanation' of wisdom from God is expressing the same possibilities of participation as were previously offered under the image of walking with Lady Wisdom on the paths of the sun.

Reading the wisdom literature should encourage a paradigm change in Christian theology, from mediation to participation. Wisdom as spirit in the Wisdom of Solomon hints at a complexity within God's life that is later to flower fully in the Christian doctrine of the Trinity. It is not that either Lady Wisdom or spirit can be simply equated with persons of the Trinity as the church later articulated them—whether Son or Holy Spirit. There is no question of imposing a cryptic Trinity upon Judaism. The point is that similar insights into movements of personal life within and from God, inviting participation, are later to be expressed in the Christian concept of Trinity. The Son or Logos comes forth from the Father, as does the Spirit, not to link a remote God with the world as in the mediation model, but so that the world

---

[186] Eusebius, *Oratio de Laudibus Constantini* 2.
[187] Aquinas, *Summa Theologiae* 1a.9.1.2.

can share in the movements of self-giving within God, participating in the flowing movement of love between the Father and the Son in the ever-surprising newness of the Spirit.[188] When 'persons' in the Trinity are understood as nothing more or less than relationships, as I have been urging,[189] the continuity here between wisdom thinking and trinitarian thinking becomes compelling, enabling us to read each in terms of the other. What persists is not some kind of equivalence of 'agents' in God (wisdom, spirit, Son, Holy Spirit), leading to an argument—for instance—that the Christian *logos* should properly be gendered as female because it inherits the Hebraic concept of wisdom which is feminine. Rather, what persists is an experience of participation in *movements* of love, creativity, and justice which include and transcend both genders or any transition between them.

WHOLE-BODY SEEING

Both wisdom thinking and the triune symbol thus assure us that the vision of God is not a dominating gaze; this is because created beings share in it, without any implication of thereby receiving an authority that comes from mediation. The fullness of divine life in which human beings are invited to participate is not beyond, but in, the world, transcendent in the sense that it is self-existent, uncreated and more inexhaustible in its depths and resources than any human reality. There is a seeing that is an embracing of the world in all its bodily reality, not a standing over against the world in a polarization of mind and body that (as Derrida points out) the Platonic sun encourages. This leads us to a second reason why 'seeing the world' need not mean domination. That is, vision can be re-thought as including 'touch' or immersion into the bodily life of the self and others. In a recent study on *Seeing Things*, Stephen Pattison has urged the recovery of a 'haptic' mode of sight, or a 'touching vision', connecting the eye with the body and its other senses. Deriving from the Greek verb *haptein* (to seize, grasp or touch), the term 'haptic vision' emphasizes 'the holistic, embodied, and relational aspects of seeing',[190] and Pattison argues that cultivating a tactile vision will 'allow visual experience to be richer and more nuanced, [so that] deeper relationships with visual artefacts might then be developed'.[191]

---

[188] Cf. Dietrich Bonhoeffer: "There are not two realities, but only one reality, and that is God's reality revealed in Christ in the reality of the world," *Dietrich Bonhoeffer Works, Vol. 6, Ethics*, trans. R. Krauss (Minneapolis: Fortress, 2005), p. 58.

[189] See Chapter 5, the section called 'The Complex Being of the Triune God'.

[190] Pattison, *Seeing Things*, p. 19.

[191] Pattison, *Seeing Things*, p. 41.

Levinas, in his attack on a visual culture, urges not only the alternative of the spoken word, but also the use of touch. Ethical interaction, he suggests, manifests itself in the sense of touch whereas visual relations with others foster manipulation; most benign is the 'caress' which does not lead to fusion with the other, but has a quality of 'seeking' without knowing what it seeks.[192] Other thinkers, however, do not set sight and touch in opposition, but seek to integrate one into the other. Notably, Merleau-Ponty writes about 'palpating' others with our look, 'because the gaze itself envelops them, clothes them with its own flesh'.[193] This perception belongs in the context of his phenomenological perception (modifying Husserl's emphasis on sight) that body is about participating in the widest possible space, and engaging in self-giving relations with others rather than protecting our own boundaries. As Merleau-Ponty puts it, bodiliness is about touching and being touched, about being 'enfolded' in a kind of embrace which has no horizons, and where the divisions between our body and the 'flesh of the world' collapses.[194] The eye is embodied in the 'chiasm' or confluence of the body and the senses where subjective experience and objective existence are fused,[195] so that 'seeing' is inseparable from the sensuous body that connects with others in a dance of reciprocity. The significance of the aspect of touch is that it opens up the possibility of mutuality, where seeing which is not embodied cultivates a mere detachment; so Roland Barthes finds a reciprocal relation with others can be sustained precisely by the gaze: 'by gaze I touch, I seize, *I am seized*'.[196]

As Pattison demonstrates, there is a long history of the 'haptic' gaze in Christian faith and practice, where pilgrims and worshippers have often not distinguished between visual and tactile piety.[197] Significant for our own enquiry is the thought of Nicholas of Cusa, for whom God's sight does not just observe everything but holds everything in being. Cusa thought that *theos* (God) and *theoria* (vision) had the same etymological root, so that God's vision is 'providence, grace and life eternal'.[198] 'Seeing' includes all the other senses that we might attribute in an analogical way to God: 'In Him sight is not other than hearing, or tasting, or smelling, or touching, or feeling, or understanding.'[199] This haptic vision is understood by Cusa to be a kind of movement, which accompanies all human movement:

---

[192] Levinas, *Time and the Other*, p. 51.

[193] Maurice Merleau-Ponty, *Basic Writings*, ed. Thomas Baldwin (London: Routledge, 2004), p. 249.

[194] Maurice Merleau-Ponty, *Visible and Invisible*, trans. A. Lingis (Evanston: Northwestern University Press, 1969), pp. 248–9.

[195] Merleau-Ponty, *Visible and Invisible*, pp. 130–55.

[196] Roland Barthes, 'Right in the Eyes' in *The Responsibility of Forms. Critical Essays on Music, Art and Representation*, trans. R. Howard (New York : Hill and Wang, 1985), p. 238.

[197] Pattison, *Seeing Things*, pp. 42–3.

[198] Nicholas of Cusa, *The Vision of God*, trans. E. S. Gurney (New York: Cosimo, 2007), Chapter 8 (p. 38), cf. Chapter 4 (p. 14).

[199] Nicholas, *Vision of God*, Chapter 3 (p. 12).

Thou, Lord, art the companion of my pilgrimage; wheresoever I go Thine eyes are always upon me. Now with Thee seeing is motion. Therefore Thou movest with me and never ceasest from motion as long as I move.

This might be a threatening and intrusive vision, were it not reciprocal with human vision: 'In beholding me thou givest thyself to be seen of me, Thou who art a hidden God.'[200] The face of God can be seen first in all human faces, though there it is veiled. Further, however, God's face can be seen unveiled in itself, although God is like the sun; we can 'see' the face of *this* sun because light invisible can *only* be seen in the 'silence, mist, darkness, cloud or ignorance' when the human mind travels beyond concepts.[201] The 'denser' the mist appears, by so much the more are we attaining to the light of God. Here is a response from the apophatic tradition of Christianity to the 'tyranny' of the blazing sun of rationality and intellect; this understanding of 'seeing' also makes clear that (as Kant was much later to insist), God cannot be known as an object, even by the 'eyes of the mind'. I intend to return later to the place—or strictly the 'no-place'—of the negative way, but for the moment, I want to draw attention to the insight that God's vision is a 'movement' in which we can participate. Cusa himself does not relate this movement to processions in the Trinity (though he does think that we can 'see' God only because the Trinity is a relational communion of love),[202] but the pictures of the movement of wisdom through the world in the three poems we have been reviewing can prompt us to do so. The idea of 'haptic' sight, together with Cusa's relation of sight to all other senses, may then lead us to experience the movement of relations which is God not only as a seeing, but as a speaking, a hearing, a touching and a relishing of human life. Moreover, we shall find these movements embodied in the rhythms of human relations and the cycles of the natural world. Though we have begun with the metaphor of seeing, the movement of the divine life cannot be exhausted by any images.

SEEING AS READING

Seeing, and especially the 'seeing' attributed to the divine wisdom, does not dominate human life because it does not imply mediation of a higher principle, and because it involves the whole body. But there is also a third reason we may draw from our three poems. In these portrayals, wisdom is both subject and object at the same time. What lies under wisdom's eye is *also*

---

[200] Nicholas, *Vision of God*, Chapter 5 (p. 19). Michel de Certeau emphasizes this mutual seeing in 'The Gaze: Nicholas of Cusa', trans. C. Porter, *Diacritics* (Fall, 1987), pp. 23–7.

[201] Nicholas, *Vision of God*, Chapter 6 (pp. 26–7).

[202] Nicholas, *Vision of God*, Chapter 17 (pp. 80–7).

wisdom, a body of knowledge waiting to be discovered and co-extensive with the world; this wisdom can be recorded in the written texts of the wise. So human beings and God are not only *co-observers* of the world; they are *co-readers* of the world as text. Nicholas of Cusa again perceives this: celebrating the vision of God which sees all things, he affirms that 'Thou readest with them that read... for with Thee *to see is to read*. Thou from eternity has seen and read... all written books and those that can be written...'[203] To be sure, Cusa lives with the tension I identified above, between a God who exists in pure Being and yet is present in the world of Becoming; he proposes that God *both* reads all books in one simultaneous moment, *and* reads them 'one after another with all who read... in time'. This is appropriate to a God who is both in motion and at rest. My own proposal is to avoid this tension with a trinitarian theology of a God in movement, thoroughly committed to reading the signs of the world in the process of time alone. But Cusa has made the interesting suggestion that a compassionate God, accompanying creatures on their 'pilgrimage' through history, will be a 'reader' of books and the world.

The significance of this may be drawn, perhaps curiously, from our late-modern times. Derrida suggests that when 'seeing' is understood as 'reading', the dominance of the observer begins to be undermined. Unlike Levinas, who wants to replace the eye with the voice, Derrida suggests that a protest against the oppressive self can be mounted from *within* the paradigm of seeing. The world is a vast network of signs and signifiers, everything giving out its own particular message and pointing away from itself to something else. The signs which are there to be read take their meaning from their difference from each other, and so the reader must always be open to their otherness. The reader must especially be open to the narratives of other lives. The world can no longer be constructed around the self, and observation becomes sympathetic participation. Further, because all signs in the world can inscribed in written texts, their meaning will change and develop in different circumstances when texts are read.

Thus, in his lecture 'The Double Session', Derrida takes issue with the theory of *mimesis* advanced by Plato, that that there is a stable and reliable relationship between representations of the world and the way that things are—between the image and the 'thing'. This would mean that the word, the book or the painting merely 'double up' what is simple in itself. Writing displaces this closure of mimesis by 'doubling the mark' in a never-ending chain of signification.[204] This does not mean there is no representation at all, or no reference beyond a particular text; after all, argues Derrida, in a kind of 'eye-graft' each written text both refers to itself and to other texts,

---

[203] Nicholas, *Vision of God*, Chapter 8 (p. 36).
[204] Derrida, 'Double Session', pp. 187–8, 193–4.

including extra-literary texts such as writing expressed by the movements of the body.[205] We should not be self-confident that we know what is 'inside' or 'outside' a text. But truth cannot be sought merely in a relation of *adequate resemblance* between a thing and its re-presentation. Rather than trying to get mastery over the world in this way, the reader will recognize that he or she is being read by the text as much as reading it. Derrida raises questions about the reader: 'Is the initiative of reading his? Is he the acting subject who knows how to read what he has to write? One could indeed believe that... he at least has the active freedom to choose to begin to read... or even that you, dear everyreader, retain the initiative of reading all these texts and hence... mastering [them]?'[206] Nothing could be less certain, replies Derrida. The reader[207] 'is both read and reading, written and writing, existing between the two, in the suspense of the hymen' (the 'hymen' being a symbol for what is 'between' the inside and outside). So, between the pages and the eye, as Mallarmé writes, a surprise awaits, 'there reigns a silence still, the condition and delight of reading'.[208]

True 'seeing' is thus an open adventure of reading. Moreover, as Jay observes, this is a haptic seeing since Derrida takes pleasure in texts 'as tactile textures with hinges, breaks and crevices' so that the reader is 'touching with the eye'.[209] Theologically, we can find this 'delight of reading' in the divine wisdom, as Cusa does. Derrida rejects a solar imagery in which human beings identify themselves with the sun on its circuit, on the grounds that this simply supports regularity and 'more of the same', suppressing difference. But in the poems about Lady Wisdom, to participate in her walking of the path of the sun is to share in her vision of the inexhaustibility and sheer excessiveness of the world, always overflowing in abundance. Her vision has something open-ended about it, inviting a never-completed process of interpretation of the world, in being read by creation as well as reading it.

In the solar imagery of Aquinas, what is seen in the light of the intellect is the universal essence of things, which the mind extracts from the particular form of a sensual image. But the wisdom poems encourage us rather to follow Duns Scotus, whose final interest is in the *haeccitas* or 'thisness' of all things.[210] What is to be seen is the manifold variety of the world, each thing relished for its particularity and delighted in. It is no wonder that the poet

---

[205] Derrida, 'Double Session', pp. 202–3.

[206] Derrida, 'Double Session', p. 224.

[207] In context, this reader is a mime-artist, writing his mime newly in each performance on the basis of what he has read in the mime-script.

[208] Derrida, 'Double Session', p. 226.

[209] Jay, *Downcast Eyes*, p. 512.

[210] Scotus, *Opus Oxoniense* (Oxford Commentary on the *Sentences* of Peter Lombard), 2.3. q.1, q.6.

Gerard Manley Hopkins preferred Scotus to Aquinas,[211] sensitive as he was to the distinctnesses, othernesses and differences of the world, or what he called its 'inscapes':

> Glory be to God for dappled things! . . .
> All things counter, original, spare, strange;
>   Whatever is fickle, freckled (who knows how?)
>   With swift, slow, sweet, sour; adazzle, dim;
> He fathers-forth whose beauty is past change:
>   Praise him.[212]

As Hans Urs von Balthasar comments, Hopkins is able to read the glory of God not only in the world of light; the poet rejoices because 'the "single eye" of the parable is capable of the highest: to interpret the formlessness and un-formable chaos of the night as form'.[213]

We should not interpret Derrida's question 'is he the acting subject who knows how to read?' as an implied denial of any active subjectivity at all, but only the rejection of the kind of activity that claims 'mastery' over the text rather than opening the subject to the joyousness of reading. This does not, however, require that God in God's self should be a subject or a Supreme Self. Using the metaphor of God as a 'reader' of the world is to draw attention to a life-enhancing movement which is *like* that of reading, of following a line of words on a page. The image of the Trinity tells us that the human joy of reading the world comes from participating in a God whom we can only speak about as a polyphony or *perichoresis* of movements – like the journey of wisdom on its travels, the motion of an eye scanning a text, or the flowing of love between a father and a son or between a mother and a daughter. As we relate to others in compassion and empathy, as we become sympathetic readers with God, so we find our true self. Observers who identify themselves with the figure of divine wisdom are thus not validating their *control* of the world, as little mortals grasping at a cosmic authority; they are gaining assurance that as she lives, so will they.

---

[211] *The Sermons and Devotional Writings of Gerard Manley Hopkins*, ed. Christopher Devlin (London: Oxford University Press, 1959), pp. 151, 341–3.

[212] 'Pied Beauty', in *The Poems of Gerard Manley Hopkins*, Fourth Edition, ed. W. H. Gardner and N. H. Mackenzie (London: Oxford University Press, 1967), p. 70.

[213] Hans Urs von Balthasar, *The Glory of the Lord: A Theological Aesthetics*. 7 volumes (Edinburgh; T & T Clark, 1982–9), vol. 3, *Studies in Theological Style: Lay Styles*, trans. A. Louth, J. Saward, M. Simon, R. Williams (Edinburgh: T & T Clark, 1986), p. 399.

7

Hidden Wisdom: A Theology
of Presence and Place

PROBLEMS OF PRESENCE AND PLACE

We are facing today the twin problems of our 'presence' in the world and our 'place' in the world. It is a characteristic feature of our late-modern age that these are sensed as being not simply equivalents, although being deeply intertwined. There is a sense of regret about the loss of identity with a local 'place' as global markets, international travel, and the Internet immerse us into a larger 'space', even if, ironically, that space becomes increasingly compressed.[1] But there is an increasing awareness that to find a 'place to be', or to be 'at home' in the world will not result from merely asserting human presence. In fact, to impose a presence might actually be to destroy the nature of the world as a place where we can dwell. At the beginning of this book I suggested that our quest for 'wisdom' today shows up something significant: we are aware that in the pursuit of mere knowledge we have allowed the human self to dominate the world with damaging results. We are, for instance, destroying the environment and exploiting the poor. Postmodern philosophers have re-cast this problem in terms of a human insistence on 'full' presence. At the same time, having a place and being present do seem closely associated, as the sense of being at home (*heimlich*, as the German Romantic poets put it) implies that we are comfortable about being present, and that our presence is welcomed and affirmed.

If our picture of the human subject is of someone controlling the world around, and treating other things and persons as mere objects to be subdued, then what it means to 'be' is a capacity to be *present*. 'Beingfulness' is the ability to impose our presence immediately on others. They are

---

[1] See the beginning of Chapter 4. Scott Lash and John Urry, *Economies of Signs and Space* (London: Sage, 1999), pp. 12–15, draw attention to an 'emptying out' of objects and places as 'things and people become disembedded'.

going to have to take account of the fact that we are there—in their space, and in their face. Moreover, for us 'to be' means a being present to ourselves: we are aware of ourselves, conscious of ourselves, controlling our own inner space. The human consciousness is thus directly present to itself and to the phenomena of the world, which in turn have being because they present themselves to the mind as sense-impressions or as essences abstracted from these impressions. This leads to a view of time in which 'presence' is confused with 'the present', and only the present is regarded as real, since the past is no longer present and the future is not yet present.[2]

A criticism then can be brought against the idea of God. God is, in a classic theological picture, the great controller who imposes 'his' presence everywhere; in fact 'he' is *omnipresent* in an eternal present tense, and also supremely present to himself, perfectly self-conscious (the gendered pronoun is deliberate and significant). So, runs the criticism, he is the absolute subject, validating human subjectivity by giving it communion with the eternal mind. On this reckoning, as Jacques Derrida puts it, 'God is the name and the element of that which makes possible an absolutely pure and absolutely self-present self-knowledge.'[3] Talk about God, then, seems to be about a cosmic controller who supports human—and especially male—domination of others. Problems of the postulated 'vision' of an all-seeing God are compounded by divine presence.

It is this simple equation of 'being' with 'presence' that has been challenged in the mood of thinking that is often called 'postmodern'. Postmodern thinkers point out that our presence to ourselves and others is never direct: it is always mediated through others and through the system of signs we use, among which words are the most powerful. Signs in our culture are given meaning by their difference from each other, so we are entangled in an endless chain of signifying, and meaning is bound to be open and unfinished. Instead of an immediate presence there are only 'traces' of presence. As Derrida expresses it, 'Nothing is ... anywhere either simply present or absent. There are only, everywhere, differences and traces of traces.'[4] In dialogue with Freud about the nature of the self, Derrida insists that all reference to a self must happen by way of detour through an other, and so presupposes an original self-effacement. Not only is there nothing more than a trace of presence, but the trace itself can be effaced or erased. The interplay between the self and the other both *makes* a trace and *erases* it; otherwise there is a claim to a sanctioning divinity.

---

[2] See Derrida's critique of Husserl, discussed in the first section of Chapter 6.
[3] Derrida, *Of Grammatology*, p. 98; cf. Derrida, 'Plato's Pharmacy', pp. 75–84.
[4] Derrida, *Positions*, p. 26.

An unerasable trace is not a trace, it is a full presence, an immobile and uncorruptible substance, *a son of God*, a sign of parousia and not a seed, that is, a mortal germ.[5]

The notion of a trace is a kind of flickering between presence and absence which applies to the human self in the world. Religious thinkers who have been influenced by this mood are also likely to speak of God as paradoxically both absent and present at the same time, or present in the mode of absence.[6] Towards the end of this chapter I shall be asking whether this is a helpful re-imaging of God or not. Does it meet the objection to a dominating presence of God to remove God from the scene?

There is then a contemporary hesitation about our presence in the world. This is accompanied by a cautious quest for a *place*. If our presence is uncertain, we nevertheless look for a place to occupy, or at least a place that will give us some sense of our bearings. There are many evidences of people's concern today to find a place to dwell. Diverse examples are the widespread interest of people today in tracing their family history, a 'regionalism' which challenges the nation-state,[7] the popularity of individualizing standard units of accomodation through home-design and DIY, and a preference for home-care over institutions. All this shows our desire to have a place to be, a place to call home.

Heidegger is helpful here in both distinguishing between the notions of 'place' and 'space', and in identifying an ambiguity about feeling 'at home'. For Heidegger, to 'dwell' is to be at 'home', to be in the world as in a *Heimat*, to be in it not as a foreign place, but as a homeland.[8] In his later work he suggests that a place is truly a 'dwelling-place' when it shows up as a 'fourfold' reality, or as a kind of enclosed courtyard (*Geviert*) which has four 'sides'—the earth, the sky, the 'godly ones', and mortals. That is, dwellers dwell 'on' the earth (the totality of things in nature), 'under' the sky (the rhythms of the planets, the seasons, the weather), 'before' the divinities (the ethos and heritage of the community) and 'with' mortals (human beings living in the face of death).[9] To be a dwelling-place, a location 'gathers' the fourfold; when Heidegger

---

[5] Derrida, *Writing and Difference*, p. 230.

[6] See e.g. Dorothee Sölle, *Christ the Representative*, trans. D. Lewis (London: SCM Press, 1967), pp. 134–40; Gordon Kaufman, *God the Problem*, (Cambridge, MA: Harvard University Press, 1972), pp. 84–8, 97, 113; Mark Taylor, *Erring: A Postmodern A/theology* (Chicago: University of Chicago Press, 1984), pp. 26–8, 68–74, 159–60; cf. John D. Caputo, *The Weakness of God. A Theology of the Event* (Bloomington: Indiana University Press, 2006), pp. 269–77.

[7] Lee Cuba and David M. Hummon, 'A Place to call Home: Identification With Dwelling, Community, and Region', *The Sociological Quarterly*, 34 (1993), pp. 111–31.

[8] Martin Heidegger, *The Question Concerning Technology and Other Essays*, trans. W. Lovitt (New York: Harper and Row, 1977), p. 49.

[9] Heidegger, *Poetry, Language, Thought*, pp. 149–50, 178–9. See Julian Young, 'The Fourfold', in Charles B. Guignon (ed.), *The Cambridge Companion to Heidegger*. Second Edition (Cambridge: Cambridge University Press, 2006), pp. 373–92.

writes that there 'poetically man dwells',[10] he means that the place shows up as 'holy', that this place grounds our experience of living in the face of 'the mystery of Being itself'.[11] Here we find our responsibility of 'looking after' or 'taking care' of a place. Place is about proximity, belonging, unveiling, and gathering. Although this language of place (mainly *Ort* or *Ortschaft*) appears explicitly in Heidegger's later work, it can be argued that similar ideas appear in his earlier *Being and Time*, implied in the constellation of terms *Dasein* ('being there'), *Situation*, *Lage* (both of which can be translated 'situation'), *Welt* (world), *Umwelt* (environing world), and *Ereignis* (happening or event).[12] In contrast to a metaphysics of presence which concentrates on the 'present' moment, the temporal concept of *Ereignis*, as Jeff Malpas argues, especially carries with it some of the same sense of gathering and disclosing as the later *Ort*.[13]

Looked at as mere physical objects, places are specific locations *within* a measurable expanse that we call 'space'. Space is then primary, and we think of it as a kind of receptacle, being filled with items such as places. This is the modern scientific concept of space as potentially infinite extension (*extensio*). But if 'place' is where we dwell, a place that shows up as 'holy', then space is the interval (*spatium*) between places, and it is only by abstraction that space becomes a realm of extendedness. We cannot begin from the mathematical idea of extension, but only from places where we dwell, such as beside the old stone bridge at Heidelberg which gathers together the earth, sky, gods, and mortals. For Heidegger, space then is always subsequent to place, as the 'nearness and farness', or 'orientation and distance'[14] which relates dwelling-places. It is relations that make space, whether the relation of the human being to a particular place or places to each other: 'Man's relation to locations, and through locations to spaces, inheres in his dwelling.'[15] A dwelling-place is thus already spatial in itself; it is a 'broad place', a place of gathering:

> Space (*raum*) means a place cleared or freed for settlement or lodging. A space is something that has been made room for . . . namely within a boundary. Space is in essence that for which room has been made . . . Accordingly spaces receive their being from locations and not from 'space'.[16]

---

[10] Heidegger, *Poetry, Language, Thought*, p. 213.

[11] Heidegger, *Question Concerning Technology*, p. 25; *Poetry, Language, Thought*, p. 178; *Hölderlin's Hymn 'Andenken'*, ed. Curd Ochwalt (Frankfurt am Main: Klostermann, 1992), p. 193.

[12] So Jeff Malpas, *Heidegger's Topology. Being, Place, World* (Cambridge, Mass. : MIT Press, 2006), pp. 30–3.

[13] Malpas, *Heidegger's Topology*, pp. 215–19, 230–5.

[14] Heidegger's terms are *Ausrichtung* and *Entfernung*; see Heidegger, *Being and Time*, pp. 136–8.

[15] Heidegger, *Poetry, Language, Thought*, p. 155.

[16] Heidegger, *Poetry, Language, Thought*, p. 152.

Places which are dwelling-places or places for relations (say, the Old Bridge of Heidelberg as opposed to a motorway bridge) are also 'spaces'–giving room for dwelling–and these separate spaces are related to each other by a more extensive 'space' which derives from them, not they from it.

However, we note that 'space' includes the element of 'farness' or 'distance' as well as proximity and orientation. Space is the area of dispersal as well as gathering, and this alerts us to an ambiguity about 'place'. Heidegger observes that it is endemic to human existence as *Dasein* ('being there') to feel *unheimlich* as well as *heimlich*, to have the sense that the world is not really home at all. *Unheimlichkeit* or 'the uncanny' (a term inherited from Freud) is a 'mood' by which *Dasein* is revealed to itself, and this 'unsettlement' is the opposite of what is homely, familiar, and understood: 'Everyday familiarity collapses . . . Being-in enters into the existential 'mode' of the "not-at-home".[17] Such anxiety is 'always latent in "Being-in-the world"', so that we need to be open to the strange and the foreign even in familiar places. *Unheimlichkeit* appears both because human beings live under the horizon of death, and because Being is veiled in the very moment of being unveiled. Heidegger is replacing the metaphysics of presence with a new kind of ontology, based on the *difference* between Being and beings. Beings have their nature in *Dasein*–being there in the everyday world–and the experience of anxiety reveals to them that they have no secure grounding. To put it metaphorically, the manner of their 'arrival' in the world through Being is concealed. Being which gives itself to beings in an 'overwhelming' and 'unconcealed' way is nevertheless usually forgotten by beings which set out to establish their identity through such means of control as modern technology. The difference between Being and beings creates a kind of 'clearing' in space and time, a 'differential tension' (Graham Ward's expression)[18] or an 'open region' (Heidegger) to which beings are exposed:

> The difference of Being and beings, as the differentiation of overwhelming and arrival, is the perdurance (*Austrag*) of the two in *unconcealing keeping in concealment*. Within this perdurance there prevails a clearing of what veils and closes itself off—and this its prevalence bestows the being apart, and the being toward each other, of overwhelming and arrival.[19]

Being thus 'appears primordially in the light of concealing withdrawal'.[20] We cannot think Being itself, but we can think the difference and we can explore the space in which Being itself has a hidden presence. We can (as we have

---

[17] Heidegger, *Being and Time*, pp. 233–4.

[18] Graham Ward (ed.), *The Postmodern God: A Theological Reader* (Oxford: Blackwell, 1997), p. xxxii.

[19] Martin Heidegger, *Identity and Difference*, p. 65.

[20] Martin Heidegger, 'On the Essence of Truth' in David Krell (ed.), *Heidegger: Basic Writings* (London: Routledge & Kegan Paul, 1978), p. 140.

already seen in exploring Hannah Arendt's debt to Heidegger) think of this hiddenness as the difference between the self-revealing 'world' and the self-concealing 'earth'.[21] The 'place' in which we dwell is where we are grounded in the world and in Being Itself, and so can become the 'clearing' for Being; it is the space for both the 'holy' and the 'uncanny'.

Like Hannah Arendt, Heidegger thinks that the 'public' sphere can dispel uncanniness and restore a sense of 'being at home' in the world. He understands publicness in terms of a shared mythological world-view and a culturally determined daily routine, whereas Arendt understands it as shaped by political action, and perhaps this is why he takes a more negative view of public space: 'Entangled flight into the being-at-home of publicness is flight from not-being at home, that is from the uncanniness which lies in Dasein'.[22] The familiar 'being-in the-the world' *can* be a tranquilized state, failing to face up to the anxiety in which Being is disclosed and which must never be suppressed alongside a proper *heimlichkeit*. If then, we are to be cautious about issues of 'presence' in the world, we also need to be cautious about investing in place.

For all these warnings, Heidegger tends to root place in presence—the presence of *Dasein* in dwelling in the world, and the self-presencing of Being. He does recognize that there is no fulness of presence, as witnessed by the human sense of *unheimlichkeit* and the phenomenon of the concealment of being.[23] Nevertheless, he has been criticized for making presence too dominant a factor, and so other thinkers have looked for another root of dwelling. Jacques Derrida, Julia Kristeva, and Luce Irigaray among others point to a mysterious space,[24] just as other writers in the past have imagined a Utopia. The word 'Utopia', literally meaning 'no place' or 'not a place', has been employed in depicting imaginary places where everything is perfect, or at least where human damage is limited; these are no-places which cannot actually be visited. Now, the late-modern thinkers I have mentioned envisage a place which is not actually a place, which cannot be inhabited even in imagination. This place which is not-a-place is not a place of perfection as in the classic Utopia; rather, it remains a constant challenge and keeps us restless. This 'place' is a non-foundational origin of flickering presence, as well

[21] See Chapter 4, the section called 'The Self-Revealing World and the Self-Concealing Earth'.
[22] Heidegger, *Being and Time*, p. 222.
[23] See Heidegger, *Poetry, Language, Thought*, p. 182, on the relation between absence and presence of 'God and the divinities'.
[24] Luce Irigaray, 'Place, Interval', in *An Ethics of Sexual Difference*, trans. C. Burke and G. C. Gill (Ithaca: Cornell University Press, 1993), pp. 34–40; Irigaray, *Sharing the World* (London: Continuum, 208), pp. 115–30; *Speculum*, pp. 177–9. See also Judith Butler, *Bodies That Matter: On the Discursive Limits of Sex* (New York: Routledge, 1993), p. 37; Elizabeth Grosz, 'Woman, Chora, Dwelling', in *Space, Time, and Perversion: Essays on the Politics of Bodies* (New York: Routledge, 1995), p. 24; Catherine Keller, *Face of the Deep: A Theology of Becoming* (London: Routledge, 2003), pp. 13–14, 16–59.

as the source of all difference; it is an otherness that continually punctures attempts to establish either full presence or full absence; it breaks open boundaries and upsets rigid ideas as to what is 'inside' or 'outside' the reality established by language. It is a place or 'primordial space' which cannot be reached, touched or established as a cause. Those who appeal to such a no-place draw the name *chōra* ($\chi\omega\rho\alpha$, also transliterated by some as *khōra*) for it from Plato, who uses it in the *Timaeus* for the space which is neither being nor non-being, but a kind of interval between, in which the 'forms' of things in the world were originally held.[25]

THE DISTURBANCE OF A 'NO-PLACE'

We might, I suggest, put Heidegger's concerns for *heimlichkeit* alongside the *chōra* in this way: physical locations will only become dwelling-places when we become aware of an existential place which is not a literal place at all. There is perhaps just a trace of this thought in Heidegger's own brief references to *chōra*, but it is not developed.[26] Derrida refers to Heidegger's comment that 'the khora means the place' and then cites his elaboration that Plato 'thus poses the question of the wholly other place of Being, by comparison with that of beings.'[27] Derrida concludes that *khōra* stands for a place which escapes all philosophical analysis, which is impossible to speak about but which 'dictates an obligation by its very impossibility: *it is necessary* to speak of it.'[28] In all his work Derrida is fascinated by the 'wholly other' which arrives to shock all horizons and prompts the crossing of all boundaries. Unlike the 'wholly other' in Emmanuel Levinas, this wholly other is always *within* the sign-network of language; there is an infinite alterity in the text since all signifieds are wholly other to other signs; yet this otherness points to the 'impossible possibility' of something outside and inside *at the same time*, and (purporting to follow Heidegger) Derrida gives this 'singularity' the name of the *khōra* (using this transliteration).[29] As John Caputo aptly summarizes it in his commentary on Derrida, talk about the *khōra* is 'discourse about a desert, about a barren and

[25] Plato, *Timaeus*, 50A–51B.

[26] Martin Heidegger, *An Introduction to Metaphysics*, trans. R. Manheim (New Haven: Yale University Press, 1959), p. 66; Heidegger, *What is called Thinking?* trans. J. Gray (New York: Harper and Row, 1968), pp. 245ff.

[27] Derrida, 'How to Avoid Speaking', p. 123, citing Heidegger, *What is called Thinking?* (see preceding note).

[28] Derrida, 'How to Avoid Speaking', pp. 123–6.

[29] Derrida, 'How to Avoid Speaking', pp. 123–6. It seems that Derrida uses other terms for essentially the same idea, such as 'hymen' and 'the cut' (*taille*); see 'Double Session', pp. 212–15 and 'Parergon', pp. 121–37.

naked place, a pure taking place, an empty place'.[30] It is a place which is no-place. Derrida denies that the *khōra* is equivalent to the God of negative theology, despite the similarity that speaking about both is experienced as an 'impossible possibility'; his main reason is that the *khōra* is not 'the giver of good gifts'. While giving a gift initially breaks open the power-games of commercial exchange, the gift is soon entrapped within that same process, and with it the giver as well. Thus, one must refrain from saying that the *khōra* gives anything at all, except perhaps that it 'gives place', as it receives all, but this is a gift 'without the least generosity', entailing neither debt nor exchange.[31] Here he takes issue even with the self-presencing of Being in Heidegger, expressed in the phrase 'there is/gives Being' (*es gibt Sein*).[32]

Derrida suggests that the *khōra* in Plato points in fact to a more radical kind of negation than negative theology, for which he also finds the point of departure in Plato. He thus identifies two strands of negative theology in the Greek tradition. The first, which continues within Christian theology, finds the idea of the Good to be 'beyond being'; but, comments Derrida, this is not actually *non*-being, despite assertions in the apophatic tradition. This 'being-beyond' (hyper-being) is super-eminent being, so that negation is at the same time affirmation. Here he quotes Pseudo-Dionysius addressing God as 'beyond being, beyond divinity, beyond goodness' and notes that he begins his prayer 'O Trinity!'. A 'Trinity beyond being' is, Derrida concludes, a 'hyper-essential Trinity',[33] and the same implication is to be found in Meister Eckhart's equation of 'super-essential nothingness' with 'super-eminent Being'.[34] Negative theology simply becomes positive theology, the affirmation of a being beyond being. In this way of thinking, the believer enters a 'place' which is Being itself: as Eckhart expresses it: 'we apprehend God in his *parvis* [sanctuary], for Being is the parvis in which he resides.'[35] Derrida is not altogether opposed to the usefulness of the language of Being, particular as used by Heidegger in a way that eludes all categories, that 'thinks Being outside the existent',[36] and which does not present Being as a totalizing power.[37] His objections here to *hyperousia* seem to be that talk of Trinity imposes a dogmatic framework on what should be infinitely other, and that 'super-essentiality' is understood as an extension from worldly being and so as absolute presence. Further, the 'no-place' ceases to be the challenge of otherness when it is *reduced* to the concept of a house of Being, so that the symbol of

---

[30] Caputo, *Prayers and Tears*, p. 37.
[31] Derrida, 'How to Avoid Speaking', pp. 106–7.
[32] Derrida, 'How to Avoid Speaking', p. 106.
[33] Derrida, 'How to Avoid Speaking', pp. 111, 116.
[34] Derrida, 'How to Avoid Speaking', p. 120.
[35] Derrida, 'How to Avoid Speaking', p. 121, quoting Eckhart (n. 22).
[36] Derrida, *Writing and Difference*, p. 144.
[37] See Chapter 5, the section called 'The Complex Being of the Triune God'.

Being is allowed to become all-embracing. Towards the end of this chapter we will return to Derrida's expressed objections to the doctrine of the Trinity.

The second strand of negative theology identified by Derrida is a more radical negativity, a reference to an Otherness which cannot be categorized either as being or non-being, and *this*—he argues—can be expressed by the strange spacing of the *khōra*. As the space into which, according to Plato, the Demiurge introduces the images of the forms that are essential to creation, it is neither eternal nor temporal, neither intelligible nor sensible, neither existent nor non-existent. For our thinking today it can, Derrida asserts, mark the margin of the 'neither/nor'.[38] This strange 'something' which is altogether Other from us, involves a negativity that escapes both positive and negative registers.

Yet the Totally Other is there (*il y a*), says Derrida, and it is necessary to speak about it, since it haunts the chain of signifiers and keeps open the promise at the heart of difference.[39] The tone of utter negation carried by *khōra* is here brought into tension with the positive associations of promise; the no-place is somehow (but not simply) associated with a 'place of promise', like the Jerusalem where the Apostles were told to wait for the promise of the Spirit.[40] This is, for instance, a promise that any piece of writing can always be repeated with new meaning in forseen and unforseen contexts, and that it will retain its performative power to change lives when a reader 'choose[s] to have him or herself addressed there'.[41] Promise is also a mode of relation to others, asking for their trust and implying that one will be faithful to one's word: 'it renders possible every present discourse on presence'[42] (though not, of course, a full presence). Moreover, the promise reaches beyond even the web of language, undermining any distinction between the 'inside' and the 'outside'; it is always excessive, in a kind of quasi-transcendence since it creates an open-ended *desire* for the primordial 'yes' to which 'we slowly, moving in circles around it, return'.[43] In this phrase Derrida reflects on the final 'yes' of Molly Bloom in James Joyce's *Ulysses*, expressing a desire that cannot be confined; the project of deconstruction is to loosen and unlock rigid structures of meaning and authority, and—as Caputo discerns—'above all to say yes, *oui, oui*, to something whose coming eye hath not seen nor ear heard'.[44]

---

[38] Derrida, 'How to Avoid Speaking', p. 105.

[39] Derrida, 'How to Avoid Speaking', pp. 98–9.

[40] Derrida, 'How to Avoid Speaking', p. 118, citing Pseudo-Dionysius.

[41] Kevin Hart, 'Jacques Derrida: Introduction' in Ward (ed.), *Postmodern God*, p. 163.

[42] Derrida, 'How to Avoid Speaking', p. 84.

[43] Jacques Derrida, 'Ulysse Gramaphone: Deux Mots pour Joyce' in Peggy Kamuf (ed.), *A Derrida Reader* (Hemel Hempstead: Harvester Wheatsheaf, 1991), p. 596.

[44] Caputo, *Prayers and Tears*, p. 18.

Derrida is thus not denying an outside to language, for 'the outside penetrates and thus determines the inside'.[45] What worries him about any theological designation of this outside, and particularly of the *khōra*, is that it easily leads to a totalizing concept of presence which undermines the mediation of language. This danger he even finds in Heidegger's talk about the 'Voice of Being' which sounds out in the space of difference.[46] The *khōra*, as a destabilizing, differentiating source is not to be described in either theological or a-theological language, while traces of it operate as hints and promises of transcendence that puncture all systems built on complete immanence. The trace which undermines all pretensions to full presence also promises the possibility of some kind of presence. The 'margin of play of difference, of opening' forbids only that anything, including God, 'be present in and of itself, referring only to itself'.[47]

Moreover, the 'indestructible desire' (Derrida's phrase)[48] generated by différance and deconstruction is quite other than the will-to-power which Nietzsche saw as the motivation behind the textual nature of the world with its 'necessary fictions'.[49] Feminist thinkers such as Luce Irigaray and Julia Kristeva have adopted the language of the *chōra* (their preferred transliteration), and have developed the concept as a womb-like, nurturing space of origin; in doing so they have resisted the Nietzschian association of desire with violence and have evoked a longing for presence which is characterized by relationships of love. Kristeva, for example, blending psychoanalysis with semiotics, understands the *chōra* as the pre-linguistic receptacle of sub-conscious drives and archetypal relations with the mother and the father. The *chōra* (she writes) 'precedes and underlies figuration and . . . is analogous only to vocal or kinetic rhythm'.[50] The *chōra* is a place 'constituted by movements'.[51] This is the space of the 'semiotic', preceding linguistic symbols which are shaped by a patriarchal culture. The *chōra* contains traces of an experience of a love which is prior to the Oedipal order of relations, and which can break through the signifiers of language, especially in two experiences: that of poetry and that of the maternal body. Both poetry and motherhood shatter the symbolic discourse which is shaped by patriarchal culture. While Kristeva's understanding

---

[45] Derrida, 'Afterword', in *Limited Inc.*, pp. 152–3.

[46] Derrida, *Memoirs of the Blind: The Self-Portrait and Other Ruins*, trans. P. Brault and M. Nauss (Chicago: University of Chicago Press, 1993), pp. 139–42; also 'How to Avoid Speaking', pp. 127–9, where Derrida concludes that for Heidegger (against his protestations), Being is effectively God.

[47] Derrida, *Positions*, p. 26.

[48] Derrida, 'Afterword', p. 116.

[49] See for example F. Nietzsche, *The Will to Power*, vol. 2:12, aphorisms 480–1, 490507 in Levy (ed.), *Complete Works of Nietzsche*, vol.15.

[50] Julia Kristeva, *Revolution in Poetic Language*, trans. M. Waller (New York: Columbia University Press, 1984), p. 26.

[51] Kristeva, *Revolution in Poetic Language*, p. 25.

of *chōra* as a womb seems remote from Derrida's 'desert-place', it is more consonant with Derrida's talk about 'promise' which provides a constructive balance to his negative language of *khōra*.

Kristeva has come under strong criticism from feminist writers for her stress on motherhood and the maternal body. The critique runs like this: if the maternal body belongs to the *chōra*, to a pre-linguistic semiotic realm rather than to the order of symbolism, then women are relegated to a position outside culture, and male hierarchies can never be subverted. In fact, the identifying of women with a pre-cultural, pre-linguistic maternal body may be exactly what satisfies male fantasies.[52] Two replies may be offered to this criticism. First, Kristeva is advancing an account of language in which the semiotic (or pre-discursive) and the symbolic are always interweaving, thereby challenging the split between subject and object. She insists on a heterogeneity in which the choric rhythm is *sublated* (in a Hegelian sense of inclusion). As one commentator puts it, 'the semiotic is both a presymbolic and postsymbolic moment'.[53] The semiotic *chōra* is a fictional place, a no-place, alerting us to the moments of undecidability and transformation working within the subject and the culture. Second, Kristeva does not identify the *chōra* exclusively with the maternal body, despite her own lapses in referring in a shorthand way to the 'maternal chora'. Clearly, according to Kristeva both poetry and the maternal body have the potential to disrupt language as a social code, through splitting symbolization in a strange way. The maternal body shatters the symbolic inscription of the body with a radical alternity; it is a space of 'othering' which is resistant to the signifying subject, since it is about carrying another within one's own identity. Kristeva is not fostering the myth of the archaic mother, but finds the maternal body to be a site of radical otherness, in which the semiotic otherness of the *chōra* breaks surface.

It seems that thinkers who are critical of the old metaphysics of presence— including Heidegger, Derrida and Kristeva—nevertheless find themselves embarked, as Graham Ward puts it, on a 'journey towards another city, a new corporeality, a new spacing in which the other is housed, affirmed'.[54] We should indeed, I suggest, be uneasy about imposing our presence on others and asserting our self-presence at their expense. We are right to object to a picture of a God who sanctions this kind of presence. But we still long for a place to dwell, even while we recognize that that this very desire for *heimlich-keit* might be tranquillizing us against recognizing the anxieties that properly belong to our existence. In this situation it seems to several late-modern

---

[52] See Judith Butler, *Gender Trouble, Feminism and the Subversion of Identity* (London: Routledge, 1990), p. 93.

[53] Ewa Ziarek, 'At the Limits of Discourse: Heterogeneity, Alterity and the Maternal Body in Kristeva's Thought', *Hypatia* 7 (1992), p. 96.

[54] Ward (ed.), *Postmodern God*, p. xli.

thinkers that the image of a 'no-place' which cannot be reached or lived in like any other dwelling-place in the world might nevertheless leave us traces of its presence to provoke us, unsettle us from complacency and open a horizon of promise.

These desires for a healthy presence and a satisfying place in the world find their fulfilment, I want to argue, in a relationship with God. Further, despite Derrida's objections to a 'hyper-essential Trinity', I want to maintain that it is the image of a triune God that actually resolves problems of both presence and place. To explore these theological issues I turn to some passages from Israel's wisdom literature which present wisdom as being hidden, and which—in doing so—reflect on the 'place' of wisdom. Mainly in view is the poem of Job chapter 28, but alongside this I am putting two further passages—a poem at the beginning of the Wisdom of Jesus Ben Sira (1:1–10) and another from Baruch 3:9–4:4 which both show a knowledge of the Job poem. These passages about a hidden wisdom are to be distinguished from those which present wisdom as available (see Chapter 6) and those which portray wisdom as 'vanished' or disappeared (see Chapter 11).

So we begin with a question which seems curiously prescient of our discussion about the problems of presence and place:

> But where shall wisdom be found?
> And where is the *place* of understanding?

This question, placed by the final editor in the mouth of the unfortunate Job (Job 28:12), appears to enquire about a particular *place* where wisdom might be located. It is looking for the place that everyone wants to find, the place where we can get the wisdom to be truly present in the world. When we hear the answer in v.13, 'Mortals do not know the way to it', we appear to be denied entrance to this mysterious place. Moreover, since it is divine wisdom which is in view, the questioner is also apparently faced by the remoteness of God. Human beings are, it may seem, faced by an absolute transcendence excluding them from the dwelling-place of God's wisdom. Only 'God understands the way to it' (v. 23).

However, I want to suggest that this is not the point of the passage at all. The question 'where shall wisdom be found?' is in fact a riddle, and the answer is both surprising and playful as all riddles are. In his study of the literary form of the poem, Claus Westermann has helpfully drawn attention to its genre as an expansion of a short proverb which has the form of a riddle, consisting of question (vv. 12, 20) and answer (v. 23).[55] But what is the point of the riddle? Its solution points us towards a 'place' which—like the philosophers' *chōra*—is not literally a place at all. Like the *chōra* it disturbs neat human schemes of

---

[55] Claus Westermann, *The Structure of the Book of Job* (Philadelphia: Fortress Press, 1981), p. 135.

control of the world, yet unlike the philosophers' *chōra* this 'no-place' points towards a real presence of a God who is hidden, but not absent, and not inaccesssible. To get to this point some patient exploration of the wisdom poems is necessary.

JOB 28: WISDOM AS OBJECTIFICATION, NOT PERSONIFICATION

What kind of wisdom is Job 28 all about? Scholars have a widespread habit of referring to a 'personification' of wisdom in this poem.[56] That is, they suppose that wisdom (*hokmah*) is pictured here as the attractive and enticing 'Lady Wisdom', whose path we have already explored in such passages as Proverbs 8, Ben Sira 24, and Wisdom 6–9. There, however, she is not hidden from human beings; she is available, out on the road of life, inviting those who are foolish to come and live with her and learn in her school. That wisdom played on the earth at the beginning of creation; she delighted in the company of newly created human beings, and the implication is that she still takes pleasure in them. If Job 28 is referring to a personified wisdom, some explanation has to be found as to why this ever-present and welcoming figure has become inaccessible, apparently living remote from human beings in her own dwell-ing-place:

> Mortals do not know the way to [wisdom],
> and it is not found in the land of the living.

For some scholars, following Bultmann, this poem is evidence of the sup-posedly ancient 'wisdom myth' in which wisdom descends from heaven, searches for a home on earth, is rejected by all and so returns to heaven where she now dwells hidden from mortal beings.[57] The answer to the question, 'where is the place of wisdom?' would be 'in heaven, with God'. But I have already suggested that we should take separately, in their own right, passages which present wisdom as either available, hidden, or vanished, rather than forcing a single mythological framework on them all. Only in the late text of 1 Enoch 42 is the outline of the story as proposed apparently visible with main features intact and (as we shall see in due time) there might be a good

---

[56] e.g. Gustav Hölscher, *Das Buch Hiob: Handbuch zum Alten Testament* (Tübingen: Mohr, 1952), pp. 68–9; E. Dhorme, *A Commentary on the Book of Job*, trans. H. Knight (London: Nelson, 1967), p. 414; Crenshaw, *Old Testament Wisdom*, p. 81; S. Schroer, 'Weise Frauen und Ratgeberinnen in Israel: Literarische und historische Vorbilder der personifizierten Chokmah', *Biblische Notizen* 51 (1990), p. 48; Judith Hadley, 'Wisdom and the Goddess' in Day, Gordon, and Williamson (eds), *Wisdom in Ancient Israel*, pp. 240–1.

[57] See Chapter 6, the section called 'No Wisdom Myth: Ben Sira 24:1–22.

reason for this other than a widespread ancient myth. The desire to find such a myth simply assumes a metanarrative of mediation between heavenly and earthly spheres.

Other readers of the poem who identify Lady Wisdom in the text (or at least lurking behind it) find other reasons for the apparently stark contrast between such a secluded figure and the figure of wisdom in Proverbs, offering instruction to travellers on the road of life. It may, for instance, be explained by a sense of crisis in Israelite faith; the sapiential expectation that life is predictable and ordered, and that piety will be rewarded, has been shaken. Some find this to be an internal development of scepticism, while some find it to be prompted by the event of exile from the homeland, disturbing confidence in providence. Roland Murphy is sceptical about such a sudden crisis in the wisdom tradition, and has simply seen the paradox of transcendence and immanence in a figure who can be available one moment and inaccessible the next.[58] But in all these versions, wisdom is hidden because she is supposedly a transcendent being, abiding alone with God. The figure of wisdom, as Burton Mack argues, is a mythological expression of transcendence: she stands for 'a category of knowledge which does not belong to human beings on the basis of observation of experience but which stands over against them.'[59]

This kind of conclusion assumes that Job 28 draws a distinction between two sorts of wisdom. On the one hand, there is a 'practical' or experiential wisdom which *is* available to human beings. On the other hand, it is supposed that there is a 'theological' or 'divine' wisdom which is not, and which is symbolized by the hidden Lady Wisdom, dwelling in heaven, out of the reach of human wisdom. Now, the first part of the poem is indeed a celebration of practical and educational wisdom; it is about the use of human skills in the mining of precious stones and ores, and portrays people as exploring hidden tracks and paths. It vividly portrays some human mastery over the world:

> Surely there is a mine for silver,
> and a place for gold to be refined . . . .
> Miners put an end to darkness
> and search out to the farthest bound
> the ore in gloom and deep darkness.
> They open shafts in a valley . . .
> That path no bird of prey knows,
> and the falcon's eye has not seen it . . .
> They cut out channels in the rocks,
> and their eyes see every precious thing. (vv. 1–10).

---

[58] R. E. Murphy, 'The personification of Wisdom' in Day, Gordon, and Williamson (eds), *Wisdom in Ancient Israel*, p. 233.

[59] Mack, *Logos und Sophia*, p. 52.

Commentators then propose that this practical wisdom is being contrasted with *a totally different kind* of wisdom in the second part of the poem. As Ringgren puts it, 'evidently wisdom has here (vv. 12–22) a special meaning . . . [as] divine wisdom'.[60]

> But where shall wisdom be found?
> And where is the place of understanding?
> Mortals do not know the way to it,
> and it is not found in the land of the living.
> The deep says, 'It is not in me',
> and the sea says, 'It is not with me'.
> It cannot be gotten for gold. . . . . (vv. 12–15)

The next move of thought is to claim that this distinctively 'theological' wisdom is expressed in the form of a personified wisdom figure who is elusive to human beings, dwelling at the side of Yahweh alone. Personification, as Lady Wisdom, is thus a tool for expressing transcendence.

But we cannot begin to see the point of the riddle in Job 28 unless we resist any temptation to force wisdom here into a personification. Not only are any features of personification absent, but in the third part of the poem, wisdom is clearly treated as an *object* of some kind which God surveys, counts, establishes, and searches out:

> God understands the way to it,
> and he knows its place.
> For he looks to the ends of the earth,
> and sees everything under the heavens.
> When he gave to the wind its weight,
> amd apportioned out the waters by measure:
> when he made a decree for the rain,
> and a way for the thunderbolt;
> then he surveyed it and counted it;[61]
> He established it, and searched it out. (vv. 23–7)

Moreover, if the reader attends to what the poem actually says, it is impossible to find two *kinds* of wisdom here. The wisdom God possesses (vv. 23–4) is of a completely practical sort. It is like the wisdom of the wise, in being a matter of observing and handling the world, just as in the activities of vv. 1–11.[62]

---

[60] Ringgren, *Word and Wisdom*, p. 93, n.4, 94, n.5. Others who propose two kinds of wisdom include S. R. Driver and George Buchanan Gray, *A Critical and Exegetical Commentary on the Book of Job*. International Critical Commentary (Edinburgh: T & T Clark, 1921), p. 234; Robert Gordis, *The Book of Job* (New York: Jewish Theological Seminary, 1978), pp. 538–40; John E. Hartley, *The Book of Job*. New International Commentary (Grand Rapids: Eerdmans, 1988), p. 384.

[61] My translation of this line. NRSV: 'then he saw it and declared it'.

[62] Observing this, Stephen A. Geller, '"Where is Wisdom?": A Literary Study of Job 28 in its Settings' in J. Neusner, B. Levine, E. Frerichs (eds), *Judaic Perspectives on Ancient Israel*

Wisdom is depicted as an object of God's activity, and as an entity separate from him, because his surveying of wisdom is synonymous with his operation upon the world in creation. It was when God gave 'weight', 'measure', 'decree' and 'way' to the elements (vv. 25–6) that he did corresponding things to wisdom: he 'surveyed' it,[63] 'counted' it,[64] 'established' it, and 'searched it out' (v. 27). The two sets of activities are not even cause and effect: they are identical. When God gave proportion to the world, that *was* his searching out of wisdom.[65] To know wisdom is to handle the world successfully.

Human beings, we notice, are not excluded from this wisdom. Commentators have repeated so many times that the poem asserts that human beings can know *nothing* about wisdom, that the reader might assume it to be the case without paying regard to the force of the words themselves. But the poem does not say that human beings do not know wisdom: it actually denies that they know the *way* to wisdom or the *place* of wisdom. The riddle question 'But where shall wisdom be found?' is explained by the parallel phrase 'and where is *the place* of understanding?' and is then followed by the statement 'mortals do not know *the way* to it'.[66] The significant terms 'place' and 'way' have already appeared in the first section of the poem which colourfully portrays the human achievements of mining and exploration, and they are repeated in the later section about God's grasp of wisdom. Precious stones and metals can be found in a 'place' and there is a 'way' or path to them which human beings can tread (vv. 1–11). But wisdom cannot be found in any place like that, and there is no simple way to it. Instead, God knew wisdom when he gave a 'way' to the elements in creation (v. 26).

THE POINT OF THE RIDDLE

Now we can see the point of the riddle. The question is, 'where shall wisdom be found?' The solution is that, unlike jewels and ores buried in the earth, there is no single *place* where wisdom is located and no *path* that can be followed to

---

(Philadelphia: Fortress, 1987), pp. 164–5 has argued that the human enterprise in vv. 1–11 is only a parody of divine activity in creation.

[63] The Hebrew *rā'ah* (ראה) 'saw' will bear the meaning I give it: cf. Ezek. 21:21 ('inspect'). The translation 'surveyed' might also be more appropriate for Gen. 1:31.

[64] Instead of the Piel form ספר ('declare') reading the Qal form meaning to 'count' or 'number'; so Gordis, *Book of Job*, p. 311.

[65] Scott L. Harris, 'Wisdom or Creation? A New Interpretation of Job XXVIII 27', *Vetus Testamentum* 33 (1983), pp. 419–27, proposes that the object of the four verbs in v. 27 is *only* the creation; but this oddly moves the subject of the poem away from wisdom.

[66] Reading דרכה ('its way') with LXX and most commentators and translators, against the MT ערכה ('its value').

find it. Wisdom can only be found in *exercising* it.[67] God originally exercised it in creating the world, and continues to exercise it in knowing the world. Wisdom as *ḥokmah*, as we have often seen, is not only a subjective faculty—*being* wise; it also has objective identity as a body of knowledge corresponding to the world. It is the wisdom which is out there, waiting to be discovered. So God knows the 'place' of wisdom and the 'way' to it. This is not because God knows a heavenly hiding-place where Lady Wisdom is concealed. It is because God has a total knowledge of *all* places in the world and sees the paths for all the elements in the world, such as the wind, the waters, the rain, and the thunderbolt:

> then he surveyed it and counted it;
> he established it and searched it out.

Wisdom is thus presented as an object that God knows well because it is the world itself as an object of study and activity. There is no need to postulate here, with David Clines, a wisdom whose 'character is ingrained in the fabric of the world . . . as fixed as a law of nature'.[68] To know the fabric of the world *is* to know wisdom, and the order of the world might not be 'fixed' at all.

Clines, however, comes close to my reading of the passage when he affirms that 'wisdom is not an object that can be obtained, but an experience one comes to through appropriate behaviour in religion and ethics'.[69] Indeed, he cites my observation that the answer to the question 'Where shall wisdom be found?' is 'in exercising it'.[70] He adds that 'Wisdom is not "located" anywhere, it is not something to be "found", for its nature has already been disclosed to humans by God.'[71] However, he bases his conclusion on his acceptance of

---

[67] I first proposed this solution to the riddle in my unpublished D.Phil. thesis, *The Hiddenness of Wisdom in the Old Testament and Later Judaism* (Oxford, 1976), pp. 140–52, and published the substance of the idea in ' "Where Shall Wisdom be Found?" Job 28 as a Riddle for Ancient and Modern Readers' in John Barton and David Reimer (eds), *After the Exile: Essays in Honour of Rex Mason* (Macon: Mercer University Press, 1996), pp. 171–90. Since 1976, a similar solution has been suggested by J. Gerald Janzen, *Job*. Interpretation Bible Commentary (Atlanta: John Knox, 1985), pp. 197–8: 'true wisdom is found "in" the creative act; and the "way to" wisdom is entry into such an act'; Carole Newsom has followed Janzen, stating that 'wisdom's place is not a location; wisdom is found in an act of creativity': Newsom, 'The Book of Job' in *The New Interpreter's Bible*, ed. L. E. Keck et al. Vol. 4 (Nashville: Abingdon, 1996), p. 532; also Newsom, 'Dialogue and Allegorical Hermeneutics in Job 28:28' in Van Wolde (ed.), *Job 28*, p. 303; similarly, Greenstein, 'The Poem on Wisdom in Job 28' in Van Wolde (ed.), *Job 28*, p. 274, citing Newsom. Clines, *Job 21–37*, pp. 992–3, cites Newsom and Janzen.

[68] David Clines, *Job 21–37*. Word Biblical Commentary (Nashville: Nelson, 2006), p. 920; cf. Newsom, 'The Book of Job', p. 533: 'Wisdom is in the world, woven into its very fabric'; also Norman C. Habel, *The Book of Job* (London: SCM, 1985), pp. 400–1: 'mystery . . . the fundamental principle'.

[69] Clines, *Job 21–37*, p. 922.

[70] David Clines, ' "The Fear of the Lord is Wisdom" (Job 28:28). A Semantic and Contextual Study', in Van Wolde (ed.), *Job 28*, p. 78, fn.46, referencing my ' "Where Shall Wisdom be Found?" ', p. 176.

[71] Clines, *Job 21–37*, pp. 922–3.

v. 28 as the original climax to the poem: 'And he said to humankind, "Truly the fear of the Lord, that is wisdom; and to depart from evil is understanding."' This, in his view, is the behaviour in which wisdom is known. But there is good reason to suppose that verse 28 is an addition to the poem, breaking in with the portentous announcement 'And he said to man.'[72] If it is the original climax, the whole poem is not only a riddle, not only deliberately misleading, but self-contradictory as—in the light of this disclosure—wisdom is not actually hidden at all. This undermines the clear implication of the poem that there is something elusive about wisdom. Clines is right to affirm that the poem does not exclude human beings from exercising wisdom, but misses the element of hiddenness that still remains in wisdom, even at the end of the poem and the solving of the riddle.

The reason for this hiddenness is indicated by the parallel form of the riddle. The riddle asks 'Where shall wisdom be found?', and the answer to which the reader is invited to come is 'in exercising it'. The parallel question is: 'where is the *place* of wisdom?' and the answer is: 'wisdom lies in knowing every place'.

> God understands the way to [wisdom],
> and he knows its place.
> For he looks to the ends of the earth
> and sees everything under the heavens. (vv. 23–4)

The phrase 'he looks to the ends of the earth' cannot mean that God literally sees a place on the earth where wisdom is, since the poet has already told us that it has no dwelling place in the land of the living or the deeps of the sea. The phrase celebrates the perfect observation of God, as is made clear by the occurrence of the idea elsewhere (Ps. 19:6, Ps. 33:13–14, Isa. 40:27–8). Unlike any human wise person, God has knowledge of every part of the vast creation; his vision is total. Wisdom cannot be found *somewhere*, because in its fulness it is the comprehending of *everywhere*. There is certainly then a huge difference between the wisdom of the wise and the wisdom of God. But—as can also be seen in passages about an available, personified wisdom[73]—it is a difference of scope and extent, not a different kind of thing altogether. Human beings can use a certain amount of wisdom in digging jewels and ores out of the earth and opening up paths to secret places that even the birds of the air cannot see. But wisdom itself cannot be simply mined out of the earth like a precious stone or purchased like a commodity. The riddle question 'But where shall *wisdom* be

---

[72] Commentators who find v. 28 to be an addition include Dhorme, *Job*, p. 414; Georg Fohrer, *Hiob*, Kommentar Zum Alten Testament (Gütersloh: Ferd Mohn, 1963), p. 392; von Rad, *Wisdom*, p. 148. Rowley, *Job*, p. 234, defends its inclusion and (extraordinarily) judges that without it the poem is a piece of 'unrelieved agnosticism'. My own exegesis of the verse stands in Chapter 10, the end of the section 'Wisdom as Torah'.

[73] See Chapter 6, the section called 'Wisdom as Observer: Proverbs 8:22–31'.

found?' means there is no short cut to wisdom, and that human beings can never possess it entirely.

This was in fact a lesson deeply rooted in the wisdom tradition. From early on the wise in Israel had a sense of caution and humility in handling the world. For all their confidence that they could steer their way through life, they recognized their limitations because of the multiplicity and inexhaustible extent of the world. As time went on and wisdom became more religious, this caution was expressed as the fear of Yahweh. *God* has possession of wisdom because he has a grasp of all the complexities of the world. Every element and item in the whole range of nature lies open to his observation, and he can therefore steer his way through creation with complete certainty. This theme which appears through the images of 'way' and 'place' in Job 28 receives magnificent elaboration in chapters 38–41 with its repeated questions about God's familiarity with the many ways and places of the world:

> Have you entered into the springs of the sea,
> or walked in the recesses of the deep? . . .
> Where is the way to the dwelling of light,
> and where is the place of darkness,
> that you may take it to its territory
> and that you may discern the paths to its home?
> Have you entered the storehouses of the snow?
> What is the way to the place where the light is distributed,
> where the east wind is scattered upon the earth?
> Who has cut a channel for the torrents of rain,
> and a way for the thunderbolt? (38:16, 19–20, 22–24)

Unlike God, human beings are often baffled by a world which is vast in its extent, complicated in its contents, and intricate in its details. There is a dimension of hiddenness in wisdom (though it is never entirely hidden), but this is not because wisdom is a transcendent reality dwelling in heaven. It is not because Lady Wisdom has taken up her residence in a secret place. It is because of the expansiveness of the world order. Some detail will always elude the wise and trip them up when they think that they have sorted the situation out. The boundary upon human wisdom is not the transcendence of a 'theological' wisdom, but the boundlessness of the area to be explored. Here is the heart of the riddle: God knows wisdom because God knows the world in its inexhaustibility, while human beings know wisdom in a lesser way because they are limited in knowing the world.

There was a particular temptation in Israel to forget this 'fear of the Lord', or religious humility, in employing guidelines which reflected cause–effect linkages ('if you do A, B will follow'). In the collections of Proverbs we find about thirty-five times the guideline that the righteous will be rewarded in this life, and the wicked will punished. As an observation of cause and effect in particular circumstances this has a certain truth. In many situations acting wickedly brings its own disaster, and acting righteously brings its own well-being. But there is no necessary connection, and the wise should have been humble enough to abandon the rule when confronted by events that failed to fit it. However, faced by the complexities of experience, there was a tendency for these empirical statements to rigidify into the principle of retribution. If people were prospering, God *must* be rewarding them for being good. If people were suffering calamity, God *must* be punishing them for being evil. If people behaved well, God *must* favour them with material blessings.

It is this hardening into dogma that the Book of Job protests against. It tells the story of a righteous man who still meets disaster—losing his wealth, his family, his reputation in a series of terrible events. The book bursts through the hardened arteries of dogmatic wisdom to return the flow of wisdom to its original well-spring. It recalls the early openness of wisdom to the shock of new experience. Chapters 38–41 achieve this by listing scores of items in the world that the wise can never grasp, from whose creation they were absent and which continue without reference to them (the hippopotamus and the crocodile, for example), so showing the absurdity of judging anyone's situation. The poem of Job 28 does the same thing by posing a riddle: 'where can wisdom be found'? That is, it challenges those who have been trying to find a single 'place' where wisdom dwells, and so have been attempting to box God up in a container of dogma. The friends of Job represent one example of this, by insisting that Job's suffering must be the consequence of wickedness, even if they find increasingly sophisticated ways of stating the connection. But Job also ascribes to a dogma of retribution: he insists that God must release him from suffering because he is righteous (13:13–28); God, he demands, must meet him in a courtroom confrontation, and reward him for his goodness. This is why the poem presents Job as repenting; he does finally confront God, and finds it is enough to know that God is present with him (42:5).

Dramatically, therefore, Job 28 cannot be envisaged as spoken either by Job or any of his friends. In the final editing of the book it appears to be the second part of a speech begun by Job in chapter 27, but it shows an insight into the problem which Job has not attained, and does not grasp until the brief confession of 42:5. David Clines has urged that it should be assigned to Elihu and placed later in the dialogues,[74] but Elihu still clings to a dogma of retribution, although he has refined it to be a means of divine self-communication rather than simple punishment (33:19–27). The poem is thoroughly in place in the whole work, but as an intermezzo or 'meditative interlude',[75] awakening all the participants to areas of mystery and the unknown. It might be argued that the final verse of chapter 28 sums up this kind of 'fear of the

---

[74] Clines, *Job 21–37*, pp. 908–9.
[75] So Newsom, 'The Book of Job', p. 528.

Lord', and so is part of the original poem, but I believe that it is a sign of something else altogether—the transfer of 'fear of the Lord' language from humility to observance of Torah, a point I shall argue later.

In the book of Job as he have it, a poetic dialogue about suffering (dating somewhere between the sixth and second centuries BCE) has been been inserted into an older narrative framework, perhaps a folk tale. The prose beginning and ending (1:1–2:13; 42:7–17), portraying the accusation of the Satan in the heavenly council about the motives for Job's righteousness, God's decision to test Job and his final restoration of his servant to all the goods of life, sets up undeniable tensions with the poem which there is no opportunity to pursue in this study. Crenshaw's judgement that dramatically 'the epilogue can be dispensed with altogether'[76] attracts assent, since Job has already reached the climax of his meeting with God, and his subsequent reward for faithfulness appears to vindicate the principle of retribution against which the poem has been protesting. However, we might applaud the skill of the ancient editor in doing his best to integrate the prose and the poetry, in carrying through the basic themes that no rational explanation can be found for suffering, and that neither God nor wisdom can therefore be boxed up in one conceptual 'place'. The Satan's challenge 'does Job fear God for nothing?' (i.e. for nothing to be gained—1:9) is a powerful assault on reliance upon retribution. Moreover, Job is never actually told of the wager God has made in heaven; in terms of the participants in the drama this is not available as an explanation and so for readers who empathize with Job a theory of divine testing is not available to them either. It might be argued too that, in the light of the whole poem, Job's good fortune in the epilogue is one more deliberate dissonance, refusing the reader's desire for closure by adding one more dimension to a complex exploration of the question.[77] But the plot-mechanism creaks.

PLACES AND DIMENSIONS OF THE WORLD

The poem of Job presents us with a riddle. The 'place' where wisdom is to be found turns out not to be a literal place at all, not a place that is the object of geographical science. There is no *single* place either on earth or in heaven which wisdom inhabits. Lady Wisdom is not hiding herself away somewhere in a place that we could find if we only we were God. The place of wisdom is not a place like that; it is strictly a 'no-place'. The riddle thus presents a *certain sort* of transcendence of wisdom. Wisdom transcends or 'goes beyond' the

---

[76] Crenshaw, *Old Testament Wisdom*, p. 89.
[77] So Newsom, 'The Book of Job', p. 634.

grasp of the human mind in its inexhaustible extent, and divine wisdom transcends human wisdom because God alone comprehends this complexity. This can be expressed poetically by affirming that 'God knows the place of wisdom' (v. 23), but it is strictly a 'no-place'. Presenting wisdom as a personification, a welcoming woman (notably in Proverbs 8, Ben Sira 24 and Wisdom 6–9) is a way of affirming the availability of wisdom to human beings, as an invitation to sharing in a communion of life. Presenting wisdom as a complex object to be 'surveyed' (as in Job 28) is a way of expressing its elusiveness, alongside its potential for exploration. Both stories are true: wisdom is accessible—she is there to be enjoyed—but wisdom can never be entirely possessed: we can never finally analyse this fascinating object.

My exegesis of Job 28 fits in with a literary trope that can be found widely in the Hebrew Bible, that of the threefold dimensions of the world, its height, depth, and breadth. When associated with a figure of wisdom who makes herself available, these dimensions encompass the path of a wisdom who follows the track of the sun; they are a stage-setting for her appearance. In many other texts, the dimensions of the world are presented as a scene that escapes comprehension because of its extensiveness;[78] despite the variations between them, all examples of the trope relate this ungraspable mass in some way to the hiddenness of a wisdom or a knowledge which is *objectified* as something that cannot be fully explored. Thus, wisdom is identified with the inexhaustible scope of the world. In Job 28, for instance, wisdom is:

> concealed from the birds of the air (height).
> Abaddon and death say,
> 'We have only heard a rumour of it with our ears' (depth);
> But God looks to the ends of the earth (breadth).

Isaiah 40 presents an example from outside the wisdom literature, but apparently influenced by wisdom ideas,[79] since the prophet asks who has instructed God 'as his counsellor,' or has 'taught him knowledge' (vv. 13–14). Especially significant is the question 'Who has showed him the *way* of understanding?' As in Job 28, this 'way' turns out to be an ability to survey the three dimensions of the world, implying that human beings are limited in their own capacity to 'measure' anything (and especially the spirit of Yahweh—v. 13):

---

[78] I propose the following classification of these 'world dimension' texts: (1) *Hidden wisdom as an objective entity*: Job 28:13–14, 21–4; Baruch 3:29–30; Ben Sira 1:1–3; Ben Sira 24:28–9. (2) *Other examples of hidden wisdom*: Job 11:5–12, Job 9:5–9, Job 26:5–8; Job 38:12–21; Eccl. 1:5–7; Eccl. 7:23–4; Prov. 25:3; Prov. 30:4; Ben Sira 16:18; Wisd. 9:16; (3) *Similar passages outside wisdom writing*: Deut. 30:12–13; Ps. 139:8–9; Isa. 40:12; Isa. 55:8–9; 2 Baruch 48:5; 4 Esdras 4:7–8; 1 Enoch 93:12–14.

[79] So McKane, *Prophets and Wise Men*, pp. 81–2, envisaging the prophet as offering a polemic against the claims of Israelite statesmen.

> Who has measured the waters in the hollow of his hand (depth)
> and marked off the heavens with a span, (height)
> enclosed the dust of the earth in a measure, (breadth)
> and weighed the mountains in scales,
> and the hills in a balance? (Isa. 40:12)

In Ecclesiastes 1:5–7 human wisdom is baffled when faced by a world of perpetual motion in all three dimensions:

> The sun rises and the sun goes down....
> round and round goes the wind....
> All streams run to the sea.

Thus, the 'dimensional' formula does not depict boundaries *beyond* which wisdom dwells (or else personified wisdom could not appear in the earthly arena), but it shows the limits on human wisdom that arise from the expanse *within* the boundaries. The trope does not portray the transcendence or remoteness of wisdom, but the inexhaustible extent of the world, and thus of wisdom. The sage Ben Sira envisages that someone might plead 'what is my life compared with the measureless creation?', and so foolishly think that he will escape God's notice; he then goes on to refer to the 'heaven, the abyss and the earth', concluding 'what human mind can grasp this or comprehend God's ways?' (Sir. 16:18–20). Similarly, there is an earlier piece from Proverbs 30:1–4:

> Thus says the man: I am weary, O God,
> I am weary, O God, I am spent...
> I have not learned wisdom,
> Nor have I [the] knowledge of the Holy One.
> Who has ascended to heaven and come down?
> Who has gathered the wind in the hollow of the hand?
> Who has wrapped up the waters in a garment?
> Who has established all the ends of the earth?[80]

We notice that various parts of the world might express height, breadth, and depth; for example, the sea can express either breadth or (as in this example) depth. Surveying these dimensions, the poet is not claiming that wisdom is hidden anywhere in particular. He is asserting that wisdom is hard to get hold of because of its sheer extent, as large as the world, a scene that escapes full comprehension by anyone except God. Moreover, the poet is 'weary' because the dimensions do not simply represent distance, but the number of items within them. Of great significance for the elusiveness of the world order is that these dimensions are not simply distance, but stand for the multiplicity of items within extremities: a 'measureless' creation is an 'uncountable' creation, and the wisdom writers are grappling with a world that is for them infinitely

---

[80] NRSV, using translations of the Hebrew from the margin.

extended not in empty distances, but in the inexhaustibility of objects that make up the distances. The very idea 'world' is often conveyed in the Old Testament by the phrase 'the heavens and the earth *and all that is in them*',[81] or simply 'the all' or 'the whole', 'the totality of things' (Prov. 16:4).[82] As Luis Stadelmann suggests, 'the Bible does not distinguish container from contents . . . space never appears as an inert, lifeless receptacle'.[83]

Like late-modern concepts of space, the wisdom idea of space is not an empty expanse which is subsequently filled with 'places'; rather, the dimensions of the world cannot be envisaged without relation to specific places in the world. Within the trope of the world dimensions, extent and multiplicity always belong together, as is readily seen in the favourite equation of 'searching out' with 'counting up.' So in Job 28:27 God 'counted [wisdom] up' and 'searched it out'.[84] Again, Job 9:10 celebrates God

> who does great things and unsearchable,
> marvellous things without number.

A similar equation of 'searching' and 'counting' is found in the Greek wisdom books, in the use of 'trace out' (*exichniazein* ἐξιχνιάζειν) in the context of 'numbering' items in the world. Thus in Ben Sira 18:4–6:

> Who can trace out his mighty deeds?
> Who can count up [the instances of] his majestic power?
> Who shall add up his mercies to tell the full account?
> No one can substract from them or add to them,
> nor trace out the wonderful acts of the Lord.[85]

The pattern here is: trace out—number—number—number—trace out. In another dimensional scheme, Wisdom 9:15–16 considers how difficult it is for the mind which 'muses upon many things' to 'trace out' what is 'on earth, close at hand and in heaven' (cf. 6:22). Ben Sira 24 considers that the thoughts of wisdom which are to be 'traced out' are vaster in number than water in an ocean. Most obviously, Ben Sira 1:1–3 equates the 'tracing out' of the height, breadth, and depth of the world with the 'numbering' of its items—the 'sand of the sea, the drops of rain, and the days of unending time'. No one, reflects the sage later on, can 'measure' the marvels of God's creation, and either increase or diminish them: 'when someone comes to the end of them he is still at the

---

[81] e.g. 1 Chr. 29:11, Ex. 20:11, Gen. 2:1, Ps. 146:6, Jer. 51:48.

[82] Also Eccl. 1:2, 3:11, 11:15, 12:8, cf. Ps. 119:91, Jer. 10:16, Isa. 44:24. For wisdom in Jer 10:16 see von Rad, *Wisdom*, p. 179; for wisdom in Isa. 44:24 (context) see McKane, *Prophets and Wise Men*, pp. 94–7. Non–sapiential instances are Ps. 145:9, 1 Chr. 29:11.

[83] Luis J. Stadelmann, *The Hebrew Concept of the World* (Rome: Pontifical Biblical Institute, 1970), pp. 1–2. However, he makes a too easy contrast between 'Hebrew' and 'Greek' conceptions of spatiality.

[84] Cf. Prov. 25:3, Baruch 3:17–18.

[85] My translation.

beginning' (18:7). Earlier a Psalmist had confessed that when he tried to count
the creative thoughts of God 'they are more than the sand' (Psalm 139:17–18).

Another major trope for expressing the multiple nature of the world is a list
of elements, modelled on the Egyptian onomastica. The influence of this
Egyptian form for classifying natural phenomena[86] is discernible in hymnody
of the Hebrew Bible, and in particular in the wisdom poems.[87] There is a
distinctive pattern in the Egyptian onomastica which rehearse the wonders of
the created world in a set order: heavenly items—meteorological items—
earthly items (including inhabitants).[88] The categorizing of the Egyptian list
thus differs from the Hebrew tripartite world scheme of three dimensions: the
basic pattern of the onomasticon is that it works around to the earth by means
of meteorological phenomena, and deals with the sea and water formations as
part of the earth rather than as a separate dimension. Of the four most
extensive instances of the widespread influence of this form in Hebrew
poetry[89] (Job 38f, Ben Sira 43, Psalm 148 and 'The Song of the Three Children'
in Daniel 3:52–90 LXX), two follow this sequence quite closely (Ben Sira 43
and 'The Song'), but the other two show a notable variation, accommodating
them to the three-dimensional trope.

This is most clearly seen in Job 38–39, which already seems uniquely to
combine two forms found in Egyptian literature, the onomasticon (for
example the Onomasticon of Amenemope) and an ironic use of the catache-
tical code of instruction (as found in the 'Satirical Letter' preserved in Papyrus
Anastasi I).[90] At the beginning of chapter 38 the pattern of three dimensions is
repeated twice, with regard both to creation in the past and God's activity in
the present. The thought of the writer moves as follows:

- earth = breadth, in the past ('who stretched out the line upon it? vv. 4–7)
- sea = depth, in the past ('who shut in the sea with doors?' vv. 8–11)
- heavens = height, in the past and present ('have you commanded the
  morning?' vv. 12–15)
- sea = depth, in the present ('have you entered into the springs of the
  sea?' 'Have you seen the gates of deep darkness?' vv. 16–18)

---

[86] Texts in Alan H. Gardiner, *Ancient Egyptian Onomastica* 2 Volumes (London: Oxford
University Press, 1947), who insists they were not merely spelling lists (vol. 1, pp. 3–4, 35ff).

[87] So von Rad, 'Job xxxviii and Ancient Egyptian Wisdom' in Problem of the Hexateuch,
pp. 281–91; E. Richter, 'Die Naturweisheit des Alten Testaments im Buche Hiob', *Zeitschrift für
die Alttestamentlichen Wissenschaft* 70 (1958), pp. 1–20.

[88] Pointed out by von Rad, 'Job xxxviii and Ancient Egyptian Wisdom', pp. 285, 291, n.14.

[89] The debt is also visible in e.g. Gen. 1:1–2:4a; Sir. 39:26, 4Esdras 7:39–42; Eccl. 1:5–7; Song
2:11–13a, 3:9f; Pss. 8:8f, 147; Job 24:5–8, 14–16a and in the Elihu speeches of Job: so Fohrer,
Hiob, p. 497, who also however offers examples that belong to the tripartite scheme rather than
the onomastic form.

[90] 'A Satirical Letter', ANET, pp. 475–9; Erman, *Literature of the Ancient Egyptians*, pp. 214–34.

- earth = breadth, in the present ('Have you comprehended the expanse of the earth?' v. 18)

The usual sequence of an onomastic list is thus interrupted from 38:4–18, and then the expected order returns: the heavens (light, picking up from vv. 12–15)—meteorological phenomena (snow, hail, wind, rain, thunderbolts, ice, hoarfrost, clouds)—earth (lion, raven, mountain goat, wild ass, wild ox, ostrich, horse, hawk, and so on). Similarly in Psalm 148 it seems quite natural to move from the heavens (vv. 1–6) to the earth (v. 7a) to the sea-depths (v. 7b) before returning to the pattern in meteorological and finally earthly items. The familiar dimensional scheme evokes the expanse of the world order, an effect underlined by the writer of Job 38 when he draws attention to measurement in vv. 5, 10, and 18 ('who determined its measurements... prescribed bounds... comprehended the expanse?'). The result of this pattern, combining the dimensions with the list, is to bring together extent and multiplicity, 'surveying' and 'counting.' The list of items is presented as filling out the dimensions, as making clear that the outlines of the world can only be understood as containing a mass of elusive detail, not as empty space.

THE 'PLACE' OF WISDOM IN BEN SIRA AND BARUCH

The relation between 'space' (world-dimensions) and 'many places' in wisdom literature makes clear that the world is elusive to human survey because of its inexhaustible nature. God, on the other hand, is aware of all its complex detail and is present to it. A riddle-like way of stating the same truth in Job 28 is that human beings do not know the 'place' of wisdom, but that God does; the place of wisdom must, however, literally be a 'no-place', or the effect of the riddle is lost. There is further support for this exegesis of Job 28 in the fact that two later poems which refer to the earlier poem apparently understand it in this way.

The poem of Ben Sira 1:1–10 appears to contain verbal echoes of both Proverbs 8 and Job 28, and we are thus not surprised to find that it presents wisdom in ways that recall both a personified figure and an impersonal object.

1 All wisdom is from the Lord;
   wisdom is with him for ever.

2 Who can count the sand of the sea,
   the drops of rain, or the days of unending time?

3 Who can trace out the height of the sky,
   the breadth of the earth, or the depth of the abyss?

4 Wisdom was created before all things;
   intelligent purpose has been there from the beginning.

6 To whom has the root of wisdom been uncovered?
  And who has understood her subtleties?

8 One there is who is wise, greatly to be feared,
  the Lord, sitting upon his throne.

9 It is he who created her, surveyed and numbered her
  and poured her out upon all his works.

10 To all humankind he has given her in some measure
  but in plenty to those who love him.[91]

The portrayal of objectified wisdom is to the fore here, while personified wisdom appears as only a shadowy image. In slight support of a personification are the references, reminiscent of Proverbs 8, to wisdom's being 'with God' (v. 1 = Proverbs 8:30) and being the first created reality (v. 4 = Proverbs 8:22). Perhaps the most significant feature in favour of a personification would be a reference to 'subtle thoughts' (*panourgeumata*/πανουργευματα) of wisdom (v. 6), if this were the correct translation. Ringgren's cautious judgement is, nevertheless, correct: 'In the passage 1:1–10 wisdom cannot be said to appear as a personal being.'[92] The feminine gender of the Greek noun *sophia* (wisdom) and associated personal pronouns cannot of course in themselves denote a female figure in the absence of personal characteristics. In contrast to this shadowy presence of a personification of wisdom is the obvious character of wisdom as an impersonal object of investigation, and the poet shows he has solved the riddle of Job 28 in equating this wisdom with the extent of the world order.

A ringing declaration about God's faculty of wisdom—potentially personified—in verse 1 is followed immediately by the description of a world in threefold dimensions (v. 3) whose content is uncountable (v. 2), which is both the object of investigation by wisdom (vv. 1–3) and analogous to the extent of wisdom itself (vv. 6–9). We thus move from considering wisdom as a faculty of mind to wisdom as a body of knowledge, a transcript of the world order. The glossator who added 'or wisdom'[93] to the second line of verse 3 (so giving 'Who can trace out . . . wisdom?') has, therefore, correctly understood the intention of this portrayal of the world: the absurdity of measuring the height, breadth, and depth of the *world* is equivalent to the impossibility of measuring *wisdom*. The reason for the hiddenness of wisdom is the extent and multiplicity of the area of knowledge with which it has to deal: the 'numbering' (verb *exarithmeō*/ἐξαριθμεω) of the *world* in v. 2 is recalled in the 'numbering' (*exarithmeō*) of *wisdom* in v. 9, and the 'tracing out' of the *world* in v. 3 is recalled in the 'surveying' of *wisdom* in v. 9. Further, the 'depth' (*abussos*/ἀβυσσος) of the *world* in v. 3 is juxtaposed with the depth image expressed by the 'root' of wisdom in v. 6.

---

[91] vv. 1, 2, 10 NEB; other verses my translation. Other textual witnesses add two extra verses (vv. 5, 7) omitted here with NEB.

[92] Ringgren, *Word and Wisdom*, p. 107.

[93] G., omitted in Syriac, Old Latin.

The question 'to whom has the root of wisdom been uncovered?' recalls the central question of Job 28, 'where shall wisdom be found?' Rather than wisdom being hypothesized as a precious object to be digged out of the ground, it is postulated as an organic, growing thing (perhaps alluding to the mythical tree of wisdom)[94] which is rooted in the ground. But wisdom cannot be uncovered, either like a buried precious stone or the root of a plant; God knows its place because he has 'surveyed' and 'numbered' wisdom (v. 9), overtly recalling Job 28:27. Thus, when Ben Sira wishes to speak of the inscrutability of wisdom, he depicts it as an object which is complex and expansive, as wide as the world. He evokes the hiddenness of wisdom by enquiring who can count the endless grains of sand, drops of rain, or days of time; he demands to know who can trace out 'the height of the sky, the breadth of the earth or of the deep'. In an echo of Job 28, the poet asserts that only God can do this fully, since he has 'created, surveyed and numbered' wisdom and 'poured her out upon all his works'. Wisdom, as the riddle tells us, is known in exercising it.

But, as in Job 28, this does not mean that wisdom is *totally* inaccessible to human beings. In an echo of Proverbs 8 the poet asserts that the wisdom (personified) who is 'with the Lord for ever' has been 'given to all humankind *in some measure*' (v. 10a, cf. Prov. 8:31 'delighting in the human race'). It is not a contradiction to affirm that wisdom is both hidden and available; human beings are not shut out from wisdom altogether, but need a good dose of humility. The poem is a stage beyond Job 28 (at least vv. 1–27) in assuming that wisdom is to be identified with Torah, so that wisdom has been given 'in plenty to those who love him' (v. 10b); but those who do not have the Torah still have *some* possession of wisdom (v. 10a). It seems a measure of desperation to find a 'myth of hidden wisdom' here, as does Felix Christ, following Bultmann;[95] he reads an implicit rejection of wisdom by human beings between the lines of 10a and 10b, so that after being given to all humankind she is rejected, returns to heaven and returns only to 'those who love' God. But this is pure speculation. Wisdom is not concealed by being located in a place with God in heaven, but because of its extent and complexity, which leaves some access open to all.

Mention of the 'subtleties' (*panourgeumata*/πανουργευματα) of wisdom in 1:6 brings together, to a certain extent, the personification and the objectification, the availability and the hiddenness of wisdom. The term might apply either to the 'subtle thoughts' of a personified wisdom, or to the complexities of a body of knowledge. We have already seen, in fact, that the thoughts of a wise person can be envisaged as a kind of objectification, corresponding to the

---

[94] cf. Lambert, *Babylonian Wisdom Literature*, p. 327 (a tree with its roots in the underworld); cf. Sir. 1:20, 14:26f.

[95] Christ, *Jesus Sophia*, p. 31.

reality that lies 'out there' in the world. While some commentators confidently translate *panourgeumata* (πανουργευματα) as 'her subtle thoughts',[96] the personification is not as obvious as this, and 'subtleties' is placed in parallel to the clearly impersonal 'root of wisdom' in v. 6a. Thus the writer of *panourgeumata* in 1:6 is most likely to have intended the meaning of 'secrets'[97] or 'subtle structures', having in mind the proportions of objective wisdom in v. 9. However, the possibility is still there of giving *panourgeumata* the personal spin of 'subtle thoughts', and in that case there would be a convergence of availability and hiddenness in wisdom: a personified wisdom shares her thoughts with those who seek her, but they can never grasp *all* their implications and profundities.

The wisdom poem in Baruch 3:9–4:4[98] also identifies wisdom with the Torah, but draws a different conclusion: wisdom dwells among people who have the Torah, but others have no wisdom at all. The poem therefore differs from Job 28 and Ben Sira 1 in denying wisdom totally to human beings outside the knowledge of Torah. But the poet still shows an understanding of the riddle in Job 28, by finding the same *reason* for the hiddenness of wisdom to people in general—not an ascent of wisdom to heaven (as Bultmann and Wilckens propose),[99] or a seclusion in some mysterious place on earth, but the expansiveness and inexhaustibility of the world.

Wisdom in this poem is clearly hidden, the poet asking 'Has any man discovered the dwelling-place of wisdom or entered her storehouses?' (3:15), and concluding 'No one can know the path or conceive the way that will lead to wisdom' (3:31). Beyond an evident general debt of the poem to Job 28 (among many other texts from the Hebrew Bible), we may observe that the section on the hiddenness of wisdom (vv. 15–35) is even structured in basically the same way:

- Human beings display remarkable achievements, but fail to discover 'the way of wisdom' (3:15–28; cf. Job 28:1–12);
- No human person can find or purchase wisdom (vv. 29–31; cf. Job 28:12–22);

---

[96] So G. H. Box and W. O. E. Oesterly, 'Sirach' in Charles (ed.) *Apocrypha and Pseudepigrapha*, vol. 1, p. 318; Revised Version, 'her shrewd counsels'. Cf 42:18 with regard to human thoughts.

[97] Cf. Rudolf Smend, *Die Weisheit des Jesus Sirach* (Berlin: Reimer, 1908), p. 8, 'Klugheit, oder vielmehr objectiv das *Geheimnis*'.

[98] The Book of Baruch, probably translated from Hebrew, is mostly concerned with issues of the exile, restoration, and return, and a date in the mid-first century BCE seems likely; see D. G. Burke, *The Poetry of Baruch* (Atlanta: Scholar's Press, 1982), pp. 20–3.

[99] Bultmann, *Exegetica*, p. 15; so also Wilckens, Art. σοφία, p. 509. Christ, *Jesus Sophia*, p. 45, argues that wisdom is hidden here because of its nature, not because it is rejected, but still finds that the poet draws on a myth of rejected wisdom for colour.

- Only God knows the way to wisdom (in the present) and utilized it in creation in the past (vv. 32–35; cf. Job 28:23–27).

Further, the final stage of the identification of wisdom with Torah in Baruch 3:36ff ('she is the book of the commandments of God') corresponds in position to the addition of v.28 to the poem of Job 28, and it appears therefore that the Baruch poet at least understands the 'fear of the Lord' in Job 28:28 as the Torah.

We notice immediately that there is a far more negative judgement upon human achievement than in Job 28. Mortals are not simply ignorant of the way 'to' wisdom, but the way 'of' wisdom. Thus any possibility of a life shaped by wisdom's patterns of behaviour is entirely denied to human beings. To some extent the expression 'the way of wisdom'[100] has by now become a faded, if not a dead metaphor. But the mythological picture of a personified wisdom who walks the circuit of the earth is also just still visible. We should not over-dramatize her appearance: the figure of wisdom is hardly more personal than in Job 28. The *Jerusalem Bible* makes a correct interpretation when it translates the literal 'her ways' as 'the paths she treads' (in vv. 21, 23) but it is wrong to make the personification so unambiguous. There is a deliberate blurring of a personal figure so that, as Ringgren judges, 'Wisdom is...not very clearly shaped as a personal being.'[101] There is certainly no question of a myth of *hidden* wisdom, in which this figure has secluded herself in heaven. The point is that humans fail to grasp a wisdom that *has* ways, who is out on the open roads of the world: 'They did not learn the way of knowledge, or discover its paths; they did not lay hold of it' (v. 21). In Job 28 the affirmation that nobody knows the way to wisdom underscores the impossibility of possessing wisdom in a particular 'place'. This idea is repeated here (v. 15: 'has any one discovered the dwelling-place of wisdom?), but there is added the failure of humans to see or understand the paths that wisdom *does* tread in the world.

In so far as personified wisdom is visible in vv. 20–3, she remains in theory 'available'. Humans have just failed to take advantage of her presence in the world. This statement of an all too-tragic fact does not explain *why* human beings have failed to find her. In giving the reason *why* wisdom is hidden the poet leans more directly on the 'riddle' approach of Job 28, concentrating on the 'place' of wisdom and the point that to know wisdom is to exercise it. The impossibility of finding a 'place' of wisdom (*topos*, v. 15) is developed in terms of being baffled by the whole living-space of the world; the strong, typified as giants, fail to cope with the measureless extent of the world, despite their skill in war (vv. 24–9):

---

[100] cf. Proverbs 2:9–22, 15:10, 24, 14:8, 22:6.
[101] Ringgren, *Word and Wisdom*, p. 114.

Israel, how great is God's dwelling–place and how vast the extent [or 'place', *topos*] of his domain! Great it is, and boundless, lofty and unmeasurable! (Bar. 3:24)

Even the giants lack the practical wisdom to steer their way through the world that confronts them. This description of the measureless and boundless world is a key to the intention behind the trope of the dimensions of the world (vv. 29–31): humans are perplexed by the multiplicity that confronts them—or in other words, wisdom is hidden.

The next stage of the poem (vv. 29–31) follows Job 28 (vv. 12–22) more closely. No one has found the location of wisdom among the dimensions of the world (vv. 29–30a = Job 28:12–14) or has bought it/her for gold (v. 30b = Job 28:15–18): no one knows the way to wisdom (v. 31 = Job 28: 13). There is certainly a difference between the way the questions about the location of wisdom are framed:

Job 28:12   But where shall wisdom be found?
            And where is the place of understanding?

       13   Mortals do not know the way to it . . . .
       14   The deep says, 'It is not in me', and the sea says, 'It is not with me'. It cannot be gotten for gold . . .
Baruch 3:29 Who has gone up into heaven and taken her and brought her down from the clouds?
       30   Who has gone over the sea and found her, or has bought her for fine gold?
       31   No one can know the path or conceive the way that will lead to her.[102]

The Job question ('where?') expects the answer 'nowhere' and the Baruch question ('who?') 'nobody'. But there is no reason to suppose that the Baruch poet actually believes that wisdom is ready to be found in heaven or beyond the sea, any more than he thinks that she could be bought if people had enough money. The poet here cleverly echoes Deuteronomy 30:12–13, which affirms that the commandments of God are *not* hidden somewhere in the sky or across the seas, but are clear and plain in the Torah. This anticipates the claim that wisdom is to be found in the Torah, but here also underlines that wisdom cannot be found in any particular place in the world.

The Baruch poet continues to follow Job closely in form. God alone knows wisdom (v. 32 = Job 28:23) because he knows all things (v. 32a = Job 28:24) and he has created all things (v. 32b = Job 28:25–26). God has 'found' wisdom in so far as he exercises knowledge and creative power, and to exercise wisdom in that way is to know her . The listing of God's creative activities does not, in

---

[102] NEB, modified.

content, at all follow the list in Job 28, although there is a link in the key-word 'established' (in Baruch 3:32 God establishes the earth; in Job 28:27 God establishes wisdom). A correspondence can be discerned instead with Job 38:

32	Only the One who knows all things knows her;	
	his understanding discovered her.	
	He has established the earth for evermore	(Job 38:4)
	and has filled it with four–footed beasts	(Job 38:39–39:30; 40:15)
33	He that sends forth the light	(Job 38:19, 24)
34	and the stars shone in their places	(Job 38:7, 31–33)[103]

We recollect also the 'storehouses' of wisdom (3:15, cf. Job 38:22). As in Job 38 two ways of describing the expansiveness of the world are brought together— the dimensional trope and the onomastic list.

In summary, then, in Job 28, Ben Sira 1 and Baruch 3 the reason for the hiddenness of wisdom lies in the expansiveness and inexhaustibility of the world order. Correspondingly, God's knowledge of wisdom's 'place' is God's comprehension of the world. For this reason, the personified wisdom figure is subordinated to an objective one. Where personified wisdom appears (most notably in Proverbs 8:22f, Ben Sira 24 and Wisdom 6–9)[104] she is available to human beings. The divine authority of wisdom is stressed in order to encourage people to grasp wisdom teaching, and so she offers herself to mortals and dwells among them. In contrast, where wisdom is described as permanently hidden by its very nature, it is treated as an impersonal object to be measured or fathomed. In Job 28 and Ben Sira 1 all this does not amount to a total denial of wisdom to human beings, but Baruch is further along the sliding scale of the obscurity of the world order to human beings, and does deny all wisdom, with the Torah in mind as the place where wisdom becomes accessible (v. 36 'The whole way of knowledge').

THE SEARCH FOR A 'NO-PLACE'

Job 28 presents us with a riddle: where is the place of wisdom? The 'place' where wisdom is to be found turns out not to be a literal place at all; it is strictly a 'no-place', but asking the riddle-question alerts us to some essential features of living in the world. Asking it tells us that human wisdom is always going to be defeated by the inexhaustible extent of the world, while God's wisdom comprehends it. There is no *single* place which wisdom inhabits and which human ingenuity could possess. But equally, wisdom is not secluded in a place that only God knows. Divine wisdom is not absolutely transcendent,

---

[103] NEB, modified.   [104] See Chapter 6.

not totally other from us; God's wisdom is not like a divine agent who dwells remotely in a place in heaven. We can exercise wisdom in tune with God: this is implied in Job 28, and in Ben Sira 1 (and even in Baruch 3), alongside the riddle of wisdom's place, we discern the shadowy outline of Lady Wisdom who invites us to communion with her.

At the beginning of this chapter I remarked that it is characteristic of the late-modern age for us to search for a place to dwell in the world, while having an uneasy conscience about the damage that human presence has caused to our surroundings. Postmodern philosophers warn us that our *Heimat* cannot be a place where we impose our being on others, where we force our presence on them, where *we* are present in the world at the expense of others. We shall only find our proper place, some suggest, when we give attention to a kind of no-place, a *chōra* in which we cannot dwell but which challenges the ambitions of the conscious mind to dominate the arena of society and symbolic language. Now, Job 28 also speaks about a no-place, a place which is unlike any other place in the world. It is not a place which we defend with hard dogmas. Like the *chōra* of the philosophers, the 'no-place' of Job 28 acts as a symbol of transcendence. It breaks open the confidence of the wise that they have complete control of the world through their linguistic codes and meta-narratives, such as the dogma of retribution; it affirms a hiddenness at the heart of reality.

In their talk about finding a place, the wisdom writers are concerned with human ability to steer one's way through the world, to make a success of resolving the tangle of things and events with which a vast world presents us. They are not afflicted with the late-modern anxiety to find our home in a world from which our technical prowess seems to have alienated us. There is, however, a considerable overlap between these concerns, ancient and late-modern. Heidegger tells us, for instance, that to be at home in a place is to 'care' for it, using what is 'to hand';[105] 'caring' for the dwelling-place and guarding it as a 'shepherd of Being' seems close to a 'steering' through life (Prov. 1: 5). Yet for all this, the 'place' of wisdom—both human and divine— differs from the *chōra* in at least one respect. The *chōra* of the philosophers is a no-place that can never be inhabited. In the wisdom poems the 'place' of wisdom is literally a no-place, but it becomes a metaphor for standing in the world with wisdom and with God. While it is 'not a place' (having no particular geographical location) it has a kind of spatiality given to it. The patient pursuit of wisdom by human beings, seeing the world with caution and humility, brings them into a wide open space where they can know the presence of God. Sometimes this presence can even be direct and unmissable,

---

[105] Martin Heidegger, *Pathmarks*, ed. and trans. William McNeill (Cambridge: Cambridge University Press, 1998), p. 252; Heidegger, *Poetry, Language, Thought*, p. 184.

as expressed finally in the theophany of chapter 38:1, when God speaks to Job out of the whirlwind.

This is a space that is made by relations (as in the modern concept of space),[106] and which can shape a human approach to all the places of the world. It is a wide space where the wise can learn to see the world as God sees it, to live in tune with God's wisdom, and to know the many places in the way that God knows them. Humans can never possess wisdom completely, but can act in its spirit, and in this sense can find the 'place' of wisdom. Using the language of personified wisdom—which is not actually part of Job 28, but which hovers behind Ben Sira 1 and Baruch 3—those who are wise can meet and love Lady Wisdom who is really present in the world.

Derrida and Kristeva, appealing to the 'no-place' of the *chōra*, refuse to identify it with God, even the God of negative theology. To associate the *chōra* with God, in their view would run the danger of supporting an oppressive presence of the self in the world; it would imply a divine self who dominates all, and would validate the human subject in its pretensions to mastery. A totalitarian concept of presence like this would also undermine the mediation of language in our relation to the world, and close down the expansion of meaning. The challenge posed by the concept of the non-theological *chōra* is thus whether we can maintain its disturbing effect in a theological form. If the 'no-place' of wisdom is to point towards a space where God is present, as I have been proposing, we need to speak of a presence which is *not* oppressive, and which does not foster the split between subject (the thinking mind) and object (the world).

Some self-declared 'postmodern a-theologies' at this point have confined themselves to an immanent 'void' that has opened up within the self, asserting the pure absence of any transcendent reality; as Mark Taylor states, 'The very search for presence testifies to the absence of presence and the 'presence' of absence.'[107] Rather than resorting to a paradoxical language of a God who is present in absence, I suggest that we should be speaking about a *hidden* presence of God. In thinking about a God who is present but who veils or conceals God's-self in humility, we might begin to see how we too can be present without oppressing others. Following the paradigm of Job 28 we should look for ways of expressing a space in which we can walk humbly with God's own wisdom, rather than striving to grasp a place where we can simply be secure. The metaphor of a 'place' which is 'not a place' has in fact proved helpful to a range of theological thought in attempting to speak of the

---

[106] See Chapter 9, the sections called 'The Sense of a Whole in the European Tradition' and 'A Whole which is not Oppressive'.

[107] Taylor, *Erring*, p. 72. Cf. Thomas Altizer, *Genesis and Apocalypse: A Theological Voyage Toward Authentic Christianity* (Louisville: Westminster/John Knox Press, 1990), p. 182: 'the absence of all nameability whatsoever [is] an absence that is a necessary and inevitable absence for a full and total apocalyptic enactment.'

hidden presence of a God who does not legitimate the subjective project of the human self. These concepts express a transcendence, breaking open the circle of human immanence, yet a transcendence which is not absolute but an accessible Otherness.[108]

The first, and most far-reaching, idea of a no-place is that there is a space in God. In creation, it can be affirmed, God has opened up room within God's own being for created beings to dwell. This idea can be found in the Jewish kabbalistic tradition of *zimsum* (contraction), which affirms that there can be nothing outside God, if God is indeed all in all. So if God is to create things from nothing, this nothing cannot be outside God either. God must 'withdraw' or contract deeply into the recesses of the divine being in order to make a space of nothingness in God's self from which creation can emerge. This mystical concept of a primordial space, as formulated by Isaac Luria, has been popularized in the twentieth century by Gershom Scholem[109] and has been adopted and adapted by several theologians including Sergius Bulgakov and Jürgen Moltmann.[110] As Scholem summarizes Luria's thought, 'God makes room for the world by, as it were, abandoning a region within himself... in order to return to it in in the act of creation and revelation.'[111]

This scheme associates creation with the humility of God. In voluntary self-humiliation, God limits God's self in bringing into being a world of created beings within the divine life. In Luria's notion of 'contraction', however, there is a deep ambiguity. Does God dwell in the space God has enabled? Alternatively, does it remain as a space from which God has withdrawn? God might be conceived as dwelling there, either simply because the space remains in God (it cannot be anywhere else), or because God has 'returned' to it and suffused into it—in Luria's theory—the divine creative light. If God does dwell in the world, and the world mutually dwells in God, then it would be consistent for God's dwelling to take the form of a hidden, patient, and suffering presence, persisting with created persons in their growth and development, and acting in persuasive and sacrificial love rather than coercion. If God has created a living-

---

[108] The remainder of this section follows closely my article, 'The Quest for a Place which is "Not-a-Place": The Hiddenness of God and the Presence of God' in Oliver Davies and Denys Turner (eds), *Silence and the Word: Negative Theology and Incarnation* (Cambridge: Cambridge University Press, 2002), pp. 35–60.

[109] Gershom Scholem, *Major Trends in Jewish Mysticism* (London: Thames and Hudson, 1955), pp. 260–4; Scholem, *Kabbalah,* Library of Jewish Knowledge (Jerusalem: Keter, 1974), pp. 129–35.

[110] Jürgen Moltmann, *God in Creation*, trans. M. Kohl (SCM Press, London, 1985), pp. 86–9; Moltmann, *The Coming of God*, trans. M. Kohl (London: SCM Press, 1996), pp. 297–302; Sergius Bulgakov, *The Lamb of God*, trans. B. Jakim (Grand Rapids: Eerdmans, 2008), p. 223. For a different critique of *zimsum* from mine, see Alan Torrance, '*Creatio ex nihilo* and the Spatio-Temporal Dimensions' in Colin E. Gunton (ed.), *The Doctrine of Creation* (Edinburgh: T & T Clark, 1997), pp. 88–93.

[111] Scholem, *Major Trends in Jewish Mysticism*, p. 261.

space for creation through humble self-limitation, then God's presence in the world will have the same character. However, the opposite conclusion could be drawn from the image of divine contraction, and Levinas draws it. Ethicizing the metaphysical idea of *zimsum* he declares that God withdraws, puts God's self at a distance, to create a space where responsible human action is possible. As Levinas puts it, 'God is real and concrete not through incarnation but through law'. God hides his face in the Warsaw Ghetto so that his people should 'love the law more than God'.[112] In Psalms of lament one is thrown back on oneself to find meaning; it is in lamentation that we become aware of a responsibility which only the self can bear.

Moltmann takes a somewhat middle view. He concludes from the notion of *zimsum* that while creation is 'in' God, God is not 'in' creation but remains 'over against it' until the moment of future new creation when the universe will be filled with the presence of God. Until the eschaton, he asserts, 'Only God can be the space of the world, and the world cannot be God's space.'[113] However, Moltmann finds that he cannot deny indwellings of God in the world during the course of history altogether; he thus describes them as 'special presences', temporary acts of self-humiliation, rather than a 'general presence'.[114] He conceives them as transient hidden presences in which the Shekinah Glory of God is 'homeless' in the world, awaiting redemption; the pre-eminent instance of this presence, anticipating the eschaton, is Christ himself.

This view of the hidden presence of God as a series of temporary stop-gaps for an absent God comes ironically from one of the group of theologians who opposed the 'death of God' movement in the 1960s. This latter movement, observing a loss of awareness of God within cultural consciousness in the West, proposed various forms of absence of God from the world. One version, advocated for example by Dorothee Sölle, suggested that the suffering Christ 'represents the absent God by giving him time to appear . . . Because God does not intervene to establish his cause, Christ appears in his place.'[115] We can keep a sort of doubting faith in the absent God whom we no longer experience, because Christ the representative stands in for him in the world. It was the German 'theologians of the cross', including Moltmann (also Eberhard Jüngel and Hans Urs von Balthasar) who insisted that God was not dead—that is, not absent from the world and irrelevant to it—precisely because God suffered death.[116] Sharing empathetically in the human condition of alienation,

---

[112] Levinas, *Difficult Freedom*, p. 145. On *zimsum*, see his *Beyond the Verse*, pp. 161–3.
[113] Moltmann, *The Coming of God*, p. 302.
[114] Moltmann, *The Coming of God*, p. 303.
[115] Sölle, *Christ the Representative*, p. 137.
[116] See Moltmann, *The Crucified God*, pp. 253–6; Eberhard Jüngel, 'Vom Tod des lebendigen Gottes. Ein Plakat', in *Unterwegs zur Sache* (Munich: Chr. Kaiser, 1972), pp. 105–25; Jüngel, *God as the Mystery of the World*, pp. 43–63, 94–104.

oppression, and death, this was a God who was alive to a world where human suffering had become an overwhelming problem for belief in God.

The idea of the world as occupying space in God is a version of a 'no-place', since this space cannot be located geographically, or in any intersection of space and time. It has the capacity for portraying a mutual indwelling of God and the world, and so for expressing a hidden presence of God in the world where God acts in vulnerability and humility. The metaphor of 'contraction' (*zimsum*), however, tends to emphasize withdrawal and absence, rather than presence. An alternative to contraction is a 'making room' within a triune life of God, when the place that God opens can be envisaged as being within the interweaving and inter-penetrating fellowship (*perichōrēsis*) of Father, Son, and Spirit. Through creation human beings participate in the relationships of ecstatic love, of mutual giving and receiving, within God. While Catherine Keller does not associate the place we can inhabit in God with a space within the *perichōrēsis* of the Trinity, she does identify it as the *chōra*, to be understood not as a barren and uninhabited desert but as a fecund matrix, a womb of possibilities; she writes that we can envisage 'the unspeakable deity itself as the abode of the universe', so that 'God becomes... the House built by She-Wisdom' (citing Proverbs 24:3: 'with wisdom the house will be built').[117]

A second approach to this 'place' which is not-a-place moves the focus from the mutual indwelling of God and the whole cosmos to the individual person. It has been a part of the apophatic 'mystical' tradition in Christianity to find an overlap between a hidden ground of the self and the God who is hidden in light which is so bright it causes a sense of profound darkness. There is a 'place' in which it is not possible to articulate in words the difference between God and the soul. So, for example, the Lady Julian of Norwich in an apophatic mood declares that 'I saw no difference between God and our essential being, it seemed to be all God.'[118] As Denys Turner has pointed out, this is not a simple affirmation that the soul is God or that the soul has been totally absorbed into God, but that it is not possible to 'see' or 'name' the difference with our resources of language.[119] Using spatial imagery, the journey of 'descent' into this inward place in the soul is at the same time an 'ascent' to God,[120] so that both the divine nature and the innermost 'refuge' of the self can be named as an 'emptiness' or 'silence' or a 'desert place'.[121]

---

[117] Catherine Keller, *Face of the Deep*, p. 167.

[118] Julian of Norwich, *Revelations of Divine Love*, trans. E. Spearing (Harmondsworth: Penguin Books, 1998), ch. 54, p. 130. While Julian is usually classified as a 'kataphatic' mystic, it is better to regard all medieval Christian mysticism as an integration of apophatic and cataphatic aspects.

[119] Denys Turner, *The Darkness of God: Negativity in Christian Mysticism* (Cambridge: Cambridge University Press, 1995), pp. 160–3.

[120] Turner explores the influential merging of these two spatial images in Augustine's thought: ibid., pp. 74–81, 92–101.

[121] For this terminology see Sermon 9 in Meister Eckhart, *The Essential Sermons, Commentaries, Treatises and Defence*, trans. and ed. E. Colledge and B. McGinn (London: SPCK, 1981).

The breakdown in language at this place of union with God is naturally understood by such mystical writers as Denys the Areopagite, Meister Eckhart, and the author of 'The Cloud of Unknowing' in terms of the Neoplatonist tradition within which they stand. First, the inability to 'see' the difference between God and the 'empty place' in the soul stems from the incomparability of God with all beings, so that there is no point of comparison from which a distinction can be observed. Second, it is not possible to 'see' anything cognitively because God as pure intellect will be apprehended as totally 'simple' essence and so as formless, featureless, a desert place, and 'nothingness'. As Turner exegetes Eckhart's thought, this is the divine *esse indistinctum*, and in so far as we are intellect, we are also *esse indistinctum*.[122]

Throughout my discussion I have opposing this second kind of argument, based on divine simplicity, in favour of an idea of God as a complex interaction of relationships. However, it is important to listen to the witness of the apophatic theologians about a 'place' of encounter with God in the self in which God is so near to us that we cannot distance God as an 'object' over against us.[123] This 'no-place' where both God and the self are hidden and which can therefore be metaphorically designated as an 'empty place' can, I aim to show, be rooted in a trinitarian theology of relationships, rather than in a concept of purely intellectual essence. This may also help to avoid the tendency of apophatic theology to focus on the individual self— although the self is certainly negated in the process – rather than the self in relationship.

A third kind of 'no-place' through which the hidden presence of God can be known is thus the space opened up between the self and other selves, or between ourselves and our neighbours. There is a place created 'between' persons when we allow others to enter our world and challenge us to recognize their particular identity and needs. This is a theme central to the thought of Emmanuel Levinas, who finds that the infinite Other—God—turns our world upside down by inserting a 'space' in time and materiality,[124] setting the stage for our encounter with other persons and so calling us to limitless responsibility for our neighbour. For Levinas, and significantly for our own theme, we can find traces of the infinitely Other in the 'face' of our neighbour, not because the face is a static model of God, but because it becomes a means by which we can 'find ourselves in his trace'.[125] To this extent, Levinas is concerned with *participation* in the transcendent and not observation or objectification of it.

---

[122] See Turner, *The Darkness of God*, pp. 164–5.

[123] Cf. Julian of Norwich: 'God is nearer to us than our own soul, for he is the ground on which our soul stands.' *Revelations*, ch. 56, p. 133.

[124] Emmanuel Levinas, 'Meaning and Sense', p. 62; cf. Levinas, 'God and Philosophy' in *Of God who Comes to Mind*, pp. 67–70.

[125] Levinas, 'Meaning and Sense', p. 65.

However, for Levinas the space between persons, the 'stage' set by the irruption of the infinite, is not a place where God is now present; what is present is a trace of the God who has always 'passed by'. Here Levinas employs the imagery of Exodus 33:22–3, understanding Moses' vision of the back of God to mean that 'Someone has already passed'; this is in accord with Levinas' use of Luria's concept of divine 'withdrawal'. But rather than speaking—as Levinas does—of an 'absent infinite', we must, I suggest, try to speak of the God who is hidden and so present in the 'between' of relations.

A fourth and final kind of 'no-place' comes rather close to the Job poet, who finds divine wisdom, not in one literal place, but as exercised in all places. We may say that God is present in a hidden way because God takes the many places of the world as a place for encounter and self-revelation. As Karl Barth points out, created objects are totally unsuitable means for the communication of the divine glory because of the finitude and sinfulness of the world, and so 'the veil is thick';[126] in the very moment of self-unveiling God will be veiled, and God is hidden precisely because God is revealed. However, Barth is less helpful when he proposes that in encountering God in this mediated immediacy we are really sharing in the 'primary objectivity' of the divine self-knowledge, that we participate in God's own knowledge of himself as an object.[127] If we are ever to escape from a dualism of subject and object in our knowledge of God we must think more radically about the nature of participation than this.

The 'place' which is not literally a place, but which evokes the hidden presence of God may thus be understood as (a) a place in God, (b) a place in the self which is inseparable from—but not identical with—the being of God, (c) a place between persons and (d) a place concurrent with many objects in the world which mediate the immediacy of God. As I have been hinting, these aspects of the place which is 'not-a-place' may all best be understood in terms of participation in the triune God.

PARTICIPATING IN TRIUNE SPACES

In an earlier chapter I suggested that the symbol of the Trinity expresses a complexity in God that matches the complexity of the world.[128] I wrote of our participating in the relationships in which the life of God consists, sharing in a flow or rhythm of relations. Since a key relation in human life is that of a parent and a child, and since Jesus of Nazareth called God 'father', a central—

---

[126] Barth, *Church Dogmatics*, I/1, p. 165.
[127] Barth, *Church Dogmatics*, II/1, pp. 49–50.
[128] See Chapter 5, the sections called 'Complexity, Wisdom and God' and 'The Complex Being of the Triune God'.

but not exclusive—image for a relational God in the Christian tradition will be that of a father and a son in the the openness of the Spirit. We enter into a movement like a father sending forth a son on a mission of compassion, into a movement like a son giving obedience and honour to a father, and into a movement like a breath or wind which is always opening up these relations to new depths and a new future. These movements are 'transcendent' in the sense of being before us and ahead of us, as well as being more expansive and inexhaustible than our own relationships; they are immanent in that they are found in the world, encountered in and through the network of relations which constitutes an organic universe. Trinity is not a mathematical puzzle. It is all about a God who lives in relationship and is in movement.

Participating in a triune God like this is standing in the 'no-place' of wisdom, and out of this 'choranic' experience we learn to treat the many places of the world as dwelling-places, to find them as a 'homeland' which is to be cared for and not exploited. Earlier I argued that understanding the three *hypostases* ('persons') of the Trinity as nothing more or less than relations (in a new version of 'subsistent relations') prevents the concept of God from becoming oppressive, as we are thinking of neither one nor three supreme individuals, and neither one nor three super-minds.[129] This, I believe, begins to answer the concerns of Derrida and others that an omni-presence of God in the world would be totalitarian, or would encourage the widening of a gap between mind and nature. Now I want to add that only a view of divine *hypostasis* ('person') as relation sustains the image of a 'no-place'.

As long as we are thinking of three persons as divine agents who *have* relations, it is impossible to conceive the universe as being 'in' God (a world-view often called 'panentheism', or 'everything in God', as distinct from 'pantheism', or 'everything as God'). Questions of physical location of these personal agents will inevitably arise, even if we think of the universe as being held in relations between them, in what is sometimes called a 'social Trinity'. The place in God has ceased to be a 'no-place'. Only the idea of divine hypostases as personal *relations* is an adequate image for the immersion of the whole created universe into God, remembering of course two things. The first is that all language for the mystery of God is analogy and metaphor, and we are looking for the least inadequate language available. The second is that talk of God as an interweaving of relationships is language of participation: it does not attempt objective knowledge of God, but describes what it is like to *engage* in God.

When we invoke God by name (Father, Son, Spirit), this is a means of drawing us into *movements* of divine love and justice, which cannot be reduced to a relationship between a subject and an object. As Julian of Norwich discovered, she could not 'see' the difference between herself and

---

[129] See Chapter 5, the section called 'The Complex Being of the Triune God' and Chapter 6, the section called 'Seeing as Reading'.

God, not because there *was* no difference, but because of the infinite degree of participation of one in the other. It is like, says John of the Cross, the inseparability of the light from the windowpane through which it passes.[130] The 'negative theologians' such as John make clear that all our speech about God must be a constant oscillation between positive and negative, affirmations and denials, word and silence: talk about God and address to God must be an interaction between the 'kataphatic' and the 'apophatic'. Speaking of the divine persons *as relations* precisely shows this double aspect of saying and un-saying. Revelation and experience lead us positively to characterize these relations as, for instance, 'sending', 'obeying', 'glorifying,' 'opening up' and 'unifying'. But since we cannot observe these relations, even in a conceptual way in the mind and imagination, we are immediately plunged into silence. We are not thinking of personal subjects who *have* relations, but only movements of relation themselves which defeat all attempts at observation and objectification.

In his poems John of the Cross depicts the mutual indwelling of Father, Son, and Spirit as marked by such an excessive love, overflowing to draw created persons in, that the names of the persons are best to be understood as pointing to *movements* of relational love. In one poem John takes up the image—used by the early Church Fathers—of the Trinity as fount (or spring), river and stream. In the 'dark night' of the soul where God both eludes our possession and is intimately present, John finds himself in a 'no-place' where he is immersed in this flow of divine life like water. Thus he writes, as translated by a modern poet:[131]

> The spring that brims and ripples oh I know
>   in dark of night.
>
> Waters that flow forever and a day
> through a lost country – oh I know the way
>   in dark of night....
>
> Bounty of waters flooding from this well
> Invigorates all earth, high heaven, and hell
>   in dark of night.
>
> A current the first fountain gave birth to
> is also great and what it would, can do
>   in dark of night
>
> Two merging currents of the living spring –
> from these a third, no less astonishing
>   in dark of night....
>
> This spring of living water I desire,
> here in the bread of life I see entire
>   in dark of night.

---

[130] St. John of the Cross, *Ascent of Mount Carmel*, 2.5.7; in *The Complete Works of St. John of the Cross*, transl. E. Allison Peers (London: Burns & Oates, 1964), p. 78.

[131] *The Poems of St. John of the Cross*, trans. John Frederick Nims (Chicago: Chicago University Press, 1979), 'Song of the Soul', pp. 43–5.

The triune life of God is evoked here as three currents or movements of 'delight', which intermingle and can nevertheless be distinguished from each other. The fluidity recalls Kristeva's description of the *chōra* as a 'rhythmic space' which 'has no thesis and no position', which is formed by drives or 'energy charges' and is 'full of movement'.[132] This rhythm, she affirms, is a constant semiotic challenge to the old law of the symbolic realm of society, and it is embodied in the revolutionary power of poetry. So, I suggest, we can only think of God in terms of our participation in rhythmic, triune movements of love and justice which are greater than we are: like the *chōra*, the movements that open the space for us to dwell cannot be objectified. Kristeva herself does not use trinitarian imagery to describe the *chōra*, but she does appeal to the symbol of the Trinity when she is describing a phase of the growth of the human psyche closely associated with the primordial nurturing of the *chōra*.

According to Kristeva, at the moment of dawning consciousness, on the verge of acquiring language and so of separating from the mother, the self imagines an image of an *other*, a father who belongs to the earliest, pre-linguistic life of the individual.[133] This resembles the 'father of pre-history' in Freud's theory of psychic development, and is not yet a gendered figure, representing both parents. But the key move that Kristeva makes as a psychoanalyst is to privilege *this* kind of 'father' or 'mother-father' over the definitely *male* father who appears subsequently in Freud's famous oedipal triangle. Unlike the theories of Freud and Kristeva's mentor, Jacques Lacan, *this* is the decisive moment in the emerging of human subjectivity, not an oedipal pact which seems to concern only fathers and sons, and which is based on violence. The image of the father-mother that arises in the drama of the growing consciousness is not the demanding Freudian super-ego, but a self-giving figure. The subject, says Kristeva, enters the realm of 'trinitary logic'.[134] As the subject has to face the agony of separation from the mother, it shares in an exchange of gifts of love with the 'other', which is symbolized in the mutual self-giving of the persons of the Trinity. This is a self-offering that has separation at its heart, since the story of the cross of Jesus tells us that a splitting or 'hiatus' enters into the relationship between the father and the son in the Trinity (here Kristeva refers to the trinitarian theology of Hans Urs von Balthasar).[135]

---

[132] Kristeva, *Revolution in Poetic Language*, p. 25; Kristeva, *Black Sun. Depression and Melancholia*, trans. L. S. Roudiez (New York: Columbia University Press, 1989), p. 264.

[133] Julia Kristeva, *Tales of Love* (New York: Columbia University Press, 1987), pp. 23–30, 42–50.

[134] Kristeva, *Black Sun*, p. 135. This must be a reference to Von Balthasar's 'trinitarian self-giving'; see her footnote 42.

[135] See Kristeva, *Black Sun*, p. 132: 'a caesura, which some have called a "hiatus"'. See further Kristeva, *Black Sun*, p. 272, n.28. Kristeva references Balthasar, *La Gloire et La Croix* (1975), 3:2 = *Glory of the Lord*, vol. 7, *Theology: The New Covenant*, trans. B. McNeil; she mentions no pages, but relevant sections are on 'Self-abandonment' (142–61), 'The time of discipleship' (pp. 188–201: see 'hiatus', p. 190), and 'Trinitarian self-giving' (pp. 391–8).

For Kristeva the drama of the developing self is thus a story of love, and in later life the self can draw on the reserves of this early psychic drama, similarly becoming aware of others, and sharing imaginatively in an interchange of love and forgiveness with them.[136] Though she does not count herself a Christian, she thinks that the process of exchange can be assisted by empathetic identification with the story of the crucified Christ and the sacred drama of the Trinity. Empathic forgiveness, she proposes, is symbolized by the doctrine of the Trinity, the 'motion of the trinitarian knot' in which there is 'a permanent instability of identity between the persons...each person of the Trinity identified with the others in an erotic fusion'.[137] From reading Kristeva, we can conclude that for Christian theology, the 'no-place' of the Trinity can function in a similar way to the *chōra* of the philosophers, while it can be inhabited in a way that the *chōra* cannot. More than this, we can be drawn into the life of the Trinity in those experiences of life, early and adult, that the *chōra* may illuminate.[138]

To speak of the Trinity as a 'no-place' where relationships create a spatiality in which we can dwell is to use a number of analogies, especially that of relationship. I am arguing, however, that the analogy between human community and divine communion lies in the relationships themselves, and not in the 'persons' who are named. Christian thinkers who want to affirm that there are three persons in God in some sense of three conscious, acting subjects will of course lay stress on the relational nature of a human person. They will rightly affirm that as persons we are not 'isolated' or 'self-sufficient' individuals, but are constituted by our networks of relationships and our openness to each other. According to this analogy, persons in God differ from human persons in the degree of their mutual openness and involvement in each other; the love of the divine persons for each other is said to be so perfect and their relationships so intimate that they are one God in a way that we can never be one with each other.[139] But however much this 'social doctrine' of the Trinity is based on the relational nature of the human person, it is doubtful whether we can ever get beyond a kind of tritheism in which threeness in God overbalances the oneness, and in which a quasi-physical location is implied.

By contrast, an analogy of relationships draws a comparison between relations in God and a wide range of relations in the world, such as that between a mother and the baby in her womb, between children and parents, between wife and husband, between humans and objects in their environment,

---

[136] Kristeva, *Tales of Love*, p. 140.

[137] Kristeva, *Black Sun*, p. 211.

[138] Wyschogrod is thus surely incorrect to classify Kristeva with Deleuze as 'ecstatic postmodernists' who entirely evaporate the self, as opposed to 'differential postmodernists'; see *Saints and Postmodernism*, pp. 222–3, 243–52.

[139] For an example of social Trinity, see Moltmann, *Trinity and the Kingdom of God*, trans. M. Kohl (London: SCM Press, 1981), p. 175.

and between members of various communities—not just religious communities such as churches but secular communities such as hospitals. The analogy lies in the relationship itself, not with those who exercise it. This is a personal analogy, but not an analogy of persons, and it is why trinitarian language can be extended beyond the relations of 'Father, Son, Spirit' into other relations that are appropriate for certain contexts.

Inadequate too, I judge, are attempts to draw an analogy between what may be called 'postmodern' concepts of a de-centred person and 'persons' in God. This is the path taken by David Cunningham (in an otherwise excellent and imaginative book on the Trinity) who draws attention to the thought of the philosopher Calvin Schrag about the self as a 'space of subjectivity'.[140] Schrag—like other thinkers I have reviewed in this book—is critical of the portrait of the human subject developed in the Enlightenment, as a free, self-sufficient and independent centre of consciousness. Yet Schrag also recognizes that acts of communication (including speaking and writing) come from somewhere, and we need to answer the questions 'Who is speaking?', 'Who is writing?' and 'Who is acting?'. His solution is to restore the idea of a subject as speaker, author, and actor, but no longer to understand this subject as being the *foundation* for communicative activities. This would continue the theme of the dominance of the human subject over objects around it. Instead, the subject is *implied* by the network of communication, emerging along with it and with other subjects. For this role of the self Schrag uses the phrase 'space of subjectivity', indicating that the subject is 'not an entity at all, but rather an event or happening that continues the conversation'.[141]

This approach may, I suggest, be placed alongside the projects of Derrida, Levinas, and Kristeva in preserving a responsible subject in relation to others while moderating Enlightenment arrogance about the human ego. But it is not helpful to draw on this view of human persons to illuminate, by analogy, the concept of 'persons' of the Trinity, and even to explain the nature of subsistent relations (to which Cunningham appears to subscribe). Here Cunningham seizes on Schrag's phrase that the subject is 'not an entity', to draw a parallel with persons in God as 'relations without remainder'.[142] Divine persons, he claims, are also 'locutionary spaces'; they are named for their communicating with and relating to human life, such as God's self-naming as 'Yahweh' in connection with the event of the exodus (Exodus 3:15). But unfortunate results will come from comparing relationships in God with a view of the human subject as the 'whence' of communication. Either we end up by undermining human particularity, or we revert to treating the divine persons

---

[140] Calvin O. Schrag, *Communicative Praxis and the Space of Subjectivity* (Bloomington: Indiana University Press, 1986), pp. 137–8; cited in Cunningham, *These Three are One*, pp. 220ff.

[141] Schrag, *Communicative Praxis*, p. 121.

[142] Cunningham, *These Three are One*, p. 65, 221–5, cf. pp. 208–9.

as some kind of individual subject. On the one hand, applying the idea of the divine persons as 'relations without remainder' to *human* subjects means that it is difficult to take seriously the notion that they have 'emerged out' of relationships and communication, and so have at least a relative—though not of course isolated—individuality. A 'subsistent relation' applied to human beings seems then to be distinctly less of a subject than Schrag and others want to affirm; the human person evaporates into a mere bundle of relationships and fragmentary experiences. On the other hand, to affirm this 'emerged' identity and to apply it to the *divine* Three means that the latter will be regarded as 'persons constituted by relations' rather than being simply relations.

All this means that, even at its best, the analogy between human and divine 'persons' is a remote one. While there are echoes and hints which should not be disregarded, a trinitarian theology cannot be built on these. Because humans are created, finite beings there will always be personal subjects with at least a relative individuality who exercise relationships, and 'between' whom the relationships exist. By contrast, because God is uncreated and unique, the language of 'persons' will be a way of drawing human beings into the personal relationships which embrace them and within which God makes room for them (and the whole universe) to dwell. The least inadequate analogy for God is that of relationships, forming a space that is strictly a 'no-place'.

It may be said that 'subsistent relations' would have no ability to *act* in a particular way. How, it may be protested, can we think of a relationship as doing anything?[143] Surely, action can only be ascribed to an agent who *has* relationships. The objection has been levelled that if the 'persons' are no more and no less than relations then they will end up being absorbed into one single acting Subject who acts in an undifferentiated way within the world. A supreme individual Subject acting in the world has then all the potential for dominance and for sanctioning human totalitarian rule which we we are trying to avoid in the first place. Only, it is asserted, three persons *constituted* by relations, but not simply *equivalent* to relations, can avoid this relapse into monarchianism.[144]

It is because Wolfhart Pannenberg wants to ascribe particular activity to the three persons that he explains he is compelled to 'cling to the idea of subject[s]' in God, which he also describes as 'living realizations of separate centres of action'.[145] He begins with the concrete, historic happening of Jesus of Nazareth, who shows his identity in the act of bearing witness to God his

---

[143] Miroslav Volf, *After Our Likeness: The Church as the Image of the Trinity* (Grand Rapids: Eerdmans, 1998), pp. 71, 205–6; cf. Moltmann, *The Trinity and the Kingdom of God*, pp. 171–4.

[144] See Gunton, *The Promise of Trinitarian Theology* (Edinburgh: T & T Clark, 1991), pp. 40–2, 94.

[145] Wolfhart Pannenberg, *Systematic Theology*, 3 Volumes, trans. G. Bromiley (Grand Rapids: Eerdmans, 1988–98), vol. 1, p. 319 and 319, n.183.

Father. In pointing away from himself to the Father ('Why do you call me good? There is none good but God alone', Mark 10:18) he thus distinguishes himself from the Father, and Pannenberg concludes that in God there must be a Son who is eternally a separate person because he actively distinguishes himself from the Father who begets him; his identity is not just established by being passively begotten. This in turn leads Pannenberg to the insight that all three persons have real identity (*hypostasis*) because of active self-distinction from each other.[146] For instance, the Father hands over the kingdom to the Son for the course of history, and the Son hands back the kingdom to the Father at the end of time; the Spirit glorifies the Son, and the kingdom of the Father in him, by raising Jesus from the dead. There is, he claims, still one God since this self-distinction is a mutual process.

What can we say in response to this challenge about affirming a diversity of divine actions? Instead of Pannenberg's vision of three 'living realizations of separate centres of action', I have been commending something like 'three living realizations of movements or directions of action', and these can equally be conceived as distinguishing themselves from each other. We can identify active aspects of these movements ('sending', 'responding', 'opening up') in which Pannenberg finds the self-distinction of the persons, alongside passive ones ('being a father', 'being begotten', 'being breathed out'). As we live in the 'no-place' of relations we become *engaged* in movements of love and pain which (as Pannenberg describes them) are like a handing over of a kingdom to another, a returning it to its giver, and a raising from the dead. In these active movements the *hypostases* distinguish themselves from each other. Jesus of Nazareth is of course a subject as a human being, but he is to be confessed as one with God, not because he is somehow united with a divine subject (and especially not with a cosmic 'mediator'), but because his actions are completely identified with these divine movements as ours are not. In his response and engagement in mission he shows himself to be inseparable from a movement of mission and response in God that we can appropriately call 'sonship'. Thus, these movements of relationship in God 'act' in the world, not through some mechanical process of cause and effect, but because the world is caught up in an environment, or a 'place', where worldly actions are influenced and shaped.[147]

If we are to experience the world as the place for which we long, a place where we are at home despite its inexhaustibility and multiplicity, we must learn to live in tune with God's wisdom, and so to stand in a place which is not literally a place. This is best understood, I am urging, as 'situated' in the space created between the movements of relationship in God. The symbol of the Trinity announces that God has opened up an interval between the interweaving movements of giving and receiving which make up God's own being. The

[146] Pannenberg, *Systematic Theology*, pp. 309–14.
[147] See chapter 5, the section 'The Complex Activity of the Triune God'.

universe exists in this space, which is formed by relationships, and its inhabitants are called to enter more deeply into it. The presence of God in the world will always be hidden, because we cannot observe God like other objects in the world. Neither wisdom nor the God of wisdom can ever be boxed up in a single place, as the riddle of Job 28 makes clear. But we can participate *in* the God who is never absent.

Indeed, all four instances of a 'no-place' in the Western religious tradition identified above are illuminated by the notion that we share in the 'no-place' of the Trinity. First there is the 'no-place' opened up for created beings in God by the divine humility, according to the Jewish tradition of *zimsum*. We now see that this space is more than the nothingness from which creation comes: it is a space which is filled with love and joy. It is not a space from which God has withdrawn, but a space which is embraced and inter-penetrated by movements of giving and receiving in love. This means that it is full of presence, but not of domination and a striving for mastery. There is no absolute subject here to legitimate human subjectivity, but only communion.

Second, there is the 'no-place' we find deep down in our selves where we meet God in the darkness, and where we find that God becomes anonymous in humble self-effacement. We now see why it can be almost impossible to 'observe a difference' between ourselves and God (though of course one remains). We are being taken into the very relations that form God, identified with the movement between the Father and the Son in the breath of the Spirit. As the spiritual writers have pointed out, God is not the *object* of our desire, a thing to be desired, but the one *in whom* we desire the good.[148] We are truly *in* love. God offers a movement of desire in which we can share.

Third, there is the 'no-place' between ourselves and our neighbours, a space made by the demand of our neighbour upon our care and responsibility, a space which prevents our absorbing others and making them just an extension of ourselves. We now see that *this* space is being held within the space in God which is opened up between the divine relations, and this is why God is present between us and others in a hidden way.[149] The 'trace' which Levinas rightly discerns is actually (differing from Levinas) the divine presence. And finally, there is the 'no-particular-place' which is concurrent with the many places of the world through which God is unveiled and veiled at the same time. God is present in every place, and can potentially disclose God's self in every place, since the whole universe is held in the space made by the interweaving relationships of the Trinity. God is always committed to the physical signs of creation, and we cannot conceive of a Trinity of relations which can be separated from relations within the world.

---

[148] Turner, *The Darkness of God*, pp. 183–5.
[149] Cf. Dietrich Bonhoeffer, *Life Together*, trans. J. Doberstein (London; SCM, 1965), pp. 12–15.

What is our place in the world? It is to live in an open space, through wisdom, in which we can know a God who is hidden but not absent. This is a presence which never imposes, and where we can learn to be present to others without forcing ourselves on them. The poet of Job 28, observing the complexity of the world, tells us that there is no single, specified place where *ḥokmah* is guaranteed to be, or in which wisdom is contained. Heidegger prompts us to see the way in which a place can become, or fail to be, a space in which to live fully, while Derrida and Kristeva alert us to the transformative power of the 'no-place'. A wisdom theology for today will maintain that at any moment, anywhere, any place can become holy. It can become the 'no-place' where wisdom is encountered, opening up a space in which there is room to dwell.

Part Three

Wisdom in the World

8

Metaphor and Mystery in the Interpretation of Wisdom

THE WORLD AS A BOOK

In Shakespeare's play *As You Like It*, the good Duke Senior is exiled to the forest of Arden to live with his faithful followers like Robin Hood of legend. There he reflects that he can learn more from nature than from the court from which he has been banished. He announces:

> . . . this our life, exempt from public haunt,
> Finds tongues in trees, books in the running brooks,
> Sermons in stones, and good in everything.[1]

The idea that nature is a kind of book which is there to be read is rooted deeply in the Jewish and Christian tradition. It derives from the belief that God has created the world by the divine word, so that all things in the world point to their author. As the Duke sits in the forest glade, so the composer of Psalm 19 looks up into the sky:

> The heavens are telling out the glory of God
> and the firmament proclaims his handiwork.
> Day to day pours forth speech,
> and night to night declares knowledge.

There is no language being audibly spoken, affirms the Psalmist, yet 'their voice goes out through all the earth/ and their words to the end of the world.' In Christian tradition, the book of nature has been set alongside the book of Scripture as dual testaments to the creator God. Origen reflected that 'I think that He who made all things in wisdom so created all the species of visible things upon the earth, that He placed in some of them some teaching and

---

[1] Shakespeare, *As You Like It*, II.1.15–18.

knowledge of things invisible and heavenly'.[2] Augustine first used the phrase 'book of nature'[3] and confessed that 'you have stretched out the firmament of your book "like a skin", that is your words which are not mutually discordant', and that in the heavens 'there is testimony to you, "giving wisdom to infants".'[4]

Now, in our time the idea of the world as a kind of text has been promoted by the philosophy of signs (or semiotics) without any appeal to God. All persons and objects are understood to be signs, pointing beyond themselves, representing and communicating themselves, and emptying themselves out in the direction of others; while these signifiers can be inscribed in written words or symbols, text is not to be limited to what is written down on paper or other materials. The whole world is a system of signs that can be read by those who look at it. As Derrida puts it, the world is 'a space of inscription, as the opening to the emission and spatial distribution of signs, to the play of their differences'.[5]

There is, to be sure, a potential clash between this late-modern semiotic world-view and the earlier Judaeo-Christian understanding. The clash is most severe when philosophers, such as Baudrillard, maintain that signs can only refer to other signs within their immediate network of connections, and to nothing outside it, so that 'the real' is replaced by 'hyper-real' *simulacra*.[6] As Lyotard wearily concludes, as we wander aimlessly through the world's picture-gallery of images, all we can do is to reflect on their 'opacity'.[7] It would follow that objects in the world cannot operate as signs to point to God, if God is envisaged as standing *beyond* all signs as their origin and creator, as seems to be implied by much of the Christian tradition. It appears that the book of the world is a closed system, that we cannot read God out of the text of the world, and that the heavens cannot declare the glory of God.

On first appearance it may appear that Derrida is likewise in iressolvable conflict with Augustine and other Christian thinkers, maintaining as he does that there is a never-ending chain of signifying, in which the signifier having done its work becomes itself something to be *signified* in its turn, and so final meaning is always postponed. Unlike Baudrillard, however, he does think that there is an 'outside' to any particular constellation of signs. In fact, he appeals

---

[2] Origen, *The Song of Songs: Commentary and Homilies* trans. R. P. Lawson (London: Longmans, Green and Co., 1957), p. 220.

[3] Augustine, *Contra Faustum Manichaeum* 32.20.

[4] Augustine, *Confessions*, trans. Chadwick, XIII.15.16–17 (pp. 282–3), citing Isa. 34:4, Ps. 103:28, Ps. 8:3–4.

[5] Derrida, *Of Grammatology*, p. 44. See See Chapter 5, the section called 'The Complexity of Signs in the World'.

[6] Jean Baudrillard, 'Simulacra and Simulations' in *Selected Writings*, ed. Mark Poster (Stanford; Stanford University Press, 1988) p. 167.

[7] Jean-François Lyotard, 'Philosophy and Painting in the Age of their Experimentation' in *The Lyotard Reader*, ed. Andrew Benjamin (Oxford: Blackwell, 1983), p. 193.

to the paradoxical relation of the inside and the outside, symbolized by the hymen. The biological hymen, writes Derrida, stands between the inside and outside of a woman's vagina. It is thus a symbol for the 'undecidability' of the relation between an image and the thing represented in any text, the two coming together in a 'supreme spasm', upsetting any simple establishing of truth by *mimēsis*. The hymen of a text (writes Derrida), 'eliminates the exteriority, anteriority, or independence of the imitated, the signified or the thing'.[8] It overcomes a difference which nevertheless remains: 'At the edge of being, the medium of the hymen never becomes a mere mediation: it outwits and undoes all ontologies.'[9] Derrida thus allows us to reformulate the issues and discover where any actual dissonance with Christian belief might lie.

The point, for Derrida, is that it is an illusion to try and escape from the sign, to postulate any supreme reality which is *signified* by the world but which is not entangled in the world of signs. His objection is to involving the sign in any separation between intelligible and physical realms, and this—it seems to him—is what Christian theology has done with the concept of the *logos*, as 'thought' or 'word' which mediates between two worlds. Saussure had proposed that a sign had two dimensions, the 'signifier'—or the physical form of the sign—and the 'signified'—or the idea in the mind to which the sign referred.[10] Derrida sees this structure of the sign as falling into the trap of a metaphysic according to which there are two separate realms of reality: a higher realm of 'being' as the location of truth is posited over against the lower physical world, and 'signifieds' in the human mind participate in this absolute truth (or a 'transcendental signified') through an intermediary *logos*. The logos, or principle of meaning, thus acts as a mediator in two ways: it mediates between mental thoughts and the world of supreme being, and it mediates between the idea and the form in a sign: 'The signified has an immediate relation with the logos, and a mediated one with the signifier.' This logos is identified by Derrida with the theological idea of the Christ as Son of God through whom God is mediated to the physical world: it is 'the logos of a creator God',[11] and 'a passage of the infinite to the finite, the finite to the infinite'.[12] Derrida concludes that 'This absolute logos was an infinite creative subjectivity in medieval theology. The intelligible face of the sign remains turned toward the word and the face of God.'[13]

---

[8] Derrida, 'Double Session', pp. 209–10.

[9] Derrida, 'Double Session', p. 215.

[10] Saussure, *Course in General Linguistics*, pp. 65–70, 101–2.

[11] Derrida, *Of Grammatology*, p. 15.

[12] Jacques Derrida, *Glas*, trans. J. P. Leavey, and R. Rand (Lincoln: University of Nebraska Press, 1986), p. 39.

[13] Derrida, *Of Grammatology*, p. 13.

In this system of 'ontotheology'[14] the spoken voice is given a privileged place, as being the closest signifier to the *logos* as the expression or presence of the transcendent realm, while 'writing' is demoted as being bound up inevitably with the inferior state of the mundane and the bodily: as Derrida explains, writing was degraded as an

> eruption of the outside within the inside, breaching into the interiority of the soul, the living self-presence of the soul within the true logos, the help that speech lends to itself . . . writing, the letter, the sensible inscription, has always been considered by Western tradition as the body and matter external to the spirit, to breath, to speech, and to the logos.[15]

The 'voice of God' in the mind (or conscience) was easily identifiable with a 'good' kind of writing or spiritual writing within, echoing Paul's distinction between the 'spirit' and the 'lettter' in 2 Corinthians 3:3–6: 'the good and the natural is the divine inscription in the heart and soul; the perverse and artful is technique, exiled in the exteriority of the body'.[16] Derrida, then, is deeply suspicious of a certain constellation of concepts—being, presence, participation, mediation. His alternative is to make writing, rather than the voice, the pre-eminent linguistic sign. As Shira Wolosky judges:

> The theory of the trace does not deny a relation between signified and signifier, seemingly freeing the sign from its 'meaning' into limitless ambiguity. Rather, it denies that there is a 'signified' separable from a 'signifier'.[17]

Meaning is generated through the interplay of inscribed 'signifiers' or traces, not from a source in some realm of 'being' where ideas exist in spendid isolation from signs. The source of differential interaction is instead an ultimate Other, beyond the world of beings, which remains hidden and can never be signified, but which is felt through the trace;[18] the idea of *khōra* as a 'no-place', as we have seen, helps us to articulate this Other. Now, the inexhaustible interplay of inscribed signs of which the world consists can be conceived, according to Derrida, by analogy with the Torah, the Jewish sacred Book. In Jewish thinking, Scripture, like the world, is immeasurable; Derrida here cites Rabbi Eleazar: 'if the sky and earth were parchments, and if all human beings practised the art of writing—they would not exhaust the

---

[14] See Chapter 2, n.145 and Chapter 5, the beginning of the section called 'The Complex Being of the Triune God'.

[15] Derrida, *Of Grammatology*, p. 34.

[16] Derrida, *Of Grammatology*, p. 17.

[17] Shira Wolosky, 'Derrida, Jabès, Levinas: Sign-Theory as Ethical Discourse', *Prooftexts* 2 (1982), pp. 283–302 (p. 289). I am indebted to Wolosky for several insights that appear in this section of the chapter.

[18] Derrida, *Of Grammatology*, p. 46.

Torah'.[19] Commenting on *The Book of Questions* by the Jewish poet Edmond Jabès, Derrida extends the analogy, asserting in agreement with Jabès that:

> Being is a Grammar; and that the world is in all its parts a cryptogram to be constituted or reconstituted through poetic inscription or deciphering; that the book is original, that *everything belongs to the book* before being and in order to come into the world; that any thing can be born only by *approaching* the book, can die only by failing in sight of the book; and that always the impassable shore of the book is first.[20]

The Jewish Kabbalistic idea, drawn on by Jabès, that the Torah is prior to the world and acts as a model for the creation of the world, is re-employed by Derrida to assert the priority of writing, and especially its status above the voice-sign: 'For Jabès the book is not in the world, but the world is in the book',[21] so that 'there has never been anything else but writing'.[22] To live in the book of the world means that existence is 'an interrogation of signs' for both Jabès and Derrida. But the Author of the book can never, for Derrida, be signified. For Jabes, God is the 'middle which is the void of the circle' of the letters of the divine Name;[23] similarly, for Levinas, the world is the space between the 'square letters' (consonants) of the divine Name, 'a precarious dwelling from which the revealed Name is already withdrawn'.[24] Derrida agrees that the writing of the world is inscribed in the space made by divine withdrawal, or (appealing to the Kabbalistic concept of *zimsum*) the separation of God from God's self.[25] We are only in 'the trace of God', which is not a state of participation.[26] Derrida is also in agreement with Levinas that there can therefore be no communion between the finite mind and the transcendent 'Other' which has absented itself; commenting on Levinas he approves of the view that relation between the sign and the other is 'without intermediary and without communion, absolute proximity and absolute distance'.[27] Here Derrida makes a contrast with Christianity: 'The Christian God manifests a concrete spirit which remains veiled and abstract in Judaism. As the Son is infinite [...] he gives to God his image.'[28]

While, for Levinas, God is always the Other who has 'withdrawn', he nevertheless differs from Derrida in understanding this absent God to exert

---

[19] Derrida, *Of Grammatology*, p. 16; cf. *Glas*, pp. 268–9.

[20] Derrida, *Writing and Difference*, p. 76; cf. 'Parergon', p. 146: 'the cipher writing on the surface of nature'.

[21] Derrida, *Writing and Difference*, p. 76.

[22] Derrida, *Of Grammatology*, p. 159.

[23] Edmond Jabès, *Le Livre des Questions* (Paris: Gallimard, 1963–5), p. 85.

[24] Levinas, *Beyond the Verse*, p. 119.

[25] Derrida, *Writing and Difference*, p. 67; on *zimsum*, see Chapter 7, the section called 'The Search for a No-Place'.

[26] Derrida, *Writing and Difference*, p. 108.　　　[27] Derrida, *Writing and Difference*, p. 90.

[28] Derrida, *Glas*, p. 39.

some positive force within the world, especially in the ethical demand made upon the self by the other.[29] While direct sight of the face of God is hidden (as it was to Moses), we do encounter the divine face indirectly through being face to face with another, so that (as Derrida summarizes him) 'the face of God *commands* while hiding itself'.[30] Derrida is critical about any such statement of 'positive infinity' or 'positive plenitude', which attempts to 'expel negativity from transcendence'.[31] The question I am addressing in this chapter is whether we can say even *more* about this 'positive' impression of God upon the world and presence to the world. It is whether we can, in some sense, understand the signs of creation as signifying God, so that creation does indeed 'tell out the glory of God'. The language of participation in God, I suggest, does not necessarily entail the view of mediation rejected by Derrida and Levinas; indeed, I have already argued that the figure of Lady Wisdom in the Hebrew wisdom writings gives no grounds for the concept of ontological mediation, and that in Christian theology Christology does not depend on such mediation either. Derrida assumes that 'participation' must imply the 'exclusion' of a physical from an intelligible realm;[32] in fact, while mediation does imply exclusion, there is no reason to think that participation must also do so. Indeed, it might even be an image for inclusion.

Derrida has already taken a qualified view of the uselessness of the language of 'being'. Although he insists that the category of being (or indeed non-being) cannot be used for the 'infinitely Other', when this affirmation is pressed it becomes clear that what he is rejecting is that Being is some kind of entity, 'a super-being' that presences itself, or that it is an intelligible and static reality which can be separated from the physical, dynamic, and sensible world.[33] Otherwise, language about Being still has some place in thinking about the meaning of 'difference'. My aim is to show that one can similarly take a modified view of 'participation' and 'signification' which will meet Derrida's concern that there can be no exemption from entanglement in the world of signs. Unlike Baudrillard (and, in some moods, Lyotard) Derrida does not exclude transcendence when he affirms that 'there is nothing outside the text of the world'; he means that what is outside is always inside at the same time. It might then be possible, against Derrida but working in his own mood, to affirm some kind of 'transcendental signified', and to read God out of the book of the world.

If there is some disagreement between psalm and semiotics, there is however also common ground. Both views of the world as a book find that that the

---

[29] This is a point stressed by Wolosky, 'Derrida, Jabès, Levinas', p. 299.

[30] Derrida, *Writing and Difference*, p. 108; so Levinas, *Beyond the Verse*, p. 141.

[31] Derrida, *Writing and Difference*, p. 114.

[32] Derrida, *Of Grammatology*, p. 71.

[33] See Chapter 5, the section called 'The Complex Being of the Triune God', and Chapter 7, the section called 'The Disturbance of a "No-Place"'.

signs are elusive and always open in meaning. The wisdom literature of Ancient Israel had already, long ago, conceived of the world as a kind of text. Wisdom as *ḥokmah* is not only *subjectively* the faculty of knowing ('my wisdom'), and it is not only *objectively* the collection of thoughts in the mind ('the wisdom in my head'); its objectivity also consists in being a body of knowledge waiting to be discovered, equal in extent to the world. This wisdom is potentially ready to be inscribed in a written text by the wise. The book of the world is thus endlessly complex, multivalent in expression, and evading exact formulations.

THE UNFATHOMABLE TEXT OF THE WORLD

Writers of ancient Jewish wisdom would judge that the Duke in Shakespeare's play was rather too over-confident and moralistic in thinking that the sermon can be so easily extracted from the stones. There is a hiddenness about the world which requires us to be humble as we live within it. In chapter 4 I explored the way that wisdom writers admitted the limits of their under-standing, when faced by the complexity of the world, and recognized that God was supremely wise in a way that they were not. In puzzling over the riddle of Job 28, we realize that the reason for the hiddenness of wisdom is not its concealment in some place or other, whether on earth or in heaven, but rather its resistance to being completely surveyed or fathomed. The personification of wisdom vividly portrays its accessibility to human beings; by contrast, when its elusiveness is being stressed (as in Job 28), it appears as an unfathomable object. Wisdom (*ḥokmah*) can never be entirely possessed, and so we can never finally analyse this fascinating phenomenon. The widespread trope of a three-dimensional world, with its height, breadth, and depth full of uncount-able items, makes clear that wisdom cannot be fully explored because it is equivalent to the whole expanse of the world.[34] Echoing the three dimensions of the world surveyed in Job 28, at the beginning of his book Ben Sira confesses:

> All wisdom is from the Lord;
> wisdom is with him for ever.
> Who can *count* the sand of the sea,
> the drops of rain, or the days of unending time?
> Who can measure the *height* of the sky,
> the *breadth* of the earth or the *depth* of the abyss? (1:1–3)

---

[34] For examples, see Chapter 7, the section called 'Places and Dimensions of the World' and Chapter 7, n.78.

Now, the wise could generally live with not being able to come to the end of the count, and could put up with tentative solutions. There is at least one case of a wise man, the one named Koheleth, who *does* refuse to put up with it and insists on knowing the 'whole'; he is brought to despair, and we are to look at his case in the next chapter. But for the most part, the hiddenness of the world order is a stimulation for discovery. Without a veiling of wisdom there can be no unveiling. Without elusiveness, there can be no interpretation. As we contemplate the way that the height, length, and depth of the world escape the observer's grasp, we have a perspective from which to view the human situation. The elusive world draws in the human interpreter and acts as a signpost to the creator.

The book of Job itself exemplifies this method, as speakers in the dramatic dialogue in turn appeal to the unfathomable nature of the tripartite world and draw various conclusions for human life from it. In the first place the friends appeal to an elusive world order to support their argument that Job should not contradict God's apparent verdict upon him (11:7–9):

> 'But oh that God would speak,
> and open his lips to you,
> and that he would tell you the secrets of wisdom!
> For wisdom is many-sided.
> Know then that God exacts of you less than your guilt deserves.
> Can you find out the deep things of God?
> Can you find out the limit of the Almighty?
> It is higher than heaven – what can you do?   (height)
> Deeper than Sheol – what can you know?   (depth)
> Its measure is longer than the earth,
> and broader than the sea.'   (breadth)

The 'many-sided'[35] wisdom of God corresponds to the manifold world. The lesson the friends draw from an expansive world is that God alone knows the true state of affairs in the world—'the secrets of wisdom'—and so he alone knows Job's guilt. For the most part the friends are not accusing Job of hypocrisy. Their argument is that God must be seeing sin that human eyes cannot see, either sin that has gone un-noticed or behaviour that is sin unknown to humans.[36] This is reminiscent of the confession of the 'Babylonian Job', that 'what is good in one's own sight is evil for a god'.[37] Significantly, this piece of Babylonian wisdom draws an analogy from the dimensions of the world to illustrate the unfathomable divine purpose:

---

[35] RSV. There is no need to emend the difficult כפלים to כפלאים 'wonders' with Clines, *Job 1–20*, p. 254 and Fohrer, *Hiob*, p. 221. Dhorme, *Job*, p. 159, aptly suggests a plural of כפל ('two-fold'), and so 'ambiguous matters', supporting the RSV rendering.

[36] Job 11:4–6; so also 4:17–19; 15:14–15; 25:3–6.

[37] See Snaith, *Book of Job*, p. 234.

> Who can understand the counsel of the gods in the midst of heaven?
> The plan of a god is deep waters, who can comprehend it?

The friends come closer to an accusation of hypocrisy when they imply that God sees sin *unadmitted* by Job, by citing a hypothetical case of a man who says that God cannot see him since the clouds block God's vision, although God 'walks on the vault of heaven' (22:12–14); this evokes the image of God's vision as being like the sun, a picture which we have seen to be typical of wisdom. The friends thus urge Job to make his confession (11:13–18), using a 'doxology of judgement', a hymn of praise to God's justice such as takes form in the 'Babylonian Job'.

Job, however, finds a different lesson in the elusiveness of the world. He complains that he cannot win his case against God, proving his innocence and requiring God to improve his present condition, because God will not answer his summons to appear in court. The complexity of the world thus demonstrates the arbitrary behaviour of God, of which his treatment of Job is one more example. Nobody can be totally pure, and it is unreasonable of God to use his superior vision of the world to condemn him.

> If one wished to contend with him,
> One could not answer him once in a thousand . . .
> He is wise in heart and mighty in strength . . .
> he shakes the earth out of its place . . . (breadth)
> who alone stretched out the heavens   (height)
> and trampled the waves of the sea. . . . (depth)
> who does great things beyond understanding
> and marvellous things without number . . . .
> Who will say to him, "What are you doing?" (9:4–10).

If, with a scholarly consensus, we take chapter 26 as a fragment of Bildad's speech which has become misplaced,[38] then we also find the friends drawing another conclusion from the dimensions of the world: these demonstrate not only God's superior vision but his naked power, illustrating Bildad's claim that 'dominion and fear are with God', and his question, 'the thunder of his power who can understand?'

> Sheol is naked before God,
> And Abaddon has no covering. (depth)
> He stretches out the North over the void
> and hangs the earth upon nothing . . . (breadth)
> The pillars of heaven tremble. (height) (Job 26:6–8)

Bildad's deduction differs from Job's in that, while they both discern divine power, Job finds it arbitrary and Bildad altogether just.

---

[38] So Clines, *Job 21–37*, p. 629; Dhorme, *Job*, p. 368; Newsom, 'Book of Job', p. 516.

Finally, the poem itself appeals to the hiddenness of the world to put *both* the friends and Job in the wrong, first in chapter 28 on the hiddenness of wisdom, and then in chapters 38–41 with God's series of ironic questions which traverse the dimensions of the world:

> Where were you when I laid the foundations of the earth? . . . (breadth)
> Who determined its measurements? . . . .
> Or who shut in the sea with doors
> when it burst out from the womb? . . . . .   (depth)
> Have you commanded the morning since your days began,   (height)
> and caused the dawn to know its place? . . . .
> Have you entered into the springs of the sea,   (depth)
> or walked in the recesses of the deep? . . .
> Have the gates of death been revealed to you?
> Have you comprehended the expanse of the earth?   (breadth)
> (Job 38:4–18)[39]

Since the world cannot be totally fathomed, the friends should not be so certain that retribution will always be visible. Nor can Job, though innocent, demand that the dogma of just retribution should operate in his favour and that he should be vindicated. The inexhaustible expanse of the world tells us that reasons for suffering, or release from it, cannot be easily identified. The very fact that the trope of a three-dimensional world can be used to yield different applications only underlines the hiddenness of the world.

BRINGING THE HIDDEN TO LIGHT: METAPHOR AND SIMILE

It is not only the big picture of a tripartite world from which lessons for human existence can be drawn: the wise are working on the basis that individual items within it can also be interpreted in a way that applies to everyday life. Analogies for particular human experiences can be found in natural events, which are therefore treated as object lessons. The making of these similes is understood to be a *discovery*. It assumes that there is a hidden order which is being brought to light. The wise presume that there is a similar process secretly at work in human and natural events, and so human experience can be illuminated by comparing it with natural phenomena.

The hidden nature of the world thus prompts the making of a simile. For example, from the Book of Proverbs: 'The dread wrath of a King is like the growling of a lion' (20:2); 'Like a sparrow in its flitting, an undeserved curse

---

[39] See further Chapter 7, the section called 'The Point of the Riddle'.

goes nowhere' (26:2); 'Like the cold of snow in the time of harvest are faithful messengers to those who send them' (25:13); 'Like a dog that returns to its vomit is a fool who reverts to his folly' (26:11); 'A wife's quarrelling is like a continual dripping of rain' (27:15). Each of these compares something in nature with a human experience. A favourite device is a 'class saying' in which a series of objects are brought together in one implied simile, the significant one being the human event: for example, in Proverbs 30 we read:

> Three things are never satisfied; four never say 'Enough':
> Sheol, the barren womb,
> the earth ever thirsty for water,
> and the fire that never says, 'Enough'. (Prov. 30:15–16)

This example, about four insatiable things, also catches the inexhaustible nature of the world which is the constant theme of the wise, and it is a saying to which we shall return.

Another form of comparison is the metaphor, in which the analogy is implied. 'Wisdom has set out her table', for example (Prov. 9:2), is a metaphorical account of wisdom, implicitly comparing the offer of wisdom to a generous hostess. While the simile, with its explicit comparator 'like', tends to have an experimental and even provisional mood, inviting further comparisons to be made, in a metaphor meanings are fused in a 'dramatic, absolute and intuited identification of two phenomena'.[40] By comparing one thing with another, all similes and metaphors show an underlying unity between things in the world, but also put them together in new ways. The maker of a metaphor—often a poet—is asking 'have you noticed that this is like that?' and so also brings something *new* out of the verbal signs. By bringing two signs together in a single image, new levels of meaning are given to both. Between the objects compared, often named the tenor and the vehicle,[41] there is room for vibrations of undertones and undertones. In older rhetorical theory metaphors could be seen as simply 'substituting' a figurative expression for a literal one, but in recent theory the 'interaction' between the two terms has been emphasized, a clash between semantic frames generating an imaginative force that can create a new world for the consciousness. Thus, metaphor and simile can actually construct reality, or 'redescribe' reality.[42]

---

[40] Roger Fowler (ed.), *Dictionary of Modern Critical Terms* (London: Routledge and Kegan Paul, 1973), p. 172.

[41] So I. A. Richards, *The Philosophy of Rhetoric* (New York: Oxford University Press, 1936), p. 96.

[42] Max Black, *Models and Metaphors* (Ithaca: Cornell, 1962), pp. 38–44; Paul Ricoeur, 'Metaphor and the Central Problem of Hermeneutics' in his *Hermeneutics and the Human Sciences*, ed. John B. Thompson (Cambridge: Cambridge University Press, 1981), p. 181; cf. Ricoeur, *The Rule of Metaphor* (London: Routledge and Kegan Paul, 1986), pp. 110–20.

As they note correspondences between things, the wise tend to lay stress on finding regularities, in uncovering a hidden connection, in order to predict successful action in the future. These comparisons belong to what might be identified as 'root metaphors', or images which act as organizing centres of tradition, using imagination to carry the most important and cherished understandings of a community.[43] But the wise are also open to finding the new and unexpected insight that disrupts the world as they think they know it. Thus metaphor and simile can offer what Ricoeur called a 'predicative impertinence, as the appropriate means of producing a shock between semantic fields'.[44] All metaphor will contain, to some degree, both the ingredients of unification and dislocation, both the consolation of form and the challenge of the new. In the saying about four things that can never be satisfied, for example (Prov. 30:15–16), there is a sense of satisfaction in cataloguing four similar phenomena, but there is also something disturbing about the inclusion of the barren womb alongside Sheol, earth, and fire. Why is the barren womb never satisfied? Is the woman who cannot conceive hungry for children, or for sexual acts that might lead to conception,[45] or for *something else altogether*? Through use of the simile, her dissatisfaction demands many levels of understanding.

A more far-reaching example of a disturbing metaphor is the very image of wisdom as a woman that has concerned us for much of this study. Leo Perdue suggests that this metaphor belongs to a cluster of images about the place of fertility in the origins and maintenance of the world. The metaphor, he suggests, constructs a world-view in which wisdom is the Queen of Heaven, the lover and consort of God, who brings life, fertility, and blessing to those who love her.[46] This, I agree, would fit in with views of the religious origins of the world and society in the Ancient Near East at the time, and might well qualify as a 'root metaphor'. However, I have already brought evidence against the view that Lady Wisdom is cast in the role of a goddess and (in Perdue's phrase) a 'mediator between God and humanity'.[47] The portrayal of wisdom as a cosmic observer who walks in the path of the sun and is at the same time a wisdom-teacher and an attractive woman is more disturbing, more open-ended than the image of a divine consort, less amenable to being labelled

---

[43] David Tracy, 'Metaphor and Religion: The Test Case of Christian Texts' in *Critical Inquiry*, 5 (1978), pp. 91–2, 95; cf. George Lakoff and Mark Johnson, *Metaphors We Live By* (Chicago: University of Chicago Press, 1980), pp. 3–7.

[44] Ricoeur, 'Imagination in Discourse and Action' in *From Text to Action*, pp. 168–87 (p. 172); cf. Eva Feder Kittay, *Metaphor: Its Cognitive Force and Linguistic Structure* (Oxford: Clarendon Press, 1987), p. 24: 'metaphor breaks certain rules of language'.

[45] So McKane, *Proverbs*, p. 656.

[46] Perdue, *Wisdom and Creation*, p. 330.

[47] Perdue, *Wisdom and Creation*, p. 330. For my critique of mediation, see Chapter 6, the section called 'Participation not Mediation'.

and classified, constructing a world in which one is being summoned to live in tune with wisdom in a surprising diversity of ways. One more example of the disruptive metaphor is that of human kingship, the royal position of humanity in creation which is celebrated in wisdom texts and other Hebrew literature (e.g. Psalm 8, Job 36:7, Ben Sira 16:24, 18:14); this serves as a consoling root metaphor, but becomes more disturbing when qualified by the image of humanity-as-slave, whether in Job's parody of Psalm 8 (Job 7:17–21) or in Koheleth's experience of being a philosopher-king who is also a slave to the contingencies of space and time (Eccl. 1:12–13).

In finding correspondences, whether stable or shocking, the wise are bringing what is hidden to light, and interpreting the signs of the world. There is a parallel to this wisdom process in the way that the prophets of Israel employ object lessons from the natural world. A natural event may be drawn upon for a literary metaphor (Israel is 'a wild ass wandering alone',[48] for example), but it may also take the form of a prophetic sign where an immediately observed object, whether or not in a vision, gives rise to an oracle.[49] Amos, for example, sees a succession of objects which tell him that Israel is on the brink of disaster—locusts, fire, a plumb-line, a basket of summer fruit. With 'observed signs' like this, there is the assumption that a hidden meaning has been uncovered by the prophet who sees the object and finds a correspondence between the natural event and the human situation. There is some evidence that such signs were called a *māšāl* (מָשָׁל)[50] which is also the general term for a wisdom-saying; the etymology of the word suggests two meanings, 'rule' and 'comparison', the first pointing to the project of the wise to master the world that confronted them, the second to the analogical approach to the world we are now exploring.[51] Both elements could be applicable to a prophetic sign, especially if the first meaning were understood more generally as a 'word of power'.

There is, however, a difference between the wisdom simile and the prophetic sign: the wisdom saying uncovers a general truth about human experience (whether reassuring or disturbing) which lies hidden in the orders of the world, while the prophetic oracle gives a word of revelation for a particular moment in the nation's history, usually including a prediction for the immediate future.[52] The prophetic examples tend to be uniformly disruptive, laying

---

[48] Hosea 8:9.

[49] Examples are Amos 7:1–3, 7:4–6, 7:8–9, 8:1–3; Jer. 1 :11–12, 1:13, 18:1–11, 24:1–5; Ezekiel 1:4–5, 21:1–5 (MT), 24:3–13.

[50] Ezek. 21:5 (MT), 24:3, cf. Hos. 12:10; see Aubrey Johnson, 'מָשָׁל', Noth and Thomas (eds), *Wisdom in Israel*, pp. 2–9, who argues for dual wisdom and prophetic use on the basis of the meaning of 'likeness'.

[51] See Perdue, *Wisdom and Creation*, p. 64.

[52] See P. von der Osten-Sacken, Die *Apokalyptik in Ihrem Verhältnis zu Prophetie und Weisheit* (München: Kaiser, 1969).

stress on a new and often shocking insight. For instance, Hosea presents God as comparing himself to moth and dry rot in the house of Israel (Hosea 5:12). In Job 13:28 we read that human beings are afflicted by rot and eaten by moths, but not that God *is* the moth and the rot; in Proverbs 15:20 we read that moth and worm is like *sorrow*, but not like *God*. Wisdom sayings are not without a disturbing element, as we have seen, but the dissonant element is applicable to any time and place. In the use of such comparisons the prophets nevertheless seem to share a common technique of learning with the wise. We cannot be sure how much actual influence the wise had on prophecy, but it is likely that the question and answer dialogue which accompanies some of the prophetic signs is derived from the usual teaching methods of the wisdom schools.[53] For example, Amos reports:

> And the Lord said to me, 'What do you see?' And I said, 'A plumb line'. Then the Lord said, 'See, I am setting a plumb-line in the midst of my people Israel . . .' (Amos 7:8).

The question, 'What do you see?' represents the approach to the world which the wisdom pupil was encouraged to adopt, but whereas the wise person says '*I saw*' (Proverbs 24:32, 7:7), drawing a lesson from his experience ('I saw a field', 'I saw a foolish youth') the prophet says 'The Lord showed me' so claiming divine revelation (here, v. 7, 'This is what he showed me: the Lord was standing beside a wall . . .').[54] Both prophet and wise person are, however, interpreting what is observed for the benefit of human experience.

Both traditions are later to converge in the 'vision-discourse' of Jewish apocalyptic literature, where the seer sees an object and holds a dialogue about it with an angelic interpreter, who may have first have instructed him to 'look' at it. For example, in 1 Enoch chapters 2–5 the seer first instructs his hearers to 'observe' a number of natural phenomena, an observation from which he draws a *sapiential* conclusion about the stability of the natural order, and then offers a *prophetic* prediction that because his hearers have not been similarly steadfast they will meet punishment in an imminent catastrophe. The apocalyptic idea of the 'heavenly tablets' where the secrets of the future are written also draws upon both prophecy and wisdom; it combines the prophetic sense of hearing words spoken in the heavenly council of God, and the wisdom idea of scribal writings which record the mysteries of the world order. The two ideas may converge in the very term *sōd* (סוד) which, as Raymond Brown argues, shows a semantic shift from 'council' to 'secret'.[55]

---

[53] So J. Lindblom, 'Wisdom in the Old Testament Prophets' in Noth and Thomas (eds), *Wisdom in Israel*, p. 202. Examples are Amos 7:8, 8:2; Jer. 1:11, 24:3; Zech. 4:2, 5:2.

[54] Also, Amos 7:1, 7:4, 8:1.

[55] Raymond Brown, *The Pre-Christian Semitic Concept of Mystery* (Philadelphia: Fortress/Facet Books, 1968), pp. 14–15.

A simile, whether used by the wise or by prophets, often begins with the natural event and then moves to the human experience: for example, 'Like clouds and wind without rain is a person who boasts of a gift he does not give' (Prov. 25:14). By beginning with the event in nature, makers of metaphors are in effect hiding again what has been discovered, so that the hearer has the stimulation of the initial difficulty of understanding. The simile is taking a riddle form: 'What is like clouds and wind that appear without any rain following them?' Answer: 'a person who is always boasting about his generous giving without actually making any gifts.' The person who asks the riddle knows the answer, but is hiding it.

Apocalyptic writing creates hidden meaning like this, building ingeniously devised symbols out of observed objects and requiring the reader to solve puzzles and apply codes. But, in a less acute way, the making of all metaphors and similes is an act of concealment. To compose them requires a previous moment of discovery, the uncovering of some connection between things. But then in their form they add a further hiddenness to the world, and so in turn *enable* new discovery to take place, allowing new correspondences, disclosures, and associations to arise which cannot be controlled by the writer. There is an awareness of this in a saying in Proverbs 25:

> It is the glory of God to conceal things,
> but the glory of kings is to search things out.
> Like the heavens for height, like the earth for depth,
> so the mind of kings is unsearchable. (vv. 2–3)

In finding what God has hidden, the mind of the interpreter (here the king in an exemplary but not exclusive way)[56] shares in the unsearchable nature of the world, and itself becomes hidden to others: this mind 'has its heights and depths, with a range and subtlety and complexity which baffles those who would study it as an object to be described, analysed, and definitively explained'.[57] In this compressed saying, we find the familiar thought that the world order, here portrayed in two dimensions of height and depth, is the thing that is concealed because of its complexity. The saying is also an example of using metaphor to speak of God; while most of the similes we have considered take two known phenomena in the world as vehicle and tenor, the wise extend the use of the figure to God as an otherwise mysterious 'tenor'. In this case, God is compared to a human wise person who uses riddles and proverbs to hide meaning as an enticement to search for it. After Kant's epistemology, it is even clearer to us today that God cannot be known like

---

[56] The wise person could assume the pose of a king renowned for wisdom, as in Eccl. 1:12; in Eccl. 12:10 the sage 'searches things out' (*ḥēqer*) as in Prov. 25:2. See Crenshaw, *Old Testament Wisdom*, p. 43.

[57] McKane, *Proverbs*, p. 579, who however limits the mind to that of the literal king.

an object in the world, that literal language of God is thus impossible and that all God-talk must be metaphorical.

HIDDENNESS AND INTERPRETATION IN MODERN THOUGHT

We have seen that for the Israelite wise, the hiddenness of meaning in the world prompts a search for meaning, and summons the observer to interpret the signs of the world. This approach to the world is taken up, it seems, by prophets and apocalypticists. In our late-modern age, in envisaging the world as a text, we have as vivid a sense of the hiddenness of meaning as had the wise of old—perhaps even more so. For the wise this was largely due to the multiplicity of the world order under the gaze of God, and the limits of all human words that attempt to encapsulate it. To this we can add two more factors from recent thought that intensify the element of hiddenness: first the relation between text and author, and second the frailty of the sign.

First, in any written text, the human author is both absent and present. While the author has absented herself from her work by producing the artefact of a text, she remains present within it to a limited extent, in so far as it exhibits her intentions as the author. But this intention has to be related to the internal authority of the text itself, and to the interpretation which the reader brings to it. It is an 'intentional fallacy' to suppose the meaning of a text is exhausted by, or even subordinate to, the purpose of the author. In some (not all) 'deconstructive' literary theory, the absence of the author is stressed to the point of excluding her presence and intentions altogether. The author is completely banished from the text; it no longer belongs to her but only to itself and to us who read it. A more nuanced view hears the voice of the author as still present in the text, but diffused through a collection of signs which require to be given further meaning. Ricoeur thus maintains that writing 'frees itself' from its author, but offers the clarification: 'Not that we can conceive of a text *without* an author; the tie between the speaker and the discourse is not abolished, but distended and complicated.'[58]

Christian theology conceives of God as—in some sense—the author of the text of the world, while aware that 'author' is a metaphor. Derrida proposes that if, with Levinas, we want to continue to speak of God and not simply an absolute 'Other', then it is proper (taking issue with Levinas) to think of God primarily as *writer* of a world rather than *speaker* within it, since this Other must be absent:

---

[58] Paul Ricoeur 'The Model of the Text: Meaningful Action considered as Text' in *Hermeneutics and the Human Sciences*, pp. 201–2.

The writer absents himself better, that is expresses himself better as other, addresses himself to the other, more effectively than the man of speech . . . The thematic of the trace . . . should lead to a certain rehabilitation of writing. Isn't the 'He' whom transcendence and generous absence uniquely announces in the trace more readily the author of writing than of speech?[59]

Christian theology will, however, question this insistence on absence. With human authors we must certainly say that they are present and absent from their texts at the same time. With regard to God as author, however, we cannot speak of a duality of presence with *absence*, since a Creator must indwell creation in a more immediate way than any artist does her painting, sculpture, or book.[60] As I suggested in a previous chapter, theology must think rather of God's *hidden* presence. God is always present, but hidden even as God reveals God's self, veiled at the same time as unveiled.[61] If any shadow of a human author's intentions are present in a text, then they are hidden; like and yet unlike a human author, not only God's intentions for life but God's own self are *hidden* in the text. This is the meaning that, from a late-modern perspective, we may give to the ancient text, 'It is the glory of God to conceal things' (Prov. 25:2).

God is present in the world through signs, filling them to bursting with the divine glory, so that they seem infinite, unfathomable, and inexhaustible. But the creator remains hidden within them, veiled as well as unveiled, because they are still finite and created things. As the Hans Urs von Balthasar puts it, 'no appearance of God is more overwhelming than this non-appearance'.[62] The worldly form irradiates a fascination, which stimulates discovery, but at the same time the uncovering of the meaning of the text by the human interpreter will include the interpreter's own hiding of significance, his or her own thoughts and words adding to the mystery of the world; for, as the proverb puts it, the mind of the one who searches things out is itself 'unsearchable' (Prov. 25:3). To the mystery of a world in which the divine beauty is hidden there is added the mystery of persons who perceive it.

Another facet of hiddenness will be the *weakness* of a sign, as something temporary and passing away. The wise were well aware of the frailty of words as signs of the world; they knew that correspondences could break down.[63] From a modern science of signs we can add that, because all signs point beyond themselves, to something other—what is signified—they are always

---

[59] Derrida, *Writing and Difference*, p. 102.

[60] So Hans Urs von Balthasar, *Glory of the Lord*, vol. 1, *Seeing the Form*, trans. E. Leiva-Merikakis, pp. 443–4.

[61] cf. Karl Barth, *Church Dogmatics* I/1, 168–76.

[62] Hans Urs von Balthasar, *Theo-Logic: Theological Logical Theory*. 3 Volumes (San Francisco: Ignatius Press, 2000–5), vol. 1, *The Truth of the World*, trans. A. Walker, pp. 235–8.

[63] See Chapter 4, the section called 'Cautiousness and God in the Sentence Literature of Proverbs'.

'poised on the brink' of emptying themselves out or *vanishing* for the sake of the other.[64] This applies to all signs, whether they are inscribed in documents or are objects in the world outside the medium of books and paper. Physical things (trees, brooks, and stones to quote Shakespeare's Duke) are signs, and on the other hand signs are always embodied. This is true of words inscribed in a document, which have a physical form made from elements like paper, ink, wood, or stone. It is also true of human beings, as interpreters of signs and as constellations of signs in their own bodies. All signs are fragile or are mere 'traces'; even their interpreters are always on the verge of vanishing in face of the transient nature of signs, appearing to be what Hegel called a 'surface-show'.[65]

Our project to discover how an elusive world might witness to a God who is the author of its signs thus inevitably includes the puzzle of the human self. How can we bring together the theological perception that earthly signs are crammed full of the glory of God, with the semiotic perception that signs—together with the self as interpreter and embodiment of signs—are fragile and prone to vanish? I want to approach an answer by following up a trail from the use of words by the wise and the prophets—that is, the capacity of a simile or metaphor to disturb.

DISRUPTION AND EMPATHY

In capturing correspondences between the natural world and human experience, a metaphor or simile can be unexpected, disrupting the world as we know it. In Coleridge's words, the imaginative making of images 'dissolves, diffuses, dissipates, in order to re-create'.[66] Some metaphors are more dislocating than others, but they all have a disturbing aspect to them. The metaphysical poets of the seventeenth century use imagery in an especially radical way, choosing a vehicle for the metaphor which seems to have no obvious emotional association with the object to which it is linked. John Donne, for example, uses scientific and geometrical imagery for human experiences; he compares lovers to the twin legs of a compass, love to experiments in alchemy, tears to coins minted by the face, and the body to a map.[67] In modern times T. S. Eliot inherits the use of these devices, comparing for

---

[64] So Oliver Davies, *The Creativity of God: World, Eucharist, Reason* (Cambridge: Cambridge University Press, 2004), p. 141.

[65] Hegel, *Phenomenology of Spirit*, p. 87.

[66] S. T. Coleridge, *Biographia Literaria*. 2 Volumes, ed. J. Shawcross (London: Oxford University Press, 1954), vol. 1, p. 102.

[67] John Donne, 'A Valediction: forbidding Mourning'; 'A Nocturnall upon S. Lucies Day'; 'A Valediction: of Weeping'.

example the evening sky and the gathering darkness to 'a patient etherized upon a table.'[68] This led to an amusing versified comment by C. S. Lewis:

> For twenty years I've stared my level best
> To see if evening – any evening – would suggest
> A patient etherized upon a table;
> In vain. I simply wasn't able.[69]

Despite Lewis' protest, unexpected imagery like this can awaken new meaning within us. Using similes to bring signs in the world together in unexpected ways creates a kind of 'hermeneutical gap'.[70] It points to a lack of information: *how* is x like y? How is the evening sky like a patient under anaesthetic? How is God like moth and dry rot? How is an empty womb like a raging fire? How is wisdom like a woman? The comparison arouses curiosity, and makes the reader try to fill the gap in a creative way. Just because the strange associations do not carry emotional weight in themselves, they call for a move of empathy, the involvement of the whole person and not just the reason, challenging the tradition that it is rationality (*ratio*) that connects the sign and the thing.[71]

As signs in a written text, similes can thus create deeper participation in the world—involving interest, wonder, respect, and responsibility—or deeper participation in the life of another person—involving mutuality, demand, obligation, and love. They direct us to the mystery within the objects that we hold within our mind; although we are apparently able to survey these objects with our intellect, the sign prompts the experience that (in the words of Balthasar) we are 'flooded by something that overflows our knowledge', or in other words 'the awareness of participating in something that is infinitely greater in itself than what comes to light in its disclosure'. We sense, says Balthasar, that the subject 'lays hold of only a fraction of the object's depth and richness'.[72] Another person will, especially, always remain mysterious; even when opening himself or herself to another, a depth of personal identity will remain, a mystery which goes on calling for empathy and the engagement of the whole person.

Above all, when we use signs to point to God, making a comparison between things in the world and their creator (speaking, for example, of God as a father, a mother, a rock, a refuge, or a redeemer), then we are

[68] Eliot, 'The Love Song of J. Alfred Prufrock', *Complete Poems and Plays*, p. 13.

[69] C. S. Lewis, *Poems*, ed. Walter Hooper (London: Bles, 1964), p. 1.

[70] See, extensively, Karl F. Morrison, '*I am You*'. *The Hermeneutics of Empathy in Western Literature, Theology and Art* (Princetown: Princeton University Press, 1988), pp. 34, 81, 224–7, 272–3.

[71] See Ricoeur, 'The Metaphorical Process as Cognition, Imagination and Feeling' in Mark Johnson (ed.), *Philosophical Perspectives on Metaphor* (Minneapolis, University of Minnesota Press, 1981), pp. 228–47.

[72] Balthasar, *Theo-Logic*, vol. 1, p. 140, taken together with pp. 234–6.

being moved to a deeper participation in God, the mystery in whom all mysteries in the world are grounded. The intrinsic meaning of signs 'depends on their being a participation in God and his revelation' through them.[73] The Jesus of the Gospels uses similes and parables like this,[74] stepping into a rich heritage of the use of sign in wisdom, prophecy, and apocalyptic. Jesus is 'both sage and revealer of God's inbreaking dominion'.[75] His comparisons use surprising images, which often run counter to the prevailing culture. The Kingdom of Heaven is like a shepherd who abandons the rest of the flock for the sake of one wandering sheep (which seems careless); or it is like a woman who uses a day's labour in searching for a coin of very little worth (which seems wasteful); or the kingdom is like leaven rising in bread (which seems immoral because leaven was usually taken by the religious to be a symbol of evil). Famously, a rich man getting to heaven is like a camel passing through the eye of a needle (which seems absurd).[76] Jesus brings contraries together in a way that dissolves the familiar; we are startled, perhaps offended, and our empathy is required to close the gap, enabling us to see through the world to the purpose of God. As Ricoeur puts it, proverbs and parables about the Kingdom in the Synoptic Gospels 'reorient us by disorienting us'.[77]

The wise of old knew that the hiddenness of the world prompts us to discover meaning, sometimes through the to and fro of poetic dialogue (as in Job), but often through the making of metaphors and similes. These figures of speech disturb and challenge us, inviting us to participate in the deepest realities of the world, and finally in God. Now we can close the hermeneutical circle. If God is the final (though collaborative) author of the text of the world, and is present in the text in a hidden way, it is empathetic participation in the movement of the triune God that actually enables us to interpret the signs of the world. The wise of old tell us through the image of Lady Wisdom, an observer like the sun, that to see things properly human interpreters must see as God sees, and measure as God measures. Balthasar maintains that finite minds do not just 'see' objects, but measure them—that is, perceive them with a creative judgement. Self-conscious minds can measure, but only because everything is being measured by God[78]—whom, wisdom writers would add, alone knows the measureless creation fully. To participate in the measuring of God (Job 28:25) means sharing in the eternal relations of the Trinity, since the love between the Father and the Son in the fellowship of the Spirit is 'the

---

[73] Balthasar, *Theo-Logic*, vol. 1, p. 236.
[74] Claus Westermann, *The Parables of Jesus in the Light of the Old Testament*, trans. F. Golka and A. Logan (Minneapolis: Fortress, 1990), pp. 182–3, argues that parables are extended similes but addressed to a historical situation rather than being timeless truths.
[75] Witherington, *Jesus the Sage*, p. 202.
[76] Lk. 15:4–7; Lk. 15:8–10; Mt. 13:33; Mt. 19:24.
[77] Ricoeur, *Figuring the Sacred*, p. 59.
[78] Balthasar, *Theo-Logic*, vol. 1, pp. 60–1.

measure of all measures'.[79] All interpretation enters into the rhythms of the divine life.

This is because, as the theologian Eberhard Jüngel puts it, God is always speaking the truth about God's self and interpreting God's self. 'The doctrine of the Trinity is the interpretation of God's self-interpretation.'[80] According to the symbol of the Trinity, the Father eternally sends out the Son from his being in the power of the Spirit, a doctrine called 'eternal generation'. This is a story about the self-expression of God, about God's speaking out a word of creative love and costly reconciliation. In this Word who is the Son, God interprets what God is as creator and redeemer of the world. All true human interpretation of the world must share in this act of divine self-communication. For the Jewish scholar Gerschom Scholem, the contraction of God into God's self (*zimsum*) was the movement that was 'the original source of all linguistic movement',[81] as first Torah and then creation is inscribed in the space opened by the divine withdrawal. In the doctrine of the Trinity the source of all signs lies in a different kind of movement, in a rhythm of mission ('sending') which makes room for the world.

This movement also, however, involves a self-emptying (*kenōsis*) of God. With Sergius Bulgakov, Balthasar, and the poet Gerard Manley Hopkins we may discern three moments of *kenōsis* or self-sacrifice in God: in eternal generation, creation, and the cross of Jesus.[82] The metaphor of a father eternally begetting a son points to a self-emptying in affirming another, an abandoning of isolation for the sake of the other. The movement of letting others be continues in the creation of a finite world with its signs over against God, and comes to a climax as the Father sends out the Son into the world and into the most remote depths of human life in the death of the cross. Thus, the movement of self-interpretation is also a self-emptying or self-limitation for the sake of others. The human interpreter of signs empties herself in the direction of others; this human self-emptying, we can now see, is held within the love of the triune God. Just as God does not lose God's self in self-emptying, but becomes more truly God, so the human self becomes itself even as it gives itself away. Here we can bring together the perception of semiotics that signs are always vanishing into something else (an object, another sign) and the theological affirmation that the signs of the world are

---

[79] Balthasar, *Glory of the Lord*, vol. 1, p. 432.

[80] Eberhard Jüngel, *God's Being is in Becoming*, trans. John Webster (Edinburgh: T & T Clark, 2001), p. 29.

[81] Gershom Scholem, 'The Name of God and the Linguistic Theory of the Kabbala', *Diogenes* 79/80 (1972), p. 181.

[82] Balthasar, *Theo-Drama: Theological Dramatic Theory*. 5 Volumes (San Francisco: Ignatius Press, 1988–98), vol. 2, *Dramatis Personae: Man in God*, trans. G. Harrison, pp. 262–6; vol. 4, *The Action*, trans. G. Harrison, pp. 313–14, 323; Bulgakov, *Lamb of God*, pp. 213–28; Hopkins, *Sermons and Devotional Writings*, p. 197.

bursting with divine presence and glory. Both can be true, because they share in the trinitarian movement of a vanishing for the sake of another. Not only the interpreter, but created signs themselves exist in the self-giving movement of God. Thus they witness to the glory of God, not by denoting God as an object or describing God literally. They signify God by drawing the interpreter to participate in a God who is communicating and giving God's own self.

TRINITY AND DISTURBANCE

If we are to take this vision of participation seriously, we must read the symbol of the Trinity carefully. As I have been proposing throughout this study, Trinity is not about three individual beings who *have* relations as a kind of property or activity. It is about persons who *are* relations. Some readers who are not theologians will no doubt be surprised, even shocked, by the idea that the divine 'persons' are nothing more or less than movements of relationship, because this means we cannot form a mental image of them as being like persons in the world. We cannot project an image of the ideal father we never had, or the ideal son or daughter we would like to be. Many theologians will likewise be disturbed by the identification of persons with relations, as we have seen, arguing that only persons who are constituted *by* relations can secure diversity in God.[83] But God is unique and cannot be classed with any finite being; we need metaphors to speak of God, and when we speak of divine persons *as* relations we are using a metaphor which is disruptive, challenging mere rationality. This is precisely in accord with the character of metaphor as 'disorientating' and dissonant, yet calling for empathy and participation. We cannot *see* a relation which is like a father sending forth a son, or a daughter responding in love to a mother, but we can engage in it, making divine movements of mission and response our own. Like all metaphors, the element of surprise creates empathy and involvement to close the hermeneutical gap. The metaphor of persons *as* interweaving relations is not only apophatic but subversive.

Using the word 'interweaving' makes clear that we need a wide range of metaphors to express participation in God. The ancient term *perichōrēsis* offers the metaphors of interweaving, inter-penetrating, and indwelling, applied first to the persons of the Trinity among themselves and then to our sharing in the divine life. A later play on words led to *perichōrēsis* being understood as a divine dance in which created beings could be dancers too.[84] In *this* dance the partners not only encircle each other and weave in

---

[83] See Chapter 5, the section called The Complex Being of the Triune God'.
[84] See Chapter 5, the section called 'The Complex Activity of the Triune God'.

and out between each other as in human dancing; in the divine dance, so intimate is the communion that they move in and through each other so that the pattern is all-inclusive. Applied to the divine 'persons', I suggest that the image of the divine dance is not about individual dancers but about the patterns of the dance itself, an interweaving of ecstatic movements; yet we cannot think about this dance without the participation of human dancers. A related image is that of the rhythms of music to which we can be attuned, to which von Balthasar is making playful allusion in his term 'measure'.[85] St John of the Cross takes up (as we have already seen) the image of different streams of water, and another mediaeval spiritual writer, Jan van Ruusbroec, also uses a liquid image for expressing the way that created beings participate in a relation which is like that between a Son and a Father: created beings share in 'an eternal going-out, this eternal life which we have and are within God' as part of 'an eternal out-flowing through the birth of the Son into an otherness with distinction'.[86] More traditionally, the relational movements in God might be pictured as speech, a plurality of voices or speech patterns, so that 'from all eternity the divine "conversation" envisages the possibility of involving a non-divine world in the Trinity's love'.[87]

All these images, we notice, derive from things that can be observed in the world, and which become the basis for metaphors which express a knowing of God. These metaphors—interweaving, indwelling, dancing, the rhythms of music, the flowing of water, the interchange of conversation—are not just accidental ways of approaching the darkness of God. The images work because they are signs in the world to which God has commmitted God's own self, as creator and redeemer. God is not a 'transcendental signified' according to Derrida's accusation, if this means existing beyond signs, beyond the text; God desires always to be related to the signs God has made. At the same time, the strangeness (the wildness) of the similes makes clear that we can never possess God through them. God is more than textuality, but never without it.

All talk of God as Trinity, as a divine communion characterized by relationships, only arises from our experience of God in the world of physical signs. We only think of speaking about a second 'person' distinct from the Father, and a third who proceeds from both, because of our experience of God's work of salvation and renewal in the world. It is because of what we want to say about God manifest in time and space, focused in Jesus of Nazareth, that we are driven to speak of God in God's self as complex being and not merely undifferentiated unity. Thus human beings and their salvation

---

[85] I expand this musical metaphor in my final chapter.

[86] Jan van Ruusbroec, *The Spiritual Espousals*, trans. H. Rolfson (Collegeville: Liturgical Press, 1995), pp. 116–17.

[87] Balthasar, *Theo-Dramatik*, vol. 5, p. 509. Thus also Barth, *Church Dogmatics* I/1, pp. 139–41, 295–306.

are from the very beginning included within our thought of God as Trinity. Karl Rahner urges that 'there *must* be a connection between Trinity and man [*sic*]. The Trinity is a mystery of *salvation*, otherwise it would never have been revealed.... The "economic" Trinity is the "immanent" Trinity, and the "immanent" Trinity is the "economic" Trinity.'[88] Similarly, Barth insists that 'in the free decision of his love God is God in the very fact ... that he does stand in this relation, in a definite relationship with the other', so that 'we cannot go back on this decision if we would know God and speak accurately of God'.[89] Again, he underlines that 'we cannot go back behind this event'[90] of God's gracious choice of humanity as covenant partner in the representative man, Jesus. Taking these theologians somewhat further than they go themselves, I suggest that God does not 'need' the world in the sense that there is some intrinsic necessity in the divine nature, binding free choice, but that God does need the world in the sense of having freely *chosen to be in need*.[91]

This affirmation of the eternal will and desire of God provides a strong theological foundation for the idea that the material universe coexists eternally with God, though of course this does not apply to any particular form it takes (such as in our own world). For some religious thought, such as process philosophy, the coexistence of God and the universe derives from the ultimate value of creativity.[92] The absolute factor of the creative process requires both God and other actualities as necessary component parts. It is for this reason that there can be no literal creation *ex nihilo*. But if we follow through the clue of the desire of God, then there is a different basis for an eternal coexistence of God and the universe: it derives from the good pleasure of God, in which there can be no 'otherwise'.[93] Creation is *ex nihilo*, but only in the sense that it is ultimately 'from nothing except' God's will and love, not in the sense that there ever 'was nothing except' God. This means that there was no 'point', often defined as marking the beginning of time,[94] when reality external to God began. Rather, the universe is dependent upon God as existing and being held above nothingness by God's will, while God also is dependent upon the universe by God's own desire. That primordial will or desire means a longing for a cooperative enterprise at all stages of creation, including a fellow-working with humankind in due time, so that in another sense creation is 'from' God

[88] Rahner, *Trinity*, pp. 21–2.

[89] Barth, *Church Dogmatics*, II/1, p. 6.

[90] Barth, *Church Dogmatics* II/1, p. 281.

[91] See my *Creative Suffering of God*, pp. 66–8.

[92] Whitehead, *Process and Reality*, pp. 528–9; see John Cobb, *A Christian Natural Theology for our Time* (London; Lutterworth, 1966), pp. 203–14.

[93] *Contra* Barth, who maintains that in principle God could have done otherwise than creating, though *in fact* there is no otherwise in the divine decision: *Church Dogmatics*, I/1, p. 434; II/1, pp. 280–1.

[94] So Augustine, *Civitas Dei* 12.15.

and creatures. To this conjunction we may apply the words of the wedding rite: 'What God hath joined together let no man put asunder'. We can thus agree with Derrida that there can be no 'transcendental signified' which exists without textuality and signs, while adding that there can be a transcendental signified which is inseparable from signifiers in the world.

We can also agree that there can be no privileging of a voice of God above writing. For Derrida, 'our writing, certainly, but already His . . . starts with the stifling of his voice,'[95] in the withdrawal of God from the world. However, a trinitarian perspective means that many metaphors for relations in God and for the mutual participation of God and the world will be valid, including (but not prioritizing) the voice. Derrida is right to object that a privileging of the divine voice has often belonged to a concept of mediation between two worlds, and so a final detachment of God from the sign. Perhaps the most accomplished account of this association, offered in full awareness of modern semiotics, is to be found in Oliver Davies' book *The Creativity of God*. According to Davies, the 'primal text' of the world precipitates from the plural speech of God, just as any text (in his view) 'crystallizes' from the speech-processes of human culture. This primal text is the bedrock of spatio-temporal existence and is manifested in the complex inter-textualities of the world we observe and touch.[96] Like a human text, the world contains the author's voice in encoded form, and does so in a way that requires interpretation. The voice exists in the text in an 'alienated' form. Christ, then, as the incarnate Word 're-voices' the text; in Christ the divine word meets us as the personal address of a living voice, not simply as encoded.[97] The body of Christ is the point where the originary trinitarian voice and the text are unified, since it is through bodies that we participate in the world-text (and ultimately, in the primal text). The voiced body of Christ thus 'mediates' between the voice of God, author of creation, and the text that is the body of God's world.[98] The world resonates with the speaking voice of Jesus, made present for us in the incarnation and in a particular way in the Eucharist. With this moment, the world becomes divine body, animated by a spirit-filled speaking breath.

The sweep and grandeur of this vision is extraordinary. There is much to be learnt from Davies' account of the divine voice inhabiting the body of the world, and especially from his insistence (similar to mine) that:

> the nature of the sign as referring is held ultimately in the act of Trinitarian address: signs only refer because they are part of a world which is itself consti-tuted as the issue or outflow of an act of communication between God and God.[99]

[95] Derrida, *Writing and Diffference*, p. 67.
[96] Davies, *Creativity of God*, pp. 104–19.
[97] Davies, *Creativity of God*, pp. 111–14.
[98] Davies, *Creativity of God*, pp. 155–6.
[99] Davies, *Creativity of God*, p. 140.

However, there is no need to privilege voice over text as Davies does. Voice is only one metaphor for the movement of self-giving in God; there is voice to be heard in the text, because voices involve a pattern of relations, but it is only one pattern. More fundamentally, the portrayal of Christ as an *intermediary* voice (although embodied) between God and world plays into trap of the Patristic logos-doctrine whose logic is finally to separate God—at least in God's immanent being—from the physical sign. Moreover, it is hard to see how the voice of one individual mediator, Christ, can embody the 'plural voices' of the Trinity as Davies wants.[100] As I have been arguing throughout, we need to replace mediation by participation. We should think of the world as text because it is *in God*, its network of signs being formed and impressed by the movements of the divine relations. One metaphor for this reality, but only one, is being included in a divine conversation, in an interchange of plural voices. In a late-modern situation when the author is often excluded from the text, Davies has asserted the presence of the divine 'author' by conceiving of the world-text as a deposit from the spoken Word. My own proposal is that that, with regard to the world, we should think of the world-text as being held in the 'author', the triune God. Here we may recall our exploration of wisdom in ancient texts: wisdom as a subject ('Lady Wisdom') does not appear as a cosmic mediator, while wisdom as an object is inexhaustible as the text of the world.

SIGN AND REFERENCE

There is one further aspect of this mysterious world of signs in which we live. At the beginning of this chapter I observed that late-modern thought can be sceptical about whether the signs in any particular inscribed text—a story, a poem, a sculpture, a film—refer to anything in the everyday world. In extreme views, it may be said that a particular text is not strictly about anything except itself. It is a self-contained world from which the outside world is absent, since the signs of the text (say, the words of a story) gain their meaning only from their relation to each other within their own immediate constellation of signs. Since the environment of the world is itself composed of signs, the question is what the relation might be between the world *of* the text and the world *as* text. Now, no creative work in words or other symbols can be a mere imitation (*mimēsis*) of the world; all writers are aware of this, from poets to physicists observing the mysterious world of quanta. There is a gap between the word and the world, of which the wisdom writers of old were well aware.

---

[100] Davies, *Creativity of God*, pp. 84–90.

Derrida does not deny the capacity of a text to refer beyond itself, but warns us against the confidence of supposing that we can determine the difference between the inside and the outside, whether of a particular text or the whole world as text; he brings us up against the paradox of the 'hymen'.[101] Yet if we follow a semiotics of the Trinity, both signs and human interpreters share in the movements of a God who is interpreting God's self. It must then be possible to refer both to God (in the participatory sense I have outlined above) and to the wider world beyond any particular sign-system. Interpretation will, however, always be needed—as both Gadamer and Ricoeur affirm[102]—together with a Derridean sense of caution. With these qualifications, if God refers to the world in creation and redemption, then so can a human interpreter who shares God's vision. Perhaps we should say that we can refer to the world *as it can be*. This is supported by the perception of Ricoeur, that the world of the written text is referring to a world less 'behind' the text than 'in front' of it.[103]

Written texts, Ricoeur proposes, express possibilities. They describe not so much how things are now, but how they *might be*. Writers and readers together do not just imitate reality but discover and change it, in imaginative ways. So the true world lies in front of the text, always ahead of it. Human existence is always full of possibilities that are not confined by how things actually are here and now.[104] For Ricoeur, human being is *possibility itself*, and out of this fecund capacity the imagination can create genuinely new possibilities which are not simply repetitions of the past and present; symbol and myth refer to a reality which is yet to come and which they help to create. 'Fiction changes reality', maintains Ricoeur, 'in the sense that it both "invents" and "discovers" it.'[105] Imagination offers possibilities to the will which adopts them and forms *projects* which not dependent upon conditions in the present. Such projects are not unreal just because all the conditions for them do not exist here and now, as the world includes 'what *is to be done* by me'. Human existence means that 'the possible precedes the actual and clears the way for it'.[106] There are obvious affinities here with *The Principle of Hope* of Ernst Bloch, as Bloch speaks of 'the ontology of the not yet' and 'real-possibilities' as the objects of hope.[107]

---

[101] See the begining of this chapter.

[102] See William Schweiker, 'Mimetic Praxis in Gadamer, Ricoeur, and Derrida', *Journal of Religion* 68 (1988), pp. 21–38.

[103] Paul Ricoeur, *Interpretation Theory: Discourse and the Surplus of Meaning* (Fort Worth: Texas Christian University Press, 1976), p. 87.

[104] Paul Ricoeur, *Freedom and Nature: The Voluntary and the Involuntary*, trans. E. V. Kohak (Evanston: Northwestern University Press, 1966), pp. 48, 54.

[105] Paul Ricoeur, 'The Function of Fiction in Shaping Reality', *Man and World* 12 (1979), p. 127.

[106] Paul Ricoeur, *Freedom and Nature*, pp. 48, 54.

[107] Ernst Bloch, *The Principle of Hope*. 3 Volumes, transl. N. Plaice, S. Plaice, and P. Knight (Oxford: Blackwell, 1986), vol. 1, pp. 235–49.

Mimēsis then is the '*creative* imitation' of reality.[108] The 'the world of the text' is referring to a world which 'the text unfolds before itself'.[109] In this context, Ricoeur can take up the old dispute between those who find the meaning of the text to be in its autonomy, and those who find it to be open in meaning and made ever anew through the participation of the reader. There is room in interpretation for both objective analysis of the text in its own right ('explanation') *and* for existential involvement ('understanding').[110] In a hermeneutics of suspicion the critic unmasks the ideologies that lie hidden in the text, and in a hermeneutics of retrieval the critic is willing to listen to the symbols that lead to truth. As Ricoeur puts it, 'the idols must die, so that the symbols may live'.[111] On the basis of analysis of the text (explanation), the reader joins in the play of the text in developing new possibilities for human existence (understanding), which can then affect the reader's self-understanding here and now through evoking feeling (appropriation). The world of the text *refers* to future reality and not to the present, but it *transforms* human reality here and now.[112]

Ricoeur greeted Jürgen Moltmann's book on *The Theology of Hope* with great enthusiasm, commending the theologian's stress upon a religion of promise rather than a religion of presence; he strongly approves Moltmann's finding of revelation to consist in the giving of a promise which opens up the future rather than in an epiphany of eternal being.[113] In this he is in agreement with Derrida's resistance to an ontology of absolute presence. Ricoeur takes Moltmann's emphasis upon promise and fulfilment into his own focus upon the 'surplus' in language and human being. Moltmann points out that in the Jewish-Christian experience, history is generated by the expectation of fulfilment, and when the fulfilment of promise comes it is perceived as being not an end of the promise but a renewal of it; Ricoeur comments that 'this designates an increase, *a surplus*, a 'not yet' which maintains the tension of history'.[114]

Above all, the resurrection of Jesus does not close off the promise of God when it fulfills it, but opens our expectations by directing our hope to the

---

[108] So Ricoeur pairs together *mimēsis* (imitation) and *muthos* (composition): *Time and Narrative*, Vol. 1, pp. 32–7. On this pairing, see James Fodor, *Christian Hermeneutics: Paul Ricoeur and the Refiguring of Theology* (Oxford: Clarendon Press, 1995), pp. 185–91.

[109] On the 'world of the text', see Paul Ricoeur, 'Towards a Hermeneutic of the Idea of Revelation', pp. 98–100.

[110] Ricoeur, *Interpretation Theory*, pp. 87–8.

[111] Paul Ricoeur, *Freud and Philosophy: An Essay on Interpretation*, trans. D. Savage (New Haven: Yale University Press, 1970), p. 531.

[112] Ricoeur, 'The Function of Fiction', pp. 134–9.

[113] Moltmann, *Theology of Hope*, pp. 42–5; Ricoeur, 'Freedom in the Light of Hope', pp. 404–8.

[114] Ricoeur, 'Freedom in the Light of Hope', trans. R. Sweeney, in Ricoeur, *Conflict of Interpretations*, p. 405; Moltmann, *Theology of Hope*, pp. 194–7, 124–33.

future resurrection from the dead.[115] Ricoeur finds 'freedom in the light of hope' to be 'the meaning of my existence in the light of the Resurrection, that is, as reinstated in the movement which we have called the future of the Resurrection of the Christ'. This hope is a 'living contradiction' of reality as it is; the superabundance of the 'how much more' (Rom. 5:12–20) is 'in spite of' death. So Ricoeur finds the cross of Jesus symbolizes a denial of everything in present reality that hope transcends; it is, as it were, God's judgement upon present actuality.[116] We note, however, that (unlike Moltmann) Ricoeur finds possibilities to be located in the 'surplus' of human life in the present, as well as in new possibilities that emerge unexpectedly in the future.

Ricoeur does not explicitly locate these possibilities in our participation in God, but it can be readily seen how they belong there. In God there is not only a relationship like a father sending forth a son, but a movement which continually opens up this relationship to new depths and to an open future, which we call Spirit. The God who is in movement is on the move towards the goal of the divine purpose, and calls human beings to contribute to this journey in making the world. It is the hiddenness of signs, and the hiddenness of God within the signs, that is always the stimulation for discovery and new creation.

For Ricoeur, the making of a 'life plan', or 'aiming at the good life' with and for others, must involve the exercise of *phronēsis* or Aristotle's practical wisdom.[117] The projection of a world 'in front of the text' requires the interpretation, not only of written texts and of the proposed action (which is thus a kind of text), but of *oneself* as a text: 'the agent, interpreting the text of an action is interpreting himself or herself'. The identity of the self, Ricoeur maintains, 'is greatly enriched by this relation between the interpretation of the text of action and self-interpretation'.[118] Now, in this hermeneutic wise judgement is required because there is always something hidden in a situation. On the one hand there will be an excess of possibilities for the future to be sorted out, and on the other the human self can only achieve partial, fragmentary knowledge. Following Gadamer,[119] Ricoeur thus appeals to the exercise of *phronēsis* in interpretation, a judgement to be exercised when there are uncertainties in a situation. Ricoeur, however, tends to keep the phronetic judgements of philosophy quite separate from his phronetic judgement in religion, the latter being a wager on faith and a future that is opened up by the resurrection of Christ. I am suggesting that the Hebrew *ḥokmah*, rather than Aristotelean *phronēsis*, points to an integration of practical judgement and

---

[115] Ricoeur, 'Freedom in the Light of Hope', p. 406; cf. Moltmann, *Theology of Hope*, p. 85.
[116] Ricoeur, 'Freedom in the Light of Hope', pp. 409–10.
[117] Ricoeur, *Oneself as Another*, pp. 174–6.
[118] Ricoeur, *Oneself as Another*, pp. 179, 290–1.
[119] Gadamer, *Truth and Method*, pp. 278–89, 377–8.

knowledge of God, and that this is finally expressed in the Christian idea of participating in the triune God.

We must finish, then, with a correction of Shakespeare's Duke, who finds object-lessons in the trees, the rivers, and the stones, rather like messages left lying around by a universal teacher. This is the classical view of a natural theology in which the universe shows traces of a creator who is standing *outside* it. The picture is, ironically, echoed later when Orlando leaves his love-poems to Rosalind pinned and carved on every tree he can find, thereby spoiling good trees with bad rhymes, as his companions point out.[120] God has not—as it were—just pinned love-letters to the world. Through seeing the world and reading its text, prompted by metaphors, we know God through participation. The signs of the world are traces of God because the Creator is *present* in a hidden way, actually speaking, loving, giving, and drawing us into the dance of life.

---

[120] Shakespeare, *As You Like It*, III.2.160–4, 255–6.

9

Wisdom as a Search for the Sum of Things

THE PROTEST AGAINST A WHOLE

In our present age, there is a widespread suspicion about attempts to include everything in one all-encompassing whole. At an intellectual level this is likely to be called a postmodern resistance to metanarratives, a rejection of the 'large story' or the universal theory, in favour of small narratives and limited explanations which are relative to each other. At a popular level one can see this happening in such phenomena as a preference for single-issue social campaigns over an allegiance to political parties with comprehensive programmes. Recent examples in the UK have been protests against the growing of genetically-modified crops, against the raising of fees for university education, against the siting of a high-speed rail network, and against extra runways at airports. Even the imposing of value added tax on hot pasties in 2012 produced a greater surge of protest across the nation than a large-scale economic policy of cutting public funding. An unwillingness to deal with large, structural issues is also demonstrated by the rapid movement and overlapping of visual images on television, unsettling the eye and attentiveness, especially in advertising. This is the culture of the disposable image and sound-bite.

Our discussion of the late-modern mood (in Chapter 2) should have made us familiar with three ingredients in this rejection of a 'whole' or a metanarrative. First, there is the suspicion that all the 'wholes' proposed—whether scientific, religious, political, or economic explanations of the world—turn out to be concealed ideologies which are being employed by some powerful group to oppress others for its own benefit. This suspicion has been notably advanced by Jean-François Lyotard in his report, *The Postmodern Condition*. He sees a state, for example, as appealing to a grand narrative of human 'freedom to pursue knowledge' every time it assumes direct control over the education of the people to 'point them down the path of progress'. The aim of educational development (*Bildung*) will be that of 'relating everything to an ideal', and 'unifying this principle and ideal in a single Idea' which may be defended on purely philosophical grounds but which turns out to be convenient to government.[1] He concludes his report with the stirring appeal, 'Let us wage a war on totality.'[2]

Second, there is the fear that a total explanation, a universal theory, suppresses differences and otherness in society and in personal relations. If people are to be treated as the distinct realities they are, and if the ethical demands they make on us are to be recognized, then there is a mystery and a strangeness about others which cannot be reduced to some common ground into which the self and the other are absorbed. Difference must not be swallowed up in sameness. This protest against 'the whole' has been powerfully advanced by Emmanuel Levinas, making a target of such totalities as Reason, Spirit and Being (even in its Heideggerian form). As Levinas expresses it: 'I, you—these are not individuals of a common concept. Neither possession nor the unity of number nor the unity of concepts link me to the Stranger, the Stranger who disturbs the being at home with oneself.'[3] The 'infinity' of the Other is an absolute moral demand upon us and is a 'breach of totality'.[4]

Third, an awareness that the world is a system of signs of one kind or another suggests that there can never be one exhaustive meaning which covers everything. Derrida does not entirely agree with Levinas that sameness with the other and difference from the other cannot co-exist, nor that the concept of 'Being' has to be a totalizing unity.[5] He finds the danger of 'the whole' in its denial of the possibility of repetition with variation, urging that since signs can at any point be inscribed in a written text which is liable to interpretation and re-interpretation in new contexts, there must be an openness of meaning in which final explanation is always being deferred. Meaning, moreover, arises in the difference *between* verbal signs, so that there is always a 'surplus' or 'excess' of meaning.[6] Writing, then, contests any claim to 'the whole': 'literature is the exception in the whole, the want-of-wholeness in the whole'. The *différance* embodied in writing cannot be a ground of totality: 'the wholly other' is 'the other incommensurate with the the whole'.[7] Derrida takes the example of the *Mystical Theology* of Pseudo-Dionysius, which begins with a prayer to God; because Dionysius is quoting his prayer for the benefit of his disciple, Timothy, through repetition his act of making the prayer interrupts a full presence of either God or Timothy, or indeed the reader of the prayer now, and the writing 'stands in the space' or the 'hole' in totality made by the turning aside of discourse from one addressee to another.[8]

---

[1] Lyotard, *Postmodern Condition*, pp. 32–3.
[2] Lyotard, *Postmodern Condition*, p. 82.
[3] Levinas, *Totality and Infinity*, p. 39.
[4] Levinas, *Totality and Infinity*, p. 40.
[5] See Chapter 5, the section called 'The Complex Being of the Triune God'.
[6] Derrida, *Writing and Difference*, pp. 278–94.
[7] Derrida, *Dissemination*, p. 56.
[8] Derrida, 'How to Avoid Speaking', pp. 116–17; cf *Dissemination*, pp. 56–7.

I want to bring into dialogue with these late-modern concerns the author of the book in the Hebrew Bible often known among Christian readers by its Latin name *Ecclesiastes*, but which in Hebrew is named *Koheleth* or 'The Teacher'.[9] This book is generally reckoned to be a late (probably third century BCE) product of the wisdom movement that flourished in Israel. As we proceed, I will be situating Koheleth, through its content, in relation to the earlier tradition. This writer is in fact often treated as uncharacteristic of the mainstream Israelite wisdom tradition, but—as will become clear in the discussion—I believe that his concerns *are* in continuity with those of his predecessors, and that he differs more in taking them to extremes than in breaking away altogether. The interest of Koheleth for our modern situation is his repeated assertion that it is impossible to find 'the whole' of things, expressed in Hebrew either as *hakkōl* (הכל), which is 'all' (*kōl*) with the definite article *ha-*, or simply as *kōl* (כל). Here for instance is his conclusion in 8:17:

> Then I saw all (*kol*, כל) the work of God, that no one can find out what is happening under the sun. However much they will toil in seeking, they will not find it out; even though those who are wise claim to know, they cannot find it out.

Earlier he had reflected upon the right time to do things, and had come to the verdict: 'God has made everything (*hakkōl*, הכל) suitable for its time ... yet people cannot find out what God has done from the beginning to the end.' (3:11) Why Koheleth thinks finding 'the whole' is impossible, why he thinks that human beings should not occupy themselves with pursuing it, and how he associates God with the whole are all—I suggest—questions of interest to us in our late-modern situation of a fragmented culture.

THE WHOLE AS A SUM

The first question to be asked is: what is this whole (*hakkōl* or *kōl*), which cannot be found? In the first place, it is simply everything that there is. *Hakkōl* means both everything and the whole. So the 'whole' is not a pre-existent, transcendent idea or constellation of ideas, some universal reality which will be substantiated in particulars. It is not the absolute One of Neoplatonism, from which the many are diffused and to which they must return. The whole is all things that are to be observed, that lie under the sun, in the world of nature and in human society. At the beginning of his book Koheleth sets out his aim, which is common to the wisdom enterprise in ancient Israel: 'I applied my

---

[9] The name is also often transliterated in English as Qoheleth, Qohelet, or Kohelet.

mind to seek and to search out by wisdom all (*kōl*) that is done under heaven'
(1:13).

But the wisdom project is not simply to see and record everything. The
manifesto 'to search out *by wisdom*' makes clear that there is a point in this
exploration. The wise observe the events and objects of the world in order to
find patterns of meaning, to establish regularities that can offer guidance to
those who are willing to listen to their teaching. This is what Koheleth neatly
calls 'the sum' (חשבון, *ḥešbōn*), a term which he uses in parallel to 'the whole'.
The quest for the whole is the search for what things amount to when they are
added together, and this is what Koheleth cannot find:

> I turned my mind to know and to search out and to seek wisdom and the *sum* of
> things (*ḥešbōn*) . . . See, this what I found, says the Teacher, adding one thing to
> another to find the sum, which my mind has sought repeatedly, but I have not
> found (7:25, 27–8).

His book thus opens with a reflection on the endless movement of natural
phenomena, which yield no object lessons to the human observer. They
present a blank face to interpretation.

> The sun rises and the sun goes down
> and hurries to the place where it rises.
> The wind blows to the south,
> and goes round to the north;
> round and round goes the wind . . .
> All streams run to the sea,
> but the sea is not full:
> to the place where the streams flow,
> there they continue to flow. (1:5–7)

Some commentators find Koheleth to be complaining here that the movement
of the natural world is *intrinsically* without purpose, its component parts
achieving no goal in their circular course.[10] But the point of the passage is
that the world only *appears* to the human gaze as a monotony of repetition. It
is not futile in itself, but is silent to the enquiry of human wisdom; as Martin
Hengel puts it, 'the whole world *becomes* an insoluble riddle, and nature and
history *appear* to human beings as an apparently meaningless circle'.[11] When
the Teacher complains: 'there is nothing new under the sun', the situation is
not that events repeat themselves in such a way that nothing new *happens*; the
basic problem is that nothing new can be *learned*: 'these phenomena lie

---

[10] George A. Barton, *Ecclesiastes*. International Critical Commentary (Edinburgh: T & T
Clark, 1908), p. 69; Hans Wilhelm Hertzberg, *Der Prediger*. Kommentar zum Alten Testament
(Gütersloh: G. Mohn, 1963), pp. 70, 72; Scott, *Proverbs-Ecclesiastes*, p. 210.
[11] Hengel, *Judaism and Hellenism*, vol. 1, p. 120. My italics.

outside human grasp'.[12] When the wisdom teacher turns the attention of his pupil to some natural phenomenon, saying 'look at this' (1:10), there is nothing new, no new step of progress in knowledge.

At this point the Teacher is offering two reasons for the human failure to obtain a sum. The first is the extension of the world in space, which faces the observer with an intricacy and complexity which he cannot fathom (1:5–8); as he reflects later, 'I said, I will be wise, but it was far from me. That which is, is far off, and deep, very deep. Who can find it out?' (7:23). The second is the extension of the world in time, in which the memory of events is lost: 'the people of long ago are not remembered' (1:11). Because we have no basis of recollection from which to start we cannot find out what is new in events as they repeat themselves. In a later chapter (3:1–15) the Teacher expands his reflection on time, and this confirms our exegesis that the problem is one of interpretation, of finding the sum, not one of intrinsic futility. Everything, complains the Teacher, has its appropriate time in which it happens, or should happen.

> For everything (*kōl*) there is a season and a time for every matter under heaven: a time to be born and a time to die; a time to plant and a time to pluck up what is planted; a time to kill and a time to heal; a time to break down and a time to build up . . .

So the Teacher goes on, naming twenty-eight different 'times' for things. Everything has its time, but whereas the technique of wisdom is traditionally designed to enable a person to act at the right time, here it is lamented that we can never know what that time is. Thus, like the course of nature in chapter 1, the course of time only *appears* to be blank to the human gaze: intrinsically, every component is beautifully in order, but the order is only known to God (3:11). It is in this context that Koheleth gives us the classic expression of his failure to find the whole:

> God has made everything (*hakkōl*) suitable for its time; moreover, he has put a sense of time as a whole (*hā'ōlām*) into human minds, yet so they cannot find out what God has done from the beginning to the end (v. 11).[13]

How to translate (or emend) the term *hā'ōlām* (העלם), often translated 'eternity' is a vexed question. In view of the context of the right 'times' for events (v. 11a, cf. vv. 1–8) and the wise person's inability to find the right time (v. 11c), a meaning for *hā'ōlām* which accords with 'time' seems perfectly appropriate.[14] Moreover, since we are concerned with the attempt of human

---

[12] Crenshaw, *Ecclesiastes: A Commentary*. The Old Testament Library (Philadelphia: Westminster Press, 1987), p. 66.

[13] My translation.

[14] i.e. retaining reading of the MT and rejecting the reading 'world' offered by LXX and Vulgate.

beings to perceive the right times for events, either a purely past tense for
hāʿōlām, such as 'memory',[15] or a future tense, such as an eternity to come,[16] is
too limited: it is observation of present and past events which leads to the
anticipation of coming events. Thus a satisfactory meaning for *hāʿōlām* seems
to be 'eternity' as comprising the whole span of time, as the New English Bible
aptly translates, 'He has given man a sense of time, past and future'; I have
translated 'He has put a sense of time as a whole into human minds', which is
similar to A. H. McNeile's rendering 'a conception of the sum total of the
times'.[17] Thus human beings have sense of there being a whole but cannot find
it out (v. 11c) and so also cannot find out its individual parts. They know that
the various 'times' make up a whole and it is complete (3:14a 'nothing can be
added to it or taken from it'), but they cannot count its component parts and
cannot find the particular time (vv. 1–8) that bears upon them at any moment.

Similarities can certainly be found between these ideas of Koheleth and
Greek thinking of his period. But what impresses in a reading of these two
passages (1:1–11, 3:1–15) is that Koheleth comes to ideas that might have some
formal similarity to Greek ones within the particular framework of Israelite
wisdom thinking. The picture of the world in cycles of motion does not reflect
a Heraclitean flux or a Stoic cycle of ages, but the characteristic wisdom picture
of a world that cannot be fully grasped because of its extent and multiplicity.
The description in 1:5–7 models a three-dimensional world order, as in much
other wisdom literature, within which there are numerous items which cannot
be entirely classified or reduced to order by the wise: the sun here represents
height, the winds breadth, and the streams which run down to the sea, depth.
This three-fold world is elusive because human vision is limited.

Our explorations of the sense of limit recognized by wisdom teachers from
the earliest period shows that there is nothing novel about Koheleth's perception that human beings cannot know the whole, *hakkōl*. What is distinctive
about this writer is his conclusion that we cannot therefore know *the sum*, or
what things amount to. In previous wisdom thinking, one might know enough
of the sum to make predictions about the results of behaviour in the present.
Even if one did not know the whole, and this fact must always make one
humble and cautious, one could glean *enough* from patterns in the natural

---

[15] James Barr renders 'consciousness of memory' in his *Biblical Words for Time* (London:
SCM 1969), p. 124, n.1.

[16] So Carl Siegfried, *Prediger und Hoheslied.* Handkommentar zum Alten Testament (Göttingen: Vandenhoeck & Ruprecht 1898), p. 41. Equally limited is Harold L. Ginsberg's referring it to
immediate future, reading 'the striving', in 'The Quintessence of Koheleth' in Alexander Alt-
mann (ed.), *Biblical and Other Studies* (Cambridge, Mass.: Harvard University Press, 1963),
p. 50.

[17] A. H. McNeile, *An Introduction to Ecclesiastes* (Cambridge: Cambridge University Press,
1904), pp. 62, 99; cf. Walter Zimmerli, in Ringgren and Zimmerli, *Sprüche. Prediger*, p. 172
'weiten Zeitverlauf'; Roland Murphy, *Ecclesiastes.* Word Biblical Commentary (Dallas: Word
Books, 1992), p. 34, 'the whole of duration'; Jerusalem Bible, 'time in its wholeness'.

world and patterns of human behaviour to produce guidelines for living. For Koheleth, enough is *not* enough. He is unwilling to compromise with uncertainty. So we find in reading his book that there are sections where he gathers together a large number of sayings from the past tradition, which in themselves go no further than issuing a caution, warning about the limitations of wisdom. He then adds to these some sayings of his own which show that even this sense of limit is not radical enough to reflect the reality of life. In view of the obscurity of events to interpretation, there is a total blight on the capacity to plan for the future.

In saying this, I have taken a view on the composition of the book. I suggest it follows the programme set out in a postscript (by a pupil) in 12:9, that the Teacher 'weighed, studied and arranged many proverbs'. It is not all his own work, but it is mostly his own compilation, with the exception of two postscripts which try to solve the problem of 'knowing the whole' in two different ways (12:9–12, 13–14); these I do not intend to explore in this chapter, but will return to in the next. Here I draw attention to just one collection within the book[18] which gathers together earlier, cautious wisdom and then twists the knife of scepticism even deeper.

The collection of sayings in 9:13–11:6 contains a large amount of material which resembles, and does not in itself exceed, the admissions of limitation upon wisdom found elsewhere in the wisdom tradition. For instance, wisdom is better than strength, but the wisdom of the poor man is despised (9:13–16). Wisdom is better than the shouting of a ruler, and better than weapons of war, but one mistake can destroy a whole mass of wisdom rather as dead flies make perfume smell bad (9:17–18, 10:1). Many skilful enterprises are uncertain, such as digging a pit, breaking through a wall, quarrying stones, splitting logs, using an axe, and charming a snake; so wisdom is always vulnerable to the materials on which it works (10:8–11). None of these observations amount to the total futility of life, as long as wisdom is thought to be strong enough to counteract or absorb the limitations in technique. That further step of thought is only explicitly taken by Koheleth when he adds (10:14b):

> No one knows what is to happen
> and who can tell anyone what the future holds?

Similarly, in 11:1–3 a number of sayings are gathered together which point out that there is always an element of the incalculable in any action, whether it is done haphazardly—like scattering bread on the water—or done prudently—like dividing resources seven or eight ways. You never know where a full rain cloud will discharge, or which way a tree will fall. These cautions do not in themselves deny the possibility of any wisdom enterprise, but Koheleth takes a

[18] Another of the same sort is 7:1–8:1 on theme of 'what is good', with Koheleth's own conclusion in 7:23–9.

further step in v. 5, as in 10:14b. Two incalculable factors are appealed to—the blowing of the wind and the growing of bones in the womb—as a basis for a more far-reaching statement of limitation: human beings cannot know God's work at all.

> Just as you do not know the way of the wind or the mysteries of a woman with child, no more *can* you know the work of God who is behind it all (*hakkōl*).[19]

It is not only that human beings must reckon with the *unpredictable* in their planning; there is no evidence on which to form plans for the future at all.

This saying echoes the earlier one in 8:17–18: 'Then I saw the whole (*kol*) of the work of God, that no one can find out what is happening under the sun.' Von Rad has objected that no wise man ever did claim to know 'the whole', and so Koheleth is attacking a man of straw when he continues, 'even though a wise man claims to know, he cannot find it out' (8:17).[20] There is something in this objection. What the wise laid claim to discover was 'the work of God', in the sense of the *sum* of things, which they believed they could find with a *partial* certainty. It is Koheleth who introduces the idea of knowing the 'whole', asserting that the 'work of God' cannot in fact be discovered because the whole cannot be known. Others may be content with knowing less than the whole, but Koheleth cannot be. But, when someone demands to know the whole, in the sense of knowing everything (*hakkōl*) and nothing less than the whole, the answer will be nothing. Here, as John Jarick has ingeniously suggested, there is a play on words between the Hebrew 'everything' (*hakkōl*) and 'nothing' (*hebel*):

> In Hebrew, 'everything' is הכל, made up of the letters he, kaph and lamedh. But if the poetic imagination takes a pen and adds the smallest of marks at the heart of this word—that is to say, an extra stroke is added on to the bottom right corner of the letter kaph, transforming that letter into a beth—an entirely different word appears: the word הבל, 'a breath, transience, futility, nothingness.'[21]

So Koheleth delivers his famous verdict, in a refrain repeated five times, that 'the whole is absurd' or 'futile' (*hebel*) (1:2, 1:14, 2:17, 3:19, 12:8),[22] to which we may add, 'the whole is wearisome' (1:8). This does not mean that every single thing is futile, taken by itself; it does not deny that there is a limited, local significance. But the pieces do not add up to a whole that has any meaning; events taken as a whole are absurd.

---

[19] Jerusalem Bible.

[20] Von Rad, *Old Testament Theology*, vol. 1, p. 457.

[21] John Jarick, 'The Hebrew Book of Changes. Hakkōl Hebel and Lakkōl Zᵉmān in Ecclesiastes', *Journal for the Study of the Old Testament* 90 (2000), p. 79.

[22] On the meaning of *hebel*, see Douglas B. Miller, 'Qohelet's Symbolic Use of הבל', *Journal of Biblical Literature* 117 (1998), pp. 437–54.

WHY CANNOT THE WHOLE BE FOUND?

Why, according to Koheleth, can the whole not be known? Why cannot the sum be found and so interpretation fails?

The first and obvious answer, arising out of our reading of Koheleth so far, is that some parts are hidden and cannot be found. He complains that he cannot find the 'sum' (7:25, 27 cf. 3:14, 9:10) by adding one piece of experience to the other because he does not have every single one of the pieces: he notes in this connection that 'What is missing cannot be counted' (1:15b, cf. 7:13). This compressed phrase says both that if a thing is not present to the view it cannot be included in the sum, and that no one can count how many pieces *are* missing if they are not there. So one commentator paraphrases, 'An untold number of things are lacking.'[23] Michael Fox suggests that in this search for pieces of experience, Koheleth differs from his predecessors. They assumed that wisdom was a reality pre-existing the sage's investigation, and 'once you have found wisdom you need only embrace it, hold to it. Wisdom is and always has been out there, waiting for your embrace'; Koheleth by contrast, he proposes, understands wisdom to be the product of thought and discovery, and the product is unfortunately defective.[24] Koheleth thus continually lays stress on what he 'sees' (1:14, 2:13, 2:24, 3:10, 3:16, 3:22, 4:1 and so on). But if wisdom as *ḥokmah* is both subject and object, as I have been suggesting, the wise have always been aware of a subtle relationship between 'wisdom out there' (equivalent to the scope of the world) and wisdom as a product of enquiry by the mind. Koheleth finds the sum of things to be absurd, not because he—for the first time—understands wisdom as the product of what he sees in the world, but because he demands a *totality* in what he sees.

A second reason why the whole cannot be found involves another key technical term of Koheleth, which is 'profit' or 'gain' (*yitrōn*, יתרון). The whole, understood as the sum, must also be a 'gain'. These three terms—*hakkōl*, *ḥešbōn*, and *yitrōn*—interact. Koheleth's complaint is that there is no adequate remuneration for the work invested in life: he follows his opening theme 'the whole is absurd' with the question, 'what do people *gain* from all the toil at which they toil under the sun?' (1:3) In short, the sum (*ḥešbōn*) is not a gain (*yitrōn*). The word *yitrōn* can be used in a comparative sense, to mean that something has an advantage over something else, and Koheleth is prepared to concede this: wisdom has an advantage over folly, for instance (2:13, cf. 7:11–12, 10:10); having a king is, all things considered, an advantage over not having one (5:9). But when *yitrōn* is used in an absolute sense, to mean a net gain in an enterprise, then humanity is certainly deprived of it. Four times

---

[23] Barton, *Ecclesiastes*, p. 79.
[24] Michael V. Fox, *A Time to Tear Down and a Time to Build Up. A Rereading of Ecclesiastes* (Grand Rapids: Eerdmans, 1999), pp. 79–83.

Koheleth repeats that there is 'no gain', and especially no gain from hard work (1:3, 2:11, 3:9, 5:16). People work hard, using their wisdom and skill, and then death comes and they have to leave the fruits of their labours to someone else who has not worked for it at all. The conclusion of 'no gain' seems most poignant in the case of pleasure. Koheleth thinks that the best chance of gain is in the combination of pleasure and work, pleasure that comes as a reward *for* work and pleasure that is to be found *in* work itself (2:9–11). But even this kind of pleasure is finally unsatisfying, and does not lead anywhere. Even toil plus pleasure does not equal the sum of profit.

Koheleth's thinking about this failure is not entirely a matter of rationality, such as the fact that any gain is destroyed by death. It is also a matter of subjective impression; Koheleth is telling us what he discovered in his experience (8:16–17). He is offering us a kind of introspective biography, a report on himself; the 'I' or ego which speaks in the book is not only observing objects in the world, but observing its own 'heart' or consciousness as it receives the impact of objects and events in the world. As Fox puts it, 'he is his own field of investigation'.[25] As we have seen, late-modern thinkers warn us of the illusions that arise when we try to establish the self by inner observation, and perhaps Koheleth stands as a startling example of this.

The complaint that 'there is no gain' belongs to a belief in the dogma of retribution or just recompense. It is with a sense of shock that Koheleth finds that there is no outworking of credit in events: it is just not the case that the wise and the good prosper while the wicked come to disaster. He protests: 'There is an absurdity that takes place on earth; that there are righteous people whose reward is like the recompense of the wicked, and there are wicked people whose reward is like the recompense of the righteous' (8:14). This perception is not quite the 'breach with ancestral belief' that one commentator suggests it is.[26] The earlier practitioners of wisdom knew that connection between act and reward was not inevitable. In the face of uncertainties, the theory of just recompense was only a guideline and not a rigid law of life. It was in later thinking, such comes under critique in the Book of Job, that the guideline was hardened into dogma, and here too Koheleth seems to be *assuming* an inflexible rule. Unlike the author of Job he does not, however, simply abandon the dogma as a restriction on the freedom of God. Accepting that it *is* the case, he protests that in his actual experience it does not work out. He thus feels (as Fox has pointed out) that he is living in a world of contradictions. There are 'unresolved tensions' between one observation and another, a 'violation of sensibility'.[27] The link between things has broken

---

[25] Fox, *A Time to Tear Down*, p. 77.

[26] Kurt Galling, 'Kohelet-Studien', *Zeitschrift für die Alttestamentlichen Wissenschaft* 50 (1932), pp. 293ff.

[27] Fox, *A Time to Tear Down*, p. 3.

down, and Koheleth feels that certain things *should not* happen. He believes in the rule of divine justice and so injustices are offensive to reason. We should therefore not too quickly dismiss as a later gloss the phrase 'I know that it will be well with those who fear God . . . and that it will not be well with the wicked' (8:12); this is what Koheleth 'knows' intellectually—it is his belief in how God *should* act—but it is challenged by actual observation.

Koheleth assumes that the parts of the whole can only be unified *for the human observer* through a law of just recompense; so they are in conflict with each other, and the whole cannot be found. The sum is an absurdity. The multiplicity of disjointed deeds and events cannot be connected into a coherent narrative; life cannot be read by human readers, though it exists as a whole to God. Koheleth in fact appears to think that the failure of the reading is exactly what God intends, since it results in fear, and this is what God desires: 'God has done this so that all should stand in fear before him' (3:14). The earlier 'fear of the Lord' among the wise, which was a humility tempering confidence, has become a fear born of the complete shattering of confidence, a collapse of the whole.

A third reason why the whole cannot be grasped is that, for Koheleth, language itself has become confused. Since the component parts of experience can never make up 'the whole', the words of wisdom in which experience is captured share the same diffuseness and amplify it. Words themselves, the tools of human mastery of the world, share the world's obscurity and complexity, and only complicate the issues they are trying to analyze. 'In much wisdom there is much vexation' (1:18); 'the more words there are, the more absurdity' (6:11); 'when dreams increase, empty words are multiplied' (5:7). If we return to Koheleth's conclusion that he cannot find the 'sum' of things, we find that this failure extends into the handling of words; according to 7:29–8:1:

> See, this alone I have found, that God made human beings straightforward, but they have searched out many subtleties. Who is wise enough for all this? And who knows the interpretation (*pēšer*) of a word (*dābār*)? Wisdom indeed can light up a person's face, but [in fact] grim looks disfigure it.[28]

Koheleth testifies that he has searched for wisdom by adding pieces of his experience together to make up the sum (*ḥešbōn*, 7: 27). In this case, in an attempt to find the difference between wisdom and folly, he has tried to add together the phenomena of a prostitute and a virtuous man, considering each carefully to draw some kind of conclusion (sardonically, he remarks that a male paragon is very rare, and a perfect female non-existent). But, in an ironic play on words, he records that instead of a sum (*ḥešbōn*, חשבון) he has found only a mass of subtleties (*ḥiššᵉbōnōt*, חשבנות, 7:29). In their originally created state human beings are 'straightforward', but as soon they begin their

---

[28] My own translation of this disputed passage.

intellectual search they lose that simplicity. 'Man may not be able to straighten what God has twisted, but it seems that he can twist what God has made straight' (Fox).[29] The saying about the wise man in 8:1 therefore follows on from this sombre reflection; it is not an admiring comment ('who is like the wise man?')[30] but the sceptical question, 'who is wise like this'?[31]—expecting the answer, 'no-one'. The very next phrase gets to the heart of the wisdom enterprise, expressing it in one compact term, *pēšer*,[32] but only in order to counter it: 'Who knows the interpretation of anything?' The 'thing' (*dābār*) to which interpretation is applied here may mean either a 'saying' or an 'event', and both are relevant because events in the world become the stuff of words in wisdom sayings; the wise person is meant to seek out happenings in the world and fix them in words. 'Who knows the interpretation of an event?' 'Who knows the interpretation of a word?'[33]

According to 8:1, no interpretation or 'meaning' (*pēšer*) is finally possible because the very multiplicity of words ('many subtleties') results in confusion, and this arises out of the extent of the material under enquiry. The result will be, not a face shining with confidence, but grim looks (8:1b).

A POSITIVE APPROACH TO LIFE: THE PORTION

Koheleth is clear that the multiple pieces of experience cannot be added together to produce the 'whole' or 'sum' on which he insists. Some pieces cannot be found, the law of retribution fails to unify the whole, and words add to confusion and increase weariness. So if a solution cannot be found in *addition*, it must be found in the *reduction* of the scope of experience. Here Koheleth in his typical way finds another large abstract concept to express this, which is the 'portion' (*ḥēleq*, חלק) (2:10, 3:22, 5:18, 5:19, 9:6, 9:9):

> This is what I have seen to be good: it is fitting to eat and drink and find enjoyment in all the toil with which one toils under the sun the few days of the life God gives us; for this is our portion (*ḥēleq*) (5:18).[34]

[29] Fox, *A Time to Tear Down*, p. 272.

[30] So Crenshaw, *Ecclesiastes*, p. 149.

[31] Re-pointing the consonants; so L.H. Brockington, *The Hebrew Text of the Old Testament* (Oxford: Oxford University Press, 1973), p. 170.

[32] An aramaic loan-word, *hapax legomenon*, but found in the Aramaic of Daniel, and frequently in the Qumran literature.

[33] Cf. 1:8, 'all things (*dᵉbārīm*) are wearisome', which can be translated 'all words are wearisome' (RSV margin).

[34] RSV, but changing 'lot' to 'portion'.

The portion is not something 'gained' through wisdom; it is neither profit (*yitrōn*) nor sum (*ḥešbōn*). The question about the human 'gain' (*yitrōn*), as has been pointed out,[35] is ultimately a question about the 'place' of human beings in the world, and this acquires particular significance against the background of the creation story, alluded to several times in the book, in which humankind is given a place in dominion over the animal kingdom and the natural world.[36] Koheleth concludes that human beings do not occupy the place in the world that older wisdom thought would have been secured by the techniques of 'steering' through experience. A place in the world cannot be found by reckoning up the multiple objects of enquiry. The place that Koheleth offers is the enjoyment of what we already have in our grasp, what is already 'given'. Here is not an addition ('adding one thing to another' 7:27) but a reduction of multiple possibilities or eventualities to a comprehensible scope, what lies to hand. Put in theological terms, a human being knows what is ordained by God not by enquiry, but simply by what God has given for the process of daily living. Together with these prevenient gifts comes the power from God to enjoy them. If this second element is lacking then the emptiness is deep indeed (6:1–6), but Koheleth thinks that the very fact they are given entitles us to assume that we should be enabled to enjoy them. A portion then is 'good' in the sense of being an advantage, but does not win a profit. One can derive satisfaction from it, but not be fully satisfied.

This basic givenness is expressed mostly with the term *ḥēleq*, applied to pleasure in work (three times—2:10, 3:22, 5:18–19), eating and drinking, bread and wine (5:18, 9:7), life with one's wife (9:9), and 'whatever your hand finds to do' (9:10). Other phrases underline the sheer givenness of these phenomena: they are 'from the hand of God' (2:24–5), 'what is good' (5:18, 8:15) 'the gift of God' (5:19) and 'what God has long ago approved' (9:7). The will of God is apparent, not in any attempt to find it by distinguishing the proper times (3:1–8) or interpreting events, but by accepting the necessities of life that lie to hand. The notion of the 'portion' is the substance of Koheleth's so-called 'hedonism', and it differs from the more careless attitude of those whom the author of the Wisdom of Solomon (Wisdom 2:1–9) quotes with disapproval; while there is reason to believe that his school unintentionally encouraged later hedonists, Koheleth himself is urging his readers actively to *take* their portion, to be courageous in the face of contradictions, and to embrace life's possibilities.

We must also distinguish Koheleth's recommendation to act upon one's portion from the advice of earlier wisdom to compromise with uncertainty. The early wisdom sayings urged that the element of uncertainty

---

[35] Schmid, *Wesen und Geschichte*, p. 188, von Rad, *Wisdom*, p. 231.
[36] See Zimmerli, 'The Place and Limit of Wisdom', pp. 323–4.

should not prevent a wise person from using the wisdom project to master and anticipate experience: enough could be known to 'steer' one's way. But Koheleth is simply advocating that one should find one's way of life in what one already has: any attempt to master and manipulate the world will be futile, or absurd. Wisdom for Koheleth is hidden for any practical purposes; he *has* some wisdom, indeed, and this will be useful negatively in keeping him from the presumption and arrogance of the fool, but it does not amount positively to anything that might enable him to control the course of his life. Nevertheless, we may judge that Koheleth is not as much on the fringes of the wisdom movement as has often been supposed. His work is grounded in the characteristic recognition of uncertainty within wisdom, taking to a remorseless conclusion what is checked and balanced elsewhere, insisting that one must obtain 'the whole' if the wisdom method is to be of any use. He presents wisdom as effectively hidden, but this is in continuity with a partial hiddenness which is recognized elsewhere, rooted in the complexity and expansiveness of the area of enquiry (wisdom as object). It is in accord with this understanding of the elusiveness of wisdom that he recommends the way forward—not to try and master experience by calculation, but to accept a reduced span of experience in 'what is given'.

THE SENSE OF A WHOLE IN THE EUROPEAN TRADITION

While Koheleth warns severely agains a search for 'the whole', he accepts that there *is* a 'sense of the whole' in human consciousness, that this whole *does* exist in reality and not just in the human mind, that it is known to God, and that it is in some way 'the work of God'. Now, there is a long tradition in European thought which generally agrees with Koheleth in his presuppos- itions, though not with his advice. More explicitly than Koheleth, it has maintained that a sense of a whole is needed to understand the fragments of life with which human beings are faced, and to cope with them. A classic way of conceiving this whole is as a *unity of being*, and this has never been better worked out than by Thomas Aquinas.

In his view of human perception of the world, Aquinas stands in the line of Aristotle. The human mind, as an active intellectual agent, turns its attention to the material phenomena of the world and abstracts, or extracts, from objects their form or species: that is, the mind finds the universal idea in the material appearance, and the form which exists in the material (*species sensibilis*) becomes a form existing immaterially (*species intelligibilis*) in the mind.[37] The mind thus shines out upon the world the light of reason which it possesses because it participates in the uncreated light of God by analogy and by the effect of divine causation.[38] When we add that being (*esse*) is the actuality of the form, and that through participating in created being all creatures participate in the one uncreated being of God, it seems that everything is being subjected to a principle of unity. It appears that the whole is prior to all the parts, and that the thinking subject masters the objects of the world around because it shares uniquely as intellect and will in that wholeness which is God. Aquinas writes, 'The perfections of everything exist in God' and approves of the statement of Pseudo-Dionysius that 'God possesses primordially in himself all being.'[39] To cap it all, it seems that the unity of God as pure and simple being is more important than Trinity, since the whole is one substance.

Aquinas, to be sure, tries to retain a rich diversity of being. His approach might even be said to be a challenge to totalizing views of being, in so far as the common being in which creatures *directly* participate (*ens commune*) is *created*, and so different from the pure being of God. Employing the concept of unity of being as a way of thinking 'the whole' does enable us to bring God and the world into one perspective and to bring together uncreated and created realities; through the idea of the analogy of being it might be claimed that we can do this without absorbing the world into God or God into the world. Further, Aquinas' view of perception is less that of an intellectual subject which projects significance on valueless objects around, than that of potentially significant objects which actualize intellectual capacities. The object, as 'objective-participant', awakens the intellect and prompts it to the process of abstraction as the intellect runs up against it.[40] Finally, the unity of God is balanced by diversity. While God is one *esse subsistens* this is an *act* of being, and the three persons are constituted by distinct acts of relationship within one overall act; they are, in Aquinas' famous phrase, 'subsistent relations'. As Fergus Kerr judges, God is 'more event than entity'. God is less a substance which has various activities, than 'activity which has at the same time something of the character of a substance'.[41] The three persons, as subsistent relations, are thus also 'action-based';[42] they are constituted by the actions of being mutually related. 'There can be no real relationship in God except founded in action,' comments Aquinas.[43]

---

[37] Aquinas, *Summa Theologiae,* 1a. 84.7 *contra*.
[38] For this idea of participation, see Chapter 6, the section called 'Participation not Mediation'.
[39] Aquinas, *Summa Theologiae* 1a.4.2.
[40] So Fergus Kerr, *After Aquinas: Versions of Thomism* (Oxford: Blackwell, 2000), p. 27.
[41] Kerr, *After Aquinas*, p. 190.
[42] Kerr, *After Aquinas*, p. 198.
[43] Aquinas, *Summa Theologiae* 1a.28.4.

For all this, however, the balance between 'whole' and 'particularities', or between the 'one' and the 'many' in Aquinas is tipped towards the whole and the one, and the suspicion of a dominating totality (or 'Parmenidean' oneness)[44] remains. Since the act of perception abstracts the universal from its exemplification in a particular object, the question must arise whether this really allows for things and persons in their singularity to make an impact on the observing mind. This tendency of thought gains further momentum through Aquinas' concept of 'transcendentals', aspects which are characteristic of being everywhere, wherever it is displayed. Five transcendentals, which give a clue as to what reality is anywhere and at any time, and which are applicable to God as well as creatures, are identified by Aquinas as being, unity, particularity, goodness, and truth.[45] Inevitably, these transcendentals tend to focus on unity (*unum*), despite the inclusion of particularity (*aliquid*). Colin Gunton points out that 'neither beauty nor plurality is believed to be a necessary—transcendental—mark of being'.[46] By contrast he argues for 'open transcendentals', provisional ways of thinking of universality which emerge from the image of the Trinity, and which he identifies as perichoresis, substantiality (or particularity), and sociality.[47]

Later in European thought, Kant turned away from a metaphysics of being and subjectivized the sense of a whole; the mind, he proposed, in engaging with phenomena certainly needs the concept of a whole to make sense of them, but it creates this out of its own self-transcendence. In its drive towards unity, on the way to extract universal laws from particulars, it generates the ideas of the world as a totality, the thinking subject ('I') as a unified self and God as creator of the whole; but these are ideas which merely regulate our perception of the world, giving us an incentive (for example) to investigate phenomena.[48] For Kant, such noumena do not in any way constitute reality and they cannot be known. The German Romantic poets (followed by the English poet Coleridge) proposed that the 'all', or the 'universe as a whole' could in fact be intuited through poetic metaphors and symbols, and Schleiermacher—addressing the poets—found the essence of religion to be such a 'feeling', immediate sense, or consciousness of unity with 'the Whole': so he urges that 'Your whole life is such an existence for self in the Whole.'[49] We should, I suggest, agree with Kant that we cannot know the whole as an object of perception, as we do objects in the world; the Romantics, however,

---

[44] Gunton, *The One, the Three and the Many*, pp. 139–40.

[45] Res, unum, aliquid, bonum, verum; see Aquinas, *de Veritate* 1.1–2; cf. *Summa Theologiae* 1a.16.

[46] Gunton, *The One, the Three and the Many*, p. 139.

[47] Gunton, *The One, the Three and the Many*, pp. 149–54.

[48] Kant, *Critique of Pure Reason*, trans. N. Kemp Smith, pp. 556–62.

[49] F. Schleiermacher, *On Religion, Speeches to Its Cultured Despisers*, trans. J. Oman (New York: Harper and Row, 1958), Second Speech, p. 43.

open up the possibility of participating in the whole by some other means of knowing.[50]

In our current age, 'the whole' is more likely to be thought of in scientific terms as a unity of 'space-time', and among those who have put this into theological context is Wolfhart Pannenberg. He points out that Kant had in fact already sided with Samuel Clarke, a close friend of Isaac Newton, in maintaining that our experience of space and time presumes an infinite whole.[51] Space as a whole must underlie the perception of different places, and time as a whole must be the framework for our experience of passing time.[52] In Kant's earlier work he had followed Clarke in regarding the infinite whole of space as an expression of God's omnipresence, and the infinite whole of time as expressing God's eternity. But in writing the *Critique of Pure Reason* he took the turn to the subject, in asserting that the infinite whole is only the experience of the human mind. It is human reason that drives the mind all the time towards a synthesis of unity. He now took the part of Leibniz in regarding space-as-a-whole as the epitome of relations between physical bodies or other spaces, which for him (but not for Leibniz) was only a concept within the thinking subject. In contrast, Pannenberg notes Clarke's insistence that that the whole of space was what was prior to all divisions and prior to all relations which link things that are divided, and that this was identifiable with the immensity of God.[53]

Pannenberg has proposed that we keep *both* definitions of space. One describes the geometric or Euclidean space of the finite world, divided by points, lines, surfaces, and bodies; this is the space-time of Einstein's General Theory of Relativity. The other is *undivided* and infinite space-time, and is 'the immensity and eternity of God'.[54] We must be careful not to confuse the two kinds of space, or we end either with the pantheism of Spinoza, in which the totality of geometric space is the mind of God, or with Newton's view of 'absolute space' as an empty receptacle for all finite things. Pannenberg is, one must remark, ambiguous about the kind of identity that exists between this 'infinite and undivided space-time' and God. He does not speak directly of God as the 'whole' of space-time, but of this wholeness as being equivalent to the 'immensity and eternity' of God, as if applying to God's attributes or energies but not to God in God's self. God—for Pannenberg—is certainly an 'undivided and infinite whole', but the identity of this 'whole' with the 'whole'

---

[50] See S. T. Coleridge, *Aids to Reflection*, ed. John Beer (Princeton: Princeton University Press), Aphorism VIIIb, p. 234, 'an Intuition or immediate Beholding' of universal truth; cf. p. 234, n.60, 'all being a Whole'.

[51] Pannenberg, *Systematic Theology*, vol. 2, p. 86.

[52] Kant, *Critique of Pure Reason*, pp. 76–91.

[53] Pannenberg, *Systematic Theology*, vol. 2, pp. 86–8.

[54] Pannenberg, *Systematic Theology*, vol. 2, p. 89.

of space and time is less clear. Nevertheless the distinction between finite and infinite space-time corresponds roughly to the Thomistic distinction between created and uncreated being, but has some advantages over it, as we shall see.

Pannenberg now refers to the theory of 'field' in modern physics. According to relativity theory, physical objects are not the final reality of the universe; they are only effects of 'fields' for which (according to Einsten) the only requirements are space and time. Earlier, Michael Farady had developed a view of 'field' which was a 'field of *force*', so that 'bodies [are] manifestations of force-fields'.[55] Pannenberg still prefers this concept as it corresponds to the theological idea of the power (*dynamis*) of God and aligns with the biblical concept of the 'Spirit' of God as breath and wind in movement.[56] He does, however, recognize that Einstein's use of 'field' separated it from the notion of force, despite the fact that physicists identify four basic types of force in the physical world – gravity, electromagnetism, and weak and strong forces within the nucleus of the atom.

Combining insights from the structure of space-time and field theory, Pannenberg argues that if bodies are the *result* of the operation of fields (of force), we can think of the creator God, whose immensity and eternity is expressed in infinite and undivided space-time, as an infinite field of force. God as Spirit is not to be understood as 'mind' (*nous*), but as a dynamic field structured in a trinitarian way.[57] The persons of the Trinity, he proposes, are singularities or instantiations of the field which is God, in a way analogous to the way that solid bodies emerge in a finite field characterized by space-time, but without the divisions typical of finite space-time. We notice that plurality and complexity in God are thus inherent within the very notion of a field, which is an advantage over the notion of God as pure being.

Pannenberg, we should observe, is not claiming that the spirit of God is simply equivalent to the field (of force) known to physicists. Interpreting God in this way functions as a '*key*' to understanding the omnipresence of God in the world and the activity of the Spirit of God within the world. To think of God as a field of force is a metaphor, but 'not a vague analogy'.[58] The divine field is both different from and similar to the scientific use of the term. It is similar in that space and time are the *only* basic requirements of the field concept in the General Theory of Relativity, and these can be associated with divine attributes of immensity and eternity; it is different in that the field of the divine spirit is immaterial. We do not thus have to rely on any specific field

---

[55] Pannenberg, *Systematic Theology*, vol. 2, p. 101.
[56] Wolfhart Pannenberg, 'God as Spirit—and Natural Science', *Zygon* 36 (2001), pp. 791, 793, n.9.
[57] Pannenberg, *Systematic Theology*, vol. 1, pp. 382–4.
[58] Pannenberg, 'God as Spirit', p. 790.

theory that scientists produce. The similarity between the field of force in space-time and the infinite and undivided whole that is God's Spirit 'makes intelligible how the divine Spirit works in creation through the creative reality of all natural fields and forces', and 'constitutes and penetrates all finite fields that are investigated and described by physicists.'[59]

We notice that Pannenberg understands the wholeness of time which belongs to God's 'eternity' as a 'simultaneity'. He claims that the tenses of past, present and future are preserved in this view of eternity, and that 'simultaneity' is not a Plotinian view of an unchanging present (*nun stans*) but includes time.[60] I suggest, however, that the concept of 'simultaneity' is not in fact helpful, as it seems to leave no room for growth and development which must be in view if—as Pannenberg himself says—the destiny of created beings is a participation in God in which finitude is not lost. It is better to speak of the 'harmonization' of time rather than simultaneity. In life, persons are broken through the passing of time because they are unable to hold past, present, and future together. They try to escape into the future through wish-fulfilment, or try to flee from the future in fear; they try to remain in the past in nostalgia, or try to blank it out in guilt. We might thus conceive of eternity as a passing of time in which time is always being brought into a whole, but not in one simultaneous moment.

Indeed, one advantage of conceiving of 'the whole' in terms of space-time, rather than a Thomistic unity of being, is that the future becomes 'the field of the possible'.[61] 'Life is characterized by self-transcending openness' to the new; there is contingency in each event as it comes. When the whole that takes precedence over the parts is the field of the divine Spirit coming from the future of God, then the possible has a priority over the actual. Pannenberg draws attention to indeterminacy at the quantum level, as a sign of this open possibility. The occurrence of microevents at each moment is a manifestation of the future. Thus the force field which has priority over every kind of material manifestation is 'a field of the possible'.[62] Perhaps this, muses Pannenberg, is responsible for the fact that the processes of nature offer space for the rise of new structures of increasing differentiation and complexity, despite the fact that they are marked by entropy, or the breaking down of distinctions. In the face of the possibility-field of the future, entropy appears only as a parasite on new events, just as evil has no ontological standing on its own but is merely parasitic on the good.[63]

[59] Pannenberg, 'God as Spirit', p. 790.
[60] Pannenberg, *Systematic Theology*, vol. 2, pp. 90–4.
[61] Pannenberg, *Systematic Theology*, vol. 2, p. 97.
[62] Pannenberg, *Systematic Theology*, vol. 2, p. 98; 'God as Spirit', p. 792.
[63] Pannenberg, *Systematic Theology*, vol. 2, pp. 97, 101.

Scientific objections can be brought against Pannenberg's scheme, and John Polkinghorne has been most articulate here.[64] Pannenberg, he comments, seems to assume that fields are immaterial or even 'spiritual', but they are in fact carriers of energy and momentum which are material. Further, Pannenberg, he objects, is joining together field theory, which belongs to quantum mechanics, with space-time structure which belongs to general relativity. Einstein, like Faraday, wanted a unified field theory but failed to attain it; though there seems high potential in contemporary 'string theory', the question is still open. Finally, Polkinghorne observes that there is no natural connection between field theory and contingency. Like Pannenberg, he has theological reasons for wanting to see the universe as constantly open to new possibilities, in response to the prompting of the Spirit of God, but he thinks it seems better to draw out the implications of quantum indeterminacy and chaos theory[65] than to locate the power of the future in fields of force.

Pannenberg responds, with some justice, that what matters is not the detail of scientific field theory, but finding a language to speak about the presence of God to creation and the involvement of divine Spirit in its development.[66] This however, is precisely where his use of 'fields of force' and the 'wholeness of space-time' seems to falter. It is certainly *suggestive* about the intimate relation between God and the world, but his use of metaphor is not at all clear. What kind of identity exists between God as an 'infinite and undivided whole' and the wholeness of space-time? How does this wholeness actually make an impact upon the divided space and divided time that we experience? There seems more potential in analogies of field and space-time than in an analogy of being, but they also seem to remain unfulfilled. How might Koheleth be convinced that the search for a whole is not just a 'chasing after the wind', and that the repetition of events in nature (1:5–7) has the possibility within it of openness to the new?

A WHOLE WHICH IS NOT OPPRESSIVE

We have reviewed the long European tradition that a sense of the whole is necessary to make sense of the fragmentary appearance of life, whether that wholeness is envisaged as a unity of being, a universal generated by the mind, an intuition available in poetic image, or as an infinite and undivided space-

---

[64] John Polkinghorne, 'Wolfhart Pannenberg's Engagement with the Natural Sciences', *Zygon* 34 (1999), pp. 151–8; cf. 'Fields and Theology: A Response to Wolfhart Pannenberg', *Zygon* 36 (2001), pp. 795–7.

[65] See chapter 5, the sub-section called 'Complexity arising from uncertainty'.

[66] Pannenberg, 'God as Spirit', pp. 788, 790–1.

time. Kant's argument that the sense of a whole is needed against which to 'measure' particularities remains persuasive and true to experience, as is Pannenberg's insight that the whole is a future reality, only to be found at the end of all things, and so opening us to new possibilities.[67] Ricoeur similarly reflects on Job's encounter with God that, while he receives no explanation for his particular experience of suffering, he is consoled by seeing 'the grandeur of the whole', leading the reader to exclaim, 'I renounce my viewpoint; I love the whole as it is.'[68]

Aquinas, Kant, Schleiermacher, and Pannenberg stand *with* Koheleth in believing that there is a whole (*hakkōl*), though *against* him in his belief that there is no point in pursuing it. Others today are *with* Koheleth on the futility of the quest, but *against* him in his assumption that the whole exists. We began this chapter with some reference to protestors against whole systems of thought and practice. They might well take up some of Koheleth's observations and turn them against his own assumption of a whole. We have seen that Koheleth has a vivid sense of a world full of tensions and contradictions. Human lives are not congruent, conforming to a simple law such as that of just rewards; neither natural nor human events can be simply classified and categorized. Some have thus read Koheleth as an early existentialist, comparing him with Sartre and Camus, translating the key-word *hebel* as absurdity, and reading 'the whole is absurd'.[69] Like the existentialists, Koheleth does experience a sense of estrangement of the self from the world. Like the existentialists, facing the tensions of life and the sense of estrangement, Koheleth commends an attitude of courage, in actively taking the portion (*ḥēleq*) or what lies to hand. Those who make this comparison have to recognize, however, that Koheleth departs from the existentialists in one key point: he does not think that the courageous act of choosing the 'portion' is an assertion of human freedom and rebellion, like Sisyphus scorning the gods on the way down the mountain side which he is eternally condemned to climb, rolling his boulder.[70]

Koheleth seems closer to the mood of late modernity in which thinkers such as Levinas, Lyotard, and Derrida are concerned to recognize the difference of 'the other'. Koheleth tells little narratives of the lives of others—the poor man who saves a city by his wisdom and is ignored, the person who works hard and

---

[67] W. Pannenberg, 'On Historical and Theological Hermeneutic' in *Basic Questions in Theology*, Vol. 1, transl. G. Kehm (London: SCM Press, 1970), pp. 137–81; Pannenberg, *Anthropology in Theological Perspective*, pp. 238–42.

[68] Ricoeur, *Conflict of Interpretations*, pp. 351, 461.

[69] William Brown, *Character in Crisis* (Grand Rapids: Eerdmans, 1996), pp. 131–9; Eric Christianson, 'Qoheleth and the Existential Legacy of the Holocaust', *The Heythrop Journal* 38 (1997), pp. 36–9, 42–3; Fox, *A Time to Tear Down*, pp. 8–11, 30–1.

[70] Albert Camus, *The Myth of Sisyphus and Other Essays*, trans. J. O'Brien (New York: Knopf, 1955).

then leaves his wealth to others, the sinner who is trapped by the deceitful woman, the wise youth who replaces an old and foolish king and yet is soon forgotten, and so on. But he cannot find any all-embracing system that will explain these stories, or reconcile them to his own experience of seeking a profit from work and pleasure. He makes no attempt to interpret the narratives of others in the light of his own story, but lets them stand as instances of the impossibility of finding the whole.

There are, then, two moods about a sense of the whole in modern thought. The first urges the necessity of a vision of a whole if the fragments of everyday life are to be understood. The second protests against oppressive totalities which assert ideology, suppress the other, and close down the expansion of meaning. The question is whether these two perspectives can converge. I suggest that this conjunction is indeed possible, and may meet at least some of the bewilderment of Koheleth, if the world is envisioned as existing *within* the communion of a triune God, being given room by God within interweaving relationships which are like those between a Father, Son, and Spirit.

If we take up the analogies developed by Pannenberg in dialogue with science we may spell out the programme like this: the divided and finite space-time with which we are familiar exists *within* a God who can be conceived, in metaphorical terms, as infinite space-time. The epithet 'undivided', however, has all the resonances of classical 'simplicity' and so is best avoided.[71] More clearly than Pannenberg, we may take 'space' as a metaphor for the immanent life of God. It does not just express 'immensity and eternity'. Space is essentially relational, as Leibniz perceived, and so finite spaces which are formed by relations may exist within an infinite space which is itself constituted by relations. As Heidegger maintained, 'space' is not an abstract concept but arises from the relation of places to each other, and from the relations that exist within a place.[72] This does not mean that finite space is just the *same* as the divine life, which would be pantheism, but that it is *included* within a triune space which always more than our space-time, exceeding and challenging it, crossing the boundaries set up within geometric space.

Pannenberg proposes that the divine persons can be considered as singularities of the divine field of Spirit, comparable to the way that material entities are 'excitations' within the finite field of force, so that they are conceivable as 'personal centres' or distinct *subjects* of action.[73] I suggest that if we are to use the metaphor of a field, then the 'persons' in God are better thought of as *movements* or 'momentums' within the field. Since space is formed by relations, then it is also conceivable to think of these movements as relational.

---

[71] See Chapter 5, the section called 'Complexity, Wisdom, and God'.

[72] See my discussion in Chapter 7, the section called 'Problems of Presence and Place'.

[73] Pannenberg, 'God as Spirit', p. 792; *Systematic Theology*, vol. 1, p. 383.

Human beings may indeed be seen as *subjects* in their instantiation of relationship or as by-products of relationality, but this classification cannot be foisted on God. Following through the insight of Aquinas that the divine persons are subsistent relations, but making this more radical, the persons may be considered as nothing more or less than relationships which are activities within a God whose whole being is event. As I have been arguing, we cannot envisage such movements of relationship as if they were objects of our vision, but we can know them through participating in them. This is a participation which is more than the kind of participation envisaged by Aquinas, which is limited to reflecting the being of God through analogy. It is an actual sharing in divine activity, and being shaped by it.

As finite relationships fit into divine relations, so created space fits into divine space without any idea of a receptacle. This means that the 'whole' is *in one sense* a 'sum' which results from adding one thing to another, as Koheleth supposes. Finite relationships accumulate within the relationships of the Trinity, so that many relationships of giving and receiving are held within the divine life and attain a kind of critical mass of love. The 'whole' is not a set of pre-existing ideas, but an interaction between God and the world. Yet there is always more than an arithmetical total or 'sum' (a *ḥešbōn*) because the triune relations in God are richer, deeper, and more open to the future than created ones. Thus the sum does not yield a 'profit' (*yitrōn*) in the sense of a just reward for labour; 'profit' is the 'more' that comes when parts are added together. In both the finite world and in God, it is not just that parts make their contribution to a summative whole, but the whole—with its 'more'—has an effect on the parts.

Koheleth here has a limited view in supposing that parts must be bound together into a whole by a kind of law—the principle of retribution—and that this makes any 'profit' there might be. While law, or regularity is a binding feature at the lowest level of created reality, even here the whole is always more than the strict sum of the parts. There is always excess, always something more. In atomic and sub-atomic particles parts are bound together in such a way that new properties are brought into being through their interaction: for example, the mass of a nucleon is more than the masses of three separate quarks. In the biological world, composite wholes are more than chemical interactions; something new emerges out of spatial relations, and the new thing is self-organization. In the animal world there are newly emergent functions of communication and interpretation which are more than simply the interchange of atoms or energy. In human societies, the whole includes not only features of common life shared with animal societies (such as kinship, communication, nurturing behaviour, and a degree of self-sacrifice), but also a shared commitment to values and beliefs, expressed in symbols and stories. The 'more' of profit (*yitrōn*) is there in the sum, not just because relations in finite space-time *reflect* or *manifest* the 'more' in God's triune life, but because they share in that life, and so are shaped by the creative influence of God.

If Koheleth's preoccupation with 'sum' and 'profit' has taken a new form in the modern world, the same is true of his urging his hearers to be content with their 'portion', and actively to take hold of it. We have already considered the suggestion that this has some similarity with the existentialists' encourage-ment to the self to assert its freedom, either in the secular form of an act of metaphysical rebellion, or in the religious form of a leap of faith. But neither of these seem to accord with Koheleth's mood. Much closer is the perception of the early Heidegger, that in its primordial experience the self can resist the urge to organize experience in objective terms, and instead it can become 'attuned' to the world that is just there, presenting itself to the one who waits and listens.[74] The primordial experience of Being is not as a collection of objects, but as a 'being-available'. Entities in the world other than Dasein are 'present to hand' (*vorhanden*), calling for attention.[75] This *Vorhandenheit* seems a striking echo of Koheleth's 'portion', or 'whatever your hand finds to do' (9:10). In this pre-conceptual experience the self finds that it does not stand outside the world but is thoroughly immersed within it, self and world united in a reciprocal movement of participation. As he puts it in an early lecture, 'The "world" is something within which one can live, while one cannot live in an object'.[76] Heidegger believes that such attunement of the self will reveal a lifeworld which is not mute or chaotic, since life in its facticity is not aimless or arbitrary but follows rhythms and patterns. Here he extends the principle of *Vorhandenheit* further than Koheleth, who restricts it to some basic experiences (largely because of his assumptions about retribution and reward), but they are united in thinking that something is *given* to the observer of the world without need for an aggressive posture of taking control.

Now, like Koheleth, Heidegger also takes up the language of 'seeing'; the self cares for the world, 'being-out-towards' it, in a circumspection (*Sichumsehen*)–a looking after and around oneself. This is not a theoretical knowing (*eidenai*), but a looking around to notice what is of concern to the self, what matters.[77] What is *Vorhandenheit* (presence to hand) is then also experienced as *Zuhandenheit*, or 'readiness to hand': 'equipment is here, ready to hand' (*zuhanden*), and things are 'handy' (*handlich*).[78] It seems, then, that the

---

[74] Heidegger, *Being and Time*, pp. 172, 176–7, 321–2, 384.

[75] Heidegger, *Being and Time*, pp. 48, 103–4, 140.

[76] Martin Heidegger, *Phänomenologie des religiösen Lebens* (Frankfurt am Main: Vittorio Klostermann, 1995), p. 11.

[77] Martin Heidegger, 'Wilhelm Dilthey's Research and The Struggle for a Historical World-view' (1925) in John Van Buren (ed.), *Supplements. From the Earliest Essays to Being and Time and Beyond* (New York: SUNY, 2002), pp. 170–1; also Heidegger, 'The Problem of Reality in Modern Philosophy' (1912), in *Supplements*, pp. 45–8.

[78] Heidegger, *Being and Time*, pp. 102–7, 137–40.

description of the self in the world, in a pre-conceptual state, does not in the end escape from the tendency to manipulate the world. Even though Heidegger avoids a subject-object structure of self and world, he speaks of the concern of the self for the world as a 'use' of the world. It is a practical 'know-how', in which the self is immersed in the world; but it is also a circumspection which is a 'possession' of the world, in which the world is meaningful because it is an integral part of the self which aims to take care of itself. This kind of 'looking around' seems to fall under the accusation of Levinas, that the self looks for like-minded people who are a reflection of itself, its needs and wants. As Levinas charges, 'Since Heidegger we are in the habit of considering the world as an ensemble of tools', and this does not allow the self to break with the immanence of its own material subjectivity.[79] We might say that wisdom as observation has suppressed wisdom as participation, both of which are properly contained within *ḥokmah*. Using a picture from Israelite wisdom, the observer is neglecting the 'being available' (*Vorhandenheit*) of Lady Wisdom, to whose movements through the world our observation, or 'looking around' at the world, can be attuned.

Heidegger's insight into the 'being-available' of Being, its sheer givenness, together with the 'presence to hand' of entities in the world (Koheleth's 'portion') needs to be retained in a new context, one in which the self is always challenged by the other. Again, I suggest, this is the case if selves are immersed into a world which itself is immersed into Trinity, into a rhythm of relationships which are just there, disclosing a pattern of mutual giving and receiving. Finally, God is the portion which Koheleth recognizes.

Using Koheleth's vocabulary, we may say that the 'whole' is nothing other than the 'portion', given without the need to manipulate or control. The Trinity, the story of a Father sending out a Son, a Son responding in obedience to the Father, and a Spirit who brings ever-new surprises to this relationship, is the supreme metanarrative. This is not oppressive for a number of reasons: because there are no subjects here to reinforce the power of human agents; because the patterns are those of mutual self-giving; because there is no synthesis but only a continual opening to the future; and because we can only know the narrative by participating in it and so bringing something to it ourselves. It is a 'sum', but not a totalitarian total. It is a 'profit' in which there is always more to be gained.

---

[79] Levinas, *Time and the Other*, pp. 62–3.

10

The Text of the World and the Comprehensiveness of Wisdom

A PARTICULAR TEXT AND THE WORLD

In the recent debate in the Church of England about human sexuality, it has been striking that all sides have wanted to affirm that they are being faithful to Holy Scripture.[1] In such matters it seems that above all a wisdom is needed which is more than information about the world, more than a synthesis of biology and sociology, and claims to possess such wisdom often centre on a particular sacred text. Some text is privileged above other texts, as a repository of a wisdom that may often challenge the prevailing mood of the culture around. The notion of a canon is important here, as a boundary which fences in a certain text as privileged. A territory is being marked out among all written texts in the world as having a distinct authority.

Yet we have seen in past chapters that wisdom is about connectedness, about living in tune with a world which is created by God. We have explored the relation between texts written on a page and the nature of the whole world as a kind of text, a network of signs; this has given us a context for thinking about what it means to participate in God through observing the world. The wisdom of Ancient Israel has been a significant partner in this enterprise. Now, is it possible to bring together a fidelity to a *particular* text and still regard the whole world as a text which has been brought into being by God? The theologian Elisabeth Schüssler Fiorenza has contrasted two pictures: on the one hand there is scripture as an enclosed garden, shut off from the fields and meadows around; on the other hand there is the 'open cosmic house of divine wisdom' which appears in the wisdom literature, a habitation with no walls and where 'the spirit of fresh air is allowed to blow where it will'.[2] Much

---

[1] See 'Homosexuality and Biblical Teaching' in *Some Issues in Human Sexuality: A Guide to the Debate* (London: Church House Publishing, 2003), pp. 119–68.

[2] Elisabeth Schüssler Fiorenza, 'Transgressing Canonical Boundaries' in Fiorenza (ed.), *Searching the Scriptures*. Vol. 2, *A Feminist Commentary* (London: SCM Press, 1995), p. 11.

of the attraction of an appeal to wisdom in our present age is that of its universal scope: must we leave this behind for a more secret, esoteric kind of wisdom in focusing on a particular sacred text?

This question of particularity has been raised by Michel de Certeau, a philosopher who understood 'from the inside' the Christian attachment to Holy Scripture, as a one-time Jesuit priest. At the same time he was a founding member of Jacques Lacan's Freudian School in Paris, and his work resounds with characteristic preoccupations of late-modernity: the deconstruction of metanarratives, the overturning of a metaphysics of presence, the impossibility of evading linguistic signs, and the centrality of 'otherness'. In his essay, 'How is Christianity Thinkable Today?' (1971) he challenges the idea that Scripture provides any unified and self-contained authority. He has in mind the claim that there is a 'world' of Scripture that absorbs the everyday human world into itself and simply shapes it from within the particular space of the text.[3] Rather, every form of authority in Christian society—whether Scripture, tradition, or councils—is 'stamped by the absence of that which founds it'. The founding event of Christ thus implies a plurality of authorities, leaving behind a 'multiplicity of signs, a historical network of interconnected places, rather than a hierarchical pyramid'.[4] In this network of texts, which is interconnected but not unified, the plural is maintained and 'differences permit the other'. In the New Testament, for instance, each apostolic text offers a distinct treatment by speaking in its own way of faith in the dead and risen Jesus. This plurality of narratives is increased by interaction with the reader, which undermines attempts by authority to own the 'letter' of the text;[5] it also exists in a world of many narratives:

> From morning to night, narrations constantly haunt streets and buildings...Captured by the radio (the voice is the law) as soon as he awakens, the listener walks all day long through the forest of narrativities from journalism, advertising, and television, narrativities that still find time, as he is getting ready for bed, to slip a few final messages under the portals of sleep.[6]

This insight about heterogeneity of authority is accompanied by another in de Certeau's thought. In his *Practice of Everyday Life*, he considers the way that the powerless evade the mechanisms of control over their lives by the tactical use of everyday practices. The marginalized employ skill and cunning in

---

[3] What he was opposing was shortly to appear in print in the approaches of Hans Frei, *The Eclipse of Biblical Narrative: A Study of Eighteenth and Nineteenth Century Hermeneutics* (New Haven: Yale University Press, 1974), pp. 29–36 and George Lindbeck, *The Nature of Doctrine. Theology and Religion in a Postliberal Age* (London: SPCK, 1984), pp. 118–24.

[4] 'How is Christianity Thinkable Today?', trans. F. C. Bauerschmidt and C. Hanley, in Ward (ed.), *The Postmodern God*, p. 148.

[5] Michel de Certeau, *The Practice of Everyday Life*, trans. S. Rendall (Berkeley: University of California Press, 1988), p. 172.

[6] De Certeau, *Practice*, p. 186.

developing practices to resist the strategies of totalizing systems; they create 'spaces' (not places to remain) at whose boundaries the 'other' is encountered. They are not mere consumers, but adopt a 'hidden poesis' in the way they appropriate their consumption.[7] While for de Certeau a 'place' is a geographical point, a 'space' is a human 'ensemble of movements deployed within it', and many spaces can be layered over the same place. These spaces are always in flux; through alternative practices, different spaces can be enacted in the same place. Narrative—storytelling—is one important function of space-making, since through stories we write and read an everyday practice. Stories tell us what one can do in a place, and how to make a space out of it.[8] Even, he writes graphically, in bedrooms 'so small that "one can't do anything in them"', human space can be made.[9]

This relation between 'space' and 'place' has some similarity to the way that I myself have employed the concepts of 'place' and 'space' in a previous chapter, especially the making of space through 'movements' of relationship. However, I have also suggested that a certain kind of place can be discovered which is not a geographical or literal place at all, but a kind of 'no-place', alerting and inducting us into the life-giving space within the 'ensemble of movements' of the triune God. This is an idea to which I want to return in this chapter. What we must notice now is that de Certeau brings together his treatment of Scripture, authority, and space. If Christianity is to be thinkable, it has to be open to spaces beyond its own narrative sources. It must admit its limitations, recognizing that there are other spaces which are open to encounter with the 'other' and which belong to different discourses from Scripture. Christianity, he affirms, must make 'an essential covenant . . . with the unforseeable or unknown spaces which God opens elsewhere and in other ways'.[10] The question is whether such a view undermines the particular place of Scripture among other texts, the particularity of scriptural narrative among other narratives. Or might attention to one text in fact help us to understand *how* the world as whole comes to have the nature of a text? To answer this question we return to our exploration of ancient wisdom literature.

WISDOM AS TORAH

Fiorenza draws an image from the wisdom literature of the Hebrew Bible—wisdom building her house (Prov. 9:1–3)—in order to express a breadth of knowledge beyond canonical boundaries:

---

[7] De Certeau, *Practice*, pp. xii–xix. [8] De Certeau, *Practice*, pp. 120–3.
[9] De Certeau, *Practice*, p. 122. [10] De Certeau, *Practice*, p. 150.

> Wisdom has built her house,
> she has hewn her seven pillars,
> She has slaughtered her animals,
> she has mixed her wine,
> she has also set her table.
> She has sent out her servant girls;
> she calls from the highest places in the town,
> 'You that are simple, turn in here!'

On the basis that the 'seven pillars' symbolize the seven planets,[11] Fiorenza suggests that wisdom is building a house as big as the universe, on a cosmic scale, with room for all.[12] There are no boundaries here to the wisdom writings. However, Fiorenza's stark contrast between such a universal habitation and the narrow space of Scripture needs to be treated with caution. We should notice that in the later period of the wisdom movement, wisdom is actually *equated* with the limited texts of *Torah*, the written law-codes of Israel. Torah comes to be identified with true *ḥokmah*, and there are—ironically—already signs of this happening in the very passage of instruction in which the picture of the house is set, as we shall see.

The moment when this change occurs is not at all clear. However, we can see it beginning to take place in some of the instruction material now included in Proverbs 1–9, passages that I designated as 'B' material in my earlier analysis (chapter 4)[13] and—at that point—largely left on one side. In these passages, possibly later than the other instruction in these chapters, wisdom is presented as a personification or a precious object, and is said to belong to Yahweh and to be *taught* by Yahweh (1:20–33, 2:1–15, 3:13–20, 8:1–36, 9:1–12, together with 1:7[14]). In this complex of ideas, the old phrase 'the fear of Yahweh' takes on new meaning. In the earlier sentence literature of Proverbs, and in the instruction material of Proverbs 1–9 I have designated as 'A',[15] it simply means a cautious and humble approach to life. But it now appears to be re-applied to observation of the religious law. It is strongly implied[16] that to 'fear the Lord' is to read, meditate upon, and keep the law—the Torah—that the Lord has given to Israel. 'Fear of the Lord' is now *equated* with heeding 'instruction' given by God, rather than being a *motivation* for listening to the instruction of the wise, and it is this that is identified with wisdom (1:7, 1:29,

---

[11] Presuming that the house is modelled on an astral temple: see Albrecht Albright, 'Canaan-ite-Phoenician Sources of Hebrew Wisdom' in Noth and Thomas (eds), *Wisdom in Israel*, pp. 8–11.

[12] Fiorenza, 'Transgressing Canonical Boundaries', pp. 11–12.

[13] See Chapter 4, the section called 'Cautiousness in the Instruction Literature of Proverbs'.

[14] The introduction (1:1–7) must represent final editorial work, when Torah piety is established in wisdom.

[15] See footnote 13.

[16] McKane, *Proverbs*, pp. 262–5 is perhaps over-confident in distinguishing between 'old' (secular) and 'new' (Yahwistic) vocabulary of wisdom.

2:5, 9:10).[17] This new use of 'fear of the Lord' marks a shift from viewing Yahweh's activity as a limitation on human wisdom, to affirming Yahweh as the teacher of wisdom. Thus in Proverbs 2:5–6:

> Then you will understand the fear of the LORD
> and find the knowledge of God.
> For the LORD *gives wisdom*:
> from his mouth come knowledge and understanding.

Similar is the admonition from Proverbs 9:9–10, in the context of the invitation of wisdom to her open house:

> Give instruction to the wise, and they will become wiser still...
> The fear of the LORD is the beginning of wisdom,
> and the knowledge of the Holy One is insight.

Two aspects of this new sense of 'fear of Yahweh' may be discerned. In the first place, it means that the wisdom teachers were claiming the authority of Yahweh for their teaching, in the same way as prophets claimed it for their word, and priests for their torah. As Whybray proposes, where Wisdom speaks in the 'I'-form (1:20ff, 8:1ff and 9:1ff) she lays claim implicitly to divine authority by this stylistic device.[18] I suggest that where the personification of wisdom appears without first-person speech, wisdom teaching is underlined by divine authority through adding sayings that equate 'fear of Yahweh' with 'knowledge of/from God'.

In the second place, covenantal Torah begins to be included within the interests of wisdom teaching, a process apparently reflected in the extended passage on the 'fear of Yahweh' in 2:5–15.[19] 'Fear of Yahweh' (v. 5) is, it seems, being used in the sense of fidelity to covenant demands as in the Deuteronomic work:

> [the king] shall have a copy of this law written for him in the presence of the levitical priests. It shall remain with him and he shall read in it all the days of his life, so that he may learn to fear the LORD his God, diligently observing all the words of this law and these statutes. (Deut. 17:18–20, cf. 2 Kings 17:25–8)[20]

The close affinity between Deuteronomy and Proverbs 1–9[21] suggests that while wisdom contributed much to the ethical motivations and didactic style

---

[17] In the nine examples of 'fear of the Lord' in the sentence literature of Proverbs 10 onwards, two further examples in the instruction literature of 22:17–24:22 (23:17, 24:21) and one in the poem on the ideal wife (31:30), only one (15:33) associates wisdom with instruction (*mūsār*, מוסר 'discipline' or instruction, cf. 1:3).

[18] Whybray, *Wisdom in Proverbs*, pp. 78–82.

[19] See McKane, *Proverbs*, pp. 181–3; Barucq, *Proverbes*, pp. 53–5; Whybray, *Wisdom in Proverbs*, pp. 97–8.

[20] See the discussion by Weinfeld, *Deuteronomy*, pp. 274–81.

[21] See footnote 13.

of Deuteronomy,[22] wisdom scribes began to take a reciprocal interest in covenantal Torah as an object of study and teaching.[23] I argued in chapter 4 that certain expressions in the 'A' sayings of Proverbs 1–9, bearing as they do no implications of instruction in the covenant law, show us that wisdom had a shaping influence on Deuteronomic thinking.[24] Now in the 'B' sayings we can see the influence beginning to move the other way. The undoubted post-exilic relationship between wisdom and Torah may therefore have its beginnings even in the earlier period of the Deuteronomic movement immediately before the exile.

The phrase 'fear of the Lord' certainly refers to observing religious Torah by the time of Ben Sira:

> The fear of the Lord brings honour and pride,
> cheerfulness and a garland of joy.
> The fear of the Lord gladdens the heart;
> it brings cheerfulness and joy and long life.
> The essence of wisdom is the fear of the Lord;
> wisdom is created with the faithful in their mother's womb,
> she has built an everlasting home among human beings. . . .
> If you long for wisdom, *keep the commandments*,
> and the Lord will give it you in plenty.
> For the fear of the Lord is wisdom and discipline. (1:11–15, 26–7, my italics)

There is no hint here that 'fear of the Lord' means simply a cautious approach to life; 'fear of the Lord' brings the same joy and delight as does the law according to the Psalms (eg. Pss. 118: 14–16, 33–5; 19:7–10).[25] Ben Sira parallels law and the fear of the Lord in numerous passages. As Eckhard Schnabel shows, sometimes he begins from an inner disposition of fear of the Lord and then concretizes it in observance of the law (e.g. Sir. 6:37, 15:1, 23:27, 37:12, 39:1); at other times his thought begins with practical obedience to the law and then progresses into the inward, comprehensive principle of the fear of the Lord (e.g. Sir. 1:26–7, 9:15–16, 21:11, 32:14–16, 32:24–33:1).[26]

Now, it has been quite widely maintained that wisdom comes to be identified with Torah as a result of a supposed problem of the 'transcendence' of wisdom. The proposed story runs like this. Wisdom was originally envisaged as a mediator between heaven and earth, personified as Lady Wisdom. Then true wisdom—the kind possessed by God as opposed to the merely practical

---

[22] This direction of influence is emphasized by Weinfeld, *Deuteronomy, passim*.

[23] So McKane, *Prophets and Wise Men*, pp. 102–8, who adduces Jeremiah 8:8–9 as strong evidence.

[24] See footnote 13.

[25] The influence of Deuteronomy on Ben Sirach is argued by Perdue, *Wisdom and Creation*, pp. 262–3; Schnabel, *Law and Wisdom*, pp. 34–5.

[26] Schnabel, *Law and Wisdom*, pp. 45–6.

wisdom of human beings—was believed to have become distant in heaven.[27] Perhaps this conviction grew, the speculation runs, in the crisis of the exile and the diaspora, when it seemed that the wisdom understood by human beings, such as a system of observable retribution, had failed to account for the situation.[28] This belief in the absolute transcendence of wisdom was backed up by the circulation of an ancient 'wisdom myth'—or at least wisdom motifs—in which wisdom searches for a home on earth and, rejected by all, returns to heaven.[29] Thus the Torah was honoured as a new mediator, making wisdom accessible on earth.[30] Now, in previous chapters I have strongly contested both the notion of wisdom as a cosmic mediator in the period of the biblical writings, and the existence of a 'wisdom myth'. There is no evidence to suppose that one mediator between God and the world—wisdom—is being replaced by another which is closer to hand—Torah.

Indeed, in the light of our study so far the story seems completely different: the problem is not so much one of transcendence as complexity. As we have often seen, at the roots of the wisdom movement wisdom (*ḥokmah*) is perceived as hidden because of its extent; it is elusive because of its immeasurable and inexhaustible scope, equivalent to the expanse of the world. So I suggest that the reason for the identification of wisdom with Torah corresponded to this real perplexity. That is, the Torah was seized upon as a convenient contraction of knowledge to a manageable span. Torah is a reduction of the vastness of wisdom to boundaries that can be grasped. The boundless text of the world is condensed, as it were, into one text with universal application.

This is surely the point of a scheme that is found a number of times in the later wisdom writings. I have already drawn attention to the trope of the dimensions of the world—height, breadth, and depth, or heavens, earth, and abyss—which may be associated either with the journey of Lady Wisdom or the secrets of wisdom.[31] Now, in a variation, the expansive world is invoked and then Torah is praised as the sure guide to life. The seeds of this way of thinking are to be found in Deuteronomy, which shows a growing interest of Torah scribes in wisdom. Perhaps the regarding of the Torah as a kind of wisdom opened up an understanding of what Torah might be really all about; regarded as a piece of wisdom, it was not merely a set of laws but a guide to

---

[27] See e.g. Hadley, 'Wisdom and the Goddess', pp. 240–1; Leo G. Perdue, 'Wisdom in the Book of Job' in Leo G. Perdue, Bernard B. Scott, and William J. Wiseman (eds), *In Search of Wisdom: Essays in Memory of John G. Gammie* (Louisville: Westminster/John Knox, 1993), p. 96.

[28] See Mack, *Logos und Sophia*, pp. 42, 46–7; cf. Crenshaw (though without reference to myth), 'Popular Questioning of the Justice of God', pp. 389–94.

[29] See Chapter 6, the beginning of the section called 'Wisdom as Observer: Proverbs 8:22–31'.

[30] e.g. Rylaarsdam, *Revelation in Jewish Wisdom Literature*, pp. 74–98.

[31] See Chapter 6, the section called 'Wisdom as Observer: Proverbs 8:22–31', and Chapter 7, the section called 'Places and Dimensions of the World'.

right living.[32] Perhaps too the identification carried the promise of making Torah appear more universal, in a situation of an Israel dispersed among foreign nations. An influential passage in this development was Deuteronomy 30:11-12. Here the word of the Torah is celebrated as something accessible and easily grasped, in contrast to the thoughts of God ('the secret things which belong to the Lord our God') which are as elusive as the dimensions of the world:

> Surely, this commandment that I am commanding you this day is not too hard for you, nor is it too far away. It is not in heaven, that you should say, 'Who will go up to heaven for us, and get it for us, so that we may hear it and observe it?' Neither is it beyond the sea, that you should say, 'Who will cross to the other side of the sea for us, and get it for us, so that we may hear it and observe it?' No, the word is very near to you. (Deut. 30:11-12)

There is a similar sequence of thought in Psalm 19, which shows an interesting convergence of Deuteronomic and wisdom motifs:

> The heavens are telling the glory of God;
> and the firmament proclaims his handiwork.
> Day to day pours forth speech
> and night to night declares knowledge.
>
> The law of the Lord is perfect, reviving the soul;
> the decrees of the Lord are sure, making wise the simple....
> the fear of the Lord is pure, enduring for ever;
> the ordinances of the Lord are true. (Ps. 19:1-2, 7-9)

The opening verses of the Psalm celebrate the witness of the vast world to its maker, under the eye of the watchful sun (a wisdom image). Its speech overflows with a lesson which is abundant and intricate, and which escapes human understanding. But this lesson is contracted into the span of the Torah which is 'perfect' and reliable ('sure'). It may also, we notice, be equated with 'fear of the Lord'. In Deuteronomy 30:11-14, written from the perspective of the scribes of Torah, it is affirmed that the decree of God is not hidden but is easily available. Probably we do not as yet have the idea that *wisdom is* hidden while Torah is available.[33] This move, however, is definitely taken in a redaction of a wisdom saying in Proverbs 30:1-6. The frustration of coping with the vastness of creation is well expressed in this late collection, headed 'Sayings of Agur'. Here (as we observed in a previous chapter),[34] the wise observer of the

---

[32] R. E. Clements, 'Wisdom and Old Testament Theology' in Day, Gordon, and Williamson (eds), *Wisdom in Ancient Israel*, 283-4.

[33] Against Joseph Blenkinsopp, 'Wisdom in the Chronicler's Work' in Perdue, Scott, and Wiseman (eds), *In Search of Wisdom*, p. 23, who argues that the Deuteronomist is exalting the Mosaic law against 'foreign wisdom' (cf. Deut. 29:28).

[34] See Chapter 7, the section called ' Places and Dimensions of the World'.

world exclaims that he is 'weary and worn out', and that it is impossible for a mortal being to explore the heights and the breadth of the cosmos (Prov. 30:1–4). He lacks God's grasp of the world order and so is exhausted by the extent of the material he has to deal with:

> I have not learned wisdom.
> nor have I [the] knowledge of the Holy One.[35]
> Who has ascended to heaven and come down?
> Who has gathered the wind in the the hollow of the hand?
> Who has wrapped up the waters in a garment?
> Who has established all the ends of the earth?
> What is the person's name?

Another scribe then enters the text and offers his solution to the problem.[36] How can we succeed in surveying the huge expanse of wisdom (*hokmah*)? The answer given is that we should read the Torah, and not add anything to it:

> Every word of God proves true;
> he is a shield to those who take refuge in him.
> Do not add to his words, or else he will rebuke you,
> and you will be found a liar. (vv. 5–6)

The contrast is not between uncertain cosmological wisdom and certain religious wisdom (as Weinfeld suggests),[37] but between the vast and the comprehensive. The fixed text of Torah is to stand over against a world where boundaries cannot be measured.

This desire to contract the expanse of wisdom to a limited scope of reliable words is also expressed at the end of Koheleth, in two consecutive post-scripts.[38] The first editor (Eccl. 12:9–12) reflects on the baffling complexity of the world from which the weary Koheleth has drawn no meaning, and urges the reader to restrict wisdom to a limited number of tried and tested sayings rather than multiplying books:

> The sayings of the wise are like goads, and like firmly fixed nails are the collected sayings that are given by one shepherd. Of anything beyond these, my child, beware. Of making many books there is no end, and much study is a weariness of the flesh. (Eccl. 12:11–12)

---

[35] Reading NRSV margin.

[36] The new scribal voice is recognized by R. B. Y. Scott, *Proverbs-Ecclesiastes*. The Anchor Bible (New York: Doubleday, 1965), pp. 176–7 and McKane, *Proverbs*, p. 643, but neither give my explanation.

[37] Weinfeld, *Deuteronomy*, pp. 258–60.

[38] Most modern commentaries take vv. 9–14 as editorial addition. Two scribal postscripts are found by Barton, *Ecclesiastes*, p. 197 and Crenshaw, *Ecclesiastes*, pp. 189–90, but Scott, *Proverbs-Ecclesiastes* and Fox, *A Time to Tear Down*, pp. 373–5 find a single epilogist.

This editor is probably from the School of Koheleth, and regards his master's own words as quite enough for a scribe to satisfy himself with (vv. 9–10). The 'collected sayings' are probably those of Koheleth himself. Koheleth, we recall, had reduced the vast scope of wisdom ('the all'—*hakkōl*) to the everyday blessings God has given human beings, their 'portion'. His pupil reduces wisdom to the teachings of his master, his own 'shepherd'. But now a second editor makes his appearance, right at the end. He re-defines the restricted material in which wisdom is available as the Torah, and associates it with fear of the Lord: 'fear God and keep his commandments.' In contrast to Koheleth's favourite phrase 'the all (*hakkōl*) is futility', the 'all' or the 'sum' of the multiplicity of life is to keep the commandments, for Torah is the completeness of wisdom:

> This is the conclusion of the matter: let us hear the whole (*hakkōl*):
> fear God and keep his commandments,
> for this is the 'all' (*kol*) for humanity. (Eccl. 12:13–14)[39]

In the light of the postscripts in Proverbs 30:5–6 and Ecclesiastes 12:13–14, it seems most likely that there is a similar intention in the added postscript to Job chapter 28,[40] a poem about the elusiveness of wisdom:

> And he said to humankind,
> 'Truly, the fear of the Lord, that is wisdom;
> and to depart from evil is understanding' (Job 28:28)

As in Proverbs 30:5 and Koheleth 12:13, the measureless extent of wisdom in the world (which has been explored in the preceding poem) is being contracted to something which the writer here calls 'the fear of the Lord', and in commenting on Job 28 the writer of the later book of Baruch is probably right to understand this as observing the Torah. After referring to the riddle question of Job 28, he appeals to the Torah as the place where wisdom can be found, also ingeniously re-using the rhetoric of Deuteronomy 30:11–14, and interpreting Torah there as wisdom:[41]

Has any person discovered the dwelling-place of wisdom or entered her storehouses? . . . Has any man gone up to heaven to gain wisdom and brought her down from the clouds? Has any man crossed the sea to find her or bought her for fine gold? No one can know the path or conceive the way that will lead to her. Only the one who knows all things knows her . . . The whole way of knowledge

---

[39] My translation.

[40] For a discussion of its addition, see Chapter 7, the section called 'The Point of the Riddle'.

[41] The re-use of Deut. 30:11–14 is commented on by Schnabel, *Law and Wisdom*, p. 248, and Gerald T. Sheppard, *Wisdom as a Hermeneutical Construct: A Study in the Sapientializing of the Old Testament* (Berlin: W de Gruyter, 1980), pp. 90–3. James Dunn, *Christology in the Making* (London: SCM, 1980), pp. 185–7 proposes that Paul draws on Deut. 30 for a wisdom Christology, possibly with reference to Baruch.

[God] found out and gave to Jacob his servant. Thereupon Wisdom appeared on earth and lived among men. She is the book of the commandments of God, the law that stands for ever. (Baruch 3:15, 29–4:1)

As elsewhere, therefore, in Job 28:28 a later Torah scribe is adding his own solution to the hiddenness of wisdom.

CONTRACTION AND EXPANSION

We have thus found a variety of ways of expressing the contraction of wisdom into the Torah: it is 'perfect' (Ps. 19:7) or 'the whole' (Eccl. 12:13) or 'the whole way of wisdom' (Baruch 3:26), and nothing can be added to it (Prov. 30:6). Now comes another step of thought; in turn, the limited text of the Torah takes on the spaciousness and expansiveness of the world order to which it is providing the key. In the poem of Ben Sira 24, personified wisdom has a mastery and a vision of the dimensions of the world, making a circuit of the sky and traversing the depth of the abyss. When Ben Sira interprets her dwelling in Jerusalem as the gift of the 'covenant book of God most high', then the Torah is depicted as being like a fertilizing river in flood flowing through the landscape and finally becoming an ocean which fills the world:

> All this is the covenant-book of God Most High,
> the law which Moses enacted to be the heritage of the assemblies of Jacob.
> He sends out wisdom in full flood like the river Pishon
> or like the Tigris at the time of firstfruits;
> he overflows with understanding like the Euphrates
> Or like Jordan at the time of harvest.
> He pours forth instruction like the Nile,
> like the Gihon at the time of vintage.
> No man has ever fully known wisdom;
> from first to last no one has fathomed her;
> for her thoughts are vaster than the ocean
> and her purpose deeper than the great abyss. (Sir. 24:23–9)

So the unsearchable and immeasurable quality of wisdom is now transferred to Torah. Ben Sira records his experience as a wise man interpreting Torah to his disciples, that his teaching begins by being a small canal watering flower beds, but he then finds it becoming a river and then a sea (vv. 30–1). Some solution to the problem of the elusiveness of wisdom is nevertheless being achieved because Torah can be recognized as a limited core of material—a covenant book; it is boundless, yet within bounds. The multiplicity of wisdom need not be a cause of despair. There is a compact area of wisdom to which to turn.

For Ben Sira and other wisdom writers (such as the author of the Wisdom of Solomon), this does not lead to an absolute, exclusive view of Torah as the *only* deposit of wisdom. The openness of the wisdom approach has not been lost. As Ben Sira puts it:

> To all humankind God has given wisdom in some measure,[42]
> but in plenty to those who love him. (1:10)[43]

At this point in the development of wisdom thinking, Torah is not portrayed as a cosmic mediator, bridging heaven and earth, but as a unique condensation of wisdom, the vastness of wisdom contracted to a span. A mediator of knowledge would be exclusive, but a concentration implies the existence of a more expansive field of knowledge to be concentrated. In the latter idea there is room for wisdom elsewhere, though—as the Wisdom of Solomon points out—collecting it may well be a laborious pursuit, inducing weariness, mistakes, and even idolatry: 'With difficulty we guess even at things on earth, and laboriously find out what lies before our feet; and who has ever traced out what is in heaven? Who ever learnt to know your holy purposes, unless you had given him wisdom and sent your Holy Spirit down from heaven on high?' (Wisd. 9:16–17; cf. 13:6–9).

We should notice, however, that another temper of mind *could* make Torah absolute, and there is an example of this in the passage about hidden wisdom in the Book of Baruch (3:9-4:4), based—as we have seen—on the poem in Job 28. Since the writer clearly understands the 'fear of the Lord' in Job 28:28 as referring to Torah, his piece falls into the familiar shape of first depicting the vastness of the world and then celebrating wisdom as Torah. 'How great is God's dwelling-place, how vast the extent of his domain! Great it is, and boundless, lofty and immeasurable' (3:24). Only God knows the 'place' of wisdom,[44] because unlike the giants of old he lives comfortably in the house of the world, and enters all its storehouses. Wisdom has been rejected, but not by humanity in general. It has been refused by the very people to whom God has given it in the form of 'the book of the commandments of God', as a compression of 'the whole way of knowledge'. The passage thus begins with a reproach that Israel has abandoned Torah, 'the fountain of wisdom' (3:12); the writer's argument is that because wisdom is hidden by its very nature, it is foolish to reject the one place where wisdom becomes accessible. Unlike the Job poet, Ben Sirach, and the Wisdom of Solomon, the writer of Baruch believes that wisdom is otherwise totally unavailable to humankind, but this

---

[42] Greek: 'according to his gift'.

[43] Perhaps we should follow some versions (G miniscules, Syriac) and read 'to those who fear him', underlining the fullest gift of wisdom to those who keep the law: so Schnabel, *Law and Wisdom*, p. 24; Marböck, *Weisheit*, p. 21.

[44] See my discussion on the meaning of 'place', in Chapter 7, the section called 'Places and Dimensions of the World'.

restriction to Torah seems to be for the purpose of underlining the stupidity of Israel which has got itself into a crisis, rather than complimenting his nation on a piece of exclusive property.

When it was cut away from the context of the wisdom enterprise (which is not yet the case, even in Baruch), the assertion that Torah was complete and inexhaustible as wisdom could make remorseless demands on every part of life: it could lead to a tedious legalism, and this would be reinforced by making Torah into a transcendent, heavenly entity and an intermediary. But the wisdom movement in its basic mood was resistant to making Torah either transcendent or mediatorial between God and the world. Such an idea *is* expressed in the later Rabbinic idea that the Torah was the model in heaven which God consulted in making the world,[45] but there seem to be several strands woven into this development. Alongside the genuinely wisdom idea of the reduction of the field of investigation from the whole world to the Torah there run two other influences from apocalyptic writings. First, the development of angels as intermediaries gave a similar opportunity for the Torah to become a mediator, and second the idea of the heavenly 'tablets of destiny' could be applied to the Torah as stored in heaven as well.

Within the mainstream of the wisdom movement itself there were thus two strategies for dealing with the hiddenness of wisdom. *First* there was an attunement with with the spirit of wisdom—'walking in the paths of Lady Wisdom'—an idea I have explored in previous chapters. The *second*, we can now see, is a contraction to the limited text of the Torah.

ONE TEXT AND MANY TEXTS IN LATE-MODERN THINKING

Torah becomes the focus of wisdom for Judaism, but Torah does not have to be wisdom exclusively (as Ben Sira and The Wisdom of Solomon show). Its authority lies in its compactness, its concentration of wisdom, but this need not exclude other sources of knowledge. While giving a sense of having firm bearings, and relieving the frustration of a Koheleth (at least in the mind of an epilogist), it still leaves an openness to the world. This ancient conclusion has some affinity with our late-modern situation, where we are uncomfortable about making an *absolute* distinction between a particular sacred text and all other texts. Ancient wisdom, with its emphasis on the Torah as the 'whole' or the 'complete' in the face of inexhaustible phenomena is a spatial approach to a text which we shall also find to be significant in our own context. We might,

---

[45] See e.g. *Pirke Aboth* 5:25, 6:3; '*Erubin* 13a; *Ber. Rabb.* 1:1, 1:4.

I suggest, carry through the spatial notion of concentration and comprehensiveness without the same claim to completion.

We can begin to understand the relation between the *one* text that is regarded as Holy Scripture, and the *many* other texts in the world, if we consider the way that the self always reads signs in the world through empathy with others. In his reflections on *Oneself as Another*, Paul Ricoeur perceives that an authentic encounter with a text occurs when the reader meets with another *person* through it, and reads the text *through other eyes*. In general, he affirms, we only come to understand ourselves by understanding others, by internalizing other people, their stories, and the signs they present us with.[46] This is also true of reading texts: 'hermeneutics is thus, explicitly or implicitly, self-understanding by means of understanding others'.[47] As we have already seen, in his self-imposed role as a philosopher Ricoeur can only raise the *question* as whether the other he encounters is more than just another person whom he can look in the face, or whether finally the Other must be named as God, 'the living God, the absent God'.[48] While he can go further as a believer, as a philosopher he is faced with an impasse from which he cannot rule God out. He cannot deny that the reading through the eyes of another human being may become at any moment reading with 'the eyes of' an infinitely greater Other.

Now, taking up this insight, we may say that, reading Holy Scripture, we meet with other persons through the text, and read with their eyes. And, if we are believers, we gain the impression that the human authors of Scripture have been writing not only as themselves but also as an infinitely Other. They have moved—vibrated, trembled—in sympathy with the one who is creator and not created. Reading them, there are moments when we too find ourselves addressed and summoned by Another. Within the wide open spaces of the text we find ourselves suddenly in a place of encounter, when our life flourishes in a new way, and our compassion for others is deepened. Geographical or bibliographical space becomes a 'place' (or, as in my previous discussion, a 'no-place') which is holy, and which gives us entry into a space which transcends (but is not separable from) physical dimensions; we may speak of this as revelation—something, someone, is being unveiled. At such moments we find that we are reading both as the human other and as the infinitely Other; while we are internalizing the author, we are *being* internalized by the gracious act of the triune God. We stand in the place of the other—historian, prophet, poet, priest or wise man—and we find ourselves in the place which God has made for us within the space of God's own self. Such occasions are called 'hearing the word of the Lord' by the Hebrew prophets, and from the

---

[46] Ricoeur, *Oneself as Another*, p. 4.
[47] Ricoeur, *Conflict of Interpretations*, p. 17.
[48] Ricoeur, *Oneself as Another*, p. 355.

perspective of Christian theology when we read as an infinitely Other like this we are actually sharing in a divine conversation that is already going on within the triune life of God, as if a father is speaking with a son.

But word and voice are only one image for this encounter. The wise of Israel remind us of the role of seeing; when we read as an infinitely Other we are also seeing with new eyes, sharing in the vision of God. As we see the world around, reduced and focused into the area of this particular text, we find ourselves—using the imagery of the Israelite wise—summoned to move beyond observation to live with Lady Wisdom.

This brings us to the relation of Holy Scripture to other writings. What we notice in reading Scripture *must* be true in some way of all texts. When we read as another, seeing with their eyes and hearing their voices, we can suddenly find that we are reading as an infinitely Other. The impasse to which Ricoeur draws attention cannot be restricted to a single text, and there are several reasons for this. The first is the nature of revelation itself: if revelation is the disclosure of a self-revealing God, then this God must be free to unveil the divine self (or utter the divine word) wherever God wills, and this means through a variety of textual media.[49] Second, as Ricoeur himself stresses, the referent of all textual worlds—including Scripture—is God, who is 'at once the coordinator of these diverse discourses and the vanishing point, the index of incompletion, of these partial discourses'.[50] Third, if the 'other', including the 'other' we meet in literary texts, is understood in an ethical way as making an *unlimited* demand upon us and upon our responsibility for others, then we touch at least a trace of the 'infinitely Other' in and through all others, and in all 'faces'.[51] Yet for all this, a unique role can be claimed for Holy Scripture, an inclusive uniqueness within a wider field. Here is an intensity, an accumulation of texts where the human voice has been shaped by rhythms of divine speech, and eyes have been sharpened by divine vision. With the earlier wisdom writers we can recognize a concentration of wisdom in one text.

There are advantages to establishing frontiers and drawing limits to a 'canon' of sacred texts. In the first place, the boundaries create a textual space, within which the reader or hearer can discover the 'places' of disclosure I have mentioned. Further, the identity of a community is shaped by owning and transmitting a certain, defined body of material, and especially significant narratives;[52] thus members of the community have an obligation to engage with it. They cannot ignore it. The boundary marks out an area, sets up a

---

[49] Barth recognizes this in *Church Dogmatics* I/1, 55, although he stresses that it is not the task of the Christian theologian to build a religion on these other 'texts' in the world.

[50] Ricoeur, 'Philosophical Hermeneutics and Biblical Hermeneutics', in Blamey and Thompson (eds), *From Text to Action*, p. 97 (89–101). Here Ricoeur regards Scripture as a regional case of general hermeneutics.

[51] See Levinas, *Otherwise than Being*, pp. 114–26.

[52] So Lindbeck, *Nature of Doctrine*, pp. 16–20.

space, in which exploration is required. With regard to the Christian community, as long as people count themselves part of it they have a demand laid
upon them to read, interpret and wrestle with its canon in a manner that no
other texts ask from them. Other literature—whether the apocrypha, the
writings of St John of the Cross or the poetry of Gerard Manley Hopkins—
can produce the impression upon readers that they have been written by the
author 'writing as himself/herself and as a wholly Other', but Christians are
not *obliged* to study them and draw them into their lives. The canon of
Scripture does create such a requirement, but it is *not* an obligation to accept
the words of the writers of Scripture as correct or infallible: it is to enter into
relation with them. It is to stand where they stand, to attempt to enter with
empathy into their 'otherness', and to hear the word of God in company
with them. To some extent this will be an experience of what John Macquarrie
calls 'repetitive revelation',[53] or what Barth identifies as the 'contingent con-
temporaneity of the Word',[54] where the Word of God spoken in the past is re-
actualized in the present. But the openness of God to human response within
divine purposes, and God's continual creative originality, means that the word
of God will also take new form and new direction in new times.

   Indeed, the *written human word* of Scripture itself is subject to the judgement of the divine word and the verdict of the divine vision, as are all other
texts. As the text becomes a 'place' of disclosure in which the reader is
standing, the Word of God may be heard sounding in accord or discord
with the sentiments in the text. Barth puts it like this:

> Theology responds to the Logos of God, when it endeavours to hear and speak of
> him always anew on the basis of his self-disclosure in the Scriptures. Its searching
> of the Scriptures consists in asking the texts *whether and to what extent* they
> might witness to him; however, *whether and to what extent* they reflect and echo,
> in their complete humanity, the Word of God is completely unknown before-
> hand... 'What stands there,' in the pages of the Bible, is the witness to the Word
> of God, the Word of God in this testimony of the Bible. *Just how far it stands
> there*, however, is the fact that demands unceasing discovery, interpretation, and
> recognition.[55]

In passages of the Hebrew Bible, for example, in which God is portrayed as
requiring wholesale slaughter or genocide of Israel's enemies, the theologian
has a responsibility to discern whether the divine Word might be heard in
criticism of the writer's world-view.[56] However, this means that no text in the

---

[53] Macquarrie, *Principles of Christian Theology*, pp. 90–6.
[54] Barth, *Church Dogmatics* I/1, pp. 145–9.
[55] Karl Barth, *Evangelical Theology: An Introduction*, trans. G. Foley (London: Weidenfeld
and Nicolson, 1963), pp. 34–6. My italics.
[56] By contrast, the belief that the divine Word *may* accord with the text means that the Old
Testament is not to be read simply as an account of human failure, as suggested by Rudolf

canon may be dispensed with, none dealt with by cutting it out. It is only through the obligation to stand with the writer and enter into his or her feelings, arguments, vision, mistakes, and prejudices that the word of promise for human life can be heard.

The boundary of a canon also invites comparison of this particular text with literature beyond its frontiers. The enclosure of a certain body of material by a community should not result in reading it in *exclusion* from other texts, but always in reading it in *relation* to others. The notion of canon obliges us, not only to explore the material so marked off, but to bring it into conjunction with other territories. It is as if *all* writings are near neighbours, all lie on the immediate further side of the boundary, and their proximity cannot be ignored. In de Certeau's understanding of the Christian canon of Scripture, its internal differentiation and plurality open it to other later texts which multiply its meaning beyond the control of ecclesiastical authorities:

> If the corpus of the testament is closed (i.e. limited) it is because it has to allow, *outside* of itself and after itself, other compilations: patristic, liturgical, theological and so forth, which will become multiple and often more and more different. The 'closing' of the New Testament makes such differences possible and even preserves the necessity of such differences.[57]

However, de Certeau is apparently referring here only to other texts within the Christian community. He views the 'limit' of the Christian community and its canon as a sign of 'lack' (the Lacanian echoes are evident), and a recognition that there are 'unknown spaces' beyond which have no connection with the Christian space. My own proposal is that the limit of the canon precisely links it with all other texts in the world-archive. Derrida perceives that every text is potentially connected with every other; its 'hymen' or boundary always opens its inside to the outside, and to a universal 'grafting' of one text onto another (whether a text written on a page or on a body).[58] The Christian claim for Scripture is that, in the myriad ways of inter-connecting the different members of the world-archive of texts, the canonical text is always to be included where this involves the 'flourishing' of human life. Until quite recently this has in fact been the position of the canon of the Hebrew-Christian Scriptures in Western culture; it has been, in the words of William Blake, 'the great code of art', the text by which all creative works are to be interpreted.[59] David Ford writes that

---

Bultmann, 'Prophecy and Fulfilment' in Claus Westermann (ed.), *Essays on Old Testament Interpretation*, trans. J. L. Mays (London: SCM, 1963), pp. 72–4.

[57] De Certeau, 'How is Christianity Thinkable Today?', p. 149.

[58] Derrida, 'The Double Session', pp. 202–3. In this piece the text of the body is the face of the silent Pierrot.

[59] See Northrop Frye, *The Great Code: The Bible and Literature* (London: Ark, 1983), pp. xii–xvi.

a Christian wisdom (*sophia*) is always in dialogue with the text of Scripture, and that a sapiential approach to exegesis means that:

> Nothing can be ruled out as unrelated to scripture and its understanding—no people, experience, history, culture, event, institution, sphere of knowledge or religion. How they might figure in the process of the Spirit leading into all truth is not predictable... The confidence is that the Word is already involved with them.[60]

In the way that the borders of a particular written text link it with other writings in the world, we may find an analogy with the human body. Both written text and body are networks of signs; both have boundaries which bestow an individual identity and create a density of meaning within their enclosures;[61] and in both the boundaries also open and connect this identity with others. As Merleau-Ponty puts it, the body is about touching and being touched, about being 'enfolded' in a kind of embrace which has no horizons, and where the divisions between our body and that of others collapse.[62] Through the body we participate in the widest possible space, and engage in self-giving relations with others rather than protecting our own boundaries. Merleau-Ponty here conceives of a difference between 'anthropological space' and 'geographical space'. According to a phenomenology of being in the world, while there is one, fixed 'geographical' space, there are as many 'anthropological' spaces as there are spatial experiences. One must therefore 'reject as an abstraction' any view of bodily space which takes account only of its geographical position; the image we have of our bodies is dynamic, and its spatiality is its situation 'in the world'.[63]

The analogy between a text written on a page and the body runs deep. On the one hand, when we write a text we put ourselves into it as a kind of extension of our body. On the other hand, our body is also a kind of text, an unwritten text, which nevertheless carries the marks of the society in which we live; we bear the impressions of the pleasures and the dangers of our community. As Mary Douglas expresses it: 'Just as it is true that everything symbolizes the body, so it is equally true that the body symbolizes everything else'.[64] I have been arguing throughout this study for the textuality of the physical world, envisaging the whole world as a complex system of signs. Within this network there seems an especially close affinity between the 'text'

---

[60] Ford, *Christian Wisdom*, p. 57.

[61] On density of meaning in scripture, see Daniel Hardy, 'Reason, Wisdom and the Interpretation of Scripture', in Ford and Stanton (eds), *Reading Texts*, pp. 76–9.

[62] Merleau-Ponty, *Visible and Invisible*, pp. 248–9.

[63] Maurice Merleau-Ponty, *Phenomenology of Perception*, trans. C. Smith (London: Routledge, 2002), pp. 114–16.

[64] Mary Douglas, *Purity and Danger: An Analysis of Concepts of Pollution and Taboo* (London: Routledge & Kegan Paul), p. 122.

of a written document and the 'text' of the human body. This in turn, for the Christian theologian leads to the conviction that the world-text ('the Book of the World') should also be conceived as the body of the triune God.

I have already suggested that understanding the whole world as a text does not just mean seeing it as a collection of references to its creator: it is the space in which we find ourselves addressed, where we can hear the Word of God and see as God sees. To understand how this happens it is not enough with some theologians to designate the world as the body of (simply) 'God', or even (with Sallie McFague) the body of God filled with life-giving Spirit, or the 'inspirited body of the universe'.[65] The world, we must say, is the body of the *Trinity*. It is not that God has a body in the same sense that creatures do, but that God uses all bodies in the world to hold us in the embrace of the relations that make up God's triune life. Bodies are the means by which we connect with the world and participate in God, sharing in the interweaving relations of Father, Son, and Spirit. To repeat an earlier argument, the world is a network of signs that signify because it is held in and shaped by the flow of relations which are God, not because the world is some kind of deposit from a mediatorial Logos spoken by God.[66]

CHRIST AS FOCUS OF WISDOM

A sacred text, such as the Torah or the Christian Bible can—as we have seen—provide an entrance into this whole world text. Above all, however, the New Testament presents Christ as the wisdom of God, replacing the Torah in this function. No longer a book but a person, a bodily text, is the key to the universe (1 Cor. 2:6–10, Col. 1:15–17 with 2:2–4). We have seen that the identification of wisdom with Torah was not in the interests of making Torah into an intermediary between earth and heaven. Wisdom is not hidden because it has disappeared into heaven: there is no wisdom myth. Wisdom (*ḥokmah*) is elusive because of its immeasurable and inexhaustible scope, equivalent to the expanse of the world. Torah makes wisdom available by contracting its spaciousness into its own bounds, and thereby acquiring its own spacious quality. It is just in this way, declare New Testament writers, that Christ is wisdom contracted to a span. According to the author of the Fourth Gospel,

---

[65] Sallie McFague, *The Body of God: An Ecological Theology* (London: SCM, 1993), pp. 144, 149–50.
[66] See Chapter 8, the section called 'Trinity as Disturbance'.

In the beginning was the Word, and the Word was with God, and the Word was God. He was in the beginning with God. All things came into being through him... *The Word became flesh and dwelt [or 'pitched his tent'] among us*, and we have seen his glory, the glory as of the father's only son, full of grace and truth. From his fullness we have all received, grace upon grace. The law indeed was given through Moses; grace and truth came through Jesus Christ. No one has ever seen God. It is the only Son, who is close to the Father's heart, who has made him known. (John 1:1–3, 14, 16, 18)

Commentators are widely agreed that 'the word' here owes more to Hebrew ideas of wisdom than to the *logos* of Greek philosophy.[67] When this author writes that 'the word became flesh and dwelt (or 'pitched his tent', *skēnoun*) among us', he is recalling the exodus story of making a tent or tabernacle for God to dwell among the people of Israel (Exodus 25:8–9). The term *miškān* (tent) was used in the Hebrew Bible and rabbinic texts as a reverent metaphor to indicate the divine presence, based on this 'tent of presence' in the wilderness wanderings (e.g. Lev. 26:11, cf Ezek. 37:27) and later took the form of the 'shekinah' in rabbinic texts. But the author is also echoing passages in the wisdom writings about the dwelling of personified wisdom among human beings, and notably the song of wisdom in Ben Sirach 24:6–10:

> *I am the word* which was spoken by the Most High. . . .
> every people and nation were under my sway.
> Among them all I looked for a home:
> In whose territory was I to settle?
> Then the Creator of the Universe laid a command upon me;
> He that created me decreed *where my tent should be*.
> He said 'Let your tent be in Jacob; find your heritage in Israel'.
> Before time began he created me,
> and I shall remain for ever. (Ben Sirach 24:3, 6–10)[68]

I suggest that the Johannine Prologue is affirming that the divine word or wisdom is incarnate in Christ because this Son comprehends in himself the multiplicity of God's works and attributes. In 'one' Son (v. 18) there is the 'fullness' of the many (vv. 14, 16), just as wisdom is 'unique' yet also 'multiple' (Wisdom 7:22). In case we miss this idea that the complexity of divine wisdom has been contracted into a human person, the author of the Prologue makes reference immediately to Torah: 'the law indeed was given through Moses; grace and truth came through Jesus Christ.'

---

[67] e.g. Raymond E. Brown, *Gospel According to John*, I–XII, pp. cxxii–cxxv; Rudolf Schnackenburg, *The Gospel According to St John*. 3 Volumes, trans. K. Smyth (New York: Crossroads, 1990), vol. 1, pp. 228–49, 256–61; J. N. Sanders and B. A. Mastin, *The Gospel According to St John*. Black's New Testament Commentaries (London: A & C Black, 1968), pp. 67–70.

[68] NEB, except v. 8. My Italics.

Thus Christ in his body in the world ('the Word became flesh') offers access into the infinite diversity of the triune life of God. Origen rather later was to say that 'in so far as Christ is the wisdom of God, he is called a multiplicity'[69] and that 'Jesus is many in accordance with the *epinoiai* [aspects]'.[70] As he explains in his own commentary on John 1, the eternal Son makes visible in his aspects, names and titles (*epinoiai*) all the many transcendent perfections of the Father, enabling us to grasp the God who would otherwise be ineffable.[71] We could not comprehend a pure unity and so—like light refracted through a prism[72]—we see the one God through the multiplicity of a finite existence which is many in one.

Feminist theologians, such as Sallie McFague and Grace Jantzen are troubled by the particularity thus assigned to Christ (by transfer from Torah). They consider the universe to be the body of God in the sense that *all bodies* are God's body.[73] The basis of the metaphor is in the universal, not in one particular body, such as the body of Jesus of Nazareth or even its historical extension in the church. God is incarnate in the whole cosmos, and Jesus is only a subsequent paradigm of what we find everywhere. The sacramental presence of God is in all bodies, insists McFague, in 'the bodies of the sun and moon, trees and rivers, animals and people'.[74] She has, we may judge, legitimate concerns. She worries that beginning with the particular will result in the imposing of one kind of body as the measure and standard for all— namely the male, human body. Diversity, she warns, will be lost. Moreover, she thinks that other bodies will not be given intrinsic value as holy in themselves, valued for what they are as the body of God. They will be treated only instrumentally, as a means to the end of the life of the body of the church. The unity of the whole cosmos, she emphasizes, does not come from expressing the life of one particular, ideal, body; it comes from the common creation story which all bodies share, their one ultimate origin, which modern science tells us is the 'Big Bang' and consequent expansion of the universe. It comes from the organic inter-connections of many bodies which is the character of creation.[75]

While, of course, other religions will begin with integrity from their own particularities, all I wish to maintain here is the Christian belief in the

---

[69] Origen, *In Lib. Iesu Nave (On the Book of Joshua)*, Homily VII.7.

[70] Cit. Aloys Grillmeier, *Christ in Christian Tradition*, Volume 1. Second Revised Edition, trans. J. Bowden (London: Mowbrays 1975), p. 143.

[71] Origen, *Comm. in Ioannem* I.20.

[72] An anachronistic image for Origen, of course. Origen himself uses the example of a small statue making visible the many details ('every line of limbs and features') of a statue as large as the cosmos and so too great to be seen: Origen, *De Principiis* I.2.8 (Latin text).

[73] McFague, *Body of God*, pp. 130–5; Grace Jantzen, *Becoming Divine: Towards a Feminist Philosophy of Religion* (Manchester: Manchester University Press, 1998), pp. 151–2, 270–5.

[74] McFague, *Body of God*, p. 134.

[75] McFague, *Body of God*, pp. 35–46.

particularity of Christ as a 'bodily text' does not exclude the presence of God in the world through all bodies. As the canon of Scripture must be brought into relation with all written texts, so the body of Christ must be related to all bodies. The Christian claim is that the 'movement' of the life of Jesus fits more exactly into the movements in God than other finite lives, but that all life shares to some extent in this same dynamic. So all the speech of Christ, all the ways he sees the world, all his acts fit exactly into the movement in the Trinity that we recognize as being like a son relating to a father. The relation of the human person Christ to the one whom he calls his heavenly father can be mapped exactly onto the relation in God which is like that between a son (or daughter) and a father (or mother). His prayer, saying 'Abba, Father', his hearing of a father's speech to him at the baptism and transfiguration, saying 'this is my beloved son', his cry of desolation, 'My God why have you forsaken me' and his offering a welcome to the outcasts of society: all these fit into the movements of the Trinity which are like speech, suffering, and generous love. But when we recognize this, we can find the same patterns in all other bodily life.[76]

If there is comprehensiveness in Christ, there is also the spaciousness of wisdom. There is an elusiveness about the person of Jesus in the Gospel records, and the narratives have to resort to a whole multiplicity of metaphors in order to identify him. As John Milbank points out, 'Jesus is the way, the word, the truth, life, water, bread, the seed of a tree and the fully grown tree, the foundation stone of a new temple and at the same time the whole edifice.' These metaphors, we notice, are essentially spatial. We can say (again with Milbank) that Jesus is the 'comprehensive space' and 'our total situation' in the sense that the total shape of his actions and words can be realized again and again in new situations.[77] Divine personhood is 'an instruction to go on re-narrating and re-realizing Christ'. De Certeau similarly comments that 'Jesus effaces himself to give rise to different but faithful communities, which he makes possible... the process of the death (the absence) and the survival (the presence) of Jesus continues in each Christian experience: What the event makes possible is different each time.'[78]

It is only possible to 're-realize Christ' in ever new situations because Christ is the 'comprehensive space' where we have access to the inexhaustible depths and multiplicity of the divine wisdom. We may say that Christ is the normative 'place' which enables participation in God, and which includes within its span all the complexities of loving relationships which are in the image of God. There will also be a relation between the body of Christ and all written texts. Some texts, as we have seen, appear to the communities which live by them to

---

[76] See chapter 12, the section called 'Tuning to the Body of Christ'.

[77] See John Milbank, *The Word Made Strange. Theology, Language Culture* (Oxford: Blackwell, 1997), pp. 149–50.

[78] De Certeau, 'How is Christianity Thinkable Today?', p. 145.

be a clue to the textuality of the whole world. For Christians this means the Hebrew Bible and the New Testament. But since Christ is the primary place where the cosmic spaciousness of wisdom is concentrated, all texts—including these sacred texts—stand under the judgement of Christ. Scripture, as I suggested earlier, is liable to the judgement of the Word of God. This means, we can now see, being measured by the shape of the story of Christ which reflects the character of God and God's project in creation. 'Sapiential' readings of the Old Testament in the Christian tradition have always, as David Ford emphasizes, worked with 'the interplay between Jewish scriptures and the testimony to Jesus Christ.'[79]

So Christ is the bodily text which gives the clue to whole text and body of the world. This is not because he is a cosmic mediator, bridging a gap between two worlds, but because the pattern visible in the actions and words of Christ is the rhythm in which the world comes to its fulness.

---

[79] Ford, *Christian Wisdom*, p. 58.

11

The Process of Learning and the Rejection of Wisdom

In an article called 'Towards a Postmodern Pedagogy', Deborah Kilgore describes how she arranged a university seminar in which both teacher (herself) and students wore blindfolds throughout the discussion. Her avowed aim was to destabilize the usual relation of power between teacher and pupil; the strategy, she believes, 'helped pull us out of our usual ways of taking up social positions in the adult education classroom, with the teacher either leading the way or delegating leadership roles in an orderly fashion to students'.[1] Postmodernism, she asserts, involves a recognition that knowledge is multifaceted: 'there is more than one way to know something and more than one thing to know about it' so that 'the teacher's authority to know only exists within an authority-granting institution and by the will of the members who play by its rules.' Beyond the games of power, the postmodern learner is 'always becoming, always in process'.[2] Such considerations will require us, she concludes, to consider 'the death of the teacher, the subversion of the student, and the diffusion of power'.[3]

A similar awareness of power structures and the multiple dimensions of meaning in education is shown by Henry Giroux in his article 'Border Pedagogy and the Politics of Postmodernism'. But rather than abandoning the social position of the teacher, instead he urges the teacher to transform his or her authority into an emancipatory practice, encouraging the student to 'cross borders'. 'Border pedagogy', or learning *on* the borders and *across* the borders, means creating

---

[1] Deborah Kilgore, 'Towards a Postmodern Pedagogy', *New Directions for Adult and Continuing Education* 102 (2004), p. 45.

[2] Kilgore, 'Towards a Postmodern Pedagogy', p. 47.

[3] Kilgore, 'Towards a Postmodern Pedagogy', pp. 46, 48–50.

conditions that allow students to write, speak and listen in a language in which meaning becomes multi-accentual, dispersed, and resists permanent closure. This is a language in which one speaks with rather than exclusively for others . . . challenging existing boundaries of knowledge and creating new ones, border pedagogy offers the opportunity for students to engage the multiple references that constitute different cultural codes.[4]

There are resonances here with the opening of the border between a canon of sacred texts and all other texts, which I was commending in the last chapter. Borders, Giroux stresses, are 'forged in domination', and he is not only concerned with the borders created by 'Eurocentric, patriarchal, racist and class-specific interests' which are legitimated by existing 'canons' of approved texts. He also points to the kind of borders which are set up by different disciplines of knowledge, preserving their own influence.[5] Students should be allowed to 're-write difference' through the process of moving into 'borderlands criss-crossed with a variety of languages, experiences and voices'.[6] Underlining the need to 'speak *with* rather than *for* others' he portrays education as a means of the formation of persons who are learning to participate in lives other than their own: 'as teachers we can never speak inclusively as the Other . . . but we can certainly work with diverse Others'.[7]

These late-modern approaches to education, and others like them, owe a great deal to the thought of Foucault who, as Keith Hoskin observes, 'really discovered something very simple . . . the centrality of education in the construction of modernity'.[8] The question of the self is for Foucault, he urges, 'an educational mystery'.[9] It is Foucault's treatment of relations of power that has caught the interests of a number of educationalists. His book *Discipline and Punish*, although mainly about the rise of the modern system of prisons, explores the development of several strategies and sites of disciplinary power in the seventeenth and eighteenth centuries—not only the prison, but the barracks, the hospital and the school—so that systems of domination (exemplified in Bentham's 'panoptikon') infiltrated the whole social fabric. Society became a 'carceral' or 'disciplined' society, setting 'normalization' and efficiency as its primary concerns.[10] Foucault himself, however, contested the view that his main goal had been to analyse the phenomenon of power in itself,

---

[4] Henry A. Giroux, 'Border Pedagogy and the Politics of Postmodernism', *Social Text* 28 (1991), pp. 52–3.

[5] Giroux, 'Border Pedagogy', p. 52.

[6] Giroux, 'Border Pedagogy', p. 62.

[7] Giroux, 'Border Pedagogy', p. 64.

[8] Keith Hoskin, 'Foucault under Examination: The Crypto-Educationalist Unmasked' in Stephen Ball (ed.) *Foucault and Education: Disciplines and Knowledge* (London: Routledge, 1990), p. 29.

[9] Hoskin, 'Foucault under Examination', pp. 29, 37–9.

[10] M. Foucault, *Discipline and Punish The Birth of the Prison*, trans. A. Sheridan (Harmondsworth: Penguin, 1991), pp. 170–83, 300–7.

or trace its genealogy: this work was only by way of his main interest, he explained, which was to explore 'the different modes by which, in culture, human beings are made subjects'.[11] It is, as Kenneth Wain has proposed, his insight into the formation of the self or subject in modernity that should interest educationalists just as much as his exposure of the structures of power that characterize educational institutions.[12] Indeed, the two themes are intertwined.

Foucault is interested in the way that the human subject is constituted by entering 'games of truth', understanding 'game' as a collection of rules for the production of what is claimed to be truth.[13] These games might take the form of the scientific enterprise, in which human beings are formed as subjects extracting knowledge from the world, or they might be found in institutions which have various practices to categorize or 'normalize' someone—distinguishing, for example, the sick from the healthy or the insane from the sane. Structures of power support these 'games', and Foucault views the development of distinct academic disciplines as practices which create truth- and power-games and make human subjects into participants in them.[14] The enlightenment ideal of education as producing 'rational autonomy' is thus an illusion.

It seems that human freedom from systems of domination, including those that characterize education, is impossible. Critics of Foucault, such as Charles Taylor, suggest that Foucault can have no notion of freedom because he has narrowly identified 'power' with '*power over*' or 'domination'; Taylor objects that Foucault fails to consider other dimensions of power such as empowerment, 'power to do things', and power as freedom.[15] Wain, however, argues that this is a misunderstanding, at least of Foucault's last period of thought. He draws attention to Foucault's own protest that 'one cannot impute to me the idea that power is a system of domination which controls everything and which leaves no room for freedom'.[16] Rather, in line with his professed aim to examine the formation of the self in the modern period, and despite tendencies elsewhere to undervalue the self, he intends 'to promote new forms of

[11] Hubert L. Dreyfus and Paul Rabinow, *Michel Foucault: Beyond Structuralism and Hermeneutics*. Second Edition (Chicago: University of Chicago Press, 1983), p. 208.

[12] Kenneth Wain, 'Foucault, Education, the Self and Modernity', *Journal of Philosophy of Education*, 30 (1996), pp. 345–60.

[13] James Bernauer and David Rasmussen (eds), *The Final Foucault* (Massachusetts: MIT Press, 1988), p. 1.

[14] Foucault, *Order of Things*, pp. 74–5, 219–20, 358–9, 382–3. For futher reflection on interdisciplinarity, see the section called 'Wisdom Pedagogy and the Puzzle of Rejection'.

[15] Charles Taylor, 'Foucault on Freedom and Truth' in: *Philosophy and the Human Sciences, Philosophical Papers Vol 2* (Cambridge; Cambridge University Press, 1985), p. 153.

[16] Bernauer and Rasmussen (eds), *The Final Foucault*, p. 13. This and the following quotations from late interviews with Foucault are cited by Wain, 'Foucault, Education, the Self and Modernity', pp. 358–9.

subjectivity through the refusal of [the] kind of individuality which has been imposed on us for several centuries'.[17] His view of true education is to acquire 'the techniques of management . . . the ethos, the practice of self, which would allow these games of power to be played with a minimum of domination'. The problem is to know the difference between the legitimate use of power, and the domination which will 'put a student under the power of an abusively authoritarian professor'. Rather like de Certeau's commendation of 'tactics', Foucault suggests that through education one should gain 'relational techniques of government and of ethos, of practice of self and of freedom'.[18]

As Wain argues, in his last interviews Foucault proposes that these practices involve regarding one's own life as a work of art, and engaging in a 'care of self' that belongs with regarding it in this way. It is important to register that Foucault distances himself from the kind of self-creation that is to be found in Sartre,[19] saying that 'We should not have to refer the creative activity of somebody to the kind of relation he has to himself, but should relate the kind of relation one has to oneself to a creative activity'.[20] What Foucault calls 'care for the self' is not a kind of Cartesian absorption in oneself, but an activity on and within the world. This means that care for oneself must include care for the other. Indeed, the practices that he commends to form the self are 'not something that the individual invents by himself', but are 'patterns that he finds in his culture . . . his society, and his social group'.[21]

Thus Foucault finds at the heart of true education an awareness of patterns of practice in the world which enable one to care for oneself and the other, to evade the games of power that education might easily become, and to develop techniques to exercise empowerment, not domination. Foucault himself is opposed to metaphysics; his understanding of these patterns is simply 'a creative activity' which is 'on and with the world'.

Israelite wisdom writers, I suggest, had the same sense of a 'creative activity' to which the self can be related, and which can be known in and through the process of education. However, their understanding of this activity is what we would now call 'metaphysical', though it is not *separated* from nature (*phūsis*). Alongside the learning (probably by rote) of proverbs and instruction from the teacher, handed on from past generations, there was a participation in an activity, a wisdom that indwelt and moved through the world; this was often personalized as 'Lady Wisdom', and she in turn was inseparable from the creative activity of God. In the developed concept of *ḥokmah* the learned

---

[17] Interview in Hubert Dreyfus and Paul Rabinow, *Michel Foucault: Beyond Structuralism and Hermeneutics* (Chicago: Chicago University Press, p. 217).

[18] Bernauer and Rasmussen (eds), *The Final Foucault*, pp. 18–19.

[19] See Chapter 2, the section called 'The Self and the World in Postmodernity', (c) 'The world as a threat to the self'.

[20] Interview in Dreyfus and Rabinow, *Michel Foucault*, p. 237.

[21] Bernauer and Rasmussen (eds), *The Final Foucault*, p. 11.

wisdom of observation was intertwined with the wisdom of participation, and this always placed a check against the tendency of the self to control the world. Wisdom could not be detached from the teacher, from the envoy of wisdom, but neither was it identical with the teacher. If wisdom were simply equivalent to the learning of the teacher, then the educational process would become the kind of domination, the rational reception and communication of information, to which the late-modern critics of education object. Education, these critics insist, is more than learning how to 'represent' things in mind and language, which reduces a text to a container of information. Foucault criticizes the modern educational movement for substituting 'representation' as a universal system in place of a receptivity to the diversity of analogies and correspondences that the world offers.[22] Transcending mere representation, true education involves an empathy and identification with others beyond the immediate social circle of the pupil, requiring the absorption of attitudes which are different from either the student or the teacher. This 'otherness' is what the wisdom writers find embodied in Lady Wisdom, and finally in the creator God of whom she is is an extension. In the end the teacher effaces himself and allows a relationship of the self with a wisdom that is greater than he.

This inseparability of wisdom *from* the teacher, and yet at the same time the non-reducibility of wisdom *to* the teacher, can be explored through examining a cluster of wisdom texts to which we have not yet turned our attention. So far we have been considering two sorts of material about wisdom when it is portrayed either as a person or as a precious object. In one group of texts (wisdom as 'available'), a personified wisdom offers herself freely to human beings, and is depicted as travelling on a circuit of the world following the path of the sun: examples are in Proverbs Chapter 8, Ben Sirach 24 and the Wisdom of Solomon 7–8.[23] In another group of texts (wisdom as 'hidden'), wisdom is presented as an object which is elusive to investigation, and this is because wisdom is equivalent in extent to a world which is complex and inexhaustible: examples are in Job 28, Ben Sirach 1, and Baruch 3–4.[24] Wisdom as *ḥokmah* (continuing as the Greek *sophia*) is both available and hidden, both subject and object, making clear that the wisdom enterprise will always have its limits, and to know this is the fear of the Lord. I have been contesting the accepted theory that these texts fit together to make up an ancient wisdom myth, in which wisdom descends from heaven to find a home on earth, is rejected and returns to hide herself in heaven again—with, it is proposed, a special Israelite appendix in which she reappears to the elect people as the Torah. I have been arguing that in the classic wisdom movement the hiddenness of wisdom is due to its expanse, not its transcendence.

[22] Foucault, *Order of Things*, pp. 53–5.
[23] See Chapter 6, the section called Wisdom as Observer: Proverbs 8:22–31.
[24] See Chapter 7, the section called 'Places and Dimensions of the World'.

But there is a third group of texts in Jewish wisdom and apocalyptic writings (wisdom as 'vanished') in which wisdom is hidden because it has been *rejected*, and it is these that have provided the strongest evidence for the so-called myth of hidden wisdom. To these we now turn. In this analysis we shall not only be examining and deconstructing a postulated wisdom myth; at the same time we will have the opportunity to explore the relation between teacher and wisdom, and to find a dimension that seems to be missing in late-modern critiques of education.

A PROGRESSIVE PROCESS OF EDUCATION

First, in the poem recorded in Proverbs 1:20–33, there appears the figure of a personified wisdom who calls to people, inviting them to share her thoughts, and threatening to hide herself if she is rejected:

> Wisdom cries out in the street;
> in the squares she raises her voice.
> At the busiest corners she cries out;
> at the entrance of the city gates she speaks:
> 'How long, O simple ones, will you love being simple?
> How long will scoffers delight in their scoffing
> and fools hate knowledge?. . . .
> Because I have called you and you refused,
> have stretched out my hand and no one heeded. . . .
> I also will laugh at your calamity;
> I will mock when panic strikes you. . . .
> Then they will call upon me, but I will not answer;
> they will seek me diligently, but will not find me.
> Because they hated knowledge
> and did not choose the fear of the LORD.'

Some commentators find the whole postulated myth of hidden wisdom reflected here,[25] while others find some basic fragments of it.[26] But we notice that there is no mention here of either a descent of wisdom from heaven, or a return to heaven; indeed, wisdom is not a cosmic figure at all, unlike the passages where she travels a circuit of heavens and earth. She speaks of her rejection in a way that has been shaped by the theme of the rejection of the prophets in Deuteronomy and Deuteronomic redaction of prophetic writings, when judgement is declared to have fallen upon Israel for not hearing the prophets as messengers of Yahweh.[27] Other Deuteronomic touches we

---

[25] So Bultmann *Exegetica*, pp. 17–18; also Wilckens, Art. σοφία, p. 491.

[26] E.g. F. Christ, *Jesus Sophia*, p. 23, finds four motifs from the supposed myth.

[27] So Kayatz, *Studien*, pp. 125–6.

notice are the theme of 'seeking and finding',[28] linked with 'calling and being answered',[29] and the accusation that 'no one heeded'.[30] Just as the rejection of the prophets was a rejection of the word of Yahweh, so here the rejection of wisdom cannot be separated from the rejection of the wise, the teachers who are in view between the lines of the text as those who stand in the city gates and invite the simple to learn in their schools. Wisdom stands for her envoys on earth, and her withdrawal is actualized in the turning away of the teacher who then observes, hidden, the self-destruction of the fool. It seems that the wise here have borrowed a motif from the Deuteronomic scribes, as those scribes in turn had borrowed from the wise in depicting Torah as a kind of wisdom. It is likely that this mutual influence means that the reference to the 'fear of Yahweh' here is to the inclusion of religious Torah in the curriculum, as an object of interpretation.[31]

The kind of judgement which wisdom threatens is related to the nature of practical wisdom. While the Deuteronomic writers and the prophets warn of invasion from foreign armies and failure in harvest, wisdom threatens to mock at fools and not to answer them. This seems remarkably weak in comparison with the typically ferocious judgement speech of the prophets, although we recall the derisive laughter of Yahweh in Psalm 2:4, observing from heaven the revolt of heathen kings.[32] The wise withdraw and observe the fate of the obstinate, such as the teacher in Chapter 7 who tells of looking out from the window of his house and seeing the foolish youth take the path to the prostitute's house with inevitable results. This allowing things to take their own course has an unattractive aspect to it; it lends itself to a certain *Schadenfreude* or even smugness about being proved right (just a hint of 'that will teach you'), and I am by no means suggesting that modern teachers should follow the example of their ancient counterparts. However, we might observe that this ancient pedagogical strategy of leaving the scene did lessen the possibility of domination by the teacher, and was an alternative to an

---

[28] The motif of 'seeking and finding' God appears in Deut. 4:29, Jer. 29:11–13 (Deuteronomic redaction), Isa. 55:6 (Deuteronomic). For the negative 'seeking and not finding', see Hos. 5:6 (cf. 2:7), Amos 8:12.

[29] For the motif of 'calling and being heard', see Deut. 4:7, Jer. 29:11–13 (Deuteronomic redaction), Isa. 55:6 (Deuteronomic), cf. Zech. 13:9. For 'calling and not being answered', see the Deuteronomic redaction in Jer. 11:11; cf. Zech. 7:13 (Deuteronomic) and Micah 3:4, Ezek. 8:18.

[30] The accusation that 'they/you have not heard' is found in exilic and post–exilic prophetic material, particularly in the Deuteronomic redaction of Jeremiah (7:13, 11:10f, 17:23, 22:2–5, 25:4f). See Mack, *Logos und Sophia*, p. 45, n.80, Christ, *Jesus Sophia*, p. 22, n.37.

[31] So I have identified this passage as a 'B' passage in Proverbs 1–9, showing evidence of a merging of wisdom with observance of religious Torah: see Chapter 10, the section called 'Wisdom as Torah'.

[32] The laughter of the heavenly observer is found again in Psalm 37 (v. 13), generally reckoned to be a wisdom Psalm; see R. N. Whybray, 'The Wisdom Psalms', in Day, Gordon, and Williamson (eds), *Wisdom in Ancient Israel*, p. 158.

institutional imposition of punishment which Foucault describes and rejects in his book *Punishment and Discipline*. At the same time, the 'death of the teacher', or the removal of the teacher from the classroom, is seen as a disaster for the pupil, rather than the positive advantage envisaged by some modern educationalists such as Deborah Kilgore, with whom we began.

The warning of wisdom in Proverbs 1 corresponds to the experience of the wise who set out to educate others. They discover that some people make themselves incapable of learning, or finding wisdom; even when they want to do so they cannot because they have previously made a habit of rejecting it.[33] Just as wisdom is progressive, requiring patience and persistence, so folly is also progressive and a teacher can only be advised to turn away from the one whose folly is ingrained:

> Do not rebuke the scoffer;
> teaching a fool is like reasoning with a person who is drowsy. (Prov. 9:8)

Other passages which portray wisdom as hiding herself fall into this pattern of experience, rather than reflecting a cosmic myth. There is a weaker mode of rejection which is accepting a failure to persist, and this is in view in Ben Sira 4:11–19. We read here that any initial hiddenness is a temporary device, requiring discipline and eliciting patient trust from the one who wants to learn: 'At first she will lead him by devious ways' and then 'she will reveal her secrets to him'. But if someone fails to persist, she will leave him and 'abandon him to his fate'. We notice that the disciple is urged to rise early for the sake of wisdom, and then two chapters later a learner is commanded to rise early to visit the wise teacher (6:36), showing again that the envoy of wisdom stands behind the figure of wisdom herself. In this latter passage, in which the learner is advised to place his neck under the yoke of wisdom, it is said that: 'wisdom is just like her name/ but to most people she is not plain'. The name or nature of wisdom is to be clear and straightforward (Prov. 8:6–8), but what she offers only appears plain to those who have the proper attitude and desire to learn (Prov. 8:9a).

Beyond failure to persist there lies the worse state of becoming an outright scoffer, and in this case Ben Sira judges that wisdom 'holds herself aloof', and 'men of arrogance shall not see her' (14:20ff). In the Wisdom of Solomon, wisdom is presented as fleeing from those who err in their thinking because they are 'hostile to righteousness' (1:1–5); the holy spirit of reason 'cannot stay in the presence of unreason'. There is no need to find a fragment here of a supposed myth of wisdom leaving the world for a hiding-place in heaven.[34] The book itself supplies a commentary in a later chapter, when those who

---

[33] E.g. Prov 1:32, 14:6, 17:16, cf. 23:23.

[34] As e.g. Mack, *Logos und Sophia*, pp. 74, 383; cf. Schnackenburg, *St John*, pp. 256–61.

rejected wisdom during many periods of Israel's history are said to have been '*disabled* from recognizing the things that are good' (10:8).

Despite the variety of these examples, there is the constant feature that wisdom will appear hidden to those who reject her: she will not be found, she abandons people, she is not plain, she is unseen, unreachable, and far off, and she flees the scene. This is not a myth, but the practical experience of those who teach and learn. We are talking about an educational process. In this process the wise are rejected along with wisdom, and the withdrawal of wisdom is a pictorial means of expressing the withdrawal of her envoys, the teachers. Yet there is a point in portraying the withdrawal of 'wisdom' herself rather than directly describing the response of teachers: we are reminded that wisdom is a 'creative activity' (Foucault's phrase) which is more than the teacher. Warnings about the result of rejecting wisdom belong within a view of education which is about the formation of the self.

REJECTED AND HIDDEN WISDOM IN APOCALYPTIC

It is this interlocking of wisdom and her rejected messengers that takes on a new form in the apocalypses of the Second Temple Period, writings that unfold the secrets of the last times in world history. Here, in 1 Enoch 42, for the first time in our study of Israel's literature, we find a figure of wisdom who is indeed hidden in heaven as the result of being rejected by human beings.

1. Wisdom found no place where she could dwell, and her dwelling was in heaven.[35]
2. Wisdom went out in order to dwell among the sons of men, but did not find a dwelling; wisdom returned to her place and took her seat in the midst of the angels.
3. And iniquity came out from her chambers; those whom she did not seek she found, and dwelt among them, like rain in the desert, and like dew on parched ground.[36]

This passage has been greeted as the golden key for those who propose an ancient myth of hidden wisdom.[37] Here at last seems to be the myth in its fulness, the complete shape that lies behind the fragments about the

[35] Or: 'then a dwelling place was assigned her in the heavens': so R. H. Charles, 'Book of Enoch' in *Apocrypha*, vol. 2, p. 213.

[36] Translation M. A. Knibb (with the assistance of Edward Ullendorff). *The Ethiopic Book of Enoch: A New Edition in the Light of the Aramaic Dead Sea Fragments.* 2 Volumes (Oxford: Clarendon Press, 1978), vol. 2, p. 130.

[37] e.g. Bultmann, *Exegetica*, p. 16; Wilckens, Art. σοφία p. 508; Christ, *Jesus Sophia*, p. 51; Mack, *Logos und Sophia*, pp. 60–2. Even Kayatz, who rejects a myth elsewhere, finds it here; *Studien*, p. 128, n.2.

hiddenness of wisdom in earlier wisdom writings. The proposed appendix in which wisdom reveals herself to Israel is missing, but there *is* a sequence of descent, search, rejection, and return to heaven. An ancient wisdom myth, it is claimed, is being turned to eschatological use. But another possibility offers itself, that the whole sequence is first emerging in an eschatological setting. Since there are no previous examples of all these phases in the myth occurring together, it seems more likely that the sequence here has been created for the first time, or at least reflects a recent formulation. The picture that exists from earlier wisdom writings is of a cosmic wisdom who walks the circuit of the world and offers herself freely to all, coming to make her home with those who receive her. This, I have suggested, is an image of wisdom as a faculty of observation, inviting people to walk in sympathy with her own paths of life. To this the writer of 1 Enoch now adds an *ascent* of wisdom, which like earlier instances depicts the withdrawal of messengers of wisdom, but now in a more dramatic way. The wise and the just do not simply, as in Proverbs, retire to their houses and schools when they are rejected; in the last days they are to be persecuted and killed. and so leave the land of the living. In this they are following in the footsteps of the wise people of the past, notably Enoch and Elijah who are believed to have ascended to heaven.

The context of Chapter 42 in these Similitudes is, in fact, a Deuteronomic view of Israel's history; it reminds the reader that a rejection of righteousness and of the prophets has led to judgement in the past, and predicts that the pattern will be repeated in the near future with the end of all things.[38] Dividing world history into weeks, the scheme for the sixth week—the time of the two kingdoms of north and south in Israel—has been the rejection of wisdom, the ascent of Elijah as the rejected prophet and wise man, and the consequent judgement of the exile. Putting matters in a fictional future, Enoch predicts that there will be a 'forgetfulness of wisdom and . . . a man will ascend (93:8)'. Now, in the last days of the seventh week, people are urged to hold fast to righteousness and wisdom. The scheme of the sixth week is repeated: there will be a rejection of wisdom by the mass of people, the rejection and death of just men, and an ensuing judgement ushering in the messianic kingdom of the eighth week. The just who are to be killed have accepted wisdom (99:10), specifically the wisdom contained in the present book of Enoch (93:10, 100:6) and so like Elijah are rejected envoys of wisdom. There are only two references to the withdrawal of wisdom in this drama of the sixth and seventh weeks: one is associated with the ascent of Elijah (93:8) and the other with the death of the martyrs (94:6), where it is said that 'no place will be found for wisdom' (94:5).

In other apocalyptic books there is a similar binding together of the ascent of wisdom and the withdrawal of her envoys, the just and wise. For instance, in

---

[38] The closest affinity to Chapter 42 (which is perhaps an insertion into the Similitudes of Enoch) is the Paraenetic Book of Chapters 91–104, 105, 108.

4 Esdras 5:9–10 the disappearance of wisdom from the earth is one of the signs of the end-time: we read 'then wisdom shall withdraw to its chamber'. It may be claimed that this is another example of an ancient wisdom myth turned to eschatological use, but we have to read this passage in the context of the preceding chapter, where the righteous are waiting in *their* 'chambers' (graves) for their vindication. Similarly in 4 Esdras 14:17, the declaration that 'Truth shall withdraw further off' is in the context of the taking up to heaven of the righteous and wise man, Ezra (14:9–14).

It is more usual to speak of those who die as going *down* to Sheol, but 1 Enoch declares 'the portals of heaven will be opened' for them, in accord with the widespread view in apocalyptic material that after temporary sojourn in Sheol the just would be received into heaven. Certainly, the figure who *represents* the righteous community in Israel, the Son of Man, is portrayed as ascending to the throne of God to act as judge of the nations, as in the Book of Daniel (Dan. 7:13–14). This scene, we notice, appears in 1 Enoch immediately before the passage about the ascent of wisdom in Chapter 42. The Son of Man is finally identified (in Chapters 70–71) with one righteous man, Enoch, and like Enoch is a supreme bearer of wisdom. So the ascent and exaltation of various envoys of wisdom—Enoch, Elijah, the Son of Man and finally all the righteous martyrs—finds expression in the ascent of wisdom herself. It is their destiny that has shaped the story of wisdom, not the other way around.

The basic reason for the hiddenness of wisdom within the earlier wisdom tradition, its complexity and extent, is continued in apocalyptic alongside the theme of rejection. We find the familiar scheme of a three-dimensional world that eludes investigation:

> And is there any man who could know what is the breadth and length of the earth? And to whom have all its measurements been shown? Or is there any man who could know the length of heaven, and what is its height, and on what it is fixed, and how large is the number of the stars, and where all the lights rest? (1 Enoch 93: 13–14)[39]

Chapter 42, with its piece about rejected wisdom, is inserted into a section describing cosmological wonders, such as 'storehouses' for the winds, hail, mist, and clouds, and including the course of the sun which comes forth from its chamber:

> And I saw the chambers of the sun and moon, whence they go out and whither they return, and their glorious return.... And the sun goes out first and completes its journey [or 'traverses his path'][40] at the command of the Lord of Spirits. (41:5–6)[41]

---

[39] Knibb, *Enoch*, vol. 2, p. 226.
[40] Charles, 'Enoch', p. 212.
[41] Knibb, *Enoch*, vol. 2, p. 129.

It may be a recollection of the old tradition that wisdom treads the path of the sun that has prompted the placing of the passage about rejected wisdom at this point. In 4 Esdras 4 an angelic interpreter divides the world up into things with which human beings are familiar from their everyday life (fire, wind, and time) and those which are beyond their experience; the point is that they cannot even understand properly the things that are close at hand, let alone those those far off, so that they cannot hope to know the purposes of God which are 'formed without measure' (v. 11). In categorizing the world in this way, we notice that the angel lays stress upon multiplicity, and the way that things are beyond calculation, weighing, and measuring. The seer laments that the things closest to him — especially suffering and death—are mysteries he cannot comprehend (v. 23):

> I have never descended into the abyss,
> nor as yet gone down into Hades,
> or even ascended into heaven.

The failure of humans fully to grasp the expanse of the world—unlike wisdom, observing all things like the sun on its course—leads in 1 Enoch to warning about the folly of neglecting the places where wisdom *is* available: this means, as in previous wisdom writings, the Torah, but this apocalyptic text now adds another source of revelation—the secrets of the Book of Enoch itself, which is called 'instruction concerning his whole creation' and whose words the reader is bidden not to change or subtract from (104:11–13). This is, of course, a claim from this apocalyptic circle to be themselves the rejected envoys of wisdom.

This brings us back to the mysterious figure of the Son of Man. For the writer of 1 Enoch, as God's appointed judge at the last time he takes over the features of two wise men who belong to the beginning of all things–the first man, Adam, and the Primal Man. Adam's wisdom had been shown in his naming the animals (Genesis 2:20). In the mythology of the Ancient Near East the Primal Man was a man created *before* the world who was supremely wise because he witnessed all the marvels of creation as they happened and so knew all the secrets of the world order.[42] Now the Son of Man is predicted to appear on the stage of history as champion of the righteous in Israel, and it is this glorious figure, identified also with the supremely wise Enoch, whose revelations the readers have in their hands, who is to lead the martyrs in their ascent to heaven. In apocalyptic, the mysteries that belong to wisdom are thus twofold: first, they are the eschatological secrets of what is shortly to happen at the end of the age, and which have been heard or seen in the council of God in heaven; second, they are the traditional wisdom mysteries about the way

---

[42] Sigmund Mowinckel, *He that Cometh*, trans. G. W. Anderson (Oxford: Blackwell, 1956), pp. 376, 430.

that the world is constructed and the manifold items it contains. Heeding wisdom is both eschatological and sapiential: it is both expecting a decisive event in history and living every day in tune with the flow of life. Disaster will follow if wisdom is rejected, and wisdom is both inseparable from its envoys and irreducible to them.

CHRIST, THE WISDOM OF GOD

Now, the rejected envoy of wisdom in whom Christian faith is most interested is Jesus Christ. He is portrayed in the Gospels as both sage and prophet, standing in the double tradition of wisdom and apocalyptic. Since his extensive use of parables (*mᵉšalīm*) is more typical of the prophet than the wise man, he might appropriately be called a 'prophetic sage'.[43] He is certainly rejected as prophet, as envoy of wisdom and—we shall see—as wisdom herself.

In the material that scholars call 'Q', a collection of sayings of Jesus which is presumed to underlie Matthew and Luke, Jesus is presented as the rejected last and greatest messenger of wisdom.[44] He is supremely one of those of whom the Wisdom of Solomon says '[Wisdom] enters into holy souls, and makes them God's friends and prophets.'[45] For instance, after the incident in which Jesus is criticized for his lifestyle of enjoying good food and wine, compared with the ascetic John the Baptist, he remarks: 'Wisdom is vindicated by all her children' (Lk. 5:35 = Mt. 11:19). In dispute with the lawyers he recalls: 'Therefore the wisdom of God said, "I will send them prophets, sages and scribes, some of whom you will kill and crucify"' (Lk. 11:49; parallel with variation Mt. 23:34). As M. J. Suggs argues, Jesus here distinguishes himself from wisdom herself, to whom the oracle is assigned.[46]

However, Matthew in his Gospel takes a step beyond Q. Even if Q were *implying* that Jesus is more than a mere envoy of wisdom,[47] Matthew makes clear that Jesus is also wisdom in person. Wisdom is not now vindicated 'by her children' (her envoys), but 'by her deeds', namely those of Jesus (Mt. 11:19). In the saying about wisdom sending her messengers cited above, Matthew has adapted the Q text to make Jesus himself the one who sends them out: 'Therefore, I send you prophets, sages . . .' Further, the saying is attached to Jesus' lament over Jerusalem (Mt. 23:37–9), the city in which wisdom desires to dwell (Sir. 24:10–12) and which is rejecting him just as

---

[43] So Witherington, *Jesus the Sage*, pp. 117–18, 158–9.
[44] M. Jack Suggs, *Wisdom, Christology and Law*, pp. 27–8, 40–8.
[45] Wisd. 7:27; see Suggs, *Wisdom, Christology and Law*, p. 39.
[46] Suggs, *Wisdom, Christology and Law*, p. 18.
[47] This is Witherington's view, *Jesus the Sage*, p. 217.

wisdom has a long history of being rejected. Jesus laments that he would have gathered its inhabitants as a hen gathers its brood 'under her wings', recalling the Jewish idea of the maternal wings of the Shekinah, often connected with wisdom.[48] When Jesus promises that his yoke will be easy on the shoulders of his disciples (Mt. 11:28–30), he is claiming what is promised of wisdom herself in Ben Sira: 'Put your head into her collar . . . In the end you will find the relief she offers . . . Her yoke is a golden ornament' (Sir. 6:24–30).[49] The Fourth Gospel similarly makes a firm identification, when Jesus is portrayed as 'pitching his tent' among us, as did wisdom in Jerusalem according to the poem in Ben Sira 24.[50]

Lives of Jesus have veered between two extremes, depicting either the wise teacher of humanity, or the apocalyptic prophet of Israel's dreams—the first more nineteenth century, and the second more twentieth century. The same duality attaches to understanding the nature of the kingdom which Jesus proclaims: it may be seen as either the wide open space of living under God's rule, or the crisis which is about to break in. Those scholars who today stress the wisdom aspect of Jesus' ministry, however, now tend to assimilate it to apocalyptic, concentrating on Jesus as the revealer of an eschatological secret— the coming of a kingdom which will mean a reversal of all human judgements and human status. This is said to be a kind of wisdom running counter to the traditional wisdom of the wise in Israel, which is conceived as always supporting the present order of things and seeking stability in finding general patterns of life.[51] So revelation is placed over against observation, the disturbing against the prudential, and Jesus against James.[52] A key text which is appealed to here is Matthew 11:25–27, placed in this Gospel just before the 'easy yoke' saying, and deriving from the Q document:

> At that time Jesus said, 'I thank you Father, Lord of heaven and earth, because you have hidden these things from the wise and the intelligent, and revealed them to infants . . . no one knows the Son except the Father, and no one knows the Father except the Son and anyone to whom the Son chooses to reveal him.'

This, it is proposed, sets 'revealed' wisdom over against the wisdom of those who are conventionally wise.[53] The Apostle Paul apparently continues this

---

[48] For evidence, see Suggs, *Wisdom, Christology and Law*, pp. 66–7. Suggs argues that the pericope was a saying of Wisdom in Q.

[49] Celia Deutsch, Hidden *Wisdom and the Easy Yoke. Wisdom, Torah and Discipleship in Matthew 11:25–30* (Sheffield: JSOT Press, 1987), pp. 130–2.

[50] See Chapter 10, the section called 'Christ as Focus of Wisdom'.

[51] Witherington, *Jesus the Sage*, pp. 156–7, 161–2, 202–3. Similarly, James Dunn, 'Jesus: Teacher of Wisdom or Wisdom Incarnate?' in Barton (ed.) *Where Shall Wisdom be Found?*, pp. 85–91, refers to an 'eschatological plus' and 'subversion' in Jesus' wisdom teaching.

[52] Witherington, *Jesus the Sage*, pp. 236–47 argues for correlation between James and Q.

[53] Witherington, *Jesus the Sage*, pp. 360–1; Deutsch, *Hidden Wisdom*, pp. 28–33; Christ, *Jesus Sophia*, pp. 84–6.

theme, regarding the death of Jesus on the cross as a revelation of God's wisdom that baffles the 'wise, the scribe, the debator of this age' (1 Cor. 1:20). What is rejected, the argument runs, is a revealed wisdom that disturbs the wisdom that works through observing the world and its evident patterns. Those who take this view also assume that from the earliest days of the wisdom movement there are two kinds of wisdom in view—a transcendent wisdom which belongs only to God, and a wisdom immanent in the world that can be practised by human beings; there is a hidden kind of wisdom, and an available kind. The wisdom of Jesus, and Jesus as wisdom, fits into the transcendent kind of wisdom that needs to be revealed by a special act of God.

But in our study we have found no evidence for this transcendent wisdom in the classical wisdom movement: where wisdom (*ḥokmah*) is said to be hidden, it is because of its extent, not its location in heaven. The idea of heavenly secrets begins with prophecy, and emerges with full flower in apocalyptic, and even here we have seen that the old wisdom sense of hiddenness is not cancelled out but continues on. Just as apocalyptic contains both wisdom mysteries about the order of the world and eschatological mysteries, the sayings of Jesus shift in a startling way between observations about the way the world is, and insights into events that are going to come. The Sermon on the Mount is full of sayings like this: 'come to terms quickly with your accuser while you are on the way to court' (Mt. 5:25) is a piece of advice about conducting law-suits, but also refers to the coming judgement of God. 'The meek shall inherit the earth' (Mt. 5:5) is a saying which runs counter to people's attitudes in the present, yet it discloses a truth about life here and now as well as the life to come.

Some of the most disturbing sayings of Jesus are about God's order in creation; like classical wisdom, those who are truly wise should be open to having their sense of the pattern of things broken open by the unexpected, to be able to see God's creation clearly. So the sabbath is made for human beings, not human beings for the Sabbath; those who lose their life will gain it; a true father welcomes back a dissolute son with unconditional love; a generous landowner will give full wages even for a short day's work—and God is above all the true father and the generous landlord.[54] The order of creation is thus full of novelty and the surprising. Today, we can even see that Paul's revealed mystery of the cross fits in with the course of life as we know it to be: the creator of a world that has come into being through a long and sacrificial process of evolution is likely to be a patient God who shares the suffering of creation.

In seeing Jesus as the rejected envoy of wisdom we must therefore resist setting a wisdom that is about seeing the world against a special, revealed wisdom. Those who reject Jesus are not just those who practise traditional

---

[54] Mk. 2:23-8, Mk. 8:34-7, Lk. 15:20-4, Mt. 20:1-16.

wisdom: they are those whose wisdom has solidified into dogmas, inflexible formulas, just like Job's friends of old.

CHRIST THE REJECTED WISDOM

The idea of a transcendent wisdom is often supported by appeal to the so-called wisdom myth, the story of a wisdom that is God's mediator in creation, comes from heaven to humanity, is rejected, and returns to heaven to hide herself from mortal beings in general and reveal herself only to the faithful few. This is the pre-existing shape into which, it is urged, the career of Jesus fits. This is supposedly the myth by which the early Christians tried to make sense of the story of Jesus.[55] The V-shaped curve of descent and ascent, associated with Jesus as wisdom, is variously discerned in such texts as John 1:1–18, Philippians 2:6–11, Colossians 1:15–20, 1 Tim. 3:16 and Hebrews 1:2–4. Even if a coherent myth is not in view, it is urged that the shape of Jesus' career is at least taking up 'mythical patterns' in which a rejected wisdom figures.[56]

Now, I have been arguing that there is no ancient myth of hidden wisdom lying behind the classical wisdom literature of Israel, though such a myth does emerge within apocalyptic circles, and particularly in 1 Enoch 42; there it expresses the withdrawal of wisdom's envoys, which *is* an old theme. It is not impossible that, in groping towards a Christology, the New Testament writers are drawing on this relatively new myth, emerging at about the same time as the first New Testament writings. But it seems more likely that what we find in the New Testament is the same process as in 1 Enoch 42—a compilation of two existing themes. There is first the theme of a wisdom who comes to human beings, offering herself freely to those who want to learn, searching for a dwelling; and there is second the theme of the exaltation to heaven of the rejected messenger(s) of wisdom. One of the earliest themes in hymns about Christ is that of the exaltation of Jesus as Lord, ransacking the Old Testament for texts which might throw light on what the early Christians believed to be the vindication and resurrection of the dead Messiah. Psalms 2 and 110 were highly influential here (along with Psalm 8), presenting scenes of the coronation and exaltation of God's chosen king, whom the nations oppose and reject. These, I suggest, were combined with traditions about the

---

[55] See Jack T. Sanders, *New Testament Christological Hymns* (Cambridge: Cambridge University Press, 1971), p. 136; Deutsch, *Hidden Wisdom*, p. 104; Hamerton-Kelly, *Pre-existence*, pp. 177–8, 206–9 (though he sees Phil. 2:3–11 as modelled on the myth of the Primal Man); Witherington, *Jesus the Sage*, pp. 253–6, 260–2, 268, 275, 279–80, 288.

[56] See Elisabeth Schüssler Fiorenza, 'Wisdom Mythology and the Christological Hymns of the New Testament', in Robert L. Wilken (ed.), *Aspects of Wisdom in Judaism and Early Christianity* (South Bend: University of Notre Dame Press, 1975), p. 29 (17–41).

Son of Man who is presented before the throne of God and given judgement and dominion. I have already drawn attention to the depiction of the Son of Man as supremely wise, and this might help to account for the association of this mysterious figure with Jesus in the Gospels. Modern scholarship has proposed that the title indicates not a supernatural figure coming *from* heaven, but the righteous and faithful of Israel who will ascend to be vindicated before God.[57]

Among the Christ-hymns, the motif of rejection is strongest in John 1, and it is in fact from this passage that Bultmann launched his theory of an ancient wisdom myth, finally reading it back as far as the Book of Proverbs:

> He was in the world, and the world came into being through him; yet the world did not know him. He came to what was his own, and his own people did not accept him. (John 1:10–11).

Here the *logos* or wisdom is said to be rejected by those to whom he came in a pre-incarnate form, since we have not yet reached the affirmation, 'The Word became flesh'. This is likely then to be a portrayal of the rejection of the *envoys* in whom wisdom/logos has come to Israel over the years, namely in prophets and wise men.[58] Logos is described as 'the true light that enlightens everyone', just as in the Wisdom of Solomon wisdom is a light 'more radiant than the sun' which 'enters into holy souls and makes them God's friends and prophets' (Wisdom 7:27–9). Wisdom/logos has been rejected insofar as those whom she indwells have not found acceptance. This reading is in accord with the view of the 'Q' material in the Synoptic Gospels about the 'children of wisdom' whose message is ignored,[59] and who include John the Baptist who has just been mentioned according to the final form of this hymn. John and the earlier envoys are said here to be *witnesses* to the light of wisdom, but not *the light itself* (v. 7). Christ, however, is the word and light of wisdom become flesh (v. 14), so that we have seen his glory. There is no trace here, then, of a myth of hidden wisdom; in this hymn, indeed, there is no mention of the return to heaven of Christ as wisdom itself.

Why should it matter that there is no ancient myth of rejected and hidden wisdom? Why have I made so much of this? First, it matters that there be no ancient myth of hidden wisdom, or even an ancient myth of a mediator between earth and heaven, because it reinforces—it may even create—the myth of Christ as a cosmic mediator that I have already dissented from in this study. It matters that this kind of metanarrative should be deconstructed,

---

[57] See Morna D. Hooker, *The Son of Man in Mark* (London: SPCK, 1967), pp. 166–73, 189–96.

[58] This is the view of C. H. Dodd, *The Interpretation of the Fourth Gospel* (Cambridge: Cambridge University Press, 1953), p. 270.

[59] Lk. 7:34–5 = Mt. 11:18–19; Mt. 12:38–42 = Lk. 11:29–32; Mt. 23:34–6 = Lk. 11:49–51.

for it has the seeds of domination within it as it invites other, more human powers to step into the chain of mediation set up by the myth.

Second, to resort to a myth means that we fail to see the location of the rejection of wisdom within an educational process. The difference between wisdom and her envoys (in all wisdom writings before narratives about Jesus in the Gospels) diminishes the danger of the teacher's use of education as a form of institutional power, while at the same time drawing attention to patterns of life ('wisdom') which can be liberating for the self. Two of Foucault's concerns are thereby met, though admittedly with a metaphysic that he would not welcome. At the same time, Hebrew wisdom has added an insight about rejection of wisdom, which is not found in late-modern accounts of pedagogy. The Book of Proverbs tells us that persistent rejection of wisdom carries the terrible penalty of disabling someone from recognizing what truth is. Jesus hints at this in his explanation of why he speaks always in parables: they are a form of speech that requires the sympathetic engagement of the listener, a willingness to be drawn into the story and contribute something to the meaning. Without this attunement, the result is that 'they may indeed look, but not perceive' (Mk. 4:12). Folly is progressive, and so is wisdom. Jesus re-uses the language of Deuteronomy, as the wise poet of Proverbs 1 had done before him, urging that 'everyone who asks receives, and everyone who searches finds' (Mt. 7:8).

However, we see that Jesus goes to endless lengths to prevent this sealing of the heart against wisdom from happening. His parables about seeking the lost echo the statements in Proverbs about the way that wisdom and her envoys appeal to the simple on the streets, in the city gates, and in the marketplace, but the search commended by Christ is far more generous than that of the wisdom depicted in Proverbs and Ben Sira, who is rather prompt to withdraw.[60] The parables are actualized in the entrance of Christ into infinite human depths of human lostness at the cross and in his journey into death on Holy Saturday. Christian theologians will thus want to claim that the identification of wisdom with Jesus produces no pedagogical domination. The multiplicity of wisdom, as I have proposed in the last chapter, is 'contracted to a span' in Christ, so that it is appropriate to present Christ as wisdom herself. However, this is set in the context of a person who gives himself totally away in love for others. It is also significant that he himself makes no claim to be Holy Wisdom in the Gospel accounts, speaking in an allusive style which leaves this decision to be made by the hearer. Matthew has come to his own conclusion, but he writes in a style that leaves readers to reach it for themselves.

---

[60] This is a contrast perceived by Schnackenburg, *St John*, p. 269.

WISDOM PEDAGOGY AND THE PUZZLE
OF REJECTION

A major concern of late-modern approaches to pedagogy is to resist the reduction of education to making either teacher or pupil a mere master of information (the 'representative' approach), who simply reinforces the structures and boundaries of power in the institutions of learning. A related concern is the formation of a person through the process of learning, whose 'care of self' includes a sensitivity to others. These are aims we have seen to be reflected, in their own way, in the urging of ancient wisdom towards relation with wisdom (*ḥokmah*) herself, and then in the New Testament towards relation with Christ. All this also has affinities with the traditional Christian understanding of wisdom (*sophia*), whose story we traced in the very first chapter of this study. Peter Candler has found a 'grammar of participation' in mediaeval Christian approaches to the reading of texts, which he opposes to a modern 'grammar of representation', here deliberately picking up echoes from Foucault.[61] Reading, Candler argues, was understood by the mediaeval Christian mind as a process of 'manuduction', being led by the hand on a journey rather than processing information, and the typical expression of this itinerary was a manuscript with glosses added by the many guiding 'voices' of readers.[62] Theological reading, either of the Scriptures or patristic commentaries on them, was a process of being led into participation in God, or sharing the wisdom of God.[63] To this account I would only want to add, in the light of our previous chapter, that the reading of all texts whatever can surely become a journey into God.

In his reflections on 'interdisciplinary wisdom' in universities today, David Ford has similarly placed a stress on the development of the person, on the aim of 'forming wise people committed to the common good'.[64] He points out that the University of Berlin in the nineteenth century hoped to achieve this formation by a strategy of allowing as much individual intellectual freedom as possible, students choosing their own path within an overall field. His judgement is that this tended to foster isolation, and he prefers the formation of students through learning in the kind of community that is found in the colleges of the University of Cambridge, with socially embedded values of learning built up over the generations.[65] In line with the late-modern critique (including that by Foucault) of the boundaries set up by the various academic

---

[61] Peter M. Candler, *Theology, Rhetoric, Manduction. Or, Reading Scripture Together on the Path to God* (Grand Rapids: Eerdmans, 2006), p. 31.

[62] Candler, *Theology, Rhetoric, Manduction*, pp. 35–9.

[63] Candler, *Theology, Rhetoric, Manduction*, pp. 49–51.

[64] Ford, *Christian Wisdom*, p. 322.

[65] Ford, *Christian Wisdom*, pp. 311–14, 319–23.

disciplines to preserve their own power, he maintains that the forming of wise persons requires an inter-disciplinary approach of learning from the resources of all traditions that 'seek wisdom and have developed overall frameworks and core convictions'.[66] The University of Berlin in its origin attempted some interdisciplinarity in the idealist philosophy that united the various *Wissenschaften*, so that at its heart was a vision of teaching and research conducted in faculties that were differentiated yet interrelated. The result, however, Ford judges to be a stress on the separate nature of disciplines.[67] This, he suggests, can only be rectified by learning in multi-disciplinary collegial communities, and by setting up deliberate conversations between all traditions of wisdom within the university where they can 'negotiate' with each other about what constitutes learning for the common good. The aim would be an 'inter-faith and secular settlement' with which the whole university could identify. Christian theology must participate in seeking wisdom in this way, he urges, because God is already involved in all sources of wisdom.[68]

Our present study has affirmed exactly such an engagement of God in all human wisdom, and the participation of all human wisdom in God. What both Jewish wisdom and Gospel narrative add to this vision, however, is a warning about the consequences of rejection of wisdom in the process of learning. It is such a severe warning that some modern scholars have even turned it into a mythology, postulating an 'ancient myth of rejected and hidden wisdom'. However, a question arises when we wish to develop a wisdom theology for today which understands life as an educational process, leading us into the lives of others and ultimately into God. A central theme of our exploration of wisdom has been that human beings exist in a space which is opened up within the movements of God's triune life, where domination is overcome. But there seems to be a tension here with the idea of rejection. If all persons are held within God's being, then how is it possible to reject either God or the 'patterns' (Foucault's word) of the world around that foster life and well-being? How *can* we reject wisdom?

The theologian Karl Barth concludes that rejection and denial is simply not possible. While he does not envisage the world as being 'within' God in quite the way I have been doing, he does think that we live in a kind of 'moral space' which is shaped by the self-revealing of God and the the history of Jesus in his life, death, and resurrection.[69] To find what is good we must conform to the reality which is already there before us and around us in Christ. In fact, to be truly human we cannot do anything else. There is, thinks Barth, a 'necessity of

---

[66] Ford, *Christian Wisdom*, p. 341.
[67] Ford, *Christian Wisdom*, pp. 312, 330–3.
[68] Ford, *Christian Wisdom*, pp. 347–9.
[69] See John Webster, *Barth's Ethics of Reconciliation* (Cambridge: Cambridge University Press, 1995), p. 216.

faith', or a necessity of saying 'yes' to God. Since the divine 'yes' to humanity has been spoken in Jesus Christ, and only Christ has suffered the impact of the divine 'no',[70] then 'the root of human unbelief... is pulled out... For this reason unbelief has become an objective, real and ontological impossibility.'[71] It is a little hard to see, however, how Barth squares this theological vision with the apparent fact that people *do* have unbelief. Unbelief might be explained as a temporary phenomenon that will finally and inevitably be swept away, but Barth himself is reluctant to assert universal salvation as a *dogma* for fear that this would damage the freedom of God.[72] Human repudiation of God, he is driven to say in a wrenching of language, seems to be an 'impossible possibility'.[73]

The important point that Barth is making is that saying 'yes' and 'no' to God are not equivalent actions, not equal possibilities set before us, given that we live in a sphere of reality shaped by the actions of the triune God, or in 'the room of the Gospel'. He concludes that saying 'no' is impossible, despite the strains on language this produces. Karl Rahner agrees that 'yes' and 'no' are not parallel responses, but suggests another approach: we can say *both* at once, because 'every "no" always derives the life which it has from a "yes"'. By our very existence, we are open to the transcendent, to a final mystery which is God. In fact we are only open to this infinite horizon because *God* is open to us, communicating and offering God's self to us. Human freedom, given by God, is the capacity to become ourselves, and this involves openness to the mystery that transcends us. We *must* then affirm God in all our knowledge of the world and our actions within it; all human beings say 'yes' to God, though this is at root a 'yes' without categories and concepts; it is a 'non-thematic' yes.[74] But if we are truly free to become what we are, we must also be free to say 'no' to the self-offer of God, to choose to become the kind of persons who are closed in upon themselves. Saying 'yes' to God in exercising freedom is thus the only foundation for saying 'no', though it involves us in a self-contradiction.[75] The 'no' is one of freedom's possibilities, but (says Rahner) 'this possibility of freedom is always at the same time abortive, something which miscarries and fails'. Rejection of God and the way that the world is constructed is, according to Rahner, impossible but still a reality; it is 'a real impossibility' which cannot be fully explained, but which belongs to the mystery of evil.[76] This echoes Barth's language, but from the perspective of a mixed 'yes' and 'no'.

---

[70] Barth, *Church Dogmatics* II/2, pp. 122–3.

[71] Barth, *Church Dogmatics* IV/1, pp. 746–7; cf. II/1, pp. 97–126 on 'man in the cosmos'.

[72] Barth *Church Dogmatics* II/2, p. 147. For the relation between election, time and eternity in Barth see Robert Jenson, *God After God* (Minneapolis: Fortress, 2010), pp. 28–30.

[73] Barth, *Church Dogmatics* II/2, p. 86; IV/3, pp. 178, 463.

[74] Rahner, *Foundations*, p. 98.   [75] Rahner, *Foundations*, pp. 99, 102.

[76] Rahner, *Foundations*, p. 102.

Han Urs von Balthasar carries through this blend of 'yes' and 'no' in our response to God, but takes a step beyond human self-contradiction as well as offering a more trinitarian vision than Rahner. Since 'there is nothing outside God', there is only one place where our 'no' *can* be spoken, and that is— ironically—within the glad response of the divine Son to the Father. Just as our 'yes' to God leans upon the movement of thanksgiving and obedience that is already there in God, like the relation of a son to a father, so we speak our pain-giving 'no' in the same space. Our 'no' is a kind of 'twisted knot' within the current of love of the Son's response.[77] So Balthasar says, 'The creature's No, its wanting to be autonomous without acknowledging its origin, must be located within the Son's all-embracing Yes to the Father, in the Spirit.'[78] The drama of human life can only take place within the greater drama of the divine life. Our dance of relationships, we may say, can only happen within the patterns of the larger dance.

Our freedom is more than an openness to the infinite, in Balthasar's vision. It is a participation in the freedom of God, and this means sharing in the free self-surrender of the Father in sending forth the Son. Only this 'yes' makes the creaturely 'no' possible. 'The creature's No (says von Balthasar) resounds at the "place" of distinction within the Godhead.'[79] That is, there is already an infinite distance between the Son and the Father through the pouring forth of the Son from the being of the Father. What greater distance could there be than a giving away of Godness by the Father in begetting the Son? While the Father does not cease to be God, such an infinite self-gift amounts to a gulf of 'Godlessness'. This distance has room for all the distances between persons that there are within the world of finitude, including those of sin.[80] There is room here to burden the Lamb of God with 'the unimaginable load of all the world's No to divine love'.[81]

These three theologians all envisage human beings as living in the continuous presence of God. Rejecting God and the way the world is created is an impossibility for Barth, whatever semantic complications this plunges Barth into; for Rahner it is a 'real impossibility' of yes and no; for Balthasar it is a tragic possibility just *because* created beings live in God. For Barth, the forsakenness of Christ at the cross has made sin impossible: God has turned away from humanity once for all in Christ so that he will always say 'yes' to us. For Balthasar, it is the very forsakenness of the cross that makes it possible for humans to turn away from the divine self-offer, by bringing rejection into

---

[77] Balthasar, *Theo-drama*, vol. 4, *The Action*, p. 330.
[78] Balthasar, *Theo-drama*, vol. 4, p. 329.
[79] Balthasar, *Theo-drama*, vol. 4, pp. 333–4.
[80] Balthasar, *Theo-drama*, vol. 4, pp. 323–4.
[81] Balthasar, *Theo-drama*, vol. 4, p. 334.

God. Both Rahner and Balthasar envisage the human 'no' to God as shaping the human person, belonging to a person's self-formation and freedom to 'become themselves' in the way that the ancient wisdom writers conceived it.

But in the light of the Gospel picture of Christ as the divine wisdom we must surely affirm with Balthasar that rejection is not the end of the story. We must hold to at least a 'hopeful universalism', the hope and the possibility that all created beings will be reconciled to God.[82] As Barth, after his semantic wrestling with impossibilities puts it, 'it can only be a matter of the unexpected work of grace . . . for which we can only hope.'[83] In his obedience the Son of God has followed to the end the path that leads humanity away from God, assuming and surpassing in an extravagant way the journey of Lady Wisdom through the world. It is a path depicted in another image, in the parable of the shepherd who unfailingly sets out to find a lost sheep. 'Wherever people are pursuing some path, he is there . . . even those who do not want to will assuredly meet him as they journey,' says Von Balthasar, quoting the mystic Adrienne Von Speyr.[84] Those who try to choose complete forsakenness, opting for the total loneliness of living only for themselves—trying to say an absolute 'no'—will find themselves confronted by the figure of someone even more absolutely forsaken than themselves.[85] There is every hope that this companionship will, through patient persuasion, open the hard shell of all those who have rejected the divine wisdom.

---

[82] So Fiddes, *The Promised End*, pp. 194–6.
[83] Barth *Church Dogmatics* IV/3:1, p. 477.
[84] Balthasar, *Theo-Dramatik*, vol. 5, *The Last Act*, p. 311.
[85] Balthasar, *Theo-Dramatik*, vol. 5, p. 312.

Coda

12

Attunement to Wisdom: From Observation to Participation

ATTUNEMENT AND THE BODY

Awake, my lute, and struggle for thy part
With all thy art.
The cross taught all wood to resound his name,
Who bore the same.
His stretchèd sinews taught all strings, what key
Is best to celebrate this most high day.

In this hymn for Easter Day, George Herbert depicts the cross of Jesus as a musical instrument, with the body of Jesus as the strings, stretched tightly between the wooden frame. This was not a bizarre conceit of his own. Church Fathers such as Augustine and Cassiodorus had compared the suffering body of Jesus to a harp, giving out a song of love that sounded through the whole world.[1] Here they were influenced not only by the myth of Orpheus, but also by the Easter Psalm 57, which contains the words 'Awake, my glory, awake psaltery and harp.' The risen Christ, the harp of love, has awoken indeed. But Herbert, as he often does, extends the traditional image. These vibrating strings of Christ's body can awaken vibrations in all other bodies. All stringed instruments can be attuned to this one, not only wooden lutes, but the 'lute' which is Herbert's own body, employing the art of poetry. His art will be 'stretched' to the utmost to meet the demands of the Easter theme.

Herbert thus suggests that the human body can be attuned to Christ, as one vibrating string is brought into tune with another. Similarly, John Donne in his 'Hymn to God my God, in my Sickness', imagines that he is about to become part of the choir of saints which does not just *play* God's music, but *is* God's music; so he writes, 'As I come/ I tune the Instrument here at the door'.

---

[1] Augustine, *Enarrationes in Psalmos* (Psalm 57), in *Patrologia Latina* 36.671–2; Cassiodorus, *Expositio Psalmorum* (Psalm 57) in *Patrologia Latina* 70.404.

But behind this image is an even more wide-embracing idea, which is not quite visible in either of these poems. Christ himself on the cross is attuned to the music of creation (*musica mundana* in mediaeval musicology), the music of the spheres, the music that holds the whole universe together; and he brings everything discordant into harmony with this music. An illumination from a German manuscript of the eleventh century shows Christ on the cross, surrounded by four numbers whose ratios make up the intervals of music which Boethius identifies in his de *Arithmetica* as foundational of the numerical order of the universe.[2] Also around the cross are clustered images of opposing principles—the sun and moon, grace and law, church and synagogue, life and death—showing that the crucified Christ brings all these polarities into a cosmic unison.

Augustine offers us one further step in a theology of music: beyond even the music of the spheres there is the music of God's own being. The numerical measure of music can be applied to God's own self, Augustine proposes, because of the relationality between the persons of the Trinity. So (as Catherine Pickstock suggests),[3] he can create the widest vision of attunement: the individual human body in its own musical ratios (*musica humana*) can be attuned to the suffering body of Jesus on the cross, which brings the whole universe into harmony (*musica mundana*) because it is attuned perfectly to the rhythms of the Trinity. For Augustine, the discordance of human suffering can be transfigured into a rightly ordered music through participation in the sufferings of Christ, and here, in his discussion of the restoring of harmony in a world whose musical ratios are distorted, Augustine significantly adopts the designation of Christ as wisdom: 'the highest wisdom of God designed to assume this wound'.[4] Clement of Alexandria also relates the wisdom of God embodied in Christ to the healing power of music:

> A beautiful, breathing instrument of music the Lord made man, after His own image. And He himself also surely, who is the supramundane Wisdom, the celestial Word, is the all-harmonious, melodious instrument of God.[5]

Much of what is ascribed to wisdom in the Jewish wisdom literature is, in fact, atttributed to music in both Augustine and Clement. As Clement expresses it,

---

[2] Crucifixion from the Gospel Book of Regensburg (produced for the Abbess Uta of Niedermünster), c.1025. The intervals are the perfect fifth, perfect fourth, and octave. See Nicolas Bell, 'Readings and Interpretations of Boethius's *De Institutione Musica* in the Later Middle Ages' in Gunilla Iversen and Nicolas Bell (eds), *Sapientia et Eloquentia* (Turnhout: Brepols, 2009), pp. 336–8.

[3] Catherine Pickstock, 'Soul, City and Cosmos after Augustine' in John Milbank, Catherine Pickstock and Graham Ward (eds), *Radical Orthodoxy: A New Theology* (London: Routledge, 1999), p. 243–77 (esp. pp. 246–9, 264–5).

[4] Augustine, *De Musica* VI.4.7.

[5] Clement of Alexandria, *Exhortation to the Heathen*, Chapter. I, translation Roberts and Donaldson (eds), *Ante-Nicene Fathers*, vol. 2, p. 172.

the 'new song' which is embodied in Christ 'composed the universe into melodious order, and tuned the discord of the elements'.[6]

The image of 'attunement' is one that I have used throughout this study, to describe the relation of human beings to wisdom. It is an apt metaphor for living in sympathetic engagement with the wisdom immanent in the world, personified as Lady Wisdom, which in the end is God's own wisdom. As Jeremy Begbie puts it, 'wisdom is directed towards a life-style thoroughly "in tune" with God . . . that resonates aptly with the Creator's intentions for us and his world'.[7] The actual metaphor of attunement, drawn from the practice of music, is not to be found in Israelite wisdom literature, although Ben Sira recognizes music as one of the skills which belong to wisdom, using a term for musical composition (*ḥuq*, חק: Sir. 44:5) which is also applied to God's ordering of items in creation and Torah.[8] 'Attunement' is a metaphor which I have adopted as central to a Christian wisdom-theology, at the intersections of ancient wisdom, modern Christian doctrine, and late-modern thought. This attunement finds expression in wisdom literature in the image of walking with wisdom on her circuit through the cosmos, and—as we saw in our last chapter—those who reject her invitation run the danger of disabling themselves from meeting her again, so that she appears to have hidden herself. It is as if, we may say, they can no longer sing or play properly in tune in the world with the instrument of their bodies (*music humana*).

In Augustine, Herbert, and Donne, a particular place is given to Christ in the process of participating in the music of the cosmos although—as I have stressed with regard to wisdom—we must understand the uniqueness of Christ here as inclusive. Christians will understand Christ's own attunement as universally enabling for others, but all human beings are, their own way and to varying degrees, attuned to wisdom and to God. This is an insight developed by the theologian Alois Gügler, leader of the Romantic school in Lucerne, in his incomplete work *The Sacred Art; or, the Art of the Hebrews* (written between 1814 and 1836), and which has been picked up by Hans Urs von Balthasar in his own project of theological aesthetics. For Gügler, as cited by Balthasar:

man is encompassed and determined [Ger. *bestimmt*, i.e. voiced or tuned] by God . . . [in] a living commerce between God and man, a real spiritual equating of the two, or a 'tuning' . . . This tuning (*Stimmung*) is . . . the living process whereby the tuner (*der Bestimmende*) and the tuned (*der Bestimmte*) are made equal . . . When the relationships of a string of the instrument to the different resonances of the air have been established in being by tightening the string, and so forth, then the string is tuned.[9]

---

[6] Clement, as footnote 5.

[7] *Resounding Truth: Christian Wisdom in the World of Music* (Grand Rapids: Baker Book House, 2007), p. 20, although Begbie thereafter uses 'wisdom' only in a general sense, and makes no attempt at engaging with the Israelite or Christian wisdom tradition.

[8] On the Hebrew text here, see Schnabel, *Law and Wisdom*, pp. 36–7.

[9] Balthasar, *Glory of the Lord*, vol. 1, p. 99.

Balthasar combined this metaphor of 'attunement' with another musical metaphor derived from the thought of the English poet Gerard Manley Hopkins, that of the 'pitch' or distinct tone of a personality which is known only to God.[10] He is wary of the Romantic direct equation of human spirit with divine Spirit, but thinks that Gügler's notions can be adopted as long as human and divine freedom are preserved. Grace is not effective regardless of human response to its call, and so attunement (*Stimmen*) is a matter of reciprocity, because the person who is to brought to tune must be flexible enough to undergo the process of tuning, which depends on the nature of the materials of the instrument. The created spirit will never be God, but one's degree of participation in and with God can increase to infinity. God's self-gift of grace is at work in all persons, often unnoticed and beneath the surface, but all persons respond in varying degrees to the offer of grace. People have different 'dispositions' (states of being tuned) towards the event which is the correct 'pitch'—the life, death, and resurrection of Christ.[11] God sets the standard of pitch in Jesus Christ, and we are attuned through contemplating this revelation in the Gospels.

If, however, we are to adopt the metaphor of 'attunement' for Christian wisdom thinking, then we must recognize some possible problems with this image to which 'postmodern' approaches to music alert us. Within the classical Christian tradition about the music of the cosmos there can be an emphasis on the transcendent quality of music, its unison with eternity, which neglects the realities of embodiment and dissonance. Both the latter aspects have been stressed in postmodern accounts of the operation of music, and both will be significant for an account of wisdom.

First, music is embodied in physical instruments of wood, string, brass— and of human flesh and blood. Music is made through the interaction of the body with musical instruments and, in the case of singing, by the human body itself as the singer finds the physicality of sound through vocal cords and breathing. Begbie, laying stress on the bodily nature of music cites the experience of a classical pianist who struggled to play jazz until he discovered that the body had to 'find a place to go', and that listening was as much to do with the hands' 'tactile knowledge' of the keyboard as the ear.[12] The Christian tradition has, however, often spiritualized music in a way that has downgraded its bodily forms; feminist musicologists have, in particular, reacted strongly against a dichotemizing of spirit and body in which music was associated with

---

[10] Balthasar, *Glory of the Lord*, vol. 3, p. 375. So Hopkins writes of being 'pitched beyond pitch of grief', *Poems*, p. 100.

[11] Balthasar, *Glory of the Lord*, vol. 1, p. 468; cf. pp. 241–8.

[12] Jeremy S. Begbie, *Theology, Music and Time* (Cambridge: Cambridge University Press, 2000), pp. 226–7.

the passions, sexuality, and the female body, and thus held under deep suspicion.[13] The use of the musical metaphor for the ordering of the body and the cosmos was often reduced to the abstraction of mathematics in terms of number, measure, and oratio, and was detached from the actual physical body producing music. Even Augustine, despite his vision of a musical universe, and notwithstanding his support of singing in church, regards music as a potential temptation to the soul. He confesses to God that

> The pleasure of the ear had a more tenacious hold on me, and had subjugated me; but you set me free and liberated me. As things now stand, I confess that I have some sense of restful contentment in sounds whose soul is your words, when they are sung by a pleasant and well-trained voice . . . But my physical delight, which has to be checked from enervating the mind, often deceives me when the perception of the senses is unaccompanied by reason . . .[14]

In the early twelfth century it was, after all, church authorities who held a strong theology of the music of the spheres who banned liturgical singing by women in nunneries. As Heidi Epstein recounts, they prompted the redoubtable Abbess Hildegard of Bingen to a kind of musical rebellion. In her hymn to the Virgin Mary, she affirms that it was only through the musical instrument of a woman's body that Jesus, as the song of God, could enter the world, writing 'For your womb held joy/ when all the harmony of heaven resounded from you.'[15]

In general, late-modern philosophical thought has stressed the immersion of the self into the physical world,[16] and rejected any detachment of a logos or 'idea' from physical signs: writing, including the signifiers of musical notes, cannot be separated from embodiment in the particularities of time and place.[17] Roland Barthes suggests that it is the body of the performer and not some supposedly higher factor such as 'soul' or 'heart' which explores and creates the multiple meanings of a musical text which exceed the intentions of the composer. The activity is 'above all manual (and thus in a way much more sensual)' and 'kneadingly physical'; the performance of an amateur, for one's own pleasure and that of friends, is

---

[13] See Heidi Epstein, *Melting the Venusberg: A Feminist Theology of Music* (New York: Continnum, 2004); Susan McLary, *Feminine Endings: Music, Gender and Sexuality* (Minneapolis: University of Minnesota Press, 1991).

[14] Augustine, *Confessions* X.33.49, trans. Chadwick, p. 208.

[15] Epstein, *Melting the Venusberg*, p. 125, citing Hildegard, 'Hymn to the Virgin', trans. Barbara Newman, *Symphony of the Harmony of Celestial Revolutions* (Ithaca: Cornell, 1998), pp. 123–5.

[16] See Chapter 2, the section called 'Self and the World in Modernity', sub-section (a) 'Immersion in the world'.

[17] See above, Chapter 8, the section called 'The World as a Book'.

muscular music . . . as though the body were hearing—and not 'the soul'; a music which is not played 'by heart': seated at the keyboard or the music stand, the body controls, conducts, coordinates, having itself to transcribe what it reads, making sound and meaning, the body as inscriber and not just transmitter, simple receiver.[18]

In her psychotherapeutic version of phenomenology, Julia Kristeva has emphasized the grounding of musical rhythm in the body prior to the progression of the self to separation from intimate union with the mother and its entering into the state of using propositions and symbols. The rhythmic experience of this early period in development, a rhythm which is the essence of the primordial *chōra*,[19] re-emerges later in music, and like the rhythms in poetry has the energy to overturn oppressive symbolic structures in social life. In the 'modality' of 'oralization' which is characteristic of much poetry and music, the mother's body 'is no longer viewed as an engendering, hollow, and vaginated, expelling and rejecting body, but rather as a vocalic one—throat, voice and breasts: music, rhythm, prosody'.[20]

In the second place, if we are to use the metaphor of attunement, we must pay attention to the late-modern perception that music contains discord and dissonance that cannot be smoothed away. A stress on the unity and order of music, in tune with a single cosmic system of numbers, can result in an overconfidence that all discord will be harmonized. For Augustine, discordant noise is inevitable in a fallen world, but true harmony will resound through it in the end. He discerns affinities between the ontological dialectic of being and non-being in creation and the alternation of sounding note and rest (caesura) in music.[21] When this dialectic is applied to the tension between concordance and discordance, however, there is the danger of overlooking the sheer intractability and irreducibility of human suffering, as all pain is seen as sublimated in its harmonization with the passion of Christ on the cross. This, as we have seen, is not the message of Job.

Some postmodern theory of music not only insists that the difference between harmony and dissonance remain, but that noise is actually prior in the order of being to music, so that music is only mitigated noise.[22] Less extreme is postmodern practice in music which employs a mixture, montage, or bricolage of unassimilated and unresolved styles. In popular music this often takes the form of 'sampling', and Peter Manuel gives the example of the influential 'hip-hop' hit entitled 'Pump up the Volume', produced by the

---

[18] Barthes, *Image, Music, Text*, pp. 149–50.
[19] See Chapter 7, the section called 'The Disturbance of a No-Place'.
[20] Kristeva, *Revolution in Poetic Language*, p. 153.
[21] Augustine, *De Musica* VI.4.7, VI.10.37, VI.14.46, VI.17.56.
[22] Jacques Attali, *Noise The Political Economy of Music*, trans. B. Massumi (Minneapolis: University of Minnesota Press, 1985), pp. 3, 20–5.

group M.A.R.S.S. in 1987.[23] The song employed more than thirty samples (digitally-reproduced excerpts from prior recordings), set over a steady disco rhythm, interspersed with a vocal refrain, itself a second-hand sample. Towards the end of the song, an even more heterogeneous element is introduced when a passage of synthetically altered traditional Arabic singing can be heard over the steady beat. Manuel points out that in modernist pieces of music, when fragments are borrowed from other compositions or cultures, they are woven seamlessly into the host genre. Here, he judges, 'the expressive meaning of the passage's incorporation derives precisely from its audible *difference*', and this is also true of the other samples.[24] In rap songs too all kinds of sampled sounds appear, 'from screeching tyres to flushing toilets and other examples of stray audio-technological trash'. The result is not mere 'noise', but it is a deliberate 'juxtaposition and combination of elements from disparate discourses', and the sampled passages 'function as simulacra, as free-floating signifiers' in a 'characteristically postmodern exhilaration of surfaces'.[25]

Another musicologist, Jann Pasler, notes that in modernist musical works pieces are often 'borrowed' from other compositions in an attempt to 'overcome and surpass one's predecessors',[26] and in his view this applies to quotations from Stravinsky and Messiaen in Pierre Boulez' work *Le Visage Nuptial* (written between 1946 and 1989). In works that might be designated 'postmodern', whether classical or popular, he detects a different intent; as expressed by the composer John Cage, incorporating the work of other artists is making 'an alphabet by means of which we spell our lives'.[27] That audiences come to works built of musical allusions (such as Luciano Berio's *Sinfonia*) is evidence of their own search for identity. Both commentators suggest that the incorporation of unassimilated and unharmonized elements is a sign that the makers and consumers of such works are engaged in what I earlier designated as a 'quest for the self' in postmodern culture.[28] Manuel judges that, in popular music, 'subcultures construct their own gerrymandered sense of identity out of imagerial *objets trouvees*'.[29] At the same time, this kind of music is rooted in the body and physical life, since samples or quotations prompt the memory of a whole range of bodily experiences, both individual and scattered across different cultures. Works like 'Deep Listening' by Pauline Oliveros, judges Pasler, 'expect listeners to start with 'knowledge and experience of the human body... beginning with their own breath'. They are

---

[23] Peter Manuel, 'Music as Symbol, Music as Simulacrum: Postmodern, Premodern, and Modern Aesthetics in Subcultural Popular Musics', *Popular Music* 14 (1995), pp. 227–39.

[24] Manuel, 'Music as symbol', p. 232.

[25] Manuel, 'Music as symbol', p. 233.

[26] Jann Pasler, 'Postmodernism, Narrativity, and the Art of Memory', *Contemporary Music Review* 7 (1993), p. 7.

[27] Pasler, 'Postmodernism', p. 27.   [28] See earlier in this section.

[29] Manuel, 'Music as symbol', p. 230.

catalysts for 'increased awareness of self and other through the medium of sound'.[30] In the culture of hip-hop, we are reminded of the body by the frequent inclusion in samples of a human grunt or cry.[31]

In our time the idea of living 'in tune' with reality has become increasingly attractive.[32] But if we are to use the image of 'attunement' for a Christian wisdom-theology in this late-modern context, I suggest that we have to qualify it by late-modern perceptions about the music from which the metaphor is drawn, which are in the end insights into human experience generally. We will have to take account of the actuality of the body and its passions, together with the reality of what must remain unharmonized. Indeed, the two aspects belong together. It is because human life is embodied that dissonance is bound to arise; taking the body seriously means that its chaotic elements have to be accepted and even welcomed.[33]

At its best, the wisdom movement of Ancient Israel held these elements together in the polyvalent concept of *hokmah*, as has become apparent throughout this present study. Wisdom affirms the life of the body; it is concerned with observation of the world *as it is*, the recording of patterns of events, and the deduction of guidelines for living from this immersion into practical experience. Wisdom is the art of reading the signs of the world. It exercises this skill, not in an attempt to dominate, but in a humility which is aware of a complexity which undermines neat formulas, and which is open to being disturbed. The wise know that some aspects of the world will always escape explanation and assimilation into harmony. But through this very process of observation there is the possibility of being attuned to a wisdom which invites relationship, empathetic involvement, and a whole way of life. Personified as Lady Wisdom, to be open to her journey through the world is to find oneself in a 'place' which is not a literal place but where one can participate in God's own wisdom. One can know God only through seeing the world. Taking up this Hebrew idea into a Christian wisdom theology, the 'no-place' of wisdom opens into a wide 'space' in which we can participate more fully in the rhythms of the triune God. Thus the movement of wisdom through the world is revealed to have the depth of relational movements of self-giving and other-receiving in love. Recalling the terms of our first chapter, we may say that the idea of *hokmah* offers the scope for *phronēsis* to evoke the 'always more' of *sophia*.

---

[30] Pasler, 'Postmodernism', p. 47.

[31] E.g. in Hey D's 'Silky'; cit. Manuel p. 233.

[32] 'Attunement' is a favourite concept of 'new age' spirituality, but is also used in psychological studies of the interaction of parents with infants and educational studies of the interaction of teachers with children: see the discussion of 'good enough attunement' in E. M. Leerkes, A. N. Blankson, and M. O'Brien, 'Differential Effects of Maternal Sensitivity to Infant Distress and Nondistress on Social-Emotional Functioning', *Child Development*, 2009, Vol. 80, pp. 762–75.

[33] This is at the heart of Epstein's musical theology: see *Melting the Venusberg*, pp. 173–6.

In exploring the way that attunement to wisdom is rooted in the life of the body—not only the bodies of individual persons but the body of the world—an important contribution was made by a group of Russian Orthodox theologians in the early part of the twentieth century. Although the concept of 'harmony' (in the cosmos, Trinity, and Christology) was fundamental to their work, these 'sophiologists' did not use the actual term 'attunement', but they were gripped by the idea that the divine wisdom or Sophia who invites relationship with her should be called the *body* of God. A brief account of their ideas will both underline some conclusions about wisdom to which we have already come, and open up some new insights.

WISDOM AS GOD'S BODY

The bodily nature of wisdom, even its female embodiment, was expressed poetically by the elder statesman of these theologians of Sophia, Vladimir Solov'ev. He relates in a poem how he met the divine Sophia three times in his life. The first and third times are where you might expect a mystical encounter—the former while attending the orthodox liturgy in Russia, in front of the open sanctuary, the latter in the deserts of Egypt. The second experience was a little more out of place, in the reading room of the British museum while researching Hindu and Gnostic philosophies. Each time there was an experience of a figure clothed in azure blue, and a radiant, beautiful face. In the third, he claims to have seen 'all' of her ('I saw all of you there in the desert'):

> Your eyes full of an azure fire,
> Your gaze was like the first shining
> Of universal and creative day.
>
> What is, what was, and what ever will be were here
> Embraced within that one fixed gaze . . .
> > The seas
> And rivers all turned blue beneath me, as did
> The distant forests and the snow-capped mountain heights.
>
> I saw it all, and all of it was one,
> One image there of beauty feminine
> The immeasurable was confined within that image
> Before me, in me, you alone were there.[34]

The natural interest of critics in these mystical moments can obscure the rigorous philosophical and theological thought underlying the embodiment of

---

[34] Vladimir Solov'ev, 'Three Meetings' in *Vladimir Solovyov's Poems of Sophia*, trans. and ed. Boris Jakim and Laury Magnus (New Haven: Variable Press, 1996), pp. 22–39.

wisdom in Solov'ev and other sophianic theologians. As poems to or about Lady Wisdom are juxtaposed with more reflective theology in Ben Sira, Proverbs 1–9, and the Wisdom of Solomon, so the poems put into personified form theological convictions about Sophia as 'the all' of the world, the 'embodiment' of Sophia both in the Trinity and creation, and the concentration of wisdom within one image.

First, we notice that in Solov'ev's thought wisdom crosses the boundaries between subject and object, as in the Hebraic concept of *ḥokmah*. He begins by observing, along with such philosophers as Schelling, that human persons are conscious of their own nature: as well as *who* they are (the 'I' or ego) there is *what* they are, which is something other to the 'I'.[35] The person is both subject and object to itself. So the three-personal God knows what God is, the divine nature, and because the nature or essence of God is love, God knows the love that God is.[36] Love is always lovable (as Augustine commented), so God loves the divine essence which is Sophia.[37] Moreover, the being of God can be nothing other than pure activity, so Sophia herself loves with infinite ardour, even as she is loved. As the act of God she is the self-revelation of all three persons; as the manifestation of the Spirit she is glory, and as the manifestation of the Logos she is wisdom. Sophia is a kind of divine 'world',[38] or the environment in which the three persons exist, a world composed of all things in unity, an 'organism' that holds together all God's ideas about everything. Sophia is both the Other of God and the All-Unity. She and the divine Logos together form the eternal Christ, with the word of God producing unity, and with Sophia as the 'produced unity'.[39]

We can readily see how this concept of Sophia as loving and loved, knowing and known, corresponds to the ancient idea of wisdom as both subject and object, the knowing subject and the whole range of ideas in the mind. The concept is conditioned here by idealist philosophy, but with the idea of a divine 'world' which is constituted by a mutual self-revelation of all three divine persons as self-giving love, so forming a trinitarian spatiality, Solov'ev has moved beyond the self-differentiating Absolute of Hegel and Schelling (even though they use trinitarian language for this differentiation).

This divine world could simply be a version of Plato's world of ideal forms, abstract thoughts detached from the messiness of the physical world. Solov'ev

---

[35] Vladimir Solov'ev, *The Philosophical Principles of Integral Knowledge* [1877], trans. V.Z. Nollan (Grand Rapids: Eerdmans, 2008), pp. 147–50.

[36] Vladimir Solov'ev, *Lectures on Divine Humanity* [1887–91], trans. P. Zouboff, rev. ed. Boris Jakim (New York: Lindisfarne Press, 1995), pp. 63–4, 102–3, 116–17; *Philosophical Principles*, pp. 114–17.

[37] Solov'ev, *Lectures*, pp. 128–32.

[38] Solov'ev, *Lectures*, pp. 118–19, cf. 109, 112; So Bulgakov, *Lamb of God*, pp. 101–3; cf. 112, 126.

[39] Solov'ev, *Lectures*, pp. 107–8, 113.

and his successors now emphasize that Sophia, as love and wisdom, is a kind of *body*. 'Sophia is God's body, the Matter of Divinity, permeated with the principle of divine unity.'[40] In the first place, the divine wisdom is a *spiritual* body because she organizes and connects all the divine thoughts, as a body does for a human person.[41] She is also the location and manifestation of love, as a human body is. But beyond this quasi-corporeality, Sophia as the divine nature encloses and houses all the bodies of the *created* world. These theologians cannot think of God without a world in which God exercises a searching love;[42] the nature of God from eternity is to be kenotic, giving God's self away in an outpouring of excessive and sacrificial love.[43] The eternal sending forth of the Son from the Father is itself a kenotic act, echoed in the creation of human persons and in the desolation of the cross on Calvary. Sergii Bulgakov, Solov'ev's successor in wisdom theology, thus identifies three moments of kenosis (generation, creation, crucifixion) in which the triune God empties God's self.[44] From eternity, then, the bodies of the world have certainly been held in the divine Sophia as unrealized concepts. As Bulgakov, puts it, Sophia as the divine world, divine body, and All-unity is 'the pan-organism of ideas, the organism of the ideas of all about all and in all'.[45] But the thought of Bulgakov exceeds Schellingian *Potenzen* or Platonic ideas. Like the persons of the Trinity, Sophia too gives herself away, allows herself to be diminished, as a *created Sophia* comes into being along with the creation of the physical universe. This created Sophia is actually embodied in the world, and the two Sophias—created and uncreated, in the world and in God, are somehow, mysteriously, one: 'the all in the Divine World, in the Divine Sophia, and the all in the creaturely world, in the creaturely Sophia, are one and are identical in content (although not in being).' The biblical image for this oneness, he suggests, is the picture of wisdom in Proverbs 8, in the world and at the side of God in creation.[46]

Further to describe the activity of created wisdom Bulgakov employs a musical metaphor, deriving from Augustine, as well as making clear that the two Sophias are the same:

> Therefore, in the life of nature, we have both the shining of the *creaturely Sophia*, the revelation of paradise, and the seething of the blind element, natural chaos . . . Nature follows the path of its sophianization, in which Providence is accomplished . . . It only helps nature to become itself, to actualize its proper image, implanted in it by the Creator. Nature is *nascens natura*, the symphony of

---

[40] Solov'ev, *Lectures*, p. 108.
[41] See Sergei Bulgakov, *Sophia. The Wisdom of God. An Outline of Sophiology*, trans. P. Thompson, O. Fielding Clarke and X. Braikevitc (New York: Lindisfarne Press, 1993), p. 56.
[42] Solov'ev, *Lectures*, p. 119 and 119, n.2.   [43] Solov'ev, *Lectures*, pp. 60–1.
[44] Bulgakov, *Lamb of God*, pp. 213–28.   [45] Bulgakov, *Lamb of God*, pp. 135, 148.
[46] Bulgakov, *Lamb of God*, p. 126.

the world that seeks the harmony of the spheres and to overcome its own dissonances.... The relation between Divine guidance and creaturely freedom is expressed here as the incessant introduction into the life of creation of its own principles, accessible to but unactualized by it.... In this sense, one can say that God's providence in the natural world is the *Divine Sophia* herself, acting in the natural world as a force of internal movement.[47]

There is no space here to try and unravel the tangled and—it must be said—confusing relations between the divine and created wisdom.[48] What is important is that the divine world, the environment of God, must always include created bodies. While Bulgakov has made explicit what is latent in Solov'ev's thought with his own idea of the created and divine Sophias, neither can think of the wisdom in God's nature without the whole scope of the world in all its diversity and multiplicity, as the outworking of God's thoughts. Sophia, with the attractiveness of a personification links—in a kind of theological poetry – the divine world of the Trinity and the everyday physical world. The world is the body of wisdom, indwelt and suffused by wisdom; but (and this is a new concept), wisdom is also the body of God. Bulgakov here resists the over-rationalization to which he thinks Solov'ev is prone in his reliance on Schelling; the relation of the two Sophias is an antinomy, and 'at this point the fiery sword bars the way to our reason'.[49] In ancient wisdom thinking, the 'body' of ideas in the wise person's mind is inseparable from the wisdom that lies out in the world, a corpus of knowledge waiting to be gleaned from experience. For these theologians, this must also be true in some way of God. This is why Bulgakov has a vision of the divine Sophia as 'the real and *fully realized* divine idea', and so as a kind of 'divine self-art', an endless collection of beautiful images which are not just ideal but actualized. This is why Sophia, for both thinkers, is the the eternal 'Godmanhood', or the fulness of reality.

This engagement of God with embodiment also coheres with another insight of ancient Israelite wisdom we have already explored, namely that divine wisdom and the wisdom exercised by human beings are essentially the same; in Bulgakov's terms, divine and created Sophia are the same wisdom. Bulgakov, indeed, in a commentary on Proverbs 1–9 explains that 'The word *wisdom* is used here undoubtedly in a double sense: in a metaphysical and a moral-practical sense, signifying at one time a certain rational essence, at another time a human quality, now wisdom itself, now a participation in it or its works. Both shades of meaning of course are connected and mutually

---

[47] Sergius Bulgakov, *The Bride of the Lamb*, trans. Boris Jakim (Grand Rapids: Eerdmans, 2002), pp. 200–1.

[48] In particular, I am omitting the dispute over whether Sophia, envisaged as the soul of the world by both Solov'ev (earlier) and Bulgakov, is fallen.

[49] Bulgakov, *Sophia*, p. 61. The guarding of Paradise as an image for inaccessibility to the 'coincidence of opposites' is taken from Nicholas of Cusa, *The Vision of God*, pp. 43–4.

conditioned.'[50] While the sophianic theologians work out these notions in the context of the idealist philosophy of their time, though always stretching and transgressing its bounds (especially with regard to 'body'), I have suggested in the context of late-modern thought that we may think of the creator God as always committed to a world of signs, never floating above physical signifiers as a transcendent mind.

The vision of Sophia as body and divine world leads to another aspect which is significant for our project. She is living and personal, but not in the sense of being a personal *subject* or personal *agent*. Using the technical term 'hypostasis', Bulgakov says that she is *not* a hypostasis herself but has '*hypostaticity*' (Russian: *ipostasnost*).[51] She is the state of 'reciprocating orientation', or 'receiving and reciprocal love',[52] without being either a self or subject. However, despite this conviction, Bulgakov is always in danger of thinking about Sophia as a 'fourth hypostasis', or 'fourth person', and in one notorious instance he actually refers to her in this way, so apparently augmenting the Trinity by one (and by one too many).[53] If she *is* a hypostasis, then she also seems to be an extra redeemer figure for the world, over and above the Son. This was not just a danger which emerges in a theologian's study: it led, in 1935, to the condemnation of Bulgakov (an émigré in Paris) by the Russian Church, and to the moving of his spiritual home from the Patriarchate of Moscow to Constantinople.

I suggest that this problem arises because Bulgakov thinks of the three divine *hypostases*, Father, Son, and Holy Spirit, as 'persons' in the sense of being personal subjects, selves, or agents. When Sophia is regarded as personal, it seems that she must have the same kind of identity (at least 'in the image of a hypostasis'),[54] and so we end up with the danger of four persons. But in envisaging Sophia as the *event* of receiving and reciprocating love, Bulgakov has surely opened up the true meaning of divine personality. I have been arguing throughout this study for an understanding of persons in the Trinity as movements of reciprocal relationship rather than subjects; to take up the musical analogy we could speak of *rhythms* of being, in relationship with each other.

---

[50] Sergei Bulgakov, *The Burning Bush*, trans. and ed. T. Allan Smith (Grand Rapids: Eerdmans, 2004), Excursus 2: 'The Old Testament Doctrine of the Wisdom of God'.

[51] This is the translation of Anastassy Brandon Gallaher, and Irina Kukota, 'Protopresbyter Sergii Bulgakov: Hypostasis and Hypostaticity: Scholia to The Unfading Light', *St Vladimirs Theological Quarterly* 49 (2005), p. 14. Rowan Williams (ed.), *Bulgakov: Towards a Russian Political Theology* (Edinburgh: T & T Clark 1999), p. 165, suggests something akin to 'hypostaseity' and Boris Jakim, in Bulgakov, *Bride of the Lamb*, p. xiv, suggests 'Hypostasizedness'.

[52] Bulgakov, 'Hypostasis', p. 29 and 29 n.46.

[53] In Bulgakov *Svet Nevechernii* [1917], trans. as 'Sergej Bulgakow—Kosmodizee' in Nicolai Bubnoff and Hans Ehrenberg, ed., *Östliches Christentum Dokumente—II Philosophie* (München: C. H. Becksch Verlagsbuchhandlung, 1925), p. 135. He corrects this in 'Hypostasis', pp. 27–8.

[54] Bulgakov, 'Hypostasis', p. 29.

By speaking of 'Father', we mean a relationship like that of a Father sending out a son on mission into the world; by 'Son' we mean a relationship like that of a son (or daughter) responding in glad obedience to a father (or mother); and by 'Spirit' we mean a movement opening up these relationships to new depths of love and to new events in the future. We cannot observe these relationships, but we can participate in them, like engaging in measures of music.

This does not mean that Sophia is a 'fourth movement', but within this concept of hypostasis we can think of 'hypostaseity' more easily, with Sophia as the divine world, the environment created by these movements, the rhythmic space opened up by these relationships, within which all created beings find a home. I suggest that this corresponds to what Wolfhart Pannenberg calls the divine 'field of force', as we have seen in a previous chapter. Within the area of Sophia's loving there are indeed 'hypostases' in the sense of distinct identities, three distinct movements of giving and receiving love within a field, yet not three subjects. Unfortunately, Bulgakov makes it difficult to draw this conclusion because, in an attempt to deny that Sophia is herself a hypostasis, he maintains that her love within the Trinity is not active like the Logos; while he stresses that 'she too loves',[55] he understands this love as purely passive, receptive, and self-surrendering, and this is the kind of love that he characterizes as 'eternal femininity'.[56] Here he differs not only from Solov'ev, but from his own portrayal of the activity of Sophia in the world.

Reflecting on the sophianic projects of Solov'ev and Bulgakov, the question inevitably arises as to whether the created world is necessary for God. Bulgakov thinks that his predecessor has capitulated to idealism in this respect, and for himself urges a bare 'antinomy' between God as Absolute and as Relative to the world (or Absolute-Relative). There is simply a paradox here that reason cannot unravel. As Absolute, God is an apophatic mystery, the 'NOT-is'; but as the one who relates to the world, 'God needs the creation of the world in order to love . . . outside himself'.[57] God both is not, and is, in need of the world. However, I suggest that the Russian theologians' presentation of the divine Persons as eternally self-emptying might lead us to catch some glimpse as to how the two sides of the paradox might converge. For these theologians, the Father gives his being away in 'free self-emptying' in freely begetting the Son; the Son is 'utterly emptied' in freely consenting to be the Word of another, his Father; and the Spirit lives in self-renunciation in freely accepting that he (*sic*) will not proclaim himself but only what the Son says in the name of the Father. This eternal self-surrender within the Trinity is continually resolved in 'the bliss of the offered and mutually accepted sacrifice',[58] and it

---

[55] Bulgakov, pp. 105–6.   [56] Bulgakov, 'Hypostasis', p. 29.
[57] Bulgakov, *Lamb of God*, p. 120.   [58] Bulgakov, *Lamb of God*, p. 99.

might lead us to suppose that while no necessity can be forced on God from outside, from all eternity God is freely *willing to be in need*.[59]

God freely puts God's self, we may say, in need of a created world, so consummating the self-giving to others that is the very nature of the Trinity. God freely determines the kind of God that God wills to be. As Karl Barth puts it, 'God's being is . . . his willed decision.'[60] We might regard creation as being part of God's self-definition, an integral factor in God's own self-determination, since God chooses to be completed through a created universe—or perhaps several universes. The philosopher Vincent Brümmer puts it this way: 'God needs our love, because he is the loving God that he has freely decided to be.'[61] This perspective might be argued to be implicit in the thought of Bulgakov's identifying of the uncreated with the created Sophia. It is certainly essential for my own insistence in this study that God's wisdom consists in always being committed to physical signs in the world.

The Russian theologians' picture of Sophia has the poetic power that theology often has when it dares to live out on the margins. Like the personifications of wisdom in ancient literature, their Sophia—with azure blue eyes and a radiant smile, to be met in the church, the library, and the desert—invites attunement to her ways of love. She offers the possibility of empathy with herself. But this is not attunement to a transcendent and dominating subject: it is alignment to movements of self-giving which are like those of a father, son, and spirit of love.

TUNING TO THE BODY OF CHRIST

Against this background we might now see more clearly what it can mean to confess Jesus Christ as wisdom incarnate, and be attuned to the the music made by the broken body of Christ on the cross. There seems an enormous potential for Christology in the way that wisdom crosses the boundaries between divine and human, which the Russian Sophiologists are constantly exploring, not least with the idea of the 'body' of wisdom, but a convincing conclusion seems tantalizingly out of reach. Building on Solov'ev, Bulgakov proposes that in the incarnate Christ the two natures, divine and human, are a unique synergy or harmony between the uncreated and created Sophias.[62] But,

---

[59] I work this idea out fully in my book *The Creative Suffering of God*, pp. 63–71, under the heading 'The freedom of God to be in need'. See also Fiddes, 'Creation out of Love' in Polkinghorne (ed.), *Work of Love*, pp. 168–84.

[60] Karl Barth, *Church Dogmatics*, II/1, pp. 271–2.

[61] Vincent Brümmer, *The Model of Love* (Cambridge University Press, Cambridge, 1993), p. 237, citing and commending the approach that I had developed in my book *The Creative Suffering of God*, pp. 66–8, 74.

[62] Bulgakov, *Lamb of God*, pp. 226–30; his debt to Solov'ev is clear on pp. 193–211.

as Brandon Gallaher has pointed out, since the divine Sophia is—in Bulgakov's view—the same as the created Sophia, then the result seems to be a monophysite Christology, identifying the person of Christ simply with a single divine nature.[63]

A better wisdom Christology can be formed, I suggest, if we abandon the language of 'two natures' from Chalecedon, which is an accommodation to philosophical concepts of the time, and focus rather on the repeated Chalcedonian doxological assertion of the person of Christ as 'one and the same Son'.[64] This is the proposal of Wolfhart Pannenberg, who affirms that the human son, Jesus, shows that he is the 'same' as the eternal Son through his dedication to the will of God, his self-sacrifice for God, and openness to the world and the future. Pannenberg proposes that in the 'function of his message' and the activity related to the message, he relates to God the Father in such a complete way that he is 'indirectly' one with the eternal Son of God within the Trinity.[65] This community of activity with the Father is also a union of being since, Pannenberg avers with reference to Hegel, 'the truth of personality is to win it through this submerging, being submerged in the other' so that 'personal community is essential community'.[66] Further, the particular sonship of Jesus is the fulfilment of all human personality, since all human beings can become sons and daughters of God through Jesus.[67] This account of Christology, I suggest, becomes even more convincing when we understand the human Jesus to be 'indirectly one' with the *wisdom* of God. In fact, in Matthew 11:25–30 there are three sayings of Jesus grouped together which bring together ideas of 'sonship' with wisdom.

As we have already seen in the last chapter, the first two of these sayings come from the Q source, and the third from some source familiar to Matthew alone.[68] In the first, Jesus first exclaims:

> 'I thank you, Father, Lord of heaven and earth, because you have hidden these things from the wise and the intelligent and have revealed them to infants.'

Those who receive wisdom, which is both knowledge of the world and of the purposes of God, are called 'children' of wisdom and contrasted with 'the (so-called) wise' from whom wisdom is hidden. Then in a second saying, Jesus

---

[63] Brandon Gallaher, 'The Christological Focus of Vladimir Solov'ev's Christology', *Modern Theology* 25 (2009), pp. 634–5.

[64] 'We all confess our Lord Jesus Christ one and the same Son, the same perfect in Godhead, the same perfect in manhood, truly God and truly man ... one and the same Christ, Son, Lord, Only-begotten ... one and the same Son and only-begotten God, Word, Lord, Jesus Christ.' Text in J. Stevenson (ed.), *Creeds, Councils and Controversies* (London: SPCK, 1973), p. 337.

[65] Wolfhart Pannenberg, *Jesus—God and Man*, trans. L. Wilkins and D. Priebe (London: SCM Press, 1968), pp. 334–5.

[66] Pannenberg, *Jesus*, p. 336.

[67] Pannenberg, *Jesus*, p. 337.

[68] So Deutsch, *Hidden Wisdom*, pp. 47–53.

identifies himself both as a special envoy of this wisdom and as a unique 'Son of God':[69]

> 'All things have been handed over to me by my Father; and no one knows the Son except the Father, and no one knows the Father except the Son and anyone to whom the Son chooses to reveal him.'

There is something hidden about wisdom, as there is something mysterious about Jesus, but human beings are not excluded from it altogether; there is no need to suppose that some myth about wisdom being hidden in heaven is being applied to Jesus here. Finally, in a third saying, a Matthean supplement to Q, Jesus identifies himself as wisdom itself, claiming what is promised of wisdom herself in Ben Sira:[70] 'Take my yoke upon you and learn from me . . . and you will find rest for your souls.' In earlier Jewish literature the yoke is the wisdom writings and especially the Torah. Studying them is hard labour, and requires the obedience of a disciple; yet it also brings reward, delight, and rest. Children of wisdom are now to be disciples of Jesus. Thus, by bringing these three sayings together, Matthew makes the creative step of identifying the yoke of wisdom as nothing other than sharing in the relationship between 'the Father and the Son'. If we were to apply the musical image of attunement, we might say that the yoke is the rhythm or melody of mission in the life of God. At the heart of all music is tension and release, sound and silence, and so it is here with the rhythm of work and rest attributed to the yoke. Further, the identification of Christ and wisdom in the third saying has an effect on the second and its reference to 'all things'. Wisdom, we have often seen, is elusive because it reflects the complexity of the world and the multitude of the loving purposes of God; 'all' this has been contracted into a span in Christ as comprehensive wisdom: 'all things have been handed over to me by my Father'. As in the saying of John 1:16, 'from his fulness we have all received'. Only the Father knows the depths of this wisdom, and so only the Father knows the Son perfectly.

Jesus Christ is thus so perfectly attuned to the love, wisdom, and glory of God that he can be called wisdom itself. But this is not because he is *indwelt* by some divine wisdom 'principle'.[71] Wisdom is not a divine 'nature' to be added onto a human nature. The relationship of this human son with the one whom he calls his heavenly Father exactly fits over the relationship in God which is like that between a father and a son. As Hans Urs von Balthasar puts it, there is perfect 'attunement/concordance (*Übereinstimmung*) between the mission of

---

[69] The title of 'Son' is not in itself a claim to divinity, as many wise and prophetic figures in Judaism were called 'sons of God'. The immediate claim is for unique intimacy. See Dunn, *Christology*, 12–29.

[70] See above, Chapter 11, the section called 'Christ, the Wisdom of God'.

[71] Against Balthasar, *Glory of the Lord*, vol. 1, p. 475, who presents Jesus as a man so dynamically *inhabited* by God that he is attuned to God and speaks with the same voice.

Christ and his existence; these two things are *in tune* with each other', and so—as man—'Christ is identical with the task given him by the Father.' They fit, he says, 'like a glove'. The acts of power of Christ in word and deed in the early part of his ministry, the increasing failures, isolation, scandal, desolation, and death: all these are in perfect tune with the movement in God, which is like a father sending out a son and a son responding in obedience to a father. Being, task, and relationship resound together in harmony. Emphasis here on 'movements' or 'rhythms' in God is, I am contending, more cogent than the conception of divine persons as some kind of agents or supra-individuals. We should thus modify Pannenberg's proposal that the human son is indirectly identical with an 'eternal son': in less skilled hands than Pannenberg's, this kind of language would run the danger of implying the idea of 'two sons', rejected by the early church under the name of 'Nestorianism'.[72] Rather, we may say, this human son is indirectly identical with the movement in the being of God that is like *sonship*, or a relation between a father and a son. This leaves it open for us to add that the relation can also be conceived and experienced as like that between a mother and a daughter.

The activity and relations of the man Jesus are indirectly identical with wisdom, because the movement of his 'sonship' occupies space within the 'field of force' in God which *is* wisdom (rather as in Solv'ev and Bulgakov), and occupies it so well that Christ's life, death, and exaltation become the means for all human participation in God. The particularity of Christ means that Christians will find a tighter 'fit' between the life of Jesus and the wisdom of God than in other human persons. Christians will believe that created beings depend in some way upon *this* particular flow of relationship as they engage in the complex and inexhaustible communion of God's life. The pattern of life of Christ is mapped so exactly over the patterns of self-giving in God, that Christ himself becomes the space for all people into which wisdom is concentrated.[73]

The New Testament image for this attunement is a sharing in 'the body of Christ', laying stress precisely on the fleshly, material aspect of the instrument of divine music. In Scripture the phrase 'body of Christ' has a threefold reference—to the glorious resurrection of the body of Christ, who is to be identified with the earthly Jesus of Nazareth, to the church, and to the

---

[72] Nestorius himself always denied he had taught 'two sons', but he certainly taught two natures which he thought must each be complete with their own *hypostasis* (distinct reality) and *prosōpon* (person), within one '*prosōpon* of union' as object of honour and worship: see Nestorius, *Liber Heraclidis*, ed. F. Nau, *Le Livre d'Héraclide de Damas* (Paris: Letouzey et Ane, 1910), paras. 210–12, 219, 250–2, 304–7, 422). This ancient tangle about 'natures' is best entirely avoided.

[73] This might be regarded as a kind of 'mediation', though not between two ontological realms; cf. Dietrich Bonhoeffer's concept of mediation, in his *The Cost of Discipleship*, trans. R. H. Fuller (London: SCM, 1959), pp. 85–90.

eucharistic bread in which the community shares.[74] In addition, we will want to speak of the embodiment of Christ in the world beyond the walls of the church, if he is indeed Lord of the cosmos and the wisdom at the heart of the universe. In the words of Dietrich Bonhoeffer, Christ 'takes form' in the world;[75] we may discern the form of Christ, for example, in the actions of a group which is working for racial equality, or providing refuge for women who have suffered violence from their husbands, or offering medical care in refugee camps. Different dimensions of the body of Christ—incarnate, eucharistic, ecclesial, and secular—are related but not simply identical.

With the vision of a God who makes room for us in God's self, we can begin to see the connection and difference between the various forms of the body of Christ. There is first the body of Jesus of Nazareth, the whole physical being of the Jesus who was born from the body of a woman, who walked the dusty roads of Galilee, whose feet were washed by the tears and perfumed by the ointment of a woman, whose body was fixed to a cross and laid in a tomb. The person who was fully embodied in this way offered an obedient response to the one whom he called God his Father which was exactly the same as the movement of responsive love within God's dance of life. Further, then, individual believers can occupy this space in God which is shaped like a child's relation to a parent; because the space is Christ-shaped, they are—in the words of the Apostle Paul—'in Christ'. *Together* in community they are limbs making up the whole body; so the life of the church, mapped onto the life in God, is not just *like* a body–it *is* the body of Christ.[76] Likewise the actions of breaking of bread and the pouring of wine fit into the movement of self-breaking and self-outpouring within God, becoming the place where the self-giving of Christ can be encountered in depth.

Wherever, too, in the world any people give themselves to others or sacrifice themselves for others, these actions match the movement in God which is like a son going forth on mission in response to the purpose of a father; their acts share in the patterns of love in God, and so in them the body of Christ is discernible. The whole natural world responds in its own way to the creativity of God, singing God's praises by just being what it is (Psalm 19:1–4), and this response too fits in with a divine movement which is like a giving of glory to the a father by a son. So different bodies in the world—the individual bodily form of Jesus Christ, the sacraments of bread, wine, and water, the eucharistic community, groups in society, and all the variety of matter in nature—are all related to a common space. The space they occupy in God is not a kind of

---

[74] E.g. (i) Rom. 7:4; Phil. 3:21; Jn. 2:21; (ii) 1 Cor. 6:15; 12:4–31; Rom. 12:3–8; Eph. 4:1–16; Col. 1:18; (iii) 1 Cor. 10:17, 24, 27, 29.

[75] Dietrich Bonhoeffer, *Ethics*, pp. 97–100, cf. p. 58.

[76] This point is made by John A. T. Robinson, *The Body: A Study in Pauline Theology* (London: SCM Press, 1953), p. 51.

container, but a reality characterized by relationships, and in this way Christ can be embodied in all of them; his form can be recognized in them, and in all of them he can take flesh.

The body of the world is thus shaped and formed by the relational movements in God, so that it takes on the form of a text, a pattern of signs which point towards its creator. The world is a text, a semiotic or sign-bearing reality because it indwells the creator whose 'body' is wisdom. This is how the body of Christ, broken on the cross, renews the body of the world. We may say, poetically, that the breaking of bread and the pouring of wine in the eucharist re-creates the physical universe; but when we ask how, this is not because one kind of body has been infused into another. Rather, eucharist and universe are both, in their own way, attuned to the body of Christ.

Such attunement should lead us to a sympathy with all the bodies in the universe, overcoming the divide between the self and world. In the divine Sophia, according to Solov'ev, there is a perfect unity of subject and object, a simultaneity between loving and being loved, knowing and being known. This cannot be so intensely the case in the created world, since created persons are finite subjects with their own core of individual identity. But participating in the divine wisdom should enable us to close the gap between subject and object in everyday experience—to increase empathy and compassion, and to reduce domination and alienation. This we might learn not only from the Orthodox *Sophia* but from the Israelite *ḥokmah* which is always crossing the boundaries between the seer and the seen.

We began this study by lamenting the way that powerful trends of thought in the Enlightenment split the subject from the object, making the world the plaything of the individual conscious mind. An alternative epistemology is proposed by Balthasar, in finding a mutual disclosure between subject and object. There is, he maintains, a mutual self-opening and self-revealing between the two in all their particularity, a kind of communion in which each finds a completion.[77] This is the case even when the object is something without consciousness, such as a tree. Even unconscious objects, suggests Balthasar, need the space inside a subject to be themselves. Even a tree needs a space created by the senses in which to 'unfurl' itself; without that space, it would not be what it is. It finds its completion only outside itself, in a world of subjects; from its own existence it radiates into the space of the knower, in order to exhibit itself there. And, re-writing Aquinas' theory of the 'turning' of the mind towards the 'phantasm',[78] if the object must be in the subject, the subject must also be in the *object*, needing the object to unfold itself and find its own truth.

---

[77] Balthasar, *Theo-Logic*, vol. 1, pp. 61–71.

[78] The image arising from sense perception. See Aquinas, *Summa Theologiae* 1a.84.7.1ff; cf. 1a.75.2.3., 1a.76.1, 1a.79.4.

A wisdom theology finds that at the root of this participation in others there is participation in God. Observing an object or another person without trying to control them is a sharing in the flow of love in the triune life of God. The 'turning' of the self to an object takes part in the eternal movements in God that we can call the mission of the Father and the obedience of the Son and—against Aquinas—these are inseparable from the turning of God towards created beings.[79] God is thoroughly 'converted' to the worldly phantasm. In the poetic imagery of the Russian sophiologists, the divine Sophia is the created Sophia. In the poetic image of the Israelite wise, Lady Wisdom is already walking on our daily path. In the practice of *ḥokmah*, the wisdom of observation is always participation. Wisdom theology finds that a person can only make space within his or her mind for another because they both already occupy space in God.[80] Thus, seeing the world properly *is* knowing God.

In many different areas of life, the call today for 'wisdom' includes the elements of attunement and an attention to the bodily life of others.[81] I began this study by appealing, for example, to current talk about the place of 'wisdom' in medicine, to supplement 'evidence-based medicine'. In the evidence-based approach, hard statistics are accumulated through clinical trials about the effects of drugs and surgical interventions; these are ordered into patterns and the best practice determined. But alongside this welcome scientific approach there is felt to be the need for other non-technical factors. These include the development of a doctor's judgement through experience, an awareness of limits to knowledge, a sensitivity to the experience and feelings of the patient, and the holistic bringing together of experience, cognition, values, and emotions to make good decisions. Such aspects are usually grouped together under the heading of 'wisdom'.

In fact, the ancient wisdom of *ḥokmah* we have been exploring *includes* an 'evidence-based approach', the organizing of observations into patterns from which guidelines can be drawn by the reflective reason. But such wisdom is also aware of the need for the leap of empathy or intuition that I have been calling 'attunement'. Examples of this attunement in medicine would be the detection of child abuse, which might require more than a physical examination; or a decision to limit surgical intervention and leave some things to the healing power of nature; or a decision in psychiatry about the borders between mood disorders and schizophrenia. Some doctors will simply regard these judgements as attunement to nature, while others will openly speak of

---

[79] See above, chapter 6, the section called 'Participation not Mediation'.

[80] This is a more panentheistic form of Balthasar's principle that the human subject with its agent intellect 'displays an analogy to the divine subject' in knowing an object: *Theo-Logic*, p. 53.

[81] Flyvbjerg, *Making Social Science Matter*, pp. 158–9 stresses that as a research method *phronēsis* must be embodied, drawing on established concepts of 'embodied learning' and 'situated learning': see Jean Lave and Etienne Wenger, *Situated Learning: Legitimate Peripheral Participation* (Cambridge: Cambridge University Press, 1991).

attunement to a divine wisdom that transcends the empirical. It would be worrying, however, if it were ever separated from attention to the actual bodies of others.

THE BODY, MUSIC, AND WISDOM

Giving attention to the bodies of the world is to be aware that they live and develop through time. Just as we can never find a self which is hidden beyond the signs of the world, so we cannot escape time. Many late-modern thinkers reject the idea of God as a 'transcendental signifier' because they assume this means a supernatural subject who inhabits an eternal present moment, exempt from the passing of time, dwelling in the 'simultaneity' of past, present, and future which Christian theology has often attributed to eternity.[82] This seems the worst example of a subject imposing its undifferentiated presence on others, neglectful of the differences that make persons and objects what they are. But *presence* is not the same thing as an eternal *present*. The God whose triune nature I have been exploring has presence in the movement of time. Time indeed must mean something to a divine wisdom that provides a space for the world and shapes the signs of the world by embracing them.

A God who exists in the differences of interweaving rhythms of relationships will allow for new possibilities to emerge in the future—not only possibilities created by God alone, but those arising in the creative interaction between God's self and the world. Such a God will be supremely wise— omniscient—in the sense of knowing everything there is to be known, perfectly related to all the reality there is at any moment. It is in this sense that we should return for the last time to the confession of the ancient wisdom writers that God – like the over-watching sun—sees all things. Taken as the ability to see everything simultaneously in the past, present, and future, this would be a domination that undermines human freedom. Despite the attempt of some philosophers to detach foresight from predestination,[83] I agree with those who conclude that they cannot be separated.[84] If God knows from eternity what I will do tomorrow, it seems inevitable that I will do it. But we may re-define omniscience as God's knowing 'everything there is to be known',[85] and so

---

[82] See the first section of this chapter, 'Attunement and the Body'.

[83] Classically, by Boethius, *De Consolatione Philosophiae*, 5.4.

[84] E.g. Anthony Kenny, *The God of the Philosophers* (Oxford: Clarendon Press, 1979), pp. 51–90; Swinburne, *The Coherence of Theism*, pp. 216–22.

[85] So, though not uniformly, H. Owen, *Concepts of Deity* (London: Macmillan, 1971), pp. 30–3; Swinburne, *The Coherence of Theism*, pp. 175–8; Keith Ward, *Religion and Creation* (Oxford: Clarendon Press, 1996), pp. 275–7.

appropriate the confession of the Israelite wisdom writers. There will be events in the future which cannot be seen or known, since they have not yet come into existence. When they exist God will infallibly know them, but in humble patience God waits for them to come into being. Unlike us, however, such a God will always be able to harmonize the past, present, and the future, as I have already suggested in considering what it means to talk about the 'whole' of time.[86] God is not at the mercy of time, since God can indwell the many time-scales that belong to the many spaces in the universe, and can always heal their moments, but this does not mean that they are unreal to God. There is testimony to this in the rhythmic movement of the Holy Spirit in God, opening up the other persons to a new future.

So we return to the image of music, which we experience as a healing of time, but not its abolition. Music has the power to harmonize passing moments, so that we may even say, 'time stood still!' as we listened. But in fact, the effect of music *depends* on time, with music's build up of tension and its release in rest. Begbie asserts that temporality in music is manifest through the blending of rhythm (articulated in tones) with metre (set by the time signature): 'rhythmic patterns ride the metrical waves'.[87] Time is an inter-connectedness of tones and beats, and different temporal modes interpene-trate each other. According to his analysis, in the wave patterns of metre, past waves 'live on' in successive waves, so that past musical events are not lost forever. In melody, tones are internally connected to each other, so that there is a 'carrying from' and a 'reaching beyond' sensed in each present moment. He concludes that in music, 'past, present and future are, in some sense, interwoven' and that 'this comes very close to something that might be called 'redeemed time'.[88]

Moreover, the temporality of music is closely tied to its bodily nature. Begbie asserts that 'the production and reception of music deeply implicates physical realities and these realities are themselves time-laden'.[89] Time frag-ments human life as we know it, and so listening to music means giving full attention to the discords in the world, to the ragged edges of suffering, to the actual crosses of men and women today. 'Attunement' to wisdom means standing in the place of suffering; in music this may take the form of the hammer blows of chords in Beethoven's setting of 'crucifixus', or the recalling of pain in the blues or the Celtic lament. So we enter the rhythms which create the space of the Trinity, which is wisdom itself. The musical image does not merely 'illustrate' the Trinity: engaging in the rhythms of music is one place where we actually *encounter* the rhythmic movements of the love of God and

---

[86] See chapter 9, the section called 'The Sense of a Whole in the European Tradition'.
[87] Begbie, *Theology, Music and Time*, p. 41.
[88] Begbie, *Theology, Music and Time*, p. 61.
[89] Begbie, *Theology, Music and Time*, p. 31.

where talk of the Trinity comes alive. This is, of course, only one place among the signs of the world where we can meet and walk with Lady Wisdom, but it is a peculiarly intense place as it depends on the involvement of persons with their bodily life and the interactions of their bodies.[90]

While I was preparing the lectures on which this book is based, a young German composer named Jorg Widmann gave the world premiere of a piece of music for string quartet and soprano, called 'Attempt at a Fugue'. The four stringed instruments busily work away at constructing the interweaving of voices that belong to a classical fugue, and never quite succeeding, while a woman's voice soars above them, singing words of wisdom from the book of Ecclesiastes in Latin: 'Futility of futility—all is futility . . . there is nothing new under the sun.' As the attempt at a fugue proceeds, different kinds of noises are heard: bowing near and on the bridge, musicians swiftly whipping their bows in the air, loud breaths. In a typically 'postmodern' way there is a montage of dissonant sounds. Just as the fugue appears to have got itself together, it is broken again by an onset of instrumental noises, and the soprano's text switches from ecclesiastical Latin to the vernacular German: 'Fern ist der Grund der Dinge und tief; gar tief, wer will ihn finden?': 'That which is, is far off, and deep, very deep; who can find it out?' (Eccl. 7:24).

The music echoes the sense of the hiddenness of wisdom in the biblical text, and the composer explains that in our world today, only an *attempt* at a fugue is possible. Yet one commentator concludes: 'the fugue has failed so that the piece may succeed'.[91] The very rhythms and the relationships between the voices in Widmann's piece bear witness that attunement to wisdom is always possible. This is the conviction of the 'wise' in Ancient Israel, and their witness speaks effectively into our late-modern world.

---

[90] See David Ford, *Self and Salvation* (Cambridge University Press, 1999), pp. 126–9, on polyphony and the self in congregational singing.

[91] From a programme note by Christopher Cerrone, performance at the Carnegie Hall, 2012.

Select Bibliography

Arendt, Hannah, *Between Past and Future: Six Exercises in Political Thought*. Enlarged Edition (New York: Viking, 1968).

——*The Human Condition*. Second Edition (Chicago: University of Chicago Press, 1998).

Augustine, *Confessions*, trans. Henry Chadwick (Oxford: Oxford University Press, 1992).

Bakhtin, Mikhail M., *Speech Genres and Other Late Essays*, ed. C. Emerson and M. Holquist, trans. V. W. McGee (Austin: University of Texas Press, 1986).

Balthasar, Hans Urs von, *The Glory of the Lord: A Theological Aesthetics*. 7 volumes (Edinburgh; T & T Clark, 1982–89).

——*Theo-Drama. Theological Dramatic Theory*. 5 Volumes (San Francisco: Ignatius Press, 1988–98).

——*Theo-Logic: Theological Logical Theory*. 3 Volumes (San Francisco: Ignatius Press, 2000–5).

Barth, Karl, *Church Dogmatics*, trans. and ed. G. W. Bromiley and T. F. Torrance. 14 Volumes (Edinburgh: T & T Clark, 1936–77).

Barthes, Roland, 'Struggle with the Angel' in Barthes, *Image/Music/ Text*, trans. Stephen Heath (London: Collins/Fontana, 1993), pp. 125–41.

Barton, Stephen C. (ed.), *Where Shall Wisdom be Found?* (Edinburgh: T & T Clark, 1999).

Barucq, André, *Le Livre des Proverbes* (Paris: Gabalda, 1964).

Baudrillard, Jean, *Simulations*, trans. P. Foss, P. Patton, P. Beitchman (New York: Semiotext(e), 1983).

Begbie, Jeremy S., *Theology, Music and Time* (Cambridge: Cambridge University Press, 2000).

Brown, Raymond E., *The Gospel According to John*, I–XII, Anchor Bible (New York: Doubleday, 1966).

Bulgakov, Sergei, *Sophia: The Wisdom of God: An Outline of Sophiology*, trans. P. Thompson, O. Fielding Clarke, and X. Braikevitc (New York: Lindisfarne Press, 1993).

——*The Lamb of God*, trans. B. Jakim (Grand Rapids: Eerdmans, 2008).

Bultmann, Rudolf, 'Der Religionsgeschichtliche Hintergrund des Prologs zum Johannesevangelium', originally in *Gunkel-Festschrift* 2 (1923), pp. 3–26 = *Exegetica. Aufsätze zur Erforschung des Neuen Testaments*, ed. Erich Dinkler (Tübingen: Mohr Siebeck, 1967), pp. 10–35.

——*The Gospel of John*, trans. G. R. Beasley-Murray (Oxford: Blackwell, 1971).

Camp, Claudia, *Wisdom and the Feminine in the Book of Proverbs* (Sheffield: Almond, 1985).

Caputo, John, *The Prayers and Tears of Jacques Derrida: Religion without Religion* (Bloomington: Indiana University Press, 1997).

Certeau, Michel de, *The Practice of Everyday Life*, trans. S. Rendall (Berkeley: University of California Press, 1988).

Certeau, Michel de, 'How is Christianity Thinkable Today?', trans. F. C. Bauerschmidt and C. Hanley, in Ward (ed.), *The Postmodern God* (Blackwell Publishers, 1997), pp. 142–55.

Charles, R. H. (ed.), *Apocrypha and Pseudepigrapha of the Old Testament*. 2 Volumes (Oxford: Clarendon Press, 1913).

Christ, Felix, *Jesus Sophia: Die Sophia-Christologie bei den Synoptikern* (Zürich: Zwingli Verlag, 1970).

Clements, R. E., *Wisdom in Theology* (Carlisle: Paternoster, 1992).

Clines, David, *Job 1–20*. Word Biblical Commentary (Dallas: Word Books, 1989).

——*Job 21–37*. Word Biblical Commentary (Nashville: Nelson, 2006).

Conzelmann, Hans, 'The Mother of Wisdom' in James M. Robinson (ed.), *The Future of our Religious Past* (London: SCM, 1971), pp. 230–43.

Coward, Harold and Foshay, Toby (eds), *Derrida and Negative Theology* (Albany: State University of New York Press, 1992).

Crenshaw, James L. (ed.), *Studies in Ancient Israelite Wisdom* (New York, KTAV, 1976).

——*Ecclesiastes: A Commentary*. The Old Testament Library (Philadelphia: Westminster Press, 1987).

——*Old Testament Wisdom: An Introduction*. Revised and Enlarged (Louisville: Westminster/John Knox, 1998).

Cunningham, David, *These Three are One: The Practice of Trinitarian Theology* (Oxford: Blackwell, 1998).

Davies, Oliver, *The Creativity of God: World, Eucharist, Reason* (Cambridge: Cambridge University Press, 2004).

Day, John, Gordon, Robert P., and Williamson, H. G. M. (eds), *Wisdom in Ancient Israel: Essays in Honour of J. A. Emerton* (Cambridge: Cambridge University Press, 1998).

Derrida, Jacques, 'Differance', trans. D. Allison, in Derrida, *Speech and Phenomena* (Evanston: Northwestern University Press, 1973), pp. 129–60.

——*Speech and Phenomena and Other Essays on Husserl's Theory of Signs*, trans. D. Allison (Evanston: Northwestern University Press, 1973).

——*Of Grammatology*, trans. G. C. Spivak (Baltimore and London: Johns Hopkins University Press, 1976).

——*Writing and Difference*, trans. A. Bass (London: Routledge & Kegan Paul, 1978).

——*Positions*, trans. A. Bass (Chicago: University of Chicago Press, 1981).

——'The Double Session', in Derrida, *Dissemination*, trans. B. Johnson (Chicago: University of Chicago, 1981), pp. 173–286.

——'Différance', trans. A. Bass, in Derrida, *Margins of Philosophy* (New York: Harvester, 1982), pp. 1–28.

——*Margins of Philosophy*, trans. A. Bass (New York: Harvester, 1982).

——'White Mythology: Metaphor in the Text of Philosophy', in Derrida, *Margins of Philosophy* (New York: Harvester, 1982), pp. 207–72.

——*Glas*, trans. J. P. Leavey, and R. Rand (Lincoln: University of Nebraska Press, 1986).

——'Parergon' in Derrida, *The Truth in Painting*, trans. G. Bennington and I. McLeod (Chicago: University of Chicago Press, 1987), pp. 15–148.

——'Afterword', in Derrida, *Limited Inc.* (Evanston: Northwestern University Press, 1988) pp. 111–54.

——*Limited Inc* (Evanston: Northwestern University Press, 1988).

——*Of Spirit: Heidegger and the Question,* trans. G. Bennington and R. Bowlby (Chicago: University of Chicago Press, 1991).

——'Of an Apocalyptic Tone Newly Adopted in Philosophy', trans. J. Leavey, in Harold Coward and Toby Foshay (eds), *Derrida and Negative Theology* (Albany: State University of New York Press, 1992), pp. 25–72.

——*On the Name,* ed. and trans. Thomas Dutoit (Stanford: Stanford University Press, 1995).

——*The Gift of Death,* trans. D. Wills (Chicago: University of Chicago Press, 1995).

Deutsch, Celia, Hidden *Wisdom and the Easy Yoke: Wisdom, Torah and Discipleship in Matthew 11:25–30* (Sheffield: JSOT Press, 1987).

Dhorme, E., *A Commentary on the Book of Job,* trans. H. Knight (London: Nelson, 1967).

Dunn, James, *Christology in the Making* (London: SCM, 1980).

Epstein, Heidi, *Melting the Venusberg: A Feminist Theology of Music* (New York: Continnum, 2004).

Fiddes, Paul S., 'The Hiddenness of Wisdom in the Old Testament and Later Judaism', DPhil Thesis, University of Oxford, 1976.

——*The Creative Suffering of God* (Oxford: Clarendon Press, 1988).

——*The Promised End: Eschatology in Theology and Literature* (Oxford: Blackwell, 2000).

——*Participating in God: A Pastoral Doctrine of the Trinity* (London: Darton Longman and Todd, 2000).

——'Creation out of Love' in Polkinghorne (ed.), *The Work of Love* (Grand Rapids: Eerdmans, 2001), pp. 167–91.

Fohrer, Georg, *Hiob,* Kommentar Zum Alten Testament (Gütersloh: Ferd Mohn, 1963).

Ford, David and Stanton, Graham (eds), *Reading Texts, Seeking Wisdom* (London: SCM, 2003).

Ford, David, *Self and Salvation: Being Transformed* (Cambridge: Cambridge University Press, 1999).

——*Christian Wisdom: Desiring God and Learning in Love* (Cambridge: Cambridge University Press, 2007).

Foucault, Michel, *The Order of Things,* English translation (London: Routledge, 2002).

Fox, Michael V., *A Time to Tear Down and a Time to Build Up: A Rereading of Ecclesiastes* (Grand Rapids: Eerdmans, 1999).

Gadamer, Hans-Georg, *Truth and Method,* English translation (London: Sheed & Ward).

Gallaher, Anastassy Brandon and Kukota, Irina, 'Protopresbyter Sergii Bulgakov: Hypostasis and Hypostaticity: Scholia to the Unfading Light', *St Vladimirs Theological Quarterly* 49 (2005), pp. 5–46.

Gemser, Berend, 'The Spiritual Structure of Biblical Aphoristic Wisdom' in *Adhuc Loquitur: Collected Essays,* ed. A. van Selms and A. S. van der Woude (Leiden: Brill, 1968), pp. 138–149.

Gese, Harmut, *Lehre und Wirklichkeit in der alten Weisheit: Studien zu den Sprüchen Salomos und zu dem Buche Hiob* (Tübingen: Mohr, 1958).

Gordis, Robert, *The Book of Job* (New York: Jewish Theological Seminary, 1978).

Hamerton-Kelly, R. G., *Pre-Existence, Wisdom and the Son of Man: A Study of the Idea of Pre-Existence in the New Testament* (Cambridge: Cambridge University Press, 1973).

Hartshorne, Charles, *A Natural Theology for our Time* (La Salle: Open Court, 1967).

Hegel, G. W. F., *The Phenomenology of Mind*, trans. J. Baillie (London: George Allen & Unwin, 1949).

——*The Christian Religion: Lectures on the Philosophy of Religion Part III*, trans. P. C. Hodgson. American Academy of Religion, Texts and Translations 2 (Missoula: Scholars Press, 1979).

Heidegger, Martin, *Being and Time*, trans. J. Macquarrie and E. Robinson (Oxford: Blackwell, 1973).

——*Poetry, Language, Thought*, trans. A. Hofstadter (New York: HarperCollins/Perennial, 2001).

——*Identity and Difference*, transl. J. Stambaugh (Chicago: Chicago University Press, 2002).

Husserl, Edmund, *Ideas Pertaining to a Pure Phenomenology and to a Phenomenological Philosophy*, trans. F. Kersetn (Dordrecht: Kluwer Academic Publishers, 1983).

Jay, Martin, *Downcast Eyes: The Denigration of Vision in Twentieth-Century French Thought* (Berkeley: University of California Press, 1994).

Jüngel, Eberhard. *God as the Mystery of the World*, transl. D. Guder (Edinburgh: T & T Clark, 1983).

Kant, Immanuel, *Critique of Pure Reason*, trans. N. Kemp Smith (London: Macmillan, 1933).

——*The Critique of Judgement*, trans. J. C. Meredith (Oxford: Clarendon Press, 1952).

Kayatz, Christa, *Studien zu Proverbien 1–9* (Neukirchen-Vluyn: Neukirchener Verlag, 1966).

Keller, Catherine, *Face of the Deep: A Theology of Becoming* (London: Routledge, 2003).

Kelsey, David, *To Understand God Truly: What's Theological about a Theological School* (Louisville: Westminster/John Knox, 1992).

——*Eccentric Existence: Theological Anthropology*, 2 Volumes (Louisville, Westminster/John Knox, 2009).

Knox, W. L., 'The Divine Wisdom', *Journal of Theological Studies* 38 (1937), pp. 230–237.

Kristeva, Julia, *Black Sun: Depression and Melancholia*, trans. L. S. Roudiez (New York: Columbia University Press, 1989).

Levinas, Emmanuel, *Totality and Infinity: An Essay on Interiority*, trans. A. Lingis (Pittsburgh: Duquesne University Press, 1965).

——*Time and the Other*, trans. R. A. Cohen (Pittsburgh: Duquesne University Press, 1987).

——*Difficult Freedom: Essays on Judaism*, trans. Seán Hand (Baltimore: Johns Hopkins University Press, 1990).

——*Nine Talmudic Readings*, trans. A. Aronowicz (Bloomington: Indiana University Press, 1994.

——'Meaning and Sense' in A. Peperzak, S. Critchley, R. Bernasconi (eds), *Levinas: Basic Philosophical Writings* (Bloomington: Indiana University Press, 1996), pp. 33–64.

——*Otherwise Than Being. Or Beyond Essence*, trans. A. Lingis (Pittsburgh: Duquesne University Press, 1998).

——'Postface: Transcendence and Evil', in Philippe Nemo, *Job and the Excess of Evil* (Pittsburgh: Duquesne University Press, 1998), pp. 165–82.

——*Existence and Existents*, trans. A. Lingis (Pittsburgh: Duquesne University Press, 2001).

——*Beyond the Verse: Talmudic Readings and Lectures* , trans. G. D. Mole (London: Continuum, 2007).

Lyotard, Jean-François, *The Postmodern Condition: A Report on Knowledge*, trans. G. Bennington and B. Massumi (Manchester: Manchester University Press, 1986).

McFague, Sallie, *The Body of God: An Ecological Theology* (London: SCM, 1993).

Mack, Burton L., *Logos und Sophia: Untersuchungen zur Weisheitstheologie im hellenistischen Judentum* (Göttingen: Vandenhoeck & Ruprecht, 1973).

McKane, William, *Prophets and Wise Men* (London: SCM, 1965).

——*Proverbs: A New Approach* (London: SCM, 1970).

Macquarrie, John, *Principles of Christian Theology*. Revised Edition (London: SCM, 1977).

Marböck, Johann, *Weisheit im Wandel: Untersuchungen zur Weisheitstheologie bei Ben Sira* (Bonn: Peter Hanstein, 1971).

Merleau-Ponty, Maurice, *Visible and Invisible*, trans. A. Lingis (Evanston: Northwestern University Press, 1969).

Moltmann, Jürgen, *Theology of Hope: On the Ground and Implications of a Christian Eschatology,* trans. J. W. Leitch (London: SCM, 1967).

——*The Crucified God: The Cross of Christ as the Foundation and Criticism of Christian Theology,* trans. R. A. Wilson and J. Bowden (London: SCM, 1974).

Morenz, Siegfried, *Egyptian Religion*, trans. A. E. Keep (London: Methuen, 1973).

Murdoch, Iris, *Metaphysics as a Guide to Morals* (London: Chatto & Windus, 1992).

——'The Sublime and the Good' in Murdoch, *Existentialists and Mystics*, ed. Peter Conradi (London: Chatto & Windus, 1997), pp. 205–20.

Murphy, R. E., 'The Interpretation of Old Testament Wisdom Literature', *Interpretation* 23 (1969), pp. 289–301.

——*The Tree of Life: An Exploration of Biblical Wisdom Literature* (Grand Rapids: Eerdmans, 1996).

Nemo, Philippe, *Job and the Excess of Evil*, trans. M. Kigel (Pittsburgh: Duquesne University Press, 1998).

Newsom, Carole, 'The Book of Job' in *The New Interpreter's Bible*, ed. L. E. Keck et al. Vol. 4 (Nashville: Abingdon, 1996), pp. 319–637.

Nicholas of Cusa, *The Vision of God*, trans. E. S. Gurney (New York: Cosimo, 2007).

Nietzsche, F. *Complete Works of Nietzsche*, ed. O. Levy, 18 Volumes (London: Allen & Unwin, 1909–13).

Noth, Martin and Thomas, D. Winton (eds), *Wisdom in Israel and the Ancient Near East* (Leiden: Brill, 1955).

Pannenberg, Wolfhart, *Jesus—God and Man*, trans. L. Wilkins and D. Priebe (London: SCM Press, 1968).

——*Systematic Theology*, 3 Volumes, trans. G. Bromiley (Grand Rapids: Eerdmans, 1988–98).

Pattison, Stephen, *Seeing Things: Deepening Relations with Visual Artefacts* (London: SCM, 2007).

Perdue, Leo G., *Wisdom Literature: A Theological History* (Louisville: Westminster John Knox, 2007).

——*Wisdom & Creation: The Theology of Wisdom Literature* (Eugene, Wipf, and Stock, 2009).

——Scott, Bernard B., and Wiseman, William J. (eds), *In Search of Wisdom: Essays in Memory of John G. Gammie* (Louisville: Westminster/John Knox, 1993).

Polkinghorne, John, *Belief in God in an Age of Science* (Yale: Yale Univesity Press, 1998).

——(ed.) The *Work of Love: Creation and Kenosis* (Grand Rapids: Eerdmans, 2001).

Pritchard, J. B. (ed.), *Ancient Near Eastern Texts Relating to the Old Testament*. Second edition (Princeton, Princeton University Press).

Rad, Gerhard von, *Old Testament Theology*, trans. D. M. G. Stalker. 2 Volumes (Edinburgh: Oliver and Boyd, 1962).

——*Wisdom in Israel,* trans. J. D. Martin (London: SCM, 1972).

Rahner, Karl, *The Trinity*, trans. J. Donceel (London: Burns & Oates, 1975).

——*Foundations of Christian Faith: An Introduction to the Idea of Christianity*, trans. W. V. Dych (London: Darton, Longman and Todd, 1978).

Reese, J. M., *Hellenistic Influence on the Book of Wisdom and its Consequences* (Rome: Biblical Institute, 1970).

Ricoeur, Paul, *The Symbolism of Evil*, trans. E. Buchanan (Boston: Beacon Press, 1969).

——*The Conflict of Interpretations*, ed. Don Ihde (Evanston: Northwestern University Press, 1974).

——'Freedom in the Light of Hope', trans. R. Sweeney, in Ricoeur, *The Conflict of Interpretations* (Evanston: Northwestern University Press, 1974), pp. 402–24.

——'Towards a Hermeneutic of the Idea of Revelation' in *Essays on Biblical Inter-pretation*, ed. and trans. Lewis S. Mudge (Philadelphia; Fortress Press, 1980), pp. 73–118.

——*Time and Narrative*, 3 Volumes, trans. K. McLaughlin, K. Blamey, and D. Pellauer (Chicago and London: University of Chicago Press, 1984–88).

——*From Text to Action: Essays in Hermeneutics II*, trans. K. Blamey and J. B. Thompson (Evanston: Northwestern University Press, 1991).

——*Oneself As Another*, trans. K. Blamey (Chicago: Chicago University Press, 1994).

Ringgren, Helmer, *Word and Wisdom: Studies in the Hypostatization of Divine Qual-ities and Functions in the Ancient Near East* (Lund: H. Ohlssons Boktrycken, 1947).

Rylaarsdam, J. Coert, *Revelation in Jewish Wisdom Literature* (Chicago: University of Chicago, 1946).

Sartre, Jean-Paul, *Being and Nothingness: An Essay on Phenomenological Ontology*, trans. H. E. Barnes (London: Routledge, 2003).

Saussure, Ferdinand de, *Course in General Linguistics*, trans. R. Harris (London: Duckworth, 1983).

Schleiermacher, Friedrich, The Christian Faith. Second Edition, trans. H. R. Mackin-tosh and J. S. Stewart (Edinburgh, T & T Clark, 1928).

Schmid, H. H., *Wesen und Geschichte der Weisheit* (Berlin: de Gruyter 1966).

Schnabel, Eckhard J., *Law and Wisdom from Ben Sira to Paul: A Tradition Historical Enquiry into the Relation of Law, Wisdom and Ethics* (Tübingen: Mohr Siebeck, 1985).

Schnackenburg, Rudolf, *The Gospel According to St John*. 3 Volumes, trans. K. Smyth (New York: Crossroads, 1990).

Scott, R. B. Y., *Proverbs-Ecclesiastes*, The Anchor Bible (New York: Doubleday, 1965).

——*The Way of Wisdom* (New York: Macmillan, 1971).

——'Wise and Foolish, Righteous and Wicked' in *Studies in the Religion of Ancient Israel*. Supplement to *Vetus Testamentum*, vol. 23 (Leiden: Brill, 1972), pp. 146–65.

Solov'ev, Vladimir, *Lectures on Divine Humanity* [1887–91], trans. P. Zouboff, rev. ed. Boris Jakim (New York: Lindisfarne Press, 1995).

——*The Philosophical Principles of Integral Knowledge* [1877], trans. V. Z. Nollan (Grand Rapids: Eerdmans, 2008).

Suggs, M. Jack, *Wisdom, Christology and Law in Matthew's Gospel* (Cambridge: Harvard University Press, 1970).

Swinburne, Richard, *The Coherence of Theism* (Oxford: Clarendon Press, 1977).

Taylor, Charles, *Sources of the Self: The Making of Modern Identity* (Cambridge: Cambridge University Press, 1989).

Thiselton, Anthony C., *Interpreting God and the Postmodern Self: On Meaning, Manipulation and Promise* (Edinburgh, T & T Clark, 1995).

Tillich, Paul, *The Courage to Be* (London: Collins/Fontana, 1962).

——*Systematic Theology*. Combined Volume (London: James Nisbet, 1968).

Treier, Daniel J., *Virtue and the Voice of God: Towards Theology as Wisdom* (Grand Rapids: Eerdmans, 2006).

Turner, Denys, *The Darkness of God: Negativity in Christian Mysticism* (Cambridge: Cambridge University Press, 1995).

Ward (ed.), Graham, *The Postmodern God: A Theological Reader* (Oxford: Blackwell, 1997).

Weeks, Stuart, *Early Israelite Wisdom* (Oxford: Clarendon Press, 1994).

Weinfeld, Moshe, *Deuteronomy and the Deuteronomistic School* (Oxford: Clarendon Press, 1972).

Whitehead, A. N., *Process and Reality: An Essay in Cosmology* (New York: Macmillan, 1967).

Whybray, R. Norman, *Wisdom in Proverbs: The Concept of Wisdom in Proverbs 1–9:45* (London: SCM, 1967).

——*The Intellectual Tradition in the Old Testament* (Berlin: de Gruyter, 1974).

Wilckens, Ulrich, Art. αοφια, *Theological Dictionary of the New Testament*, ed. Gerhard Kittel, Geoffrey Bromiley, and Wilhelm Friedrich. 10 Volumes (Grand Rapids, Eerdmans, 1964–76), vol. 5, pp. 496–516.

Witherington, Ben III, *Jesus the Sage: The Pilgrimage of Wisdom* (Minneapolis; Fortress, 2000).

Wolde, Ellen Van (ed.), *Job 28: Cognition in Context* (Leiden: Brill, 2003).

Wyschogrod, Edith, *Saints and Postmodernism: Revisioning Moral Philosophy* (Chicago; University of Chicago Press, 1990).

Zimmerli, Walther, 'The Place and Limit of the Wisdom in the Framework of the Old Testament Theology', *Scottish Journal of Theology* 17 (1964), pp. 146–58.

Index of Names

Index of Subjects

action in the world, God's 13, 19, 21, 39–40, 47, 98–9, 112–13, 117, 120, 122, 124, 130, 161–5, 252, 262–3, 350
Ahikar, Wisdom of 105 n. 67, 117, 125, 126
alienation 33 n. 27, 36, 38, 87–9, 90, 91–3, 95, 127, 128, 152, 155, 165, 166, 253, 392
Amen-em-het, Instruction of 111, 115 n. 100
Amen-em-Opet, Instruction of 16, 111, 112 n. 85, 113, 114 n. 94, 115, 122, 125
analogy 47, 89, 96, 97, 98, 137, 147, 154, 167, 201, 213, 244, 257, 272, 273, 276, 279, 281, 313, 316, 320–1, 341, 351, 393
analogy of being 159, 205, 318
analogy of relationship 152, 260–2, 385
Ani, Instruction of 111, 115 n. 103, 116 n. 105
attunement 12, 112, 116, 139, 291, 322, 323, 336, 364, 373–4, 375–6, 378, 380–1, 387, 389, 390, 392, 393–4, 396

being 12, 25, 39, 58, 70, 80, 92, 156–7, 158–9, 169–71, 208, 218–19, 221–3, 224, 225–6, 227, 273, 274, 300, 322–3
see also God, as Being-Itself
body 31–2, 47, 62, 68, 70, 75, 98, 138–9, 163, 168, 172, 212–13, 214, 216, 227–8, 272, 340, 341–2, 346, 376–8, 379, 380, 391, 394

Chalcedon 388
Cappadocian Fathers 150
chōra (khōra) 158, 224–5, 226–30, 250–1, 254, 257, 259–60, 272, 378
church 9, 13, 37, 47, 88–9, 153, 211, 261, 344, 377, 391
complexity 15, 23, 57, 96, 108, 110, 120, 127, chapter 5 passim, 167, 169, 203, 236–8, 239, 243, 245, 256, 265, 275, 277, 283, 293, 303, 309, 312, 316–17, 330, 332, 341, 345, 351, 357, 380, 389
see also God the Trinity, and complexity
covenant 13, 53, 123, 124, 164, 196, 292, 326, 328–9, 334
creation See God, as creator

dance, image of 161 n. 146, 164, 166, 213, 290–1, 368, 391
deconstruction 28, 38–40, 46, 47, 48, 53, 54, 55, 63, 132, 146, 164, 216, 217, 274, 315, 342, 353

desire 7–8, 41, 42, 45, 52, 55, 60, 62–3, 65, 128, 140, 142, 149, 165, 220, 226–7, 228, 229, 264, 291–2, 354
différance 48, 141–3, 156, 158, 173, 227, 300
difference 4, 48, 50, 55, 58–9, 62, 69, 69, 72 n. 59, 131, 140, 141–3, 145, 153, 157, 172–4, 206, 215, 217, 219, 222, 224, 226, 227, 270, 271, 274, 295, 300, 325, 340, 348, 379, 394

empathy 4, 35, 72, 154, 217, 253–4, 260, 286–90, 337, 339, 351, 380, 387, 392, 393
Enlightenment, the 3, 28–30, 61, 74, 76, 81, 87, 141, 171, 261, 349, 392
Enoch, First Book of 175, 230, 355–63
see Index of Scripture and Inter-Testamental Books for all references
eschatology 205, 356–9, 360, 361
evil 32, 37, 46, 50, 68–9, 70, 71, 237, 276, 317, 367

forgiveness 24, 95, 260
Fourth Gospel (John) 194 n. 226, 362–3, 343–4 see Index of Scripture and Inter-Testamental Books for all references
futility 19, 303, 305, 306, 319, 333, 396

God
as Being-Itself 58 n. 145, 65, 147–9, 149–154, 157–60, 169, 215, 220, 225–6, 390
'body' of 293, 342, 344, 381–4
as creator 12, 47, 58, 110, 128, 135, 138–9, 147, 149, 161–2, 188, 194, 211, 269, 270, 271, 276, 285, 287–8, 289, 291, 298, 314, 316, 337, 342, 351, 361, 375, 383, 385, 392
desire of 149, 291–2
as hidden 156, 214, 251–6, 264–5, 272, 274, 285, 297–8
kenōsis of 289, 383
as knowing potentialities and actualities 148–9
as observer 113, 115–16, 122–3, 138, 181–4, 184–6, 203, 213–14, 217, 232, 235, 236, 353–4
as participating in the world 25, 65, 149, 188, 293, 366

Index of Scripture and Inter-Testamental Books

Printed and bound by CPI Group (UK) Ltd, Croydon, CR0 4YY